DATE			

DICTIONARY
OF
FIRST NAMES

The Jonathan David

DICTIONARY
OF
FIRST NAMES

ALFRED J. KOLATCH

jD | JONATHAN DAVID PUBLISHERS
MIDDLE VILLAGE, N.Y. 11379

**DICTIONARY
OF
FIRST NAMES**

Copyright © 1980
by
ALFRED J. KOLATCH

No part of this book may be reproduced in any manner without written permission from the publishers. Address all inquiries to:

JONATHAN DAVID PUBLISHERS, INC.
68-22 Eliot Avenue
Middle Village, New York 11379

Library of Congress Cataloging in Publication Data

Kolatch, Alfred J.   1916-
    Dictionary of first names.

    1. Names, Personal--English--Dictionaries.
2. English language--Etymology--Names.   I. Title.
CS2367.K64   929.4'0917'521   79-21411
ISBN   0-8246-0247-1

Printed in the United States of America

TO
THELMA
WITH LOVE
on our fortieth
wedding anniversary

Acknowledgements

A great many people have been helpful in the preparation of this manuscript, and I must recognize my indebtedness to them. Aside from all those who wrote to me in response to notices in various magazines, I especially want to thank David Kolatch for his very capable editing of the entire manuscript; Mercedes Bowen of San Jose, California, for the detailed information about the unique names of the members of her family; Sherre Lipton and Mere Racule of Hawaii for their help with Hawaiian names; Professor Donald Hook, Trinity College, Hartford, Connecticut, and Professor Richard Spears, Northwestern University, Evanston, Illinois, both language experts, for reading the manuscript and making invaluable suggestions. Florence Weissman and Mary McGee for helping in the proofreading and typing of the manuscript.

The following correspondents have supplied useful information, much of which has been incorporated in the body of this work:

Mr. William Aalbue, Pueblo West, CO; Garland G. Aaron, Laurel Bay, SC; Cindy Abato, Branchville, NJ; Yvonne Abner, Blanchester, OH; Libby B. Abramson, Somervill, NJ; Terry Afshargadeh, Chico, CA; Retha Elsie Daniell Alarid, Carmichael, CA; Iora Alexander, Andover, MA; Brenda Allen, Wichita, KS; Virginia Pauline Allen, Trenton, OH; Tricia Andrew, LaCrescents, CA; Rebecca Andrews, Los Angeles, CA; Flora Jane Anutinora, Phoenix, AZ; Mrs. Karyl Aronoff, Dallas TX; Mrs. Yetive Matthews Ashcraft, Uniontown, PA; Zna Atherton, Las Vegas, NV; Richia Eliza Atkinson, Palm Beach, FL; Mrs. Eloise Auwae, Haetselle, AL; Reja Elise B, Gulfport, MS; Mrs. Cynthia Babiak, Boulder, CO; Mrs. Blandina F. Badger, Folsom, CA; Maralee Baker, Raleigh, NC; Rita Baker, Euclid, OH; Mrs. Chris Bannigan, Diamond Bar, CA; Mrs. Jennilee Barnhart, Neapolis, OH; Mrs. V. Baro, Imola, CA; Mrs. Richard J. Barrett, Palo Alto, CA; Honorable Birch Bayh, Washington, D.C.; Inza Aleph Beasley, Nederland, TX; Mrs. John Beckman, Phippsburg, CO; Geraldine V. Beatty, Zephyhills, FL; Marijune Belt, Wilmington, NC; Tresella Benson, Louisville, KY; Reneise Deliz Bentley, Capistrano Beach, CA; Karen Berendsen, Strongsville, OH; Icyl D. Berg, Marietta, OH; Warrene Berge, Phoenix, AZ; Mrs. Tawana Bernard, Irving, TX; Mrs. Shirley Berry, Nacaville, CA; Dorelle Bishop, Sallis, MS; Dorinda Bishop, San Francisco, CA; Mrs. Lillus Black, Laguna Beach, CA; Kathy Blagrove, Maybrook, NY; Ms. Azora P. Blair, Bridgeport, CT; Hila Blair, California, PA; Caprice Blasingame, Carenco, LA; Mrs. Ellice Blazon, Concord, NH; Mrs. D. Blyston, Crestline, CA; Mernie Bochoff, Sandpoint, ID; Mrs. Sunny Jean Bond, Red Bluff, CA; Mrs. Roneel G. Bowden, Linden, TX; Vyonne Bowers, Huntington Beach, CA; Ms. Mercedes M. Bowen, San Jose, CA; Brillane K. Bowman, Burke, VA; Blythe Bowne, Columbia, MS; Mrs. James William Boyce, Atlanta, GA; Mrs. Mary C. Brand, Huntington Beach, CA; Mrs. Fred Braun, Grand Rapids, MI; Zudy Brier, San Leandro, CA; Parilee Brinkerhoff, Gainesville, FL; Izellah Bristow, Brea, CA; Brin Britton, Knoxville, TN; Delpha Brosseau, Milford, MI; Jordan Brown, Yellow Springs, OH; E. Bruggeman, Elmira, NY; Linita Brumfield, Jackson, MS; Mrs. Woodren Buchan, Apple Valley, CA; Reida Buehler, Las Vegas, NV; Zelpha N. Bulow, Hinsdale, IL; Agnes J. Bundy, Northmapton, MA; Leslie Burk, Napa, CA; Miss Bryn Burns, Buffalo, NY; Mrs. Lodemia H. Burroughs, Randolph, MA; Roanne Stradcutter Butier, Oakland, CA; Mrs. Mary Casquilho Cabral, Hanford, CA; Susan Alvera Capie, Santa Barbara, CA; Mrs. Vincent Caporizzo, Pittsburgh, PA; Arvelle Carey, Memphis, TN; Alfred Carney, Columbia, MS; Mr. John T. Carr, Ctr. Tuftonboro, NH;

Joanne Carson, Beaumont, TX; Roselyn Carter, San Bernardino, CA; Kirsti Cates, Minot, AFB, ND; Phila Wolcott Chackerian, Downey, CA; Alison Chaiken, Doylestown, PA; Janerette Chamberlain, Somerset, NJ; Onze Chapman, Burnsville, MN; Urilla M. Cheverie, North Reading, MA; Danice Chisholm, Plymouth, MI; Jereva Christensen, Ann Arbor, MI; Sharol Clark, Groveport, OH; Rebecca Codd, Los Angeles, CA; Cleta Cohen, Artesia, CA; Richanda Conley, Duncansville, PA; Mrs. James Connors, Redford, MI; Mrs. Versie B. Cook, Ashland, KY; Shirley Loris Pennington Cooper, Los Angeles, CA; Rolleen Cord, Wakefield, RI; Elena R. Corum, Henderson, KY; Merta Cota, Bend, OR; Mrs. E. Covey, Oakland, CA; Irene E. Craig, Temple City, CA; M. E. Crandall, Springville, UT; Mr. Hume Cronyn, New York, NY; Mrs. Gail Crook, Atlanta, GA; Betty Ann Crotts, Mountain City, TN; Mrs. Gene Cullum, Quinlan, TX; Mrs. Gerald D. Cullum, Marlow, OK; Miss Neigy P. Cupoli, Newton, MA; Mrs. Indi Carlana Curreri, Dover, NH; Toyah M. Dafft, Carrollton, TX; David & Donna Dame, Concord NH; Nancy Reece Darby, San Diego, CA; Jobyna Davis, San Gabriel, CA; Ruth Evanne DeAmicis, Bellefontaine, OH; Wilandra S. Dean, Little Rock, AR; D. Dusty Deane, New York, NY; Delores Deese, Phoenix City, AL; Renee Delahunty, Southington, CT; Mrs. Zathara Delaney, Lancaster, CA; Mrs. Louis Delcioppo, Syracuse, NY; Ms. Linda DeLia, Lansdowne, PA; Mrs. Sherran M. Denkler, Key West, FL; Stana Lee Dennis, Walla Walla, WA; Irene Derendal, Windsor, CT; Shona DeSilva, Oak Bluffs, MA; Lucinda Lee DeWeeese, Cincinnati, OH; Mrs. Paul T. Diehl, La Porte, TX; Anne Dietmeyer, Madison, WI; Mrs. Aldyne Dilling, Eureka, CA; Doreen Dinzes, Passaic, NJ; Mrs. C.R. Doering, El Cajon, CA; Miss Nira Lynnn Dolan, Livonia, MI; Anabeth Judy Placo Dollins, Pittsburgh, PA; Miss Eda Ann D'Onofrio, North Brunswick, NJ; Jocelyn Donway, Maple Valley, WA; Fortunata Dota, Holiday, FL; Mrs. G.L. Dowler, Escondido, CA; Mrs. Linnea Peterson Downen, San Diego, CA; Ms. Rhonda M. Draper, Martinsville, VA; Voncile Draper, Covina, CA; Mrs. Trula, M. Dresser, Santa Ana, CA; Z.H. Duffy, Vancouver, CA; Ginger Dunn, Buckeye, AZ; Crisann Dunnington, Connersvill, IN; Mrs. Ruth Dunfee, Guysville, OH; Mrs. Emmett Dunp, New Foundland, Canada; Oriente Tegla Dunskis, Vandergrift, PA; Norene Durham, Columbus, OH; Doretta Durnil, Knightstown, IN; Marlea M. Dutt, Webster, NY; Mrs. Lee Jo Dykstra, Pasadena, CA; Lynette Eads, Twain Harte, CA; Mrs. M. Eckenfelder, Westport, CT; Mary Edsall, So. Portland, ME; Nell Eleam, Longmont, CO; Mrs. Stephen Ellison, Poway, CA; Mrs. Harold G. Emrick, Indianapolis, IN; Mrs. Lera Nell England, Garland, TX; Martylu Estrada, Venice, CA; Sandra Simmons Evans, Corpus Christi, TX; Dr. Eulalia Fagan, Hollidaysburg, PA; Mrs. Nelda Faust, Pairborn, OH; Mrs. Elsena Felker, Princeton, KY; Jerriann Feola, Santa Ana, CA; Adele Fergus, Pope AFB, NC; Mrs. Linette J. Filipek, Tuba City, AZ; Vondra Lynne Day Finley, Stocton, CA; Mrs. Bronwyn M. Flanagan, Boulder Creek, CA; Waurene Flannigan, Batesville, MS; Lawrence R. Fleischer, Granada Hills, CA; Faylenea C. Flint, Miami, FL; Sister M. Trinita Flood, Miami Shores, FL; Marge Mason Ford, Newark, NJ; Romaine Forsythe, Jacksonville, FL; Carlia Itasta R. Foster, Opeleka, AL; Osma Foster, Hollywood, FL; Ottalie Foster, Lake Montezuma, AZ; Laureem Francksen, Salt Lake City, UT; Brailey Franco, Newhall, CA; Eviene C. Fulginti, Cupertino, CA; Vivian D. Fulk, Mt. Pleasant, MI; Carol Ann Furnish, Spokane, WA; Vena Garrett, New Port Beach, CA; Mrs. Albina H. Gautreau, Gardner, MA; Ronaele Kelly Gaynor, Philadelphia, PA; Sharlea S. Gilcrease, Pineville, GA; Gleanus Serepta Gilliam, Hendersonville, NC; Jeancie Ginn, Grass Valley, CA; Joslyn Ginn, Palm Beach Gardens, FL; Joella Ruth Giradin, Auburn, ME; Honorable Mills E. Godwin, Jr., Richmond, VA; Marlene M. Gogne, So. Hadley, MA; Mrs. George H. Goodale, San Leandro, CA; Mary Ann Goodburn, Powell River, BC; Mrs. Charles Goodenough, Honolulu, HI; Orion Smith Gosnell, Barnwell, SC; Mrs. Manetta Gould, El Segundo, CA; Tavi Granger, Marysville, CA; Melane Zoe Grayson, Culver City, CA; Mrs. Starlit D. Grazulis, Aliquippa, PA; Cezanne Greene, Ann Arbor, MI; Maretta M. Grego, Moore, MT; Mrs. R. B. Gruenenfelder, Woonsocket, RI; Dearaine J. Turner Gubbins, Burt, MI; Mrs. Jamese Ann Gucciardi, Detroit, MI; Fredannette Hackler, Carrollton, TX; Mrs. William H. Ham, Sr., Staunton, VA; Lisa Hammel, Brooklyn, NY; H. Idane Hanlyn, Seattle, WA; Kathryn Hanson, Chino, CA; Janice Harden, Decatur, GA; D. Harris, Sacramento, CA; Mrs. Jenale J. Harris, Glendale, CA; Rando Harris, Safford, AZ; Suella G. Hart, Roanoke, VA; Rivers Ann Hatchett, No. Jackson, OH; Ivana Hays, Norfolk, VA; Naida Hearn, Huntington Beach, CA; Mrs. Jinx Heaton, Carmel, IN; Pam Hefner, Catawala, NC; Mrs. R.W. Heidgerd, Wallingford, CT; Lucile Henegar, Nashville, TN;

VIII

Artemisa Ireta Hicks, Alburquerque, NM; Mrs. Meltha E. Higgins, Yale, MI; Mrs. A.L. Hight, Grand Haven, MI; Miss Norma E. Hill, Pacific House, CA; Nola Hinton, Matton, IL; Mrs. Julia Hise, Pleasanton, CA; Garniata Hiss, Tarzanna, CA; Mrs. Elaine M. Ho, Ewa Beach, HI; Michaela Holey, Milwaukee, WI; Mrs. Warren L. Holland, Sr., Portsmouth, VA; Mrs. Leo E. Hollenbeck, Brea, CA; Dellene E. Hornsby, Austin, TX; Mrs. O.K. Houck, Houston, TX; Mrs. Harold E. Hubbell, Denver, CO; Trudy A. Hugie, Fairbanks, NC; Look Kathleen Huland, Halliston, MA; Michona E. Hummel, Phoenix, AZ; Sudy Hurst, Tucson, AZ; Tauba Ingenthron, St. Louis, MO; Melvene Iverna, Glen St. Mary, FL; Mrs. A.K. Jackson, Durham, NC; Mrs. Evelyn Jackson, Houston, TX; Mrs. Joset Jackson, Jackson, MI; Merrita Jackson, Huntsville, AL; Z. Jeannette, Mission Viejo, CA; Mrs. John Stevens Jenkins, Wayne, IL; Mrs. Robert L. Jewett, Amhurst, NH; Richard Jochinsen, Lolo, MT; Mrs. Louis Joffe, Knoxville, TN; Wacil Johnson, Bainbridge Island, WA; Mrs. Jaredene Lee Johnston, Fullerton, CA; Nanella L. Jones, Little Rock, AR; Jalene Kalbaugh, Redding, CA; Bluma Jeri Kallio, MPLS, MN; Jetta E. Katowitz, New Port Richie, FL; Miss Nadie T. Kaufmann, Tustin, CA; Mrs. Pat Keenan, Connersville, IN; Kendai Kay Walker Kehrer, Louisville, KY; Ms. Aintre B. Keliner, St. Louis, MO; Bronwyn Anne Kelly, Export, PA; Jymie Kelly, Butler, PA; Mrs. Frances H. Kemp, Covina, CA; Carol Kennedy, Houston, TX; Poppy Kepford, New Canaan, CT; Gulnare Kergel, Woodland, CA; Stellise Kiek, Beverly, MA; Chester Kiekintveld, Jr., Scottsdale, AZ; Silver A. Kim, Pleasanton, CA; Hazelle Kimberlin, Santa Ana, CA; Mrs. Lora W. Kinch, Orlando, FL; Ruby N. King, Bladensburg, MD; Dorrit A. Kirk, Newport Beach, CA; Mrs. E.J. Klandrud, Evanston, IL; Mrs. Val Klindt, San Jose, CA; Angeles Knebel, S. Marina Del Rey, CA; Mr. & Mrs. James Loenigseker, Toledo, OH; Ms. L.L. Kositzke, Minneapolis, MN; Kaki Kozelek, Mexley, OH; Laura Krause, Independance, MO; Linda Krause, Mattawan, MI; Mary E. Krol, Southgate, MI; Donita Labas, Solon, OH; A.G. LaBush, Pittsburgh, PA; Kimet M. Laidlaw, Stratton Mt., VT; Miss Honey Lamb, Dallas, TX; Mrs. Eglah McGurie Lambert, La Mesa, CA; DeVee Lange, San Diego, CA; Mrs. Felta Lanpher, Newport, ME; Eugenia M. Lanzetta, Vineland, NJ; Mrs. Brilliant Laurie, Finleyville, PA; Mrs. Marcia Lawson, Huntington Beach, CA; Miss Marion L. Leary, Garden Grove, CA; Teresa May Le Brado, Newark, CA; Martha W. LeCroy, Finleyville, PA; Leabel C. Lees, San Diego, CA; Mrs. Cynthia Leffler, Ventura, CA; Ms. Betsy Legner, Columbus, OH; Ms. Lida Levine, Boston, MA; Mrs. Mardi Lewis, Pueblo, CO; Margene Libertino, Long Branch, NJ; Ms. Pia Lindstrom, New York, NY; Mrs. R.M. Lindvig, Potter Valley, CA; Mrs. Leilani Livermore, El Cajon, CA; Joneda Loftus, Kansas City, MO; Kristin Loney, Santa Ana, CA; Mrs. Lilo Lorentz, Brooklyn, NY; Kem Lowen, Phoenix, AZ; Sheri Lucterhand, Chicago, IL; Milah Faith Lynn, Santa Ana, CA; Mrs. Lois MacDonald, Taunton, MA; Anna Maria Maloy, Bakersfield, CA; Mrs. Rudolph L. Mappus III, Richardson, TX; Candy Martin, Mannington, WV; Lassie A. Martin, Clarksville, TN; Sharman Lee Key Martin, Lubbock, TX; Mrs. Henry Mastalerz, Cumberland, RI; Monte Mathews, New York, NY; Mrs. Roseltha Mathews, North Branch, MI; Liala Caroline Matthews, Oakmont, PA; Mrs. Norma Jean McBride, Pasadena, CA; Mrs. Iryl McClintock, Elizabeth, PA; Charel McCulley, Ogden, UT; Cyrilla McDowell, International Falls, MN; Jenny Lind Erickson McGaha, Brevard, NC; Vinetia McGreeary, Cadiz, OH; Mrs. Deborah K. McIntosh, Castro Valley, CA; Tyann McIntyre, Rensselaer, IN; Pauline McLaughlin, Matteson, IL; LaDean McMahan, Van Nuys, CA; Mrs. Peggie J. McNatl, Ashland, AL; Ms. Marise Meier, Seatecket, MA; Berneta Metcalf, Christiansburg, VA; Lauve Metcalfe, Tallahassee, FL; Mrs. Cheryle Meyncke, Windfall, IN; Sarayn Miceli, New York, NY; Mrs. G.L. Middleton, Holden, MA; Mrs. Christine Miller, Wellsburg, WV; Ms. Kaye-Rose Miller, Dallas, TX; Graylen Milligan, Webster, NY; Miss Cheryl Minor, Toledo, OH; Jean S. Mitchell, Susanville, CA; Mauraine Mitchell, Sodus, NY; Mrs. Varuma J. Mitchell, Marin, CA; Mrs. Carolyn Monck, Orangevale, CA; Kristie L. Montgomery, Pekin, IL; Jocqui Moone, Vacaville, CA; Steuer Moore, Brooklyn, NY; Alcina Morais, Pawtucket, RI; Mrs. Anemone Morgan, Edmond, OK; Mrs. Peter Mortzos, Saxonburg, PA; Mrs. Elaine F. Munck, Camarillo, CA; Mrs. Vida B. Musielak, Chicago, IL; Llda Jean Myers, Pitcarin, PA; Mrs. Linda L. Nance, San Antonio, TX; Kayo Boles Nash, Ladysmith, WI; David Nelson, San Rafael, CA; Ainslie Newton, Ruston, LA; Laris Nichols, Rockingham, NC; Julie Nowinski, Interlocken, RI; Dr. Dallin U. Oaks, Provo, UT; Michael Ann O'Neal, Santa Ana, CA; Gail O'Neil, Windsor, Ontario; G. Ortlieb, New Orleans, LA; Burma G. Orton, Tucson, AZ; Miss Anka Ostojic, Montreal, Quebec; Honorable Varner

L. Paddack, Hagerstown, MD; Mrs. A.C. Paintz, Canton, OH; Antonette Parish, Dallas, TX; Ms. Petra Park, Coldwater, MI; Sarah L. Parker, Cheasapeake, VA; Honorable Weldo Parkhill, Great Prairie, TX; Belva Parsons, Webster, NY; Mrs. Falba Patrick, Corpus Chrisit, TX; Honorable Caliborne Pell, Washington, DC; Mrs. Theryl Sensing Penney, Hillsboro, TX; Elissa Lewis Peries, Wilmington, NC; Mrs. Robin Petrillo, Everett, MA; Denette L. Pike, Springville, UT; Dorann Pohmurski, Warren, OH; Mrs. Ronald M. Pote, Franklin, IN; Shasta L. Powers, Murells Inlet, SC; Laurelen J. Pratts, Avon, New York; Mrs. R.H. Preston, Marshall, NC; Petite J. Proutsos, Sparks, NV; Donna M. Quagliano, North Bellmore, NY; Al Quaintance, Englewood, CO; Miss Yasmin L. Ratchliff, Norfolk, VA; Elsie Alcina Rathert, Long Beach, CA; Sister Joel Read, Milwaukee, WI; Jeff Ready, Columbia, MS; Mrs. Virginia M. Reagan, Naples, FL; Ronsy Reaner, Toronto, Ontario; Harvina Redd, Arcadia, IN; Trilby S. Redford, Richmond, VA; Lester Reecy, Dell Rapids, SD; Mrs. Patricia L. Reed, Cape May, NJ; Mrs. Bridget Ann Reston, Haverhill, MA; Mrs. P.E. Richardson, Magna, UT; Z. Richardson, Oceanside, CA; Mrs. Edward C. Richmond, Redwood City, CA; Mrs. Cheera L. Roadarmel, Warner Robins, GA; Mrs. Jeffrey D. Roberts, Longmeadow, MA; Ms. Prescovia Robinette, Alderson, WV; Mrs. L.L. Robinson, Quitman, LA; R. Rosenberg, Roslindale, MA; Jolea Noel Rucker, Huntington Beach, CA; Davalyn Ruggles, San Bernaidino, CA; Mrs. Floyd Rupert, Blanchard, PA; Lauren K. Ryon, Kentwood, MI; Frances Salorio, South Salem, NY; Aurie Salpen, Weiser, ID; Julinda G. Sanders, Shoals, IN; Sandra A. Sangiuliano, Louisville, KY; Penny Sanko, Walled Lake, MI; Santina Santoro, Heuief, CA; Arolyn Sargent, Concord, NH; Norella J. Scarborough, Virginia Beach, CA; Mrs. Marlene Schaefer, Santa Ana, CA; Marina Schindler, New Albany, IN; Debera Schlesinger, Wilmette, IL; Palmer A. Schneider, Evart, MI; Marva Achoen, Annapolis, MD; Markay Schroeder, Escondido, CA; Mrs. Verena Schubert, Hidden Hills, CA; Darlene Schnuff, Chicago, IL; Howard Schnuff, Chicago, IL; Mrs. Lena J. Seibert, Santa Ana, CA; Vila SeVall, Robbins, CA; Bobette Seymour, Bellevue, OH; Mrs. Karen Shannon, Pacifica, CA; Mrs. Cassandra M. Herod, Honolulu, Hawaii; Mrs. Candance K. Shoppell, Carmel, IN; Roanne Shriver, New York, NY; Mrs. Jean Shroyer, No. Attleboro, MA; Earla Silva, Long Beach, CA; Sharon Simcak, Cypress, TX; Darla Simmons, El Salvador, C.A.; Penn Simpkins, Fremont, OH; Mrs. Loqueta Sinclair, Norwalk, CA; Mrs. John Skinner, New Bedford, MA; LaJuan Slaton, Idalou, TX; Penelope J. Dunn Smalley, Rawlins, WY; Jennelle Smart, Versailles, KY; Moniece Charlton Smiley, Sunnyvale, CA; Dorma Smith, Three Rivers, MI; Mrs. Gaylord Smith, Sioux City, IA; Gussie Smith, So. San Francisco, CA; Mrs. Lynda E. Smith, Lewisburg, PA; Kacy Soper, Dearborn, MI; Mrs. Robert Sorensen, Vallejo, CA; Onetha South, Arlington, VA; Demelda Southard, Ventura, CA; Jorel Stallones, Woodside, CA; Mardell W. Stansberry, Los Angeles, CA; Wilenda Staselavag, Spartanburg, SC; Manila D. Stead, Santa Cruz, CA; Miss Norma Steinbeck, Newport, KY; Mrs. Alsace Lorraine Stewart, Conroe, TX; Mrs. Jan Stewart, Amherst, OH; Elizabeth Stikis, Weenhawken, NJ; Mrs. T.W. Stoner, Hilo, Hawaii; Carol Strauss, Corona Del Mar, CA; Barb Stroupe, Lynchburg, VA; Lasca Lynne Stucki, Holyoke, MA; Ms. Judith E. Sturgill, Lima, OH; Fleur H. Sullivan, Augusta, GA; Karloun Summers, Chicago, IL; Zella Sutton, Elizabethtown, KY; Dreane Swanson, New London, CT; Reba Swicegood, Rockwood, TN; Arue Szura, Castro Valley, CA; Devlynn L. Tanner, Xenia, OH; Pama Tavernier, San Diego, CA; Mrs. Maralou Taylor, Littleton, CO; Ms. Caryn Tens, West Patterson, NJ; Lilybeth K. Teske, Bay Village, OH; Jerry & Lynnea Terrill, Deadwood, SD; Thana, San Diego, CA; Mrs. Harva George Thomas, Kodak, TN; Zoe Oma Thompson, Amarillo, TX; Mrs. Thyra Thomson, Cheyenne, WY; Mrs. Ruth Tobler, Pleasant Hill, CA; Tamara Sue Tomkinson, Ventura, CA; Albina Tomsha, LaSalle, IL; Jenise S. Trammell, Woodstock, CA; Philena Trompeter, Lakeside, CA; Ja Donne Tulla, Ft. Worth, TX; Mrs. Patricia Lois Turcotte, Bar Harbor, ME; Hollis M. Turnage, Columbia, MS; Jean Tutt, Southampton, NY; Miss Allison Tyler, Memphis, TN; Mrs. Dicie M. Utsey, Red Level, AL; Mrs. Herbert Valentine, Newton, MS; Miss Edlyn Vancina, Los Angeles, CA; Mrs. M. Van Ostrand, Kailua, Hawaii, Tuanette Van Winkle, Billings, MT; Ms. Gail S. Vare, Middletown, CT; Wendi Varsoke, Dover, DE; Mrs. G.L. Verplank, Boulder, CO; Lucia Vidal, Stamford, CT; Dora Villarreal, Watsonville, CA; T.M. Wade, Phoenix, AZ; Sherrie-Dee Schubert Wagner, Methuen, MA; Mrs. Patia Waggoner, Indianapolis, IN; Callis E. Walker, Glendale, CA; Ila Walker, Farrell, PA; Petie Walters, Winston-Salem, NC; Laudonna Watkins, Lancaster, OH; Novenda

Watkins, Newark, OH; E. Wasileski, Bridgeville, PA; Thelma Weatherly, Warsaw, NC; Miss Neeta Webb, Mount Airy, NC; Mrs. Huela Winifred Webber, Phoenix, AZ; Rolene Wehr, Waterloo, IA; Richard D. Weigel, Bowling Green, KY; Mrs. Orma Weil, Dallas, TX; Ms. Dahtee Maree West, Boston, MA; Junez Whitehill, Morro Bay, CA; Mrs. Daomi Williams, Coats, NC; Mrs. Frances J. Williams, Santa Rosa, CA; S. Salene Williams, Pittsburgh, PA; Twila Williams, Lincoln, NE; Linda Lee Wiley, Arlington, TX; Mrs. Ronna Wilson, Garden Grove, CA; Sheila Marie Witkowski, Fairport, NY; Nyla J. Witmore, Acton, MA; Lurchel Fontenst Wittler, Lake Charles, LA; Mrs. Janey S. Wolfe, Savannah, TN; Rowan Wolnick, Van N; Noelle Wolter, Penfield, NY; Pennoky E. Wood, Columbus, OH; Susan Wood, Hampton Bays, NY; Kimberley Worthington, Chattanooga, TN; Kate Sadler Wright, Lakewood, NJ; Naia Dawn Wright, Lincolnton, NC; Mrs. Cuba Fay Yetman, Houston, TX; Mrs. Steven P. Young, San Diego, CA; Carnei Zaccaro, Reseda, CA; Merla Zellerbach, San Francisco, CA;

Introduction

I

Origins of the English Language

Sir William Jones, an Englishman, and Rasmus Rask, a Dane, working independently, came to the same conclusion: most European languages are derived from one source—the family of languages known as Indo-European. The primary groups within this family—those that have had the greatest influence on English—are Greek, Celtic, Italic, and Germanic.

Except for Greek, each has produced many sub-languages. From the Celtic have emerged principally Welsh, Gaelic, and the now obsolete Manx. From the Italic group has emerged Latin, which in turn has fathered Italian, French, Spanish, Portuguese, and Romanian. And the Germanic group has given us various forms of High and Low German, from which are derived Dutch, Flemish, and Yiddish. English itself is considered a member of the Low Germanic group.

The Slavic languages, which are also part of the family of Indo-European languages, and which include Russian, Polish, and Czech, have not had much influence on the English language and our nomenclature.

Another family of languages, totally unrelated to Indo-European, is known as the Afro-Asiatic family. The most prominent group in this family is the Semitic group, which includes Akkadian, Phoenician, Aramaic, Ethiopic, Arabic, and Hebrew.

As we aim to define and etymologize the names presented in this *Dictionary of First Names*, it is important to note that except for Hebrew, and to a lesser extent Arabic, the languages of the Afro-Asiatic group have had practically no influence on the development of the English language and English nomenclature.

Attempts have often been made to connect Hebrew root names, etymologically, to Greek, Celtic, Italic, or Germanic root names, but such suggestions are invalid because all names of Hebrew origin have a source totally independent of Indo-European names. Some of the most prestigious authors in the field of nomenclature have attempted, from time to time, to make such connections, but they have no scholarly basis.

Sophy Moody, in her *What Is Your Name?* (1863), does this with the name Theresa. She tries to associate this name, which is clearly of Greek derivation meaning "to reap" with the Hebrew name Tirzah, meaning "to be willing." Even the knowledgeable Charlotte M. Yonge, perhaps the greatest authority in the field, whose book *History of Christian Names* has been the bible of nomenclature for almost 100 years, was so tempted occasionally. She suggested, for example, that a name such as Emily, from a Latin root meaning "industrious," may be associated with the Hebrew root *amal*, meaning "work." True, there is a closeness in sound and meaning, but it is hardly likely that Emily, which is an Indo-European Latin name, can be related to a name with roots in an Afro-Asiatic language.

Although this dictionary is concerned only with names and their meanings, a bit more should be said about the history and influence of the languages from which our names have been derived. It is valuable to be able to place the various languages in the proper time frame.

West Germanic, as we have pointed out, is the basic language upon which English has been built. The Scandinavian languages and Dutch, being closely linked to German, have had their influence on the development of the English language. And, finally, at one point, the Italic languages, principally Latin and French, have made their influence felt. All of these languages, and more, have played a role in what has emerged as present-day English language.

The following chronology should be helpful in tracing these various influences:

The Celtic Influence

The Celts were a tribal people living in various parts of Europe, primarily in what is today southeastern Germany. They spoke many dialects but had one language in common. The Celts invaded England about the year 1000 B.C., and many of the invaders settled there. Their influence was strong. In 55 B.C. the Celts living in continental Europe were attacked by Julius Caesar's Roman legions; many Celts were killed while many fled to England. Large numbers of these Celts settled in England in various localities, carrying with them their various Celtic dialects. One group, which spoke Gaelic, was the forerunner of the groups known as the Irish, the Manx, and the Highland Scots. A second group consisting of the Welsh, the Cornish, and the Bretons spoke Brythonic. A third group consisted of the Gauls. Cornish, Manx, and Gaulish are now obsolete languages.

The Welsh word *mor* (from which the name Morgan comes), means "sea." It is cognate with the Latin *mare,* the Gothic *marei,* the Germanic *meer,* and the Spanish *mar.*

The Roman Influence

About 43 A.D. the Romans, under Emperor Claudius, invaded the British Isles and placed the Celts under Roman rule. This accounts for the strong influence of Latin on the English language.

From this point on Celt influence began to diminish. Their language gradually disappeared, and today no more than 50 or 60 Celtic words are part of the English language.

The Romans remained in Britain until the year 410, when troops were pulled back to Italy to defend the country.

The Anglo-Saxon Period

The year 410 marks the beginning of the British period, or the Anglo-Saxon period. The Roman conquerors had left Britain after almost 400 years of occupation. During these four centuries the Latin influence had made itself felt on the development of the English language. During this period, and for the next 600 years, the language spoken in England was called Old English. Consequently, the terms Old English and Anglo-Saxon are used interchangeably.

Old English, or Anglo-Saxon, is basically a Germanic language. The Anglo-Saxons were a European Germanic people who, over a period of 100 years (from 450 to 550 A.D.), conquered England and settled there. They consisted of three primary tribes: the Angles, the Saxons, and the Jutes. The dominant tribe was the Angles, from which England got its name. England means "the land of the Angles." The Anglo-Saxon word for English is *englisc*.

Anglo-Saxon was not a very prestigious language at the outset. It was an earthy language. The more commonplace, vulgar words in the English language are of Anglo-Saxon origin.

The Nordic Influence

By the ninth century the Anglo-Saxons of Britain had become united and powerful under the leadership of Alfred the Great (849-899), king of the West Saxons. An able general, he saved England from being conquered by the Danes. Wars between the Danes and the English continued for many years, however, and by 1017 the Danes were victorious and King Canute of Denmark and Norway ruled England. The Danish presence in England added a Nordic influence to the English language. But King Canute's rule did not last long.

The Norman-French Period

In 1066 William, Duke of Normandy, invaded England with his Norman-French army and made serfs of the Anglo-Saxons. This is referred to as the Norse Invasion, as a result of which the Germanic influence was brought to bear on English, which contained strong French and Scandinavian elements.

The Norman-French ruled England for 300 years. French was used by the upper classes, the courts of law, and in the school systems until the fourteenth century. Anglo-Saxon (Old English) continued as the spoken language of the masses during this period of French influence.

The Middle English Period

Between the twelfth century and the sixteenth century English began to emerge as a literary language once again. Having absorbed a great many French words, there was a need for the natives of England to express their cultural independence. In the period that followed, therefore, the English people gradually turned to sources other than French for enrichment.

The Modern English Period

A period of tremendous growth in the English language began with the sixteenth century. During this century and those that followed, a great many Greek, Latin, and Italian words were added to the language. The English-speaking people also borrowed words from many other sources, such as *moccasin* and *wigwam* from the North American Indians, *canoe* and *hurricane* from the people of the West Indies, *chocolate* and *tomato* from the people of Mexico, and *boomerang* and *kangaroo* from the Australians. Such types of accretion to the English language will be found in the newer nomenclature.

LANGUAGES REFERRED TO

Aside from the familiar languages (Hebrew, Greek, Latin, French, Dutch, etc.) referred to in the text of this dictionary, the following lesser-known languages are often mentioned as the source of names:

Anglo-Saxon is the Germanic language that was used by the three Teutonic tribal groups living in England before the Norman Conquest (1066): the Angles, the Saxons, and the Jutes. It is used synonymously with Old English.

British is the language that was used by the ancient Britons beginning about 400 A.D. It includes many of the Celtic languages.

Celtic refers to a family of languages used in the British Isles dating back to 1000 B.C. It includes Erse, Scottish, Gaelic, Irish Manx, Breton, Cornish, Scottish, and Welsh.

Danish is the Germanic language spoken in Denmark.

Erse is synonymous with Irish Gaelic.

Gaelic is a subbranch of the Celtic family of languages.

Irish Gaelic is the Celtic language of Ireland.

High German consists of the upland (southern) German dialects. Standard German arose in the south and is, therefore, basically High German.

Low German consists of lowland (northern) German dialects.

Middle Latin is the form of Latin used in Europe from about 700 to 1500 A.D. It is also called Medieval Latin.

Middle Low German, the language that succeeded Old Low German, was used in the northwestern European lowlands (the Rhine and Elbe areas) from the twelfth to the fifteenth century.

Middle High German succeeded Old High German. It was used in the highlands of south and central Germany from the twelfth to the sixteenth century.

Middle Irish, which succeeded Old Irish, was used in Ireland from the twelfth to the fifteenth century.

Old English is the Germanic language (or dialect) of the Anglo-Saxons spoken in England from the fifth to eleventh century. It is used synonymously with Anglo-Saxon.

Old French is the language used in France from the ninth to sixteenth century, after which modern French emerged.

Old High German was the language spoken in southern Germany from the eighth to twelfth century. It is the basis of Middle High German.

Old Italian is the language of Italy as recorded from the tenth century A.D. onward.

Old Irish designates the Gaelic and Celtic languages as used in Ireland from the eighth to the twelfth century.

Old Latin was used in written and spoken form from the sixth to the first century B.C.

Old Low German is the language that was used in the northern part of Germany and in the Netherlands from the eighth to the twelfth century.

Old Norse is the language that was used in Denmark, Iceland, and Norway from the eighth to the fourteenth century.

Scotch Gaelic is the Celtic language of Scotland.

Scottish, a variant form of Scotch, is the dialect of the English language used in Scotland.

Slavic is a subbranch of the Indo-European family of languages and includes Polish, Czech, Slovak, Serbo-Croation, Slovenian, Bulgarian, Russian, and Ukranian.

Slavonic is used synonymously with the word Slavic.

Yiddish is a dialect of High German with a mixture of Hebrew, Russian, and Polish, plus words from other East European languages.

II

Where Do Our Names Come From?

Old Testament Names

The earliest personal names on record are found in the Bible. Many are still in use in their original form. For the most part, biblical names are easy to understand because their roots are easily traced, usually to the Hebrew; in fact, many are explained in the Bible itself.

The Hebrew root of the name Cain, for example, is *kanoh*, meaning "to acquire, to buy." The verse in Genesis (4:1) explains it: "And she [Eve] conceived and bore Cain, and said, "I have *acquired* a man [Cain] with the help of the Lord."

Adam and Eve's third son was named Seth. In Genesis (4:25), Eve says, "For God has given me another seed [child] instead of Abel; for Cain slew him." The name of this child, Seth [Shes], in Hebrew, has the meaning "to give, to put, to appoint."

Abraham and Sarah named their son Isaac. Abraham was 100 years old at the time, and when Sarah was told she was to bear a child, she said, "Everyone who hears about it will *laugh*." The Hebrew root of the name Isaac, *tzachok*, means "laughter."

Jacob and Leah were excited over the birth of their first son, so they named him Reuben. The Hebrew form of Reuben is *re'u ben*, meaning "Behold, a son!"

Scores of such examples can be found in the pages of the Bible. Clearly, names given to offspring were usually derived directly from the personal lives and experiences of parents.

Old Testament names can be broken down into the following categories:

1. Names describing a characteristic of the person or a peculiarity of the body. For example, Laban means "white"; Korah means "bald"; Harim means "flat-nosed."

2. Names inspired by experiences in the life of the parents or newborn child. For example, Moses was so named by Pharaoh's daughter because she "*drew* him out of the water" (Exodus 2:10). Eve was so named "because she was the mother of all *living* beings" (Genesis 3:20).

3. Names of animals. For example, the name Deborah literally means "a bee"; Jonah means "a dove"; Hulda means "a weasel." These names may have been adopted because the child's appearance resembled the animal, or perhaps the parents loved the animal, or the child may have been born in a locality where the animal was common.

4. Names of plants and flowers. For example, the name Susan means "rose"; Tamar means "palm." We can speculate that in biblical times parents named their children after plants and flowers for reasons similar to those used for choosing animal names.

5. Theophoric names, in which part of the name is the name of God used as a prefix or suffix. Jehoiakim, for example, means "God will establish." Isaiah means "salvation of the Lord."

6. Names which express hope for the future or for a desired condition. For example, Joseph means "to add" or "increase." When the biblical Joseph was born, his mother Rachel said, "May the Lord *add* to me another son" (Genesis 30:24).

Christian Names

Christians of the first centuries used Old Testament Hebrew names. In time, however, these were abandoned by many New Testament figures as a form of protest against Judaism. Thus, the man once known as Simon bar Jonah came to be called Peter, and Saul of Tarsus became known as Paul.

During those early centuries many Christian parents followed the pattern of choosing names associated with mythology and idolatry, even though they abhorred both. Phoebe, Olympius, and Jovianus were commonly used. The seventh-century Bishop of Seville was outraged by the use of these names. In his *Etymologiae* he wrote of the significance of biblical names, urging Christians to use them, but to no avail.

The Reformation

Not until the Reformation, in the 1500s, when as a rebellion against the Catholic church and its authority Protestantism came into being, did biblical names—particularly Old Testament names—again become popular. In seventeenth-century Puritan England, where the Reformation turned into a crusade against all church dogma and ceremonials, New Testament names in particular were renounced in favor of Old Testament names.

Many Puritan extremists, even those living as late as the eighteenth and nineteenth centuries, went so far as to use the most obscure and odd-sounding names they could find; they even took phrases from Scripture and used them—in their entirety—as names. Ernest Weekley, in his book *Jack and Jill*, reports that at the beginning of the twentieth century there was a family with the names Asenath Zaphnath Paaneah, Kezia Jemima Keren Happukh, and Maher Shalal Hashbaz.

Additional strange appellations used by Puritans include Free-gift, Reformation, Earth, Dust, Ashes, Delivery, Morefruit, Tribulation, The Lord is Near, More Trial, Discipline, and Joy Again. One Puritan parent names his child If-Christ-had-not-died-for-you-you-had-been-damned-barebones, but his acquaintances, becoming weary of its length, retained only the last part, Damned-Barebones. The average Puritan, however, was satisfied with Old Testament names as well as those derived from abstract virtues, such as Perseverance, Faith, Hope,

Humility, Charity, and Repentance. A pair of twin girls born to the English Wycliffe family in 1710 were named Favour and Fortune.

Opposition to New Testament Names

The Quakers (Society of Friends), like the Puritans, preferred Old Testament names and despised the nomenclature of the New Testament, probably as part of their protest against the Church of England, with whom they broke in 1648. The Quakers disapproved of the elaborate ceremonies of the established church.

The life of John Bunyan (1628-1688), author of *Pilgrim's Progress*, epitomizes the conflict between the Quakers and Puritans and their opponents. In his early years Bunyan was an antagonist of the Quakers. For this reason he named his children Mary, John, Thomas, and Elizabeth—all but the last being New Testament names. By the time of Bunyan's second marriage his philosophy had changed. No longer an opponent of the Quakers, he had become intensely opposed to the established church and its bishops. His children by his second wife were named Joseph and Sara, after the Old Testament figures.

Names From Places

Many first names, like surnames, have been borrowed from the names of places. The Bible, of course, has many such examples.

Efrat is the place where Rachel died and was buried; Efrata is the name of Caleb's wife in the Book of Chronicles. Beer Sheba, a local name in the Book of Genesis, later became a masculine and feminine first name. Afra, the name of a city in the Book of Joshua, is also a masculine first name. Ur, a place-name in the Book of Genesis, is a masculine first name that appears in the Book of Chronicles.

Other first names that have their origin in place-names are Sharon, Carmel, Carmela, Shomrona, and Yeshurun.

In more recent times we find Judge Kenesaw Mountain Landis (1866-1944), the brother of evangelist Fred Landis, an excellent example of a name drawn from a place. Kenesaw Landis, whose father was a medical officer, was the first of his family born after the Civil War. His father was wounded while performing an amputation during the Battle of Kenesaw Mountain; he named his son after that mountain.

Myrna Loy, the actress, was named after the whistle-stop Myrna, a name her father found intriguing. Portland Hoffa, the radio comedienne and wife of Fred Allen, was named after Portland, Oregon. Florida Edwards is the name of a radio actress. Actress Tallulah Bankhead was named after her grandmother, who in turn was named after Tallulah Falls, Georgia. Philadelphia Levy was the daughter of a Philadelphia family prominent at the end of the eighteenth century.

Although throughout history places have been named by early settlers or by explorers who first discovered them, many first names have come from places already named. Here are a few examples which have been submitted by our correspondents:

● *Mrs. O.K. Hauck, Houston, Texas*: "My great-grandfather named his daughters after states he had visited: Ohio, Virginia, Nebraska, Indiana."

● *Kimberley Worthington, Chattanooga, Tennessee*: "In 1949 my mother was visiting her father in Cape Town, South Africa, and was taken on a tour of the great Kimberley Diamond Mine. She was impressed with the name and promised herself that she would name her daughter Kimberley."

● *Michona E. Hummel, Phoenix, Arizona*: "Trying to think of an original name, my father came upon the idea of combining the first part of Michigan (where he and my mother originally came from) and the last part of Arizona (where I was born), and named me Michona."

● *Manila Dewey Stead, Santa Cruz, California*: "I was born on May 5, 1898, five days after Admiral Dewey captured Manila Bay, and was named Manila Dewey."

● *Marne Caparizzo, Pittsburgh, Pennsylvania*: "When I was born, the headlines in newspapers were all about the famous World War I Battle of the Marne, when the Germans were pushed back. My father liked Marne for a name and decided that was to be my name."

● *Alsace Lorraine Stewart, Conroe, Texas*: "My daddy—now nearing 90 years of age—was a foot soldier during World War I. In 1917, while in Germany in Alsace Lorraine, he became ill from the effects of mustard gas. He recovered and was grateful! I was born on June 14, 1921, and my mother and daddy named me Alsace Lorraine."

Nature Names

Nature has always been a prime source for our nomenclature. The Bible abounds in such names, as does the mythology of all early peoples. The practice continues to this day. Here are some samples submitted by our correspondents:

● *Silver A. Kim, Pleasanton, California*: "My Mom told me she often watched the leaves as the wind blew the leaves on a Silver Maple tree that she had planted in our backyard. She said they looked so beautiful blowing in the wind that she would name her next daughter Silver."

● *Sunny Jean Bond, Red Bluff, California*: "My name is Sunny Jean (married name Bond). My first name came about because my mother said to Sister Superior at the hospital, 'no matter whether a boy or a girl, the first name will be Sunny because for the first time in days the sun was shining.'"

● *Terry and Lynnea Terril, Deadwood, South Dakota*: "Our first daughter was named The Sunshine for leaving delicate light in our lives. Our second daughter was named Season Music so she shall have music wherever she goes."

● *Starlit Grazulis, Aliquippa, Pennsylvania*: "On the eve of my birth my mother and father took a walk and Dad commented on the starlit sky. At that precise moment a star fell brightly to earth, and Dad felt this was an indication I should be named Starlit."

● *Yvonne Abner, Blanchester, Ohio*: "My sister's name is Starla Doreen Coogan. She was named Doreen after one of the Musketeers and Starla for the Christmas star because she was born in Texas, the Lone Star State, on Christmas Day."

● *Karen Shannon, Pacifica, California*: "[My daughter] Dandylyon Rosebud Shannon was conceived in a large field of dandelions in a small town in New Mexico. It seemed only proper and fitting to name her after the flower she bloomed from."

Calendar Names

In the course of history we find that a great many of the days of the week, months of the year, and holidays have constituted a source of first names as well as surnames. Monday (spelled Munday), Tuesday (Dienstag, in German), and Saturday were commonly used as names. Friday, the famous character in *Robinson Crusoe*, is well known to all.

Although many of the months of the year have been used as surnames, they have been used to a greater extent as first names. Augustus (August) and Julia (July) were especially common in Roman days. May and June are very popular forenames today. April, a name given by actress June Havoc to her daughter, is also occasionally encountered. Howard Fast, in his book *Patrick Henry and the Frigate's Keel*, records the name of January Fernandez, a Portuguese who participated in the breaking of the British blockade in 1812.

From the Hebrew calendar the months of Nisan, Awv (Ab), and Adar have been appropriated for use as first names. Sabbatai (Sabbath) and Pesach (Passover) are popular Hebrew names to this day.

Among the Christian holidays, Easter and Christmas have long served as sources for forenames. Pentecostes was the name of a servant of Henry VIII. Easter is commonly used and can be found as a character in Lillian Smith's novel *Strange Fruit*, and Christ and Christmas are the backbone of names such as Chris, Christopher, Christine, and Noel.

One of our correspondents, Jinx Heaton of Carmel, Indiana, writes: "I was born on Friday the 13th of December, 1946 and have been called Jinx ever since."

Numeral Names

Numbers are another source for names that were used a great deal in the past and in some rare instances today. The Romans were the first to take numeral names. Among the more common are Quintus (5), Octavius (8), and Septimus (7). Among recent Tripolitan Jews in North Africa, Hmessa and Hammus, meaning five, are used as feminine and masculine personal names respectively. There was recently a family in

Michigan by the surname Stickaway that named their three boys One, Two, and Three; and their three girls, First, Second, and Third.

One of the rare present-day examples of a number being used as a personal name made its appearance recently in the case of a young rabbi who, having difficulty finding a satisfactory Hebrew name for his first daughter, decided to name her Reeshonaw (first).

It is interesting to note that the Puritans, and especially the Quakers, refrained from using the names of months and substituted numbers in their place. They believed that since most months had names of pagan origin, it would be best to avoid using them as personal names. For this reason we find, as we study some of the official records and tombstone engravings of the seventeenth century, that months are referred to by number rather than name—January referred to as 1, February as 2, etc.

One of our correspondents, Joyce Pagan of Gilroy, California, writes: "My mother was to be named Mabel, but a friend of her parents offered to buy her first pair of shoes if they would name her Nina (for "nine"). The reason: she was born on the nineteenth day of the ninth month of the year nineteen nineteen at nine A.M."

Occupational Names

Many occupational names have become first names, although the vast majority have come down to us as last names. Most fall into the category of the name Wright, which is an Old English name meaning "an artisan, a worker." It is used occasionally as a first name (e.g., Wright Morris, author), but for the most part it has remained a surname (e.g., the Wright brothers, Orville and Wilbur).

Middle English names were often occupational names. Bannister, meaning "one who draws a crossbow," and Brewster, meaning "one who brews beer," are used from time to time. Newly created names are rarely based on occupation.

Personal Preferences

A large group of names has come into being for no reason other than a mother-or father-to-be took a liking to a certain sound or was overcome by a sudden inspiration. In some cases the name was selected as a lark.

Bill Lear, a radio executive in the 1940s, named his daughter Chrystal Chanda Lear (chandelier).

Charles Fisher, in his book *The Columnist*, reports that Walter Winchell's wife wanted to call their child Reid (read) Winchell if it were a boy, while he preferred Sue Winchell in the event the offspring were a girl. Ben Bernie, who at the time was carrying on a prearranged feud with Winchell, suggested the name Lynch Winchell. In the end the boy was named Walter, Jr., but Winchell's daughter, who was born some nine years earlier, was named Walda, and was undoubtedly so named becuase it sounded very much like Walter.

Broadway publicist Spencer Hare was in a jesting mood, it would seem, when he named his daughter Hedda Hare. Recent reports tell that if he should have another daughter he would call her Lotta Hare and if a boy, Noah Hare. However, Surjit Singh, an accountant for Punjab State Electricity Board was quite serious when he named his son Skylab. Skylab Singh was born in northern India, in 1979, just a few hours after the outerspace vehicle fell to earth nearby.

Here are a few examples submitted by our correspondents:

● *Verena Shubert, Hidden Hills, California*: "My name is Verena. My mother was also named Verena. Her mother took the F off of Ferena cereal and put a V in the place of F."

● *Moniece Charlton Smiley, Sunnyvale, California*: "My parents created the name. They liked the sound of the name Denise, but since they wanted all of us to have names that began with the letter M, I was named Moniece."

● *Candy Martin, Mannington, West Virginia*: "A good friend of mine is a teacher. She has two new students this year, one named Rusty Irons and the other Penny Coin."

● *Mary Blaisdell, Auburn, Washington*: "My grandfather's name is Darius Othniel Blaisdell. Both are Bible names. His mother just opened the Bible, found Darius, turned a few pages and found Othniel."

● *Ivana Griffin Hays, Norfolk, Virginia*: "While reading a newspaper, my mother noticed a photograph of a beautiful Italian woman named Ivana who, along with her dog, was a stowaway on an American ship. Thus I got my name, Ivana Ellis (my father's name is Elison)."

● *Jeanice Ginn, Grass Valley, California*: "My name is Jeanice Ginn, and Janice Ginn is my identical twin sister. The day we were born my older sister, Suzanne, who was eight years old, went to school and told her teacher that her mom had twins but were not yet named. So, for a class project they decided to select names for us. Each pupil thought of two names, and then the class voted for the best set. My sister came home with Janice and Jeanice, and my parents liked them."

● *Marina Kay Lomax Schindler, New Albany, Indiana*: "My father was a brave man who believed in fighting for his country. He joined the Marine Corps. Mother decided to name me after something my father believed in strongly. So, my name is Marina, after the U.S. Marine Corps."

● *Mrs. Jenise S. Trummel, Woodstock, Georgia*: "My mother had a dream of giving birth to a daughter with the name Jenise. She had never heard of this name before. A few months later I was named Jenise Ann Simms."

● *Alison Chaiken, Doylestown, Pennsylvania*: "My friend Verdi Logan has an unusual first name. Before her birth, her mother was approached by a woman who said that all the females in her family were named Verdi, but she was the last of the line and had no relatives to carry on the name. She asked Mrs. Logan to name her child Verdi if it were to be a girl. Verdi's mother agreed."

- *Adele Fergus, Pope Air Force Base, North Carolina*: "My friend named their newborn Daien, because it sounded good with their last name Knight—Daien Knight. Her sisters are named Windy Knight and Gay Knight."

- *Mrs. Charles Lamb, Dallas, Texas*: "Since I had named our three boys, my husband took the pleasure of naming our fourth child. He said, 'After giving me three fine sons, this girl can't help but be a honey.' Her name is Honey Lamb."

- *Penelope J. Dunn Smalley, Rawlings, Wyoming*: "My sister's name is Nardi Ann Dunn Ferge. Our father, who is a big sports car buff, named her after a little-known Italian sports car, the Nardi (an Italian surname).

- *Jacqui Moore, Vacaville, California*: "In 1968 a television commercial for an aftershave lotion mentioned the name Joelle. That was it. We named our daughter Joelle, and Joey is her nickname. A few years later I discovered when visiting my hometown that one of my friends gave her daughter the same name. She had seen the same commercial!"

- *Nilda M. Faust, Fairborn, Ohio*: "Just before I was born, my mother read a short story, and the name of the heroine was Nilda. The character was a very sweet, lovable person, and she hoped her daughter would be like that fictitious person. So, she gave me that name."

- *Rilla-Luretta Peck Hight, Grand Haven, Michigan*: "They named me Rilla after a friend. My father had been to the horse races, and when he came home he said a horse had the name Luretta and they added Luretta to my name."

Hybrid and Scrambled Names

A considerable number of new names are newly-coined names created by parents or grandparents who want to preserve part of an old name. They, therefore, scramble the letters of a name to create a new one, or they join parts of two or more names to accomplish the same purpose. We include in this category of newly-coined names acronyms, which are formed by combining the first letters of several words or names.

In Greek and Roman times it was quite common for a new name to make an appearance by the use of this simple "scrambling" procedure. Nathaniel and Elnathan consist of the same syllables and have the same meaning. Theodora and Dorothea, likewise, are the same name with their syllables rearranged.

In the Middle Ages the names of outstanding personalities, in particular, were telescoped by combining the first letters of title and name.

Thus, Rabbi Moses ben Maimon became R(A)MB(A)M and Rabbi David Kimchi became R(A)D(A)K.

During World War II America looked forward anxiously to the day of victory. The day of victory in Europe was designated as V-E day. One soldier combined the letters "V" for Victory, "E" for England, "R" for Russia, and "A" for America and named his daughter Vera.

Our correspondents have shared with us a large sampling of such name creations:

● *Pia Lindstrom*, the television newscaster and daughter of Dr. Peter Aron Lindstrom and actress Ingrid Berman, advises us that her name is a combination of *P*eter, *I*ngrid, and *A*ron.

● *Graylen Milligan, Webster, New York*: "When my parents adopted me, they wanted me to be uniquely theirs, to always feel part of them. They decided to do this by giving me a name derived from theirs. My father was Graydon and my mother Helen. I was named Graylen."

● *Marles Burrell, Dyer, Indiana*: "My name is Marles. It is made from my mother's name, Margaret, and my father's name, Leslie."

● *Kathy Blagrone, Maybrook, New York*: "My daughter, Kaela Janelle, was named for four people: KAthy (mother), LArry (father), JANet (a friend), ELLa (grandmother). The "e" was added to the first and the middle name."

● *Sister Joel Read, Milwaukee, Wisconsin*: "My father's name was Joseph and my mother's name was Ellen. The first two letters of both names were joined and I was named Joel."

● *Pennoky Wood, Columbus, Ohio*: "My father wanted an unusual name. He had worked for the Pennsylvania, Ohio, and Kentucky Railroad. And so he named me Pennoky: Penn for Pennsylvania, O for Ohio, and KY for Kentucky."

● *Nira Lynn Dolan, Livonia, Michigan*: "My name, Nira, is an acronym my grandmother made up from the National Industrial Recovery Act."

● *Reja Elise B., Gulfport, Mississippi*: "My father has four brothers: Ronnie, Elbert, John, and Alan. He took the first letter of their names, put them together, and named me Reja."

● *Reida Buehler, Las Vegas, Nevada*: "My first name, Reida, is my father's name, Reid, plus the "a" of Anna, my mother's name.

● *Judith E. Sturgill, Lima, Ohio*: "My daughter's name is Tanim. She gets her name from her great-grandmother, whose name is Minta. We wanted to give her a meaningful name, so we scrambled the five letters in Minta, which resulted in the unusual name Tanim.

● *Ronaele Kelly Gaynor, Philadelphia, Pennsylvania*: "My mother's first name is Eleanor. She named me Ronaele, which is Eleanor spelled backwards."

● *Mrs. Warren L. Holland, Sr., Portsmouth, Virginia*: "We have a granddaughter who has an original name. Her daddy's name is Rick and her mother's name is Teri Ellen. Her parents combined Rick with part of Ellen, and her name is Rickell."

● *Roneel G. Bowden, Linden, Texas*: "My name is Roneel. My parents came up with the name by scrambling the letters of my mother's name, Lorene. When my first daughter was born, I surprised my parents by naming her Eloren."

Celebrity Names

Many of our names today, as in the past, have been adopted because they were the names of celebrities or centered about events in the lives of celebrities. In this category we include not only contemporary celebrities in the fields of entertainment, sports, music, politics, etc., but also the great figures of history, political as well as religious, whose charisma was so great that parents named children after them.

When Alexander the Great entered Palestine in 333 B.C., according to the legend, all Jewish boys born in that year were named Alexander in his honor.

Hugh, originally spelled Hew, became a popular name in England after the thirteenth century because of the popularity of Hugh of Lincoln, an infant-martyr. After he was canonized by the Catholic church, his name became even more popular and gave rise to many surnames, such as Uet, Hutchins, Higgins, and Hughes.

Many Catholics are named after saints. Among the most popular is Saint Patrick (c. 387-463), whose name is often bestowed on babies born in March, particularly those born on March 17, the feast day assigned by the church to commemorate his life.

Louis Adamic, in his *The Native's Return*, tells of his uncle Yanez, who was named after his patron saint, John the Baptist (Yanez is the Slovakian form of John).

Protestants sometimes choose a famous or well-liked minister as a namesake. One can hardly doubt that the name of Luther Martin, a delegate from Maryland to the Constitutional Convention in Philadelphia, was inspired by Martin Luther. In *Get Thee Behind Me*, author Hartzell Spence tells that he was personally named after Bishop Hartzell.

Freddy Fitzsimmons, the well-known baseball player, whose middle name is Landis, was named after Fred Landis, the brother of Judge Kenesaw Mountain Landis. Fred Landis was a prominent midwestern evangelist and a friend of Fitzsimmon's father.

Many Jewish boys have been named after Theodor Herzl, the founder of modern Zionism.

Inspired by the peace treaty signed in Washington, D.C., in March 1979, between Israel and Egypt, Mr. and Mrs. Hotam El Kabassi named their triplets born on April 5, 1979, Carter, Begin, and Sadat in honor of U.S. President Jimmy Carter, Israeli Prime Minister Menachem Begin, and Egyptian President Anwar Sadat, the three principals at the signing.

Our correspondents have provided us with a wide variety of examples that fall into this category:

● *Patia Waggoner, Indianapolis, Indiana*: "I was born in 1944. In that year Tyrone Power was very popular in the movies. My mother was a very big fan of his. His mother's name was Patia Power. So, when I was born, she named me after his mother."

● *Yvonne Abner, Blanchester, Ohio*: "My name is Yvonne Deniese Abner (nee Coogan). My initials are Y.D.C., and I was named after Yvonne DeCarlo."

● *Cassandra M. Sherod, Honolulu, Hawaii*: "My daughter is of Irish, Scotch, and Japanese descent. At the time of my pregnancy I attended a movie which starred a famous Irish actress named Siobhan McKenna. I heard the name pronounced as Shevon, and it seemed to go nicely with our last name. My daughter was named Shevon Sherod."

● *Mary Blaisdell, Auburn, Washington*: "My father's name is Lytle Gaines Blaisdell. His first name is after Doctor Lytle Atherton, a good friend of the family. He got his middle name from Professor Gaines Dobbins, a teacher in the Baptist seminary his father attended."

● *Pochantas Lee Watkins, Illinois Station, Oklahoma*: "My father, William A. Watkins, was the best friend of General Robert E. Lee. He named all six of his children Lee, after the general."

● *Jenny Lind Erickson McGaha, Brevard, North Carolina*: "When my mother was five years old, she used to stand on her aunt's bed so she could see a portrait of the Swedish Nightingale, Jenny Lind. She thought she was beautiful and decided that that was the name she would give her daughter."

● *Nancy Reece Darby, San Diego, California*: "My father was a member of the U.S. Army band playing trombone and trumpet. Frank Sinatra had a new song out—'Nancy With the Laughing Face'—about his daughter. It was my father's favorite song. When he found out his first child was a girl, he decided to name me after that favorite song."

Unconventional Spellings

For the past two or three decades many new first names have come into being as a result of a desire on the part of parents to be different or distinctive. They have increasingly been taking popular names and spelling them differently.

The most common characteristic of this new fad is substituting a "y" for an "i" or adding an "e." Fannye was once Fannie, and Mollye was formerly Mollie. Likewise, Sadie has become Sadye, and Edith has become Edyth or Edythe. Shirley has become Shirlee, Shirlie, or Sherle. Sarah and Hannah have dropped the "h" and become Sara and Hanna. Esther can now be found as Ester and sometimes as Esta or Estee.

Among the many feminine names that have, because of a new spelling, made their appearance of late, are the following familiar ones:

Rosalin, Rosaline, Rosalyn, Roselyn, Roslyn, Roslyne, and Rosylin from Rosalind; Debra and Dobra from Deborah; Karolyn and Carolyn from Caroline; Alyce and Alyse from Alice; Gale from Gail; Arlyne from Arline; Arleyne from Arlene; Lilyan from Lilian; Elane and Elayne from Elaine; Ilene and Iline from Eileen; Ethyl and Ethyle from Ethel; Janis from Janice; Jayne from Jane; Madeline, Madelon, Madelyn, Madelyne, and Madlyn from Madeleine; Marilin and Marylin from Marilyn; and Vyvyan and Vivien from Vivian.

Changes in spelling also account for a large number of new masculine names. Prominent among these are: Allan, Alyn, Allyn, and Allen from Alan; Frederic, Fredric, and Fredrick from Frederick; Irwin, Erwin, Irving, and Irvine from Irvin; Isidore, Isador, and Isadore from Isidor; Laurance, Laurence, Lawrance, and Lorence from Lawrence; Maury, Morey, and Morry from Morris; Murry from Murray; and Mervyn from Mervin.

Masculine/Feminine Interchanges

A substantial number of names in contemporary use have been "borrowed" from the opposite sex, sometimes without modification, but usually after a slight change has been made.

This practice of interchanging names between the sexes is an old one. The Bible contains many examples of names common to both sexes. Athaliah was the daughter of Ahab and Jezebel in the Book of Kings, while in Chronicles Athaliah is a masculine name. Efah, the concubine of Caleb, is also used as a masculine name. Shlomith appears as both a masculine and feminine form, as do Tzivyaw, Bilgah, Chuba, Noga, Chupah, Gomer, Bunah, Beenah, Abijah, Afra, Reenah, Chaveelah, and Simchah.

Among the early Normans every name was free to be used by either sex, thus Druetta and Williametta became feminine names by simply adding a suffix (etta) to the original masculine form. In eighteenth-century national army lists, the names Lucy, Ann, and Caroline can be found recorded as masculine names. Today, more than ever, do we find male names and female names shared by the opposite sex.

On a list of army casualties published in *The New York Times* on August 10, 1943, there appeared two men named Patsy: Patsy Natale, Jr., and Patsy Demarco. Vivian, also spelled Vyvyan, is occasionally used by men, as are Carol, Dorris, and Evelyn.

A number of outstanding contemporary personalities have been given names that are characteristically feminine: polar explorer Richard Evelyn Byrd, noted author Evelyn Waugh, Congressman Clare Hoffman of Michigan, among others.

Among women's names we find a vast number adopted from the masculine forms. In many instances, the feminine name is so long established and accepted that we no longer realize that it had its origin in a masculine name. In this group the following are prominent: Alexandra and Alexandria from Alexander; Charlotte and Charleene from Charles; Davi, Davida, and Davita from David; Erica from Eric; Frederica from Frederic; Georgia, Georgine, and Georgette from George;

Harriet and Harri from Harry; Henrietta, Henri, and Henria from Henry; Herma and Hermine from Herman; Horatio (daughter of Horatio "Lord" Nelson and Lady Hamilton) from Horatio; Isaaca from Isaac; Josepha and Josephine from Joseph; Lou, Louise, and Louisa from Louis (the wife of Herbert Hoover was Lou Henry Hoover); Roberta from Robert; Stephanie from Stephan; and Willa and Willene from Will or William. Other less common feminine names of masculine origin are Alexis, Alwyn, Barnetta, Cary, Ellys, Franklyne, Freddie, Herberta, Jamie, Joelle, Merril, Merrill, Meryl, Raymonde, Roye, Simona, Simonne, and Toni.

This list is long and can be supplemented with many additional names found in this dictionary.

Patronymics and Matronymics

A patronymic is a name derived from the name of a father or a male ancestor. A matronymic (also spelled metronymic) is a name derived from the name of a mother or a female ancestor. Matronymics are comparatively rare because society of prior centuries was basically a patriarchal society. Our prime concern is therefore with patronymics.

The patronymic played a significant role in the naming of children, particularly in earlier centuries when the population was small and mobility was an unknown word. People were born, lived, and died in one village without ever traveling more than a few miles from it in the course of a lifetime. So, when John had a son, he was known as John's son (which later may have become Johnson), and he needed no other nomenclature to be properly identified.

But with the coming of the twelfth, thirteenth, and subsequent centuries, as the population grew, it became clear that greater identification was required so as not to confuse people. In its earliest form the problem was resolved by adding a descriptive appellation to a name. Thus, Richard I (1157-1199), a king of England, became Richard Coeur de Lion or Richard the Lion-Hearted (possibly because of the strength he displayed as one of the leaders of the Third Crusade). And, in a similar vein, the average citizen who may have been named John became John the Short, or John the Tall, or John from Selkirk, or John from the North, or John the Scot, or John the Potter (an occupational name).

In time, as the population grew increasingly larger, this procedure became cumbersome. By the 1500s in England, the use of patronymic forms (Davidson, MacDonald, etc.) as surnames was introduced. In time, many of these patronymic surnames came to be used as first names (CONTEMPORARY EXAMPLE: Macdonald Carey, actor).

The following list represents many of the common prefixes and suffixes that have been appended to personal names to form patronymics:

Ab	as in the Welsh AbHarry (son of Harry, which later became Barry)
Ana	as in the Basque Lorenzana (son of Lorenzo)
Ap	as in the Welsh ApEvan (son of Evan), which later became Bevan
Bar	as in the Aramaic Bar Giora (son of Giora)
Bas	as in the Hebrew Basheva and Bathsheba (daughter of Sheva)
Ben	as in the Hebrew Benzecry (son of Zechariah)
ena	as in the Basque Lorenzena (son of Lorenzo)
escu	as in the Romanian Jonescu (son of John)
ez	as in the Spanish Rodriguez (son of Rodrigo)
fitz	as in the Norman-French Fitzgerald (son of Gerald)
Ibn	as in the Arabic Ibn Daud (son of David)
ing	as in the Anglo-Saxon Cidding (son of Cidda)
ides	as in the Greek Gersonides (son of Gerson)
Mac	as in the Scotch MacDavis (son of David)
Mc	as in the Gaelic McCue (son of Hugh)
O'	as in the Irish O'Donald (son of Donald)
off	as in the Slavonic Rubinoff (son of Rubin)
ov	as in the Slavonic Pietrov (son of Peter)
ovitch	as in the Russian and Serbian Davidovitch (son of David)
s	as in the English Davis (son of David) and Edwards (son of Edward)
sen	as in the Danish and Swedish Andersen (son of Andrew)
ski	as in the Slavonic Polanski (son of Poland)
sky	as in the Slavonic Gregorsky (son of Gregory)
sohn	as in the German Mendelssohn (son of Mendel)
son	as in the Scandinavian Johnson (son of John)
vich	as in the Russian Alexandrovich (son of Alexander)
vitch	as in the Russian Rabinovitch (son of Reuben)
wicz	as in the Polish Davidowicz (son of David)
witz	as in the Russian and Slavonic Itzkowitz (son of Isaac)
zen	as in the Dutch Janzen (son of Jan or John)

Pet Forms (Diminutives)

Pet forms, often called diminutives (although, as indicated in the Preface, this is not a precise characterization of the form), make up a large portion of our contemporary first names. This group grows larger and larger as the desire for self expression grows stronger. Often, the original Christian, baptismal first name of an individual is completely abandoned and the pet name becomes the real name.

James Earl Carter, the thirty-ninth president of the United States, is a prime example. Although his original and legal name is James, Jimmy is the name he prefers and the name he has used when signing official documents.

The most common form of the pet name has evolved by dropping the last letter or syllable of the original name and adding to it "y" or "ie" or "ette." Suffixes such as these are to be found in most modern Indo-European languages. The following are some of the more common ones that are found in this dictionary:

_____chen;_____cock;_____cox;_____en;_____ella;_____ elle;_____elli;_____ello;_____et;_____etta;_____ette;____ __etto;_____ia;_____ie;_____in;_____ina;_____ino;____ __kin;_____on;_____ot;_____ota;_____ott;_____otte;____ __ucce;_____ucci;_____uccio;_____ucco;_____y;_____ye.

DICTIONARY
OF
FIRST NAMES

MASCULINE
NAMES

A

Aaron   From a variety of Hebrew roots, meaning "to sing," "to shine," "to teach," or "a mountain." Also, from the Arabic, meaning "a messenger." In the Bible, the older brother of Moses and Miriam. Aaron Burr (1756-1836) was a U.S. vice-presidential candidate. Among the antecedents of President Grover Cleveland, five Aarons appeared before the family turned to non-biblical names. VARIANT FORMS: A'alona (Hawaiian); Aharon, Ahron, Aron (Hebrew). CONTEMPORARY EXAMPLE: Aaron S. Watkins, U. S. politician. SURNAME USAGE: Aranof, Aaronson, Aarons, Aronovitch, Aronowitz. PLACE-NAME USAGE: Aaronsburg, Pennsylvania, named for Aaron Levy, town founder.

Abba   From Arabic, Syriac, and Aramaic roots, meaning "father." Commonly used in the post-biblical period. VARIANT FORMS: Aba, Abbe, Abbey, Abbie, Abby, Abbot, Abbott. CONTEMPORARY EXAMPLE: Abba Eban, Israeli statesman. SURNAME USAGE: Abbot, Abbey.

Abbas   A patronymic form, meaning "son of Abba." *See* Abba. CONTEMPORARY EXAMPLE: Abbas Kelidar, sociologist.

Abbe, Abbey   From the Old French *abaie* and the Late Latin *abbatia*, meaning "the head of a monastery, an abbot." SURNAME USAGE: Ernest Abbe (1840-1940), German physicist; Edwin Austin Abbey (1852-1911), American painter.

Abbie   A variant spelling of Abbey. *See* Abbey. Also, a pet form of Abba. Used also as a feminine name. PLACE-NAME USAGE: Abbie Lake, in Montana; Abbie Creek, in Alabama, is a short form of Yattayabba, a female Indian name.

Abbot, Abott   Derived from Abba. *See* Abba. In the Middle Ages, the head (father) of a religious order or abbey assumed the name Abbot. CONTEMPORARY EXAMPLE: Abbott Kaplan, educator. SURNAME USAGE: Lyman Abbott (1835-1922), American clergyman and author. PLACE-NAME USAGE: Abbotsford was the name Sir Walter Scott gave to the residence he built in Scotland.

Abby   A variant spelling of Abbe, Abbey, and Abbie. More commonly used as a feminine form. *See* Abby (feminine section). Also, a pet form of Abba. PLACE-NAME USAGE: Abbyville, Kansas, named for Abby McLean, the first child born in the settlement.

Abda   From the Hebrew and Arabic, meaning "servant." In the Bible, a Levite.

Abdal   A variant spelling of Abdul. *See* Abdul. PLACE-NAME USAGE: a town in Nebraska.

Abdel   A variant spelling of Abdul and Abdal. *See* Abdul.

Abdi   From the Hebrew, meaning "my servant." In the Bible, a Levite.

Abdiel   From the Hebrew, meaning "servant of God." In the Bible, a leader of the tribe of Gad. In Milton's *Paradise Lost*, Abdiel was the angel who opposed Satan in revolt against God.

Abdul, Abdullah   From the Arabic, meaning "servant of Allah." A compound of *Abd*, meaning "servant," and Allah, the Arabic name for the Supreme Being in the Mohammedan religion. Abdul is a short form of Abdullah. Abdallah is a variant spelling. CONTEMPORARY EXAMPLE: Abdullah ibn Hussein, King of Jordan, assassinated in 1951; Abdul Said, professor; Kareem Abdul Jabbar, basketball player.

Abe   A pet form of Abraham. *See* Abraham.

Abednego   An Aramaic name, meaning "servant of God Nego (Nebo)." In the Bible, the Aramaic name of Azariah, one of the three men who miraculously escaped unharmed from a blazing furnace.

Abel   From the Hebrew *hevel*, meaning "a breath" or "vapor." In the Bible, the son of Adam and Eve, brother of Cain. Often spelled Able or Abell, the name was popular among the monks of England from the fifth through the eleventh centuries. SURNAME USAGE: Abelard, Abeles, Abell, Ableson, Able.

Abelard   From the Middle English, meaning "the keeper of the Abbey's larder." Also, a variant form of Abel. *See* Abel. Pierre Abelard (1079-1142), French theologian and philosopher.

Abeles   A variant form of Abel. *See* Abel. PLACE-NAME USAGE: a town in Arkansas named for a prominent local family.

Abi   A pet form of Abraham. *See* Abraham. A feminine form in the Bible.

Abida   From the Hebrew, meaning "my father [God] knows." In the Bible, a grandson of Abraham and Ketura.

Abidan   From the Hebrew, meaning " my father [God] is judge." In the Bible, a leader of the tribe of Benjamin.

Abie   A pet form of Abraham. *See* Abraham.

Abiel   From the Hebrew, meaning "God is my father." Aviel is a variant spelling. In the Bible, King Saul's grandfather.

Abihu   From the Hebrew, meaning "he [God] is my father." In the Bible, a son of Aaron.

Abir   From the Hebrew, meaning "strong."

Abiri   From the Hebrew, meaning "my hero."

Abisha   A variant form of Abishai. *See* Abishai. CONTEMPORARY EXAMPLES: Abisha Pritchard, football player.

Abishai   From the Hebrew, meaning "my father's [God's] gift." In the Bible, a grandson of Jesse; a brother of Joab.

Abishua   From the Hebrew, meaning "my father [God] is salvation." In the Bible, a son of Phineas.

Abishur   From the Hebrew, meaning "my father [God] is a wall [strong]." In the Bible, a member of the tribe of Judah.

Abraham   From the Hebrew, meaning "father of a multitude." Abraham (Avram) was the earlier form. In the Bible Avram, the first Hebrew, was called an Ivri because he came from the "other side" (*ever*) of the Euphrates River. Abram's name was changed to Abraham when he accepted the concept of one God. (The Hebrew letter H, the symbol for God, was added to his name as a reward.) Not one rabbi in the entire Talmud is named Abraham, but after the sixth century it became popular. By the twelfth century, it was third in popularity among the Jews of England. Early Christians refrained from using the name because of its association with Judaism, although it does occur as the name of a priest in the English Domesday Book of the eleventh century. After the Reformation, in sixteenth-century Europe, the bias against the name lessened. After Abraham Lincoln's death, in 1865, the name became more popular. VARIANT FORMS: Avraham (Hebrew); Ibrahim (Persian); Ali Baba (Arabic); Bram (English and Dutch). Abra was used as a feminine form in seventeenth-century England. SURNAME USAGE: Abrahams, Abrahamson, Abramowitz, Abramovitch, Braham, Eberman. PLACE-NAME USAGE: a bay in Alaska.

Abram   From the Hebrew, meaning "father of might" or "exalted father." The original name of Abraham. *See* Abraham. Became popular among the New Englanders of Puritan stock. James Abram Garfield (1831-1881), twentieth president of the U.S. SURNAME USAGE: Abrams, Abramson. PLACE-NAME USAGE: Abrams Creek, Tennessee.

Abran   A Spanish form of Abram. *See* Abram.

Absalom   From the Hebrew, meaning "the father of peace." In the Bible, the third son of King David. Used in the thirteenth and fourteenth centuries. Chaucer used it for the jolly clerk in his *Miller's Tale*. Absolom is a variant spelling. SURNAME USAGE: Apsolon, Aspelon, Aspenlon, Asplin, Ashplant.

Ace   From the Latin *as* and the Middle English *aas*, meaning "a unit, unity." PLACE-NAME USAGE: a city in Texas, named for Ace Emanuel, its first postmaster.

Achilles   Rarely used and of doubtful etymology. Achilles was the Greek hero of Homer's *Iliad*. PLACE-NAME USAGE: Achille, Oklahoma, derived from the French form of Achilles, used as a personal name by Cherokee Indians, to whom it means "fire."

Ackley   From the Old English, meaning "a meadow of oak (*ack*) trees."

Acton   From the Old English, meaning "a town in which oak trees grow." PLACE-NAME USAGE: a town in Maine.

Adalia   From the Hebrew, meaning "God is my refuge." In the Bible, a son of Haman.

Adalric, Adelric   From the German, meaning "noble ruler." Akin to Adelbert and Richard. *See* Adelbert *and* Richard.

Adam   From the Hebrew *adamah*, meaning "earth." Also ascribed to Phoenician and Babylonian origins, meaning "man, mankind." In the Bible, the name of the first man. Not used among Christians until the seventh century, when it appears as the name of an Irish clergyman, Saint Adamman (Adam the Little), Abbot of Iona. In nineteenth-century Scotland, Adamina was created as a feminine pet form. Adan is a Spanish form. John Adams (1735-1826), second president of the U.S., is probably responsible for much of its popularity after the nineteenth century. SURNAME USAGE: Adams, Adamson, Adcock, Addison, Adking, Atkinson, MacAdam. PLACE-NAME USAGE: Adam's Grave, Missouri, in Mormon tradition the burial site of the biblical Adam; Adamana, Arizona, named for Adam Hanna, a cattleman.

Adams, Adamson   Patronymic forms of Adam, meaning "Adam's son." PLACE-NAME USAGE: Mount Adams, Washington; Point Adams, Oregon; Adams, Massachusetts, named for Samuel Adams (1722-1803), American patriot.

Adan   The Spanish form of Adam. *See* Adam.

Adar, Addar   From the Hebrew, meaning "noble, exalted." The Hebrew month that ushers in springtime. In the Bible, the son of Bela; a grandson of Benjamin.

Addi, Addie   From the Hebrew *adah*, meaning "my adornment." In the Bible, an ancestor of Joseph; the husband of Mary. CONTEMPORARY EXAMPLE: Addie Joss, baseball player.

Addis   A variant form of Addison. *See* Addison. PLACE-NAME USAGE: Addis Ababa, capital of Ethiopia.

Addison   Old English patronymic form of Adam, meaning "the son of Adam." *See* Adam. Used also as a feminine name. SURNAME USAGE: Joseph Addison (1672-1719), English essayist and poet. PLACE-NAME USAGE: Addison, Maine, named for Joseph Addison.

Ade   From the Old English *ad*, meaning "a mound, a heap." SURNAME USAGE: George Ade (1866-1944), American humorist.

Adel, Adell   A short form of Adelbert. *See* Adelbert. CONTEMPORARY EXAMPLE: Adell White, baseball player. PLACE-NAME USAGE: Adel, Oregon; Adell, Iowa.

Adelbert   A variant form of the Old High German *adal*, meaning "noble," and *beraht*, meaning "bright," hence "an illustrious person." Akin to Albert. VARIANT FORMS: Albert, Albertus, Albrecht, Ethelbert, Elbert. PET FORMS: Al, Adel, Bert.

Ader   From the Hebrew, meaning "a flock." In the Bible, a member of the tribe of Levi.

Adin   From the Hebrew *adah*, meaning "beautiful, decorative." In the Bible, a man who returned from exile with Zerubbabel. PLACE-NAME USAGE: Adin, California, named for Adin McDowell, an early settler.

Adino   From the Hebrew, meaning "His [God's] adorned one." In the Bible, one of King David's warriors.

Adir   From the Hebrew, meaning "noble, majestic." CONTEMPORARY EXAMPLE: Adir Cohen, Israeli author.

Adiv   From the Arabic, meaning "pleasant, gentle-mannered." Used in Israel.

Adlai   From the Hebrew, meaning "refuge of God." Or, from the Arabic, meaning "to act justly." In the Bible, the father of Shaphat, overseer of David's flocks. CONTEMPORARY EXAMPLE: Adlai Stevenson, American statesman.

Adlard   From the Old German Adalhard, now obsolete. VARIANT FORMS: Alard, Allard. *See* Alard. CONTEMPORARY EXAMPLE: Adlard Coles, author.

Adler   From the German, meaning "eagle." SURNAME USAGE: Alfred Adler (1870-1937), Austrian-born psychiatrist.

Admon   From the Hebrew, meaning "red." The name of the red peony flower in Upper Galilee, Israel.

Adnah   From the Hebrew, meaning "adorned." In the Bible, a member of the tribe of Judah. Adin is a variant form.

Adolf, Adolfo   Variant spellings of Adolph. Adolf is an Old High German form. Adolfo is a Spanish form. *See* Adolph. CONTEMPORARY EXAMPLE: Adolfo Philips, baseball player.

Adolph   From the Old German, compounded of *athal*, meaning "noble," and *wolfa*, meaning "wolf." In Old English, Aethelwulf was the form used until the eleventh century. VARIANT FORMS: Adolphus (Latin); Adolphe (French); Adolf (German); Adolfo (Spanish). PET FORMS: Dolph, Dolphus, Dolly. CONTEMPORARY EXAMPLE: Adolphe Menjou, actor.

Adolphe   The French form of Adolph. *See* Adolph.

Adon   From the Hebrew, meaning "lord, master." In the Bible, Adonai means "my Lord," and is used for God.

Adonis In Greek mythology, a beautiful young man, loved by Aphrodite, who was killed by a wild boar. His name became synonymous with beauty. CONTEMPORARY EXAMPLE: Adonis Terry, baseball player.

Adrian A short form of the Latin name Hadrian. From the Greek, meaning "rich." Also, from the Latin, meaning "black." The seaport of Adria, which gave its name to the Adriatic Sea, was known in ancient times for its black sand. VARIANT FORMS: Adrianus, Hadrian, Hadrianus. CONTEMPORARY EXAMPLE: Adrian Dantley, basketball player. PLACE-NAME USAGE: Adrian, Missouri, named for Adrian Talmage, son of the railroad agent.

Adriel From the Hebrew, meaning "God is my majesty." In the Bible, King Saul's son-in-law.

Adron Origin uncertain. CONTEMPORARY EXAMPLE: Adron Doran, educator.

Aelfric An early form of Alfric. *See* Alfric. The name of the Archbishop of Canterbury (died 1005).

Aeneas In Greek and Roman legend, a Trojan. The hero of Virgil's *Aeneid*. From the Latin *aeneus*, meaning "bronze-colored."

Aggrey From the Latin *ager*, meaning "a field." CONTEMPORARY EXAMPLE: Aggrey Brown, author.

Agu An African name, meaning "leopard." Popular among the Ibo tribe of Nigerians.

Ahab From the Hebrew, meaning "father's brother." In the Bible, a king of Israel, husband of Jezebel.

Aharon The Hebraic form of Aaron. *See* Aaron. CONTEMPORARY EXAMPLE: Aharon Ipale, actor.

Ahearn, Ahern From the Middle English *heroun*, meaning "a heron."

Ahmed From the Arabic, meaning "most highly adored." Akin to Mohammed. CONTEMPORARY EXAMPLE: Ahmed-El Gohary, book salesman.

Aidan From the Middle English *aiden*, meaning "to help." Saint Aidan (died 651) was the first Bishop of Lindisfarne. CONTEMPORARY EXAMPLE: Aidan Warlow, author.

Aikane From the Hawaiian, meaning "friend, friendly."

Aiken From the Anglo-Saxon, meaning "made of oak"; hence, "strong." SURNAME USAGE: Conrad Aiken (1889-1973), U.S. poet.

Ain From the Scotch, meaning "belonging to one." Used also as a feminine name.

Ainsley From the Scotch, meaning "one's own meadow, one's own field."

Ainsworth From the Old English, meaning "from Ann's estate." Or from the Scottish, meaning "belonging to Ain." *See* Ain *and* Ann (feminine section).

Akevy A Hungarian form of Jacob. *See* Jacob.

Akiba A variant form of the Hebrew name Yaakov, meaning "to hold by the heel." *See* Jacob. Akiba ben Joseph was a talmudic scholar of the first century A.D. Akiva is a variant spelling. PET FORMS: Kiva, Kiba.

Akim A Russian pet form of the Hebrew Jehoiakim. *See* Jehoiakim. CONTEMPORARY EXAMPLE: Akim Tamiroff, actor.

Akiva A variant spelling of Akiba. *See* Akiba.

Akkub A variant form of Akiba. *See* Akiba. In the Bible, a descendent of King David.

Aksel From the Old German, meaning "a small oak tree."

Al A pet name for many first names: Albert, Alfred, Alexander, etc.

Aladdin From the Arabic, meaning "height of faith." Popularized after the publication of *The Arabian Nights*, in which the story of Aladdin is told. PLACE-NAME USAGE: Aladdin, Wyoming.

Alain The French form from which Alan is derived. *See* Alan. CONTEMPORARY EXAMPLES: Alain Cote, hockey player; Alain Delon, French actor.

Alan From the Middle Latin name Alanus. Of doubtful origin, but usually taken from the Celtic, meaning "harmony, peace," or from the Gaelic, meaning "fair, handsome." Alawn was a legendary British poet of the first century. First used by the Norman-French in the form of Alain. Introduced into England in the eleventh century during the Norman Conquest. VARIANT FORMS: Allan, Allen, Alyn, Aleyn, Allwyn.

Alard, Allard Variant forms of the Old German name Adalhard. Compounded of *athal*, meaning "noble," and *hardu*, meaning "hard." Aethelheard is an Old English form. CONTEMPORARY EXAMPLE: Allard K. Lowenstein, U.S. politician.

Alaric From the Old German name Alaicus, a compound of *ala*, meaning "all," and *ric*, meaning "ruler," hence "ruler over all." VARIANT FORMS: Alarick, Ulric, Ulrich, Rich, Rick, Ricky. Several kings of the West Goths were named Alaric. Alaric I was the king who sacked Rome in 410. CONTEMPORARY EXAMPLE: Alaric C. Fraser-Lane, Glendale, Arizona.

Alasdair A variant form of Alastair. *See* Alastair. CONTEMPORARY EXAMPLES: Alasdair Clayre, author; Alasdair MacIntyre, editor.

Alastair A Gaelic form of Alexander. *See* Alexander. Alastor may be the original form of the name. In Greek mythology, Alastor personified revenge.

Alba   A variant form of Alban. *See* Alban. PLACE-NAME USAGE: a town in Michigan, named for Alba Haywood, a teacher; a town in Texas in which black people were not allowed, in keeping with the meaning of the name Alban.

Alban   From the Latin name Albanus, meaning "white." VARIANT FORMS: Alba, Alben, Albin, Alva. Saint Alban was a third-century British martyr. Used in England as far back as the seventeenth century. CONTEMPORARY EXAMPLE: Alban E. Reid, educator; Alben Barkley, a U.S. vice-president. PLACE-NAME USAGE: the capital city of New York; Albania, a country in the Balkan Peninsula.

Alben   A variant spelling of Alban. *See* Alban.

Alberic, Alberich   From the Middle High German *alb*, meaning "elf," and *rich*, meaning "leader, king." In German mythology, Alberich was king of the dwarfs and leader of the Nibelungs. Aelfric is the Old English equivalent. Introduced into England by the Normans in the form of Alberi and Auberim, which later became Aubrey.

Albert   A French form of the Old High German name Adelbrecht. Albert is compounded of the Old High German *adal*, meaning "noble, nobility," and *beraht*, meaning "bright." VARIANT FORMS: Adalbert, Adelbert, Ulbricht (German); Albertus (Latin); Aubert (French); Albrecht (German); Alberto, Albertino (Italian); Elbert (English); Bertel (Danish); Olbracht (Polish). Became popular in the mid-nineteenth century after the marriage of Queen Victoria of England to King Albert of Germany. PET FORMS: Al, Albie, Bert. Alberta and Albertine are feminine forms. SURNAME USAGE: Albright, Halbert. PLACE-NAME USAGE: Albert Lake, Uganda; Albert Canal, Belgium.

Alberti, Alberto   Italian forms of Albert. *See* Albert. SURNAME USAGE: Leon Batista Alberti (1404-1472), Italian architect.

Albie   A pet form of Albert. *See* Albert. Elbie is a variant form. CONTEMPORARY EXAMPLE: Albie Grant, basketball player.

Albin   A variant spelling of Alban. *See* Alban. PLACE-NAME USAGE: Albin, Wyoming, named for John Albin, first postmaster.

Albino   An Italian form of Alban. *See* Alban. CONTEMPORARY EXAMPLE: Albino Luciana (Pope John Paul I).

Albion   From the Latin, meaning "white, fair." The ancient name for Britain (which included Scotland), so named because of its white cliffs. In America, in 1579, Sir Francis Drake, upon noticing the white cliffs on the California coast, decided to call the area New Albion. Sir Albion Richardson was a prominent nineteenth-century Englishman. PLACE-NAME USAGE: Albion River, California.

Alboin   A variant form of Albion. *See* Albion. In the sixth century,

Alboin, king of the Lombards, conquered North Italy.

Albrecht An early Old German form of Albert. *See* Albert.

Alcander From the Greek, meaning "manly, masculine." SURNAME USAGE: Alcinder, Alcindor.

Alcot, Alcott From the Old English, meaning "old cottage." PLACE-NAME USAGE: Alcott, South Carolina, named for author Louisa May Alcott.

Alcuin Origin unknown. Akin to Alcacysm, a 600 B.C. Greek lyric poet. Alcuin was an eighth-century English theologian. CONTEMPORARY EXAMPLE: Alcuin Loehr, political leader.

Aldan A variant form of Alden. *See* Alden. PLACE-NAME USAGE: a river in Eastern Siberia.

Alden From the Middle English *elde*, meaning "old age, antiquity." VARIANT FORMS: Aldin, Aldo, Aldon, Aldous, Aldus, Aldivin, Eldon. Alda is a feminine form. CONTEMPORARY EXAMPLE: Alden Robertson, author. SURNAME USAGE: John Alden (1599-1687), a pilgrim settler in Plymouth Colony immortalized in Longfellow's poem *The Courtship of Miles Standish*.

Alder From the Old English *eald*, meaning "old"; hence "a chief, a prince, one in authority." Also, from the Middle English *alder* and *aller*, referring to a small group of trees in the birch family. VARIANT FORMS: Aldo, Aldous, Elder, Eldor.

Aldo An Old German form of Alder. *See* Alder. Popular in Italy. VARIANT FORMS: Alder, Aldous, Aldos. Alda is a feminine form. CONTEMPORARY EXAMPLE: Aldo Moro, premier of Italy.

Aldon A variant spelling of Alden. *See* Alden. CONTEMPORARY EXAMPLE: Aldon Wilkie, baseball player.

Aldous A variant form of Aldus and Aldo. *See* Aldo. CONTEMPORARY EXAMPLE: Aldous Huxley (1894-1963), English author.

Aldred Derived from the Old English name Ealdred, meaning "old, wise counsel." Eldred is a variant form.

Aldren Probably a variant form of Alder. *See* Alder. CONTEMPORARY EXAMPLE: Aldren A. Watson, artist.

Aldrich From the Old German, meaning "old, wise ruler." SURNAME USAGE: Thomas Bailey Aldrich (1836-1907), American writer.

Aldridge A variant spelling of Eldridge. *See* Eldridge.

Aldus A Latinized form of the Old German Aldo. *See* Aldo. A popular Italian name. Aldus Manutius and his family published fine editions of the classics in sixteenth-century Venice and Rome. VARIANT FORMS: Aldo, Aldan, Aldous. SURNAME USAGE: Aldiss, Aldous.

Aldwin   An Old English name compounded of *ald*, meaning "old," and *win*, meaning "friend." In use since the eleventh century. VARIANT FORMS: Aldin, Alden, Aldan.

Alec, Aleck   Short forms of Alexander, popular in Scotland. *See* Alexander. CONTEMPORARY EXAMPLE: Alec Guinness, actor. PLACE-NAME USAGE: Aleck Island, Georgia.

Aleksander, Aleksandr   Variant Russian and Slavic spellings of Alexander. *See* Alexander. CONTEMPORARY EXAMPLE: Aleksandr R. Luria, Soviet psychologist.

Aleksei   A Russian form of Alexander. *See* Alexander. CONTEMPORARY EXAMPLE: Aleksei Kosygin, Russian statesman.

Alena   The Hawaiian form of Allen. *See* Allen.

Aleron   From the Latin, meaning "one with wings."

Alessandro   The Italian form of Alexander. *See* Alexander. CONTEMPORARY EXAMPLE: Alessandro de Tomaso, industrialist.

Alex   A popular pet form of Alexander. VARIANT FORMS: Alec, Aleck, Alick.

Alexander   From the Greek name Alexandros, meaning "protector of men." According to legend, when Alexander the Great (356-323 B.C.) conquered Palestine in 333 B.C., all Jewish boys born in that year were named Alexander in his honor. The name has been popular for more than 2,000 years. In thirteenth-century Scotland, three kings were named Alexander. Alexander Nevski was a thirteenth-century Russian military hero and statesman. VARIANT FORMS: Alexandre (French); Alaster, Alysandyr, Sawney (Scotch); Allesandro, Sandro (Italian); Alejandro (Spanish); Alesksander, Aleksandr, Sacha, Sasha (Russian); Alasdair, Alastair (Gaelic). PET FORMS: Alec, Aleck, Alick, Alex, Sander, Sanders, Sandey, Sandy, Sandro, Saunder, Saunders. FEMININE FORMS: Alexandra and Alexandrina. CONTEMPORARY EXAMPLE: Alexander Woollcott (1887-1943), American author. PLACE-NAME USAGE: Alexandria, Egypt; Alexandria, Virginia; Alexander Archipelago Islands, off the coast of Alaska.

Alexandre   A variant form of Alexander. CONTEMPORARY EXAMPLE: Alexandre Dumas, French author; Alexandre Parode, French statesman.

Alexis   A variant form of Alexander. Used also as a feminine name. *See* Alexander. Alexis Mikhailovich was Czar of Russia in the seventeenth century. CONTEMPORARY EXAMPLE: Robert Alexis Green, U.S. congressman.

Alfonse, Alfonso, Alfonzo   Variant spellings of Alphonso. *See* Alphonso. CONTEMPORARY EXAMPLE: Alfonso III, king of Spain (1902-1931).

Alf, Alfeo, Alfie   Pet forms of Alfred. *See* Alfred. CONTEMPORARY EX-
AMPLE: Alf Landon, U.S. presidential candidate.

Alfred   From the Old English *aelf*, meaning "elf" (and having the connotation of wise, clever), and *raed*, meaning "counsel." Became popular
in the ninth century when the English king, Alfred the Great, curbed
Danish conquests in England. Prior to the sixteenth century, especially
in northern Europe, Alfred was one of the most popular names. VARI-
ANT FORMS: Alfric, Alfrid, Alfris, Elfrid. PET FORMS: Al, Allie, Alf, Alfie,
Fred. Alfreda is a feminine form. CONTEMPORARY EXAMPLE: Alfred
Hitchcock, movie director. PLACE-NAME USAGE: Alfred, Maine, and Alfred, North Dakota, both named for Alfred the Great.

Alfric, Alfrick, Alfris   Early English variant forms of Alfred. *See* Alfred.

Algar   A variant spelling of Alger. *See* Alger.

Alger   From the Anglo-Saxon, meaning "noble spear, noble warrior."
VARIANT FORMS: Elgar, Elger. CONTEMPORARY EXAMPLE: Alger Hiss, U.S.
government employee. SURNAME USAGE: Horatio Alger (1832-1899),
American writer.

Algernon   From the French *al grenon*, meaning "with mustache."
PET FORMS: Al, Algie, Algy. CONTEMPORARY EXAMPLE: Algernon Horatio, author.

Ali   A form of Allah, the Supreme Being of the Mohammedan religion.
Ali was the name of the fourth Calif of Islam (656-661), son-in-law of
Mohammed. Made popular with the publication of *The Arabian
Nights*, in which the famous story "Ali Baba and the Forty Thieves" ap-
pears. Also, an American Indian name, meaning "little." CONTEMPORA-
RY EXAMPLE: Ali A. Hossaini, physician. SURNAME USAGE: Muhammed
Ali, heavyweight boxing champion. PLACE-NAME USAGE: Ali Ak Chin,
Arizona.

Alic, Alick   Variant forms of Alex popular in Scotland. *See* Alex.
CONTEMPORARY EXAMPLE: Alick Rowe, author.

Alika   A Hawaiian form of Alexander. *See* Alexander.

Alistair, Allistair   Variant spellings of Alastair. *See* Alastair. May
also be derived from the Arabic *altair* (*al* plus *tair*), meaning "the bird."

Alix   A variant form of Alex. *See* Alex.

Allah   From the Arabic, meaning "God." The Moslem name for God.

Allan   Variant spellings of Alan. *See* Alan. SURNAME USAGE: Ethan
Allen (1738-1839), American Revolutionary soldier. PLACE-NAME USAGE:
Allantown, Arizona, named for Allan Johnson, a cattleman.

Allard   A variant spelling of Alard. *See* Alard.

Allen   The more common spelling of Allan. *See* Allan. PLACE-NAME

USAGE: Allentown, Pennsylvania, named for William Allen, an early landowner.

Allison A masculine name derived from Alice, meaning "Alice's son." *See* Alice (feminine section). CONTEMPORARY EXAMPLE: Allison Danzig, sportswriter. PLACE-NAME USAGE: Allisonia, Virginia.

Allistair, Allister Variant spellings of Alistair. *See* Alistair.

Allix A variant spelling of Alex. *See* Alex. CONTEMPORARY EXAMPLE: Allix B. James, educator.

Allon A variant spelling of Alon. *See* Alon. CONTEMPORARY EXAMPLE: Allon Gal, Israeli author. SURNAME USAGE: Yigal Allon, Israeli statesman.

Allston From the Old English, meaning "Al's (elf's) town." *See* Alfred. SURNAME USAGE: Washington Allston (1779-1843), artist, author.

Allyn A variant spelling of Alan. *See* Alan.

Almarine From the Scotch-Gaelic, meaning "noble, famous." CONTEMPORARY EXAMPLE: Almarine Wininger, a resident of San Jose, California.

Almeric An Old German name compounded of *amal*, meaning "work," and *ric*, meaning "ruler." In the eleventh century, the Norman-French introduced the name to England as Ameri, Amaury, and Amery.

Almon From the Hebrew, meaning "forsaken, widower." CONTEMPORARY EXAMPLE: Almon William, baseball player; Almon L. Mullen, bibliophile.

Alon From the Hebrew, meaning "oak tree." Allon is a variant spelling. Also used as a short form of Alphonso. *See* Alphonso. In the Bible, a member of the tribe of Simeon.

Alonso A variant spelling of Alphonso. *See* Alphonso.

Alonza, Alonzo Pet forms of Alphonso. *See* Alphonso. CONTEMPORARY EXAMPLE: Alonza Thomas, football player.

Aloys A short form of Aloysius. *See* Aloysius. CONTEMPORARY EXAMPLE: Aloys Senelder, inventor.

Aloysius A variant form of Loeis, which is an Old French name for Louis. *See* Louis. A sixteenth-century Spanish saint. CONTEMPORARY EXAMPLE: Aloysius J. Wycislo, clergyman.

Alpha The first letter of the Greek alphabet, meaning "the beginning." Derived from the Hebrew *aleph* and *aluph*, meaning "leader, prince."

Alphonse The French form of Alphonso. *See* Alphonso.

Alphonso From the Old High German *athal* and *adal*, meaning "noble," plus the Latin *funds*, meaning "estate"; hence "nobleman's estate." VARIANT FORMS: Alfons (German); Alphonse (French); Alonso (Spanish); Alfonso (Italian); Alonzo (English). The French Alphosine and the Spanish Alphosina are feminine forms. CONTEMPORARY EXAMPLE: Alphonso Taft, father of U.S. President Howard Taft; Alphonso Smith, basketball player.

Alpin From the Latin name Alpes (Alps), meaning "a high mountain." Akin to the Latin *albus*, meaning "white." The Alps are also called *Mont Blanc* (in French), meaning "white mountain."

Alroy From the Latin and Old English, meaning "royal ruler."

Alsie Probably a variant form of Alson. *See* Alson. CONTEMPORARY EXAMPLE: Alson J. Streeter, U.S. presidential candidate in 1888.

Alson A patronymic form, meaning "the son of Al." CONTEMPORARY EXAMPLE: Alson J. Streeter, U.S. presidential candidate in 1888.

Alston A variant spelling of Allston. *See* Allston. SURNAME USAGE: Walter Alston, baseball manager.

Alta From the Latin and Spanish, meaning "tall, high." Alto is a variant spelling. Used also as a feminine name.

Alter From the Old High German and Yiddish, meaning "the old one." Among Jews, a supplementary name given to a critically ill person so as to confuse the angel of death into thinking that the man called "old one" could not possibly be the (young) sick person he was after. CONTEMPORARY EXAMPLE: Alter Kriegel, rabbi.

Altie A pet form of Alta or Alistair. *See* Alta *and* Alistair. CONTEMPORARY EXAMPLE: Altie Taylor, football player.

Alto A variant spelling of Alta. *See* Alta. PLACE-NAME USAGE: Alto, Washington; Los Altos, California.

Alton From the Old English, meaning "old town." CONTEMPORARY EXAMPLES: Alton Carter, uncle of U.S. President Jimmy Carter; Alton Lennon, U.S. congressman. PLACE-NAME USAGE: Alton, Illinois, named for Alton Easton, son of the founder of the town; Alton, New Hampshire, named for a town in England.

Altus The Latin form of the name Alta, meaning "high." PLACE-NAME USAGE: Altus, Oklahoma; Altus, Arkansas.

Aluph From the Hebrew, meaning "head, chief."

Alva A variant spelling of Alvah. *See* Alvah.

Alvadore A short form of Salvadore. *See* Salvadore. PLACE-NAME USAGE: a town in Oregon named for Alvadore Welch, a banker.

Alvah A transposed form of the Hebrew *avla*, meaning "sin, in-

justice." In the Bible, a member of Esau's family. CONTEMPORARY EX-
AMPLE: Alvah Eaton, boxing promoter.

Alvan   From the Latin *albus*, meaning "white," or from the Old High
German, meaning "old friend" or "noble friend." In the Bible, the
name of an Edomite, not related to the modern name. Or, a variant
form of Alvah. *See* Alvah. VARIANT FORMS: Alvin, Alwin, Alwyn, Alva,
Alvah, Elva, Elvin, Elvis.

Alvar   A Norwegian form of the German Alfihar, meaning "elf army."
A variant form of Oliver. CONTEMPORARY EXAMPLE: Alvar Norgard,
football player.

Alvin   A variant form of Alvan. *See* Alvan.

Alvis   From Old Norse, meaning "wise." CONTEMPORARY EXAMPLE:
Alvis Shirley, baseball player.

Alwin, Alwyn   From the Old English, meaning "noble friend" or "elf
friend." Akin to Alvan and Alvin. VARIANT FORM: Elwin.

Alyn   A variant spelling of Alan and Alwin. *See* Alan *and* Alwin.

Alzada   Meaning uncertain. PLACE-NAME USAGE: Alzada, Montana,
named for Alzada Shelton, an early resident.

Amadeus   From the Latin and French, meaning "love of God."

Amadis   The Spanish form of Amadeus. *See* Amadeus. Amadis of
Gaul was the name of a character in a medieval romantic story written
in Spanish.

Amado   A variant form of Amadeus. *See* Amadeus. CONTEMPORARY
EXAMPLE: Amado Samuel, baseball player.

Amadore   From the Greek and Italian, meaning "gift of love."

Amal   From the Hebrew, meaning "work, toil." In the Bible, a
member of the tribe of Asher.

Amand   A French form of the Latin, meaning "worthy of love."
Amanda is a feminine form.

Amarillo   From the Spanish, meaning "yellow." CONTEMPORARY EX-
AMPLE: Amarillo Slim, professional gambler. PLACE-NAME USAGE: a city in Texas.

Amati   From the Italian, meaning "love." SURNAME USAGE: Nicolo
Amati (1596-1684), Italian violin-maker.

Ambert   From the German, meaning "bright, shining."

Ambrose   From the Greek, meaning "immortal, divine." St. Ambrose
was a fourth-century Bishop of Milan. Ambrosine is a feminine form.
CONTEMPORARY EXAMPLE: Ambrose Bierce, American author.

America, Americo, Americus   Americus Vespucius is the Latin name of Amerigo Vespucci, the Italian navigator after whom the American continent was named. CONTEMPORARY EXAMPLE: Americo Petrocelli, baseball player. PLACE-NAME USAGE: America, Oklahoma, named for America Stewart, a resident; American Township, Minnesota.

Amerigo The Spanish form of America. *See* America. CONTEMPORARY EXAMPLE: Amerigo Sapienza, football player.

Amery From the Latin, meaning "the loving one." May also be a form of the Hebrew name Amal. VARIANT FORMS: Amory, Embry, Emory, Imray, Imrie. *See* Amal.

Ames Probably from the Latin and French, meaning "love." SURNAME USAGE: Oakes Ames, a railroad official. PLACE-NAME USAGE: Ames, Iowa, named for Oakes Ames.

Ami From the Hebrew, meaning "my people." In the Bible, a servant of King Solomon. CONTEMPORARY EXAMPLE: Ami Shaked, psychologist.

Amiel From the Hebrew, meaning "God of my people."

Amihud From the Hebrew, meaning "my nation is glorious." In the Bible, a member of the tribe of Simeon. Amyhud is a variant spelling.

Amin From the Hebrew and Arabic, meaning "trustworthy." Made famous by Idi Amin, president of Uganda. SURNAME USAGE: Samir Amin, author.

Amiram From the Hebrew, meaning "my people (nation) is exalted." CONTEMPORARY EXAMPLE: Amiram Carmon, scientist.

Amitai From the Hebrew, meaning "truth." In the Bible, the father of Jonah.

Amitan From the Hebrew, meaning "true, faithful."

Ammon From Hebrew, meaning "faithful." In the Bible, a son of David. VARIANT FORMS: Amnon. PLACE-NAME USAGE: Ammon, Idaho, named after a leader mentioned in the *Book of Mormons*.

Amyhud A variant spelling of Amihud. *See* Amihud.

Amzi From the Hebrew, meaning "my strength." A descendant of Levi.

Analu The Hawaiian form of Andrew. *See* Andrew.

Anan From the Hebrew, meaning "a cloud." In the Bible, one of the Babylonian repatriates.

Anastasio A Spanish form of Anastasius. *See* Anastasius. Anastasia is the feminine form. Tacho is a pet form. CONTEMPORARY EXAMPLE: Anastasio Somoza, president of Nicaragua.

Anastasius From the Greek, meaning "resurrection." VARIANT FORMS: Anastase (French); Anastagio (Italian); Stas, Stasi (Old German). Anastatia is the feminine form.

Amnon   From the Hebrew, meaning "faithful." In the Bible, the oldest son of David. VARIANT FORM: Ammon. CONTEMPORARY EXAMPLE: Amnon Reshef, Israeli general.

Amon   From the Hebrew, meaning "faithful." CONTEMPORARY EXAMPLE: Amon G. Carter, publisher.

Amory   A variant spelling of Amery. *See* Amery.

Amos   From the Hebrew, meaning "to be burdened, troubled." In the Bible, an eighth-century B.C. prophet of Judean origin. CONTEMPORARY EXAMPLE: Amos Otis, baseball player.

Amoz   From the Hebrew, meaning "strong." In the Bible, the father of the prophet Isaiah.

Amram   From the Hebrew, meaning "a mighty nation." Also, from the Arabic, meaning "life." In the Bible, the father of Moses.

Amron   An invented name created by spelling Norman backwards and dropping the first "n." CONTEMPORARY EXAMPLE: Russel Amron McBride, Pasadena, California.

Anatole, Anatoly   From the Greek, meaning "rising of the sun," or "from the east." Anatoly is a Russian form. CONTEMPORARY EXAMPLE: Anatole Broyard, journalist; Anatoly Sharansky, Russian scientist. PLACE-NAME USAGE: Anatoly, Turkey.

Ancel   From the Old German name Ansi, meaning "a god." Ansila, used by the Normans, evolved into Ancelin and Ancelot. Ancelot later became Lancelot. Ancilla is probably the feminine form.

Ancher   From the Middle English *anker* and the Greek *ankyra*, meaning "an anchor, a hook." CONTEMPORARY EXAMPLE: Ancher Nelson, U.S. congressman.

Anders, Anderson   Patronymic form of Andrew, meaning "son of Andrew." *See* Andrew.

Andor   A variant form of Andrew. *See* Andrew. Akin to Anders. CONTEMPORARY EXAMPLE: Andor Weiss, communal leader.

Andre, Andres   The French and Spanish forms of Andrew. *See* Andrew. CONTEMPORARY EXAMPLES: Andre Previn, musical conductor; Andres Segovia, Spanish guitarist. SURNAME USAGE: Major John Andre, a British officer hanged as an American spy during the Revolutionary War.

Andreas   The Latin form of Andrew. *See* Andrew. CONTEMPORARY EXAMPLES: Andreas S. Anderson, educator; Andreas Antoniou, professor.

Andrew   From the Greek, meaning "manly, valiant, courageous." In the Bible, a disciple of Jesus; the brother of Simon Peter. A favorite name among Scandinavians and Scots. Andrew was a patron saint of Scotland and Russia. Immensely popular in the Middle Ages. More than 600 churches in England alone were dedicated to St. Andrew. VARIANT FORMS: Andreas (Latin, German, and Dutch); Anders, Andersen (Danish); Andrea (Italian); Andre, Andrien (French); Andres (Spanish); Andrei, Andrej (Russian); Andvari (Old Norse); Dandie (Scotch); Dries (Dutch); Bandi (Hungarian). PET FORMS: Andy, Tandy, Dandy, Drew. SURNAME USAGE: Hans Christian Andersen, Danish writer (1805-1959). ADDITIONAL SURNAMES: Anders, Andres, Andreyer, Tandy. PLACE-NAME USAGE: Lake Andrusia, in Minnesota, named after President Andrew Jackson; the Andes mountain range (originally Andy's mountains); Andersonville, Georgia.

Andrewes　An early English form of Andrew. SURNAME USAGE: Lancelet Andrewes (1555-1626), English theologian.

Andronicus　A Greek form of Andrew. *See* Andrew. In the Bible, a relative of Paul.

Andros　A Greek form of Andrew. *See* Andrew. SURNAME USAGE: Sir Edmund Andros (1637-1714), British governor of the American colonies.

Andy　A pet form of Andrew. *See* Andrew.

Aneurin　Probably a variant form of the Latin name Honorius, meaning "honor." A seventh-century Welsh poet. Commonly used in Wales. Aneirin is a variant spelling. Nye is a pet form. CONTEMPORARY EXAMPLE: Aneurin Bevan, author.

Angel, Angell　From the Greek, meaning "a messenger" or "a saintly person." VARIANT FORMS: Angelico, Angelo, Angelos. Angela is a feminine form. PET FORMS: Angie, Angelina. CONTEMPORARY EXAMPLE: Angel Cordero, jockey. PLACE-NAME USAGE: Mount Angel, Oregon; Angel Island, California; Angel Terrace, Wyoming.

Angelico　An Italian form of Angel. *See* Angel. SURNAME USAGE: Fra Angelico (1387-1455), Italian painter.

Angelo　An Italian form of Angel. *See* Angel. CONTEMPORARY EXAMPLE: Angelo Wells, football player.

Angelos　A Greek form from which the name Angel derives. *See* Angel. CONTEMPORARY EXAMPLE: Angelos Terzakis, novelist.

Angie　A pet form of Angel. *See* Angel. Used also as a feminine form. CONTEMPORARY EXAMPLE: Angie Leno, musician.

Angus　From the Gaelic and Irish, meaning "exceptional, outstanding." The original form was Aeneas, a Trojan hero. In Celtic mythology, Angus was the god of love. A popular name among the Scots and Irish. Gus is a pet form. CONTEMPORARY EXAMPLE: Angus Wilson, novelist. PLACE-NAME USAGE: a county in Scotland.

Ansel, Anselm　From the Old German, meaning "divine helmet of God." Saint Anselm was Archbishop of Canterbury in the eleventh century. Ansel is a variant form. CONTEMPORARY EXAMPLES: Ansel

Adams, author; Anselm L. Straus, professor.

Anson, Ansonia   From the Anglo-Saxon, meaning "the son of Ann" or "the son of Hans." *See* Hans. CONTEMPORARY EXAMPLES: Anson Dibell, author; Anson Williams, actor. PLACE-NAME USAGE: Ansonia, Connecticut; Ansonia, Pennsylvania, named for Anson G. Phelps; Anson County in North Carolina, named for Admiral George Anson, an eighteenth-century resident.

Antal   A variant form of Anatole. *See* Anatole. CONTEMPORARY EXAMPLE: Antal Dorati, musical conductor.

Anton, Antone, Antonin   Variant forms of Antony. *See* Antony. Anton is used mostly by Germans, Scots, and Slavs. CONTEMPORARY EXAMPLE: Anton Peters, football player; Antonin Sealia, professor. PLACE-NAME USAGE: San Antone Lakes, New Mexico.

Antonino   A variant form of Anthony. *See* Anthony. PLACE-NAME USAGE: Antonino, Kansas, named for Anthony Sauer, the most senior local citizen.

Antonio   The Italian, Spanish, and Portuguese form of Antony. *See* Antony. CONTEMPORARY EXAMPLE: Antonio Aguilar, boxer. PLACE-NAME USAGE: a city in Kansas named after Anthony Sauer. Antonio was used because another city in Kansas had already been named Anthony.

Antony, Anthony   From the Greek, meaning "flourishing," and from the Latin, meaning "worthy of praise." Antonius is the original form. VARIANT FORMS: Antoine, Antoni (French); Anton (Russian and Slavonic); Antonio, Tonio, Tonetto (Italian); Antal (Hungarian); Antonio (Italian, Spanish, and Portuguese). Among the earliest to use the name in some form were: the first century Roman general Marcus Antonius, also known as Mark (Marc) Antony (Anthony); Antoninus Pius (86-161), a Roman emperor; and Saint Anthony, patron of swineherds. Antony was popular in twelfth-century England. In the sixteenth century, the letter "h" was added to make it Anthony. Antonia is a feminine form. SURNAME USAGE: Susan Brownell Anthony (1820-1906), American suffragist leader.

Anwar   From the Arabic, meaning "light." CONTEMPORARY EXAMPLE: Anwar Sadat, president of Egypt.

Ara   From the Latin, meaning "altar." In the Bible, a descendant of the tribe of Asher. CONTEMPORARY EXAMPLE: Ara Parseghian, football coach.

Aram   From the Assyrian *aramu*, meaning "high, heights." The ancient name of Syria, whose language was Aramaic. In the Bible, the grandson of Noah. CONTEMPORARY EXAMPLE: Aram Saroyan, author.

Arbie   Probably from the Old French, meaning "a crossbow." CONTEMPORARY EXAMPLE: Arbie M. Dale, psychologist.

Arch   A short form of Archibald. Also used as an independent name. CONTEMPORARY EXAMPLE: Arch A. Moore, governor of West Virginia;

Arch Stokes, labor lawyer. PLACE-NAME USAGE: Arch, Oklahoma; Arch, New Mexico.

Archibald   From the Anglo-Saxon, meaning "very bold" or "holy prince." CONTEMPORARY EXAMPLE: Archibald Cox, attorney. PET FORMS: Arch, Archie, Archy.

Archie, Archy   Pet forms of Archibald. *See* Archibald. Archie has become an independent name. CONTEMPORARY EXAMPLE: Archie H. Crowley, clergyman.

Ard   Probably a short form of Addar. *See* Addar. In the Bible, a son of Benjamin.

Arda   A form of Ard or Arden. May also be from Middle High German, meaning "a heart, a deer." CONTEMPORARY EXAMPLE: Arda Bowser, football player.

Arden   From the Latin, meaning "to burn." Popularized in Shakespeare's *As You Like It*. PLACE-NAME USAGE: an area in Warwickshire, England; an area in northeastern France, southern Belgium, and Luxembourg called Ardennes; a city in South Carolina.

Ardon   From the Hebrew, meaning "bronze." In the Bible, a son of Caleb, a member of the tribe of Judah.

Arel   From the Hebrew, meaning "lion of God." Ariel is a variant form. Akin to Ariel.

Areli   A variant form of Arel. *See* Arel. In the Bible, a son of Gad.

Arend   Possibly a variant form of Arnold or Aaron. *See* Arnold *and* Aaron. CONTEMPORARY EXAMPLE: Arend Lubbers, educator.

Aretas   Origin doubtful, but may be associated with Arethusa, a nymph of the woods in Greek mythology. In the Bible, a Rabataean king. The eighteenth-century governor of the Leeward Islands was Aretas Seton.

Argus   From the Greek, meaning "bright." In Greek mythology, a giant with one hundred eyes.

Argyle   A fabric with a woven diamond-shaped design. Popular in Scotland. CONTEMPORARY EXAMPLE: Argyle Wakeman, football player. PLACE-NAME USAGE: a county in Scotland, also spelled Argyll.

Ari   From the Hebrew, meaning "a lion." Also, a pet form of Aristotle. *See* Aristotle.

Aric, Arick   Early German forms of Richard. *See* Richard.

Arie   A variant spelling of Ari. *See* Ari.

Ariel   From the Hebrew, meaning "lion of God." In the Bible, a leader who served under Ezra; also, a symbolic name for Jerusalem, David's city (Isaiah 29). Akin to Arel. In Shakespeare's *The Tempest*, a spirit who was the servant of Prospero. CONTEMPORARY EXAMPLE: Ariel Merari, Israeli professor.

Ario   A variant form of Ari. *See* Ari. Also, a variant form of Arion. *See* Arion.

Arion   From the Italian *aria* and *arioso*, meaning "songlike, melodious." In Greek mythology, a musician who was thrown overboard by pirates and was saved by a dolphin. SURNAME USAGE: Lodovico Ariostos (1474-1533), Italian poet.

Aristo   From the Greek *aristos*, meaning "the best." VARIANT FORMS: Aristotle, Aristophanes.

Aristotle   A variant form of Aristo. *See* Aristo. A foremost Greek philosopher (384-322 B.C.).

Arkady   The Russian form of Archibald. CONTEMPORARY EXAMPLE: Arkady Strugarsky, author.

Arky   A pet form of Archibald. Used also as a short form of Arkansas. CONTEMPORARY EXAMPLE: Arky Vaughan, baseball player.

Arland   A variant form of Arlando. *See* Arlando. CONTEMPORARY EXAMPLE: Arland Christ-Janer, educator.

Arlando   A variant form of Orlando. *See* Orlando. CONTEMPORARY EXAMPLE: Arlando Smith, television technician.

Arlee   A variant form of Arleigh. *See* Arleigh. PLACE-NAME USAGE: a city in Montana, named for an Indian chief.

Arleigh   A variant form of Arles. *See* Arles. May also be a variant form of Harley. *See* Harley. CONTEMPORARY EXAMPLE: Arleigh B. Templeton, educator.

Arlen   The Celtic form of Arles, meaning "a pledge." VARIANT FORMS: Arlin, Arland. SURNAME USAGE: Richard Arlen, actor.

Arles   Originally a Hebrew word, *eravon*, meaning "a pledge, a promise to pay." Arrived at its present form via Latin, French, and Middle English. VARIANT FORMS: Arlen, Arleigh, Arley, Arlie, Arlin, Arliss, Arland, Arlo, Arlyn.

Arley   A variant spelling of Arleigh. *See* Arleigh. CONTEMPORARY EXAMPLE: Arley Cooper, baseball player.

Arlie   A variant spelling of Arleigh. *See* Arleigh.

Arlin   A variant spelling of Arlen. *See* Arlen.

Arliss   A variant form of Arles. *See* Arles. CONTEMPORARY EXAMPLE: Arliss Taylor, baseball player.

Arlo   Probably from the Old English, meaning "a fortified hill." CONTEMPORARY EXAMPLE: Arlo Guthrie, folk singer.

Arlyn   A variant spelling of Arlin. *See* Arlin.

Armand   French and Italian form of the Old German name Hermann, meaning "warrior." VARIANT FORMS: Armine (French); Armando (Spanish); Armino (Italian); Herman (Dutch). CONTEMPORARY EXAMPLES: Armand Quick, scientist; Armand Hammer, industrialist.

Armando   A Spanish form of Armand. *See* Armand.

Armen, Armin   Variant forms of Armand. *See* Armand. CONTEMPORARY EXAMPLE: Armin Mandel, industrialist.

Armond   A variant spelling of Armand. *See* Armand.

Armon   From the Hebrew, meaning "castle, palace."

Armoni   From the Hebrew, meaning "castle, palace." In the Bible, a son of King Saul.

Armstrong   An Old English nickname for a strong person. A popular surname.

Arndt   A variant form of Arnold. *See* Arnold. CONTEMPORARY EXAMPLE: Arndt Jorgens, baseball player.

Arne   A short form of Adrian. Popular in the north of England in the Middle Ages. *See* Adrian. Also, a modern pet name for Arnold. *See* Arnold.

Arnesta   Probably a form of the Spanish and Italian forms of Ernest (Ernesto). *See* Ernest. CONTEMPORARY EXAMPLE: Arnesta Gaines, baseball player.

Arnie   A pet form of Arnold. *See* Arnold.

Arno   A short form of Arnold. *See* Arnold. PLACE-NAME USAGE: a city in California; a river in Italy.

Arnold   From the Old German, compounded from *aran*, meaning "eagle," and *wald*, meaning "power." Commonly used by Teutonic tribal chiefs. A popular name in northern Europe prior to the sixteenth century. VARIANT FORMS: Armand, Armant, Arnaud, Arnaut (French); Ahrent, Ahrens, Arno (German); Arnoldo (Italian and Spanish); Arend (Dutch). PET FORMS: Arne, Arny, Arnie. SURNAME USAGE: Benedict Arnold (1741-1801), the American general who became a traitor. VARIANT FORMS: Arnoll, Arnot, Arnott, Arnald, Arnall, Arnell, Arnet, Arnett, Arness.

Arny   A pet form of Arnold. *See* Arnold.

Arnon   From the Hebrew, meaning "roaring stream." In the Bible, a stream on the frontier of Moab that flowed into the Dead Sea.

Aron   A variant spelling of Aaron. *See* Aaron.

Arrigo   The Italian pet form of Harry. *See* Harry.

Arsen From the Greek *arsenikos*, meaning "manly, strong." CONTEMPORARY EXAMPLE: Arsen Darnay, novelist.

Art A short form of Arthur. *See* Arthur. PLACE-NAME USAGE: a city in Texas.

Artemas A variant spelling of Artemis. *See* Artemis. In the Bible, a companion of Paul.

Artemis Used as masculine and feminine names. In Greek mythology, the goddess of the moon, animals, and hunting.

Artemus A variant spelling of Artemis. *See* Artemis. CONTEMPORARY EXAMPLE: Artemus Allen, baseball player.

Arthur From the Gaelic *art*, meaning "a rock," hence "noble, lofty hill"; or, from the Celtic *artos*, meaning "a bear." Also, from the Icelandic, meaning "a follower of Tur (Thor)," the Norse god of war. Arthur was the legendary sixth-century king of Britain who led the knights of the Round Table. Was common in the nineteenth century, because of the popularity of Arthur Wellesley, Duke of Wellington. VARIANT FORMS: Artor, Artur, Arturo (Italian). PET FORMS: Art, Artie, Arty. Arta is a feminine form. SURNAME USAGE: Chester A. Arthur (1830-1886), twenty-first president of the U.S. PLACE-NAME USAGE: Port Arthur, Texas; Arthur Kill, New Jersey; Arthur Peak, Wyoming.

Artie Pet forms of Arthur. *See* Arthur.

Artimus A variant spelling of Artemis. *See* Artemis. CONTEMPORARY EXAMPLE: Artimus Parker, football player.

Artis A pet form of either Arthur or Artimus. *See* Arthur *and* Artimus. CONTEMPORARY EXAMPLE: Artis Gilmore, basketball player.

Artro, Arturo Variant forms of Arthur. *See* Arthur. CONTEMPORARY EXAMPLE: Artro Morris, actor; Arturo Toscanini, musical conductor.

Arty A pet form of Arthur. *See* Arthur.

Arva, Arvada From the Latin, meaning "from the coast," or from the Danish, meaning "eagle." Used also as feminine names. PLACE-NAME USAGE: Arvada, Colorado. One of the founding fathers was Hiram Arvada Haskins.

Arval, Arvala From the Latin, meaning "cultivated land." CONTEMPORARY EXAMPLE: Arvel Hale, baseball player.

Arvid, Arvin From the Anglo-Saxon, meaning "a man of the people" or "a friend of the people." PET FORMS: Arv, Arve, Arvy. CONTEMPORARY EXAMPLE: Arvin W. Hahn, educator.

Ary A variant spelling of Ari. *See* Ari.

Arye, Aryeh From the Hebrew, meaning "lion." In the Bible, one of the officers in the army of Pekah. CONTEMPORARY EXAMPLE: Arye Amyr, sculptor; Aryeh Neier, attorney.

Aryell   A variant spelling of Ariel. *See* Ariel. CONTEMPORARY EXAMPLE: Aryell Cohen, choir director.

Asa   From the Hebrew, meaning "healer." In the Bible, a king of Judah. CONTEMPORARY EXAMPLE: Asa Gray, botanist.

Asael   From the Hebrew, meaning "God has created." In the Bible, a nephew of King David. Also spelled Asahel.

Asaph   From the Hebrew, meaning "to gather." In the Bible, a Levite. PLACE-NAME USAGE: a city in Pennsylvania.

Ascanius   From the Old Norse *askr* and the Middle English *asshe*, meaning "an ash tree." In Roman legend, the son of Aeneas, hero of Virgil's *Aeneid*.

Aser   A variant form of Asher. *See* Asher.

Asgard   From the Old Norse *ass*, meaning "god," plus *garth*, meaning "yard, court." In Norse mythology, Asgard was the home of the gods and of slain heroes.

Ash   From the Old Norse *askr* and the Middle English *asshe*, meaning "an ash tree." VARIANT FORMS: Ashby, Ashbey, Ashley. PLACE-NAME USAGE: Ash Butte, Oregon.

Ashbel   From the Hebrew, meaning "the fire of [the god] Bel." In the Bible, a son of Benjamin. CONTEMPORARY EXAMPLE: Ashbel Green, educator.

Ashbey, Ashby   From the Scandinavian, meaning "from the ash tree farm." CONTEMPORARY EXAMPLE: Ashby Neusome, baseball player.

Asher   From the Hebrew, meaning "blessed, fortunate, happy." In the Bible, the son of Jacob and Zilpah, head of one of the twelve tribes. SURNAME USAGE: Asser, Anschel, Ansell, Asherson.

Ashford   From the Old English, meaning "from the ford near the ash tree."

Ashley   From the Old English, meaning "a field of ash trees." CONTEMPORARY EXAMPLES: Ashley Harvey-Walker, cricket player; Ashley Carter, author. PLACE-NAME USAGE: a river in South Carolina.

Asir   From the Hebrew, meaning "to bind, imprison." In the Bible, a son of Korah.

Asser   A variant form of Asher. *See* Asher. CONTEMPORARY EXAMPLE: Asser Levy, seventeenth-century Jewish pioneer in America.

Asun   Probably a variant form of the Arabic name Hassan. *See* Hassan. CONTEMPORARY EXAMPLE: Asun Balzola, author.

Atanasio   A variant form of Anastasia. *See* Anastasia. CONTEMPORARY EXAMPLE: Atanasio Perez, baseball player.

Athan   From the Greek, meaning "immortality." A short form of Athanasius. Saint Athanasius (293-373), a Greek church father. CONTEMPO-RARY EXAMPLE: Athan Theoharis, professor.

Athens   In Greek mythology, the goddess of wisdom and skills, the counterpart of Minerva in Roman mythology. Athena is a feminine form. CONTEMPORARY EXAMPLE: Athens Clay Pullias, educator. PLACE-NAME USAGE: the capital of Greece.

Athol   Meaning uncertain. May be related to the word "atoll," a ring-shaped island. CONTEMPORARY EXAMPLE: Athol Guy, musician. PLACE-NAME USAGE: a district in Scotland; Athol, Idaho.

Atlas   From the Greek, meaning "to bear, lift, carry." In Greek myth-ology, a Titan forced to carry the world on his shoulders as punishment for warring against Zeus. A symbol of strength. SURNAME USAGE: Charles Atlas, gymnastic. PLACE-NAME USAGE: Atlas Mountains in northwest Africa; Atlas, Texas.

Atli   An Old Norse form of the Gothic name Attila. In Norse myth-ology, a king of the Huns, killed by his wife Gudrun. *See* Attila.

Atoy   Possibly a variant form of Attila. *See* Attila. CONTEMPORARY EX-AMPLE: Atoy Wilson, figure skater.

Attila, Attilio   From the Gothic, meaning "little father." Derived from the Greek and Latin name Atta, meaning "father," and *ila*, a diminutive suffix. Attila the Hun ruled over the Goths in the fifth cen-tury. Attilio is an Italian form. CONTEMPORARY EXAMPLES: Attila Ficzere, ballet dancer; Attilio R. Frassinelli, Connecticut politician. PLACE-NAME USAGE: Attila Mountain, New Hampshire.

Aubert   From the Old German, meaning "bright ruler."

Aubin   From the Latin, meaning "fair, white." VARIANT FORMS: Alban, Albin, Auburn.

Aubrey   From the Teutonic, meaning "elf ruler." The original form was Alberic. *See* Alberic. Avery is a variant form.

Auburn   From the Latin, meaning "fair, white." VARIANT FORMS: Al-ban, Albin, Aubin. PLACE-NAME USAGE: Auburn, New York; Auburn, Wyoming.

August   German and English variant forms of Augustus. *See* Augustus. PET FORMS: Gus, Augie. August, the eighth month in the calendar, was named after Augustus Caesar, grand-nephew of Julius Caesar. CONTEMPORARY EXAMPLE: August Busch, business executive.

Augustin, Augustine   Variant forms of Augustus. *See* Augustus. CONTEMPORARY EXAMPLE: Augustine R. Marusi, industrialist. PLACE-NAME USAGE: a creek in Delaware, named for Augustine Herrman, an early settler; San Augustine, Texas; St. Augustine, Florida.

Augustus   From the Latin, meaning "revered, exalted." First used as a title of honor for the first Roman emperor, Augustus Caesar (63 B.C. to 14 A.D.). VARIANT FORMS: August, Augustin (German); Augustino

(Spanish); Augustin, Augustine, Austin, Austen (English); Agostinho (Portuguese); Agostin (Polish); Agostino (Italian). CONTEMPORARY EXAMPLE: Augustus Phillips, football player.

Aundra   Probably from Saundra, a form of Alexander. *See* Alexander. CONTEMPORARY EXAMPLE: Aundra Thompson, football player.

Aurea   From the Latin, meaning "gold, golden." VARIANT FORMS: Aurel, Orel.

Aurel   A form of Aurelio. *See* Aurelio.

Aurelio   A variant form of Aurelius. *See* Aurelius. Aurelia is a feminine form. CONTEMPORARY EXAMPLE: Aurelio Rodriquez, baseball player.

Aurelius   From the Latin, meaning "gold, golden." Marcus Aurelius (121-180), Roman statesman, was emperor of Rome (161-180). PLACE-NAME USAGE: Arles, France, probably named for Aurelius; a city in New York state.

Aurelo   A variant form of Aurelio. *See* Aurelio. CONTEMPORARY EXAMPLE: Aurelo Kolnai, author.

Aury   A pet form of Aurelius. *See* Aurelius.

Austen, Austin   English variant forms of August and Augustus. *See* August *and* Augustus. CONTEMPORARY EXAMPLE: Austin M. Patterson, editor. PLACE-NAME USAGE: Austin, Texas, named for Stephen F. Austin, a patriot; Austin, Minnesota, named for Austin R. Nicholls, an early settler.

Autrey   A variant form of the feminine Audrey. *See* Audrey (feminine section). CONTEMPORARY EXAMPLE: Autrey Howell, football player.

Av   From the Hebrew, meaning "father." Also, a pet form of Averell. CONTEMPORARY EXAMPLE: Av Weston, television executive.

Avenel   Probably a masculine form of Aveline and Evelina. *See* Aveline *and* Evelina (feminine section). PLACE-NAME USAGE: Avenel, Maryland; Avenel, New Jersey.

Averell   Probably from the Latin name Everild, a seventh-century Yorkshire saint. A compound of the Old English *oefer*, meaning "boar," and *hild*, meaning "battle." May also be from the Old English, meaning "to open," associated with spring and the "opening" of nature. VARIANT FORMS: Averil, Averill, Haverhill. CONTEMPORARY EXAMPLE: W. Averell Harriman, U.S. statesman.

Averic   From the Latin and French, meaning "truthful, honest ruler."

Averil, Averill   Variant forms of Averell. *See* Averell.

Averitt   A variant form of Everett. *See* Everett. CONTEMPORARY EXAMPLE: Averitt Bird, basketball player.

Averno   From the Latin and French, meaning "truthful." CONTEM-
PORARY EXAMPLE: Averno M. Rempel, educator.

Avery   A variant form of Aubrey. *See* Aubrey.

Avi   From the Hebrew, meaning "my father." Abi is a variant form.
CONTEMPORARY EXAMPLE: Avi Piamenta, musician.

Avidan   From the Hebrew, meaning "father of justice" or "God is
just."

Avidor   From the Hebrew, meaning "father of a generation."

Aviel   The Hebrew spelling of Abiel. *See* Abiel.

Avigdor   From the Hebrew, meaning "father protector."

Avinoam   From the Hebrew, meaning "father of delight."

Avital   From the Hebrew, meaning "father of dew." Used as a
masculine and feminine name in Israel.

Avitus   From the Latin *avis*, meaning "a bird." CONTEMPORARY EXAM-
PLE: Avitus Himsl, baseball player.

Avner   The Hebrew spelling of Abner. *See* Abner.

Avniel   From the Hebrew, meaning "God is my rock."

Avraham, Avram, Avrom, Avrum   Hebraic forms of Abraham and
Abram. *See* Abraham *and* Abram. CONTEMPORARY EXAMPLES:
Avram Fleishman, professor; Avraham Weiss, rabbi.

Axel, Axtel   Swedish names of Germanic origin, meaning "divine
source of life." CONTEMPORARY EXAMPLE: Axel Lindstrom, baseball
player; Axel Madsen, author.

Aylmer   From the Old English Aethelmaer, a compounded name
meaning "noble and famous." VARIANT FORMS: Ailemar, Eilemar,
Elmer.

Aylwin   A variant form of Alwin. *See* Alwin.

Azaria, Azariah   From the Hebrew, meaning "God is my help." In
the Bible, a king of Judah. Used in England and America by the
Puritans. CONTEMPORARY EXAMPLE: Azaria Alon, naturalist.

Azaz   From the Hebrew, meaning "strong." In the Bible, the father
of Bela.

Aziz   From the Hebrew, meaning "strong."

Aziza   A variant form of Aziz. *See* Aziz. In the Bible, a son of Zahu.
Used also as a feminine name.

Azriel   From the Hebrew, meaning "God is my help." In the Bible,
members of the tribe of Manasseh and Naphtali. CONTEMPORARY EX-
AMPLE: Azriel Eisenberg, author.

B

Babe   A common masculine and feminine nickname, Basically, a pet form of baby. Bubba is a variant form. *See* Bubba. *See also* Bambino. CONTEMPORARY EXAMPLE: Babe Ruth (George Herman Ruth), baseball star.

Babson   An English matronymic form, meaning "Barbara's son." *See* Barbara (feminine section).

Bacchus   In Greek and Roman mythology, the god of wine and revelry. His earlier Greek name was Dionysius. The son of Jupiter (and Zeus), he learned to make wine from grapes. PLACE-NAME USAGE: Bacchus, Utah, named for T.W. Bacchus, a local resident.

Badger   An occupational name for a dealer in grain. Derived from the animal known for stealing and storing grain. Brock is the Anglo-Saxon and Gaelic form, from *broc*, meaning "badger." PLACE-NAME USAGE: Badger Lake, South Dakota; Badger Creek, Arizona; Badgeworthy, in Gloucester, England, later called Badgery.

Bailey, Bayley   From the Middle English *bail* and *baile*, meaning "fortification" or "outer castle wall." CONTEMPORARY EXAMPLE: Bailey Howell, basketball player.

Bainbridge   Compounded of *bain* and *bridge*. From the Latin and French *bain*, a form of *payn*, which is a contraction of *pagan*, a common name among the Norman knights. *Bain* may also be from the Latin and French word for "bath." PLACE-NAME USAGE: Bainbridge, Georgia, named for William Bainbridge, an early hero of the U.S. Navy.

Baird   A Scottish form of Bard, meaning "minstrel." PLACE-NAME USAGE: a mountain range in Northwest Alaska named for S.F. Baird (1823-1887), ornithologist.

Bake, Bakke   From the Middle English *baken*, meaning "to bake." CONTEMPORARY EXAMPLE: Bake McBride, baseball player. SURNAME USAGE: George Pierce Baker (1886-1935), American author. PLACE-NAME USAGE: Bakersfield, California, named for Colonel T. Baker, an early settler.

Balder   In Norse mythology, the God of sun and summer, light and peace. From the Old Norse *baldr*, meaning "bold, dangerous."

Baldwin   From the Middle High German name Baldewin, meaning "bold friend." Baldewin and Baudoin are Old French forms. Baldwin I was King of Jerusalem in the twelfth century. CONTEMPORARY EXAMPLE: Baldwin Dansby, author. SURNAME USAGE: Stanley Baldwin

29

(1867-1947), British prime minister. PLACE-NAME USAGE: Baldwin, Long Island, New York, named for the prominent Baldwin family.

Balfour   From the Old English *bal*, meaning "a hill," and *far*, meaning "along the way." Balfouria is a feminine form. Adopted as a personal name in Israel, after 1917, when the Balfour Declaration was issued. CONTEMPORARY EXAMPLE: Balfour Brickner, rabbi. SURNAME USAGE: Lord Arthur James Balfour (1848-1930), British foreign secretary.

Ball   From the Middle English *bal*, meaning "a ball." Also from the Old French *baller*, meaning "to dance." Also, a pet form of Baldwin. *See* Baldwin. SURNAME USAGE: George Ball, U.S. statesman. PLACE-NAME USAGE: Ball's Bluff, Virginia; Ball Ground, Georgia.

Ballard   From the Middle English *balad* and Old French *ballade*, meaning "a dancing song."

Balor   From the Old French *bale* and *balle*, and from the Old High German *balla*, meaning "one who makes bales or packages." CONTEMPORARY EXAMPLE: Balor Libon, baseball player.

Bambino   From the Italian *bambo*, meaning "a small child." A nickname of baseball hero George Herman (Babe) Ruth.

Bancroft   From the Anglo-Saxon, meaning "bean field." Banfield is a variant form. SURNAME USAGE: George Bancroft (1800-1891), U.S. statesman.

Banet   A short form of Barnett and Bennett. *See* Barnett *and* Bennett.

Banfield   From the Anglo-Saxon, meaning "bean field." Bancroft is a variant form.

Baptist, Baptiste   From the Greek and Latin, meaning "a dipping." First used as the name of John the Baptist. The French form is Jean-Baptiste. CONTEMPORARY EXAMPLE: Baptist Thunder and Baptiste Manzini, football players.

Barak   From the Hebrew, meaning "flash of light." In the Bible, an army officer when Deborah ruled over Israel.

Baram   From the Hebrew, meaning "son of the nation."

Barber   Originally an occupational name. From the Latin *barga*, meaning "a beard." Akin to the feminine name Barbara. Barbour is a variant spelling. CONTEMPORARY EXAMPLE: Barber B. Conable, Jr., U.S. congressman. PLACE-NAME USAGE: Barber, Ohio, named for O.C. Barber, a town founder (1892).

Barbour   A variant spelling of Barber. Used in England. *See* Barber.

Barclay   A variant form of Berkely. *See* Berkeley. CONTEMPORARY EXAMPLE: Barclay Plager, hockey player; Barclay Cooke, author.

Bard   From the Gaelic and Irish, meaning "a minstrel, a poet." Shakespeare was known as the Bard of Avon. May also be from the French, Spanish, and Italian *barde* and *barda*, meaning "a leather armor" for horses.

Barden   From the Anglo-Saxon, meaning "a valley where barley grows." *See also* Borden. VARIANT FORMS: Bardon, Borden.

Bardolf, Bardolph   From the German, meaning "bright wolf."

Bardon   A variant of Barden. *See* Barden.

Baretta   Probably from the French *beret*, meaning "a cap." popularized by Tony Baretta, a character in a television series. May also be a short form of Barnett. *See* Barnett.

Bari, Barri   Variant spellings of Barrie. *See* Barrie. Also, from the Old English *bar*, meaning "gate, a fence."

Barker   An Old English occupational name. From *bire*, meaning "a birch tree," hence "a logger of birch trees." Birk is a Scottish form.

Barksdale   From the Old English, meaning "a valley where birch trees grow." CONTEMPORARY EXAMPLE: Barksdale Hamlett, educator.

Barnabas   From the Latin, Greek, and Aramaic, meaning "son of exhortation." In the New Testament, a disciple of Paul; one of the first Christian missionaries. Barnaby is a variant form. CONTEMPORARY EXAMPLE: Barnabas Sears, attorney.

Barnaby   A variant form of Barnabas. The name of a character in the television series *Barnaby Jones*.

Barnard   The French form of Bernard. *See* Bernard. CONTEMPORARY EXAMPLE: Barnard Hughes, actor. SURNAME USAGE: George Gray Barnard (1863-1938), American sculptor. PLACE-NAME USAGE: Mount Barnard, California, named in 1892 for E.E. Barnard, astronomer.

Barnes   From the Old English *beorna*, meaning "a bear." CONTEMPORARY EXAMPLE: Barnes Milan, football player. SURNAME USAGE: Harry Elmer Barnes (1889-1968), sociologist. PLACE-NAME USAGE: Barnes, Arizona, named for Will C. Barnes (1859-1936), author of *Arizona Place Names*.

Barnet, Barnett   Variant forms of Bernard. *See* Bernard. Banet is an abbreviated form. CONTEMPORARY EXAMPLE: Barnett Danson, Canadian political leader. PLACE-NAME USAGE: Barnet, Vermont, named for a town in England.

Barney   A pet form of Bernard and Barnaby. *See* Bernard *and* Barnaby.

Barnum   From the German, meaning "a storage place" or "a barn." SURNAME USAGE: Phineas Taylor Barnum (1810-1891), circus originator.

Barr, Barre   Short forms of Bernard and Barnard. *See* Bernard *and* Barnard. PLACE-NAME USAGE: Barre, Maine, named for Isaac Barre, a supporter of American independence.

Barret, Barrett   Short forms of Barnett. *See* Barnett. CONTEMPORARY EXAMPLE: Barrett Smith, football player. SURNAME USAGE: Elizabeth Barrett (Browning), poet.

Barrie   A variant spelling of Barry. *See* Barry.

Barron   From the Old High German *baro*, meaning "a man, a person of nobility."

Barry   A Welsh patronymic form of Harry (from Ap-Harry and Ab-Harry), meaning "son of Harry." *See* Harry. May also be an Old Celtic name, meaning "spear" or "marksman." VARIANT FORMS: Barrie, Barett, Barnett, Barnard. SURNAME USAGE: James M. Barrie (1860-1937), British novelist. PLACE-NAME USAGE: Barry Islands, in Wales, named after Baruch, a devout man interred there.

Bart   A pet form of Barton and Bartholomew. *See* Barton *and* Bartholomew. May also be a variant spelling of Bard. *See* Bard. CONTEMPORARY EXAMPLE: Bart Starr, football player.

Barth   A variant spelling of Bart. *See* Bart. Also, from the Anglo-Saxon, meaning "a shelter." SURNAME USAGE: Karl Barth (1886-1968), Swiss theologian.

Bartholomew   A patronymic form meaning "son of Talmai." From the Aramaic *telem*, meaning "hill, furrow." In the Bible, one of the twelve Apostles. VARIANT FORMS: Bartholomieu, Barholomee, Tolomieu (French); Bartolo, Meo (Italian); Bardo, Bartel (Danish); Bartholomaus, Bertel, Bartold, Mewes (German); Bartolo, Bartolome (Spanish); Bartley (Irish); Bartlett, Bat (English). PET FORMS: Bart, Bat, Bate, Batly, Bartle, Bartelot, Batcock, Batkin, Tolly, Tholy.

Bartlett   A variant form of Bartholomew. *See* Bartholomew. SURNAME USAGE: Josiah Bartlett (1729-1795), American Revolutionary patriot; Enoch Bartlett, Roxbury, Massachusetts, for whom the Bartlett pear was named.

Bartley   From the Anglo-Saxon, meaning "Bart's (Bartholomew's) field." *See* Bartholomew. Used in Ireland.

Barton   From the Anglo-Saxon, meaning "Bart's (Bartholomew's) town." *See* Bartholomew. VARIANT FORMS: Bart, Barth, Bartley. CONTEMPORARY EXAMPLE: Barton E. Smith, football player; Barton A. Dowdy, educator. PLACE-NAME USAGE: Barton Kansas, named for Clara Barton (1821-1912), Civil War nurse.

Baruch   From the Hebrew, meaning "blessed." In the Bible, the friend and secretary of the prophet Jeremiah. VARIANT FORMS: Bendit, Benedict, Beniton, Boruch. PET FORMS: Barrie, Barry. SURNAME USAGE: Bernard Mannes Baruch (1870-1965), American financier and statesman.

Barzilai From the Hebrew, meaning "man of iron." In the Bible, a friend of King David.

Basil From the Greek *basileios*, meaning "royal, kingly." St. Basil (the Great) was a fourth-century Cappadocian church father. VARIANT FORMS: Basile, Basilie, Basine (French); Basilio (Italian). Basilia is a feminine form. CONTEMPORARY EXAMPLE: Basil Paterson, New York political leader.

Basilio The Italian form of Basil. *See* Basil.

Basti, Bastian Old German forms of Sebastian. *See* Sebastian.

Bat An English variant form of Bartholomew. *See* Bartholomew.

Baxley From the Greek *backen* and the Middle English *baken*, meaning "to bake" or "to cook." Baked products were allowed to sit in the sun in the meadow (lee) to become dry and hard. CONTEMPORARY EXAMPLE: Baxley McQuaig, Jr., fisherman.

Baxtel A variant form of Baxter. *See* Baxter.

Baxter From the Old English, meaning "a baker." *See* Baxley. SURNAME USAGE: Richard Baxter (1615-1691), English minister and author.

Bayard From the Old French, meaning "a bay horse," normally reddish-brown in color. In medieval times, a magical horse given as a gift by Charlemagne to Rinaldo. CONTEMPORARY EXAMPLE: Bayard Rustin, professor.

Bayless From the Old French, meaning "one who leases out a bay." CONTEMPORARY EXAMPLE: Bayless Manning, educator.

Baylor From the Anglo-Saxon, meaning "one who trains horses."

Beals A short form of Beasley. *See* Beasley. CONTEMPORARY EXAMPLE: Beals Becker, baseball player.

Bear An Anglo-Saxon animal name. Often used as a nickname. CONTEMPORARY EXAMPLE: Bear Bryant, football coach. PLACE-NAME USAGE: Bear Creek, Montana, named for Benjamin Bear, an early settler. There are thousands of similar place-names in the world.

Beasley From the Old English, meaning "a field of peas." VARIANT FORMS: Beals, Peasley. CONTEMPORARY EXAMPLE: Beasley Reece, football player.

Beattie A variant form of the feminine Beatrice. *See* Beatrice (feminine section). CONTEMPORARY EXAMPLE: Beattie Feathers, football player.

Beau From the Latin and French, meaning "pretty, handsome." Popularized by Beau Brummell (George Bryan Brummell, 1788-1840), an Englishman famous for his fashionable dress. CONTEMPORARY EXAMPLE: Beau Bell, baseball player; Beau Bridges, actor.

Beaumont   From the French, meaning "beautiful mountain." SUR-NAME USAGE: Francis Beaumont (1584-1616), English dramatist. PLACE-NAME USAGE: Beaumont, Texas.

Beauregard   From the French, meaning "to be well regarded." SUR-NAME USAGE: Pierre G.T. Beauregard (1818-1893), Civil War general. PLACE-NAME USAGE: Beauregard, Louisiana, named for Confederate General P.G.T. Beauregard.

Beck   From the Middle English *bek* and the Old Norse *bekkr,* meaning "a brook." A popular surname.

Bede   From the Middle English *bede*, meaning "prayer." St Bede was an eighth-century English historian and theologian. CONTEMPORARY EXAMPLE: Bede Karl Lackner, historian.

Bedell   From the Old French *bedel* and *bidal,* meaning "a messenger." CONTEMPORARY EXAMPLE: Bedell Smith, U.S. Army general.

Bedivere   From the Latin and Middle English, meaning "to venerate in prayer." In Arthurian legend, the knight who remained with King Arthur at his deathbed.

Beebe   From the Anglo-Saxon, meaning "one who lives on a bee farm." SURNAME USAGE: Charles William Beebe (1877-1962), American explorer.

Beeson   Possibly a matronymic form, meaning "the son of Bee (Beatrice). *See* Beatrice (feminine section).

Belden   From the Anglo-Saxon, meaning "beautiful pasture-land." CONTEMPORARY EXAMPLE: Belden Hill, baseball player.

Bell   From the Latin and French, meaning "beautiful friend." SUR-NAME USAGE: Edward Bellamy (1850-1898), author of *Looking Backward*: Ralph Bellamy, actor.

Bellamy   From the Latin and French, meaning "beautiful friend." SUR-NAME USAGE: Edward Bellamy (1850-1898), author of *Looking Backward*; Ralph Bellamy, actor.

Bellini   From the Italian, meaning "beautiful." SURNAME USAGE: Gentile Bellini, Venetian painter.

Belton   From the French, meaning "beautiful town." CONTEMPORARY EXAMPLE: Belton P. Mouras, author.

Belveder, Belvedere, Belvidere   From the Italian, meaning "beautiful view." CONTEMPORARY EXAMPLE: Belveder Bean, baseball player. PLACE-NAME USAGE: Belvedere, California.

Bemus   From the Greek, meaning "a platform." CONTEMPORARY EXAMPLE: Bemus Pierce, football player.

Ben   From the Hebrew, meaning "son." In the Bible, the name of a Levite. Used occasionally as an independent name, but most often as the pet form of Benjamin. *See* Benjamin. Also, a form of the Gaelic and

Scottish *beann,* meaning "a peak." PLACE-NAME USAGE: Ben Mar Hills, California, named for Ben Mark, a real estate promoter (1920); Ben Nevis, a mountain peak in Scotland, the highest peak in the British Isles.

Ben-Ami   From the Hebrew, meaning "son of my people." In the Bible, the son of one of Lot's daughters. CONTEMPORARY EXAMPLE: Ben-Ami Lipetz, computer scientist.

Benedict   From the Latin *benedictio,* meaning "to speak well of, to bless." St. Benedict founded the Benedictine Order. Benedict Arnold (1741-1801), American Revolutionary general who became a traitor. VARIANT FORMS: Berachya (Hebrew); Bennet (English); Benito, Benedetto, Bettino, Betto (Italian); Benes (Czechoslovakian); Benet, Benoit (French); Benedicto, Benito (Spanish); Bento (Portuguese); Banko (Slavonic). PET FORMS: Ben, Benny, Dix, Dixie. SURNAME USAGE: Ruth Fulton Benedict (1887-1948), U.S. anthropologist.

Ben-Gurion   From the Hebrew, meaning "son of the lion" or "son of might." CONTEMPORARY EXAMPLE: Ben-Gurion Sekler, Israeli educator. SURNAME USAGE: David Ben-Burion (1886-1973), Israeli prime minister.

Benigno   An Italian and Spanish pet form of Benedict. *See* Benedict. CONTEMPORARY EXAMPLE: Benigno Ayala, baseball player.

Benito   An Italian pet form of Benedict. *See* Benedict. CONTEMPORARY EXAMPLES: Benito Mussolini (1883-1945), Italian dictator; Benito Ricardo, football player.

Benjamin   From the Hebrew, meaning "son of my right hand," having the connotation of favoritism. In the Bible, the youngest of Jacob's twelve sons. Among Jews, Benjamin did not become popular until the Middle Ages. Benjamin of Tudela was a famous world traveler in the twelfth century. Among Christians, Benjamin came into use after the sixteenth century. It was commonly used in England from the seventeenth to the nineteenth centuries, and then fell into disuse. In the United States it was revived and grew in popularity because of the fame of Benjamin Franklin (1706-1790). VARIANT FORMS: Berihert (Irish); Benmajee (Hindi). PET FORMS: Ben, Benji, Benjy, Bennie, Benny. SURNAME USAGE: Judah Philip Benjamin (1811-1884), lawyer.

Bennet, Bennett   Variant English forms of the Latin name Benedict. *See* Benedict. CONTEMPORARY EXAMPLE: Benett Johnston, politician. SURNAME USAGE: Enoch Arnold Bennett (1867-1931), English novelist.

Bennie   A pet form of Benjamin. *See* Benjamin.

Benno   A variant form of Benjamin. *See* Benjamin. CONTEMPORARY EXAMPLE: Benno Isaacs, author.

Benny   A pet form of Benjamin. *See* Benjamin. CONTEMPORARY EXAMPLE: Benny (Benigno) Ayala, baseball player.

Benoit   A yellow-flowered plant of the rose family. Also, the French form of Bennett. *See* Bennett. CONTEMPORARY EXAMPLE: Benoit

Gosselin, hockey player.

Benroy   From the Gaelic *beann,* meaning "a mountain peak," plus the Old French *roy,* meaning "royal"; hence "royal mountain."

Benson   A patronymic form, meaning "Ben's son." *See* Ben. CONTEMPORARY EXAMPLE: Benson L. Grayson, author.

Bentley, Bently   From the Old English *beonot,* meaning "a meadow of ben (grass)." SURNAME USAGE: Richard Bentley (1662-1742), English clergyman.

Benton   From the Anglo-Saxon, meaning "Ben's town. *See* Ben. SURNAME USAGE: Thomas Hart Benton (1782-1858), U.S. senator.

Benzecry   A patronymic form, meaning "the son of Zechariah." *See* Zechariah.

Benzi   A pet form of Ben Zion. *See* Ben Zion.

Ben Zion   From the Hebrew, meaning either "excellent son" or "a son of Zion." CONTEMPORARY EXAMPLE: Ben Zion Bokser, rabbi.

Beppe   The Italian pet form of Joseph. *See* Joseph.

Ber   From the Anglo-Saxon, meaning "a badge" or "a boundary."

Berg   From the German, meaning "a mountain." VARIANT FORMS: Bergen, Berger, Bergin.

Bergen, Bergin   From the German, meaning "one who lives on a hill or mountain." CONTEMPORARY EXAMPLE: Bergen Evans, lexicographer. PLACE-NAME USAGE: Bergen, New Jersey; Bergen, Minnesota; Bergen-op-zoom, the Netherlands.

Berger   A variant form of Burgess. *See* Burgess. Or, a form of Bergen. *See* Bergen.

Beriah   From the Hebrew, meaning "a creature." In the Bible, a son of Asher; also, a member of the tribe of Benjamin. CONTEMPORARY EXAMPLE: Beriah Green, theologian. •

Berkeley, Berkley, Berkly   From the Anglo-Saxon, meaning "from the birch meadow." Barclay is a variant form. PLACE-NAME USAGE: a city in England; Berkeley, California, named for Bishop George Berkeley.

Berlin, Berlyn   From the German, meaning "boundary line." CONTEMPORARY EXAMPLE: Berlyn Horne, baseball player. SURNAME USAGE: Irving Berlin, composer. PLACE-NAME USAGE: capital of West Germany; Berlin, Connecticut.

Bern, Berna, Berne   From the German, meaning "a bear." CONTEMPORARY EXAMPLE: Bern Keating, author. PLACE-NAME USAGE: Bern, capital of Switzerland; Bern, Pennsylvania; New Bern, North Carolina.

Bernard   From the Old High German name Berinhard, meaning "bold as a bear." Derived from *bero* or *berin,* meaning "bear," plus *hart,* meaning "hard, brave, bold." Akin to *beorn,* a common element in Anglo-Saxon names, meaning "brave, a warrior." Bernard of Menthon was an eleventh-century monk. VARIANT FORMS: Barnard (French and English); Bernadin (French); Bernardo (Italian and Spanish); Benno, Bernhard, Bernhardt (German); Bernhardi (Italian). PET FORMS: Bern, Bernie. SURNAME USAGE: Behr, Behrens, Bernardi.

Bernardo   The Italian and Spanish form of Bernard. *See* Bernard.

Bernd, Berndt   Variant forms of Bernard. *See* Bernard. CONTEMPORARY EXAMPLES: Bernd Melchers, editor; Bernd Grossman, publisher; Berndt Berglund, author.

Bernhard, Bernhardt   Variant German forms of Bernard. *See* Bernard. SURNAME USAGE: Sarah Bernhardt (1844-1923), actress.

Berni, Bernie   Popular pet forms of Bernard. *See* Bernard.

Bernis   A variant form of Bernard. *See* Bernard. CONTEMPORARY EXAMPLE: Bernis Sadler, city mayor.

Bernt   A variant form of Bernard. *See* Bernard. CONTEMPORARY EXAMPLE: Bernt Balchen, aviator.

Berry   From the Old English *berie,* meaning "a berry, a grape." CONTEMPORARY EXAMPLE: Berry Gordy, industrialist. PLACE-NAME USAGE: Berry Hill, South Carolina; a province in France.

Bert, Bertie   Pet forms of Albert, Berthold, Bertol, Bertram. PLACE-NAME USAGE: Bertie County, North Carolina, named for James and Henry Bertie (1722), property owners.

Bertell, Bertil   Swedish forms of Berthold. *See* Berthold. CONTEMPORARY EXAMPLES: Bertil Ohlin, economist; Bertell Ollman, inventor.

Berthold   From the German, meaning "bright." Akin to Bertram. Bertha is the feminine form.

Bertin   A variant form of Bert. *See* Bert. CONTEMPORARY EXAMPLE: Bertin Bisbee, football player.

Bertol   A variant form of Berthold. *See* Berthold.

Bertold, Bertolt   Variant spellings of Berthold. *See* Berthold. CONTEMPORARY EXAMPLES: Bertolt Brecht, playwright; Bertold Spuler, professor.

Berton   A variant form of Berthold. *See* Berthold. CONTEMPORARY EXAMPLE: Berton James, baseball player; Berton Rouche, author.

Bertram   From the Old High German *beraht,* meaning "bright, illustrious one." VARIANT FORMS: Bertol, Berthold (German); Bertran, Bertrand (French); Bertrando (Italian); Bertole (Hungarian).

Berwin   From the Anglo-Saxon, meaning "powerful friend."

Beryl   From the Greek, meaning "a sea-green precious stone." Also, a Yiddish pet form for Bernard. *See* Bernard. Used also as a feminine name.

Bethel   From the Hebrew, meaning "house of God." In the Bible, a city north of Jerusalem. PLACE-NAME USAGE: Bethel, Connecticut; Bethel, Vermont.

Bevan, Bevin   A Celtic patronymic form of Evan, meaning "son of Evan." *See* Evan. Bivian is a variant form.

Beverley, Beverly   From the Old English, meaning "beaver meadow." Used most often as a feminine form. CONTEMPORARY EXAMPLE: Beverley Fuller, author. PLACE-NAME USAGE: a town in England; Beverly, Massachusetts; Beverly Hills, California.

Bevis   A patronymic form of Evan, meaning "son of Evan." Also, from the French name Beuves, meaning "bull, beef." Richard Jefferies' 1882 novel, *Bevis, the Story of a Boy,* contributed to the popularity of the name.

Bezalel   From the Hebrew, meaning "in the shade of God" or "protected by God." In the Bible, the skilled artisan, in the days of Moses, who built the tabernacle.

Bid   A masculine pet form of the Irish feminine Briget and Biddy. *See* Briget *and* Biddy (feminine section). Bider is also a feminine form. CONTEMPORARY EXAMPLE: Bid McPhee, baseball player. PLACE-NAME USAGE: Biddeford, Maine, named for a town in England.

Biff   From the slang, meaning "to strike, to hit." CONTEMPORARY EXAMPLE: Biff McGuire, actor; Biff Pacoroba, baseball player.

Bildad   From the Hebrew, meaning "Bel (Baal) has loved." In the Bible, one of the friends of Job.

Bilgai, Bilguy   From the Arabic, meaning "joy." In the Bible, a priest in the time of Nehemiah.

Bill, Billie, Billy, Billye   Variant pet forms of William. *See* William. CONTEMPORARY EXAMPLE: Billye Dymally, author. PLACE-NAME USAGE: Billy Meadows, Oregon, named for William Smith, a sheep herder; Bill Point, Washington.

Bin   From the Celtic, meaning "a crib" or "a receptacle." Binnie is a feminine form. CONTEMPORARY EXAMPLE: Bin Ramke, poet.

Bing   A pet form of Bingham. *See* Bingham. Also an independent name. CONTEMPORARY EXAMPLE: Bing (ne Harry Lillis) Crosby, entertainer.

Bing, Bingham   Origin uncertain. Possibly a variant form of Bin. *See* Bin. PLACE-NAME USAGE: Bingham, Utah, named for Sandford and Thomas Bingham, cattlemen; Binghamton, New York, named for William Bingham, town developer (1855).

Bingo   Origin unknown. A chant used by eighteenth-century thieves, meaning "brandy." CONTEMPORARY EXAMPLE: Bingo Binks, baseball player.

Bion   From the Greek *bios*, meaning "to live." Bion was a Greek pastoral poet of the third century B.C.

Birch   A tree name. From the Anglo-Saxon, meaning "white" or "shine." CONTEMPORARY EXAMPLE: Birch Bayh, U.S. senator. PLACE-NAME USAGE: Birch Creek, California.

Bird, Birdie   From the Middle English *bird* and the Anglo-Saxon *bridd*. By metathesis the word became bird with its present popular meaning. Used also as a feminine name. CONTEMPORARY EXAMPLE: Bird Tebbetts, baseball player. PLACE-NAME USAGE: Bird Rock, California; Bird Butte, Oregon, named for George Bird, a forest guard; Birdseye Creek, Oregon, named for David Birdseye, a pioneer.

Birk   A Scottish form of Barker. *See* Barker.

Bishan   Origin uncertain. Probably from the French *bis*, meaning "dingy." CONTEMPORARY EXAMPLE: Bishan Bedi, cricket player.

Bishop   From the Greek *episkopos*, meaning "an overseer." A common designation applied to high-ranking Christian clergymen. SURNAME USAGE: Joey Bishop, comedian. PLACE-NAME USAGE: Bishop, California, named for S.A. Bishop, early cattleman.

Bivian   A variant form of Bevan. *See* Bevan. CONTEMPORARY EXAMPLE: Bivian Lee, football player.

Bix   Origin uncertain. Probably from the French name Beuves, meaning "bull, beef." CONTEMPORARY EXAMPLE: Bix Beiderbecke, musician.

Bjarne, Bjorn, Bjorne   Norwegian forms of Bernard. *See* Bernard. CONTEMPORARY EXAMPLES: Bjorn Johansson, hockey player; Bjorn Borg, tennis player; Bjarne R. Ullsvik, educator.

Blackstone   An Old English place-name, meaning "Black's town." Blackstone Daniel was reported to have been President Andrew Johnson's best friend.

Blackwell   Originally an Old English surname, meaning "Black's well." CONTEMPORARY EXAMPLE: R. Blackwell Smith, Jr., educator.

Blaine   From the Old English, meaning "the source of a river." CONTEMPORARY EXAMPLES: Blaine Johnson, author; Blaine Peterson, hockey player. SURNAME USAGE: James G. Blaine (1820-1893), American statesman. PLACE-NAME USAGE: Blaine, Oklahoma, named for James G. Blaine.

Blair   From the Celtic, meaning "a place." CONTEMPORARY EXAMPLE: Blair Lee, Maryland political leader; Blair Stewart, hockey player.

Blake   From the Anglo-Saxon, meaning "white." Akin to the Spanish name Blanco. Blanchard is a variant form. CONTEMPORARY EXAMPLE: Blake Edwards, movie director. SURNAME USAGE: Robert Blake, (1599-1657), British admiral.

Blanchard   A variant form of Blake. *See* Blake. CONTEMPORARY EXAMPLE: Blanchard Carter, football player.

Bland, Blandon   From the Latin and Old French, meaning "mild."

Blanton   A variant form of Blandon. *See* Blandon. May also be from the Old English, meaning "the town near the river source." Akin to Blaine. CONTEMPORARY EXAMPLE: Blanton Collier, football coach.

Blas   The Spanish form of Blase. *See* Blase.

Blase   From the Greek *basilios* and the Latin *blaesus*, meaning "flat-footed." Blasius is an early Roman form. The fourth-century St. Blasius was patron saint of wool workers. VARIANT FORMS: Blaise, Blaisot (French); Blaze (English); Braz (Portuguese); Vlass (Russian); Blas (Spanish). CONTEMPORARY EXAMPLE: Blas Monaco, baseball player.

Blaze   Most commonly used as a feminine name. *See* Blaze (feminine section).

Bligh   From the Anglo-Saxon *bliss* and *blithe*, meaning "happiness." CONTEMPORARY EXAMPLE: Bligh Angus MacDonald, Taunton, Massachusetts.

Blythe   From the Anglo-Saxon name, meaning "spirited, joyful." Used also as a feminine name. SURNAME USAGE: Anne Blythe, actress. PLACE-NAME USAGE: Blythewood, South Carolina.

Bo   A pet form of Bogart. *See* Bogart. CONTEMPORARY EXAMPLES: Bo Belinsky, baseball player; Bo Svenson, actor.

Boaz   From the Hebrew, meaning "strength." In the Bible, the second husband of Ruth.

Bob, Bobbie, Bobby   Pet forms of Robert. *See* Robert. Police in England have been nicknamed Bobbies ever since Sir Robert (Bobby) Peel served as Police Commissioner.

Bogart   From the Gaelic *bog* and the Irish *bogach*, meaning "soft, marshy ground." SURNAME USAGE: Humphrey Bogart, actor.

Bogey, Bogie   A pet form of Bogart. Popularized as nicknames after actor Humphrey Bogart's rise to fame.

Bola   From the Spanish, meaning "a ball." CONTEMPORARY EXAMPLE: Bola Ayeni, Nigerian professor.

Boliston   From the Greek *bolos*, meaning "lump of earth or clay." PLACE-NAME USAGE: a town in England.

Bolivar   A variant Spanish form of the Polish name Boleslav, meaning "strong, warlike." SURNAME USAGE: Simon Bolivar, nineteenth-century South American revolutionary soldier. PLACE-NAME USAGE: Mount Bolivar, Oregon, named for Simon Bolivar Cathcart, local surveyor; towns in Ohio, West Virginia, and Tennessee.

Bonamy   From the French *bon ami*, meaning "good friend." Used as a surname in France.

Bonaro   From the Spanish and Italian, meaning "friend." CONTEMPORARY EXAMPLE: Bonaro W. Overstreet, author.

Bonaventure   From the Italian *bonaventura*, meaning "good luck." A variant form of Bonaventura, a thirteenth-century Italian theologian.

Bond   From the Anglo-Saxon, meaning "to bind." Originally an occupational name. CONTEMPORARY EXAMPLE: Bond Gideon, actor.

Boni   From the Italian, meaning "good." Also a pet form of Boniface. *See* Boniface. CONTEMPORARY EXAMPLE: Boni Petcoff, football player.

Boniface   From the Latin *bonifacius*, meaning "welldoer." Boniface I (418-422) was the first of a series of popes named Boniface. PET FORMS: Boni, Facio, Fazio (Italian).

Boo   A nickname of uncertain origin. CONTEMPORARY EXAMPLE: Boo Johnson, publisher.

Boog   From the Anglo-Saxon *boc* and *bec*, meaning "beech tree." Booker is a variant form. *See* Booker. CONTEMPORARY EXAMPLE: Boog Powell, baseball player.

Booker   From the Anglo-Saxon *boc* and *bec*, meaning "beech tree." An occupational name for one who copies books, since parchment for books was made from the beech tree. CONTEMPORARY EXAMPLES: Booker T. Washington, educator; Booker T. Brown, football player. PLACE-NAME USAGE: Mount Booker, Washington, named for Booker T. Washington; Booker, Texas, named for B.F. Booker, a railroad engineer.

Boone   From the Latin *bonus* and the Old French *bon*, meaning "good." SURNAME USAGE: Daniel Boone (1734-1820), American frontiersman. PLACE-NAME USAGE: Boonville, Missouri.

Booth   From the Old Norse *both* and *buth*, meaning "a temporary dwelling." CONTEMPORARY EXAMPLE: Booth Tarkington, author. SURNAME USAGE: William Booth (1829-1912), founder of the Salvation Army.

Borden   From the Old French *borde*, meaning "a cottage." Or from the Anglo-Saxon, meaning "a den of boars." CONTEMPORARY EXAMPLE: Borden Deal, author.

Borg   From the Old Norse, meaning "a castle." Also, a variant form of the German *berg*, meaning "a mountain."

Boris   From the Russian, meaning "to fight." Boris III (1894-1943), a king of Bulgaria. CONTEMPORARY EXAMPLE: Boris Karloff, actor.

Borje   A variant form of Borg. *See* Borg. CONTEMPORARY EXAMPLE: Borje Salming, hockey player.

Bors   In Arthurian legend, a knight of the Round Table; a nephew of Sir Lancelot. PLACE-NAME USAGE: Borstal, England.

Bosley   From the Old English, meaning "a grove of trees, a thicket." CONTEMPORARY EXAMPLE: Bosley Crowther, author.

Boston   From the Old English, meaning "a town near the thicket." CONTEMPORARY EXAMPLE: Boston E. Witt, lawyer. PLACE-NAME USAGE: Boston, Massachusetts, named for a town in England.

Boswell   From the Old English, meaning "a thicket of willow trees." SURNAME USAGE: James Boswell (1740-1795), author.

Bosworth From the Old English, meaning "an estate surrounded by trees."

Bourbon   A name derived from Bourbon County, Kentucky, where a whiskey is made from corn. The Bourbon family was the ruling family in France for many centuries.

Bourke   From the Old English *burg* or *burgh*, meaning "a fortification" or "a hill."

Bourn, Bourne   From the French and Latin, meaning "a boundary." Also, from the Anglo-Saxon, meaning "a stream, a brook."

Bouvier   A French form of the Latin *bos* and *bovis*, meaning "an ox." SURNAME USAGE: Jacqueline Bouvier (Kennedy Onassis).

Bowen   A Celtic patronymic form, meaning "the son (or descendant) of Owen." Bowie is a pet form.

Bowie   A pet form of Bowen. *See* Bowen. CONTEMPORARY EXAMPLE: Bowie Kuhn, baseball commissioner. PLACE-NAME USAGE: Bowie, Texas, named for J.A. Bowie, prominent frontiersman.

Boyce   From the county called Powys, in Central Wales. SURNAME USAGE: three brothers: John Cowper Powys, Llewelyn Powys, and T.F. Powys—all English novelists.

Boyd   From the Celtic, meaning "yellow." CONTEMPORARY EXAMPLE: Boyd C. Patterson, educator.

Boynton   From the Celtic, meaning "a town near the Boyne River."

Brad   A pet form of Braden. *See* Braden.

Braden   From the Old English, meaning "broad." VARIANT FORMS: Braden, Bradley. CONTEMPORARY EXAMPLE: Braden Beck, football player.

Bradford   From the Anglo-Saxon, meaning "the broad ford." VARIANT FORMS: Braden, Brad. CONTEMPORARY EXAMPLES: Bradford Davis, football player; Bradford Angier, author. PLACE-NAME USAGE: Bradford, Massachusetts, named for a town in England; Bradford, Pennsylvania, named for William Bradford, U.S. attorney general (1812).

Bradley   From the Old English, meaning "a broad lea, a meadow." CONTEMPORARY EXAMPLE: Bradley Smith, author. SURNAME USAGE: Bill Bradley, U.S. senator.

Brady   From the Anglo-Saxon, meaning "broad island."

Brage   A variant form of Bragi. *See* Bragi.

Braggo   A variant form of Bragi. *See* Bragi. CONTEMPORARY EXAMPLE: Braggo Ruth, baseball player. PLACE-NAME USAGE: Braggadocio, Missouri.

Bragi   In Norse mythology, the god of poetry and eloquence. CONTEMPORARY EXAMPLE: Brage Golding, educator.

Brailey   An invented name. CONTEMPORARY EXAMPLE: Brailey Franco, Newhall, California.

Brainard   From the British *bren*, meaning "a prince."

Bram   A short form of Abraham or Abram. *See* Abraham *and* Abram. Also, from the Old English *brom*, meaning "brushwood," from which the surnames Broome and Bromley evolved. A popular name in Holland after the Reformation. CONTEMPORARY EXAMPLES: Bram Stoker, author; Bram Cavin, florist.

Bran   From the Irish *bran*, meaning "a raven." In Celtic mythology, the god of the nether world. VARIANT FORMS: Brand, Brandon, Brant, Brend, Brondan, Brent, Brennan.

Branch   From the Late Latin *branca*, meaning "a paw, a claw, an extention from a tree trunk." CONTEMPORARY EXAMPLE: Branch Rickey, baseball team owner. PLACE-NAME USAGE: Branchland, Virginia, named for Colonel Branch, coal mine operator.

Brand   A variant form of Bran. *See* Bran. Or, from the Anglo-Saxon *brand* and *brond*, meaning "a sword."

Brandi   A variant form of Brand. *See* Brand.

Brandon   A variant form of Brand. *See* Brand. PLACE-NAME USAGE: Brandon, Vermont, named in 1761 for the Duke of Hamilton and Brandon, an English political leader.

Brandt   A variant spelling of Brand. *See* Brand. CONTEMPORARY EXAMPLE: Brandt Kennedy, football player.

Brant   A variant spelling of Brand. *See* Brand.

Bravlio, Bravilio   From the Italian *bravi*, meaning "brave." CON-

TEMPORARY EXAMPLE: Bravilio Smith, jockey.

Braxton   From the Anglo Saxon, meaning "Brock's town." *See* Brock. CONTEMPORARY EXAMPLE: Braxton McKee, author.

Bray   From the Middle English *braien*, meaning "to cry out." CONTEMPORARY EXAMPLE: Bray Hammond, historian.

Braz   A Portuguese form of Blase. *See* Blase. Blaze is a variant spelling.

Breandan   A variant form of Brendan. *See* Brendan. CONTEMPORARY EXAMPLE: Breandan Oheithir, author.

Brend, Brendan   Variant forms of Bran. *See* Bran. CONTEMPORARY EXAMPLES: Brend Magnus, author; Brendan Byrne, state governor.

Brennan   A variant form of Brendan. *See* Brendan.

Brent   A variant spelling of Brend. *See* Brend. CONTEMPORARY EXAMPLE: Brent Tarter, editor.

Bret, Brett   From the Celtic, meaning "a Breton, a native of Brittany." CONTEMPORARY EXAMPLE: Brett Lunger, auto racer. PLACE-NAME USAGE: Bretton Woods, New Hampshire.

Brevard   From the Latin *brevis*, meaning "short." CONTEMPORARY EXAMPLE: Brevard S. Childs, theologian.

Brewster   An occupational name. From the Middle English *breuen*, meaning "one who brews or makes beer." SURNAME USAGE: William Brewster (1567-1644), a pilgrim who helped establish Plymouth Colony. PLACE-NAME USAGE: Brewster, New York; Brewster, Massachusetts, named (1803) for William Brewster, an early settler.

Brian   Derived from the Celtic and Gaelic name Briareus, meaning "strong." *See* Briareus. Brian Borhus (910-1014), a king and hero of Ireland. VARIANT FORMS: Bryan, Bryant.

Briand   From the French, meaning "castle." SURNAME USAGE: Aristide Briand (1862-1932), French statesman.

Briar   A variant form of Briareus. *See* Briareus.

Briareus   From the Greek *briaros*, meaning "strong." Probably the original form of Brian. *See* Brian. In Greek mythology, a 100-handed giant who fought with the Olympians against the Titans. VARIANT FORMS: Brian, Bryan, Bryant.

Brice   A patronymic form, meaning "the son of rice." *Rice* is the Anglo-Saxon form of the Middle English *riche*, meaning "rich, noble, powerful." Akin to Richard. VARIANT FORMS: Bryce, Brick.

Brigham   From the Old French and Italian *brigata*, meaning "a troop of soldiers." A hamlet or location where army troops were stationed. CONTEMPORARY EXAMPLE: Brigham Young (1801-1877), U.S.

Mormon leader. PLACE-NAME USAGE: Brigham, Utah, named for Brigham Young.

Brigman   From the Old English, meaning "a soldier." *See* Brigham. CONTEMPORARY EXAMPLE: Brigman Owens, football player.

Brindley, Brinley   From the Middle English *brended* and *brennen,* meaning "to burn," hence "having a gray or tawny color." Popular in Ireland. CONTEMPORARY EXAMPLE: Brindley Williams, Santa Rosa, California.

Bristol   A variant form of Brice. *See* Brice. CONTEMPORARY EXAMPLE: Bristol Lord, baseball player. PLACE-NAME USAGE: a city in Connecticut, Massachusetts, Pennsylvania, Rhode Island, and Tennessee. All named for Bristol in England.

Brit   A short form of Briton. *See* Briton. An early name for Wales. CONTEMPORARY EXAMPLES: Brit Hume, television news reporter.

Briton, Britton   Early forms for Britain. Used by the Celts when they inhabited the British Isles. *See also* Brit. CONTEMPORARY EXAMPLE: Britton Hadden, publisher.

Broadus   A variant form of Brad. *See* Brad. CONTEMPORARY EXAMPLE: Broadus Connatser, baseball player. PLACE-NAME USAGE: Broadus, Montana.

Brock   From the Anglo-Saxon and Gaelic, meaning "a badger," an animal that steals grain and stores it. *See* Badger. CONTEMPORARY EXAMPLES: Brock Adams, U.S. political leader; Brock Stroschein, football player. PLACE-NAME USAGE: Brockton, Massachusetts, named for Sir Isaac Brock (1769-1812), lieutenant governor of Canada.

Brockholst   A name compounded from Brock (*see* Brock) and the Old Norse *heolstor*, meaning "hiding, concealment," hence "a hiding place for badgers."

Broderick   A compounded name of Brad and Richard, meaning "rich flat land." Popularly used in Ireland. CONTEMPORARY EXAMPLE: Broderick Crawford, actor.

Bromley   From the Anglo-Saxon *brom*, meaning "brushwood," hence "a meadow or field of brushwood." Akin to Bromwell. PLACE-NAME USAGE: a city in England.

Bromwell   From Old English, meaning "the well near the brushwood field." Akin to Bromley.

Bronco, Bronko   Spanish forms of the Old German name Bruno, meaning "brown." Also independent Mexican-Spanish names, meaning "rough." CONTEMPORARY EXAMPLE: Bronko Nagurski, athlete.

Bronson   From the Old English, meaning "son of Brown." VARIANT FORMS: Bronco, Bruno, Bruns. CONTEMPORARY EXAMPLE: Bronson C. La Follette, Wisconsin political leader.

Bronte   From the Greek, meaning "thunder." Derived from the surname of the Bronte sisters, Charlotte and Emily, famous nineteenth-century authors. PLACE-NAME USAGE: Bronte, Texas, named for Charlotte Bronte (1887).

Brook, Brooke, Brooks   From the Old English *broc*, meaning "a stream." Used also as a feminine name. CONTEMPORARY EXAMPLES: Brooks Robinson, baseball player. SURNAME USAGE: Rupert Brooke (1887-1915), English poet; Geraldine Brooks, actress. PLACE-NAME USAGE: Brook Lake, Minnesota; Brooks Range, Alaska, named for A.H. Brooks, geologist; Brookline, Massachusetts; Brooklyn, New York.

Brown   From the Middle English *brown* and *broun*, meaning the color brown, but originally meaning "a bear" (most often colored brown). PLACE-NAME USAGE: Brown Deer, Wisconsin; Brownsville, Texas, named for Mayor Jacob Brown, soldier (1840s).

Bruce   A Scottish form of the French name Brieux, probably meaning "woods." Robert the Bruce (1274-1329) was a king of Scotland. May also be a variant form of Brice. *See* Brice. PLACE-NAME USAGE: Brieux, France.

Bruin   A variant form of Bruno. *See* Bruno. In Danish legend, the brown bear (Bruin) figures prominently.

Bruno, Bruns   From the Old German, meaning "brown" or "dark in appearance." Akin to Bruin. CONTEMPORARY EXAMPLES: Bruno Sammartino, wrestler; Bruno Skoggard, novelist. PLACE-NAME USAGE: Bruno, Minnesota.

Brutus   From the Latin, meaning "senseless, irrational." Marcus Junius Brutus (85-42 B.C.) was one of the conspirators who murdered Julius Caesar.

Bryan, Bryant   Variant spellings of Brian. *See* Brian. PLACE-NAME USAGE: Bryant, Iowa, named for W.C. Bryant, poet.

Bryce   A variant spelling of Brice. *See* Brice. CONTEMPORARY EXAMPLE: Bryce Jordan, educator. SURNAME USAGE: James Bryce (1838-1922), English statesman. PLACE-NAME USAGE: Bryce, Utah, named for Ebenezer Bryce, first settler.

Bryshear   A compounded name of the Greek *bryon*, meaning "moss" or "a gourd," and the German *scheren*, meaning "to cut." CONTEMPORARY EXAMPLE: Bryshear Davis, baseball player.

Bubba   From the German *bube*, meaning "a boy." The name of a tribal chief in ancient England. VARIANT FORMS: Babba, Babe, Bebba. CONTEMPORARY EXAMPLES: Bubba Smith, Bubba Dean, and Bubba Broussar, all football players.

Buck, Bucky   From the Anglo-Saxon and German, meaning "a male deer" or "a he-goat." CONTEMPORARY EXAMPLE: Buck Ewing and Bucky Dent, baseball players; Bucky Dilts, football player. PLACE-NAME USAGE:

Buck Creek, Iowa; Bucks County, Pennsylvania.

Buckminister, Buckminster   From the Old English *broc* plus minister, meaning "one who teaches the book," i.e., "a preacher." CONTEMPORARY EXAMPLE: Buckminister Fuller, educator.

Buckner   From the Anglo-Saxon, meaning "a dealer in bucks (deer)." CONTEMPORARY EXAMPLE: Buckner Melton, a Georgia political leader.

Bud, Budd   From the Anglo-Saxon *budda*, meaning "a beetle," or from the German, meaning "to swell up," as the bud on a branch. Commonly used as a slang expression for a boy or a man. *See* Buddy. CONTEMPORARY EXAMPLE: Bud (William) Abbott, comedian.

Buddy   A pet form of Bud. *See* Bud. In an early British dialect *butty* meant "companion."

Buell   A variant form of the British *bul*, meaning "a bull." Buford is a variant form. CONTEMPORARY EXAMPLE: Buell G. Gallagher, educator.

Bufford, Buford   Compound of the Old French *boef*, meaning "an ox," and the Middle English *ford*, meaning "a ford," hence "a shallow stream (ford) where the oxen cross." Buell is a variant form. CONTEMPORARY EXAMPLES: Bufford Ellington, Tennessee political leader; Buford Ray, football player.

Bunk   A Scottish form of the Danish *bank*, meaning "a bench" or "a large container." CONTEMPORARY EXAMPLES: Bunk Gardner, rock musician; Bunk Congalton, baseball player.

Bunn   An Old English form of the Latin and French words meaning "good, beautiful." CONTEMPORARY EXAMPLE: Bunn Hearn, baseball player.

Burbank   From the Middle English *burre*, meaning "a prickly coating" on the seedcoat of certain plants, hence "a mound of prickly plants." SURNAME USAGE: Luther Burbank (1849-1926), American horticulturist. PLACE-NAME USAGE: Burbank, California.

Burdette   From the Middle English *burde* and *bird*, meaning "a small bird." CONTEMPORARY EXAMPLE: Burdette Glenn, baseball player.

Burgess   From the Middle English and Old French, meaning "a shopkeeper," hence "a freeman of a borough." CONTEMPORARY EXAMPLE: Burgess Meredith, actor. SURNAME USAGE: Gelett Burgess (1866-1951), American humorist and illustrator.

Burke   An Old English form of the German *burg*, meaning "a castle." CONTEMPORARY EXAMPLE: Burke Davis, author. PLACE-NAME USAGE: Burke, Vermont, named for Edmund Burke, English supporter of the American Revolution (1782).

Burl, Burle   From the Latin *burra*, meaning "coarse hair." Or, from the Middle English *burle*, meaning "a knot on a tree trunk." CONTEMPORARY EXAMPLES: Burl Ives, actor; Burle Robinson, football player.

Burleigh   An Old English name, meaning "a field with knotted tree trunks." Akin to Burl. Burley is a variant spelling. CONTEMPORARY EXAMPLE: Burleigh Grimes, baseball player.

Burley   A variant spelling of Burleigh. *See* Burleigh. PLACE-NAME USAGE: a city in England.

Burnell   A variant form of the Old English *bourn*, meaning "a brook." Commonly used in Scotland. CONTEMPORARY EXAMPLE: Burnell Fortune, football player.

Burnham   From the Old English meaning "the hamlet near the brook." Akin to Burnell and Burnis. CONTEMPORARY EXAMPLE: Burnham Holmes, author.

Burnis   From the Scottish *burn*, meaning "a little stream." CONTEMPORARY EXAMPLE: Burnis G. Preston, industrialist.

Burr   From the Middle English *burre*, meaning "a prickly coating on a plant." Akin to Burbank. *See* Burbank. CONTEMPORARY EXAMPLE: Burr Baldwin, football player. SURNAME USAGE: Raymond Burr, actor. PLACE-NAME USAGE: Burr, Minnesota, named for a family of early settlers.

Burrell   A variant form of Burr. *See* Burr. CONTEMPORARY EXAMPLE: Burrell Shields, football player.

Burris   A variant form of Burr. *See* Burr.

Burt, Burte   Pet forms of Burton. *See* Burton. CONTEMPORARY EXAMPLE: Burt Lancaster, actor.

Burton   From the Old English, meaning "town on a hill." PET FORMS: Burt, Burte.

Bushrod   Compounded from the Old Danish *bosch*, meaning "a cluster of shrubs," and the Middle English *rodde*, meaning "a shoot" or "a stem." Akin to Buster. CONTEMPORARY EXAMPLE: Bushrod Washington, Supreme Court Justice.

Butty   *See* Buddy.

Byrd   From the Anglo-Saxon, meaning "a bird." Used also as a feminine name. SURNAME USAGE: Robert Byrd, U.S. senator.

Byrne   From the Anglo-Saxon, meaning "a coat of armor."

Byron   From the German, meaning "the cottage." Or, from the Old English, meaning "a bear." CONTEMPORARY EXAMPLES: Byron Sherwin, author; Byron Janis, pianist. PLACE-NAME USAGE: Byron, New York, named for Lord Byron, English poet (1820).

C

Cab   Possibly a short form of *cabriolet*, meaning "the drivers cabin of a truck, derrick, or train." CONTEMPORARY EXAMPLE: Cab Calloway, bandleader.

Cable   From the Old French, meaning "a rope." SURNAME USAGE: George Washington Cable (1844-1925), American author.

Cadmar   A Welsh name derived from the Greek name Cadmus, meaning "warrior." Akin to Cadmus.

Cadmus   In Greek legend, a Phoenician prince who killed a dragon sacred to Zeus. He sowed the dragon's teeth on earth, from which armed men sprang up, hence the meaning warrior. Cadmar is a variant form.

Cadwalader, Cadwallader   Variant forms of Cadmar and Cadmus. *See* Cadmar *and* Cadmus. CONTEMPORARY EXAMPLE: Cadwallader Coles, baseball player.

Cadwell   A variant form of Cadmar and Cadmus. *See* Cadmar *and* Cadmus.

Caesar   From the Latin *caedere*, meaning "to cut" and "the hairy one." The title of the emperor of Rome from Augustus to Hadrian, most notably Julius Caesar. Akin to the title Caesarea, the German Kaiser and Russian Czar. VARIANT FORMS: Cesar, Cesare. PLACE-NAME USAGE: Caesarea, Israel; Kayseri, Turkey.

Cal   A short form of Calvin or Caleb. *See* Calvin *and* Caleb. CONTEMPORARY EXAMPLES: Cal Hubbard, member of the baseball and football halls of fame; Cal Rayborn, motorcyclist.

Calbert   A variant spelling of Calvert. *See* Calvert.

Calchas   In Greek legend, a priest of Apollo during the Trojan War.

Calder   From the Celtic, meaning "from the stony river." CONTEMPORARY EXAMPLE: Calder Willingham, author. SURNAME USAGE: Alexander Stirling Calder (1870-1945), American sculptor.

Caldwell   A variant form of Cadwell. CONTEMPORARY EXAMPLE: Caldwell Jones, basketball player. SURNAME USAGE: Erskine Caldwell (1903-   ), American writer.

Cale   Possibly a pet form of Caleb. *See* Caleb. CONTEMPORARY EXAMPLE: Cale Yarborough, auto racer.

Caleb   From the Hebrew, meaning "a dog," hence the connotation of "faithful." May also be from the Assyrian, meaning "a messenger," or

49

from the Arabic, meaning "brave." In the Bible, the leader of the Israelites following the death of Moses. CONTEMPORARY EXAMPLE: J. Caleb Boggs, U.S. senator.

Calhoun   From the Celtic, meaning "a warrior." SURNAME USAGE: John Caldwell Calhoun (1782-1850), U.S. vice-president (1825-1832).

Callis   From the Latin *calix*, meaning "a cup, a chalice." CONTEMPORARY EXAMPLE: Callis E. Walker, a resident of Glendale, California. SURNAME USAGE: Charles A. Callis, Mormon leader.

Calvert   An Old English occupational name for a herdsman. SURNAME USAGE: George Calvert (1580-1632), founder of Maryland.

Calvin   From the Latin *calvus*, meaning "bald." Cal is a pet form. CONTEMPORARY EXAMPLE: Calvin Coolidge (John Calvin Coolidge) (1872-1933), thirteenth president of the U.S. (1923-1929). SURNAME USAGE: John Calvin (1509-1564), French Protestant reformer.

Cam   A short form of Cameron. *See* Cameron. CONTEMPORARY EXAMPLE: Cam Botting, hockey player.

Cameron   From the Celtic, meaning "bent nose." Cam and Camm are pet forms. CONTEMPORARY EXAMPLES: Cameron S. Moseley, publisher; Cameron Mitchell, actor. SURNAME USAGE: Richard Cameron, an eighteenth-century Scotsman who inspired the founding of the Reformed Presbyterian Church (1743).

Camillus   The original Latin form of the feminine French names Camilla and Camille, meaning "virgin of unblemished character." Its original meaning was "an attendant" (at a sacrifice), or "a messenger." Camillo is an Italian form.

Campbell   Compounded of the Latin *campus*, meaning "a field," and the French *belle*, meaning "beautiful." PET FORMS: Camp, Campy. CONTEMPORARY EXAMPLE: Campbell R. McConnell, economist. SURNAME USAGE: Thomas Campbell (1777-1844), Scottish poet.

Canute   From the Latin, meaning "white-haired." Canute II was King of England and Denmark in the eleventh century. VARIANT SPELLINGS: Knut, Knute, Cnut.

Capp   From the Old French *chapelain*, meaning "chaplain." A variant form of Caplin. SURNAME USAGE: Al Capp (Alfred Gerald Caplin), creator of the *Li'l Abner* comic strip.

Carden   From the Latin, French, and Middle English, meaning "to comb" or "brush out" fibers of wool or cotton. CONTEMPORARY EXAMPLE: Carden Gillenwater, baseball player. SURNAME USAGE: Lazaro Cardenas, president of Mexico (1934-1940).

Carew   From the Latin *currere*, meaning "to run," or *carrus*, "a two-wheeled war chariot." SURNAME USAGE: Rod Carew, baseball player; Thomas Carew, seventeenth-century English poet.

Carey From the Welsh or Cornish, meaning "rocky island." CONTEM-PORARY EXAMPLE: Carey Brewer, educator. SURNAME USAGE: Hugh Carey, governor of New York.

Carl A corrupt form of the Old English names Ceorl and Charl, variant forms of Charles. *See* Charles. Karl is a variant spelling. Carol is a feminine form.

Carleton A variant spelling of Carlton. *See* Carlton.

Carlisle From the Anglo-Saxon, meaning "Carl's island." Carlyle is a variant spelling. PLACE-NAME USAGE: Carlisle, England.

Carlo, Carlos Italian and Spanish forms of Charles. *See* Charles. Don Carlos (1788-1855), a Spanish prince, was the second son of King Charles IV. CONTEMPORARY EXAMPLES: Carlo Ponti, film producer; Carlos P. Romulo, journalist.

Carlson A patronymic form, meaning "son of Carl." *See* Carl *and* Charles. CONTEMPORARY EXAMPLE: Carlson Wade, author. SURNAME USAGE: Evans F. Carlson (1896-1947), U.S. Army general.

Carlton From the Old English, meaning "Carl's town." Carleton is a variant spelling. CONTEMPORARY EXAMPLES: Carlton Fisk, baseball player; Carlton Hollander, author. PLACE-NAME USAGE: Carlton, Oregon.

Carlyle A variant spelling of Carlisle. *See* Carlisle. CONTEMPORARY EXAMPLE: J. Carlyle Sitterson, educator. SURNAME USAGE: Thomas Carlyle (1795-1881), Scottish historian and essayist.

Carman A variant spelling of Carmen. *See* Carmen. SURNAME USAGE: William Bliss Carman (1861-1929), Canadian poet.

Carmel From the Hebrew, meaning "vineyard" or "garden." Used also as a feminine name. VARIANT FORMS: Carmen (Spanish); Carmine (Italian). PLACE-NAME USAGE: Carmel, California; Carmel, New York.

Carmeli From the Hebrew, meaning "my vineyard." Akin to Carmi.

Carmelo A variant form of Carmel. *See* Carmel. CONTEMPORARY EX-AMPLE: Carmelo Ayala, Amenia, New York.

Carmen The Spanish form of Carmel. Used also as a feminine form. *See* Carmen (feminine section). CONTEMPORARY EXAMPLES: Carmen Fanzone, baseball player; Carmen Marcantonio, soccer player.

Carmi From the Hebrew, meaning "my vineyard." Used also as a feminine name. Akin to Carmeli.

Carmiel From the Hebrew, meaning "the Lord is my vineyard."

Carmine The Italian form of Carmen. *See* Carmel. Used also as a feminine form. CONTEMPORARY EXAMPLE: Carmine DeSapio, New York political leader. PLACE-NAME USAGE: Carmine, Texas.

Carney   From the Celtic, meaning "a fighter."

Carol   Primarily a feminine form of Caroline. Used as a masculine name most often in the southern United States, and in England. *See* Caroline (feminine section). *See also* Carl.

Carolle   A form of Carl. *See* Carl. Used also as a feminine name. CON-TEMPORARY EXAMPLE: Carolle J. Carter, Irish author.

Carr   From the Scandinavian and Old Norse, meaning "marshy land." Kerr is a variant form. SURNAME USAGE: Vikki Carr, singer.

Carrol, Carroll   Variant forms of Carl. *See* Carl. Used also as a feminine name. CONTEMPORARY EXAMPLES: Carroll O'Connor, actor; Carroll Chambliss, baseball player. SURNAME USAGE: Charles Carroll, a signer of the Declaration of Independence. PLACE-NAME USAGE: Carroll, Maryland, named for Charles Carroll.

Carson   A patronymic, meaning "son of Carr." *See* Carr. CONTEM-PORARY EXAMPLE: Carson Baird, sports car racer. SURNAME USAGE: Johnny Carson, entertainer. PLACE-NAME USAGE: Carson City, Nevada, named for Christopher (Kit) Carson, famous frontiersman.

Carsten   From the Old English, meaning "a stony marsh." CONTEM-PORARY EXAMPLE: Carsten D. Leikvold, a city manager.

Carter   An Old English occupational name, meaning "cart driver." Cass is a pet form. CONTEMPORARY EXAMPLES: Carter Glass, U.S. con-gressman; Carter Hoag, baseball player. PLACE-NAME USAGE: Carter, Georgia, named for Farish Carter, a landowner; Carter, Oklahoma.

Cartha   Origin unknown. CONTEMPORARY EXAMPLE: Cartha Deloach, FBI agent.

Carvel, Carvell   From the Old English, meaning "the villa by the marsh." CONTEMPORARY EXAMPLE: Carvel Rowell, baseball player. SUR-NAME USAGE: Tom Carvel, ice cream franchisor.

Carver   An Old English occupational name, meaning "a wood carver, a sculptor." CONTEMPORARY EXAMPLE: Carver Clinton, basketball player. SURNAME USAGE: John Carver, seventeenth-century first governor of Plymouth Colony. PLACE-NAME USAGE: Carver, Massachusetts, named for John Carver.

Cary   A variant spelling of Carey. *See* Carey. CONTEMPORARY EXAM-PLE: Cary Grant, actor. SURNAME USAGE: Alice Cary (1820-1871), American poet.

Case   From the Old French *casse,* meaning "a chest, a box." CONTEM-PORARY EXAMPLE: Case Patten, baseball player. SURNAME USAGE: Clif-ford Case, New Jersey politician.

Casey   From the Celtic, meaning "valorous." Also, a pet form of Casimir *and* Cassius. *See* Casimir *and* Cassius. CONTEMPORARY EXAM-

PLE: Casey Stengel, baseball manager. SURNAME USAGE: Gene Casey, songwriter.

Cash A short form of Cassius. *See* Cassius. CONTEMPORARY EXAMPLE: Cash White, boxer. SURNAME USAGE: Johnny Cash, singer. PLACE-NAME USAGE: Cash, Texas; Cash, South Dakota, named for Casius Timmons, an early ranger.

Casimir From the Polish name Kazimier, meaning "proclamation of peace." PET FORMS: Cass, Cassy. Casimir Pulaski was a general in the American War of Independence. CONTEMPORARY EXAMPLE: Casimir Banaszak, football player.

Casius A variant spelling of Cassius. *See* Cassius. CONTEMPORARY EXAMPLE: Casius Timmons, rancher.

Caskey Probably a variant form of Cash. *See* Cash. CONTEMPORARY EXAMPLE: Caskey Swaim, actor.

Caspar From the German, meaning "imperial." VARIANT FORMS: Josper, Kaspar, Kasper. CONTEMPORARY EXAMPLE: Caspar W. Collins, Ohio cavalry officer killed in 1865.

Casper A variant spelling of Caspar. *See* Caspar. PLACE-NAME USAGE: Casper, Wyoming, named for Lieutenant Caspar W. Collins.

Cass A short form of Cassius or Casimir. *See* Cassius *and* Casimir. CONTEMPORARY EXAMPLES: Cass Michaels, baseball player; Cass Canfield, editor. PLACE-NAME USAGE: Cass Lake, Minnesota, named for General Lewis Cass.

Cassidy From the Celtic, meaning "ingenious." SURNAME USAGE: David Cassidy, actor.

Cassius From the Old Norman French *casse* and the Latin *capsa,* meaning "a box, a sheath, a protective cover." Gaius Cassius Longinus, a first–century Roman general. VARIANT FORMS: Cash, Casius, Cass. CONTEMPORARY EXAMPLE: Cassius Clay, heavyweight boxing champion (later called Muhammed Ali). SURNAME USAGE: Case, Casey, Cash.

Caster An Old English form of Chester. *See* Chester. Also, from the French and Spanish, meaning "a beaver."

Castor A variant spelling of Caster. *See* Caster. PLACE-NAME USAGE: a river in Missouri; a bayou in Louisiana.

Catfish A nickname. CONTEMPORARY EXAMPLE: Catfish (James) Hunter, baseball player.

Cavanagh A variant form of the Middle English *chubbe,* meaning "rounded, chubby."

Cazzie A pet form of Cassius. *See* Cassius. CONTEMPORARY EXAMPLE: Cazzie Russell, basketball player.

Cecil From the Latin *caecus*, meaning "blind." Caecilius was a Roman family name in medieval England. Used also as a feminine name. Cecilio is an Italian variant form. CONTEMPORARY EXAMPLE: Cecil Rhodes (1853-1902), British administrator in South Africa. PLACE-NAME USAGE: an island in the Aegean.

Cecilio An Italian form of Cecil. *See* Cecil. CONTEMPORARY EXAMPLE: Cecilio Acosta, baseball player.

Cedric From the Celtic, meaning "war chief." Probably invented by Sir Walter Scott for one of the characters in *Ivanhoe*. CONTEMPORARY EXAMPLES: Cedric Brown, football player; Sir Cedric Hardwicke, actor.

Cedro From the Spanish, meaning "cedar."

Celerino From the Latin and French, meaning "swift." CONTEMPORARY EXAMPLE: Celerino Sanchez, baseball player.

Celo From the Greek, meaning "a flame." PLACE-NAME USAGE: Celo, North Carolina, named for John Celo, a hunter.

Cesar, Cesare Variant forms of Caesar. *See* Caesar. CONTEMPORARY EXAMPLES: Cesar Gibson, baseball player; Cesar Chavez, labor leader; Cesare Maniago, hockey player.

Chad From the Celtic, meaning "battle" or "warrior." CONTEMPORARY EXAMPLE: Chad Stuart, musician. SURNAME USAGE: George Whitefield Chadwick (1854-1931), American composer. PLACE-NAME USAGE: a country in Central Africa, formerly a colony of France.

Chaim From the Hebrew, meaning "life." Among Jews, frequently bestowed as an additional name to one critically ill, in the hope that continued life will be granted. Vive is a French form. VARIANT SPELLINGS: Chayim, Chayyim, Chaym, Haim, Hayim, Haym. CONTEMPORARY EXAMPLE: Chaim Potok, author.

Chalmer, Chalmers From the Old English, meaning "king of the household." A Scottish occupational name for senior attendants to a king or nobleman. CONTEMPORARY EXAMPLES: Chalmer Harris, baseball player; Chalmer Cissell, baseball player.

Champ From the Middle English and Old French, meaning "a gladiator." Originally, from the Latin *campus*, meaning "a field, a stadium where games were played." Champion is a variant form. CONTEMPORARY EXAMPLE: Champ Clark, U.S. political leader (1914).

Champion A variant form of Champ. *See* Champ. SURNAME USAGE: Gower Champion, director-choreographer.

Chance An Americanized form of the Old English Chauncey. *See* Chauncey. CONTEMPORARY EXAMPLE: Chance O. Richardson, Mogna, Utah. PLACE-NAME USAGE: Chance, Oklahoma, named for T.C. Chance, its first postmaster; Chance, Maryland.

Chancellor   From the Middle English and Old French, meaning "keeper of records" or "secretary." SURNAME USAGE: John Chancellor, television news reporter.

Chandler   From the French, meaning "a maker or seller of candles." Chan is a pet form. SURNAME USAGE: Howard Chandler (1873-1952), American painter.

Chaney   A short form of either Chancellor, Chandler, or Channing. *See* Chancellor, Chandler, *and* Channing. Also, from the French *chaine de roches*, meaning "chain of rocks." SURNAME USAGE: Lon Chaney, actor. PLACE-NAME USAGE: Chaney Rush Creek, South Dakota.

Channing   From the Old French, meaning "a canal." CONTEMPORARY EXAMPLE: Channing Pollak, writer. SURNAME USAGE: Carol Channing, actress.

Chanticleer   From the Middle English *chauntecler* and the Old French *chantecler*, meaning "to sing aloud." The name of a rooster in *Reynard the Fox*, a medieval epic. Chantal is a feminine equivalent.

Chapin   A condensed form of the Old French *chapelain*, meaning "chaplain." Chopin is a variant form.

Chaplin   From the Old French *chapelain*, meaning "chaplain." VARIANT FORMS: Chapin, Chopin, Capp. SURNAME USAGE: Charlie Chaplin, actor.

Chapman   From the Middle English *shopman*, meaning "a trader." CONTEMPORARY EXAMPLE: Chapman Pincher, journalist. SURNAME USAGE: George Chapman (1559-1634), English poet; Lonny Chapman, actor.

Charles   A French form, from the Anglo-Saxon *ceorl* and the English *churl*, meaning "manly, strong" or, literally, "full-grown." Perhaps the earliest forms are the Old High German Karl and the Latin-French Carolus. Extremely popular in France and Germany due to the renown of Emperor Charles the Great, or Charlemagne. VARIANT FORMS: Carl (English); Karl (German); Carlo (Italian); Carlos (Spanish and Portuguese); Karol (Slavonic); Kalle (Swedish); Karel (Danish and Dutch); Carel, Carolus (Dutch); Karoly (Hungarian). PET FORMS: Charlie, Charley, Chick, Chuck, Charlot (French); Chico. FEMININE FORMS: Charlotte, Carla, Caroline, Charlene. PLACE-NAME USAGE: Cape Charles, Virginia; Charles River, Massachusetts; Charleston, South Carolina.

Charls   A variant spelling of Charles created by the mother of Washington lobbyist Charls Edward Walker. She dropped the "e" from Charles so her son would not be nicknamed Charlie.

Charlton   A French-German name derived from Charles and meaning "Charles' town." *See* Charles. CONTEMPORARY EXAMPLE: Charlton Heston, actor. PLACE-NAME USAGE: Charlton, Massachusetts, named for Sir Francis Charlton, member of the Privy Council (1755).

Chase   From Old French and Middle English, meaning "the hunt." CONTEMPORARY EXAMPLE: Chase Clements, football player.

Chauncey   A pet form of Chancellor. *See* Chancellor. Also, from the Old French *cheaunce*, meaning "chance, luck." CONTEMPORARY EXAMPLE: Chauncey Browning, Jr., West Virginia attorney general.

Chayym   From the Hebrew, meaning "life." A variant form of Chaim. *See* Chaim. CONTEMPORARY EXAMPLE: Chayym Zeldis, novelist.

Chaz   A variant form of Cassius. *See* Cassius. Akin to Kaz. CONTEMPORARY EXAMPLE: Chaz Bowyer, author.

Cheney   A variant spelling of Chaney. *See* Chaney.

Chesleigh, Chesley   From the Old English, meaning "a camp on the meadow." Used primarily in southern areas of the U.S.

Chester   From the Latin, meaning "fortress, camp." Chet is a popular form. VARIANT FORMS: Caster, Castor. CONTEMPORARY EXAMPLE: Chester Alan Arthur (1830-1886), twenty-first president of the U.S. SURNAME USAGE: George Randolph Chester (1869-1929), American author. PLACE-NAME USAGE: the oldest city in Pennsylvania, named by William Penn (1682); Chester, Texas, named for Chester A. Arthur.

Chet   A pet form of Chester. *See* Chester. CONTEMPORARY EXAMPLES: Chet Meyers, author; Chet Huntley, newscaster.

Chevy   From the British, meaning "a hunt, a chase." A name derived from the hunting cry *chivy*, in the ballad *Chevy Chase*. CONTEMPORARY EXAMPLE: Chevy Chase, actor.

Chez   From the French, meaning "at the home of." CONTEMPORARY EXAMPLE: Chez Evans, football player.

Chic, Chick   Pet forms of Charles. *See* Charles. CONTEMPORARY EXAMPLES: Chic Young, cartoonist; Chick Hafey, baseball player.

Chico   A pet form of Charles. *See* Charles. Also, from the Spanish, meaning "small." Chick is a variant form. CONTEMPORARY EXAMPLE: Chico Salmon, baseball player. PLACE-NAME USAGE: Chico, California.

Chill   A pet form of Chilton. *See* Chilton. CONTEMPORARY EXAMPLE: Chill Wills, actor.

Chilton   From the Anglo-Saxon, meaning "the town by the river." Chelton is a variant form. CONTEMPORARY EXAMPLE: Chilton Powell, clergyman. PLACE-NAME USAGE: Chilton, Texas, named for L.B. Chilton, the first storekeeper; Chilton, Wisconsin, from the English place-name Chillington.

Chip, Chipper   Derived from *Chippeu*, a tribe of Algonquian Indians. *Chip* is the echoic word for the chipping sparrow. CONTEMPORARY EXAMPLES: Chip Sheffield, football player; Chipper Mancuso, golf player.

Chon From the Greek, meaning "a grain, a cartilage." CONTEMPO-RARY EXAMPLE: Chon Gallegos, football player.

Chopin A variant spelling of Chapin. *See* Chapin.

Chris, Chrissie Pet forms of Christopher or Christian. *See* Christopher *and* Christian. CONTEMPORARY EXAMPLE: Chris Dubbs, author; Chris Harper, news reporter.

Christiaan The Dutch spelling of Christian. *See* Christian. CONTEM-PORARY EXAMPLE: Christiaan Barnard, surgeon.

Christian From the Latin *christianus,* meaning "a Christian." VARIANT FORMS: Chrestien (French); Kristian (Swedish); Christiaan, Karston, Kerstan (Dutch); Zan (Old German); Kito, Krista, Kristo (Slavonic). PET FORMS: Chris, Chrissie, Kit. FEMININE FORMS: Chris-tiana, Christina, Christine. CONTEMPORARY EXAMPLE: Christian Diro, French designer. PLACE-NAME USAGE: Christiania is the former name of Oslo, capital of Norway.

Christie A pet form of Christopher and Christian. *See* Christopher *and* Christian.

Christoff A variant form of Christopher. *See* Christopher. CONTEM-PORARY EXAMPLE: Christoff St. John, actor.

Christopher From the Greek and Latin, meaning "Christ-bearer." Popularized through the life of St. Christopher, martyred at the hands of the Romans in 250 A.D. Christian is the original form. *See* Christian. VARIANT FORMS: Christophe (French); Kester (English); Christal (Scotch); Kristofel, Kristofer (Swedish); Cristovano, Cristoforo (Ital-ian); Cristoval (Spanish); Christoph Stoffel (German). PET FORMS: Kit, Chris. CONTEMPORARY EXAMPLE: Christopher (Kit) Carson, American Frontiersman.

Christy Primary Scottish pet form of Christian. *See* Christian. SUR-NAME USAGE: Howard Chandler Christy (1873-1952), American painter.

Chubb, Chubby From the Old German *kubb,* referring to anything rounded, e.g., a rounded head of hair (*kobbe* in Flemish) or a block of wood (*kubbe* in Norwegian). CONTEMPORARY EXAMPLES: Chubby Phillips, football player; Chubby Checker, singer.

Chuck A pet form of Charles. *See* Charles. CONTEMPORARY EXAMPLES: Chuck Connors, actor; Chuck Scarborough, newscaster. PLACE-NAME USAGE: Chuck Lake, Alaska, named for Charles Forward, U.S. Forest Service.

Cicero From the Latin, meaning "the orator" or "a guide who explains the history of a place to sightseers." Marcus Tullius Cicero (100-43 B.C.) was a Roman statesman and orator. Ciceroni is an Italian form. CONTEMPORARY EXAMPLE: Cicero Murphy, billiard player. PLACE-NAME USAGE: cities in New York and Illinois.

Ciceroni   An Italian form of Cicero. *See* Cicero.

Cid   A Spanish name derived from the Arabic *sayyid*, meaning "a lord." The Cid was an eleventh-century Spanish hero and soldier of fortune. PLACE-NAME USAGE: Cid, North Carolina, named for Sidney Muffley, a local superintendent of mines.

Cimon   A variant form of Simon. *See* Simon. The earliest Cimon was the fifth-century B.C. Athenian statesman and general.

Ciro   A pet form of Cicero. *See* Cicero.

Claiborn, Claiborne   A compounded name, from the German *klee*, meaning "clover," and the French *borne*, meaning "boundary," hence "a boundary marked by clovers." CONTEMPORARY EXAMPLE: Claiborne Pell, U.S. senator (whose name was originally spelled Kleeburn). SURNAME USAGE: Craig Claiborne, culinary expert.

Clair, Claire   Short forms of Clarence. *See* Clarence. More commonly used as feminine names. CONTEMPORARY EXAMPLES: Clair Rasmusen, football player; Claire Bee, athletic coach.

Clancy   From the Gaelic and Irish *clann*, meaning "offspring, tribe." CONTEMPORARY EXAMPLE: Clancy Osborn, football player.

Claral   From the Latin *clarus*, meaning "clear, bright." Akin to Clarence. CONTEMPORARY EXAMPLE: Claral Gillenwater, baseball player.

Clare   A pet form of Clarence. *See* Clarence. Primarily a feminine form.

Clarence   From the Latin *clarus*, meaning "clear, prominent, illustrious." The name of the English Duke of Clarence (later called William IV) was derived from Clare, a town in England. Akin to the feminine Clare. SURNAME USAGE: Edward Hyde Clarendon (1609-1674), English statesman.

Clark, Clarke   From the Old English, meaning "clergyman; learned man." A clark, or clerk, was originally a member of a clerical order. CONTEMPORARY EXAMPLES: Clark Ahlberg, educator; Clarke Hinkle, footballl player. SURNAME USAGE: Ramsey Clark, U.S. attorney general.

Claron   A variant form of Clarence. *See* Clarence. CONTEMPORARY EXAMPLE: Claron Bailey, football player.

Claud   The English form of Claude. *See* Claude.

Claude   From the French and Latin *claudus*, meaning "lame." Claud is a variant English spelling. Claudio is the Italian form. CONTEMPORARY EXAMPLE: Claude R. Kirk, Jr., governor of Florida.

Claudell   A pet form of Claude. *See* Claude. Also, a name invented by combining the first and last names of Claude D. Wells, the first postmaster of Claudell, New Mexico. CONTEMPORARY EXAMPLE: Claudell Washington, baseball player.

Claudio   The Italian form of Claude. *See* Claude.

Claxton   A variant pronounciation of "Clark's town." *See* Clark. CONTEMPORARY EXAMPLE: Claxton Welch, football player.

Clay   From the German *klei*, and the Indo-European *glei*, meaning "to stick together." CONTEMPORARY EXAMPLES: Clay Felker, publisher; Clay Carroll, baseball player. SURNAME USAGE: Henry Clay (1777-1852), U.S. statesman. PLACE-NAME USAGE: Clay County, Kentucky, named for General Green Clay, prominent in the War of 1812.

Clayborn, Clayborne   Variant spellings of Claiborn. *See* Claiborn.

Clayland   From the British *clai*, meaning "a town built upon clay land." CONTEMPORARY EXAMPLE: Clayland Touchstone, baseball player.

Clayton   A variant form of Clayland. *See* Clayland. CONTEMPORARY EXAMPLE: Clayton Pachal, hockey player. PLACE-NAME USAGE: Claytonia (a Latinized form of Clayton), Nebraska.

Cleander   Compounded from the British *clee*, meaning "*the* place (of eminence)," and the name Ander, or Andrew, hence "Andrew's place."

Cleanth   Probably from the Old English *claene*, meaning "clean, pure." CONTEMPORARY EXAMPLE: Cleanth Brooks, author.

Cleavant   From the Old English *clif*, meaning "a steep bank." VARIANT FORMS: Cleeve, Cleve, Clive, Cliffe. CONTEMPORARY EXAMPLE: Cleavant Derricks, actor.

Cleavon   A variant spelling of Cleavant. *See* Cleavant. CONTEMPORARY EXAMPLE: Cleavon Little, actor.

Clem   A pet form of Clement. *See* Clement.

Clemens   A variant form of Clement. *See* Clement. CONTEMPORARY EXAMPLE: Clemens Hausmann, baseball player. SURNAME USAGE: Samuel Langhorne Clemens (1835-1910), American author who wrote under the pseudonym Mark Twain.

Clement   From the Latin *clemens*, meaning "gentle, merciful." Clementine is a feminine form. Clem is a popular pet form. CONTEMPORARY EXAMPLE: Clement Atlee, English prime minister.

Clemon, Clemmons   Variant forms of Clement. *See* Clement. CONTEMPORARY EXAMPLE: Clemon Daniels, football player.

Clendon   Possibly a variant form of Cleon. *See* Cleon. CONTEMPORARY EXAMPLE: Clendon Thomas, football player.

Cleneth   A variant form of Cleanth. *See* Cleanth. CONTEMPORARY EXAMPLE: Cleneth Markland, baseball player.

Cleo   A variant form of Clio. *See* Clio. Also, from the Old English, meaning "a hill." *See also* Cleo (feminine section). CONTEMPORARY EXAMPLE: Cleo Johnson, football player. PLACE-NAME USAGE: Cleo,

Oregon, an acronym of Oregon Export Lumber Company, with the letters reversed.

Cleomenes From the Latin, referring to members of a variety of woody, tropical plants with white, green, or purple flowers. The name of three Spartan kings from the sixth to the third centuries B.C.

Cleon A variant form of Clio. *See* Clio. An Athenian politician and general of the fifth century B.C. CONTEMPORARY EXAMPLE: Cleon Jones, baseball player.

Cleophus From the Old English *cleopian*, meaning "to call one, to address someone." CONTEMPORARY EXAMPLE: Cleophus Miller, Jr., football player.

Cletis A variant spelling of Cletus. *See* Cletus. CONTEMPORARY EXAMPLE: Cletis Boyer, baseball player.

Cletus A variant form of the British names Clay, Cle, and Clea, meaning "clay." Cletis is a variant spelling. CONTEMPORARY EXAMPLE: Cletus Fisher, football player.

Cleve From the Old English *clif*, meaning "a steep bank." Used also as a pet form of Cleveland. *See* Cleveland. CONTEMPORARY EXAMPLE: Cleve Dickerson, football player. SURNAME USAGE: P.T. Cleve (1840-1905), Swedish chemist.

Cleveland From the Old English *clif*, meaning "land near the steep bank." CONTEMPORARY EXAMPLES: Cleveland Williams, boxer; Cleveland Amory, writer. SURNAME USAGE: Grover Cleveland (1837-1908), twenty-second and twenty-fourth president of the U.S. PLACE-NAME USAGE: cities in Idaho, Utah, and Ohio. Cleveland, Ohio was named for General Moses Cleaveland, who chose the townsite in 1796.

Clever From the Old English *clifer*, meaning "a claw, a hand." PLACE-NAME USAGE: Clever, Missouri.

Cliff, Cliffe From the Old English *clif*, meaning "a steep bank." Also, a short form of Clifford or Clifton. VARIANT FORMS: Cleve, Cleveland, Clifford, Cleavant. CONTEMPORARY EXAMPLES: Cliff Stout, football player; Cliff Robertson, actor. PLACE-NAME USAGE: Cliff Lake, Montana; Cliff Island, Maine.

Clifford From the Old English, meaning "a crossing near the cliff." CONTEMPORARY EXAMPLE: Clifford D. Clark, educator. SURNAME USAGE: Clark Clifford, attorney.

Clifton From the Old English, meaning "the town near the cliff." VARIANT FORMS: Cliff, Clifton, Clifford, Cleve, Cleveland. CONTEMPORARY EXAMPLE: Clifton R. Wharton, Jr., educator. PLACE-NAME USAGE: cities in Arizona, Idaho, New Jersey, Texas, and West Virginia.

Clim A variant form of Clem. *See* Clem.

Clint A pet form of Clinton. *See* Clinton. CONTEMPORARY EXAMPLE: Clint Eastwood, actor.

Clinton From the Anglo-Saxon *klint*, meaning "hill," and *tun*, meaning "town," hence "a town on a hill." CONTEMPORARY EXAMPLE: Clinton Rossiter, a professor. SURNAME USAGE: DeWitt Clinton (1769-1828), American statesman. PLACE-NAME USAGE: a city in Massachusetts.

Clio From the Greek *kleos*, meaning "to praise, to acclaim." In Greek mythology, the Muse of history. Used also as a feminine name. VARIANT FORMS: Cleo, Cleon. PLACE-NAME USAGE: Clio, South Carolina; Clio, California.

Clive From the Old English *clif*, meaning "a steep bank." Originally a place-name in England. VARIANT FORMS: Cleve, Cleveland, Clif, Clifford, Clifton. CONTEMPORARY EXAMPLES: Clive Barnes, theater critic; Clive Cussler, author. SURNAME USAGE: Robert Clive (1725-1774), English soldier and statesman.

Clovis From the Anglo-Saxon and German, meaning "a clover," a leguminous plant. CONTEMPORARY EXAMPLES: Clovis Ruffin, fashion designer; Clovis Swinney, football player. PLACE-NAME USAGE: Clovis, New Mexico: Clovis, California, named for Clovis Cole, a local rancher.

Cloy From the Middle English *acloien*, meaning "to hamper, to harm." Also, from the Latin *clavus*, meaning "a nail." CONTEMPORARY EXAMPLE: Cloy Mattox, baseball player.

Cloyce A variant form of Cloy. *See* Cloy. CONTEMPORARY EXAMPLE: Cloyce Box, football player.

Cloyd A variant form of Cloy. *See* Cloy. CONTEMPORARY EXAMPLES: Cloyd Marshall, football player; Cloyd Boyer, baseball player.

Clure From the Latin *cluere*, meaning "to be esteemed, famous." CONTEMPORARY EXAMPLE: Clure Mosher, sports broadcaster.

Clyde From the Welsh, meaning "heard from afar." Or, from the British, meaning "a warm and sheltered place." PLACE-NAME USAGE: a river in southern Scotland; Clyde, Texas, named for Robert Clyde, early railroad builder (1881); Clyde River, Vermont.

Clydell A variant form of Clyde. *See* Clyde. CONTEMPORARY EXAMPLE: Clydell Castleman, baseball player.

Coburn From the Middle English *burne*, meaning "a little stream," and the prefix *co*, meaning "together," hence, "where the streams come together." CONTEMPORARY EXAMPLE: Coburn Jones, baseball player. SURNAME USAGE: James Coburn, actor.

Coby A pet form of Coburn. *See* Coburn. CONTEMPORARY EXAMPLE: Coby Dietrick, basketball player.

Cody From the Anglo-Saxon *codd*, akin to the Old Norse *koddi*, meaning "a cushion." CONTEMPORARY EXAMPLE: Cody Jones, football player. SURNAME USAGE: William (Bill) Frederick Cody (1846-1917), American frontiersman.

Colbert A French name from the Latin *collum*, meaning "the neck," and the Old High German *beraht*, meaning "bright," referring to "a good, bright passageway in a mountain range." CONTEMPORARY EXAMPLE: Colbert Harrah, baseball player. SURNAME USAGE: Jean Baptiste Colbert (1619-1683), French statesman.

Colby From the Old English and Danish, meaning "a coal town." Akin to Coleman. CONTEMPORARY EXAMPLE: Colby Chester, actor. PLACE-NAME USAGE: Colby, Washington, originally called Coal Bay.

Cole A pet form of Coleman or Colby. *See* Coleman *and* Colby. CONTEMPORARY EXAMPLES: Cole Porter, songwriter; Cole Hendrix, city manager. SURNAME USAGE: Nat (King) Cole, singer.

Coleman, Colman From the Middle English *col*, meaning "coal," hence "coal miner." Or, from the Middle English *cole* and the Latin *colis*, meaning "cabbage," hence "a man who farms cabbage." CONTEMPORARY EXAMPLE: Coleman Young, American politician. PLACE-NAME USAGE: Coleman Valley, California.

Colin Most often, a pet form of Nicholas, meaning "victory." Also, from the Celtic, meaning "a cub, whelp." Or, from the Gaelic, meaning "a dove," probably derived from St. Columba, patron saint of Cornish parishes. Used in England in the eighteenth century, but gained popularity after World War II because of the heroism of pilot Colin Kelly. CONTEMPORARY EXAMPLE: Colin Davis, musical conductor.

Collier From the Middle English *col*, meaning "a coal miner." Also, "a ship for carrying coal." Collie is a pet form.

Colonel From the French and Italian, meaning "a column of soldiers." CONTEMPORARY EXAMPLE: Colonel Mills, baseball player.

Colton From the Old English, meaning "coal town." Akin to Colby and Colville.

Colum From the Gaelic, meaning "a dove," or from the Latin *collum*, meaning "a hill." Akin to Columba. *See* Columba.

Columba From the Latin *columba*, meaning "a dove." St. Columba (521-597) was the apostle of the Picts. Colin is a Gaelic form. Akin to Columbia. *See* Columbia (feminine section).

Colville From the Old English, meaning "a coal town." VARIANT FORMS: Colby, Colton. CONTEMPORARY EXAMPLE: Colville Jackson, football player. PLACE-NAME USAGE: Colville River, Alaska, named for Andrew Colville, an official of Hudson's Bay Company.

Colvin, Colwyn Compounded from the Middle English *col*, meaning "coal," and the Germanic *vin* and *wyn*, meaning "friend of." Coleman is a variant form. CONTEMPORARY EXAMPLE: Colwyn Trevelgan, scholar. SURNAME USAGE: Sidney Colvin (1845-1927), English writer.

Comillo An Italian form of Camillus. *See* Camillus.

Conan, Conant   From the Middle English *connen*, meaning "to be able, to be knowledgeable." Popular in Ireland. CONTEMPORARY EXAMPLE: Sir Arthur Conan Doyle, author. SURNAME USAGE: James Bryant Conant (1893-   ), American educator.

Conn   A variant form of Conan. *See* Conan.

Connie   A pet form of Constantine and Conan. *See* Constantine *and* Conan. CONTEMPORARY EXAMPLE: Connie Zelenick, football player.

Connor, Conor   An Irish form of Conan. *See* Conan. CONTEMPORARY EXAMPLE: Conor O'Brien, author.

Conrad   From the Old High German, meaning "bold, wise counsellor." VARIANT FORMS: Kurt (German); Konrad (Swedish, Russian, and German); Conrade (French); Cort (Danish). CONTEMPORARY EXAMPLE: Conrad Aiken, poet. SURNAME USAGE: Joseph Conrad (1857-1924), English novelist.

Conroy   A variant form of Conrad. *See* Conrad.

Constant   A short form of Constantine. *See* Constantine.

Constantine   From the Latin, meaning "constant, loyal, firm." Constantine I (280-337) was the first Christian emperor of Rome. PLACE-NAME USAGE: a city in northern Algeria.

Consuel   A Spanish form of the Latin *consolatio*, meaning "consolation." Consuela is the feminine form.

Conway   A Welsh place-name, meaning "head river." CONTEMPORARY EXAMPLE: Conway Hayden, football player.

Cook, Cookie   From the Latin *conquere*, meaning "to cook." Originally an occupational surname. CONTEMPORARY EXAMPLE: Cookie Rojas, baseball player. SURNAME USAGE: James Cook (1728-1779), English writer. PLACE-NAME USAGE: Mount Cook, the highest peak in New Zealand; Cook Islands, New Zealand.

Coop   A pet name of Cooper. *See* Cooper. The nickname of actor Gary Cooper.

Cooper   From the Latin *cupa*, meaning "a cask." An occupational name for persons who make and repair barrels. SURNAME USAGE: James Fenimore Cooper (1789-1851), American novelist. PLACE-NAME USAGE: Cooper River, South Carolina, named for Sir Anthony Ashley Cooper.

Corbet, Corbett   From the Old French *corb* and the Middle English *corbe*, meaning "a raven, a cow." CONTEMPORARY EXAMPLE: Corbett Davis, football player. SURNAME USAGE: Dean Corbett, actor.

Corbin   A variant form of Corbet. *See* Corbet.

Corby   A pet form of Corbet and Corbin. *See* Corbet *and* Corbin.

Cord   From the Old French *corde* and the Latin *chorda*, meaning "a rope." A pet form of Cordell. CONTEMPORARY EXAMPLE: Cord Meyer, Jr., CIA official.

Cordas   A variant form of Cordell. *See* Cordell. CONTEMPORARY EXAMPLE: Cordas C. Burnett, educator.

Cordell   From the Old French *corde* and the Latin *chorda*, meaning "a rope." Also, the masculine form of Cordelia. *See* Cordelia (feminine section). CONTEMPORARY EXAMPLE: Cordell Hull, U.S. secretary of state.

Corey   A variant form of Cory. *See* Cory.

Corin   From the Greek *kore*, meaning "a maiden." A masculine form of Cora. Also, a variant form of Caren. *See* Caren. CONTEMPORARY EXAMPLE: Corin Redgrave, actor.

Corliss   A variant form of Carl. *See* Carl. Also, a variant form of Carlisle. *See* Carlisle. CONTEMPORARY EXAMPLE: Corliss Lamont, author.

Cormac   From the Greek *kormos*, meaning "the trunk of a tree (with branches lopped off)." A common name in Irish legend and mythology. CONTEMPORARY EXAMPLE: Cormac McCarthy, author.

Cormick   A variant form of Cormac. *See* Cormac.

Cornelius   From the Old French *cornille* and *corneille*, derived from the Latin *cornicula*, meaning "a cornell tree." Corney is a variant form. Cornelia is a feminine form. CONTEMPORARY EXAMPLE: Cornelius Walker, fooball player.

Cornell   A variant form of Cornelius. *See* Cornelius. CONTEMPORARY EXAMPLE: Cornell Green, football player.

Corney   A variant Irish form of Cornelius. *See* Cornelius.

Corwan   A variant spelling of Corwin. *See* Corwin. CONTEMPORARY EXAMPLE: Corwan Artman, football player.

Corwin   From the Latin *corvinus*, meaning "a raven." Akin to Corbet. CONTEMPORARY EXAMPLE: Corwin Clatt, football player.

Cory   From the Latin *korys*, meaning "a helmet." Corey is a variant spelling. Also, a pet form of Cornelius.

Corydon   From the Greek *korys*, meaning "a crested (helmeted) lark." Akin to Cory.

Cosimo   The Italian form of Cosmo. *See* Cosmo.

Cosmo   From the Greek *kosmos*, meaning "universe, universal." Cosimo is a variant Italian form. Cosima is a feminine form.

Cotton   From the Middle English *cotton*, referring to the cotton plant. CONTEMPORARY EXAMPLES: Cotton Clark and Cotton Davidson, football players. PLACE-NAME USAGE: cities in Montana and Oregon.

Council   From the Latin *concilium*, meaning "a group of people." CONTEMPORARY EXAMPLE: Council Rudolph, football player.

Count, Countee   From the Old French *conte*, meaning "companion." CONTEMPORARY EXAMPLES: Count Basie, band leader; Countee Cullen, American poet.

Courtenay, Courtney   From the Late Latin *curtis*, meaning "an enclosed place." PET FORMS: Court, Cort, Cortie, Corty. CONTEMPORARY EXAMPLES: Courtney Snyder, football player; Courtney Smith, educator. SURNAME USAGE: Tom Courtney, actor.

Courtland, Courtlandt   From the Anglo-Saxon, meaning "land belonging to the king (court)." VARIANT FORMS: Courtenay, Courtney. CONTEMPORARY EXAMPLE: Courtlandt Canby.

Court, Courts   From the Late Latin *curtis*, meaning "an enclosed area." Akin to Curtis. VARIANT FORMS: Courtenay, Courtney, Courtland, Courtlandt. CONTEMPORARY EXAMPLE: Courts Redford, educator.

Covert   From the Old French *covrir*, meaning "to cover." CONTEMPORARY EXAMPLE: Covert Bailey, author.

Covington   From the Anglo-Saxon *cofa*, meaning "a cove, a cave, a secret place," hence "the town near the cove." CONTEMPORARY EXAMPLE: Covington Harder, banker. PLACE-NAME USAGE: Covington, Kentucky.

Cowan   From the Middle English *coul* and the Latin *capa*, meaning "a hooded cloak," hence, a member of the clergy. Akin to Cohen, from the Hebrew, meaning "priest."

Coy, Coye   From the British *coed*, meaning "wood, a wooded area." Also, from the Old French *coi*, meaning "quiet, still." CONTEMPORARY EXAMPLES: Coy MacDonald, parachutist; Coye Dunn, football player.

Cozy   From the Scottish and Norwegian, meaning "comfortable." CONTEMPORARY EXAMPLE: Cozy Polan, baseball player.

Craig   From the Celtic and Gaelic *creag*, meaning "from the crag or rugged rocky mass." Graig is a variant form. CONTEMPORARY EXAMPLES: Craig Morton, football player; Craig Swan, baseball player.

Cram   A short form of Cramer. *See* Cramer. SURNAME USAGE: Ralph Adam Cram (1863-1942), American architect.

Cramer   From the Middle English *crammen*, meaning "to cram in, to squeeze in." Akin to Kramer. Originally an occupational name for a peddler who traveled the country with a cram (pack) on his back. CONTEMPORARY EXAMPLE: Cramer Beard, baseball player.

Crandall, Crandell   From the Old English, meaning "a dale, a valley of cranes."

Crane   From the Old English *cran*, meaning "to cry hoarsely." A member of the family of large wading birds. CONTEMPORARY EXAMPLE: Crane Davis, television executive. SURNAME USAGE: Stephen Crane (1871-1900), American novelist.

Crawford   From the Old English, meaning "the ford or stream where the crows flock." CONTEMPORARY EXAMPLE: Crawford H. Greenwalt, industrialist. SURNAME USAGE: Francis Marion Crawford (1854-1909), American novelist; Hubert H. Crawford, author.

Creighton   From the Old English *cricca*, meaning "a creek," hence "a town near the creek." Akin to Crichton. *See* Crichton. CONTEMPORARY EXAMPLE: Creighton Abrams, U.S. Army general.

Creole   A masculine form of Creola. *See* Creola (feminine section).

Creon   In Greek legend, the King of Thebes who had his niece buried alive because she disobeyed him.

Creston   From the Old English, meaning "Christ's town." CONTEMPORARY EXAMPLE: Creston Whitaker, football player.

Crichton   A corrupt form of the Welsh *crug* and the British *creeg*, meaning "a hill," hence "a town on the hill." May also be a variant form of Creighton. *See* Creighton.

Crispin   From the Latin *crispus*, meaning "curly, wavy," generally referring to crisp hair. Saint Crispin was a third-century Roman Christian martyr, the patron saint of shoemakers.

Crispus   A variant form of Crispin. *See* Crispin. CONTEMPORARY EXAMPLE: Crispus Attucks, author.

Cristobal   A compound of the French *bal*, meaning "to dance," and Christ, hence "the dance of Christ." CONTEMPORARY EXAMPLE: Cristobal Mendoza, baseball player. PLACE-NAME USAGE: a seaport in the Panama Canal Zone.

Cristobol   A variant form of Cristobal. *See* Cristobal.

Crockett   From the British *crug*, meaning "a heap, a hill." SURNAME USAGE: Davy (David) Crockett (1786-1836), American frontiersman and politician.

Croft   From the Anglo-Saxon, meaning "a field" or "appropriated land."

Cromwell   From the Welsh *crom*, meaning "bent," plus the Old English *wella*, meaning "a well, water," hence "one who lives near the winding brook." SURNAME USAGE: Oliver Cromwell (1599-1658), English statesman.

Cronan   From the Greek *chronos*, meaning "a companion." In Greek mythology, Cronus was a Titan, son of Uranus and Gaea. CONTEMPORARY EXAMPLE: Cronan Minton, author.

Crook   From the Middle English *crok*, meaning "a bend in the river, a bay." Used especially in Scotland. CONTEMPORARY EXAMPLE: Crook Graham, grandfather of evangelist Billy Graham.

Crosby   From the Anglo-Saxon, meaning "a crossroads near the town." Or, from the Middle English, meaning "the cross in the town." SURNAME USAGE: Bing Crosby, actor.

Crowell   From the Middle English *crowe* and the German *krake*, meaning "to crow, to call," hence "a cry of victory." CONTEMPORARY EXAMPLE: Crowell Kenyon, football player.

Cullen   From the Celtic, meaning "a cub, a young animal." May also be a corrupt form of Cologne (Koln) in Germany. CONTEMPORARY EXAMPLE: Cullen Bryant, football player. AS SURNAME: Countee Cullen (1905-1946), American poet.

Culley   A pet form of Cullen. *See* Cullen. CONTEMPORARY EXAMPLE: Culley Rikard, baseball player.

Culver   From the Latin *columba* and the Old English *culfer*, meaning "a dove." PLACE-NAME USAGE: Culver City, California.

Cumbert   From the Latin and Anglo-Saxon, meaning "famous."

Curley   From the Old English *ceorle*, meaning "strong." A variant form of Charlie (Charles). *See* Charles. CONTEMPORARY EXAMPLE: Curley Culp, football player.

Curran   From the Old English *ciern*, meaning "a churn," hence "a place where cheese was made."

Curt   A pet form of Curtis. *See* Curtis. Kurt is a variant form. CONTEMPORARY EXAMPLES: Curt Leviant, author; Curt Gowdy, sportscaster.

Curtell   A variant form of Curtis. *See* Curtis. CONTEMPORARY EXAMPLE: Curtell Motton, baseball player.

Curtis   From the Late Latin *curtis*, meaning "an enclosure, a court." Or, from the Old French *corteis*, meaning "courteous." Akin to Court. *See* Court. PET FORMS: Curt, Kurt. CONTEMPORARY EXAMPLE: Curtis LeMay, U.S. general. SURNAME USAGE: Charles Curtis (1929-1933), American statesman; Tony Curtis, actor.

Curvan   Possibly from the Latin *cura*, meaning "to care for, to cure." CONTEMPORARY EXAMPLE: Curvan Lewis, basketball player.

Cuthbert   An Old English variant form of Cumbert. *See* Cumbert.

Cutler   From the Middle English *cuteler*, meaning "one who makes cutlery."

Cuyler   Probably from the Irish *kyle*, meaning "chapel."

Cy   A pet form of Cyrus. *See* Cyrus.

Cyprian   From the Latin name Cyprianus, meaning "a native of Cyprus." In ancient times, a city with a reputation for licentiousness and prostitution, the place of the worship of Aphrodite, the Greek goddess of beauty and love. CONTEMPORARY EXAMPLE: Cyprian Luke, educator.

Cyril   From the Greek, meaning "lordly." Saint Cyril I (c. 315-386) was bishop of Jerusalem. VARIANT FORMS: Cyrille (French); Cyrillo (Portuguese); Cirilo (Spanish); Cirillo (Italian); Cyrill (German); Ciril, Ciro (Slavonic). Cy is a pet form. CONTEMPORARY EXAMPLE: Cyril Ritchard, actor.

Cyrus   From the Persian, meaning "sun." In the Bible, a king of Persia (c. 600-529 B.C.). Cy is a pet form. CONTEMPORARY EXAMPLES: Cyrus Adler, educator; Cyrus Vance, U.S. secretary of state.

D

Dab, Dabbey, Dabby   Variant forms of David. *See* David.

Dabney   A variant form of David. *See* David. CONTEMPORARY EXAMPLE: Dabney Coleman, actor.

Daedalus   From the Greek, meaning "a skillful worker." In Greek legend, a craftsman who invented a winged apparatus by which King Minos of Crete was able to escape from prison.

Daffy   A variant form of David. *See* David.

Dag   From the Danish and German *dag* and *tag*, meaning "day." VARIANT FORMS: Dagget, Darmon, Daymon. CONTEMPORARY EXAMPLE: Dag Hammarskjold (1905-1961), Swedish statesman.

Dagan   From the Hebrew, meaning "corn, grain." In Babylonian mythology, the god of the earth. *See also* Dagania (feminine section).

Dagget   An Anglo-Saxon form of Dag. *See* Dag.

Dago   A variant form of Diego, the Spanish form of James. *See* James. CONTEMPORARY EXAMPLE: Dago Berto Campaneris, baseball player. PLACE-NAME USAGE: an island in the Baltic Sea.

Dailey, Daily   From the Middle English *daylay*, meaning "day." Akin to Dag. Daly is a variant spelling.

Dainard   An Old English form of Dane, meaning "a bold or hardy Dane." *See* Dane. CONTEMPORARY EXAMPLE: Dainard Paulson, football player.

Dakin   A pet form of Dane. *See* Dane. CONTEMPORARY EXAMPLE: Dakin Miller, baseball player.

Dal   A variant form of Dale. *See* Dale.

Dalbert   From the German, meaning "a bright, cheerful valley."

Dale   From the Old English *dael*, and the Old Norse *dalr*, meaning "a hollow; a small valley." Dal is a variant form. CONTEMPORARY EXAMPLES: Dale Carnegie, author; Dale Learn, U.S. vice-presidential candidate (1948). SURNAME USAGE: Thomas Dale (died 1619), English colonial governor of Virginia.

Dali   A Spanish form of Dal and Dale. *See* Dale. SURNAME USAGE: Salvador Dali, Spanish surrealist painter.

Dallan   From the Anglo-Saxon, meaning "the land in the valley." *See* Dale. CONTEMPORARY EXAMPLE: Dallan Maxvill, baseball player.

69

Dallas   From the Old English, meaning "a house in the valley." VARIANT FORMS: Dal, Dalbèrt, Dale, Dallan, Dallin. CONTEMPORARY EXAMPLE: Dallas Smith, hockey player. PLACE-NAME USAGE: a city in Texas.

Dallin   From the Anglo-Saxon, meaning "from the dale." Akin to Dallan. *See* Dallan. VARIANT FORMS: Dal, Dalbert, Dallan, Dallas. CONTEMPORARY EXAMPLE: Dallin U. Oaks, Provo, Utah. SURNAME USAGE: Cyrus E. Dallin, sculptor and educator.

Dalton   From the Old English, meaning "the town near the valley." Akin to Dale. *See* Dale. CONTEMPORARY EXAMPLE: Dalton Jones, baseball player. SURNAME USAGE: John Dalton (1776-1844), English chemist.

Dalva   A form of the Old English name Dale, meaning "valley." *See* Dale. Akin to the Latin *ad vallum*, meaning "down to the valley." CONTEMPORARY EXAMPLE: Dalva Allen, athlete.

Daly   A variant spelling of Dailey. *See* Dailey.

Damian   A variant spelling of Damien or Damon. *See* Damien *and* Damon. A popular name in England from the thirteenth century onward.

Damien   From the Greek, meaning "divine power" or "fate." Also, a variant form of Damon. *See* Damon. CONTEMPORARY EXAMPLES: Joseph Damien de Veuster (1840-1889), Catholic priest and missionary; Damien Magee, auto racer.

Damon   From the Latin *daemon*, meaning "a spirit, a demon." Also, from the Danish *dag* and the Anglo-Saxon *daeg*, meaning "day." In Roman legend, the devoted friend of Pythias, hence the connotation of "friendship, devotion." VARIANT FORMS: Dag, Damien, Dayman, Daymon, Daymond. CONTEMPORARY EXAMPLES: (Alfred) Damon Runyon (1884-1946), American writer; Damon Keith, a judge.

Dan   From the Hebrew, meaning "judge." In the Bible, the fifth of the twelve sons of Jacob. Akin to Daniel. PLACE NAME USAGE: a town in northern Palestine in biblical times; Dan River, Virginia.

Dana   The feminine form of the biblical Dan. *See* Dan. CONTEMPORARY EXAMPLES: Dana Nafziger, football player; Dana Andrews, actor. PLACE NAME USAGE: Dana Point, California, named for R.H. Dana, Jr.; Dana Butte, Arizona, named for J.D. Dana (1813-1895), American geologist.

Dandie   A pet form of Andrew. *See* Andrew. Dandy is a variant spelling. A dog in Sir Walter Scott's *Guy Mannering* was named Dandie Dinmont.

Dandy   A pet form of Andrew. *See* Andrew. Dandie is a variant spelling.

Dane   The Anglo-Norse form of the Anglo-Saxon *dene* and *daene,* the original name of the inhabitants of Denmark. CONTEMPORARY EXAMPLE: Dane Clark, actor. PLACE NAME USAGE: a county in Wisconsin, named for Nathan Dane (1787), a political leader; a creek in Nebraska, named for the Danish settlers.

Dani From the Hebrew, meaning "my judge." Akin to Dan and Daniel.

Daniel From the Hebrew, meaning "God is my judge." In the Bible, a character noted for his escape from the lion's den. VARIANT FORMS: Dani (Hebrew); Danilo (Italian). PET FORMS: Dan, Dannie, Danny. Danielle is a feminine form. SURNAME USAGE: Samuel Daniel (1562-1619), English poet; Josephus Daniels (1862-1948), American statesman.

Danil A variant form of Daniel. *See* Daniel. CONTEMPORARY EXAMPLE: Danil Torppe, actor.

Danilo An Italian form of Daniel. *See* Daniel. CONTEMPORARY EXAMPLE: Danilo Donati, costume designer.

Dannie A variant spelling of Danny, a pet form of Daniel,. *See* Daniel. Used also as an independent name. CONTEMPORARY EXAMPLE: Dannie Abse, author.

Dante A pet form of the Italian name Durante. From the Latin *durans*, meaning "durable, lasting," literally, "the enduring." CONTEMPORARY EXAMPLES: Dante Alighieri (1265-1321), Italian poet, author of *The Divine Comedy* (born Durante Alighieri); Dante B. Fascell, Florida congressman (1960s). PLACE-NAME USAGE: a town in South Dakota, named for the Italian poet.

Dar From the Hebrew, meaning "pearl, mother-of-pearl." Also, from the British *dar*, meaning "an oak."

Darby From the British *dwr* and *by*, meaning "the home near the water." Also a variant form of Derby. *See* Derby. In the eighteenth century, Darby and Joan was used as an expression to describe a typical couple. PLACE-NAME USAGE: a stream in Ohio, named for an Indian.

D'arcy, Darcy From the French, meaning "of the Arsy (Oise River)" in Belgium and France, which flows into the Seine. CONTEMPORARY EXAMPLES: D'arcy Flowers, baseball player; Darcy Regier, hockey player.

Dard From the Greek name Dardanos, son of Zeus in Greek mythology. The Dardanoi were an ancient people who helped the Trojans in the Trojan War. CONTEMPORARY EXAMPLE: Dard Hunter, author. PLACE-NAME USAGE: Dardanelles (originally Hellespont), a strait joining the Sea of Marmara and the Aegean Sea.

Daren A variant spelling of Darren. *See* Darren.

Daria, Darian, Darien From the Persian *dara*, meaning "a king." Akin to Darius. *See* Darius.

Darin   A variant spelling of Darren. *See* Darren. SURNAME USAGE: Bobby Darin, singer.

Dario   An Italian form of Darren. *See* Darren. Or, a variant form of Daria. *See* Daria. CONTEMPORARY EXAMPLE: Dario Lodigiani, baseball player.

Darius   From the Persian, meaning "a king." Darius the Great was king of Persia (581-486 B.C.). VARIANT FORMS: Darian, Darien, Dario, Darin, Darren, Dorian, Darrel, Daryl. CONTEMPORARY EXAMPLES: Darius Helton, football player; Darius Kinsey, photographer.

Darlin, Darling   From the British *dar,* meaning "a grove of oak trees." Akin to Dar. Or, from the Anglo-Saxon *deorling,* a pet form of *deor,* meaning "dear, loved one." Darlin is the earlier form. VARIANT FORMS: Darol, Darrell, Daryl, Darryl. PLACE-NAME USAGE: a river in Australia.

Darlington   A variant form of Darling, meaning "the town near the oak grove" or "beloved town." CONTEMPORARY EXAMPLE: Darlington Hooper, a U.S. presidential candidate (1956). PLACE-NAME USAGE: a city in England; Darlington, Idaho, named for Wayne Darlington, an early miner.

Darnell   The name of a weed found in grain fields, resembling rye, and sometimes called rye grass. CONTEMPORARY EXAMPLE: Darnell Hillman, basketball player.

Daro   A variant form of Darrow. *See* Darrow.

Darol   A variant form of Darrell and Darlin. *See* Darlin. CONTEMPORARY EXAMPLE: Darol Delaporte, football player.

Darold   A variant form of Darrell and Darlin. *See* Darlin. CONTEMPORARY EXAMPLE: Darold Knowles, baseball player.

Darrel, Darrell   Variant forms of Darlin. *See* Darlin. CONTEMPORARY EXAMPLES: Darrell Chaney, baseball player; Darrell Porter, baseball player.

Darren   From the British, meaning "a small, rocky hill." VARIANT SPELLING: Darin, Daren. CONTEMPORARY EXAMPLE: Darren McGavin, actor.

Darring   A variant form of Darren. *See* Darren.

Darris   A patronymic form of Harry, meaning "the son of Harry." CONTEMPORARY EXAMPLE: Darris McCord, football player.

Darrol, Darroll   Variant forms of Darlin. *See* Darlin. CONTEMPORARY EXAMPLE: Darrol Ray, football player.

Darrow   From the Old English *daroth,* meaning "a spear." SURNAME USAGE: Clarence Seward Darrow (1857-1938), U.S. lawyer.

Darry   A pet form of Darryl. *See* Darryl. Or, from the French, meaning "from Harry." CONTEMPORARY EXAMPLE: Darry Edestrand, hockey player.

Darryl A variant form of Darlin. *See* Darlin. CONTEMPORARY EXAMPLE: Darryl Greenamyer, pilot.

D'Artagnan A variant French form of Arthur, meaning "from Arthur." A character in Alexandre Dumas' novel *The Three Musketeers.* CONTEMPORARY EXAMPLE: D'Artagnan Martin, football player.

Darton From the British *dwr* plus the Old English *ton,* meaning "the town near the water."

Darwin From the British and Anglo-Saxon, meaning "lover of the sea." CONTEMPORARY EXAMPLE: Darwin H. Wright, U.S. city mayor. SURNAME USAGE: Charles Robert Darwin (1809-1882), English scientist. PLACE-NAME USAGE: a seaport in Australia; Mount Darwin, California, named for Charles Darwin.

Daryl, Daryle Variant forms of Darrell. *See* Darrell. CONTEMPORARY EXAMPLES: Daryl Cumber Dance, author and professor; Daryle Lamonica, football player.

Daud The Arabic form of David. *See* David.

Dave A pet form of David. *See* David.

Daven A Scandinavian form of the British *dwy* plus *afon,* meaning "two rivers." Davip is a variant Scandinavian form.

Davey A pet form of David. *See* David. Davy is a variant spelling.

Davi A pet form of David. *See* David. Used also as a feminine name.

David From the Hebrew, meaning "beloved." In the Bible, the second king of Israel, successor to King Saul; father of King Solomon. Strangely, not one rabbi in the Talmud is named David. St. David, also called Dewi, was a sixth-century patron saint of Wales. David I (1084-1152) and David II (1324-1371) were kings of Scotland. VARIANT FORMS: Dab, Dabbey, Dabby, Dabney, Daffy, Daw, Dow (English); Daud (Arabic); Devi, Dewey, Dewi (Welsh); Dawoodjee (Hindi); Devlin (Irish); McTavish (Gaelic patronymic); Daviot, Davit (Middle English and Old French); Daveed (Russian); Dabko, Dako (Slavic). PET FORMS: Dave, Davi, Davie, Davy, Taffy. FEMININE FORMS: Davida, Vida. SURNAME USAGE: Jacques Louis David (1748-1825), French painter; Joseph Davidson (1883-1952), U.S. sculptor; Jefferson Davis (1808-1889), U.S. statesman; John William Dawson (1820-1899), Canadian geologist. Also Davids, Davies, Dawkins, Tewel, Tewels. PLACE-NAME USAGE: Davis Strait, an arm of the Atlantic Ocean.

Davidyne A variant form of David. *See* David. CONTEMPORARY EXAMPLE: Davidyne Mayleas, author.

Davie A variant form of David used as an independent name. *See* David. CONTEMPORARY EXAMPLE: Davie Napier, theologian.

Davip   A Scandinavian form of the British *dwy* plus *afon*, meaning "two rivers." Daven is a variant form.

Davis   A patronymic form of David, meaning "son of David." Akin to Davidson. Used most often as a surname. SURNAME USAGE: Jefferson Davis (1808-1889), American statesman; Moshe Davis, historian. PLACE-NAME USAGE: Davis Strait in the Atlantic Ocean.

Davit   A variant form of David. *See* David.

Davy   A pet form of David. *See* David. Davy Jones, a humorous name for sailors, represented the spirit of the sea. Davy Crockett (1786-1836) was an American frontiersman and politician. SURNAME USAGE: Humphry Davy (1778-1829), English chemist.

Davyd   A variant spelling of David. *See* David.

Daw, Dawe   From the Old English, meaning "a doe." Also, a variant form of David. *See* David. Dow is a variant spelling.

Dawes, Dawson   Patronymic forms of David, meaning "son of David." *See* David. SURNAME USAGE: Charles Gates Dawes (1865-1951), American statesman; John William Dawson (1820-1889), Canadian geologist. PLACE-NAME USAGE: Dawson Creek, a town in Canada.

Day   A variant form of Dag. *See* Dag. SURNAME USAGE: Mathias Day, founder of Daytona Beach, Florida.

Dayman, Daymon, Daymond   From the Anglo-Saxon *daeg*, meaning "day." VARIANT FORMS: Dag, Damien, Damon.

Dayton   From the Middle English, meaning "day town; bright, cheerful town." Akin to Dag. *See* Dag. CONTEMPORARY EXAMPLE: Dayton Allen, comedian. SURNAME USAGE: Elias Dayton (1737—1807), American general. PLACE-NAME USAGE: a city in Ohio named either for General Elias Dayton or for Jonathan Dayton (1760—1824), one of its founders.

Deacon   From the Greek *diakonos*, meaning "a servant, a messenger." CONTEMPORARY EXAMPLE: Deacon Jones, football player. SURNAME USAGE: Richard Deacon, actor.

Dean, Deane   From the Old French *deien*, meaning "head, leader." Also, from the Celtic *den* and the Old English *dean* and *dene*, meaning "a hollow, a small valley." CONTEMPORARY EXAMPLE: Dean Jagger, actor; Deane Jordan, journalist. SURNAME USAGE: Dizzy Dean, baseball player; Silas Deane (1717—1789), American diplomat.

DeBow   From the French *debouche*, meaning "to emerge," from which has evolved "debonair," meaning "of good breeding." CONTEMPORARY EXAMPLE: DeBow Freed, educator.

Debs   Probably a matronymic form of Deborah, meaning "the son of Deborah." *See* Deborah (feminine section). CONTEMPORARY EXAMPLE: Debs Garms, baseball player. SURNAME USAGE: Eugene V. Debs

(1885—1926), American labor leader.

Decatur From the Greek, meaning "pure." Akin to the feminine Catherine. CONTEMPORARY EXAMPLE: Decatur Jones, baseball player. SURNAME USAGE: Stephen Decatur (1779–1820), American naval officer. PLACE-NAME USAGE: a city in Illinois; a city in Alabama.

Decimus From the Latin, meaning "tenth." Used as a name for the tenth child in a family.

Dee Probably derived from the name of the river. Also, a shortened form of Dean. *See* Dean. CONTEMPORARY EXAMPLE: Dee Moore, baseball player. PLACE-NAME USAGE: a river in Scotland; a river in Wales.

Deems From the Middle English *demen,* meaning "to judge." Also, a variant form of Demetrius. *See* Demetrius. CONTEMPORARY EXAMPLE: Deems Taylor (1885-1966), American composer.

Defforest, DeForest, DeForrest From the Anglo-Saxon, meaning "to clear the land." CONTEMPORARY EXAMPLE: DeForest Covin, actor. SURNAME USAGE: Lee DeForest (1873—1961), American inventor.

Deiniol A Welsh form of Daniel. *See* Daniel.

Dekel From the Arabic and Hebrew, meaning "palm tree, date tree."

Del A pet form of Delbert, Delmar, or Delmore. *See* Delbert *and* Delmar. CONTEMPORARY EXAMPLE: Del Cogswell Brebner, novelist.

Delano From the Old French, meaning "of the night." Or from the Erse, meaning "a healthy, dark man." CONTEMPORARY EXAMPLE: Delano Williams, football player. SURNAME USAGE: Sara Delano, maiden name of the mother of Franklin Delano Roosevelt.

Delbert A variant form of Adelbert and Albert. *See* Adelbert *and* Albert. CONTEMPORARY EXAMPLES: Delbert Unser, baseball player; Delbert Mann, movie director.

Deli From the Greek name Delos, a small island in the Aegean, the legendary birthplace of Artemis and Apollo. Deli is a variant form of Delos. CONTEMPORARY EXAMPLE: Deli Sacilotto, educator.

Delius A variant form of Delos, an island in the Aegean. *See* Deli. SURNAME USAGE: Frederick Delius (1862-1934), English composer.

Delles A variant form of Dale. *See* Dale. CONTEMPORARY EXAMPLE: Delles Howell, football player.

Delmar From the Latin, meaning "of the sea." Delmer is a variant spelling. Del is a pet form. CONTEMPORARY EXAMPLE: Delmar Robinson, farmer.

Delmer A variant spelling of Delmar. *See* Delmar. Del is a pet form. CONTEMPORARY EXAMPLE: Delmer Baker, boxer.

Delmore   A variant form of Delmar. *See* Delmar. Del is a pet form. CONTEMPORARY EXAMPLE: Delmore Schwartz, poet.

Delos   A small island in the Aegean, the legendary birthplace of Artemis and Apollo. Delius is a variant form. CONTEMPORARY EXAMPLE: Delos H. Kelly, sociologist.

Delvin   From the Greek *delphin,* meaning "a dolphin." Or, an inverted form of Devlin. *See* Devlin.

Demetrius   From the Greek, meaning "lover of the earth." In Greek mythology, Demeter was the goddess of agriculture and fertility. VARIANT FORMS: Dimitri, Dmitri, Demmy.

Demian   A variant spelling of Damien. *See* Damien.

Demond   A short form of Desmond. *See* Desmond. CONTEMPORARY EXAMPLE: Demond Wilson, actor.

Demosthenes   From the Greek *demos,* meaning "democracy." A fourth-century B.C. Athenian orator.

Dempsey   From the Middle English and Old French *demerite,* meaning "deserving of blame, demerit." VARIANT FORMS: Demer, Dempster, Demester. SURNAME USAGE: Jack Dempsey (born William Harrison Dempsey), prizefighter.

Denby   From the Old Norse, meaning "a Danish settlement." Akin to Dane and Denholm.

Denholm   From the Old Norse, meaning "the home of the Dane." Akin to Denby. CONTEMPORARY EXAMPLE: Denholm Elliott, actor.

Denis   The French form of the Latin and Greek name Dionysus. In Greek mythology, the god of wine and revelry, hence the connotation of "wild, frenzied." Saint Denis was a third-century patron saint of France. Denys is a variant spelling. VARIANT FORMS: Dionis (used in Spain and in twelfth-century England); Denit, Dennit, Donnet, Diot (English); Diot and Dion (French); Diniz (Portuguese); Donogh (Irish); Tennis (Slavic). SURNAME USAGE: Denisard, Denison, Dennison, Denny, Nisard, Sard, Sardi, Sardon, Sarney, Tennyson.

Denit   A variant form of Denis. *See* Denis.

Denman   A variant form of Denis, meaning "servant of Denis (Denys)." Or, from the Anglo-Saxon, meaning "a resident of the valley (den)."

Denmark   From the Latin *dominus,* meaning "master, lord," plus *mark,* meaning "boundary," hence "the land within the master's boundary." Danmark is the Danish form. *See also* Dane. CONTEMPORARY EXAMPLE: Denmark Vesey, American anti-slavery leader (1820s).

Dennis   A variant spelling of Denis. *See* Denis.

Dennison   A patronymic form, meaning "son of Dennis." *See* Dennis.

Dennit   A variant form of Denis. *See* Denis. Also, a variant form of Denton. *See* Denton. CONTEMPORARY EXAMPLE: Dennit Morris, football player.

Deno   An Italian pet form of Dean. *See* Dean. CONTEMPORARY EXAMPLE: Deno Geanakoplos, professor.

Denton   A variant form of Dean, meaning "Dean's town." *See* Dean. PLACE-NAME USAGE: a city in Texas, named for Reverend John B. Denton, a pioneer.

Denver   From the Anglo-Saxon and Old French, meaning "green valley." CONTEMPORARY EXAMPLE: Denver LeMaster, baseball player. SURNAME USAGE: J.W. Denver (1817-1894), governor of Kansas Territory. PLACE-NAME USAGE: capital of Colorado, named after J.W. Denver.

Denys   From the Latin name Dionysius and the French form Denis. *See* Denis.

Denzil, Denzel, Denzell   Possibly variant forms of Denis. *See* Denis. CONTEMPORARY EXAMPLE: Denzil Gainer, a politician.

Derby   From the Old English *deor*, meaning "deer" or "wild animal," plus *by*, meaning "abode," hence "the place where the deer live." Or, a variant form of Darby. *See* Darby. PLACE-NAME USAGE: Mount Derby, Colorado, so named because it looks like a derby hat.

Derek   An English form of the Old High German name Hrodrich, meaning "famous ruler." VARIANT FORMS: Diederick and Dirck (Dutch); Theodoric (Old German); Derric (English). CONTEMPORARY EXAMPLES: Derek Brewer, author; Derek Jewell, author.

Derel   A variant form of Darlin. *See* Darlin. CONTEMPORARY EXAMPLE: Derel Thomas, baseball player.

Derial   Probably a variant form of Darlin. *See* Darlin. CONTEMPORARY EXAMPLE: Derial Jackson, book critic.

Derral   A variant form of Darlin. *See* Darlin. CONTEMPORARY EXAMPLE: Derral Cheatwood, author.

Derrel, Derrell   Variant forms of Darlin. *See* Darlin. CONTEMPORARY EXAMPLES: Derrel Harrelson, baseball player; Derrell Roberts, educator.

Derric   A variant form of Derek. *See* Derek.

Derland   From the British *dwr*, meaning "water," hence "land near water." Also, from the Danish and Old English, meaning "land inhabited by deer (animals)." Akin to Darlin. CONTEMPORARY EXAMPLE: Derland Moore, football player.

Dermot   From the British and Middle English, meaning "a pond surrounding a castle." Akin to Derland. CONTEMPORARY EXAMPLE: Dermot McGuigan, author.

Dero   From the British root *dwr*, meaning "water." Or, a variant form of Derry. *See* Derry. Akin to Deron. CONTEMPORARY EXAMPLE: Dero Downing, educator.

Deron   From the British root *dwr*, meaning "water." Dero is a variant form. CONTEMPORARY EXAMPLE: Deron Johnson, baseball player.

Deror, Derori   From the Hebrew, meaning "freedom" or "free-flowing." Also, the name of a bird (a swallow).

Derrek   A variant form of Derek or Derry. *See* Derek *and* Derry. CONTEMPORARY EXAMPLE: Derrek Dickey, basketball player.

Derrick, Derrik   Variant forms of Derek or Derry. *See* Derek *and* Derry. CONTEMPORARY EXAMPLE: Derrick Mercer, editor.

Derril, Derrill   Variant forms of Darlin. *See* Darlin.

Derry   From the British *deru*, meaning "oak tree." Akin to Dar and Darlin. CONTEMPORARY EXAMPLE: Derry Quinn, author.

Derwent   From the British root *dwr*, meaning "water," hence "the waters of Gwent" or "the waters of the highlands." CONTEMPORARY EXAMPLE: Derwent May, author.

Derwin, Derwyn   From the British *dwr*, meaning "water," hence "a lover of water, a sailor."

Deryck   A variant spelling of Derek. *See* Derek. CONTEMPORARY EXAMPLE: Deryck Murray, cricket player.

Des   An abbreviated form of Desmond. *See* Desmond. CONTEMPORARY EXAMPLE: Des O'Connor, entertainer.

Desi   An abbreviated form of Desiderio. *See* Desiderio. Also, a pet form of Desmond. CONTEMPORARY EXAMPLE: Desi Arnaz, actor.

Desideratus   From the Latin, meaning "desired." Akin to Desiderio.

Desiderio   From the Latin, meaning "desire." Popular in Italy. VARIANT FRENCH FORMS: Desiderius, Didon, Didot, Diderot.

Desiderius   The French form of Desiderio. *See* Desiderio. The name of the last Lombard King of Italy. Also, the name of a seventh-century French saint.

Desmond   From the French and Latin *mundus*, meaning "the world, society." PET FORMS: Des, Desi, Dezi. CONTEMPORARY EXAMPLE: Desmond Morris, anthropologist.

Detlev   Origin unknown. CONTEMPORARY EXAMPLE: Detlev W. Bronk, neurophysiologist.

Deuel   From the Hebrew, meaning "knowledge of God." In the Bible, a member of the tribe of Gad. Also spelled Reuel in the Bible, and meaning "a friend of God." CONTEMPORARY EXAMPLE: Deuel Richardson, Wesley, Massachusetts.

Devereux   A French place-name. From the Old High German Ebur-hart, meaning "a hardy, strong, wild boar." Akin to Everett. SUR-NAME USAGE: Robert Devereux (1566-1601), English soldier, known as the Earl of Essex.

Devin   From the Celtic, meaning "a poet." Probably the feminine form of *deva*, meaning "god, deity." Devi was a Hindu goddess. Also, a name invented by substituting the K of Kevin with the letter D.

Devir   From the Arabic and Hebrew, meaning "innermost room" or "holy place." Possibly related to Devin. *See* Devin. In the Bible, the king of Eglon.

Devlin   An Irish form of David. *See* David. CONTEMPORARY EXAMPLE: Devlin Williams, football player.

Dewey   A Welsh form of David. *See* David. CONTEMPORARY EXAM-PLES: Dewey Bartlett, governor of Oklahoma (1960s); Dewey Selman, football player. SURNAME USAGE: John Dewey (1859-1952), American philosopher and educator.

DeWitt, Dewitt   From the Low German, meaning "white." CONTEM-PORARY EXAMPLES: DeWitt Clinton, U.S. presidential candidate (1812); Dewitt Weaver, football player. SURNAME USAGE: Joyce Dewitt, actress.

Dexter   From the Latin *dextra*, meaning "right-hand side," connoting "skillfulness."

Dhani   A Hindi name, meaning "rich person." CONTEMPORARY EX-AMPLE: Dhani Harrison, son of musician George Harrison.

Diablito   From the Spanish, meaning "little devil." CONTEMPORARY EXAMPLE: Diablito Valdez, boxer.

Diamond   From the Latin and Greek *adamas*, meaning "a precious stone." PLACE-NAME USAGE: Diamond Head, Honolulu, Hawaii.

Dick, Dickey, Dickie, Dicky   Pet forms of Richard. *See* Richard. The basis of many surnames, including Dickens and Dickinson.

Diderot, Didon, Didot   Variant forms of Desiderius. *See* Desiderius.

Didi   From the Hebrew *yedid*, meaning "beloved." A pet form of Jedidiah. Also, a variant form of Diderot. *See* Diderot.

Diego   A Spanish form of James. *See* James. Dago is a variant form. PLACE-NAME USAGE: San Diego, California, named for Saint Didacus.

Dieter   A variant form of Dietrich. *See* Dietrich. Also, possibly a var-iant form of Peter. *See* Peter. CONTEMPORARY EXAMPLE: Dieter Har-nack, editor.

Dietrich   From the German, meaning "a rich people." VARIANT FORMS: Dierk, Dirk (Dutch); Dytrych (Polish); Ditrik (Hungarian).

Digby   From the Dutch *dijk* and the Middle English *diggen*, meaning "dike." CONTEMPORARY EXAMPLE: Digby Diehl, editor.

Digory, Diggory   Origin uncertain. Possibly from the Middle English *diggen*, meaning "dike."

Dillon   A variant form of Dale. *See* Dale. Or, a variant spelling of Dylan. *See* Dylan.

Dimitri   A variant form of Demetrius. *See* Demetrius.

Dimitrios   A variant spelling of Demetrius. *See* Demetrius. CONTEM-PORARY EXAMPLE: Dimitrios Baxes, baseball player.

Dimitry   A variant form of Demetrius. *See* Demetrius. CONTEMPO-RARY EXAMPLE: Dimitry Kabalevsky, composer. PLACE-NAME USAGE: Dimitrovgrad, a city in Bulgaria.

Dino   A pet form of the Italian name Aldobrandino. From the German, meaning "little old sword." CONTEMPORARY EXAMPLE: Dino DeLaurentis, movie producer.

Diomedes   In Greek legend, a warrior at the siege of Troy. CONTEMPO-RARY EXAMPLE: Diomedes Olivo, baseball player. PLACE-NAME USAGE: Diomede Islands in the Bering Strait.

Dion   A short form of Dionysius. *See* Dionysius. CONTEMPORARY EX-AMPLE: Dion DiMuccim, musician.

Dionysius   In Greek mythology, the god of wine and revelry. A Greek tyrant in ancient Syracuse (405-367 B.C.) VARIANT FORMS: Denis, Denys, Dennis, Dionysos.

Dirk   An English form of the Old High German name Hrodrich, meaning "famous ruler." Akin to the Latin name Rex. VARIANT FORMS: Derek, Durk. Popular in Holland. Also, the Dutch form of Dietrich. *See* Dietrich. CONTEMPORARY EXAMPLE: Dirk Bogarde, actor.

Diron   Origin uncertain. Possibly, from the Anglo-Saxon *trone*, meaning "a trench." CONTEMPORARY EXAMPLE: Diron Talbert, football player.

Diskin   A metathesized form of Dixon. *See* Dixon. CONTEMPORARY EXAMPLE: Diskin Clay, author.

Dix   A patronymic of Dick, meaning "Dick's son." A pet form of Richard. *See* Richard. Dixie is a feminine form of Dix. SURNAME USAGE: Richard Dix, actor. PLACE-NAME USAGE: Dix, Nebraska; Dix, Illinois; Dix Hills, New York.

Dixey, Dixie, Dixy   Variant forms of Dix, a form of Richard. *See* Richard. Dixie was the leading Negro character in an 1850 minstrel play. PLACE-NAME USAGE: Dixie, Maryland.

Dixon   A patronymic form of Richard, meaning "Richard's (Dick's) son." *See* Richard. SURNAME USAGE: MacIntyre Dixon, actor.

Dizzy   A nickname, but also an independent name. CONTEMPORARY EXAMPLES: Dizzy Dean, baseball player; Dizzy Gillespie, musician.

Dmitri   A Russian form of Demetrius. *See* Demetrius. Dimitri is a variant spelling. CONTEMPORARY EXAMPLE: Dmitri Shostakovich, Russian composer.

Doane   From the Celtic, meaning "dweller on the sand dune."

Dob, Dobbs   Variant forms of Robert. *See* Robert. Also, from the Czech *dobro*, meaning "to do good." SURNAME USAGE: Henry Austin Dobson (1840-1921), English poet. PLACE-NAME USAGE: Dobruja, a region on the Black Sea.

Dodo   From the Hebrew, meaning "beloved" or "his uncle." In the Bible, a member of the tribe of Issachar. Also, the name of an extinct bird that resembled a duck formerly found in Mauritius.

Dolan   From the British *dol*, meaning "a bend in a stream." Also, from the Old English *dael*, meaning "a valley." *See* Dale. CONTEMPORARY EXAMPLE: Dolan Nichols, baseball player.

Dolph   A short form of Adolph. *See* Adolph. Dolf is a variant spelling. CONTEMPORARY EXAMPLE: Dolph Honicker, journalist.

Dolphus   A variant form of Adolph. *See* Adolph. CONTEMPORARY EXAMPLE: Dolphus Whitten, educator.

Dom   A pet form of Dominic. *See* Dominic. CONTEMPORARY EXAMPLE: Dom Deluise, entertainer.

Domingo   A Spanish form of Dominic. *See* Dominic.

Dominic, Dominick   From the Latin *dominicus*, meaning "belonging to, pertaining to God." VARIANT FORM: Dominique (French); Domenico (Italian); Domingo (Spanish); Dominy (English). Often given to boys born on Sunday. Dominique is also a feminine form. Dom is a pet form.

Dominique   A French form of Dominic. *See* Dominic. More commonly used as a feminine name.

Dominy   A variant form of Dominic. *See* Dominic.

Don   A pet form of Donald. *See* Donald. Also, the Spanish form of the Latin *dominus*, meaning "master."

Donahue   A variant form of Donald. *See* Donald.

Donal   An Irish form of Donald. *See* Donald.

Donald   From the Irish form Donghal, meaning "brown stranger." Donal is a popular Irish variant form. Also, from the Celtic and Scottish, meaning "proud ruler." PET FORMS: Don, Donnie, Donny.

Donatus   From the Latin, meaning "given."

Donn, Donne   Variant spellings of Don. *See* Don. CONTEMPORARY EX-
AMPLES: Donn Arden, movie producer; Donn Clendenon, baseball
player. SURNAME USAGE: John Donne (1573-1631), English poet.

Donnel, Donnell   From the Celtic *don* and *dun*, meaning "a hill." CON-
TEMPORARY EXAMPLES: Donnel Jeffrey Carten, American Statesman;
Donnell Smith, football player.

Donnelly   A variant form of Donnel. *See* Donnel. CONTEMPORARY EX-
AMPLE: Donnelly Rhodes, actor.

Donner   A variant form of Donn. *See* Donn. CONTEMPORARY EXAM-
PLE: Donner Spencer, author.

Donnie, Donny   Pet forms of Donald. *See* Donald. CONTEMPORARY
EXAMPLE: Donnie Hickman, football player.

Donovan   A variant form of Donald. *See* Donald. CONTEMPORARY EX-
AMPLE: Donovan Leitch, musician.

Dor   From the Hebrew, meaning "a generation." Also, a French
name derived from the Latin, meaning "of gold."

Doran   From the Hebrew and Greek, meaning "a gift." VARIANT
FORMS: Dore, Dorian, Doron, Dorran.

Dore   From the Greek, meaning "a gift." Akin to Doran, Dorian, and
Doron. Often used as a pet form of Isidore. CONTEMPORARY EXAMPLE:
Dore Schary, author. SURNAME USAGE: Gustav Dore, French painter.
PLACE-NAME USAGE: a river in England.

Dorian   A variant form of Dore and Doran. *See* Dore *and* Doran. Also,
from the Greek, meaning "from the town of Doris," where one group of
ancient Greeks lived.

Dorne   From the Gaelic *dorn*, meaning "a hand." CONTEMPORARY EX-
AMPLE: Dorne Dibble, football player.

Doron   From the Hebrew and Greek, meaning "a gift." Doran is a
variant spelling.

Dorran   A variant spelling of Doran. *See* Doran.

Dorrel   A variant form of Darrel. *See* Darrel. CONTEMPORARY EXAM-
PLE: Dorrel Herzog, baseball player.

Dorris   The masculine form of Doris. *See* Doris (feminine section).

Dorset   Derived from the Old English *setu*, meaning "a tribe," and the
British *dwr*, meaning "water," hence "the tribe that lived near the water."

Dorsey   A variant form of Dorset. *See* Dorset. CONTEMPORARY EXAM-
PLE: Dorsey Carroll, baseball player. SURNAME USAGE: Joe Dorsey, actor.

Dorsie   A pet form of Dorset. *See* Dorset. CONTEMPORARY EXAMPLE:
Dorsie W. Willis, a U.S. soldier.

Doston   A metathesis of Dotson. *See* Doston.

Dotan, Dothan   From the Hebrew *dat*, meaning "law." In the Bible, a place in Palestine, north of Samaria, where Joseph found his brothers grazing their flocks.

Dotson   A matronymic form of Dorothy, meaning "the son of Dot or Dottie." *See* Dorothy (feminine section). CONTEMPORARY EXAMPLE: Dotson Rader, novelist.

Doug   A pet form of Douglas. *See* Douglas.

Dougal   A variant form of Douglas. *See* Douglas.

Douglas   From the Celtic, meaning "gray." Also, from the Gaelic, meaning "black stream." Doug is a pet form. CONTEMPORARY EXAMPLE: Douglas Bailey, political advisor. SURNAME USAGE: Stephen A. Douglas (1813-1861), U.S. politician. PLACE-NAME USAGE: counties in Georgia and South Dakota, named for Stephen A. Douglas; a river in Scotland.

Douglass   A variant spelling of Douglas. *See* Douglas. SURNAME USAGE: Frederich Douglass, U.S. Negro leader.

Dov   From the Hebrew, meaning "a bear." Also, from the Arabic, meaning "to walk gently, leisurely." CONTEMPORARY EXAMPLE: Dov Siton, scientist.

Dove   From the British *dyfi*, meaning "the stream near the valley." Also, from the Middle English *douve*, meaning "a bird of the pigeon family." Dovey is a variant form. PLACE-NAME USAGE: a river in England.

Dover   From the British *dwr* or *dwfwr*, meaning "water." PLACE-NAME USAGE: the English Channel port; cities in Delaware and New Jersey.

Dovev   From the Hebrew *davor*, meaning "to speak, whisper."

Dovey   A variant form of Dove. *See* Dove.

Dow, Dowe   Variant forms of David. *See* David. CONTEMPORARY EXAMPLE: Dow Finsterwald, golfer. SURNAME USAGE: Gerard Dow (also spelled Dou), Dutch painter (1613-1675); Ernest Dowson (1867-1900), English poet.

Down   From the Old English *dune*, meaning "a grassy hill." PLACE-NAME USAGE: a former county in northern Ireland.

Doyce   Origin unknown. Possibly a corruption of Joyce. *See* Joyce. CONTEMPORARY EXAMPLE: Doyce Schick, football player.

Doyle   From the Irish *dail*, meaning "an assembly, a gathering." CONTEMPORARY EXAMPLE: Doyle Lade, baseball player. SURNAME USAGE: Arthur Conan Doyle (1859-1930), English novelist.

Doyt   Possibly a variant form of Dwight. *See* Dwight. CONTEMPORARY

EXAMPLE: Doyt Morris, baseball player.

Drake From the Latin *draco*, meaning "a dragon." Or, from the Old High German, meaning "a male duck." CONTEMPORARY EXAMPLE: Drake Garrett, football player. SURNAME USAGE: Sir Francis Drake (1540-1596), English explorer. PLACE-NAME USAGE: a bay in California, named for Sir Francis Drake, who landed there in 1579.

Drannon From the Middle English *dreinen*, meaning "to strain off, to dry out." CONTEMPORARY EXAMPLE: Drannon Guinn, football player.

Dred Probably a short form of Aldred. *See* Aldred. CONTEMPORARY EXAMPLE: Dred Scott (died 1858), American slave.

Drew A pet form of Andrew. *See* Andrew. CONTEMPORARY EXAMPLE: Drew Pearson, journalist. SURNAME USAGE: John Drew (1853-1927), American actor.

Driscoll From the Celtic *drystan*, meaning "sorrowful." Tristam is a variant form.

Dror From the Hebrew, meaning "freedom."

Dru A variant spelling of Drew. *See* Drew.

Dryden From the Anglo-Saxon, meaning "a dry valley." SURNAME USAGE: John Dryden (1631-1700), English playwright.

Duane A variant form of Wayne. *See* Wayne. Also, a variant form of Dane, a native of Denmark. *See* Dane. VARIANT SPELLINGS: Dwane, Dwayne. CONTEMPORARY EXAMPLE: Duane Wylie, musician.

Duard A variant form of Edward. *See* Edward.

Dude From the Irish *duidin*, meaning "a little pipe." Or, from the slang expression meaning "man, boy." CONTEMPORARY EXAMPLE: Dude Esterbrook, baseball player.

Dudley From the Old English, meaning "Dodd's meadow." CONTEMPORARY EXAMPLES: Dudley Hargrove, baseball player; Dudley Pope, author. PLACE-NAME USAGE: a town in Worcestershire, England.

Duff A variant spelling of the Middle English *dough*, hence "a baker."

Dugald A variant form of Douglas. *See* Douglas.

Duke From the Latin, meaning "leader." The nickname of actor John Wayne. CONTEMPORARY EXAMPLES: Duke Snyder, baseball player; Duke Ellington, musician.

Dumont From the French, meaning "from the mountain." CONTEMPORARY EXAMPLE: Dumont F. Kenny, educator.

Dunc A pet form of Duncan. *See* Duncan.

Duncan From the Celtic, meaning "a warrior with dark skin." Duncan I and Duncan II were eleventh-century Scottish kings. Dunc is a pet form. CONTEMPORARY EXAMPLES: Duncan Grant, English painter; Duncan Crow, author.

Dunn, Dunne   From the Old English, meaning "brown." SURNAME USAGE: Finley Peter Dunne (1867-1936), American journalist.

Dunstan   From the Old English *dun*, meaning "brown," and *stan*, meaning "stone," hence "the brownrock quarry."

Dupee   From the French *dupe*, meaning "to deceive, to trick." CONTEMPORARY EXAMPLE: Dupee Shaw, baseball player.

Dur   From the Hebrew, meaning "to heap, pile up" or "to circle." Also, from the Old English *deor*, meaning "a wild animal, a deer."

Durand   The French form of the Latin *durantem*, meaning "enduring, lasting." VARIANT FORMS: Dante, Durant, Durante, Duryea.

Durant, Durante   Variant Italian forms of Durand. *See* Durant. SURNAME USAGE: Jimmy Durante, entertainer.

Duriel   From the Hebrew, meaning "my house is God's." CONTEMPORARY EXAMPLE: Duriel Harris, football player.

Durk   A variant spelling of Dirk. *See* Dirk. CONTEMPORARY EXAMPLE: Durk Pearson, actor.

Durwald   From the Old English, meaning "a forest of wild animals." CONTEMPORARY EXAMPLE: Durwald G. Hall, U.S. congressman.

Durward   From the Persian, meaning a porter, doorkeeper; a guardian." Or, from the Old English, meaning "a protective enclosure from wild animals." CONTEMPORARY EXAMPLE: Durward Kirby, entertainer.

Durwin   From the Old English, meaning "a friend of the animal world." Dirk is a pet form. CONTEMPORARY EXAMPLE: Durwin (Dirk) Blyston, Crestline, California.

Durwood   A variant form of Durwald. *See* Durwald. CONTEMPORARY EXAMPLE: Durwood Fleming, educator. PLACE-NAME USAGE: Durwood, Oklahoma.

Duryea   From the Latin, meaning "enduring, lasting." VARIANT FORMS: Dante, Durand, Durant, Durante. SURNAME USAGE: Perry Duryea, New York politician.

Dusan   Origin unknown. CONTEMPORARY EXAMPLE: Dusan Maronic, football player.

Duster   A nickname of some baseball pitchers who throw balls very close to batters. CONTEMPORARY EXAMPLE: Duster Mails, baseball player.

Dustin   A variant form of Dunstan. *See* Dunstan. CONTEMPORARY EXAMPLES: Dustin Hoffman, actor; Dustin O'Neil, Windsor, Ontario, Canada.

Dusty A pet form of Dustin. *See* Dustin. CONTEMPORARY EXAMPLE: Dusty Baker, baseball player.

Dutton From the Celtic and Old English, meaning "a fortified hill."

Dwaine A variant spelling of Duane. *See* Duane. CONTEMPORARY EXAMPLE: Dwain Knight, golfer.

Dwayne A variant form of Wayne. *See* Wayne. Also, a variant spelling of Duane. *See* Duane. CONTEMPORARY EXAMPLES: Dwayne Hickman, actor; Dwayne Crump, football player.

Dwight From the Anglo-Saxon, meaning "white, fair." CONTEMPORARY EXAMPLE: Dwight D. Eisenhower (1890-1969), thirty-fourth president of the U.S. SURNAME USAGE: Timothy Dwight, president of Yale University (1795-1817).

Dyce From the British *dy*, meaning "a house." Akin to Dyne.

Dylan From the Welsh, meaning "the sea."

Dyne From the British *dy*, meaning "a house." Akin to Dyce.

E

Eamon   The Irish form of the Old English name Eadmund, meaning "fortunate, happy warrior." Akin to Edmond. *See* Edmond. CONTEMPORARY EXAMPLE: Eamon de Valera (1882-1975), Irish statesman.

Earl   From the Middle English *erl*, meaning "a nobleman, a count." Or, from the Anglo-Saxon *eorl*, meaning "warrior, brave man."

Earland   From the Old English, meaning "the Earl's land." *See* Earl. CONTEMPORARY EXAMPLE: Earland I. Carlson, educator.

Earle   A variant spelling of Earl. *See* Earl.

Earlie   A variant spelling of Early. *See* Early. CONTEMPORARY EXAMPLE: Earlie Fires, jockey.

Early   From the Middle English, meaning "the Earl's lee (shelter)." CONTEMPORARY EXAMPLE: Early Wynn, football player. SURNAME USAGE: Jubal Anderson Early (1816-1894), Confederate general in Civil War. PLACE-NAME USAGE: Early, Iowa, named for D.C. Early, one of the first settlers.

Earvin   A variant form of Irvin. *See* Irvin. Ervin is a variant spelling. CONTEMPORARY EXAMPLE: Earvin Johnson, basketball player.

Eaton   From the Anglo-Saxon, meaning "the town near the river."

Eavan   An Irish form of Evan. *See* Evan. CONTEMPORARY EXAMPLE: Eavan Boland, Irish author.

Eban   From the Hebrew, meaning "stone." SURNAME USAGE: Abba Eban, Israeli political leader.

Eben   A short form of Ebenezer. *See* Ebenezer. PLACE-NAME USAGE: Ebensburg, Pennsylvania, named for Reverend Eben Lloyd.

Ebenezer   From the Hebrew, meaning "a foundation stone." Eben is a short form. Ebenezer Scrooge is a character in Charles Dickens' *A Christmas Carol.* PLACE-NAME USAGE: towns in Kentucky, Mississippi, New Jersey, New York.

Eberhard, Eberhart   From the Old French and High German, meaning "a strong, wild boar." VARIANT FORMS: Everard, Everhard (Norse and German); Everett (Old High German); Everette (French). CONTEMPORARY EXAMPLE: Eberhard Schneider, author.

Eberle   From the High German, meaning "wild boar." CONTEMPORARY EXAMPLE: Eberle Schultz, football player.

Ebert   A short form of Eberhart. *See* Eberhart. CONTEMPORARY EXAM-

PLE: Ebert van Buren, football player. SURNAME USAGE: Friedrich Ebert (1871-1925), first president of the German Republic (1919-1925).

Ed   A pet form of Edward. *See* Edward.

Edan   From the Celtic, meaning "fire, flame."

Edd   A pet form of Edward. *See* Edward. CONTEMPORARY EXAMPLE: Edd Byrnes, actor.

Eddie   A pet form of Edward. *See* Edward.

Eddy   From the Middle English *ydy*, meaning "a whirlpool." Also, a pet form of Edward. *See* Edward. PLACE-NAME USAGE: Eddy, Alaska.

Edgar   From the Anglo-Saxon name Eadgar, derived from *ead*, meaning "riches," plus *gar*, meaning "a spear." CONTEMPORARY EXAMPLE: Edgar Allan Poe (1809-1840), U.S. author. PLACE-NAME USAGE: Edgartown, Maine, named for Prince Edgar, son of the Duke of York.

Edison   A patronymic form, meaning "the son of Ed (Edward)." *See* Edward. CONTEMPORARY EXAMPLE: Edison Armbrister, baseball player. SURNAME USAGE: Thomas Alva Edison (1847-1931), inventor.

Edlin   From the Old High German, meaning "nobility." A variant form of Adeline.

Edlow   From the Old English, meaning "fruitful (*ead*) hill *(low)*."

Edmar   From the Anglo-Saxon, meaning "rich sea." CONTEMPORARY EXAMPLE: Edmar Mednis, chess master.

Edmond, Edmund   From the Anglo-Saxon name Eadmund. Derived from *ead*, meaning "rich, fortunate, happy," and *mund* (*mond*), meaning "warrior, protector." CONTEMPORARY EXAMPLE: Edmond Wilson, author and critic. PLACE-NAME USAGE: Edmonds, Washington, named for Senator G.F. Edmunds. The spelling of the town's name was altered.

Edom   From the Hebrew *adom*, meaning "red." Idumea is the Greek form. In the Bible, another name for Jacob's brother, Esau. Also, an ancient kingdom south of the Dead Sea.

Edouard   A French form of Edward. *See* Edward.

Edric   From the Anglo-Saxon, meaning "rich ruler."

Edsel   From the Anglo-Saxon, meaning "rich." CONTEMPORARY EXAMPLE: Edsel Ford, automobile manufacturer.

Edson   A patronymic form, meaning "the son of Ed (Edward)." *See* Edward. Edison is a variant form. CONTEMPORARY EXAMPLE: Edson Case, scientist.

Eduard   The German form of Edward. *See* Edward. CONTEMPORARY EXAMPLE: Eduard Bernstein, author.

Eduardo   The Italian and Spanish form of Edward. *See* Edward.
CONTEMPORARY EXAMPLE: Eduardo Acosta, baseball player.

Edvard   The Scandinavian form of Edward. *See* Edward.

Edward   From the Old English name Eadweard, derived from *ead*,
meaning "happy, fortunate," and *weard*, meaning "guardian, protector," hence "happy guardian." The name of eight kings of England
from the thirteenth to the twentieth century. VARIANT FORMS: Edwar-
dus (Latin); Edouard (French); Eduard (German); Eduardo (Spanish
and Italian); Edvard (Scandinavian); Duarte (Portuguese); Ede
(Netherlands). PET FORMS: Ed, Eddie, Eddy, Nedd, Neddy, Teddy.
SURNAME USAGE: Edwards, Edwardes, Edwardson.

Edwardo   A variant spelling of Eduardo. *See* Eduardo. CONTEMPO-
RARY EXAMPLE: Edwardo Figueroa, baseball player.

Edwin   From the Old English name Eadwine. Derived from *ead*,
meaning "happy," and *win*, meaning "friend." Edwina is the feminine
form. CONTEMPORARY EXAMPLE: Edwin Newman, author.

Edy   A variant spelling of Eddy. *See* Eddy. CONTEMPORARY EXAMPLE:
Edy Kaufman, author.

Efim   Origin uncertain. Possibly a variant form of Efrem (Ephraim).
See Ephraim. CONTEMPORARY EXAMPLE: Efim Etkind, professor.

Efraim   A variant spelling of Ephraim. *See* Ephraim.

Efrat   From the Hebrew, meaning "honored, distinguished." In the
Bible, a member of the tribe of Ephraim. Used also as a feminine
name in the Bible.

Efrem   A variant spelling of Efraim. *See* Efraim. CONTEMPORARY EX-
AMPLE: Efrem Zimbalist, U.S. violinist born in Russia.

Efren   A variant spelling of Efrem. *See* Efrem. CONTEMPORARY EXAM-
PLE: Efren Herrera, football player.

Efron   A variant spelling of Ephron. *See* Ephron.

Egan   From the Anglo-Saxon, meaning "formidable, strong." Egon is
a variant spelling. PLACE-NAME USAGE: Egan Range, Nevada, named
for Howard Egan, explorer of the region in the 1850s.

Egbert   From the Anglo-Saxon, meaning "bright sword." PET FORMS:
Bert, Bertie.

Egerton   From the Middle English *egge* and the German *ecke*, meaning "edge, corner of the town."

Egil   From the Old French *aiglent*, meaning "a sting, a prickle." CON-
TEMPORARY EXAMPLE: Egil Krogh, attorney.

Egmont   From the Middle English *egge*, meaning "corner," plus *mont*,
meaning "mountain," hence "corner (edge) of the mountain."

Egon   A variant spelling of Egan. *See* Egan. CONTEMPORARY EXAMPLE: Egon von Furstenburg, clothing designer.

Ehren   From the German, meaning "honored."

Ehud   From the Hebrew, meaning "union." In the Bible, a descendant of Benjamin. CONTEMPORARY EXAMPLE: Ehud Avriel, author.

Eifion   From the Dutch *ei*, meaning "water," plus the Irish hero Fionn (Finn), hence "Finn's waterway." CONTEMPORARY EXAMPLE: Eifion Jones, cricket player.

Einar   From the Old English and Dutch *ei (ey)*, meaning "water," referring to the river Nar. CONTEMPORARY EXAMPLE: Einar Olsen, educator.

Eisig   A Yiddish form of Isaac. *See* Isaac. CONTEMPORARY EXAMPLE: Eisig Silberschlag, educator.

Eitan   From the Hebrew, meaning "strong." VARIANT FORMS: Etan (Hebrew); Ethan (English). CONTEMPORARY EXAMPLE: Eitan Haber, Israeli author.

Ela   A variant form of Elah. *See* Elah. In the Bible, the father of an officer of King Solomon.

Elah   From the Hebrew, meaning "an oak tree." In the Bible, a king of Israel.

Elai   A variant form of Elah. *See* Elah. In the Bible, one of King David's warriors.

Elan   From the Hebrew, meaning "a tree," or from the British, meaning "a young deer."

Elazar   From the Hebrew, meaning "God has helped." In the Bible, a son of Aaron the High Priest. Lazarus is the Greek form used in the New Testament. Eliezer is a variant form. Lazar is a pet form.

Elbert   A variant form of Albert. *See* Albert. CONTEMPORARY EXAMPLE: Elbert Drungo, football player. PLACE-NAME USAGE: Mount Elbert in Colorado, named for Governor S.H. Elbert.

Elbie   A pet form of Elbert. *See* Elbert. Also, derived from the river Elbe that flows through Germany and Czechoslovakia. CONTEMPORARY EXAMPLE: Elbie L. Gann, educator.

Elbridge   From the Old English, meaning "old bridge." CONTEMPORARY EXAMPLE: Elbridge Gerry, U.S. vice-presidential candidate (1812).

Elder   From the Old English *eldo (eald)*, meaning "old, older." Also, a variety of shrubs and small trees. Akin to the alder. CONTEMPORARY EXAMPLE: Elder White, baseball player. PLACE-NAME USAGE: Elder, California, named for the trees and shrubs common in the area.

Elden A variant form of Elder. Akin to Eldon. CONTEMPORARY EXAMPLE: Elden W. Joersz, pilot.

Eldon From the Middle English *elde,* meaning "old age, antiquity." Akin to Alden. CONTEMPORARY EXAMPLE: Eldon B. Schuster, clergyman.

Eldor A variant form of Elder and Alder. *See* Elder *and* Alder.

Eldred From the Old English, meaning "old, wise counsel." Akin to Aldred. *See* Aldred.

Eldridge From the Old English, meaning "an old range (ridge) of hills" or "old fortification." Aldridge is a variant form. CONTEMPORARY EXAMPLE: Eldridge Cleaver, author.

Eldwin From the Old English, meaning "noble friend" or "old friend."

Eleazar A variant spelling of Elazar. *See* Elazar.

Elex A variant form of Alex. *See* Alex. CONTEMPORARY EXAMPLE: Elex Price, football player.

Elford From the Old English, meaning "the old ford (river crossing)." CONTEMPORARY EXAMPLE: Elford A. Cederberg, U.S. congressman.

Elgar, Elger From the Anglo-Saxon *el* (from *aethel*), meaning "noble," and *gar,* meaning "spear," hence "noble spear (protector)." VARIANT FORMS: Algar, Alger. SURNAME USAGE: Sir Edward William Elgar (1857-1934), English composer.

Elgin From the Old English *el* (from *aethel*), meaning "noble," and the British *gyn* and *gwyn,* meaning "white, pure." CONTEMPORARY EXAMPLE: Elgin Baylor, basketball player. PLACE-NAME USAGE: a city in Scotland; a city in Illinois.

Eli From the Hebrew *al,* meaning "on, up, high." In the Bible, a high priest, the last of the Judges. Not to be confused with Elijah or Elisha. "Get there, Eli," was a common slang expression in the nineteenth century. PLACE-NAME USAGE: a lake in South Dakota; Eli, Nebraska.

Elia A variant form of Elijah. Popular in Hawaii. The pen name of Charles Lamb (1775-1834), English essayist. *See* Elijah. CONTEMPORARY EXAMPLE: Elia Kazan, movie director and author.

Elias The Greek form of Elijah. *See* Elijah. In the Douay Version of the Bible Elijah is rendered as Elias.

Eliezer From the Hebrew, meaning "my God has helped." In the Bible, Abraham's servant; also, Moses' son.

Eligio A Spanish form of Elijah. *See* Elijah. CONTEMPORARY EXAMPLE: Eligio de la Garza, U.S. congressman.

Elihu From the Hebrew, meaning "He is my God." In the Bible, the young friend of Job. CONTEMPORARY EXAMPLE: Elihu Root, Nobel

Peace Prize winner (1912).

Elijah   From the Hebrew, meaning "the Lord is my God." In the Bible, one of the earliest of the Hebrew prophets. The New Testament spelling is Elias. VARIANT FORMS: Elia (Greek, German, and Danish); Eligio, Elio, Elisio (Spanish); Elie (French); Elia (Italian and German); Eliot, Elliot, Elliott, Ellis (English). PET FORMS: Eli, Elie, Eliot, Elliot. CONTEMPORARY EXAMPLE: Elijah Anderson, professor. PLACE-NAME USAGE: Mount Elijah, Oregon, named for Elijah J. Davidson, an early settler.

Elio   A Spanish form of Elijah. *See* Elijah. CONTEMPORARY EXAMPLE: Elio Chacon, baseball player.

Eliot   A variant form of Elijah. Also a pet form of Elijah. *See* Elijah. CONTEMPORARY EXAMPLE: Eliot Feld, choreographer. SURNAME USAGE: Charles William Eliot (1834-1926), American educator.

Eliseo   A Spanish form of Elisha. *See* Elisha. Also, from the Latin, meaning "to eliminate." CONTEMPORARY EXAMPLE: Eliseo Rodriguez, baseball player.

Elisha   From the Hebrew, meaning "God is my salvation." In the Bible, a prophet, successor of Elijah. VARIANT FORMS: Elias, Eliot, Elliot, Ellis. CONTEMPORARY EXAMPLE: Elisha Skinner, baseball player.

Elison   A variant spelling of Ellison. *See* Ellison.

Eliyahu   The Hebrew form of Elijah. *See* Elijah. CONTEMPORARY EXAMPLE: Eliyahu Kanovsky, professor.

Elizur   From the Hebrew, meaning "God is my rock." CONTEMPORARY EXAMPLE: Elizur Wright, professor.

Elkan   A Yiddish form of Elkanah. *See* Elkanah.

Elkanah   From the Hebrew, meaning "God has acquired." In the Bible, the father of Samuel. Elkan is a variant form.

Ellard   From the Old English *aler*, meaning "alder tree," plus the Old High German *ard* (from hart), meaning "hardy, strong," hence "the hardy alder tree."

Ellas   A variant spelling of Ellis. *See* Ellis. CONTEMPORARY EXAMPLE: Ellas McDaniel, rock musician.

Ellery   From the Old English *aler*, meaning "the alder tree." Akin to Ellard.

Elliot, Elliott   Variant spellings of Eliot. *See* Eliot. CONTEMPORARY EXAMPLE: Elliot Gould, actor.

Ellis   A variant form of Elisha. *See* Elisha. CONTEMPORARY EXAMPLE: Ellis McCune, educator. SURNAME USAGE: (Henry) Havelock Ellis (1859-1939), English psychologist.

Ellison   A patronymic form, meaning "son of Elijah." *See* Elijah.

Elison is a variant spelling.

Ellsworth   From the Anglo-Saxon, meaning "Ellis's homestead." Elsworth is a variant spelling. CONTEMPORARY EXAMPLE: Ellsworth Kelly, artist. SURNAME USAGE: Lincoln Ellsworth (1880-1951), American explorer.

Ellwood   From the Old English, meaning "the woods (land) of Ellis." *See* Ellis. CONTEMPORARY EXAMPLE: Ellwood A. Voller, educator.

Elly   A pet form of Elijah. *See* Elijah. CONTEMPORARY EXAMPLE: Elly Rakowitz, educator.

Elma   From the Old English, meaning "an elm tree." Also, a variant form of Elmer. *See* Elmer. CONTEMPORARY EXAMPLE: Elma Knight, baseball player.

Elman   From the Anglo-Saxon, meaning "noble man" or "noble servant." CONTEMPORARY EXAMPLE: Elman R. Service, author. SURNAME USAGE: Mischa Elman (1891-1967), violinist.

Elmer   From the Old English Aethelmaer, derived from *aethel*, meaning "noble," and *maere*, meaning "famous." VARIANT FORMS: Ailemar, Aylmer, Eilemar, Elmo. CONTEMPORARY EXAMPLE: Elmer Rice, playwright.

Elmo   A variant form of Elmer. *See* Elmer. CONTEMPORARY EXAMPLE: Elmo Zumwalt, U.S. admiral. PLACE-NAME USAGE: Elmo, Texas, named after Elmo Scott, a railroad engineer.

Elmore   A variant form of Elmer. *See* Elmer. CONTEMPORARY EXAMPLE: Elmore Stephens, football player.

Elois   Probably a variant form of Louis. *See* Louis. CONTEMPORARY EXAMPLE: Elois Grooms, football player.

Elon   A variant form of Elan. From the Latin, meaning "spirited, self-assured." *See also* Elan. In the Bible, the father-in-law of Esau; also, a son of Zebulun. CONTEMPORARY EXAMPLE: Elon Hogsett, baseball player.

Elrad   From the Hebrew, meaning "God is the ruler." Also, from the Old English and German, meaning "noble (*el*) counsel (*rat*)."

Elrod   A variant spelling of Elrad. *See* Elrad. CONTEMPORARY EXAMPLE: Elrod Hendricks, baseball player.

Elroy, El Roy   From the Latin, meaning "royal, king." The French form is Leroy. CONTEMPORARY EXAMPLE: El Roy Face, baseball player. PLACE-NAME USAGE: Elroy, Pennsylvania; Elroy, Wisconsin.

Elsdon   A hybrid Hebrew-Anglo-Saxon name, meaning "Ellis's valley." *See* Ellis.

Elsen   A patronymic form, meaning "son of Ellis" or "son of Elias." *See* Ellis *and* Elias.

Elson   A variant form of Elsen. *See* Elsen. Also, an independent name. Elson Bertan Snow was named after his grandparents Elbert and Anson.

Elston   From the Old English, meaning "noble town" or "town of the nobleman." Also, meaning "Els (Ellis's or Eliot's) town." CONTEMPORARY EXAMPLE: Elston Howard, baseball player.

Eltis   Possibly a variant form of Aldus. *See* Aldus. CONTEMPORARY EXAMPLE: Eltis Henson, educator.

Elton   From the Anglo-Saxon, meaning "from the old farm or village." Elton may also be a short form of Elston. CONTEMPORARY EXAMPLE: Elton John, entertainer.

Elul   The name of the sixth month in the Jewish calendar.

Elva   An Old English variant form of Elvin or a form of Elvert. *See* Elvin *and* Elvert.

Elvert   A variant form of Elbert. *See* Elbert.

Elvin   From the Anglo-Saxon *aelfwine*, meaning "friend (*wine*)," and "noble (aelf)," hence "noble friend." VARIANT FORMS: Elva, Elvert, Elvis, Elwin. CONTEMPORARY EXAMPLE: Elvin Skiles, educator.

Elvis   A variant form of Elvin. *See* Elvin. CONTEMPORARY EXAMPLE: Elvis Presley, singer.

Elwill   From the Old English, meaning "a noble, stately willow tree." CONTEMPORARY EXAMPLE: Elwill M. Shanahan, Kansas politician.

Elwin   A variant form of Elvin. *See* Elvin. VARIANT FORMS: Elwyn, Winn, Wynn.

Elwood   From the Old English, meaning "noble woods" or "garden of the nobleman."

Elwyn   A variant spelling of Elwin. *See* Elwin. CONTEMPORARY EXAMPLE: Elwyn Simon, paleontologist.

Ely   A variant spelling of Eli. *See* Eli. Or, from the Old English, meaning "island of eels." PLACE-NAME USAGE: Ely, Montana, named for Arthur Ely, railroad promoter; Ely, Nevada, named for John Ely, town developer.

Emanuel   From the Hebrew, meaning "God is with us." In the Bible, the name appears in Isaiah 7:14, and is said to refer to the Messiah. The name was never very popular among Christians. VARIANT FORMS: Manuel (Spanish); Manoel (Portuguese). Immanuel is a variant spelling. Manny is a pet form.

Emanuela   An Hawaiian form of Emanuel. *See* Emanuel.

Embert   From the Anglo-Saxon, meaning "bright."

Emerald   From the Middle English and Old French *smaragde*, meaning "a bright green precious stone." Used more commonly as a feminine name. CONTEMPORARY EXAMPLE: Emerald Lamme, football player.

Emerson A patronymic form, meaning "the son of Emery." *See* Emery. CONTEMPORARY EXAMPLE: Emerson Boozer, football player. SUR- NAME USAGE: Ralph Waldo Emerson (1803-1882), American philoso- pher.

Emery From the Old High German name Amalrich, meaning "work" (*amal*), and "ruler" (*rich*, *riche*). Emory is a variant spelling. VARIANT FORMS: Almericus (Latin); Emmerich (German); Amerigo (Italian). Akin to Emil. CONTEMPORARY EXAMPLE: Emery Wendell Carr, Tufson- boro, New Hampshire.

Emil From the Latin *aemulus*, meaning "to emulate, to be in- dustrious." Akin to Emery. VARIANT FORMS: Emile (French); Emilio (Italian). Emily is a feminine form. CONTEMPORARY EXAMPLE: Emil Jen- nings, actor.

Emile A French form of Emil. *See* Emil. CONTEMPORARY EXAMPLE: Emile Barnes, baseball player.

Emilio An Italian form of Emil. *See* Emil. CONTEMPORARY EXAMPLE: Emilio Gucci, fashion designer.

Emir From the Arabic *amara*, meaning "to command." CONTEM- PORARY EXAMPLE: Emir Rodriguez Monegal, author.

Emlin, Emlyn Possibly a compounded name meaning "Emil's lake." CONTEMPORARY EXAMPLE: Emlin Tunnel, football player; Emlyn Williams, actor.

Emmanuel A variant spelling of Emanuel. *See* Emanuel.

Emmet, Emmett From the Hebrew *emet*, meaning "truth." Or, from the Anglo-Saxon, meaning "an ant." CONTEMPORARY EXAMPLE: Emmet Kelly, circus clown. SURNAME USAGE: Robert Emmet (1778-1803), Irish patriot. PLACE-NAME USAGE: county in Iowa.

Emmitt A variant spelling of Emmett. *See* Emmett. CONTEMPORARY EXAMPLE: Emmitt Earl Thomas, football player.

Emmon A variant spelling of Eamon.

Emmons A patronymic form of Emmon, meaning "son of Emmon." *See* Emmon. CONTEMPORARY EXAMPLE: Emmons Bowen, baseball player.

Emmory A variant spelling of Emory. *See* Emory.

Emory A variant spelling of Emery. *See* Emery. CONTEMPORARY EX- AMPLE: Emory H. Hebard, Vermont political leader.

Endelon A masculine adaptation of Gwendolyn. CONTEMPORARY EX- AMPLE: Endelon Wininger, Mannsville, Oklahoma.

Endymion   In Greek mythology, a young handsome shepherd whom Selene loved.

English   From the Old English name Englisc, meaning an early tribe that settled on the British Isles. CONTEMPORARY EXAMPLE: English E. Jones, educator. PLACE-NAME USAGE: Englishtown, New Jersey, named for landowner James English; English, West Virginia.

Enid   Commonly a feminine name. *See* Enid (feminine section). CONTEMPORARY EXAMPLE: Enid Thomas, football player. PLACE-NAME USAGE: Enid, Oklahoma.

Ennis   A short form of Denis. *See* Denis. Also, from the Greek *ennea*, meaning "mine," possibly referring to the Nine Muses. CONTEMPORARY EXAMPLE: Ennis Oakes, baseball player.

Enoch   From the Hebrew, meaning "educated" or "dedicated." In the Bible, the son born to Cain after he killed his brother Abel. PLACE-NAME USAGE: Enoch, Utah. Named (1884) for the Mormon Order of Settlers.

Enos   From the Hebrew *enosh* and *ish*, meaning "man." The Hebrew form is Enosh. In the Bible, a son of Seth. CONTEMPORARY EXAMPLE: Enos Slaughter, baseball player.

Enrico   An Italian form of Henry. *See* Henry. CONTEMPORARY EXAMPLE: Enrico Caruso (1873-1921), opera singer.

Enrique   A Spanish.form of Henry. *See* Henry. CONTEMPORARY EXAMPLE: Enrique Cassareto, soccer player.

Ensign   From the Latin *insignia*, meaning "a badge, a symbol of authority." CONTEMPORARY EXAMPLE: Ensign Cottrell, baseball player.

Enzio   An Italian form of Henry. *See* Henry. Or, a variant form of Enzo. *See* Enzo.

Enzo   A Spanish form of Ennis. *See* Ennis. Or, a variant form of Enzio. *See* Enzio. CONTEMPORARY EXAMPLE: Enzo Hernandez, baseball player.

Ephraim   From the Hebrew, meaning "fruitful." In the Bible, one of the two sons of Joseph. Efraim is a variant spelling. Efrem is a variant form.

Ephron   From the Hebrew, meaning "a fawn." In the Bible, a Hittite who sold Abraham a burial plot. Efron is a variant spelling.

Er   From the Hebrew, meaning "guardian." In the Bible, the son of Judah

Erasmus   From the Greek *eran*, meaning "to love." Akin to Eros. Erasmios is the Greek form.

Erastus   A variant Greek form of Erasmus. *See* Erasmus. CONTEMPORARY EXAMPLE: Erastus D. Coming, mayor of Albany, New York.

Erhard   A variant form of Gerhard. *See* Gerhard.

Eri   From the Hebrew, meaning "my guardian." In the Bible, a son of Gad. CONTEMPORARY EXAMPLE: Eri Steimatzky, Israeli publisher.

Eric   From the Old Norse name Eirkir, a compound of the German *chre*, meaning "honor," and the Latin *rex*, meaning "king, ruler," hence, "honorable ruler." VARIANT FORMS: Erie (English); Erich (German); Erik (Swedish and Slavonic); Eryk (Polish). PET FORMS: Rick, Rickie.

Erich   A variant spelling of Eric. *See* Eric.

Erik   A variant spelling of Eric. *See* Eric. CONTEMPORARY EXAMPLE: Erik Bruhn, choreographer.

Erland   From the German *ehre*, meaning "honor, honorable," plus land, hence "honorable country." CONTEMPORARY EXAMPLE: Erland Josephson, actor.

Erling   A variant Norse form of Erland. *See* Erland. CONTEMPORARY EXAMPLE: Erling Larsen, baseball player.

Ermal   From the German *ehre*, meaning "honor" and the Old English *mal*, meaning "a place of meeting." CONTEMPORARY EXAMPLE: Ermal Allen, football player.

Erme   A variant form of Ermin. *See* Ermin.

Ermin   From the Old German *ermin*, meaning "universal, whole," plus *drudi*, meaning "strength." Evolved into a masculine form from the feminine Ermegarde and Emengarde, used in the Middle Ages.

Ernald   A variant form of Arnold. *See* Arnold.

Ernest   From the Old High German *ernust*, meaning "resolute, earnest, sincere." VARIANT FORMS: Earnest, Ernesto (Italian and Spanish); Ernst (German); Erno (Hungarian); Erneste (French); Ernestus (Dutch). Ernis and Erneis were forms used from the eleventh to the thirteenth centuries. PET FORMS: Ern, Ernie. Ernestine is a feminine form.

Ernie   A pet form of Ernest. *See* Ernest.

Erno   A variant Hungarian form of Ernest. *See* Ernest. CONTEMPORARY EXAMPLE: Erno Dahl, educator.

Ernst   A variant form of Ernest. *See* Ernest. SURNAME USAGE: German Max Ernst, surrealist painter.

Eros   From the Greek *eros*, meaning "love." In Greek mythology, Eros was the god of love. CONTEMPORARY EXAMPLE: Eros Barger, baseball player.

Errol   From the Latin *errare*, meaning "to wander." CONTEMPORARY EXAMPLE: Errol Flynn, actor.

Erskine   From the Middle English name Erish, meaning "Irish." Popular in Ireland and Scotland. CONTEMPORARY EXAMPLE: Erskine Caldwell, author. SURNAME USAGE: John Erskine (1879-1951), American educator and writer.

Erv   A variant spelling of Irv (Irving). *See* Irving. Or, a pet form of Ervin. *See* Ervin. CONTEMPORARY EXAMPLE: Erv Dusak, baseball player.

Erve   A short form of Herve. *See* Herve. Or, a variant spelling of Erv. *See* Erv. CONTEMPORARY EXAMPLE: Erve Beck, baseball player.

Ervin, Erwin   Variant forms of Irvin. *See* Irvin.

Eryk   A variant spelling of Eric. *See* Eric. CONTEMPORARY EXAMPLE:

Eryle   A variant spelling of Eric. *See* Eric. CONTEMPORARY EXAMPLE: Eryle Spector, textile executive.

Esau   From the Hebrew, meaning "hairy." In the Bible, the son of Isaac and Rebekah, twin brother of Jacob.

Escott   From the British name Esk (*ysc*), meaning "water, river," and the Old English *cot*, meaning "a cottage," hence "a shepherd's hut near the river." CONTEMPORARY EXAMPLE: Escott Reid, Canadian political leader.

Eshkol   From the Hebrew, meaning "a cluster of grapes." In Hebrew literature, it is a word signifying a group of outstanding scholars. SURNAME USAGE: Levi Eshkol, prime minister of Israel.

Esmond, Esmund   From the Anglo-Saxon *estmund*, meaning "gracious protector." Esmond became popular after the publication of Thackeray's historical novel *The History of Henry Esmond* (1852). PLACE-NAME USAGE: Esmond, Rhode Island.

Essex   Probably a corrupt form of Saxon, one of the early tribes that invaded the British Isles. CONTEMPORARY EXAMPLE: Essex Johnson, football player. PLACE-NAME USAGE: former East Saxon kingdom in England; a county in Maryland; a county in Massachusetts.

Esteban   The Spanish form of Stephen. *See* Stephen. May also be related to Estes. *See* Estes. CONTEMPORARY EXAMPLE: Esteban Belon, baseball player.

Estel   Probably a masculine form of Estelle. *See* Estelle (feminine section). CONTEMPORARY EXAMPLE: Estel Crabee, baseball player.

Estes   A Spanish form of the Latin *aestus*, meaning "the tide," hence "an inlet from the sea, an estuary, a bay." CONTEMPORARY EXAMPLE: Estes Kefauver, U.S. senator. PLACE-NAME USAGE: Estes Park, Colorado, named for Jel Estes, first permanent settler (1859).

Eston   From the Old English, meaning "the town near the estuary." Akin to Estes. *See* Estes. CONTEMPORARY EXAMPLE: Eston K. Feaster, educator.

Etan, Ethan   From the Hebrew, meaning "permanent, firm, strong."

Etan is the modern Hebrew spelling. In the Bible, a son of Zera; a descendant of Gershon; a Levite. CONTEMPORARY EXAMPLE: Etan Patz, New York City. SURNAME USAGE: Ethan Allen, hero of the American Revolution.

Ethelbert From the Old English name Aethelbryht, meaning "noble (*aethele*)" and "bright (*beorht*)." A variant form of Adelbert. Akin to Albert, the King of Kent (560-616).

Ethelred From the Old English *aethele*, meaning "noble," and *hreod*, meaning "reed." King of England (978-1016).

Etienne A French form of Stephen, from Estienne. CONTEMPORARY EXAMPLE: Etienne Gilson, author. SURNAME USAGE: The Estiennes were a family of fifteenth and sixteenth-century French printers and publishers.

Eubie A pet form of Eubule. *See* Eubule. CONTEMPORARY EXAMPLE: Eubie Blake, pianist.

Eubule From the Greek, meaning "one who offers good counsel." In the New Testament, one of St. Paul's companions. Also spelled Ewball.

Eucal A short form of Eucalyptus. From the Greek, meaning "well covered." A species of tree on which the buds are well covered. CONTEMPORARY EXAMPLE: Eucal Clanton, baseball player.

Euclid From the Greek *eucharis*, meaning "charming, gracious." A fourth-century B.C. Greek mathematician. PLACE-NAME USAGE: cities in Ohio, Pennsylvania, and Minnesota.

Eudo From the Old German name Eutha, derived from the Greek *eudaimonia*, meaning "happiness." Eudo is a Latinized form, which also appears as Udo. Introduced into England by the Normans in the forms Eudes and Eudon.

Euel A variant form of Ewell. *See* Ewell. CONTEMPORARY EXAMPLE: Euel Moore, baseball player.

Eugen A variant form of Eugene. *See* Eugene. CONTEMPORARY EXAMPLE: Eugen Bossard, editor.

Eugene From the Greek, meaning "well born, born lucky" or "one of noble descent." VARIANT FORMS: Eugen, Eugine. Gene is a popular pet form. Eugenie is a feminine form. PLACE-NAME USAGE: Eugene, Oregon, named for Eugene Skinner, an early settler.

Eugenio A Spanish, Portuguese, and Italian form of Eugene. *See* Eugene.

Eulis From the Greek, meaning "sweet-speaking." CONTEMPORARY EXAMPLE: Eulis Keahey, football player.

Eustace From the Greek, meaning "rich in corn" or "fruitful." CONTEMPORARY EXAMPLE: Eustace Newton, baseball player.

Evald, Evaldo From the Latin name Everildis, compounded of the

Old English *eofor,* meaning "boar," and *hild,* meaning "battle." CONTEM-PORARY EXAMPLE: Evaldo L. Kothny, editor.

Evan A Welsh form of John. *See* John. Owen is a variant form. CON-TEMPORARY EXAMPLE: Evan Hunter, author. PLACE-NAME USAGE: Evanston, Illinois.

Evander A variant form of Evan. CONTEMPORARY EXAMPLE: Evander Child, educator.

Evans A patronymic form of Evan, meaning "son of Evan." *See* Evan. SURNAME USAGE: Maurice Evans, actor.

Evel, Evelio, Evelle Variant forms of Evelyn. *See* Evelyn. CONTEMPO-RARY EXAMPLES: Evel Knievel, stuntman; Evelio Hernander, baseball player; Evelle Younger, California government official.

Evelyn Primarily a feminine name. *See* Evelyn (feminine section). The name was first used as a masculine name by Evelyn Pierrepont, Duke of Kingston (born 1665). Evelyn was his mother's name. CON-TEMPORARY EXAMPLES: Evelyn Waugh, author; Richard Evelyn Byrd, explorer.

Everard, Everhard From the Norse and German, meaning "a strong, wild boar." VARIANT FORMS: Eberhard, Eberhart (German); Ebbo (Italian); Evart (Dutch). CONTEMPORARY EXAMPLE: Everard Barrett, educator.

Everett From the Old High German name Eburhart, derived from *ebur,* meaning "a wild boar," and *harto,* meaning "hard, strong," hence "one who is strong; a warrior." VARIANT FORMS: Eberhard (German); Evert (Dutch); Everart (Old French); Devereux, Everette (French). CON-TEMPORARY EXAMPLE: Everett Colby, Everett, Washington; Everett M. Dirksen, U.S. senator. PLACE-NAME USAGE: a city in Massachusetts, named for Edward Everett; a city in Washington, named for Everett Colby.

Everette A French form of Everett. *See* Everett. CONTEMPORARY EX-AMPLE: Everette E. Dennis, journalist.

Everley From Old English, meaning "Ever's (Everett's) field."

Evo An Italian form of Ivo, derived from the French Yves. Akin to Ivan. A form of John. *See* John. CONTEMPORARY EXAMPLE: Evo Perini, football player.

Evon A variant form of Ivan. *See* Ivan. CONTEMPORARY EXAMPLE: Evon Williams, football player.

Ewald A variant form of Evald. *See* Evald. VARIANT FORMS: Evald, Evaldo, Ival, Ivol.

Ewan A variant spelling of Ewen. *See* Ewen.

Ewart From the Old French *evier,* meaning "a ewer." Probably an occupational name for "one who serves water; a butler." CONTEMporary example: Ewart (Dixie) Walker, baseball player.

Ewell   A variant form of Ewart. *See* Ewart. contemporary example: Ewell Phillips, football player. surname usage: Richard Stoddert Ewell (1817-1872), Civil War general.

Ewen   Probably a variant form of Evan, the Welsh form of John. *See* Evan *and* John. Also, a variant form of Owen. contemporary example: Ewen Akin, educator.

Ezar   From the Hebrew name Ezer, meaning "help, salvation." contemporary example: Ezar Kollet, New Delhi, India.

Ezekiel   From the Hebrew, meaning "God will strengthen." In the Bible, one of the later prophets. Zeke is a pet form. contemporary example: Ezekiel Moore, Jr., football player. surname usage: Moses Jacob Ezekiel (1844-1917), American sculptor.

Ezell   Probably a short form of Ezekiel. *See* Ezekiel. contemporary example: Ezell Jones, football player.

Ezer   From the Hebrew, meaning "help, salvation." variant forms: Ezra, Azariah, Ezri, Azur, Azrikam. contemporary example: Ezer Weizman, Israeli political leader.

Ezio   A short form of Enzio. *See* Enzio. contemporary example: Ezio Pinza, opera singer.

Ezra   From the Hebrew, meaning "help, salvation." In the Bible, a leader of the Jews in the fifth century b.c. variant forms: Ezar, Ezer, Ezri, Ezzard, Ezzret. Used also as a feminine name in Israel. contemporary example: Ezra Pound, poet.

Ezri   From the Hebrew, meaning "my help." In the Bible, one of King David's overseers.

Ezzard   Possibly a variant form of Ezra. *See* Ezra. contemporary example: Ezzard Charles, boxer.

Ezzret   Possibly a variant form of Ezra. *See* Ezra. contemporary example: Ezzret Anderson, football player.

F

Fa   From the British, meaning "a place."

Fabian   From the Latin name Fabianus, meaning "belonging to Fabius." *See* Fabius. CONTEMPORARY EXAMPLES: Fabian Kowalik, baseball player; Fabian Forte, singer.

Fabius   From the Latin *faba*, meaning "a bean, a member of the pea family of plants." In ancient Rome, members of the Fabia family were wealthy bean growers. Also, the name of a third-century Roman general who defeated Hannibal in the Second Punic War by a strategy of delay and avoidance of battle, hence the meaning "cautious, careful." VARIANT FORMS: Fabian, Fabyan. Fabia is a feminine form. PLACE-NAME USAGE: Fabius, West Virginia; Fabius, Missouri.

Fahey   Possibly from the Middle English *fain*, meaning "joyful." CONTEMPORARY EXAMPLE: Fahey Flynn, television newscaster.

Fairbanks   From the Old English *faer*, meaning "by the way," plus *bank*, meaning "a mound," hence "a mound along the path." SURNAME USAGE: Douglas Fairbanks, actor. PLACE-NAME USAGE: Fairbanks, Alaska.

Fairfax   From the Anglo-Saxon, meaning "fair-haired." PLACE-NAME USAGE: Fairfax, Virginia, named for Lord Fairfax.

Fairleigh, Fairley   From the Anglo-Saxon, meaning "the wayside place." Farley is a variant form.

Fait   Possibly from the Old French *faitor*, meaning "doer, maker." CONTEMPORARY EXAMPLE: Fait Elkins, football player.

Falconer   From the Old French *fauconnier*, meaning "one who breeds and trains falcons." VARIANT FORMS: Falkner, Faulkner. PLACE-NAME USAGE: Cape Falcon, Oregon; Falcon, North Carolina.

Falkner   A variant form of Falconer. *See* Falconer. Faulkner is a variant spelling. PLACE-NAME USAGE: Falkland Islands, South America; Falkner, Mississippi, named for Colonel W.C. Falkner, soldier and novelist, grandfather of William Faulkner (who modified the spelling).

Fallen   Possibly a short form of Farland. *See* Farland. PLACE-NAME USAGE: Fallen Leaf Lake, California.

Faramond   From the Old German name Faramund, compounded of *fara*, meaning "journey," and *mund*, meaning "protection." SURNAME USAGE: Farr, Farrimond, Farman, Fairman, Fearman.

Fardy   An Irish form of Ferdinand. *See* Ferdinand.

Farl   A short form of Farley. *See* Farley. CONTEMPORARY EXAMPLE: Farl J. Waters, scientist.

Farland   From the Anglo-Saxon, meaning "the land by the road."

Farley   From the Anglo-Saxon, meaning "the wayside place." Fairleigh is a variant form.

Farquhar   From the Gaelic name Fearchar, derived from *fer*, meaning "man," and *car*, meaning "friendly," hence "friendly man." SURNAME USAGE: George Farquhar (1678-1707), Anglo-Irish dramatist.

Farrar   From the Old French *ferrier* and the Latin *ferrarins*, meaning "a worker with iron, a blacksmith." SURNAME USAGE: Geraldine Farrar, American dramatic soprano.

Farrel, Farrell   From the Celtic, meaning "the valorous one." Or, a variant form of Farrar. *See* Farrar. CONTEMPORARY EXAMPLES: Farrel Everret Summers, Chicago, Illinois; Farrell Dobbs, politician.

Fate   A variant spelling of Fait. *See* Fait. Also, a variant form of Faye and Fayette. *See* Faye *and* Fayette. CONTEMPORARY EXAMPLE: Fate Echols, football player. PLACE-NAME USAGE: Fate, Texas, named for LaFayette Brown, local sheriff.

Fats   A nickname for a fat person that has become an independent name. CONTEMPORARY EXAMPLES: Fats Waller and Fats Domino, musicians.

Faulkner   A variant spelling of Falkner. See Falkner. SURNAME USAGE: William Faulkner (1897-1962), American Nobel Prize winner in literature.

Faunus   In Roman mythology, a god of nature, the patron of farming and animals.

Faustus   From the Latin *faustus*, meaning "fortunate." The name of a third-century Roman martyr. SURNAME USAGE: Johann Faust, a sixteenth-century necromancer.

Faxon   From the Anglo-Saxon, meaning "hair."

Faye   From the Middle English *fai* and the Latin *fata*, meaning "a fairy" or "one of the fates." Also, from the Old French, meaning "fidelity." More commonly used as a feminine name. CONTEMPORARY EXAMPLE: Faye Wilson, football player.

Fayette   A pet form of Faye. *See* Faye. Also, from the Celtic, meaning "the little raven." Used also as a feminine form. *See* Fayette (feminine section).

Fearn   A variant form of Fern. *See* Fern. PLACE-NAME USAGE: Fearn, Scotland.

Fedor   The Russian form of Theodore. *See* Theodore.

Feibush   A variant form of Feivel. *See* Feivel.

Feivel, Feiwel   The Yiddish form of Phoebus, from the Latin and Greek, meaning "bright one."

Felipe   The Spanish form of Philip. *See* Philip. CONTEMPORARY EXAMPLE: Felipe Luciano, television news reporter.

Felix   From the Latin *felix*, meaning "happy, fortunate, prosperous." The name of four popes and a number of saints. Felicia is a feminine form.

Fell   From the Old Danish, meaning "a field" or "a hill."

Felton   From the Old English, meaning "the town in the garden." CONTEMPORARY EXAMPLE: Felton Prewitt, football player.

Fenton   From the Old English, meaning "the town near the fen or marsh." CONTEMPORARY EXAMPLES: Fenton Keyes, educator; Fenton Mole, baseball player.

Ferd, Ferde, Ferdie   Short forms of Ferdinand. *See* Ferdinand. Also, from the German *pferd*, meaning "a horse." Ferdy is a pet form. CONTEMPORARY EXAMPLE: Ferde Grofe, musician; Ferdie A. Falk, business executive.

Ferdinand   From the German, meaning "to be bold, courageous." Ferdinand I, the eleventh-century king of Castille and emperor of Spain, was called Ferdinand the Great. VARIANT FORMS: Ferdinando, Fernando, Ferrando (Italian); Fardy (Irish). PET FORMS: Ferd, Ferde. FEMININE FORMS: Fern, Fernanda.

Ferdy   A pet form of Ferd. *See* Ferd. CONTEMPORARY EXAMPLE: Ferdy Mayne, actor.

Ferenc   A variant form of Firenze, the Italian name of Florence, Italy. *See* Florence (feminine section). CONTEMPORARY EXAMPLE: Ferenc Mate, essayist.

Fergus   From the Irish and Gaelic, meaning "manly." In Irish legend, a military hero who attacked Cuchulain at Ulster. CONTEMPORARY EXAMPLE: Fergus Carrick, cricket player.

Ferguson   A patronymic form, meaning "son of Fergus." *See* Fergus. CONTEMPORARY EXAMPLE: Ferguson Jenkins, baseball player.

Feridon   Origin uncertain. Possibly, a variant form of Fermin. *See* Fermin. CONTEMPORARY EXAMPLE: Feridon Erkin.

Fermin   From the Latin *feritas* and *ferus*, meaning "wild, savage." Firmin is a variant form. CONTEMPORARY EXAMPLE: Fermin Guerra, baseball player.

Fern   A pet form of Ferdinand. *See* Ferdinand. Also, from the Old English *fearn*, meaning "a leafy plant." Used as a Scottish surname. CONTEMPORARY EXAMPLE: Fern Bell, baseball player.

Fernand, Fernandas, Fernando Spanish forms of Ferdinand. *See* Ferdinand. CONTEMPORARY EXAMPLES: Fernand J. Germain, U.S. congressman; Fernando Lamas, actor. PLACE-NAME USAGE: San Fernando Valley, California.

Ferrin A variant form of Ferris. *See* Ferris.

Ferris From the Latin *ferrum*, meaning "iron." An occupational surname used in France and Ireland by blacksmiths and iron workers. Farrar is a variant form. CONTEMPORARY EXAMPLE: Ferris Beekley, football player.

Ferrol From the Old French *virole*, meaning "an iron ring on a staff." Derived from the Latin *ferrum*, meaning "iron." PLACE-NAME USAGE: El Ferrol, a seaport in northwest Spain, officially named El Ferrol del Caudillo.

Festus From the Latin *festivus*, meaning "festive, joyous." CONTEMPORARY EXAMPLES: Festus Tierney, football player; Festus Higgins, baseball player. PLACE-NAME USAGE: Festus, Missouri.

Fibber From the seventeenth-century word *fible*, meaning "a fable, a lie." A nickname also used as an independent name. CONTEMPORARY EXAMPLE: Fibber McGee, radio actor.

Fico From the Italian *fico*, meaning "a fig," connoting something worthless.

Fidel From the Latin *fidelis*, meaning "faithful." CONTEMPORARY EXAMPLE: Fidel Castro, Cuban prime minister.

Field, Fielder From the Middle English *feld*, meaning "field." An occupational name for "one who works in the fields." CONTEMPORARY EXAMPLE: Fielder Jones, baseball player. SURNAME USAGE: Cyrus West Field (1819-1912), U.S. industrialist. PLACE-NAME USAGE: Field, New Mexico.

Fielding A variant form of Field. *See* Field. CONTEMPORARY EXAMPLES: Fielding Wright, U.S. presidential candidate (1948); Fielding Dawson, writer. SURNAME USAGE: Henry Fielding (1707-1754), English novelist.

Firmin A variant spelling of Fermin. *See* Fermin. CONTEMPORARY EXAMPLE: Firmin Warwick, baseball player.

Firpo From the Middle English *firre*, meaning "the fir tree." CONTEMPORARY EXAMPLE: Firpo Marberry, freelance writer.

Fish From the German *fisch*, meaning "a fish." VARIANT FORMS: Fisk, Fiske. SURNAME USAGE: Hamilton Fish, Jr., U.S. congressman. PLACE-NAME USAGE: Fish-Eating Creek, Florida; Fisher Creek, Oregon.

Fishke A Yiddish name derived from the Old German *fisch*, meaning "fish."

Fisk, Fiske From the Old English *fisc*, meaning "a fish." SURNAME

USAGE: John Fiske, born Edmund Fisk Green (1842-1901), U.S. historian.

Flan, Flann   From the Old English, meaning "an arrow." Also, pet forms of Flannery. *See* Flannery.

Flavian   From the Latin *flavus*, meaning "yellow, blonde." Used for people with flaxen or blonde hair. VARIANT FORMS: Flavius, Flavio.

Flavio, Flavius   Variant forms of Flavian. *See* Flavian. CONTEMPORARY EXAMPLE: Flavio Tosi, football player.

Flem   A pet form of Fleming. *See* Fleming.

Fleming   From the Middle Dutch *vlaming*, meaning "a native of Flanders." Flem is a pet form. SURNAME USAGE: Alexander Fleming (1881-1955), British bacteriologist.

Fletcher   From the Old French *fleche*, meaning "an arrow," hence an occupational name for "one who makes arrows." CONTEMPORARY EXAMPLE: Fletcher Thomson, U.S. congressman. SURNAME USAGE: John Fletcher (1579-1625), British playwright.

Flint   From the Old English and Norwegian, meaning "a stone splinter." CONTEMPORARY EXAMPLE: Flint Rhem, baseball player. PLACE-NAME USAGE: a town in Wales; Flint, Michigan; Flint, Texas, named for R.P. Flynt, landowner.

Flip   A nickname for one who is glib, talkative, and impertinent. Also, from the Modern English, meaning "nimble." CONTEMPORARY EXAMPLES: Flip Schulke, author; Flip Wilson, entertainer.

Florence   From the Latin, meaning "blooming." Primarily a feminine name. *See* Florence (feminine section). VARIANT FORMS: Fiorello, Florents, Florentz, Florenz. PLACE-NAME USAGE: Florence, Italy.

Florentino   A diminutive form of Florence. *See* Florence. CONTEMPORARY EXAMPLE: Florentino Molina, golfer.

Florentz, Florenz   Variant spellings of Florence. *See* Florence. CONTEMPORARY EXAMPLE: Florenz Ziegfeld producer.

Florian   From the Latin *florianus*, meaning "flowering, blooming." Florianus was a fourth-century Roman saint. Flory is a pet form. Akin to Florence. CONTEMPORARY EXAMPLE: Florian Ackley, baseball player.

Floyd   A corrupt form of Lloyd. *See* Lloyd. PLACE-NAME USAGE: Floyd River, Iowa.

Fob   From the German *fappe*, meaning "a pocket for carrying a watch." CONTEMPORARY EXAMPLE: Fob James, Alabama politician.

Fon   A short form of Fonda. *See* Fonda. CONTEMPORARY EXAMPLE: Fon W. Boardman, Jr., author.

Fonda   From the French *fondre*, meaning "to melt." Used most often as a feminine form. *See* Fonda (feminine section). SURNAME USAGE:

Henry Fonda, actor.

Forbes From the Greek *phorbe*, meaning "fodder, a broad-leaved flowering plant." CONTEMPORARY EXAMPLE: Forbes Collins, actor.

Ford From the Old English, meaning "a road." Akin to the German *furt*, meaning "passage." Generally refering to a shallow part of a stream or river where crossing is possible. CONTEMPORARY EXAMPLE: Ford Madox (1873-1939), English writer; Ford Frick, president, National Baseball League. SURNAME USAGE: Gerald R. Ford, thirty-eighth president of the U.S.

Fordon From the Middle English *fordon*, meaning "to destroy." CONTEMPORARY EXAMPLE: Fordon Allen Basichis, author.

Forester An Old French occupational name, meaning "one in charge of a forest." VARIANT FORMS: Forrest, Forster, Foster. SURNAME USAGE: Cecil Scott Forester (1899-1966), English novelist.

Forrest From the Latin *foris*, meaning "out-of-doors, woods." CONTEMPORARY EXAMPLE: Forrest Wilson, Pulitzer Prize winner, 1942.

Forrester A variant spelling of Forester. *See* Forester.

Forster A variant form of Forester. *See* Forester.

Fortney From the Latin *fortis*, meaning "strong."

Fortune From the Latin *fortuna*, meaning "chance." Akin to the feminine Fortuna and Fortunata. *See* Fortuna *and* Fortunata (feminine section).

Foster A variant form of Forrest. *See* Forrest. CONTEMPORARY EXAMPLES: Foster S. Brown, educator; Foster Brooks, comedian.

Fountain From the Latin and Old French *fontaine*, meaning "a spring." PLACE-NAME USAGE: Fountain Green, Utah; Fountain Lake, Minnesota.

Fowler From the Old English *fugol* and the German *vogel*, meaning "one who traps fowl (birds)." VARIANT FORMS: Falconer, Falkner, Faulkner. SURNAME USAGE: Henry Watson Fowler (1858-1933), English lexicographer.

Fox From the German *fuchs*, meaning "a fox." Used by members of a tribe of North American Indians who originally lived in Wisconsin and later merged with the Sauk. CONTEMPORARY EXAMPLE: Fox Butterfield, journalist. SURNAME USAGE: George Fox (1624-1691), English clergyman. PLACE-NAME USAGE: Fox River, Wisconsin.

Foy From the Middle Dutch, meaning "a journey." Later, a Scottish name, meaning "a feast in honor of one going on a journey." SURNAME USAGE: Eddie Foy, actor.

Fraley Origin uncertain. Possibly from the Latin *frater*, meaning "a friar," and the Middle English *le*, meaning "a shelter," hence "a friar's house." CONTEMPORARY EXAMPLE: Fraley Rogers, baseball player.

Fran   A pet form of Francis. *See* Francis. CONTEMPORARY EXAMPLE: Fran Tarkenton, football player.

Francesco, Francisco   Variant forms of Francis. *See* Francis. CONTEMPORARY EXAMPLES: Francesco B. Salvadori, author; Francisco Franco (1892-1975), Spanish dictator. PLACE-NAME USAGE: San Francisco, California.

Franchot   A French form of Francis. *See* Francis. CONTEMPORARY EXAMPLE: Franchot Tone, actor.

Francis   From the Middle Latin name Franciscus, meaning "a free man." Francis I (1494-1547), king of France, was one of the earliest so named. Frank is a popular pet form. *See* Frank. France took its name from the Franks, a confederacy of German tribes who battled the Romans before settling permanently in Gaul in the fifth century. VARIANT FORMS: Francois, Franchot (French); Franco (German, Spanish, Italian); Franz (German); Francesco (Italian); Francisco (Spanish and Portuguese); Frenz (Dutch); Francie (Scotch); Frans (Swedish); Franck (Polish); Franca (Old English); Fenencz (Hungarian). Frances is a feminine form. *See* Frances (feminine section).

Franciscus   The Middle Latin form of Francis. *See* Francis.

Franco   A German, Spanish, and Italian form of Francis. *See* Francis. CONTEMPORARY EXAMPLE: Franco Harris, football player.

Francois   The French form of Francis. CONTEMPORARY EXAMPLE: Francois Mauriac, author.

Frank   A pet form of Francis. From the Old English name Franca and the Old French name Franc, meaning "a Frank," hence "a free man." *See* Francis.

Frankie   A pet form of Frank. *See* Frank.

Franklin   A Middle English form of the Late Latin name Francus plus the Germanic suffix *ling*, meaning "freeholder." Akin to Francis. *See* Francis. CONTEMPORARY EXAMPLE: Franklin D. Roosevelt (1882-1945), thirty-second president of the U.S. PLACE-NAME USAGE: Franklin, Texas.

Franklyn   A variant spelling of Franklin. *See* Franklin.

Franz   The German form of Francis. *See* Francis. CONTEMPORARY EXAMPLES: Franz Joseph I (1830-1916), emperor of Austria; Franz Kafka (1883-1924), Austrian-Czech author.

Fraser, Frazer, Frazier   An occupational name, from the French *fraisil*, meaning "charcoal cinders," hence "one who makes charcoal." CONTEMPORARY EXAMPLE: Fraser Harrison, author.

Fred, Freddie, Freddy   Pet forms of Frederick. *See* Frederick.

Frederic   A variant spelling of Frederick. *See* Frederick.

Frederick   From the Old High German *fridu*, meaning "peace," plus *rik*, a form of the Latin *rex*, meaning "king, ruler." VARIANT FORMS: Frederic (French); Fridrich, Friedrich, Fritz (German); Federico (Spanish and Italian); Frederik (Dutch and Danish); Fridrich (Russian). VARIANT SPELLINGS: Frederic, Fredric, Frederick. Frederica is a popular feminine form. PET FORMS: Fred, Freddie, Freddy, Fritzi. PLACE-NAME USAGE: Frederick, Maryland; Frederick, Texas.

Freed   A variant form of Frederick. *See* Frederick. Originally used as a surname. CONTEMPORARY EXAMPLE: Freed Hair, Santa Ana, California.

Freeman   From the Anglo-Saxon, meaning "one born free." *See* Francis. CONTEMPORARY EXAMPLE: Freeman McKee, educator.

Fremont   From the French, meaning "freedom mountain." CONTEMPORARY EXAMPLE: Fremont Kast, management consultant. SURNAME USAGE: John Charles Fremont (1813-1890), U.S. explorer. PLACE-NAME USAGE: city on San Francisco Bay.

Frenchy   A nickname for Americans of French origin. PLACE-NAME USAGE: a creek in Montana.

Friso   Probably a short form of Francisco. *See* Francisco. CONTEMPORARY EXAMPLE: Friso Henstra, illustrator.

Frits   A variant spelling of Fritz. *See* Fritz. CONTEMPORARY EXAMPLE: Frits Stall, author.

Fritz   A German variant form of Frederick. *See* Frederick. CONTEMPORARY EXAMPLE: Fritz Wunderlich, opera singer.

Froilan   Orgin uncertain. Probably akin to the French surnames Froysell and Froissart, meaning "free." CONTEMPORARY EXAMPLE: Froilan Fernandel, baseball player.

Fry, Frye   From the Middle English *frie* and the Old Norse *frjo*, meaning "a seed, an offspring." CONTEMPORARY EXAMPLE: Frye Gaillard, editor. SURNAME USAGE: Christopher Fry, English playwright; David Frye, comedian.

Fulbert   From the Old German name Filibert, compounded of *filu*, meaning "much," and *berhta*, meaning "bright." VARIANT FORMS: Fulbright, Philbert.

Fulbright   A variant English form of Fulbert. *See* Fulbert. SURNAME USAGE: J.W. Fulbright, U.S. senator.

Fulk, Fulke   From the Old German name Fulco, derived from *volk*, meaning "folk, people." SURNAME USAGE: Fawke, Fowke, Fulk.

Fuller   From the Old English *fullere*, meaning "a person whose job it is to full (shrink and thicken) cloth." A popular occupational surname. CONTEMPORARY EXAMPLE: Fuller Thompson, baseball player.

Fulton   From the Anglo-Saxon, meaning "a field near the town."

CONTEMPORARY EXAMPLE: Fulton J. Sheen, Catholic bishop. SURNAME USAGE: Eileen Fulton, actress. PLACE-NAME USAGE: Fulton, Missouri.

Furman   A variant spelling of Fermin. *See* Fermin. CONTEMPORARY EXAMPLE: Furman Owens, baseball player. PLACE-NAME USAGE: Furman, South Carolina, named for Lizzie Furman, a local resident (1901).

Fuzzy   A variant form of the Dutch *voos*, meaning "spongy, covered with down." CONTEMPORARY EXAMPLE: Fuzzy Zoeller, golfer.

G

Gab A pet form of Gabriel. *See* Gabriel.

Gabbo From the Old Norse *gabba*, meaning "to mock." CONTEMPORARY EXAMPLE: Gabbo Garvic, soccer player.

Gabby A pet form of Gabriel. *See* Gabriel. CONTEMPORARY EXAMPLE: Gabby Hartnett, baseball player.

Gabe A pet form of Gabriel. *See* Gabriel. CONTEMPORARY EXAMPLE: Gabe Pressman, television news reporter.

Gabi A pet form of Gabriel. Gabby is a variant spelling. *See* Gabriel.

Gabriel From the Hebrew, meaning "God is my strength." In the Bible, the angel seen by Daniel in a vision. VARIANT FORMS: Gabriello (Italian); Gavrila (Russian); Gabryel (Polish); Gabor (Hungarian). PET FORMS: Gab, Gabe, Gabi, Gabby.

Gad From the Hebrew and Arabic, meaning either "happy, fortunate." or "a warrior." Akin to the British *cyd*, meaning "a battle." In the Bible, one of the twelve sons of Jacob.

Gadi A variant form of Gad. *See* Gad. In the Bible, a member of the tribe of Manasseh.

Gadiel From the Hebrew, meaning "God is my fortune, my blessing." A variant form of Gad. *See* Gad. In the Bible, a member of the tribe of Zebulun.

Gael The name by which Celtics of Scotland, Ireland, and the Isle of Man were called. CONTEMPORARY EXAMPLE: Gael D. Swing, educator.

Gaeton From the Old English *gaet*, meaning "a goat," hence "goat town." CONTEMPORARY EXAMPLE: Gaeton Picon, art critic.

Gage From the Middle English and Old French, meaning "a pledge, a pawn."

Gail A pet form of Gaylord. *See* Gaylord. Also, a diminutive form of the feminine Abigail. *See* Abigail (feminine section). CONTEMPORARY EXAMPLE: Gail Henley, baseball player.

Gaines From the Middle English and French, meaning "to increase in wealth." Or, from the British *genau*, meaning "the mouth or opening of a passage." CONTEMPORARY EXAMPLE: Gaines David, football player. SURNAME USAGE: Thomas Gainsborough (1727-1788), English painter. PLACE-NAME USAGE: Gainesville, Florida.

Gaius From the Latin name Gaius. Used as a first name (praenomen)

111

in Roman times. Akin to Kay. *See* Kay.

Gal   From the Hebrew, meaning "a wave" or "a heap." Used also as a feminine name in Israel.

Galahad   In Arthurian legend, a knight of pure spirit (the son of Lancelot) who was successful in his search for the Holy Grail, hence, "a person pure and noble."

Gale   From the German *gagel*, meaning "a hardy shrub." Or, from the Greek *galee*, meaning "a weasel." Also, a variant spelling of Gail. *See* Gail. CONTEMPORARY EXAMPLE: Gale Sayers, football player. SURNAME USAGE: Zona Gale (1874-1938), American novelist.

Galen   From the Greek, meaning "still, tranquil." Claudius (Galenus) Galen was a second-century A.D. Greek physician and writer. CONTEMPORARY EXAMPLE: Galen Cisco, baseball player.

Gali   From the Hebrew, meaning "my wave." A variant form of Gal. *See* Gal.

Gallagher   From the Celtic, meaning "eager helper." CONTEMPORARY EXAMPLE: Gallagher Crook, Atlanta, Georgia. SURNAME USAGE: Kevin Gallagher, actor.

Galloway   From the Latin *gallus*, meaning "Gaul," a division of the ancient Roman Empire.

Galt   From the British, meaning "a steep, wooded area." CONTEMPORARY EXAMPLE: Galt MacDermott, author. SURNAME USAGE: Sir Francis Galton (1822-1911), English scientist.

Galvan, Galvani, Galvin   From the French and Italian, referring to "electricity produced by chemical action." SURNAME USAGE: Luigi Galvani (1737-1798), Italian physicist.

Galway   From the Old Norse *gol*, meaning "blast of wind." Also, a short form of Galloway. *See* Galloway. CONTEMPORARY EXAMPLE: Galway Kinnell, poet. PLACE-NAME USAGE: a county in Ireland.

Gamal, Gamali   From the Arabic, meaning "a camel." Jammal is a variant form.

Gamaliel   A variant spelling of Gamliel. *See* Gamliel.

Gamel   From the Old Norse *gamal* and the Old English *gamol*, meaning "old." Gemmel is a Scottish form. SURNAME USAGE: Gamble, Gambling, Gamlen, Gamlin.

Gamli   From the Arabic and Hebrew, meaning "my camel." Gamali is a variant spelling. In the Bible, a member of the tribe of Dan.

Gamliel   From the Hebrew, meaning "God is my reward." A biblical name that became popular among the Puritans. The middle name of President Warren Harding. Gamaliel is a variant spelling.

Gamul   A variant form of Gamal. *See* Gamal.

Garabed   From the Anglo-Saxon *gar*, meaning "a spear." Garo is a pet form. CONTEMPORARY EXAMPLE: Garabed (Garo) Yepremian, football player.

Garcia   From the Anglo-Saxon *gar*, meaning "a spear."

Gardell   From Old High German, meaning "a guard, a protector."

Garden, Gardener, Gardiner   From the Danish *gaard*, meaning "an enclosure, a garden." CONTEMPORARY EXAMPLE: Gardiner C. Means, author. SURNAME USAGE: Alexander Garden (1730-1791), American botanist; Samuel Rawson Gardiner (1829-1902), English historian.

Gardnard, Gardner   Variant forms of Gardener. *See* Gardener. CONTEMPORARY EXAMPLES: Gardnard Hamilton, golfer; Gardner Dickinson, golfer. SURNAME USAGE: Herb Gardner, playwright.

Gareth   A variant form of Garth. *See* Garth. In Arthurian legend, one of the knights of the Round Table. A nephew of King Arthur.

Garett   A variant form of Garth. *See* Garth. VARIANT FORMS: Gareth, Garret, Garreth, Garrett. CONTEMPORARY EXAMPLE: Garett Morris, entertainer.

Garfield   From the Old English *gara*, meaning "a promontory." CONTEMPORARY EXAMPLE: Garfield Todd, prime minister of Rhodesia. SURNAME USAGE: James Abram Garfield (1831-1881), twentieth president of the U.S.

Garland   From the Old French and Italian, meaning "a wreath of flowers." CONTEMPORARY EXAMPLE: Garland G. Aaron, Laurel Bay, South Carolina. SURNAME USAGE: Hamlin Garland (1860-1940), American novelist. PLACE-NAME USAGE: Garland, Texas.

Garlon   Probably a variant form of Garland. *See* Garland. CONTEMPORARY EXAMPLE: Garlon Godfrey, educator.

Garner   From the Middle English *gerner* and the Latin *granarium*, meaning "a granary." CONTEMPORARY EXAMPLE: Garner E. Shriver, U.S. congressman. SURNAME USAGE: John Nance Garner, vice-president of the U.S. (1933-1941).

Garnet, Garnett   From the Latin *granatum*, meaning "a grain, a seed," and literally "a pomergranate," whose seed resembles the precious red jewel named garnet. CONTEMPORARY EXAMPLE: Garnett Smith, actor.

Garo   A pet form of Garabed. *See* Garabed. Also, a variant form of Guiraud. PLACE-NAME USAGE: Garo, Colorado, named for Adolph Guiraud (pronounced Garo), town founder (1863).

Garrard   A variant form of the German name Gerhard, akin to the Old French Gerard. *See* Gerard. CONTEMPORARY EXAMPLE: Garrard

Ramsey, football player.

Garret, Garreth, Garrett   From the Old French *garir*, meaning "to watch." Akin to Garth. *See* Garth. Gary is a pet form. CONTEMPORARY EXAMPLES: Garret A. Hobart, vice-president of the U.S. (1896); Garrett Eckbo, architect.

Garrick   From the Anglo-Saxon, meaning "an oak spear." SURNAME USAGE: David Garrick (1717-1779), English actor.

Garrison   From the Old French *garison*, meaning "a garrison, troops stationed at a fort." SURNAME USAGE: William Lloyd Garrison (1805-1879), American editor.

Garson   A short form of Garrison. *See* Garrison. CONTEMPORARY EXAMPLE: Garson Kanin, author. SURNAME USAGE: Greer Garson, actress.

Garth   From the Old Norse *gyrthr*, meaning "an enclosure, a field, a garden." CONTEMPORARY EXAMPLES: Garth Lipsky, city manager; Garth Clark, author. SURNAME USAGE: David Garth, publicist.

Garton   From the Anglo-Saxon, meaning "a town near the field." A variant form of Garth. CONTEMPORARY EXAMPLE: Garton DelSavio, baseball player.

Garvey, Garvie   From the Anglo-Saxon, meaning "a spear-bearer, a warrior." Also, forms of Garth. *See* Garth. CONTEMPORARY EXAMPLE: Garvie Craw, football player. SURNAME USAGE: Steve Garvey, baseball player.

Garvin   From the Anglo-Saxon, meaning "war friend." Akin to Garvey.

Gary, Garry   Variant forms of Garvey. *See* Garvey. Also, a pet form of Garrett. *See* Garrett. CONTEMPORARY EXAMPLE: Gary Cooper, actor. SURNAME USAGE: Harold Gary, actor. PLACE-NAME USAGE: Gary, Indiana, named for E.H. Gary, a prominent attorney of the steel company that founded the city; Gary, New Mexico, named for Garrett L. Thorpe, first businessman in town.

Gascon   From the French, meaning "a person from Gascony," a former province in the southwest of France whose inhabitants were reputed to be "swaggering and boastful."

Gaspar, Gasper   From the Persian, meaning "treasure-holder." In the Bible, one of the three Wise Men. May also be variant spellings of Caspar and Casper. *See* Caspar. COMTEMPORARY EXAMPLE: Gasper Urban, football player.

Gaston   Probably a form of Gascon. *See* Gascon.

Gavan, Gavin   From the Welsh, meaning "little hawk." A popular name in Scotland. May also be a variant form of Gawain. *See* Gawain. CONTEMPORARY EXAMPLES: Gavin MacLeod, actor; Gavin Hewitt, television journalist. SURNAME USAGE: John Gavin, actor. Gavan Daws, author.

Gavvy   A pet form of Gavin. *See* Gavin. CONTEMPORARY EXAMPLE: Gavvy Cravath, baseball player.

Gawain, Gawaine, Gawen   From the Welsh, meaning "courteous." In Arthurian legend, a knight of the Round Table; a nephew of King Arthur. Akin to Gavin.

Gay   From the Old French *gai*, meaning "joyous, merry." CONTEMPORARY EXAMPLE: Gay Brewer, golfer. SURNAME USAGE: John Gay (1685-1732), English poet. PLACE-NAME USAGE: Gay Hill, Texas, named for G.H. Gay and W.C. Hill, town settlers.

Gayelord   A variant spelling of Gaylord. *See* Gaylord. CONTEMPORARY EXAMPLE: Gayelord Hauser, author.

Gaylard   A variant spelling of Gaylord. *See* Gaylord.

Gayle   A pet form of Gaylord. *See* Gaylord. CONTEMPORARY EXAMPLE: Gayle Knief, football player.

Gaylon   A variant form of Galen. *See* Galen. CONTEMPORARY EXAMPLE: Gaylon Smith, football player.

Gaylord   From the Old French *gailard*, meaning "brave." May also be a variant form of Gay. *See* Gay. Gaylard is a variant spelling. Gail is a pet form. CONTEMPORARY EXAMPLE: Gaylord Perry, baseball player.

Gayne   A variant form of Gaines. *See* Gaines.

Gaynell   A pet form of Gayne. *See* Gayne. CONTEMPORARY EXAMPLE: Gaynell Tinsley, football player.

Gaynor   From the Irish, meaning "son of the white-haired man" or "son of the light-complexioned man." CONTEMPORARY EXAMPLE: Gaynor Fitzpatrick, translator.

Gedalia, Gedaliah, Gedaliahu   From the Hebrew, meaning "God is great." In the Bible, the governor of Judea appointed by Nebuchadnezzar.

Gedalio   The Spanish form of Gedalia. *See* Gedalia.

Geddes   From the Anglo-Saxon *gad*, meaning "a javelin, a sharp-pointed stick" used in goading cattle. CONTEMPORARY EXAMPLE: Geddes MacGregor, author. SURNAME USAGE: Norman Bel Geddes (1893-1958), American industrial designer.

Gefania, Gefaniah   From the Hebrew, meaning "vineyard of the Lord." VARIANT SPELLINGS: Gephania, Gephaniah.

Gehan   A variant form of John. *See* John. CONTEMPORARY EXAMPLE: Gehan Mendis, cricket player.

Gemmel   A Scottish form of Gamel. *See* Gamel.

Gene   A pet form of Eugene. *See* Eugene.

Gennaro   An Italian form of John. *See* John. Gino is a pet form. SUR-
NAME USAGE: Peter Gennaro, choreographer.

Geno   An Italian and Greek form of John. *See* John. CONTEMPORARY
EXAMPLE: Geno Silva, actor.

Gentile   From the Latin *gentilis*, meaning "of the same gens, clan, or
race; a foreigner." CONTEMPORARY EXAMPLE: Gentile Bellini
(1429-1507), Italian painter. PLACE-NAME USAGE: Gentile Spring,
Arizona.

Geoff   A pet form of Geoffrey. *See* Geoffrey. CONTEMPORARY EXAM-
PLE: Geoff Edwards, entertainer.

Geoffrey   From the Anglo-Saxon, meaning "gift of peace." VARIANT
FORMS: Jeffery, Jeffrey. PET FORMS: Geoff, Jeff. SURNAME USAGE: Jefferies, Jefferson, Jephson, Jepson.

Geordie   A variant Scottish form of George. *See* George.

George   From the Greek, meaning "a farmer" or "a tiller of the soil."
George I (1660-1727), was king of England; George Washington
(1732-1797), was the first president of the U.S. VARIANT FORMS: Georgius
(Latin); Georgy (English); Geordie (Scotch); Jerzy (Polish); Egor, Yuri
(Russian); Georgius (Dutch); Georges (French); Georg (German),
Georgio (Italian); Jorge (Spanish); Jorge (Portuguese); Georg, Jorgen
(Danish); Jiri, Jurg (Slavonic); Seiorse (Irish). FEMININE FORMS: Georgia,
Georgiana, Georgine. Georgie is a pet form. SURNAME USAGE: Henry
George (1839-1897), American political economist. PLACE-NAME USAGE:
Georgia, a U.S. southern state named after King George of England:
Georgetown, a seaport in Malaya, and cities and counties in various U.S.
states.

Gephania, Gephaniah   Variant forms of Gefania and Gefaniah. *See*
Gefania.

Gerald   An Old French and Old High German form of Gerard. *See*
Gerard.

Geraldo   A Spanish form of Gerald. *See* Gerald. CONTEMPORARY EX-
AMPLE: Geraldo Rivera, television news reporter.

Gerard   A variant form of the Old French *gerart*. Akin to the Old
High German name Gerhart. From *ger*, meaning "spear," implying "a
warrior." VARIANT FORMS: Gerald, Garret, Jarett, Jarrett (English);
Geraud (French); Gerardo (Spanish and Italian); Gerhard (German);
Gerrit (Dutch). SURNAME USAGE: Garrard, Garrett, Garrod, Jerrard.

Gerardo   A Spanish form of Gerard. *See* Gerard. CONTEMPORARY EX-
AMPLE: Gerardo Joffe, author.

Gerbert   From the Old German, meaning "bright spear."

Gerbold   From the Old German, meaning "bold spear."

Gerhard, Gerhardt, Gerhart Variant forms of Gerard. *See* Gerard. SURNAME USAGE: Werner Gerhard, developer of EST.

Geritt A variant form of Garret. *See* Garret. CONTEMPORARY EXAMPLE: Geritt Graham, actor.

Germain The Middle English form of the Latin *germanus*, meaning "a sprout, a bud." The name of two saints.

German From the Latin name Germanus, meaning "a German." VARIANT FORMS: Germain, Jarman, Jermyn.

Germany Derived from the name of the country in Central Europe. Germain is a variant form. *See* Germain. CONTEMPORARY EXAMPLE: Germany Smith, baseball player.

Gerome From the Greek, meaning "of holy fame" or "sacred name." Jerome is a variant spelling. CONTEMPORARY EXAMPLE: Gerome Ragni, lyricist.

Geronimo A Spanish form of Gerome. *See* Gerome. PLACE-NAME USAGE: San Geronimo, California; Mount Geronimo, Arizona.

Gerrett A variant spelling of Garrett. *See* Garrett. CONTEMPORARY EXAMPLE: Gerrett Stires, baseball player.

Gerry A pet form of Gerome. *See* Gerome.

Gershom, Gershon From the Hebrew, meaning "stranger." In the Bible, Gershom was a son of Moses, and Gershon was a son of Levi. The names are often used interchangeably. Gerson is a variant form. CONTEMPORARY EXAMPLES: Gershon Scholem, author; Gershon Chertoff, clergyman.

Gerson A variant spelling of Gershon. *See* Gershon. CONTEMPORARY EXAMPLE: Gerson D. Cohen, clergyman.

Gervais, Gervase From the Old German *ger*, meaning "spear." Akin to Garvey. *See* Garvey.

Gervis A variant form of Gervais. *See* Gervais. Akin to Jarvis. *See* Jarvis.

Geva From the Hebrew, meaning "a hill." In the Bible, the name of a place.

Giacomo An Italian form of Jacob. *See* Jacob. CONTEMPORARY EXAMPLE: Giacomo Patri, author.

Gian–Carlo An Italian form combining John and Charles. Giancarlo is a variant spelling. *See* John *and* Charles. CONTEMPORARY EXAMPLE: Gian–Carlo Menotti, composer.

Gib A pet form of Gilbert. *See* Gilbert.

Gibby A pet form of Gilbert. *See* Gilbert. CONTEMPORARY EXAMPLE: Gibby Gilbert, golfer.

Gibor   From the Hebrew, meaning "strong."

Gibson   A patronymic, meaning "son of Gib (Gilbert)."

Gideon   From the Hebrew, meaning either "maimed" or "a mighty warrior." In the Bible, one of the Judges of Israel, the warrior–hero who defeated the Midianites. CONTEMPORARY EXAMPLE: Gideon Hausner, attorney.

Gidi   A pet form of Gideon. *See* Gideon.

Gifford   A variant spelling of the Middle English name Gifford, akin to the Old High German name Gebahard, meaning "to give," plus "hard, bold," hence "a worthy gift." Also, a variant form of Gilford. *See* Gilford. SURNAME USAGE: Frank Gifford, sportscaster.

Gig   From the Middle English, meaning "a horse–drawn carriage." CONTEMPORARY EXAMPLE: Gig Young, actor.

Gil   From the Hebrew, meaning "joy." Used also as a feminine name in Israel. Also, a pet form of Gilbert. *See* Gilbert.

Gilad   A variant form of Gilead. *See* Gilead. CONTEMPORARY EXAMPLE: Gilad Weingarten, Israeli sportsman.

Giladi   From the Hebrew, meaning "a man from Gilead." *See* Gilead.

Gilbert   From the Old High German name Willibehrt, meaning "to will, to desire," plus "bright" (*behrt*), hence "the will to be bright (famous)." VARIANT FORMS: Gibbon, Wilbert, Wilbur (English); Gilberto (Italian); Guilbert (French); Gilli (Flemish). PET FORMS: Gil, Gipp. PLACE-NAME USAGE: Gilbert Islands in the Pacific Ocean. SURNAME USAGE: Cass Gilbert (1859-1934), American architect; also Gibbon, Gibbs, Gibson, Gilbertson.

Gilchrist   From the Gaelic, meaning "servant of Christ."

Gilder   An Anglo-Saxon name, meaning "one who gilds." An occupational name.

Gilead   From the Arabic, meaning "hump of a camel." In the Bible, a mountainous area east of the Jordan River.

Gilean, Gileon   Short forms of Galilean, meaning "a man from Galilee." CONTEMPORARY EXAMPLES: Gilean Douglas, author; Gileon Holroyd, editor.

Giles   From the Greek *aegis*, meaning "goatskin," hence "a shield that protects." In Greek mythology, a shield or breastplate used by Zeus, and later by his daughter Athena, and occasionally by Apollo. A seventh–century saint. VARIANT FORMS: Gil, Gilean, Gileon, Gilles, Gillette. Gide is a variant French form. CONTEMPORARY EXAMPLE: Giles St. Aubyn, author. SURNAME USAGE: Bill Giles, choreographer; William Gillette (1855–1937), American actor; also Gile, Gilles.

Gilford   From the Old English, meaning "a ford near the wooded ravine." VARIANT FORMS: Gifford, Gilmore, Gilroy. CONTEMPORARY EXAMPLE: Gilford Duggan, football player.

Gili   From the Hebrew, meaning "my joy." Akin to Gil.

Gill, Gilli   Variant spellings of Gil and Gili. *See* Gil *and* Gili.

Gilles   A variant spelling of Giles. *See* Giles. CONTEMPORARY EXAMPLE: Gilles Zuispel, historian.

Gillian   A variant form of Giles. *See* Giles. CONTEMPORARY EXAMPLE: Gillian Martin, author.

Gilmore   From the Celtic, meaning "the glen near the sea." CONTEMPORARY EXAMPLES: Gilmore B. Seavers, educator; Gary Gilmore, mass murderer.

Gilroy   From the Latin, meaning "the king's faithful servant." Also, from the Old Norse *gil*, meaning "a glen, a wooded ravine," plus the Gaelic *rhu*, meaning "red," hence "a ravine with a reddish hue." SURNAME USAGE: Frank D. Gilroy, playwright.

Gino   The Italian pet form of John. *See* John. Akin to Gennaro. CONTEMPORARY EXAMPLE: Gino Cappalletti, football player.

Ginson, Ginton   From the Hebrew, meaning "a garden, orchard," In the Bible, the name of a priest who returned to Palestine after the Babylonian Exile. Ginton is the Israeli pronunciation of Ginson.

Giora   From the Aramaic, meaning "convert." Simon bar Giora was a first–century A.D. leader in the Jewish war against Rome. CONTEMPORARY EXAMPLE: Giora Ilany, zoologist.

Giorgio   The Italian form of George. *See* George. CONTEMPORARY EXAMPLE: Giorgio de Chirico, painter.

Girard   A variant spelling of Gerard. *See* Gerard.

Girault, Giraut   A French form of Gerald. *See* Gerald. VARIANT FORMS: Giralt (French); Gerwald (German). CONTEMPORARY EXAMPLE: Girault M. Jones, clergyman.

Giscard   A variant form of Guiscard. *See* Guiscard. CONTEMPORARY EXAMPLE: Valery Giscard d'Estaing, prime minister of France.

Gitai, Giti   From the Hebrew, meaning "one who presses grapes." Popular names in Israel.

Givon   From the Hebrew, meaning "hill, heights." A variant form of the biblical place-name Gibeon.

Glade   From the Anglo-Saxon *gladian*, meaning "to be glad" and "to bring light." Akin to the French *clairiere* (*clair*), meaning "a clearing in the woods." Also, a variant form of Claude. *See* Claude.

Gladstone A form of Glade, meaning "the town near the clearing in the woods." *See* Glade.

Glat A Scottish spelling of Glade. *See* Glade.

Glen, Glenn From the Celtic, meaning "a glen, a dale; a secluded, woody valley." Akin to the Welsh name Glyn. Was popularized by the writings of Sir Walter Scott in the nineteenth century. SURNAME USAGE: John Glenn, astronaut and U.S. senator. PLACE-NAME USAGE: Glen Cove, New York; Glendale, California.

Glenard Variant spelling of Glennard. *See* Glennard. CONTEMPORARY EXAMPLE: Glenard P. Lipscomb, congressman.

Glennard A variant form of Glen. *See* Glen.

Glennon A variant form of Glen. *See* Glen. CONTEMPORARY EXAMPLE: Glennon P. Flavin, clergyman.

Gloster A short form of the place-name Gloucester, a city in England. CONTEMPORARY EXAMPLE: Gloster Richardson, football player.

Glover From the Middle English *glofe*, meaning "glove, paw." SURNAME USAGE: John Glover, actor. PLACE-NAME USAGE: Gloversville, New York.

Glyn, Glynn Welsh forms of Glen. *See* Glen. CONTEMPORARY EXAMPLE: Glynn Turman, actor.

Goddard From the Old English, meaning "good in counsel."

Godfrey From the Old German name Godafrid, meaning "God's peace." Gottfried is a variant form. VARIANT FORMS: Geoffrey, Jeffrey (English); Giotto (Italian); Godofredo (Spanish); Gottfried, Gotz (German); Govert (Dutch). CONTEMPORARY EXAMPLE: Godfrey Cambridge, entertainer. SURNAME USAGE: Arthur Godfrey, entertainer.

Godric From the Old English, compounded of God and *ric*, meaning "ruler," hence "God Almighty." The Normans used it as a nickname for King Henry I and his queen Godiva. SURNAME USAGE: Godrich, Goodrich, Goodrick, Goodridge.

Godwin From the Anglo-Saxon, meaning "friend of God." CONTEMPORARY EXAMPLE: Godwin Tasie, author. SURNAME USAGE: Godin, Goding, Goddard, Godden, Godding, Godden, Goodwin.

Goel From the Hebrew, meaning "the redeemer."

Gold From the Old English, meaning "to shine," hence "yellow."

Golden A variant form of Gold. *See* Gold. CONTEMPORARY EXAMPLE: Golden Richards, football player.

Goldman An occupational name for a person dealing in gold. *See* Gold.

Goldsmith An occupational name for an artisan who fabricates ornaments of gold. Akin to Goldman. *See* Gold. SURNAME USAGE: Oliver Goldsmith (1728-1774), British poet.

Goldwin, Goldwyn From the Anglo-Saxon, meaning "a lover of gold." SURNAME USAGE: Samuel Goldwyn, movie producer; also Goulden, Goulding.

Goliath From the Hebrew, meaning "one who was exiled; a stranger." In the Bible, the Philistine giant killed by David with a slingshot.

Gomer From the Hebrew, meaning "to end, to complete." In the Bible, the son of Japhet. Also, a feminine name in the Bible: the wife of the prophet Hosea. CONTEMPORARY EXAMPLE: Gomer Jones, football coach. PLACE-NAME USAGE: Gomer, Ohio.

Gonzales A variant form of Gonzalo. *See* Gonzalo. CONTEMPORARY EXAMPLE: Gonzales Morales, football player. SURNAME USAGE: Poncho Gonzales, tennis player.

Gonzalo A Spanish form of the Anglo-Saxon name Gundulf, meaning "wolf." VARIANT FORMS: Gonslave, Gonzalve (French); Goncalo (Portuguese); Consalvo (Italian). CONTEMPORARY EXAMPLE: Gonzalo Marquez, baseball player.

Goodman From the Anglo-Saxon, meaning "the good man" or "the good servant." CONTEMPORARY EXAMPLE: Goodman Ace, actor.

Goodwin From the Anglo-Saxon, meaning "good, faithful friend." Godwin is a variant form.

Goran From the British *gor*, meaning "a choir" or "a cathedral." Also, from an Indo-European root, meaning "a javelin" or "a whip." CONTEMPORARY EXAMPLE: Goran Hogosta, hockey player.

Gordie A pet form of Gordius. *See* Gordius. CONTEMPORARY EXAMPLE: Gordie Clark, hockey player.

Gordius In Greek legend, King Gordius of Phrygia tied a knot which could be undone only by the future master of Asia. Alexander the Great, unable to untie the knot, slashed it with his sword. Hence the meaning, "a bold, quick solution to a problem."

Gordon From the Old English *gor* and *denn*, meaning "a dung pasture." May also be a form of Gordius, meaning "bold." *See* Gordius. May also be a variant form of Gorton. *See* Gorton. SURNAME USAGE: Charles George Gordon (1833-1885), British general. PLACE-NAME USAGE: a town in England.

Gore A short form of either Goran or Gordon. *See* Goran *and* Gordon. CONTEMPORARY EXAMPLE: Gore Vidal, author.

Gorham From the Old English, meaning "a hamlet built on or near the dung pasture." CONTEMPORARY EXAMPLE: Gorham Getchell, football player.

Gorrell   From the British, meaning "a thicket of trees in a marsh." Gorllyn is the original form. CONTEMPORARY EXAMPLE: Gorrell Stinson, baseball player.

Gorton   From the British, meaning "the town on (or near) the marsh." May also be a variant spelling of Gordon. *See* Gordon. CONTEMPORARY EXAMPLE: Gorton Riethmiller, educator.

Gottfried   From the German, meaning "peace of God." Godfrey is a variant form.

Gouverneur   From the Latin, meaning "to steer, to govern." Guv is a pet form.

Gover   From the Hebrew, meaning "victorious." Also, an Anglo-Saxon occupational name, meaning "one who stores corn in a barn."

Gowell   From the Old Norse *goll*, meaning "gold." A small yellow flower in the daisy family. CONTEMPORARY EXAMPLE: Gowell Claset, baseball player.

Gower   Origin uncertain. Possibly a form of Gowell. *See* Gowell. Or, from the British, meaning "crooked" (usually with reference to a coastline). May also be a form of the Anglo-Saxon name Godhere or from the Old French *goherier*, meaning "a harness maker." CONTEMPORARY EXAMPLE: Gower Champion, choreographer. SURNAME USAGE: John Gower (1325-1408), English poet.

Gozal   From the Hebrew, meaning "a young bird."

Grady   From the Latin *gradus*, meaning "a grade, a rank." CONTEMPORARY EXAMPLE: Grady Wilson, football player.

Graeme   A variant form of Gram. *See* Gram. Or, a form of Graenum. *See* Graenum. CONTEMPORARY EXAMPLE: Graeme Clark, jockey.

Graemer   Probably a corrupt form of Kramer. *See* Kramer. Or, a variant form of Graenum. *See* Graenum. CONTEMPORARY EXAMPLE: Graemer K. Hilton, industrialist.

Graenem, Graenum   From the Greek *grais*, meaning "old." Akin to Graham. CONTEMPORARY EXAMPLE: Graenem Berger, author.

Graham   From the Anglo-Saxon, meaning "the gray home." Also, akin to Gram. *See* Gram. Sylvester Graham (1794–1851), was a U.S. dietary reformer for whom the graham cracker was named. CONTEMPORARY EXAMPLE: Graham Kerr, gourmet cook. SURNAME USAGE: Martha Graham, dancer. PLACE-NAME USAGE: a city in England.

Graig   A variant spelling of Craig. *See* Craig. CONTEMPORARY EXAMPLE: Graig Nettles, baseball player.

Graily   From the Middle English *groal*, meaning "a flat dish." In medieval legend, the cup or platter used by Jesus at the Last Supper. CONTEMPORARY EXAMPLE: Graily Hewitt, calligrapher.

Gram   From the Latin *granum*, meaning "a grain." CONTEMPORARY EXAMPLE: Gram Parsons, rock musician.

Granger   From the Old French, meaning "a farm steward." CONTEMPORARY EXAMPLE: Granger E. Westberg, author.

Grant   From the Middle English and Old French, meaning "to give, to assure." CONTEMPORARY EXAMPLE: Grant Tinker, television producer. SURNAME USAGE: Ulysses S. Grant (Hiram Ulysses Grant) (1822-1885), eighteenth president of the U.S. PLACE-NAME USAGE: Grants Pass, Oregon; Grantsville, Utah; Grant Town, West Virginia.

Grantland   From the Old English, meaning "deeded land." CONTEMPORARY EXAMPLE: Grantland Rice, sportscaster.

Grantley   A variant form of Grantland. *See* Grantland.

Granville, Grenville   From the French, meaning "the big town." CONTEMPORARY EXAMPLE: Granville Hammer, baseball player. SURNAME USAGE: Harley Granville–Barker (1877-1946), English playwright. PLACE-NAME USAGE: cities in Maine and Pennsylvania, named for John Carteret (1690-1763), Earl of Granville.

Gray   From the Old English *graeg*, meaning "to shine." Also a color. VARIANT FORMS: Craig, Graig. CONTEMPORARY EXAMPLE: Gray Temple, clergyman. SURNAME USAGE: Asa Gray (1810-1880), American botanist.

Graydon   From the Anglo-Saxon, meaning "the gray town." *See* Gray. Graham is a variant form. CONTEMPORARY EXAMPLE: Graydon V. Olive, Jr., city manager.

Grayson   From the Anglo-Saxon, meaning "the son of a *greve* (an earl)." Or, a patronymic form of Gray. *See* Gray. CONTEMPORARY EXAMPLE: Grayson Pearce, baseball player.

Greco   From the Greek, meaning "the Greek." CONTEMPORARY EXAMPLE: El Greco, a Spanish and Italian painter of Greek origin.

Greeley, Greely   Abbreviated forms of the Anglo-Saxon *green-lea*, meaning "green, luxurious meadow." SURNAME USAGE: Horace Greeley (1811-1872), American journalist. PLACE-NAME USAGE: a city in Colorado.

Greg   From the Anglo-Saxon *graeg*, meaning "to shine." Also a pet form of Gregory. *See* Gregory.

Gregor   The German and Scandinavian form of Gregory. *See* Gregory.

Gregory   From the Greek, meaning "vigilant," hence "watchman." VARIANT FORMS: Gregorius (Latin); Gregoire (French); Gregor, Gregus (German and Scandinavian); Gregorio (Italian and Spanish); Gregos, Gregus (Danish); Greis (Swedish); Grischa (Russian); Gero (Hungarian). Greg is a pet form. Popularized by Pope Gregory I (the Great) (590-604), the first of sixteen popes named Gregory. SURNAME USAGE: Greig, Greg, Gregg, Gregson, Grig, Grigg, Grigson, McGregor.

Gridley   From the Anglo-Saxon, meaning "a flat meadow."

Griffin   A mythological animal with the body and hind legs of a lion, and the head and wings of an eagle. Griffin is a variant form. CONTEMPORARY EXAMPLE: Griffin Bell, a U.S. attorney general. SURNAME USAGE: Merv Griffin, entertainer.

Griffith   From the Welsh name Gruffydd, a variant form of Griffin. *See* Griffin. SURNAME USAGE: Andy Griffith, actor.

Grimbald   From the Old English *grimm*, meaning "fierce," and *beald*, meaning "bold." VARIANT FORMS: Grimbel, Grimbold. SURNAME USAGE: Grimble, Grimbly.

Grimsley   From the Anglo-Saxon, meaning "green meadow." Greeley is a variant form. CONTEMPORARY EXAMPLE: Grimsley T. Hobbs, educator.

Griswald   Compounded from the French *gris*, meaning "gray," and the German *wald*, meaning "forest."

Grosvenor   Origin uncertain. Possibly associated with the grouse, any of a number of game birds. CONTEMPORARY EXAMPLE: Grosvenor W. Cooper, musicologist.

Groucho   A nickname made popular by comedian Groucho Marx. Usually, conferred upon a person who grumbles or sulks.

Grove   From the Old English *graf*, meaning "a thicket, a group of cultivated trees." PLACE-NAME USAGE: Grove City, Pennsylvania.

Grover   From the Anglo-Saxon, meaning "one who grows or tends to trees." CONTEMPORARY EXAMPLE: (Stephen) Grover Cleveland (1837-1908), twenty-second and twenty–fourth president of the U.S.

Guerrant   From the Italian *guerra*, meaning "war." CONTEMPORARY EXAMPLE: Guerrant Scarce, baseball player.

Guido   From the Italian *guidare*, meaning "guide." CONTEMPORARY EXAMPLE: Guido Calabresi, lawyer.

Guillermo   The Spanish form of William. *See* William. CONTEMPORARY EXAMPLE: Guillermo Montanez, baseball player.

Guiscard   From the Old French *guise* and the Old High German *wisa*, meaning "a way, a manner of behavior." *See also* Giscard.

Guni   From the Arabic and Hebrew, meaning "reddish–black." In the Bible, a member of the tribe of Gad.

Gunn   From the Middle English and Old Norse, meaning "war." CONTEMPORARY EXAMPLE: Gunn McKay, U.S. congressman.

Gunnar   From the Old Norse *gunnarr*, meaning "war." In Norse legend, the brother of Gudrun and the husband of Brynhild. A popular name in Scandinavian countries.

Gunter A variant spelling of Gunther. *See* Gunther. CONTEMPORARY EXAMPLE: Gunter Grass, novelist. PLACE-NAME USAGE: Guntersville, Alabama, named for John Gunter, an early settler (1848).

Gunther From the Old German *gundi*, meaning "war." In the *Nibelungenlied*, a king of Burgundy. VARIANT FORMS: Gunn, Gunnar, Gunter. CONTEMPORARY EXAMPLE: Gunther Schuller, composer. SURNAME USAGE: John Gunther, author.

Guntur A variant spelling of Gunther. *See* Gunther. PLACE-NAME USAGE: a city in India.

Gur From the Hebrew, meaning "a young lion." In the Bible, a name by which Judah, son of Jacob, was called. Gurion is a variant form.

Gurdon From the Middle English *crud*, meaning "to curdle, to coagulate (as with milk)," hence "to crowd." CONTEMPORARY EXAMPLE: Gurdon Whitely, baseball player.

Guri From the Hebrew, meaning "my young lion." VARIANT FORMS: Gur, Gurion.

Guriel From the Hebrew, meaning "God is my lion," hence "protected by God."

Gurion From the Hebrew *gur*, meaning "a lion," hence "strong." David Ben-Gurion (1886-1973), Israeli statesman, originally David Gruen, assumed this name after settling in Palestine. VARIANT FORMS: Gur, Guri, Guriel.

Gurney From the Old French *gornart* and the Latin *grunnire*, meaning "to grunt." VARIANT FORMS: Gourney, Gornus. CONTEMPORARY EXAMPLE: Gurney York, horseshoe champion.

Gus A pet form of Gustave. *See* Gustave.

Gustaf The Swedish form of Gustavus. *See* Gustavus.

Gustav The German form of Gustavus. *See* Gustavus.

Gustave The French form of Gustavus. *See* Gustavus.

Gustavo The Italian and Spanish form of Gustavus. *See* Gustavus. CONTEMPORARY EXAMPLE: Gustavo Gutierrez, theologian.

Gustavus From the German and Swedish, meaning "the staff of the Goths." VARIANT FORMS: Gustaf (Swedish); Gustav (German); Gustave (French); Gustavo (Italian and Spanish). Gustavus I was king of Sweden from 1523-1560. Gus is a pet form.

Guthrie From the Celtic, meaning "war serpent" or "war hero." CONTEMPORARY EXAMPLE: Guthrie L. Dowler, Escondido, California. SURNAME USAGE: Arlo Guthrie, singer.

Guy From the Old French, meaning "a guide" or "a rope that guides." Also, from the Hebrew, meaning "valley." CONTEMPORARY

EXAMPLES: Guy Friddell, journalist; Guy Kibee, actor.

Gwyn, Gwynne   From the Welsh, meaning "fair, white." Used also as a feminine name. CONTEMPORARY EXAMPLES: Gwyn Richards, cricket player; Gwynne Vevers, Zoo curator. SURNAME USAGE: Fred Gwynne, actor.

Gyles   A variant spelling of Giles. *See* Giles. CONTEMPORARY EXAMPLE: Gyles Brandreth, author.

H

Haakon, Hacon   From the Old Norse name Hakon and Haakon, derived from *hag*, meaning "useful, handy." CONTEMPORARY EXAMPLE: Haakon VII, king of Norway (1905-1957). Hacon is a variant spelling.

Habakkuk   From the Hebrew, meaning "to embrace." In the Bible, a seventh-century B.C. prophet. The Latin spelling is Habacuc.

Hadar   From the Hebrew, meaning "adornment, glory." In the Bible, a king of Edom.

Hadden, Haddon   From the Old English, meaning "a heath, a wasteland." CONTEMPORARY EXAMPLE: Haddon W. Robinson, author.

Hadlai   A variant form of Hadley. *See* Hadley. Also, a variant form of Adlai. *See* Adlai. CONTEMPORARY EXAMPLE: Hadlai A. Hull, administrator.

Hadley   From the Old English, meaning "the meadow near the wasteland (heath)." CONTEMPORARY EXAMPLE: Hadley S. DePuy, educator.

Hadrian   From the Greek, meaning "rich." A Roman emperor (117-138). Adrian is a variant form. *See* Adrian.

Hafey   Origin unknown. CONTEMPORARY EXAMPLE: Hafey Clyde Jones, theologian.

Hagan, Hagen   Variant forms of Haven. *See* Haven. PLACE-NAME USAGE: Copenhagen, Denmark.

Hagood   From the Old English *haga*, meaning "a hedge." Or, from the Middle English *hagas*, meaning "a pudding." CONTEMPORARY EXAMPLE: Hagood Clarke, football player.

Haida   From the name of a tribe of Indians living in British Columbia and Alaska, meaning "people."

Haim   A variant form of Chaim, meaning "life." *See* Chaim.

Haimes   A variant spelling of Hames. *See* Hames.

Haines   A variant form of the German name Johannes, a form of John. *See* John. Also, from the Anglo-Saxon, meaning "a hedge, an enclosure."

Hakon   A variant spelling of Haakon. *See* Haakon.

Hal   A pet form of Harold or Haley. *See* Harold *and* Haley. CONTEMPORARY EXAMPLE: Hal Holbrook, actor.

Haldon   From the Old English, meaning "Hal's (Harold's) town." *See*

127

Hale. CONTEMPORARY EXAMPLE: Haldon A. Leedy, editor.

Hale   From the Old English *hal*, meaning "healthy, whole." Also, from the Hawaiian, meaning "a house, a building." CONTEMPORARY EXAMPLE: Hale Johnson, vice-presidential candidate (1896). SURNAME USAGE: Nathan Hale (1775-1776), American soldier.

Haley, Halley   Variant forms of Hale. *See* Hale. SURNAME USAGE: Jack Haley, actor.

Halford   From the Old English, meaning "Hal's (Harold's) ford (river crossing)." CONTEMPORARY EXAMPLE: Halford E. Luccock, author.

Halil, Hallil   From the Hebrew, meaning "a flute."

Hall   From the Middle English *halle* and the Old English *heall*, meaning "to cover, conceal." Originally, the great room of the king or leader. CONTEMPORARY EXAMPLE: Hall Whitley, football player. SURNAME USAGE: Charles Martin Hall (1863-1914), American chemist.

Hallberg   A compounded name, from the Old English *heall*, meaning "hall" or "that which is covered," and the German *berg*, meaning "mountain," hence "a snow capped mountain." CONTEMPORARY EXAMPLE: Hallberg Hallmundsson, translator.

Halley   A variant spelling of Haley. *See* Haley. Also, a form of Hall. SURNAME USAGE: Edmund Halley (1656-1742), English astronomer.

Hallie   A variant spelling of Halley. *See* Halley. CONTEMPORARY EXAMPLE: Hallie G. Grantz, educator.

Halsey, Halsy   From the Anglo-Saxon, meaning "from Hal's Island." Halsy is a variant spelling.

Ham   From the Hebrew, meaning "warm, swarthy." In the Bible, Noah's second son. Also used as a pet form of Hamilton. SURNAME USAGE: Mordecai Ham, evangelist.

Haman   Probably from the Persian, meaning "to rage, to be turbulent." In the Bible, the wicked prime minister of King Ahasueros who sought the destruction of the Jewish people.

Hames   From the Old Norse and Scottish *hame*, meaning "home." Haimes is a variant spelling. Hamlet is a variant form. CONTEMPORARY EXAMPLE: Hames Rosenzweig, executive.

Hamilton   A variant form of Hamlet and Hamlin. *See* Hamlet *and* Hamlin. CONTEMPORARY EXAMPLE: Hamilton Jordan, U.S. presidential aide. SURNAME USAGE: Alexander Hamilton (1757-1804), American statesman. PLACE-NAME USAGE: cities in Ohio, New Zealand, and Scotland.

Hamish   A variant form of the Gaelic name Seumas, a form of James. *See* James. Also, from the Scottish *hame*, meaning "home." Akin to Hames. A name popularized in the novels of William Block (1841-1898). CONTEMPO-

RARY EXAMPLE: Hamish Swanston, author. PLACE-NAME USAGE: Hamelin (Hameln) a city in Northwest Germany.

Hamlet   From the Low German *hamm*, meaning "an enclosed area." Also, from the Old German *haimi*, meaning "a home." Akin to Hames. *See* Hames. Let is the pet form. A Danish prince in Shakespear's play *Hamlet*.

Hamlin   From the Old English, meaning "the brook near the home." CONTEMPORARY EXAMPLE: Hamlin Garland, Pulitzer Prize winner in letters (1922). SURNAME USAGE: Hannibal Hamlin (1809-1891), President Lincoln's first vice-president.

Hammond   From the Old English, meaning "a home" or "a village." Akin to Hamlet. CONTEMPORARY EXAMPLE: Hammond Edward Fisher, cartoonist. PLACE-NAME USAGE: Hammond, Indiana, named for G.H. Hammond, local meat packer.

Hamo   A variant form of Hamon. *See* Hamon. Sir Hamo Thornycroft (1850-1925), English sculptor.

Hamon   From the Old German name Haimo, derived from *haimi*, meaning "home, house." Akin to Hamlet. *See* Hamlet.

Hampden   From the Old English, meaning "the home in the valley." SURNAME USAGE: Walter Hampden (1879-1955), actor.

Hampton   From the Old English, meaning "a town" or "a village." CONTEMPORARY EXAMPLE: Hampton Pool, football player. SURNAME USAGE: Lionel Hampton, musician. PLACE-NAME USAGE: a town in England; Hampton Roads, Virginia.

Hanan   From the Hebrew, meaning "grace, gracious." A short form of Johanan, from which John is derived. CONTEMPORARY EXAMPLE: Hanan J. Ayolti, author.

Handley   A variant form of Hanley. *See* Hanley. CONTEMPORARY EXAMPLE: Handley Daniel, baseball player.

Hanes   A variant form of Hans. *See* Hans.

Hanley   From the Old English, meaning "the field or meadow belonging to Hans or Hanes."

Hanoch   From the Hebrew, meaning "educated, trained." In the Bible, a grandson of Abraham; a son of Reuben. CONTEMPORARY EXAMPLE: Hanoch Bartov, author.

Hannibal   From the British, meaning "a steep hill." A third–century Carthaginian general who invaded Italy. CONTEMPORARY EXAMPLE: Hannibal Hamlin, vice-president of the U.S. (1861-1865).

Hans, Hanns   A short form of the German name Johannes. Dutch, German, and Swedish forms of John. *See* John. CONTEMPORARY EXAMPLES: Hans Flueck, editor; Hanns M. Schleyer, industrialist.

Hansel   A Bavarian form òf Hans. *See* John.

Hansen   A variant form of Hanson. *See* Hanson. SURNAME USAGE: A. Hansen (1841-1912), Norwegian physician.

Hanson   A patronymic form, meaning "the son of Hans (John)." Popular in Scandinavian countries. CONTEMPORARY EXAMPLE: Hanson Horsey, baseball player. SURNAME USAGE: Howard Hanson (born 1896), American composer.

Harald   A Norse form of Harold, from the Old Norse name Harivald. *See* Harold. CONTEMPORARY EXAMPLE: Harald Vocke, journalist.

Harcourt   From the Middle English, meaning an "army court or quadrangle." CONTEMPORARY EXAMPLE: Harcourt Roy, author.

Harden   A variant form of Hardy. *See* Hardy.

Hardin   A variant form of Hardy. *See* Hardy. CONTEMPORARY EXAMPLE: Hardin Barry, baseball player.

Harding   A variant form of Hardy. *See* Hardy. SURNAME USAGE: Warren G. Harding (1865-1923), twenty-ninth president of the U.S.

Hardley   From the Old English, meaning "a hardy green meadow." CONTEMPORARY EXAMPLE: Hardley Packer, baseball player.

Hardy   From the Middle English and Old French, meaning "bold, robust." VARIANT FORMS: Harden, Hardin, Harding. SURNAME USAGE: Thomas Hardy (1840-1928), English novelist.

Harel   From the Hebrew, meaning "mountain of God." In the Bible, a place-name. An Israeli personal name and surname.

Harl   A short form of Harlan. *See* Harlan. CONTEMPORARY EXAMPLE: Harl Maggert, baseball player.

Harlan   From the Middle English *herle*, and the Low German *harle*, meaning "a strand of hemp or flax." CONTEMPORARY EXAMPLE: Harlan Fiske Stone, Chief Justice, U.S. Supreme Court (1941-1946). SURNAME USAGE: John Marshall Harlan, U.S. Supreme Court Justice (1955-1971).

Harley   From the Old English, meaning "a field in which plants yielding hemplike fiber grow." Akin to Harlan. CONTEMPORARY EXAMPLE: Harley Affeldt, educator.

Harlin   A variant spelling of Harlan. *See* Harlan.

Harlow   From the Old Norse, meaning "army leader." CONTEMPORARY EXAMPLE: Harlow Estes.

Harm   A short form of Harman. *See* Harman. CONTEMPORARY EXAMPLE: Harm Steyn, fishing expert.

Harman   A form of the Anglo-Saxon name Herenan, meaning "army man, soldier." Akin to Herman.

Harmon From the Greek, meaning "peace, harmony." Or, a variant spelling of Harman. *See* Harman. CONTEMPORARY EXAMPLE: Harmon Killebrew, baseball player.

Harold From the Old English name Hereweald and the Germanic name Hariwald, meaning "leader of the army." Akin to Herbert. Harold I was king of England in the eleventh century. Hal is a common pet form.

Harper From the Old Norse *harpa*, meaning "to grip a javelin for spearing whales." CONTEMPORARY EXAMPLE: Harper Lee, Pulitzer Prize winner in letters (1961). SURNAME USAGE: Robert Harper, owner of Harper's Ferry. PLACE-NAME USAGE: city in West Virginia.

Harrell A variant spelling of Harel. *See* Harel. CONTEMPORARY EXAMPLE: Harrell E. Garrison, educator.

Harris A patronymic form, meaning "Harry's son." *See* Harry. SURNAME USAGE: Joel Chandler Harris (1848-1908), author.

Harrison A patronymic form, meaning "Harry's son." *See* Harry. CONTEMPORARY EXAMPLE: Harrison E. Salisbury, Pulitzer Prize winner in journalism (1955). SURNAME USAGE: William Henry Harrison (1773-1841), ninth president of the U.S.

Harry From the Middle English name Herry, a form of Henry. *See* Henry. English kings named Henry were called Harry by their subjects. Also, a short form of Harold. *See* Harold. Harris and Harrison are patronymic forms. Harriet is a feminine form.

Hart, Harte From the Middle English *hert*, akin to the German name Hirsch, meaning "a hart, a deer, a stag." CONTEMPORARY EXAMPLE: Hart Crane, poet. SURNAME USAGE: Bret Harte (1836-1902), American author. PLACE-NAME USAGE: Hartford, Connecticut.

Hartley From the Old English, meaning "a field in which the deer roam." Hartley Coleridge (1796-1849) was the son of Samuel Taylor Coleridge, English poet and critic. SURNAME USAGE: David Hartley, eighteenth-century English philosopher, after whom Hartley Coleridge was named.

Hartman A variant form of Hart, meaning "a man who traps or deals with deers." *See* Hart. CONTEMPORARY EXAMPLE: Hartman Oberlander, baseball player. SURNAME USAGE: David Hartman, television personality.

Hartwell A variant form of Hart, meaning "a well at which the deer drink." *See* Hart. CONTEMPORARY EXAMPLE: Hartwell Menefee, football player.

Hartwig From the Old English, meaning "the way (*waeg*) of the deer, the deer path." Akin to Hartley. CONTEMPORARY EXAMPLE: Hartwig Lohman, German pastor.

Harve A short form of Harvey. *See* Harvey. CONTEMPORARY EXAM-

PLE: Harve Presnell, actor.

Harvey   From the Old High German *herewig*, meaning "army battle." Harve is short form. Herve is a French variant. CONTEMPORARY EXAMPLE: Harvey Korman, actor. SURNAME USAGE: William Harvey (1578-1657), English physician.

Haskel, Haskell   From the Anglo-Saxon *aesc* and *ask*, meaning an "ash tree." (The aspirated "h" was added.) Also a Yiddish form of the Hebrew *yechezkayl*, Ezekiel, meaning "God is my strength." CONTEMPO-RARY EXAMPLE: Haskel Billings, baseball player.

Hassan   From the Arabic, meaning "nice, good."

Hasting, Hastings   From the Latin *hasta*, meaning "a spear." Also, from the Old English and Old Norse *husthing*, meaning "house council." CONTEMPORARY EXAMPLE: Hastings Keith, U.S. congressman. SURNAME USAGE: Warren Hastings (1732-1818), English statesman. PLACE-NAME USAGE: a city in England; Hastings-on-Hudson, New York.

Hatchen   From the Old English *haeth*, meaning "a small wasteland." CONTEMPORARY EXAMPLE: Hatchen Hughes, Pulitzer Prize winner in drama (1924).

Havelock   From the English surname of Sir Henry Havelock (1795-1857), English general serving in India, who introduced a light cloth (havelock) to cover the military cap for protection against the sun. CON-TEMPORARY EXAMPLE: Havelock Ellis (1859–1939), English psychologist. His actual first name was Henry.

Haven   From the Middle Dutch and Old English, meaning "a harbor, a port." VARIANT FORMS: Hagen, Hagan, Hogan. CONTEMPORARY EX-AMPLE: Haven Moses, football player.

Hawthorne   From the Old English *haga*, meaning "hedge," plus *thorn*, "any of a group of thorny shrubs of the rose family." SURNAME USAGE: Nathaniel Hawthorne (1804–1864), American novelist. PLACE-NAME USAGE: a city in California; a city in New York.

Hayden, Haydn   From the Anglo-Saxon, meaning "a hay pasture." CONTEMPORARY EXAMPLES: Hayden Rorke, actor; Haydn Stephens, ac-tor. SURNAME USAGE: Franz Joseph Haydn (1732-1809), Austrian com-poser.

Hayes   From the Old English, meaning "one who grows hay, a farmer." SURNAME USAGE: Rutherford Birchard Hayes (1822-1893), nineteenth president of the U.S.

Haym   A variant spelling of Haim and Chaim. *See* Chaim. CONTEM-PORARY EXAMPLE: Haym Solomon, American statesman.

Haynes   A variant spelling of Hanes. *See* Hans *and* John. SURNAME USAGE: Tiger Haynes, musician.

Hays   A variant spelling of Hayes. *See* Hayes. SURNAME USAGE: Arthur

Garfield Hays (1881-1954), U.S. civil libertarian.

Hayward   From the Middle English *hei*, meaning "a hedge," and *ward*, meaning "a guardian," hence "a protective fence or hedge." CONTEMPORARY EXAMPLE: Hayward Cirker, publisher. PLACE-NAME USAGE: Hayward, California, named after William Hayward, a local postmaster.

Haywood, Heywood   From the Old English, meaning "a hay field." Akin to Hayward. CONTEMPORARY EXAMPLES: Haywood Nelson, actor; Heywood Broun, journalist.

Hayyim   A variant spelling of Haim and Chaim. *See* Chaim. CONTEMPORARY EXAMPLE: Hayyim Schauss, author.

Hazard   From the Old French *hasard*, meaning "a game of dice" and "adventuresome." Akin to names like Chance and Lucky.

Hazen   A variant form of Haven. *See* Haven. CONTEMPORARY EXAMPLE: Hazen Cuyler, baseball player.

Heartley   A variant spelling of Hartley. *See* Hartley. CONTEMPORARY EXAMPLE: Heartley Anderson, football player.

Heath   From the Middle English, meaning "wasteland." CONTEMPORARY EXAMPLE: Heath Wingate, baseball player; Heath Larry, industrialist.

Heber   A variant form of Herbert. *See* Herbert. CONTEMPORARY EXAMPLE: Heber Ladner, Mississippi politician.

Hebert   A variant form of Herbert. *See* Herbert.

Hector   From the Greek, meaning "anchor." In Greek mythology, Hector was the son of Priam. He was slain by Achilles. CONTEMPORARY EXAMPLE: Hector Cruz, baseball player.

Hedley   From the Old English *heder*, meaning "a covering" or "a covered meadow." CONTEMPORARY EXAMPLES: Hedley Donovan, editor; Hedley Goodall, actor.

Hedric, Hedrick   From the Old English, meaning "the ruler's or rich man's house." Hendrick is a variant form.

Heiman   Probably a short form of the surname Heinemann. *See* Heine. Or, a variant form of Heimadall, who in Norse mythology is the watchman of Asgard, home of the gods.

Heine, Heinie   Variant forms of the German Heinrich and Henry. *See* Henry. CONTEMPORARY EXAMPLE: Heinie Zimmerman, baseball player. SURNAME USAGE: Heinrich Heine (1797-1856), German poet.

Heinrich   The German form of Henry. *See* Henry.

Heinz   A variant form of Hans. Also a pet form of Heinrich. *See* Hans *and* Heinrich. CONTEMPORARY EXAMPLES: Heinz Wichman, fishing expert; Heinz Becker, baseball player.

Helem   From the Hebrew, meaning "a hammer" or "to strike down." In the Bible, a member of the tribe of Asher.

Helgi   Possibly a form of Hel. In Norse mythology, the goddess of the underworld and death. CONTEMPORARY EXAMPLE: Helgi Johannson, North Dakota politician. *See also* Hel in feminine section.

Heli   From the Greek *helios*, meaning "the sun." In the Bible (Luke), the father of Joseph (Mary's husband).

Heller   An Old High German form of the Latin *helios*, meaning "the sun," hence "light, bright."

Helm   From the Old English meaning "an elm tree." The "h" is aspirated. Or, a form of Helmut. *See* Helmut.

Hellmut, Helmut   From the Anglo-Saxon name Helmaer, meaning "a helmet." CONTEMPORARY EXAMPLE: Helmut Bohme, historian; Hellmut Lehmann–Haupt, librarian.

Heman   From the Hebrew, meaning "faithful." In the Bible, a member of a family of priests.

Henderson   A variant form of Anderson, a patronymic of Andrew. *See* Andrew. CONTEMPORARY EXAMPLE: Henderson Wright, football player.

Hendric, Hendrick, Hendrik   Variant forms of Hedric. *See* Hedric. CONTEMPORARY EXAMPLE: Hendrick Smith, author.

Heneli   The Hawaiian form of Henry. *See* Henry.

Henlee   A variant form of Hanley. *See* Hanley. CONTEMPORARY EXAMPLE: Henlee Barnette, theologian.

Henri   The French form of Henry. *See* Henry. CONTEMPORARY EXAMPLE: Henri Frankfort, author.

Henrik   A variant Swedish form of Hendrik, the Dutch form of Henry. CONTEMPORARY EXAMPLE: Henrik Henriksen, fishing expert.

Henry   From the Old High German names Haimirich and Heimerich, compounded of *haimi*, meaning "house, home," and *ric*, meaning "ruler." The son of William the Conqueror was King Henry I of England (1078-1135). Also, the name of several kings of France and Germany. VARIANT FORMS: Henricus (Latin); Hal, Halkin, Harry, Hawkin (English); Henri, Henriot (French); Enrique (Spanish); Arrigo, Enrico, Enzio, Guccio (Italian); Heine, Heinrich, Heinz, Henke, Henning (German); Henrik (Swedish); Hendrik (German, Dutch, and Danish); Henryk (Polish). PET FORMS: Hal, Hank, Henny, Harry, Heriot, Herriot. Harry was the pet name of English kings named Henry. Henrietta is the feminine form. SURNAME USAGE: Harris, Harrison, Henderson, Hendy, Halkin, Hawke, Hawkins, Heriot, Herriot, Penny, Parry, Perry.

Henty A variant form of Henry. *See* Henry. Or, from the Old English, meaning "to hunt." SURNAME USAGE: George Alfred Henty (1832-1902), English author.

Herbert From the Old English *herebeorht*, meaning "bright, excellent army or ruler." PET FORMS: Herb, Herbie, Bert, Bertie. SURNAME USAGE: Victor Herbert (1859-1924), American composer.

Hercules From the Greek, meaning "glory." In Greek and Roman mythology, the son of Zeus, renowned for feats of strength. CONTEMPORARY EXAMPLE: Hercules Burnett, baseball player.

Heriot A pet form of Henry. *See* Henry.

Herman From the Old High German name Hariman, meaning "army (*heri*) man" or "soldier." Akin to Harold. VARIANT FORMS: Armand, Armant (French); Ermanno (Italian); Hermann (German); Armin (English). SURNAME USAGE: Armand, Arment, Harman, Harmon.

Hermann A variant German form of Herman. *See* Herman.

Hermanze A variant form of Herman. *See* Herman. CONTEMPORARY EXAMPLE: Hermanze Fauntleroy, city mayor of Petersburg, Virginia.

Hermes In Greek mythology, a god who served as the messenger of the gods. Akin to the Roman Mercury and connoting "speed, efficiency, eloquence." In the Bible, a friend of Paul.

Herminio A Spanish pet form of Herman. *See* Herman.

Hermus A variant form of Hermes. *See* Hermes. CONTEMPORARY EXAMPLE: Hermus McFarland, baseball player.

Hern, Herne Archaic forms of *heron* (*heroun*), the Middle English name of the cranelike bird with a hoarse cry. *See* Heron.

Herndon From the Anglo-Saxon, meaning "the valley where the herons breed."

Herod From the Greek *heros*, meaning "to watch over, protect." Herodutus was a fifth-century B.C. Greek historian. Herod the Great was a first-century B.C. king of Judea. Herodias is a feminine form.

Heron A variant form of Hern. *See* Hern. Heron of Alexandria, a third–century A.D. Greek mathmetician and inventor.

Herriot A variant spelling of Heriot. *See* Heriot.

Hersch, Hersh From the German, meaning "a deer." VARIANT FORMS: Hertz, Hertzl, Heschel, Heshel. VARIANT SPELLINGS: Hirsch, Hirsh.

Herschel, Hershel A diminutive form of Hersch. *See* Hersch. CONTEMPORARY EXAMPLE: Herschel Bernardi, actor. SURNAME USAGE: Sir William Herschel (1738-1822), German-born English astronomer.

Hertz A variant form of Hersch. *See* Hersch. SURNAME USAGE: Heinrich Rudolph Hertz (1857-1894), German physicist.

Hertzel   A variant spelling of Herzl. *See* Herzl.

Herve, Hervey   French forms of Harvey. *See* Harvey. CONTEMPORARY EXAMPLES: Herve Villechaize, actor; Hervey Garrett Smith, author.

Herzl   A diminutive form of Hirsch. From the German, meaning "a deer." Became popular as a result of the activity of Theodor Herzl (1860-1904) in behalf of the establishment of a Jewish state. His first and middle Hebrew names, Binyamin Ze'ev, also became popular.

Heschel, Heshel   Variant forms of Hersch and Herschel. *See* Hersch. SURNAME USAGE: Abraham Joshua Heschel, philosopher.

Hesketh   Probably a variant form of Hezekiah. *See* Hezekiah. May also be a form of the British Esk (*ysc*), meaning "water," the name of two rivers. CONTEMPORARY EXAMPLE: Hesketh Pearson, author.

Hevel   From the Hebrew, meaning "breath, vapor," or from the Assyrian, meaning "son." The Hebrew name of Abel, son of Adam and Eve.

Hew   A pet form of Hewlett or a variant spelling of Hugh. *See* Hewlett *and* Hugh. CONTEMPORARY EXAMPLE: Hew Sullivan, football player.

Hewlett   From the British *aewelm*, meaning "the fountainhead of a stream." The "h" is aspirated. PLACE-NAME USAGE: Ewell in England; a town in Nassau County, New York.

Heywood   From the Old English, meaning "a field on which hay is grown." CONTEMPORARY EXAMPLE: Heywood (Woody) Allen, actor. SURNAME USAGE: Thomas Heywood, seventeenth–century English author.

Hezeki   A variant form of Hezekiah. *See* Hezekiah. In the Bible, a member of the tribe of Benjamin.

Hezekiah   From the Hebrew, meaning "God is my strength." In the Bible, a king of Judah in the days of Isaiah. Hezekiahu is a variant biblical form.

Hi   A pet form for a variety of names including Hiram, Hilary, and Hyman. Used also as an independent name. CONTEMPORARY EXAMPLE: Hi Bithorn, baseball player.

Hicks, Hickson   Patronymic forms of Richard, meaning "Richard's son." Evolved from Dick and Dix. May also be variant forms of Isaac, with the aspirated "h" added.

High   From the Old English *heah*, meaning "high, a hillsite." Also, a variant form of Hi. *See* Hi. CONTEMPORARY EXAMPLE: High Salpeter, publicist.

Hilar   A pet form of Hilary. *See* Hilary.

Hilarid   A variant form of Hilary. *See* Hilary. CONTEMPORARY EXAMPLE: Hilarid Valdespino, baseball player.

Hilary   From the Greek and Latin, meaning "cheerful." Used also as a feminine name. VARIANT FORMS: Hilaire (French); Ilario (Italian); Laris (Anglo-Saxon). SURNAME USAGE: Edmund Percival, New Zealand explorer.

Hildebrand   From the Old German Hildibrand, compounded of *hildi*, meaning "battle, war," plus the Old English *brand*, meaning "a torch" or "a sword."

Hildreth   A variant form of Hildebrand. *See* Hildebrand. CONTEMPORARY EXAMPLE: Hildreth Flitcraft, baseball player.

Hill   From the Anglo-Saxon, meaning "hill, high place." Also, a pet form of Hillary. *See* Hillary.

Hillard, Hilliard   Variant forms of Hilary and Hillary. *See* Hilary.

Hillary   A variant spelling of Hilary. *See* Hilary.

Hillel   From the Hebrew, meaning "praised, famous." In the Bible, the father of a Hebrew judge. A renowned Jewish scholar, born in Babylonia about 75 B.C., who was the founder of a great academy of learning.

Hilliard   A variant form of Hillard and Hilary. *See* Hilary.

Hilly   A pet form of Hillary and Hilliard. *See* Hillary. CONTEMPORARY EXAMPLE: Hilly Rose, entertainer.

Hilmer   From the Old English, meaning "the lake on the hill."

Hilton   From the Old English, meaning "a town on the hill." CONTEMPORARY EXAMPLE: Hilton Kramer, art critic. SURNAME USAGE: James Hilton, author.

Hinkel   Probably from the Middle English *henge*, meaning "a hinge." CONTEMPORARY EXAMPLE: Hinkel Shillings, writer.

Hiraldo   A Spanish form of Harold. *See* Harold. CONTEMPORARY EXAMPLE: Hiraldo Ruiz, baseball player.

Hiram   From the Hebrew, meaning "noble born" or "exalted brother." An abbreviated form of Ahiram. In the Bible, a king of Tyre. A favorite seventeenth-century name in England. CONTEMPORARY EXAMPLE: Hiram L. Fong, U.S. senator (Hawaii, 1950s).

Hirsch, Hirsh   Variant spellings of Hersch and Hersh. *See* Hersch.

Hoagy   A pet form of Hogarth. *See* Hogarth. CONTEMPORARY EXAMPLE: Hoagy Carmichael, entertainer.

Hob, Hobs   A variant Middle English form of Rob, Robin, and Robert. SURNAME USAGE: Thomas Hobbes (1588-1679), English social philosopher.

Hobart   From the Danish *ho*, meaning "a hill," hence "Bart's hill." Bart is a short form of Bartholomew. PLACE-NAME USAGE: the capital of Tasmania.

Hobert   A variant form of Hobart, meaning "Bert's hill." *See* Hobart. Bert is a pet form of Berthold. CONTEMPORARY EXAMPLE: Hobert Landrith, baseball player.

Hobson   A patronymic form of Robert, meaning "Robert's son." Hob is a variant form of Rob, a nickname for Robert. Akin to Dobson.

Hockley   From the Old English *hock*, meaning "high," hence "a meadow (lea) in the highlands." CONTEMPORARY EXAMPLE: Hockley Clark, author.

Hod   From the Hebrew, meaning "splendor." In the Bible, a member of the tribe of Asher. *See* Hodding.

Hodding   From the Middle Dutch *hodde*, meaning "a wooden tray for carrying bricks," hence "bricklayer." Or, from the Anglo-Saxon, meaning "a heath near water." CONTEMPORARY EXAMPLE: Hodding Carter, U.S. civil servant.

Hodge, Hodges   Variant forms of Roger and Rogers, from the Old High German name Hrodger, meaning "famous spear." *See* Roger. Hodges is a patronymic form. CONTEMPORARY EXAMPLE: Hodges West, football player. SURNAME USAGE: Gil Hodges, baseball player.

Hodiah, Hodiya   From the Hebrew, meaning "God is my splendor." A masculine and feminine name. In the Bible, a member of the tribe of Judah and also the wife of Ezra.

Hoffman   From the German *haupt* or *hof*, meaning "man at court," hence a person of influence. SURNAME USAGE: Josef Hoffman (1876-1957), Polish–born composer.

Hogan   An Irish variant form of Hagan and Haven. *See* Haven. Also, from the language of the Navajo Indians, meaning "house." CONTEMPORARY EXAMPLE: Hogan Wharton, football player. SURNAME USAGE: Frank Hogan, district attorney.

Hogarth   From the Old Norse *ho* (hill) and *garthr* (garden), meaning "the garden on the hill." SURNAME USAGE: William Hogarth (1697-1764), English painter.

Hogg   A nickname for Hough and Houghton. *See* Hough.

Holbrook   From the Old English *hol*, meaning "a valley," hence "the brook in the valley." SURNAME USAGE: Hal Holbrook, actor.

Holden   From the Old English, meaning "a valley." CONTEMPORARY EXAMPLE: Holden Caufield, a character in J.D. Salinger's *Catcher in the Rye*. SURNAME USAGE: William Holden, actor.

Hollis   A variant form of Haley and Halley. *See* Haley. CONTEMPORARY EXAMPLE: Hollis Hodges, novelist. PLACE-NAME USAGE: Hollis, New York.

Holm   From the Old Norse *holmr*, meaning "an island." Holmes is a variant form.

Holmes   A variant form of Holm. *See* Holm. CONTEMPORARY EXAMPLE: Holmes Alexander, columnist. SURNAME USAGE: Oliver Wendell Holmes (1841-1935), U.S. Supreme Court Justice.

Holt   From the Old English and the German *holz*, meaning "wood," hence "a wooded area."

Homer   From the Greek and Latin, meaning "a hostage, one who is being led," hence "one who is blind." An eighth–century B.C. Greek poet, author of *The Iliad* and *The Odyssey*. SURNAME USAGE: Winslow Homer (1836-1910), American painter.

Homero   A Spanish form of Homer. *See* Homer. CONTEMPORARY EXAMPLE: Homero Blancas, golfer.

Honester   From the Old English *han*, "a stone," and the Old Norse *hein*, "to whet, to hone, to sharpen," hence "one who is engaged in sharpening tools." CONTEMPORARY EXAMPLE: Honester Davidson, football player.

Honi   From the Hebrew, meaning "gracious." Akin to the Hebrew Yochanan and Johanan, corresponding to John.

Honor, Honore   From the Middle English and Latin, meaning "dignity, esteem." Also, from the Old French, meaning "lord, nobleman." CONTEMPORARY EXAMPLE: Honore de Balzac, French author; Honor Jackson, football player.

Honus   A variant form of Hans, a short form of Johannes. *See* Johannes. Or, from the Latin *honos*, meaning "honor, dignity." *See also* Honor. CONTEMPORARY EXAMPLE: Honus Wagner, baseball player.

Hopkins   A pet form of Hob and Hobs, pet forms of Rob and Robert. SURNAME USAGE: Johns Hopkins (1795-1873), American financier.

Horace   From the Greek, meaning "to see, to behold." The Latin form is Horatius. CONTEMPORARY EXAMPLE: Horace Greeley (1811-1872), American journalist.

Horacio   The Spanish form of Horace. *See* Horace. CONTEMPORARY EXAMPLE: Horacio Rivero, American admiral.

Horatio   The Italian form of Horace. *See* Horace. CONTEMPORARY EXAMPLE: Horatio Seymour, U.S. presidential candidate (1868).

Horatius   The Latin form of Horace. *See* Horace.

Hornsby   From the Anglo-Saxon *hearn*, meaning "the place where the heron live." SURNAME USAGE: Roger Hornsby, baseball player.

Horst   From the German, meaning "a thicket." CONTEMPORARY EXAMPLE: Horst Janson, art historian.

Horton   From the Latin *hortus*, meaning "a garden." CONTEMPORARY EXAMPLE: Horton Davies, author. Hortense is a feminine form.

Hosea   From the Hebrew, meaning "salvation." In the Bible, an eighth–century B.C. prophet who prophesied in the Kingdom of Israel during the reign of King Jeroboam.

Hoshal   Origin uncertain. Possibly a form of Hosea. CONTEMPORARY EXAMPLE: Hoshal Wright, rock musician.

Hough, Houghton   From the Anglo-Saxon, meaning "a hill" and "a town on the hill." Hogg is a nickname for Hough.

Houston   From the Anglo-Saxon, meaning "the house in the town." CONTEMPORARY EXAMPLE: Houston Cole, educator. SURNAME USAGE: Samuel Houston (1793-1863), American general and senator. PLACE-NAME USAGE: a city in Texas.

Howard   From the Anglo-Saxon, meaning "guardian of the home." CONTEMPORARY EXAMPLE: Howard Jarvis, U.S. congressman. SURNAME USAGE: Sidney Coe Howard (1891-1939), American playwright.

Howden   A variant spelling of Houdan, a French breed of crested five-toed chickens. CONTEMPORARY EXAMPLE: Howden Ganley, auto racer. SURNAME USAGE: Jean Houdon (1741-1828), French sculptor.

Howe   From the Anglo-Saxon, meaning "a hill." SURNAME USAGE: Elias Howe (1819-1867), American inventor.

Howel, Howell   From the Old English, meaning "a well on the hill." CONTEMPORARY EXAMPLE: Howell M. Estes, U.S. general.

Howie   A pet form of Howard. See Howard.

Hoyle   A variant form of Hoyt. See Hoyt. SURNAME USAGE: Edmond Hoyle (1672-1769), English authority on games.

Hoyt   From the Middle English *hoye*, meaning "a vessel, a sloop." CONTEMPORARY EXAMPLES: Hoyt Axton, songwriter; Hoyt Wilhelm, baseball player.

Hub   A pet form of Hubbard. See Hubbard. Used also as an independent name. CONTEMPORARY EXAMPLE: Hub M. Harrison, publisher.

Hubbard   A variant form of Hubert and Hubbell. See Hubert *and* Hubbell. CONTEMPORARY EXAMPLE: Hubbard Law, football player.

Hubbell   A variant English form of Hubert from its early form, Hygebeohrt. Hubbard is a variant form. CONTEMPORARY EXAMPLE: Hubbell Hill, baseball player.

Hubert   From the Old High German name Huguberht, meaning "bright in mind and spirit (*hugu*)." VARIANT FORMS: Uberto (Italian); Huberto (Portuguese). PET FORMS: Hugh, Hubie. CONTEMPORARY EXAMPLE: Hubert H. Humphrey, U.S. senator and vice-president.

Hubie   A pet form of Hubert. See Hubert. CONTEMPORARY EXAMPLE: Hubie Ginn, football player.

Hudd, Hudde   Pet forms of Richard common in the thirteenth and

fourteenth centuries but long obsolete. Traces can be seen in the surnames Hudd, Hudson, and Huddleston.

Huddie Derived from the place-name Huddersfield, a city in Yorkshire, England. Originally, a form of Hudd. *See* Hudd. CONTEMPORARY
EXAMPLE: Huddie Ledbetter, musician.

Hudson A patronymic form, meaning "son of Hudd." *See* Hudd.
CONTEMPORARY EXAMPLE: Hudson T. Armerding, educator. SURNAME
USAGE: Henry Hudson (died 1611), English explorer. PLACE-NAME
USAGE: a city and river in New York.

Huey A pet form of Hubert. *See* Hubert. CONTEMPORARY EXAMPLE:
Huey Long, U.S. senator.

Hugh A pet form of Hubert. *See* Hubert. VARIANT FORMS: Hugo
(Latin and German); Huey, Hutchin (English); Hughie (Scottish);
Huet (French); Ugo (Italian); Hugi (Norwegian). CONTEMPORARY EX-
AMPLE: Hugh Heffner, publisher. SURNAME USAGE: Hughes, Huggins,
Hewes, Hewlett.

Hugo A variant form of Hugh. *See* Hugh. CONTEMPORARY EXAMPLE:
Hugo Black (1886-1971), U.S. Supreme Court Justice. SURNAME USAGE:
Victor Hugo (1802-1885), French writer.

Hulett From the Old English *hyl*, meaning "a hill." Also, a variant
form of Hugh. *See* Hugh. CONTEMPORARY EXAMPLE: Hulett C. Smith,
state governor (West Virginia).

Humbert From the Old German, meaning "bright home," or from
the Old English, meaning "a home on a hill." Most popular in Italy in
the variant form Umberto. PET FORMS: Bert, Bertie.

Humberto The Spanish form of the Italian Umberto. *See* Humbert.
CONTEMPORARY EXAMPLE: Humberto Fernandez, baseball player.

Hume From the Norse *holm* and *hulm*, meaning "a grassy hill by the
water." CONTEMPORARY EXAMPLE: Hume Cronyn, actor. SURNAME
USAGE: Holm, Holme, Holmes. The Scottish and Irish name Holme is
often pronounced Hume.

Humphrey, Humphry From the Old English *hunfrith*, derived from
the Germanic *hun*, meaning "strength," and the Old English *frith*,
meaning "peace." PET FORMS: Dumphry, Dump (from which Humpty-
Dumpty of the nursery rhyme comes). CONTEMPORARY EXAMPLE: Humphrey Bogart, actor; Humphry Osmond, author. SURNAME USAGE:
Hubert H. Humphrey, U.S. senator.

Hunfrey A variant spelling of Humphrey. *See* Humphrey.

Hunt, Hunter, Huntington From the Old English *huntian*, meaning "to search, hunt." CONTEMPORARY EXAMPLES: Hunt Winans, Sr.,
farmer; Huntington Hartford, industrialist. SURNAME USAGE: Leigh
Hunt (1784-1859), English poet; John Hunter (1728-1793), English
surgeon. PLACE-NAME USAGE: Huntington, West Virginia.

Hutchins Originally a surname derived from Hodges, a form of Roger. *See* Roger. CONTEMPORARY EXAMPLE: Hutchins Hapgood, author. SURNAME USAGE: Thomas Hutchinson (1711-1780), colonial governor of Massachusetts.

Huw A variant spelling of Hugh. *See* Hugh. CONTEMPORARY EXAMPLE: Sir Huw Wheldon, English television director.

Huxley From the Anglo-Saxon, meaning "a field of ash trees." SURNAME USAGE: Aldous Huxley (1894-1963), English writer.

Hy A pet form of Hyman or Hyland. *See* Hyman *and* Hyland.

Hyde From the Old English *hida*, meaning "a measure of land." SURNAME USAGE: Douglas Hyde (1860-1949), Irish statesman. PLACE-NAME USAGE: Hyde Park in London; Hyde Park, New York.

Hyder From the English occupational name, meaning "one who prepares hides for tanning." Or, a form of Hyde. *See* Hyde. CONTEMPORARY EXAMPLE: Hyder Barr, baseball player.

Hyland From the Anglo-Saxon, meaning "one who lives on high land," PLACE-NAME USAGE: Hyland Park, New Jersey.

Hyman From the Anglo-Saxon, meaning "one who lives in a high place, a mountaintop." CONTEMPORARY EXAMPLE: Hyman Rickover, U.S. admiral. SURNAME USAGE: Earle Hyman, actor.

I

Iain A variant Scottish spelling of Ian. *See* Ian. CONTEMPORARY EXAMPLE: Iain Douglas Hamilton, zoologist.

Ian The Scottish form of John. *See* John.

Ib An Old English form of the Hebrew *ab* (*av*), meaning "father." VARIANT FORMS: Abb, Abba, Abbot, Ebb. CONTEMPORARY EXAMPLE: Ib Melchior, novelist.

Ichabod From the Hebrew, meaning "without glory." In the Bible, a son of Phineas. CONTEMPORARY EXAMPLE: Ichabod Crane, a literary character created by Washington Irving, American author.

Ignatius From the Greek and Latin, meaning "the fiery or lively one." VARIANT FORMS: Ignace, Ignatz, Ignazio. Saint Ignatius was a first-century Christian martyr and Bishop of Antioch. CONTEMPORARY EXAMPLE: Ignatius J. Galantin, U.S. general.

Ignazio An Italian variant form of Ignatius. *See* Ignatius. CONTEMPORARY EXAMPLE: Ignazio Silone, novelist.

Igor From the Scandinavian, meaning "hero." VARIANT FORMS: Inge, Ingmar. CONTEMPORARY EXAMPLES: Igor Cassini, journalist; Igor Stravinsky, composer.

Ikaia The Hawaiian form of Isaiah. *See* Isaiah.

Ike A pet form of Isaac. *See* Isaac. The nickname of Dwight D. Eisenhower (1890-1969), thirty–fourth president of the U.S.

Ilan From the Hebrew, meaning "a tree." CONTEMPORARY EXAMPLE: Ilan Zion, a resident of Israel.

Ilbert From the Old German Hildabehrt, compounded of *hildi*, meaning "battle" and *berhta*, meaning "bright," hence "a brilliant warrior." Akin to Imbert.

Ilie A variant form of Elijah or Elisha. *See* Elijah *and* Elisha. CONTEMPORARY EXAMPLE: Ilie Nastase, tennis player.

Ilija, Ilya Variant Slavic forms of Elijah or Elisha. *See* Elijah *and* Elisha. CONTEMPORARY EXAMPLES: Ilija Mitic, soccer player; Ilya Prigogine, Nobel Prize winner in chemistry.

Imanuel A variant spelling of Immanuel. *See Immanuel.*

Imbert From the German, meaning "bright." VARIANT FORMS: Albert, Adelbert, Bert, Bertram.

Immanuel From the Hebrew, meaning "God is with us." VARIANT FORMS: Emanuel, Emmanuel, Manuel.

Imon Origin uncertain. Perhaps an abbreviated form of Simon. *See* Simon. CONTEMPORARY EXAMPLE: Imon E. Bruce, educator.

Imray Variant form of Amory and Emery. *See* Amory *and* Emery.

Imre A variant form of Imray. *See* Imray. CONTEMPORARY EXAMPLE: Imre Horvath, television producer.

Imri, Imrie From the Hebrew, possibly meaning "tall" or "eloquent." In the Bible, a member of the tribe of Judah. Imric is a variant spelling. CONTEMPORARY EXAMPLE: Imri Tel-Oren, a resident of Israel.

Inge From the Middle English, derived from the Gaelic *innis*, meaning "an island." CONTEMPORARY EXAMPLES: Inge Hammarstrom, hockey player. SURNAME USAGE: William Ralph Inge (1860-1954), English theologian.

Ingmar From the Old English *ing*, meaning "meadow," and *mare*, meaning "sea." CONTEMPORARY EXAMPLE: Ingmar Bergman, Swedish film director.

Ingo From the Danish name Ingold. Related to the Old English *ing*, meaning "a meadow." CONTEMPORARY EXAMPLE: Ingo Swam, psychic.

Ingram From the British *engylion*, meaning "angel." VARIANT FORMS: Ingra, Ingrim. Inglis is a variant form.

Ingrim A variant form of Ingram. *See* Ingram.

Inman An Old English occupational name, meaning "an innkeeper." CONTEMPORARY EXAMPLE: Inman Veal, baseball player.

Inness, Innis From the British, meaning "an island." Innis is a Cornish form.

Intrepid From the Latin, meaning "fearless."

Iona The Hawaiian form of Jonah. *See* Jonah.

Iosif A Russian form of Joseph. *See* Joseph. CONTEMPORARY EXAMPLE: Iosif Stalin (1879-1953), premier of the Soviet Union.

Ira From the Hebrew *yarod*, meaning "descend." Akin to Jordan.

Irvin, Irvine, Irving From the Gaelic, meaning "beautiful, handsome, fair." May also be of Anglo–Saxon origin, meaning "sea friend." Irvin is the original form. Irving probably originated as a British place–name. SURNAME USAGE: Washington Irving (1783-1859), American writer. PLACE-NAME USAGE: Irvine, California; Irvington, New York.

Irwin, Irwyn A variant spelling of Irvin. *See* Irvin. CONTEMPORARY EXAMPLE: Irwyn Applebaum, publisher.

Is, Isa, Issa   Diminutive forms of Isaiah. *See* Isaiah. Also, Old British names, meaning "lower than" or "below" (the woods or village).

Isaac   From the Hebrew *yitzchak*, meaning "he will laugh." In the Bible, Isaac was one of the three patriarchs: the son of Abraham and the father of Jacob. Although Abraham was not a preferred name by early Christians, Isaac was commonly used. VARIANT FORMS: Isaacus (Latin); Isaak (Greek); Yithak, Yitzchak (Hebrew); Itzik (Yiddish); Isak (German).

Isador, Isadore   Variant spellings of Isidor. *See* Isidor.

Isaiah   From the Hebrew, meaning "God is salvation." One of the most famous of the Hebrew prophets, he prophesied in Jerusalem from 740–701 B.C. VARIANT FORMS: Isaias (Latin); Esaias (Greek); Yeshaya, Yeshayahu (Hebrew). PET FORMS: Is, Isa, Issa.

Ishmael   From the Hebrew, meaning "God will hear." In the Bible, the son of Abraham and the brother of Isaac. CONTEMPORARY EXAMPLE: Ishmael Reed, author.

Isidor, Isidore   From the Greek, meaning "gift of Isis." Isis was the Egyptian moon goddess. Izzy is a common pet form.

Ismar   A variant form of Ittamar. *See* Ittamar. CONTEMPORARY EXAMPLE: Ismar Ellenbogen, historian.

Israel   From the Hebrew, meaning either "prince of God" or "wrestled with God." The name was given to Jacob, the third of the three patriarchs, after wrestling with the angel of God. Adopted as a synomyn for the Jewish nation, and as a place name for the northern part of Palestine where the ten tribes of Israel lived. CONTEMPORARY EXAMPLE: Israel Putnam (1718-1790), American Revolutionary War general.

Issa   A pet form of Isaiah. *See* Isaiah. Is is a variant form. Isa is a variant spelling.

Issachar   From the Hebrew, meaning "there is a reward." In the Bible, Issachar was the ninth son of Jacob. He was the head of one of the twelve tribes of Israel.

Itai, Ittai   From the Hebrew, meaning "friendly, companionable." In the Bible, Itai was one of David's mighty warriors.

Italo   An Italian name derived from the name of the country Italy. CONTEMPORARY EXAMPLE: Italo Chelini, baseball player.

Itamar   From the Hebrew, meaning "island of palms." CONTEMPORARY EXAMPLE: Itamar Rabinovich, professor.

Ithamar   A variant spelling of Itamar. *See* Itamar. CONTEMPORARY EXAMPLE: Ithamar Bellows, Amenia, New York.

Itiel   From the Hebrew, meaning "God is with me." In the Bible, a member of the tribe of Benjamin.

Ittamar   A variant spelling of Itamar. *See* Itamar.

Ivair   A variant form of Ivar. *See* Ivar. CONTEMPORARY EXAMPLE: Ivair Ferreira, soccer player.

Ival   A variant form of Ewald. *See* Ewald. CONTEMPORARY EXAMPLE: Ival Goodman, baseball player.

Ivan   The Russian form of John, meaning "grace." *See* John. CONTEMPORARY EXAMPLE: Ivan Nagy, Hungarian dancer.

Ivar   A variant spelling of Ivor. *See* Ivor.

Ive   From the Middle English *ivi*, meaning "a climbing vine." Ivy is a variant form.

Iver   A variant form of Ive. *See* Ive. Also, a variant spelling of Ivor. *See* Ivor.

Ives   A variant form of Ive. *See* Ive. SURNAME USAGE: Charles Edward Ives (1864-1954), American composer.

Iving   A variant form of Ive. *See* Ive.

Ivol   A variant form of Ewald. *See* Ewald. CONTEMPORARY EXAMPLE: Ivol J. Curtis, clergyman.

Ivor   From the Latin *ebur*, meaning "ivory," and the Egyptian *ab*, *abu* meaning "elephant, ivory." CONTEMPORARY EXAMPLE: Ivor Drummond, novelist. Ivar is a variant spelling.

J

Jabez   From the Hebrew, meaning "he will be put to shame." In the Bible, a member of Caleb's family.

Jacinto   A Spanish pet form of Jacob. *See* Jacob. CONTEMPORARY EXAMPLE: Jacinto Hernandez, baseball player.

Jack   A pet form of Jacob. *See* Jacob. A common nickname for John, it is probably a variant form of the French name Jackin which evolved from Johannes and Jan. It has come to mean "a man, a boy, a person," as in the phrase, jack-of-all-trades.

Jackie   A pet form of Jack. *See* Jack.

Jackman   A variant form of Jack and Jacob, meaning "a servant of Jack." *See* Jack. CONTEMPORARY EXAMPLE: Jackman Gillet, author.

Jackson   A patronymic form, meaning "son of Jack" or "son of Jacob." *See* Jack *and* Jacob. CONTEMPORARY EXAMPLE: Jackson Brown, musician; Jackson Pollack, art critic. SURNAME USAGE: Andrew Jackson (1767–1847), seventh president of the U.S. (nicknamed Old Hickory).

Jacob   From the Hebrew, meaning "held by the heel," hence "one who holds back another." In the Bible, the son of Isaac and Rebekah; the twin brother of Esau. The third of the three patriarchs, Jacob was also named Israel. The twelve tribes of Israel evolved from Jacob's twelve sons. James is the popular English form. VARIANT FORMS: Jacobus (Latin); Jakob, Jacke (German); Iago (Welsh and Spanish); Seumuis (Irish); Jakobos (Greek); Jayme (Portuguese); Diego, Jaco, Jacobo, Jago, Santiago, Yago (Spanish); Coppo, Como, Lapo, Jacopo, Giacobbe, Giacomo (Italian); Jacquot, Jacques (French); Gemmes (Old French); James, Jemmy (English); Jamie (Scotch); Akkoobjee (Hindu); Hamish (Gaelic); Jakob, Kub, Kuba (Polish); Jakov, Jascha, Jaschenka (Russian); Jaap (Dutch). PET FORMS: Jack, Jackie, Jake. SURNAME USAGE: Jackson, James, Jameson, Jacobi, Jacoby, Jacobs, Jacobson.

Jacobo   A Spanish form of Jacob. *See* Jacob.

Jacopo   An Italian form of Jacob. *See* Jacob. CONTEMPORARY EXAMPLE: Jacopo Bellini (1400-1470), Italian painter.

Jacque, Jacques   French forms of Jacob. *See* Jacob. CONTEMPORARY EXAMPLE: Jacque Mapes, movie producer; Jacques-Yves Cousteau, oceanographer.

Jaeson   A variant spelling of Jason. *See* Jason.

Jaime   A Spanish pet form of James. *See* James. CONTEMPORARY EX-

AMPLE: Jaime Benitez, educator. Used also as a feminine name.

Jaimie   A pet form of James. *See* James. Commonly used as a feminine name. Jamie is a variant spelling.

Jake   A pet form of Jacob. *See* Jacob.

Jakob   A variant spelling of Jacob. *See* Jacob.

Jakon   A patronymic form of the Hebrew name Jacob, meaning "Jack's son." *See* Jack *and* Jacob. CONTEMPORARY EXAMPLE: Jakon Thomas Hays, Norfolk, Virginia.

Jamaal   A variant form of Gamal. *See* Gamal. CONTEMPORARY EXAMPLE: Jamaal Wilkes, basketball player.

James   The English form of the Hebrew name Jacob, meaning "held by the heel, supplanter." *See* Jacob. In the Bible, a Christian apostle, the son of Zebedee; also, a brother of Jesus. A popular name of the kings of England, the first being King James I (1566-1625). VARIANT FORMS: Hamish and Seumas (Gaelic); Seumus (Irish); Jamie (Scottish). PET FORMS: Jamie, Jim, Jimmie, Jimmy. SURNAME USAGE: William James (1842-1910), American philosopher; also, FitzJames, Jameson. PLACE-NAME USAGE: a river in Virginia, North Dakota, and South Dakota; Jamestown, Virginia.

Jamie   A Scottish pet form of James. *See* James. CONTEMPORARY EXAMPLE: Andrew Wyeth, painter. Jaimie is a variant spelling. Used also as a feminine name.

Jan   Either a form of John or James. *See* John *and* James. Sometimes used as an independent name. CONTEMPORARY EXAMPLE: Jan Masaryk (1886-1948), Czechoslovakian statesman; Jan Lochman, theologian. Used also as a feminine name.

Janny   A pet form of Janus. *See* Janus.

Janus   From the Latin, meaning "gate, arched passageway." In Roman mythology, the guardian of gateways and the patron of beginnings and endings. January, the first month of the year, is a derivative of Janus.

Janvillem   Compounded of Jan and Wilhelm (William). *See* Jan *and* William. CONTEMPORARY EXAMPLE: Janvillem van de Wetering, Dutch author.

Japhet, Japheth   From the Hebrew, meaning "youthful, beautiful." In the Bible, the youngest of Noah's three sons. Yaphet is a variant form.

Jardine   From the French, meaning "a garden."

Jareb   From the Hebrew, meaning "he will contend." In the Bible, an Assyrian king.

Jared   From the Hebrew, meaning "to descend" or "descendant." In the Bible, an ancestor of Noah. Jordan is a related name. CONTEM-

PORARY EXAMPLES: Jared Ingersoll, U.S. vice–presidential candidate (1812); Jared Martin, actor.

Jaren   An invented name. CONTEMPORARY EXAMPLE: Jaren John Skinner, New Bedford, Massachusetts.

Jarib   From the Hebrew, meaning "he will contend." In the Bible, a member of the tribe of Simeon.

Jaron   From the Hebrew, meaning "to sing, cry out."

Jaroslav   From the Russian *yar*, meaning "spring grain." Originally a surname from the Galician city, now part of Russia. CONTEMPORARY EXAMPLE: Jaroslav Koch, physician.

Jarrell   A variant form of Gerald. *See* Gerald.

Jarrett   A variant form of Garret. *See* Garret. CONTEMPORARY EXAMPLE: Jarrett Hise, Pleasanton, California; Jarrett Kroll, author. SURNAME USAGE: Jerry Jarrett, actor.

Jarrod   A variant form of Jared. *See* Jared. CONTEMPORARY EXAMPLE: Jarrod Johnson, actor.

Jarvis   From the Old English name Garwig, meaning "a battle spear," hence "a conqueror." Gary is a variant form derived from the Norman-French Gervais and the Latin Gervasius. An early Christian saint name. Akin to Gervais. *See* Gervais. SURNAME USAGE: Howard Jarvis, U.S. congressman.

Jary   A pet form of Jarvis. *See* Jarvis.

Jascha   A Russian form of James or Jacob. *See* James *and* Jacob. CONTEMPORARY EXAMPLE: Jascha Heifetz, violinist.

Jason   From the Greek and Latin, meaning "healer." Jaeson is a variant spelling, In Greek mythology, a prince who led the Argonauts to get the Golden Fleece. The Greek name of Joshua, the High Priest in the second century B.C. In the New Testament, a kinsman of Paul. CONTEMPORARY EXAMPLE: Jason Miller, actor.

Jaspar, Jaspar   From the Greek, meaning a "semi-precious stone." Also, from the Persian, meaning "a treasured secret." VARIANT FORMS: Kaspar (German); Gaspard (French); Gaspar (Spanish); Gaspare (Italian); Caspar, Casper. PLACE-NAME USAGE: Jasper National Park, Alberta, Canada.

Jay   From the Old French and Latin *gaius*, referring to a bird in the crow family. Gaius is a variant form. Also, a pet form of Jason. *See* Jason. CONTEMPORARY EXAMPLE: Jay Dermer, city mayor (Miami, Florida). SURNAME USAGE: John Jay (1745-1829), first U.S. Chief Justice of the Supreme Court.

Jean   The French form of John. *See* John. Often used with another name to make a hyphenated first name. CONTEMPORARY EXAMPLES: Jean-Claude Killy, skier; Jean-Luc Ponty, musician.

Jeb Probably a pet form of Jacob. *See* Jacob. CONTEMPORARY EXAMPLE: Jeb Magruder, attorney.

Jed From the Arabic, meaning "hand." Also a pet form of Jedidiah. *See* Jedidiah.

Jedaiah From the Hebrew, meaning "God knows" or "knowledge of God." In the Bible, a member of the tribe of Simeon.

Jedidiah From the Hebrew, meaning "beloved of the Lord." In the Bible, a name of King Solomon. PET FORMS: Jed, Jeddy.

Jef, Jeff Short forms of Jeffery and Geoffrey. *See* Jeffery. Used also as independent names. CONTEMPORARY EXAMPLE: Jef Geeraert, novelist.

Jefferies A patronymic form, meaning "son of Jeffery." *See* Jeffery.

Jefferson A patronymic form, meaning "the son of Jeffers or Jeffery." Became popular as a personal name after the death of Thomas Jefferson. CONTEMPORARY EXAMPLE: Jefferson Davis (1808-1889), president of the Confederacy; Jefferson Jordan, football player. SURNAME USAGE: Thomas Jefferson (1743-1826), U.S. president.

Jeffery, Jefferey From the Anglo-Saxon, meaning "gift of peace" or "God's peace." Variant forms of Geoffrey. PET FORMS: Jef, Jeff.

Jeffie A pet form of Jeffery. *See* Jeffery.

Jeffrey A variant spelling of Jeffery. *See* Jeffery.

Jeffries A pet form of Jeffery. *See* Jeffery. CONTEMPORARY EXAMPLE: Jeffries Wyman, author.

Jeffry A variant spelling of Jeffery. *See* Jeffery.

Jehiel From the Hebrew, meaning "may God live." Yehiel is a variant spelling. In the Bible, a priest who served in the Temple when Josiah was king.

Jehoiachin From the Hebrew, meaning "God will establish." In the Bible, a king of Judah, the son of King Jehoiakim.

Jehoiakim From the Hebrew, meaning "God will establish." In the Bible, a king of Judah who was defeated by the Babylonians. Akim is a short form. Joachim is a variant form.

Jenner A variant form of John. *See* John. SURNAME USAGE: Sir William Jenner (1815-1898), English physician.

Jennings An Anglo-Saxon patronymic form of Jean, meaning "a descendant of Jean or John." CONTEMPORARY EXAMPLES: Jennings Randolph, U.S. senator; Jennings Williams, Lincoln, Nebraska.

Jephthah, Jephtah From the Hebrew, meaning "he will open," referring to the first-born. In the Bible, a judge who sacrificed his daughter to fulfill a vow he had made to God. VARIANT FORMS: Yiftach, Yiftah.

Jerald A variant spelling of Gerald. *See* Gerald. CONTEMPORARY EX-AMPLE: Jerald C. Brauer, theologian.

Jere A variant spelling of Jerry. *See* Jerry. Also, a short form of Jeremiah. *See* Jeremiah. CONTEMPORARY EXAMPLE: Jere Cunningham, novelist.

Jeremiah, Jeremias From the Hebrew, meaning "God will loosen (the bonds)" or "God will uplift." In the Bible, one of the major prophets. He began to prophecy in 625 B.C., and one of the books of the Bible bears his name. VARIANT FORMS: Jeremias (Latin); Hieremias (Greek); Yirmeeyahu (Hebrew). PET FORMS: Jere, Jeremy, Jerry.

Jeremy A pet form of Jeremiah. *See* Jeremiah.

Jerold, Jerrold Variant spellings of Gerald. *See* Gerald.

Jerome From the Greek, meaning "of holy name." A fourth–century monk translated the Bible into Latin. VARIANT FORMS: Jeromo (Spanish); Geronimo (Italian); Jeronim (Russian). Jerry is a pet form.

Jeron A variant form of Jerome. *See* Jerome. CONTEMPORARY EXAMPLE: Jeron Royster, baseball player.

Jerrald A variant spelling of Jerold. *See* Jerold. CONTEMPORARY EX-AMPLE: Jerrald Taylor, football player.

Jerram A variant form of Jerome. *See* Jerome. CONTEMPORARY EXAMPLE: Jerram Delahunty, Southington, Connecticut.

Jerre A variant spelling of Jerry used in Sicily. *See* Jerry. See also Jere. CONTEMPORARY EXAMPLE: Jerre Mangione, Italian author.

Jerrel A variant form of Jarrell and Gerald. *See* Jarrell *and* Gerald. CONTEMPORARY EXAMPLE: Jerrell Wilson, football player.

Jerrold A variant spelling of Jerold and Gerald. *See* Gerald.

Jerry A pet form of Jerold, Jerome, or Jeremiah. *See* Jerold, Jerome, *and* Jeremiah. Used also as an independent name.

Jervis A variant form of Jarvis. *See* Jarvis. PLACE-NAME USAGE: Port Jervis, New York.

Jess A pet form of Jesse. *See* Jesse.

Jessamine A variant form of Jesse. *See* Jesse. CONTEMPORARY EXAMPLE: Jessamine Milner, actor.

Jesse From the Hebrew *yishai*, meaning "wealthy" or "a gift." In the Bible, the father of David. Jess is a pet form.

Jesus From the Hebrew name Yehoshua (Joshua), meaning "God will help." Jesous is a Greek form. In the Bible, the son of Mary and Joseph. Founder of the Christian religion. CONTEMPORARY EXAMPLE: Jesus Alou, baseball player.

Jethro   From the Hebrew, meaning "abundance, riches." In the Bible, the father-in-law of Moses. CONTEMPORARY EXAMPLES: Jethro K. Lieberman, author; Jethro Pugh, football player.

Jett   A pet form of Jethro. *See* Jethro. CONTEMPORARY EXAMPLE: Jett C. Arthur, Jr., editor.

Jib   A name invented by joining part of the father's name, Bill, and the first letter of Junior. CONTEMPORARY EXAMPLE: Jib Reagan, Naples, Florida.

Jim   A pet form of James, evolved by shortening the long "a" sound. *See* James. VARIANT PET FORMS: Jimmie, Jimmy.

Jimbo   A pet form of James, probably a short form of Jimboy. *See* James. CONTEMPORARY EXAMPLE: Jimbo Elrod, football player.

Jimmie, Jimmy   Popular pet forms of James. *See* James. CONTEMPORARY EXAMPLE: Jimmy Hendrix, musician.

Joab   From the Hebrew, meaning "willing" or "God is father." In the Bible, King David's nephew; also a member of the tribe of Judah. CONTEMPORARY EXAMPLE: Joab Thomas, educator.

Joachim   From the Hebrew, meaning "the Lord will establish." In the Bible, a king of Judah. VARIANT FORMS: Jehoiakim, Yehoiakim (Hebrew); Achim, Jochim (German); Joa (Spanish); Giachimo (Italian); Akim (Russian). CONTEMPORARY EXAMPLE: Joachim Neugroschel, editor.

Joaquin   A Spanish form of Jehoiachin. *See* Jehoiachin. CONTEMPORARY EXAMPLE: Joaquin Andujar, baseball player.

Job   From the Hebrew, meaning "hated, oppressed." In the Bible, noted for his patience and faith in God.

Joce   A variant form of Joseph. *See* Joseph. CONTEMPORARY EXAMPLE: Joce Guevremont, hockey player.

Jochanan   From the Hebrew, meaning "God is gracious, merciful." A popular name in post-biblical times, which later evolved into John. *See* John. Johanan is a variant spelling.

Jody   A pet form of Joseph. *See* Joseph. CONTEMPORARY EXAMPLE: Jody Powell, U.S. presidential press secretary.

Joe, Joey   Pet forms of Joseph. *See* Joseph.

Joel   From the Hebrew, meaning "God is willing." In the Bible, one of the twelve minor prophets. SURNAME USAGE: Al Jolson, entertainer.

Joffre   The French form of Geoffrey. *See* Geoffrey. CONTEMPORARY EXAMPLE: Joffre Cross, baseball player. SURNAME USAGE: Joseph Jacques Joffre, French general.

Johanan   A variant spelling of Jochanan. *See* Jochanan.

Johannes   A Middle Latin form of John. *See* John.

John   From the Hebrew, meaning "God is gracious; God is merciful." A contraction of the Hebrew name Johanan (Jochanan). In the Bible, an apostle said to be the author of the Gospel of St. John. King of England (1199-1216) who signed the Magna Carta. Jack, a popular pet form, has taken on a generic meaning and personifies the average man. VARIANT FORMS: Jon (Middle English); Johannes (Middle Latin); Johannes (Late Latin): Joannes (Greek); Jochanan, Johanan, Yochanan (Hebrew); Johan, Jehan, Jan (Old French); Jean, Jeanno (French); Ivan (Russian); Hans, Johann, Johannes (German); Hans, Janne, Jens, Johan (Danish); Giovanni (Italian); Jan (Polish); Jock (Scotch); Juan (Spanish); Sean, Shawn (Gaelic and Irish); Iain, Ian (Gaelic); Jan, Jenkin (Welsh); Jan (Dutch); Janos (Hungarian); Janez, Jovan (Slavonic). PET FORMS: Jack, Johnnie, Johnny. FEMININE FORMS: Jane, Jean, Jeanne, Joan, Joana, Johanna. CONTEMPORARY EXAMPLE: John Paul Jones (1747-1792), American naval officer in Revolutionary War. SURNAME USAGE: Lyndon Baines Johnson, thirty-sixth president of the U.S. PLACE-NAME USAGE: Johnstown, Pennsylvania.

Johnnie, Johnny   Pet forms of John. *See* John.

Jon   A pet form of Jonathan. *See* Jonathan.

Jonah   From the Hebrew *yonah*, meaning "a dove." In the Bible, a prophet who was swallowed by a big fish, but was later spat out and saved.

Jonas   The Greek form of Jonah as used in the Latin (Vulgate) translation of the Bible. *See* Jonah. CONTEMPORARY EXAMPLE: Jonas Salk, developer of the Salk Vaccine.

Jonathan   From the Hebrew, meaning "God has given." In the Bible, the son of King Saul; friend and brother-in-law of David. PET FORMS: Jon, Jonny. CONTEMPORARY EXAMPLE: Jonathan Winters, actor.

Jonathon   A variant spelling of Jonathan. *See* Jonathan. CONTEMPORARY EXAMPLE: Jonathon L. Lazer, publicist.

Jonny   A pet form of Jonathan. *See* Jonathan.

Jophrey   A variant form of Geoffrey. *See* Geoffrey. CONTEMPORARY EXAMPLE: Jophrey Brown, baseball player.

Jordan   From the Hebrew *yarod*, meaning "to flow down, descend," hence "a descendant." VARIANT FORMS: Jori, Jory, Judd. SURNAME USAGE: David Starr Jordan (1851-1931), American educator; Jacob Jordaens (1593-1678), Flemish painter. PLACE-NAME USAGE: a river bordering on Israel and Jordan.

Jorel   A name invented by combining *Joyce* and *reuel*. CONTEMPORARY EXAMPLE: Jorel Stallones, Woodside, California.

Jorge   A Spanish form of George. *See* George. CONTEMPORARY EXAMPLE: Jorge Luis Borges, Argentine author.

Jori, Jory   Pet forms of Jordan. *See* Jordan. CONTEMPORARY EXAMPLE:

Jory Graham, columnist.

Jornel Origin unknown. CONTEMPORARY EXAMPLE: Jornel Williams, football player.

Jose A Spanish form of Joseph. *See* Joseph. CONTEMPORARY EXAMPLE: Jose Morales, baseball player.

Joseph From the Hebrew name Yosayf, meaning "He (God) will add or increase." In the Bible, the son of Jacob and Rachel. In the New Testament, the father of Jesus. VARIANT FORMS: Joses (Greek); Josce (French); Giuseppe, Beppo, Peppo (Italian); Jose, Pepe, Pepito (Spanish and Portuguese); Josko, Jaska (Slavic); Josephus (Latin); Yosayf, Yosef (Hebrew); Yussuf (Arabic); Iosif (Russian). PET FORMS: Jo, Joe, Joey, Joie. FEMININE FORMS: Jo, Josie, Josepha, Josephine. SURNAME USAGE: Josephs, Jessop, Jessup. PLACE-NAME USAGE: St. Joe, West Virginia; San Jose, California; St. Joseph, Missouri.

Josephus The Latin form of Joseph. *See* Joseph. CONTEMPORARY EXAMPLE: Josephus Daniels (1862-1948), American statesman and journalist. Josepha is a feminine form. SURNAME USAGE: Flavius Josephus (c. 30-100), Jewish historian.

Josh A pet form of Joshua and Josiah. *See* Joshua *and* Josiah. CONTEMPORARY EXAMPLE: Josh Logan, theatrical director.

Joshua From the Hebrew, meaning "the Lord is my salvation." In the Bible, the successor to Moses who led the children of Israel into the Promised Land. The original Hebrew Yehoshua, akin to Hoshayah (Hosea). The Latin form is Josue. In the post-biblical period, Joshua was one of the most frequently used names. During the Greek period, Jews in the upper strata of society originally named Joshua changed their names to the Greek Jason. Jesus is a variant form of Joshua. *See* Jesus. Josh is a pet form.

Josiah From the Hebrew, meaning "fire of the Lord." Also, from the Arabic, meaning "God has supported or protected." In the Bible, a king of Judah (637-608 B.C.). He ascended the throne at the age of eight, upon the murder of his father, Amon. Josias is the Greek form. Josh is a pet form.

Jotham From the Hebrew, meaning "God is perfect." In the Bible, the youngest of Gideon's seventy sons. Also, a king of Judah.

Jotun From the Old English *eotun,* meaning "a giant." In Norse mythology, any one of a group of giants.

Joubert A variant form of the Anglo-Saxon name Godbeohrt, meaning "praise or brilliance of God." CONTEMPORARY EXAMPLE: Joubert Davenport, baseball player. SURNAME USAGE: Joseph Joubert (1754-1824), French essayist.

Jovett A French pet form, meaning "beloved God." CONTEMPORARY

EXAMPLE: Jovett Pfiester, baseball player.

Joyce From the Latin name Jocosa, meaning "merry." More commonly a feminine name. CONTEMPORARY EXAMPLES: Joyce Pidkin, football player; Joyce Hall, publisher. SURNAME USAGE: James Joyce (1882-1941), Irish novelist.

Joyner From the Old French *joindre*, meaning "to join together." An occupational name for a carpenter who finishes and joins wood planks. Joynt is an Irish form. CONTEMPORARY EXAMPLE: Joyner White, baseball player.

Jubal From the Hebrew *yovel*, meaning "jubilee." In the Bible, a son of Lamech. Jubal Anderson Early (1816-1894), Civil War general.

Jud A variant spelling of Judd, derived from Judah or Jordan. *See* Judah *and* Jordan. Also, an independent name. CONTEMPORARY EXAMPLE: Jud Morris, author.

Judah From the Hebrew, meaning "praise." In the Bible, one of the sons of Jacob and Leah. VARIANT FORMS: Yehuda, Yehudah (Hebrew); Judas, Jude (Latin); Jud, Judd (English). Juda is a variant spelling. Judith is a feminine form.

Judas The Latin form of Judah. *See* Judah. In the Bible, Judas is a disciple who betrayed Jesus. Judas Maccabaeus led the revolt against the Syrians who ruled Palestine in the second century B.C.

Judd A variant form of Judah or Jordan. *See* Judah *and* Jordan. CONTEMPORARY EXAMPLE: Judd Hirsch, actor.

Jude A variant form of Judah. *See* Judah. In the Bible, a Christian apostle. CONTEMPORARY EXAMPLE: Jude G. Cleary, educator.

Judson A patronymic form of Judah, meaning "Judah's (or Judd's) son." *See* Judah. Popular as a surname. CONTEMPORARY EXAMPLE: Judson Welliver, U.S. President Warren Harding's political secretary; Judson Philips, novelist.

Juedon Most frequently a French surname. CONTEMPORARY EXAMPLE: Juedon Finis, Attleboro, Massachusetts.

Jule, Jules Variant forms of Julian or Julius. *See* Julian *and* Julius. CONTEMPORARY EXAMPLE: Jule Styne, composer.

Julian Origin uncertain, but probably from the Greek, meaning "soft-haired, light-bearded." Julius, derived from Julianus, is the Latin form, and is most commonly used. VARIANT FORMS: Julien, Jules (French); Giuliano, Guliano, (Italian); Julio (Spanish); Jellon (Scotch). FEMININE FORMS: Juliana, Juliet. CONTEMPORARY EXAMPLE: Julian Bond, state senator (Georgia).

Julio The Spanish form of Julian and Julius. *See* Julian *and* Julius. CONTEMPORARY EXAMPLE: Julio Morales, baseball player.

Julius   A variant form of Julian. *See* Julian. The Romans popularized it by naming the month in which Julius Caesar was born July. The Julian calendar, introduced by Julius Caesar in 46 B.C., was named after him. VARIANT FORMS: Julio (Spanish and Portuguese); Iola (Welsh); Jules, Julot (French); Giulio (Italian).

Jum   A short form of Jumbo. *See* Jumbo. CONTEMPORARY EXAMPLE: Jum C. Nunnaly, psychologist.

Jumb, Jumbo   From the African *jamba,* meaning "elephant." P.T. Barnum named his large circus elephant Jumbo.

June   From the Latin name Junius. The name of the sixth month, which honors the great Roman family Junius. More commonly used as a feminine name. *See* June (feminine section). CONTEMPORARY EXAMPLE: June Barnes, baseball player.

Junior   A contracted form of the Latin *juvenior,* meaning "young." CONTEMPORARY EXAMPLE: Junior Bridgeman, basketball player. Used also to designate a son who carries the same name as his father (abbreviated Jr.).

Junius   A variant form of the Latin Junior. *See* Junior. June is the feminine form. CONTEMPORARY EXAMPLE: Junius Brutus Booth, actor (father of John Wilkes Booth).

Jurgen   A Germanic form of George. *See* George. Akin to the Danish Jorgen. CONTEMPORARY EXAMPLE: Jurgen M. Wolff, author.

Justin   A variant form of Justus. *See* Justus. CONTEMPORARY EXAMPLE: Justin M. Saccio, San Diego, California.

Justino   An Italian form of Justus. *See* Justus. CONTEMPORARY EXAMPLE: Justino Fernandez, art critic.

Justus   From the Latin, meaning "just." Justus is the Latin form. Saint Justin was a first-century Christian martyr. Justina is a feminine form. CONTEMPORARY EXAMPLE: Justus D. Sundermann, educator.

Jut   A short form of Justin. *See* Justin. Also, perhaps a short form of Jute, an ancient German tribe that lived in Jutland in northern Europe. CONTEMPORARY EXAMPLE: Jut Meininger, author.

Juventino   From the Latin *juvenis,* meaning "young, youthful." CONTEMPORARY EXAMPLE: Juventino Villarreal, Watsonville, California.

K

Kadmiel From the Hebrew, meaning "God is the ancient One." In the Bible, a Levite.

Kahil From the Arabic, meaning "friend, lover." Also, a variant form of Kalil. *See* Kalil.

Kahlil A variant form of Kalil. *See* Kalil. In the Talmud, the father of Abaye. CONTEMPORARY EXAMPLE: Kahlil Gilbran (1883-1931), philosopher.

Kai From the Hawaiian, meaning "ocean." Also, a variant form of Kay. *See* Kay. CONTEMPORARY EXAMPLE: Kai Erikson, publisher.

Kaikane From the Hawaiian, meaning "man of the sea."

Kailil A variant form of Kalil. *See* Kalil. In the Talmud, the father of Abaye.

Kal Possibly a short form of Kalil or Kalman. *See* Kalil *and* Kalman. May also be a variant form of the German Kahl, meaning "bald." CONTEMPORARY EXAMPLE: Kal Segrist, baseball player.

Kalani From the Hawaiian, meaning "the heavens."

Kalil From the Greek *kalos,* meaning "beautiful." Akin to Kahlil. *See* Kahlil. Also, from the Hebrew, meaning "a crown, a wreath." Kailil is a variant spelling. Kalila is a feminine form.

Kallie A variant form of Kalil. *See* Kalonymos. CONTEMPORARY EXAMPLE: Kallie Knoetze, South African boxer.

Kalman A short form of Kalonymos. *See* Kalonymos. CONTEMPORARY EXAMPLE: Kalman Levitan, U.S. Army chaplain.

Kalonymos A variant form of the Latin name Clement, meaning "merciful or gracious." Popular among eminent Jewish families in Germany from the ninth to the thirteenth centuries with its origin in eighth-century Italy. Kalonymos ben Kalonymos was a fourteenth-century scholar who translated Arabic works into Hebrew and Latin for King Robert of Naples.

Kalton From the Greek *kalos,* meaning "beautiful," hence "beautiful town." CONTEMPORARY EXAMPLE: Kalton C. LaHue, editor.

Kane A variant form of Keene. *See* Keane. SURNAME USAGE: Richard Kane, football player.

Kani A variant form of Keene. *See* Keene. Or, a pet form of Kaniel.

See Kaniel. CONTEMPORARY EXAMPLE: Kani Evans, fishing record-holder.

Kaniel   From the Hebrew, meaning "a reed, a stalk," or from the Arabic, meaning "a spear."

Kaniela   The Hawaiian form of Daniel. *See* Daniel.

Kareem   From the Arabic, meaning "noble, exalted." Karim is a variant spelling. CONTEMPORARY EXAMPLE: Kareem Abdul-Jabbar, basketball player.

Karel   A variant form of Carol and Charles. *See* Charles. CONTEMPORARY EXAMPLE: Karel Husa, composer.

Karim   A variant spelling of Kareem. *See* Kareem.

Kario   A variant form of Kareem. *See* Kareem. CONTEMPORARY EXAMPLE: Kario Salem, actor.

Karl   A variant spelling for Carl, a form of Charles. *See* Charles.

Karmel, Karmeli   Variant spellings of Carmel and Carmeli. *See* Carmel *and* Carmeli.

Karmi   A variant spelling of Carmi. *See* Carmi.

Karmiel   A variant spelling of Carmiel. *See* Carmiel.

Karol, Karole   Variant spellings of Carol. *See* Carol. CONTEMPORARY EXAMPLE: Karol J. Mysels, chemist.

Kati   A pet form of Katriel used in Israel. *See* Katriel.

Katriel   From the Hebrew, meaning "the Lord is my crown."

Kaufman, Kaufmann   From the German, meaning "a buyer, a merchant." CONTEMPORARY EXAMPLE: Kaufmann Kohler, biblical scholar. SURNAME USAGE: George S. Kaufman, playwright.

Kavika   The Hawaiian form of David. *See* David.

Kay   Either from the Greek, meaning "rejoicing," or from a Germanic root, meaning "a fortified place" or "a warden." May also be derived from the Latin, meaning "gay." The Welsh converted it into Kai, akin to Caius (or Gaius), the first name (praenomen) of Julius Caesar. In Arthurian legend, one of the Knights of the Round Table, a foster brother of King Arthur. Used also as a feminine pet form of Katherine. PLACE-NAME USAGE: a county in Oklahoma.

Kayne   A variant spelling of Kane. *See* Kane.

Kaz   A pet form of Cassius. *See* Cassius. Chaz is a variant spelling.

Kean, Keane   Variant forms of Keene. *See* Keane. CONTEMPORARY EXAMPLE: Edmund Kean (1787-1833), English actor.

Kearney, Kearny   Variant forms of Kern. *See* Kern. SURNAME USAGE:

Philip Kearny (1814-1862), U.S. Army general. PLACE-NAME USAGE: Kearny, New Jersey.

Kedem   From the Hebrew, meaning "old, ancient," hence "from the East."

Keefe   An Irish form of the Arabic *kef* and *kaif,* meaning "well-being, peacefulness (induced by smoking narcotics)." SURNAME USAGE: O'Keefe, meaning "son of Keefe."

Keegan   A condensed form of the Celtic MacEgan, meaning "son of Egan." *See* Egan.

Keenan   A variant form of Keene. *See* Keene. CONTEMPORARY EXAMPLE: Keenan Wynn, actor.

Keene   From the Old English *cene,* meaning "wise, learned," and the German *kuhn,* meaning "bold." CONTEMPORARY EXAMPLE: Keene Curtis, actor.

Keever   A variant form of Keefe. *See* Keefe. CONTEMPORARY EXAMPLE: Keever Jankovich, football player.

Keir   A variant form of Kerr. *See* Kerr. CONTEMPORARY EXAMPLE: Keir Dullea, actor.

Keith   From the Gaelic, meaning "the wind." A popular name in Scotland. CONTEMPORARY EXAMPLE: Keith Carradine, actor. SURNAME USAGE: Sir Arthur Keith (1866-1955), Scottish-born anthropologist. PLACE-NAME USAGE: a town in Scotland.

Kelley   A variant spelling of Kelsey. *See* Kelsey.

Kellog   A variant form of Kelly. *See* Kelly.

Kellow   A variant form of Kelly. *See* Kelly. CONTEMPORARY EXAMPLE: Kellow Chesney, author.

Kelly   From the Old English *ceol,* meaning "a keel, a ship," and the Dutch and the Old Norse *kill,* meaning "a stream, river, inlet," hence "the ship on or near the river." CONTEMPORARY EXAMPLE: Kelly Greenbank, hockey player.

Kelo   Origin uncertain. Probably an Indian name. CONTEMPORARY EXAMPLES: Kelo Henderson, actor; Kelo Turcotte, Bar Harbor, Maine.

Kelsey   A variant form of Kelson. *See* Kelson. Kelcey is a variant spelling.

Kelson   From the Middle Dutch *kiel,* meaning "a boat." VARIANT FORMS: Keelson, Kelcey, Kelsey. Akin to Kelly. *See* Kelly.

Kelton   From the Old English, meaning "keel town," or "the town where ships are built." Akin to Kelson. *See* Kelson. CONTEMPORARY EXAMPLE: Kelton Winston, football player. Used also as a feminine name.

Kelvin, Kelwin   From the Anglo-Saxon, meaning "a friend or lover of ships." CONTEMPORARY EXAMPLE: Kelvin Bourke, jockey. SURNAME USAGE: William Thomson Kelvin (1824-1907), English physicist.

Kemp   From the Anglo-Saxon, meaning "a Saxon lord" or "royalty." Kem is a variant form. CONTEMPORARY EXAMPLE: Kemp Wicker, baseball player. SURNAME USAGE: Thomas a Kempis (c. 1380–1471), German monk and scholar.

Ken   A short form of Kenneth. *See* Kenneth. Also, an independent name from the British *cen*, meaning "a head, a headland." CONTEMPORARY EXAMPLE: Ken Auletta, author.

Kendal, Kendall   From the Celtic, meaning "ruler of the valley." Also, the name of a green wool cloth woven in Kendal, England. PET FORMS: Ken, Kenny. CONTEMPORARY EXAMPLE: Kendall Webster Sessions, author. SURNAME USAGE: Kendal, England; Kendalia, West Virginia, named after G.W. Kendall, a local resident.

Kendig   A variant form of Kendrick. *See* Kendrick. CONTEMPORARY EXAMPLE: Kendig Brubaker Cully, editor.

Kendrick   From the Anglo-Saxon *coenric,* meaning "royal." VARIANT FORMS: Kendig, Kendal, Kendall.

Kene   A variant spelling of Kenny, the pet form of Kenneth. *See* Kenneth. Or, from the Old English *cene,* meaning "brave." Akin to Keene. CONTEMPORARY EXAMPLE: Kene Holliday, actor.

Kenelm   From the Old English, meaning "king or ruler of the elms." Or, a compound of *cene* and *helm,* meaning "brave helmet (ruler)." CONTEMPORARY EXAMPLE: Kenelm Burridge, author.

Kenesaw, Kennesaw   Probably from the Old Norse *kenna,* meaning "to know." Also, an Indian (Cherokee) name of uncertain meaning. Ken is a pet form. CONTEMPORARY EXAMPLE: Kenesaw Mountain Landis, baseball commissioner. PLACE-NAME USAGE: Kennesaw Mountain, northwest Georgia.

Kenley   From the British, meaning "headland, peninsula." CONTEMPORARY EXAMPLE: Kenley Jones, television news reporter.

Kenman   From Old English, meaning "leadman, ruler."

Kenn   A pet form of Kenneth. *See* Kenneth. CONTEMPORARY EXAMPLE: Kenn Oberrecht, author.

Kennard   A variant form of Kennedy. *See* Kennedy.

Kennedy   From the old English *cyn*, meaning "royal." SURNAME USAGE: John F. Kennedy (1917-1963), thirty–fifth president of the U.S. PLACE-NAME USAGE: Cape Kennedy, Florida.

Kenneth   From the Scottish and Gaelic *caioreach,* meaning "comely, handsome." VARIANT FORMS: Kent, Kenton, Kenric, Kenrich, Kemp. SURNAME USAGE: Mackenzie, meaning "son of Kenneth."

Kenric, Kenrick   From the British *cyn* and the Anglo-Saxon *coenric,* meaning "royal." VARIANT FORMS: Kendrick, Kenwright.

Kent   A variant form of Kenneth. *See* Kenneth. CONTEMPORARY EXAMPLE: Kent Benson, basketball player. PLACE-NAME USAGE: a county in England; a city in Connecticut; Kent, Ohio, named after a family of local businessmen.

Kenton   A variant form of Kent and Kenneth. *See* Kenneth. CONTEMPORARY EXAMPLE: Kenton Boyer, baseball player.

Kenward   From the Old English, meaning "brave guard." Akin to Kenneth and Kenric.

Kenyon   A variant form of Kenneth. *See* Kenneth. CONTEMPORARY EXAMPLE: Kenyon C. Rosenberg, librarian. SURNAME USAGE: John Samuel Kenyon (1874-1959), educator.

Kerby   A variant spelling of Kirby. *See* Kirby.

Kermit   A variant form of the Dutch *kermis,* meaning "a church." CONTEMPORARY EXAMPLES: Kermit Washington, basketball player; Kermit Roosevelt, U.S. President Theodore Roosevelt's son.

Kern   From the Old Irish *ceitern,* meaning "a band of soldiers." CONTEMPORARY EXAMPLE: Kern Leslie Kemp, Covina, California; Kern Pederson, author. SURNAME USAGE: Jerome David Kern (1885-1945), U.S. composer. PLACE-NAME USAGE: Kern County, California, named after E.M. Kern, typographer and artist who accompanied Fremont in 1845.

Kerr   From the Norse, meaning "marshland." Carr is a variant form. SURNAME USAGE: William Kerr (died 1814), British botanist.

Kerry   A variant form of Kerr. *See* Kerr. Or, from the British *ceri,* one of Britain's early kings. CONTEMPORARY EXAMPLE: Kerry Reardon, football player. PLACE-NAME USAGE: a county in southwest Ireland.

Kerwin   From the Old English, meaning "a friend of the marshlands." Kerr is a variant form.

Kester   A variant English form of Christopher. *See* Christopher.

Ketti   A variant form of the Old English surnames Kettle and Kittle, meaning "cauldron (of the gods)." CONTEMPORARY EXAMPLE: Ketti Fringo, Pulitzer Prize winner in drama (1958).

Keven   A variant spelling of Kevin. *See* Kevin.

Kevin   From the Gaelic, meaning "handsome, beautiful." Coemgen is the Old Irish form. CONTEMPORARY EXAMPLE: Kevin Dobson, actor.

Key   From the Old English *caeg,* meaning "a key," hence "a protected place." VARIANT FORMS: Keg, Keigh. CONTEMPORARY EXAMPLE: Key Pittman, U.S. senator. SURNAME USAGE: Francis Scott Key (1779–1843), U.S. lawyer.

Keyes   A variant form of Key. *See* Key. CONTEMPORARY EXAMPLE: Keyes Beech, Pulitzer Prize winner in journalism (1951).

Kibby   From the British, meaning "cottage by the water." SURNAME USAGE: Guy Kibby, actor.

Kidd   From the British *cadr,* meaning "strong." VARIANT FORMS: Cad, Cade. SURNAME USAGE: Michael Kidd, choreographer.

Kildare   Compounded from the Dutch *kil,* meaning "stream, creek," and the Old English *dear,* meaning "courageous, bold." PLACE-NAME USAGE: a county in eastern Ireland.

Kile   A variant spelling of Kyle. *See* Kyle. CONTEMPORARY EXAMPLE: Kile Morgan, city mayor (National City, California.)

Kilgore   From the Dutch *kil,* meaning "stream, creek," and *gore,* meaning "warm, hot (blood of an animal, which was shed)." CONTEMPORARY EXAMPLE: Kilgore Trout, a character name invented by novelist Kurt Vonnegut.

Kilian   From the British *kil,* meaning "a cell, a retreat." Used in Scotland and Ireland.

Kilmer   From the Dutch and French, meaning "an inlet to the sea" or "a retreat near the sea." *See* Kilian. CONTEMPORARY EXAMPLE: C. Kilmer Myers, clergyman. SURNAME USAGE: (Alfred) Joyce Kilmer (1886-1918), American poet.

Kim   A pet form of Kimball or Kimberly. *See* Kimball *and* Kimberly. Used also as a feminine name. CONTEMPORARY EXAMPLES: Kim Philby, Russian spy; Kim Davis, hockey player.

Kimball   Perhaps from Cunobeline, a British king who was defeated by the Romans at Kimble, England. Probably from the Greek *kymbalon,* meaning "a hollow vessel," and *kymbe,* meaning "a boat." CONTEMPORARY EXAMPLE: Kimball King, author.

Kimberly   Used most often as a feminine name. *See* Kimberly (feminine section).

Kimo   The Hawaiian form of James. *See* James.

Kinchen   From the Old English *cynn,* and the Old Norse *kyn,* meaning "related to; family; kin." Chen is a diminutive German form, meaning "little relative." CONTEMPORARY EXAMPLE: Kinchen Ray, Oklahoma City, Oklahoma.

King   From the Anglo-Saxon, meaning "ruler." CONTEMPORARY EXAMPLE: King Hill, football player. SURNAME USAGE: Martin Luther King, Jr., clergyman.

Kingsley   From the Anglo-Saxon, meaning "from the king's meadow." CONTEMPORARY EXAMPLE: Kingsley Amis, author. SURNAME USAGE: Charles Kingsley (1819-1875), English clergyman.

Kingston From the Old English, meaning "the king's town." PLACE-NAME USAGE: capital of Jamaica; a city in New York.

Kinnaird From the Old English *cyning*, meaning "a king." Akin to Kingston. CONTEMPORARY EXAMPLE: Kinnaird McKee, educator.

Kinsey From the British *cyne*, meaning "royal." SURNAME USAGE: Alfred Charles Kinsey (1894-1956), American zoologist.

Kinta An American Indian name, meaning "a beaver." PLACE-NAME USAGE: Kinta, Oklahoma.

Kip A pet form of Kipling. *See* Kipling. CONTEMPORARY EXAMPLE: Kip Addotta, comedian.

Kipling From the Middle English *kypre*, meaning "a kippered (cured) herring or salmon." Kip is a pet form. SURNAME USAGE: (Joseph) Rudyard Kipling (1865-1936), English author.

Kirby From the Old English *ciric* and *cirice* and the Middle English *kirke*, meaning "a church." Or, from the British, meaning "a cottage by the water." VARIANT FORMS: Kerby, Kerr, Kirk. SURNAME USAGE: George Kirby, entertainer.

Kiril, Kyril Variant spellings of Cyril. From the Old English, meaning "a church." CONTEMPORARY EXAMPLES: Kiril Sokoloff, editor; Kyril Bonfiglioli, novelist.

Kirk The Scottish form of the Middle English *kirke* and the Old English *ciric* and *cirice*, meaning "a church." CONTEMPORARY EXAMPLE: Kirk Douglas, actor.

Kirkland From the Old English, meaning "church's land." Kirtland is a variant form.

Kirtland A variant form of Kirkland. *See* Kirkland. PLACE-NAME USAGE: Kirtland, northern England.

Kirtly A variant form of Kirk, meaning "the lea (meadow) near the church." CONTEMPORARY EXAMPLE: Kirtly Baker, baseball player.

Kit A pet form of Christopher. *See* Christopher. CONTEMPORARY EXAMPLE: Kit Carson (1809-1867), American frontiersman. PLACE-NAME USAGE: Kit Carson, a mountain pass in California, named by Fremont after his guide, Kit Carson.

Kitron From the Hebrew, meaning "crown."

Kivi A short form of Akiba, Yaakov, or Jacob. *See* Jacob.

Klaas, Klaus Short forms of Nicolaus. *See* Nicolaus *and* Nicholas. CONTEMPORARY EXAMPLE: Klaus Voorman, rock musician.

Klemens A variant form of Clement. *See* Clement. CONTEMPORARY EXAMPLE: Klemens Tilmann, author.

Kline From the German *klein*, meaning "small." CONTEMPORARY EX-

AMPLE: Kline Gilbert, football player. SURNAME USAGE: Benjamin S. Kline (1886–1968), American pathologist.

Knoll From the Old English *cnoll*, meaning "a round, smooth hill." Koll is a short form. Knox is a variant form. *See* Knox.

Knox From the British *knock* (*cnwee*), meaning "a bunch or swelling," hence "a hill." A variant form of Knoll. *See* Knoll. CONTEMPORARY EXAMPLE: Knox Ramsey, football player. SURNAME USAGE: John Knox (c.1505-1572), religious reformer. PLACE-NAME USAGE: Knoxville, Tennessee.

Knud An early Danish form of Knut. *See* Knut.

Knut, Knute From the Swedish *knut*, meaning "a knot." King Canute (Knut) was a Danish king who won a battle at Knutsford. CONTEMPORARY EXAMPLES: Knut Hamsun, Nobel Prize winner in literature (1920); Knute Rockne, football coach.

Koll A short form of Knoll. *See* Knoll. Knox is a variant form.

Konrad A variant spelling of Conrad. *See* Conrad.

Korah, Korach From the Hebrew, meaning "bald." In the Bible, a Levite related to Moses, who led a rebellion against the leadership of Moses and Aaron, but failed.

Kraig A variant spelling of Craig. *See* Craig. CONTEMPORARY EXAMPLE: Kraig Metzinger, actor.

Kramer A variant spelling of Cramer. *See* Cramer.

Kresten A Danish form of Christian. *See* Christian. CONTEMPORARY EXAMPLE: Kresten Nordentoft, author.

Kris, Kristian Variant forms of Christian and Christopher. *See* Christian *and* Christopher. CONTEMPORARY EXAMPLE: Kris Kristofferson, actor.

Krystian A variant spelling of Kristian. *See* Kristian. CONTEMPORARY EXAMPLE: Krystian Michallik, soccer player.

Kunta A name made popular by author Alex Haley in *Roots*. Kunta Kinte was Haley's ancestor in Africa.

Kurt A pet form of Konrad. *See* Konrad. CONTEMPORARY EXAMPLE: Kurt Vonnegut, novelist.

Kuti A pet form of Yekutiel. *See* Yekutiel.

Kyle A Gaelic form of the Old English name Kyloe, meaning "a hill where the cattle graze." Kile is a variant spelling. CONTEMPORARY EXAMPLE: Kyle Rote, sportscaster.

L

Laban   From the Hebrew, meaning "white." In the Bible, a resident of Aram Naharaim, the brother of Rebekah and the father of Leah and Rachel. In Jewish folklore, Laban, the Aramean, is synonymous with "deceiver."

Label   A pet form of the Yiddish name Leib, meaning "lion." Leibel is a variant spelling. *See* Leibel.

Labert   A French form of the Anglo-Saxon name Bert, meaning "bright." *See* Bert. Also, a metathesis of *labret*, from the Latin *labrum*, meaning "lip," an ornament of wood or bone worn by some American Indians in a hole pierced in the lip. CONTEMPORARY EXAMPLE: Labert Meyer, baseball player.

Labron   From the French *brun*, meaning "brown." A variant form of Bruno. *See* Bruno. CONTEMPORARY EXAMPLE: Labron Harris, golf player.

Lachlan   From the Old English *loc*, meaning "an enclosure, a prison," hence "enclosed land." Or, a variant form of Lakeland. *See* Lake. Or, a variant form of Lalan, the Lowlands of Scotland, where the Scottish dialect Lalan is spoken. CONTEMPORARY EXAMPLE: Lachlan P. MacDonald, publisher.

Ladd, Laddie   From Middle English *ladde*, meaning "a boy." CONTEMPORARY EXAMPLE: Ladd Marback, publisher. SURNAME USAGE: Alan Ladd, actor.

Ladimir   A variant form of the Russian name Vladimir. *See* Vladimir. CONTEMPORARY EXAMPLE: Ladimir Zemen, football player.

Laertes   In Greek mythology, the father of Odysseus. In Shakespeare's *Hamlet*, the brother of Ophelia.

Lafayette   From the Old French *fei*, meaning "faith." CONTEMPORARY EXAMPLE: Lafayette Russell, football player. SURNAME USAGE: Marquis de LaFayette (1757–1834), French statesman. PLACE-NAME USAGE: a city in Indiana.

Laffit, Lafitte   Variant forms of Lafayette. *See* Lafayette. CONTEMPORARY EXAMPLE: Laffit Pincay, jockey. SURNAME USAGE: Jean Lafitte, nineteenth–century pirate in the Gulf of Mexico.

Laird   A form of Lord, which in Scotland refers to wealthy landowners. CONTEMPORARY EXAMPLE: Laird Sutton, photographer.

Lake   From the Latin *lacus*, meaning "a pond, a lake." Loch is an Old

English form from *lager*, meaning "water." SURNAME USAGE: Veronica Lake, actress.

Lale, Lalo   From the Latin *lallare*, meaning "to sing a lullaby." SURNAME USAGE: Edward Lalo (1823-1892), French composer.

Lamar, LaMar   From the Latin and French, meaning "of the sea." CONTEMPORARY EXAMPLES: Lamar Alexander, state governor; LaMar T. Empey, professor.

Lambert   From the German and French, meaning "the brightness of the land." Lamberto is the Italian form. CONTEMPORARY EXAMPLE: Lambert C. Mims, city mayor (Mobile, Alabama). SURNAME USAGE: J.H. Lambert (1728-1777), German physicist.

Lammie   A pet form of either Lambert or Lamar. *See* Lambert *and* Lamar. CONTEMPORARY EXAMPLE: Lammie Robertson, soccer player.

LaMont, Lamont   From the Latin, French, and Spanish, meaning "the mountain." PLACE-NAME USAGE: Lamonta, Oregon.

Lance   From the Latin *lancea*, meaning "a light spear." Lancelot is a pet form. CONTEMPORARY EXAMPLES: Lance Morrow, editor; Lance Kerwin, actor. SURNAME USAGE: Bert Lance, banker. PLACE-NAME USAGE: Lance Creek, Wyoming.

Lancelot   In Arthurian legend, one of the bravest of the Knights at King Arthur's Round Table. PLACE-NAME USAGE: Lancelot Point, Arizona.

Landan   From the Anglo-Saxon *launde*, meaning "an open, grassy area; a lawn." VARIANT FORMS: Lander, Landor, Landis, Landman, Lunds, Lunt. PLACE-NAME USAGE: Landan, a city in Germany.

Lander, Landers   Possibly a short form of Flanders, once an independent country to the north of France. Or, a form of Landan. *See* Landan. SURNAME USAGE: General F.W. Lander, nineteenth–century American explorer. PLACE-NAME USAGE: cities in Nevada and Wyoming named for General Lander.

Landis   A variant form of Landan. *See* Landan. SURNAME USAGE: Kenesaw Mountain Landis (1866-1944), U.S. commissioner of baseball.

Landon   A variant form of Landan. *See* Landan. SURNAME USAGE: Alfred Landon, U.S. presidential candidate. PLACE-NAME USAGE: Lando, South Carolina, settled by Germans from Landan, Germany, in the eighteenth century.

Landor   A variant form of Landan. *See* Landan. Landon is a variant spelling. SURNAME USAGE: Walter Savage Landor (1775-1864), English writer.

Landry   A variant form of Landan and Landor. From the Old English, meaning "rough (*rih*) land." Langtry is a variant form. SURNAME USAGE: John Landry, clergyman.

Lane From the Old English *lanu*, meaning "to move, to go," hence "a narrow path between hedges; a road." CONTEMPORARY EXAMPLE: Lane Kirkland, union leader. SURNAME USAGE: Mark Lane, attorney.

Lang From the German, meaning "long." Originally a nickname, which evolved into many surnames. Largo is a Spanish form.

Langdon A compounded Old English form, meaning "long valley." *See* Lang.

Langer A variant form of Lang, meaning "tall one." SURNAME USAGE: Susanne Langer (born 1895), American philosopher.

Langford An Old English compounded form, meaning "the long river crossing." *See also* Lang. SURNAME USAGE: Frances Langford, actress.

Langhorne From the Old English, meaning "long horn." CONTEMPORARY EXAMPLE: Langhorne Bond, aviation executive.

Langley A variant Old English form of the German *lang*, meaning "the long meadow." SURNAME USAGE: Samuel Pierpont Langley (1834-1906), American astronomer. PLACE-NAME USAGE: Mount Langley, California, named after S.P. Langley.

Langston A compounded Old English name from *lang* and *ton*, meaning "a long narrow town." *See also* Lang. CONTEMPORARY EXAMPLE: Langston Hughes, author.

Langtry A variant form of Landry. *See* Landry. PLACE-NAME USAGE: Langtry, Texas, named for Lily Langtry, actress.

Lanny A pet name of a variety of names with the *lang* prefix. CONTEMPORARY EXAMPLE: Lanny MacDonald, hockey player.

Lansing An Old English patronymic form, meaning "son of Lance." *See* Lance. CONTEMPORARY EXAMPLE: Lansing Lamont, author. SURNAME USAGE: Robert Lansing, actor. PLACE-NAME USAGE: Lansing, Michigan; Lansing, New York, named for John Lansing (c.1800).

Larney From the Old English, meaning "the water in the lowlands." Also, perhaps a short form of *blarney*, from the Middle English, meaning "to blare, to talk loudly." CONTEMPORARY EXAMPLE: Larney E. Owens, publisher.

Larns A pet form of Laurence. *See* Laurence.

Larron From the French, meaning "a thief." Latheron and Lathron are corrupt forms. CONTEMPORARY EXAMPLE: Larron Jackson, football player.

Larry A popular pet form of Laurence. *See* Laurence.

Lars A Swedish pet form of Laurence. *See* Laurence. CONTEMPORARY EXAMPLE: Lars Gustafsson, author.

Larson A patronymic form of Larns or Lars. Used in Ireland. *See*

Larns *and* Lars.

Larvall, Larvell　From the Old English, meaning "the well in the lowlands." *See* Larney. CONTEMPORARY EXAMPLE: Larvall Blanks, baseball player.

Laszlo　Probably a Slovakian form of Lazarus. *See* Lazarus. CONTEMPORARY EXAMPLE: Laszlo Kovacs, cinemaphotographer.

Latham　From the Old English *leth* and *lathe*, meaning "a division, a district." CONTEMPORARY EXAMPLE: Latham Flanagan, football player. PLACE-NAME USAGE: Latham, New York.

Lather　From the Old English *lath* and *lathe*, meaning "a district, a division." CONTEMPORARY EXAMPLE: Lather A. Bannigan, Diamond Bar, California.

Latimer　From the Old English, meaning "a district near the sea." Akin to Latham.

Laurence　From the Latin, meaning "a laurel, a crown." VARIANT FORMS: Larkin, Lawrence (English); Laurent (French); Laurie (Scotch); Lorenz (German); Lorenzo (Spanish and Italian); Lanty, Larry (Irish); Lars (Danish). Laura is a feminine form. PET FORMS: Laurie, Larry. SURNAME USAGE: Laurie, Lawrenson, Lawson, Lawrie. PLACE-NAME USAGE: Laurentian Mountains, Canada.

Laurie　A pet form of Laurence. *See* Laurence. The name of a character in Louisa May Olcott's *Little Women*. More commonly a feminine name. CONTEMPORARY EXAMPLES: Laurie Calloway, soccer player; Laurie VanWinkle, Billings, Montana.

Lauriston　A variant form of Laurence, meaning "Laurie's town." CONTEMPORARY EXAMPLE: Lauriston L. Scaife, clergyman.

Lauro　An Italian form of Laurence. *See* Laurence. CONTEMPORARY EXAMPLE: Lauro Martines, historian.

Laval　A French form of Lave. *See* Lave. SURNAME USAGE: Pierre Laval (1883-1945), French statesman.

Lave　From the Old English *hlaford*, meaning "Lord." Also, from the Italian *lave* and the Latin *labes*, meaning "lava, a mountain of molten rock." Akin to Lawton. *See* Lawton.

Lavern, Laverne, LaVerne　From the French forms of the Latin *vernus*, *vernalis*, meaning "belonging to spring." Akin to the French *verd*, meaning "green." Vernon is a variant form. Used also as feminine forms. CONTEMPORARY EXAMPLES: Lavern Dilweg, Laverne Smith, LaVerne Allers, football players. SURNAME USAGE: Jules Verne (1828–1905), French author.

Lavey　A variant form of Levi. *See* Levi. CONTEMPORARY EXAMPLE: Lavey Derby, clergyman.

Lavi   A variant spelling of Levi. *See* Levi. Also, a Yiddish form of the German *loeb* or *lob*, meaning "lion."

Lavrans   A variant form of Lave or Laverne. *See* Lave *and* Laverne. CONTEMPORARY EXAMPLE: Lavrans Nielsen, author.

Lawrence   A variant spelling of Laurence. *See* Laurence. SURNAME USAGE: Ernest Orlando Lawrence (1901-1958), American physicist. PLACE-NAME USAGE: Lawrence, Massachusetts, named for A.A. Lawrence (1814-1886).

Lawton   From the Old English, meaning "a town on the hill (*hlaew*)." CONTEMPORARY EXAMPLE: Lawton Chiles, U.S. congressman. SURNAME USAGE: Henry W. Lawton (1843-1879), U.S. general. PLACE-NAME USAGE: Lawton, Oklahoma, named for H.W. Lawton.

Lazar   A pet form of Elazar and Lazarus. *See* Elazar *and* Lazarus. CONTEMPORARY EXAMPLE: Lazar Berman, Russian pianist.

Lazaro   The Italian form of Lazarus. *See* Lazarus. CONTEMPORARY EXAMPLE: Lazaro Naranjo, baseball player.

Lazarus   The Greek form of the Hebrew name Elazar, meaning "God has helped." In the Bible, the brother of Mary and Martha, raised from the dead by Jesus. SURNAME USAGE: Emma Lazarus (1849-1887), American poet.

Lazer   A Yiddish form of Eliezer. *See* Eliezer. CONTEMPORARY EXAMPLE: Lazer Goldberg, author.

Leander   From the Greek *andros*, meaning "a man." Also, possibly akin to Leon, meaning "lion." The common connotation is "brave man." In Greek legend, the lover of Hero, a man of great strength favored by the gods. Andrew is a variant form. CONTEMPORARY EXAMPLE: Leander Pedez, Louisiana politician.

Leanther   A variant form of Leander. *See* Leander. CONTEMPORARY EXAMPLE: Leanther Dalton, football player.

Leavitt   From the Middle English *levein* and the Latin *levare*, meaning "to raise, to make light." Probably from the surname meaning "a baker." Also, from the biblical Levi. *See* Levi. CONTEMPORARY EXAMPLE: Leavitt Daley, baseball player.

Lebert   A variant form of Lever. *See* Lever.

LeBron   A variant spelling LaBron. *See* LaBron. CONTEMPORARY EXAMPLE: LeBron Shields, football player.

Ledell   A masculine form of Leda. In Greek mythology, a Spartan queen. CONTEMPORARY EXAMPLE: Ledell Titcomb, baseball player.

Lee   A pet form of Leo, Leon, Leroy, Leslie, Leigh. Also, a name derived from the Anglo-Saxon, meaning "field, meadow." Also, a feminine form. CONTEMPORARY EXAMPLE: Lee Salk, child psychologist. SURNAME USAGE: Robert E. Lee (1807-1870), Civil War general.

Leek   From the Old Norse *lik* and the Old English *leac*, meaning "to bind." CONTEMPORARY EXAMPLE: Leek Tevis, football player.

Leeland   From the Old English *hleo* and the German *lee*, meaning "a shelter, a protected area." CONTEMPORARY EXAMPLE: Leeland Jones, football player.

Lee Roy   A variant spelling of Leroy. *See* Leroy. CONTEMPORARY EXAMPLE: Lee Roy Yarborough, car racer.

Legrand, Legrant   From the French, meaning "grand, great." CONTEMPORARY EXAMPLE: Legrant Scott, baseball player.

Leib, Leibel   Yiddish names from the German name Loeb, meaning "lion." Akin to Leo. Label is a variant spelling.

Leif   From the Old Norse *heifr*, meaning "beloved." Akin to Lief. *See* Lief. SURNAME USAGE: Leif Ericsson, Scandinavian explorer.

Leigh   A variant spelling of Lee. *See* Lee.

Leighland   A variant form of Leeland. *See* Leeland.

Leighton   From the Hebrew, meaning "belonging to God." CONTEMPORARY EXAMPLE: Leighton Gibson, baseball player.

Leland   A variant spelling of Leeland. *See* Leeland. CONTEMPORARY EXAMPLE: Leland Stark, clergyman.

Lem   A pet form of Lemuel. *See* Lemuel. CONTEMPORARY EXAMPLE: Lem Overpeck, South Dakota politician.

Lemar   A variant form of Lamar. *See* Lamar. CONTEMPORARY EXAMPLE: Lemar Parrish, football player.

Lemuel   From the Hebrew, meaning "belonging to God." In the Bible, an alternate name for Solomon. Lem is a pet form. CONTEMPORARY EXAMPLE: Lemuel Barney, football player.

Len   A pet form of Leonard. *See* Leonard. Also, from the Old English *len* and *leen*, meaning "a tenant house on a farm."

Lendal   From the Old English, meaning "a river near the alder tree." CONTEMPORARY EXAMPLE: Lendal H. Kotschevar, food consultant.

Lendon   From the Old English, meaning "a river near the tenant farmer's house." CONTEMPORARY EXAMPLE: Lendon Smith, physician.

Leni   A variant spelling of Lennie, a pet form of Leonard. *See* Leonard. CONTEMPORARY EXAMPLE: Leni Riefenstahl, photographer.

Lenis   From the Latin, meaning "gentle, mild." CONTEMPORARY EXAMPLE: Lenis Swinford, football player.

Lenn   A variant spelling of Len. *See* Len. CONTEMPORARY EXAMPLE: Lenn Evan Goodman, author.

Lennard   A variant form of Len. *See* Len. CONTEMPORARY EXAMPLE:

Lennard Bickel, author.

Lennart   A variant form of Len. *See* Len. CONTEMPORARY EXAMPLE: Lennart Karstorp, author.

Lennie   A pet form of Leonard. *See* Leonard. Leni is a variant spelling.

Lennon   From the Old English, meaning "the river near the tenant farmer's house." CONTEMPORARY EXAMPLE: Lennon Blackman, football player.

Lennox   From the Old English, meaning "the tenant farmer's ox." *See* Len. CONTEMPORARY EXAMPLE: Lennox Cook, author. PLACE-NAME USAGE: Lennox, Massachusetts.

Lenvil   From the Old English and French, meaning "the tenant house near the town." *See* Len. CONTEMPORARY EXAMPLE: Lenvil Elliott, football player.

Lenwood   From the Old English, meaning "a tenant house in the woods." *See* Len.

Leo   From the Latin, meaning "lion." VARIANT FORMS: Leonard (French); Leon (Greek); Lion (Middle English); Loew (German); Leonid (Russian). The name of several popes: Leo I (440-461); Leo III (795-816); Leo XIII (1878–1903). PET FORMS: Lionel (French), Leibel (Yiddish).

Leodis   A variant form of Leo. *See* Leo.

Leon   The Greek form of Leo. *See* Leo. Leona and Leonia are feminine forms. CONTEMPORARY EXAMPLES: Leon Blum (1872-1950), French statesman; Leon Trotsky (1879-1940), Russian revolutionist. PLACE-NAME USAGE: cities in Spain, Mexico, and Nicaragua.

Leonala   The Hawaiian form of Leonard. *See* Leonard.

Leonard   The Old French form of the Old High German name Lewenhart, meaning "strong as a lion." VARIANT FORMS: Leo, Leon (English); Leonardo, Lionardo (Italian); Leonhard (German). PET FORMS: Len, Lennie.

Leonardo   An Italian variant form of Leonard. Leonardo da Vinci (1452-1519), Italian painter. CONTEMPORARY EXAMPLE: Leonardo Cardenas, baseball player.

Leondaus   An Old English form of Leon, meaning "Leon's house." *See* Leon. CONTEMPORARY EXAMPLE: Leondaus Lacy, baseball player.

Leone   The Hawaiian form of Leo. *See* Leo.

Leonhard   A Germanic form of Leonard. *See* Leonard. CONTEMPORARY EXAMPLE: Leonhard Deutsch, author.

Leonid   A Russian form of Leo. *See* Leo. CONTEMPORARY EXAMPLES: Leonid Brezhnev, Russian statesman; Leonid Shamkovich, chess master.

Leonidas A variant form of Leo. *See* Leo. Leonidas was King of Sparta in the fifth century B.C. CONTEMPORARY EXAMPLE: Leonidas Lee, baseball player.

Leonis A variant Old English form of Leon, meaning "Leon's house." *See* Leon.

Leopold From the Old High German and the Old English, meaning "a bold free man." Leopold I (1640-1705), emperor of the Holy Roman Empire. VARIANT FORM: Leopoldo (Italian); Poldo (Slavic). PLACE-NAME USAGE: Leopoldville (presently Kinshasa), Africa.

Leor From the Hebrew, meaning "I have light" or "light is mine." Used in Israel as a masculine and feminine name. Lior is a variant spelling.

Leron, Lerond, Lerone From the French *rond*, meaning "round, a round object." CONTEMPORARY EXAMPLES: Leron Lee, baseball player; Lerone Bennett, author.

Leroy An Old French name of Latin origin, meaning "the king" or "royalty." Lee Roy is a variant spelling.

Lerrin Possibly a variant form of Leron. *See* Leron. CONTEMPORARY EXAMPLE: Lerrin LaGrow, baseball player.

Les A pet form of Lester and Leslie. *See* Lester *and* Leslie.

Leshem From the Hebrew, meaning "a precious stone." In the Bible, an amber stone in the breastplate of the High Priest.

Lesley, Leslie From the Anglo-Saxon, meaning "a small meadow, a dell." Lee is a popular pet form. Used also as a feminine name. Lesley is a variant spelling.

Lesser A variant form of the Yiddish name Lazer. *See* Lazer.

Lester Originally Leicester, a place-name in England. From the Latin and the Old English *caestre*, meaning "a camp, a protected area." Chester is a variant form.

Letcher An early English form of Leicester and Lester. *See* Lester. Also, a short form of Fletcher, from the Old French *fleche*, meaning "an arrow."

Lev From the Hebrew *layv*, meaning "a heart." Also, a Yiddish form of the German Loeb, meaning "a lion." Also a pet form of Levi. *See* Levi. CONTEMPORARY EXAMPLE: Lev Levite, Israeli writer. SURNAME USAGE: Aryeh Lev, clergyman.

Levander A variant form of Levant, meaning "a man from the East." *See* Levant.

Levant A Spanish and French form of the Latin *levare*, meaning "to rise." Applies to Eastern countries from the "rising of the sun." VARIANT FORMS: Lever, Levert, Lebert. CONTEMPORARY EXAMPLE: Levant Dahl, football player. SURNAME USAGE: Oscar Levant, musician. PLACE-NAME USAGE: Levant, Maine.

Le Var A French variant form of the Old English *beorna*, meaning "a bear." CONTEMPORARY EXAMPLE: Le Var Burton, actor.

Lever A variant French form of Levant, meaning "light." *See* Levant. Also, possibly a form of the Anglo-Saxon *leof*, meaning "love." VARIANT FORMS: Levert, Lebert.

Leverett A variant form of Lever. *See* Lever. CONTEMPORARY EXAMPLE: Leverett Saltonstall, former governor of Massachusetts.

Levert A variant form of Lever. *See* Lever. CONTEMPORARY EXAMPLE: Levert Carr, football player.

Levi From the Hebrew, meaning "joined to" or "attendant upon." In the Bible, the third of Jacob's sons. His mother was Leah. Descendants of Levi were the Priests and Levites who served in the Temple in Jerusalem. VARIANT FORMS: Lavey, Lavy, Lev, Levic. CONTEMPORARY EXAMPLES: Levi Watkins, educator; Levi Strauss, merchant. SURNAME USAGE: Halevi, Lewin, Levin, Levy, Levinson, Levinsky, Lebeson, Lewissohm, Low, Lowey, Lowy.

Lew A pet form of Lewis. *See* Lewis.

Lewellen The Welsh form of Lewis. *See* Lewis. *See also* Llewellyn.

Lewes A variant spelling of Lewis. *See* Lewis. SURNAME USAGE: George Henry Lewes (1817-1878), English writer. PLACE-NAME USAGE: Lewes, Delaware.

Lewi The Hawaiian form of Levi. *See* Levi.

Lewie A pet form of Lewis. *See* Lewis.

Lewis An English form of the French name Louis. *See* Louis. Also, a variant form of the Welsh name Llewellyn. *See* Llewellyn. Lewes is a variant spelling. PET FORMS: Lew, Lewie. SURNAME USAGE: Sinclair Lewis (1885-1951), American novelist. PLACE-NAME USAGE: Lewiston, Maine.

Lex From the Greek, meaning "a word, vocabulary." Lexington is a variant form. CONTEMPORARY EXAMPLE: Lex Hixon, author. PLACE-NAME USAGE: Lexington, Kentucky; Lexington, England (now spelled Laxton).

Leycester An early English form of Lester. *See* Lester. CONTEMPORARY EXAMPLE: Leycester Aulds, baseball player.

Leyland A variant spelling of Leeland. *See* Leeland.

Liam A variant form of Lian. *See* Lian. Popular in Hawaii.

Lian From the French, meaning "to bind, tie."

Liddon From the Old English *hlidan*, meaning "to hide." CONTEMPO-

RARY EXAMPLE: Liddon R. Griffith, author. PLACE-NAME USAGE: Leiden (Leyden), a city in the Netherlands; Lidice, a village in Czechoslovakia; Lido, an island in Italy.

Lie A variant spelling of Lee and Leif. *See* Lee *and* Leif. SURNAME USAGE: Trygve Lie (1896–1968), Norwegian statesman and U.N. secretary-general.

Lieber A Yiddish form from the German *lieb*, meaning "love."

Lief From the Middle English *lef* and the Old English *leof*, meaning "beloved, dear." Akin to Leif. *See* Leif. Lieb is a variant form. CONTEMPORARY EXAMPLE: Lief Johanson, tennis player.

Lin A variant spelling of Lyn. *See* Lyn.

Lincoln From the Old English *lind* and the German *linde*, meaning "lithe, bending, flexible," and referring to the trees of the linden family. Or, from the Old English and Latin, meaning "the camp near the stream." Akin to Lindsey. CONTEMPORARY EXAMPLES: Lincoln Steffens (1866-1936), American journalist; Lincoln Gordon, educator. SURNAME USAGE: Abraham Lincoln (1809–1865), sixteenth president of the United States. PLACE-NAME USAGE: Lincoln, Nebraska; Lincolnshire, England; Lincoln Park (Detroit), Michigan.

Lind, Linde From the Old English *lind*, and the German *linde*, meaning "lithe, supple, flexible," and referring to the trees of the linden and lime families.

Lindall A variant form of Lind. *See* Lind.

Lindbergh, Lindbert From the German, meaning "a mountain of linden trees." *See* Lind. SURNAME USAGE: Charles Lindbergh (1902-1974), American aviator.

Lindel, Lindell Variant forms of Lind. *See* Lind. CONTEMPORARY EXAMPLES: Lindel Jaquess and Lindell Pearson, football players.

Linden A variant form of Lind. *See* Lind. CONTEMPORARY EXAMPLE: Linden Chiles, actor.

Lindley From the Old English, meaning "the meadow near the linden trees." CONTEMPORARY EXAMPLE: Lindley M. Garrison, U.S. Secretary of the Army (1915).

Lindo An Italian form of Lind. *See* Lind. CONTEMPORARY EXAMPLE: Lindo Storti, baseball player.

Lindon A variant form of Lind. *See* Lind. Lyndon is a variant spelling.

Lindsay A variant form of Lindsey. *See* Lindsey. CONTEMPORARY EXAMPLE: Lindsay Nelson, sportscaster. SURNAME USAGE: Vachel Lindsay, poet.

Lindsey   From the Old English, meaning "the linden trees near the water."

Lindsy   A variant spelling of Lindsey. *See* Linsey.

Lindy   A pet form of Lindsey and the nickname of Charles A. Lindbergh, first to make a solo non-stop flight from New York to Paris (1927).

Lingrel   From the Old English *hlinc*, meaning "an enclosure." CONTEMPORARY EXAMPLE: Lingrel Winters, football player.

Link   From the Old English *hlinc*, meaning "an enclosure." CONTEMPORARY EXAMPLE: Link Wyler, author.

Linley   From the Old English, meaning "the meadow near the brook." Akin to Lin and Lyn. CONTEMPORARY EXAMPLE: Linley M. Stafford, author.

Linn, Linnie   Variant forms of Lin. *See* Lin. CONTEMPORARY EXAMPLES: Linn C. Baker, Utah politician; Linnie Marsh Wolfe, Pulitzer Prize winner in letters (1946).

Lino   From the French *linon*, meaning "linen, flax, a type of weave."

Linsey   A variant spelling of Lindsey. *See* Lindsey.

Linton   A variant form of Lind, meaning "the town with the linden trees." CONTEMPORARY EXAMPLE: Linton R. Massey, editor.

Linus   From the Latin *linum*, meaning "linen-colored, flaxen-colored," after the linnet, a colored songbird of the finch family. CONTEMPORARY EXAMPLE: Linus Pauling, chemist.

Linwood   A variant spelling of Lynwood. *See* Lynwood. CONTEMPORARY EXAMPLE: Linwood Sexton, football player.

Linzy   A variant spelling of Lindsey. *See* Lindsey. CONTEMPORARY EXAMPLE: Linzy Cole, football player.

Lion   A variant form of Leon. *See* Leon. CONTEMPORARY EXAMPLE: Lion Fenhtwanger, author.

Lionel, Lionello   Variant forms of Lion. *See* Lion. CONTEMPORARY EXAMPLE: Lionello Venturi, art historian; Lionel Barrymore, actor.

Lipman   A corrupt form of the German name Liebman, meaning "lover of man." *See* Leif.

Liron   From the Hebrew *li* and *ron*, meaning "song is mine." VARIANT SPELLINGS: Leron, Lyron. Used also as a feminine name in Israel.

Lisle   From the Spanish, meaning "strong cotton thread." Derived from the French city Lisle, now spelled Lille, its place of manufacture. CONTEMPORARY EXAMPLE: Lisle Blackbourn, football player.

Litton   From the Old English, meaning "little town."

Livingston   An Anglicized form of the Anglo–Saxon, meaning "Lever's town, Leif's town." CONTEMPORARY EXAMPLE: Livingston Biddle, art critic. SURNAME USAGE: Robert R. Livingston (1746–1813), American statesman.

Llewellyn   From the Welsh, meaning "in the likeness of a lion."

Lloyd   From the Welsh, meaning "grey." Floyd is a variant form. CONTEMPORARY EXAMPLE: Lloyd George, (1863-1945), English statesman (full name: David Lloyd George).

Loaird   A variant spelling of Laird. *See* Laird. CONTEMPORARY EXAMPLE: Loaird McCreary, football player.

Locadio   From the Latin *locus*, meaning "a place."

Locke   From the German *loch*, meaning "a hole" and the Old English *loc*, meaning "an enclosure." An occupational name for locksmiths. CONTEMPORARY EXAMPLE: Locke E. Bowman, Jr., theologian. SURNAME USAGE: John Locke (1632-1704), English philopsopher.

Lodge   From the Middle English *loge*, meaning "a hut." SURNAME USAGE: Henry Cabot Lodge (1850-1924), U.S. senator.

Loeb   From the German, meaning "a lion." Common as a Yiddish form. Jews use it as a middle name with Judah (Judah Loeb) because of the reference in the Bible, comparing Judah to a lion. SURNAME USAGE: Jacques Loeb (1859-1924), German physiologist.

Loewy   A variant form of Loeb. *See* Loeb. SURNAME USAGE: Raymond F. Loewy, American industrialist.

Logan   From the Middle English *logge* and the Old Norse *lag*, meaning "a felled tree." CONTEMPORARY EXAMPLE: Logan Drake, baseball player. PLACE-NAME USAGE: highest mountain in Canada (19,850 feet).

Lombard   From the Latin and German *lango* (long) and *barda* (beard). Derived from the ancient Germanic tribe that settled in the Po Valley. PLACE-NAME USAGE: a region of North Italy, bordering on Switzerland.

Lon   A pet form of Alphonso. *See* Alphonso. CONTEMPORARY EXAMPLE: Lon D. Randall, educator.

Lonas   Origin uncertain. Possibly a variant form of Lon. *See* Lon. CONTEMPORARY EXAMPLE: Lonas Bailey, baseball player.

London   From the British, meaning "a fortress of the moon." Probably a site established by the Romans where a temple was erected to worship Diana, the moon goddess. SURNAME USAGE: Jack London (1876-1916), American novelist.

Longfellow   From the Middle English, meaning "a tall person." SURNAME USAGE: Henry Wadsworth Longfellow (1807-1882), American poet.

Lonnie, Lonny   Pet forms of Alphonso. *See* Alphonso. CONTEMPO-
RARY EXAMPLE: Lonny Chapman, actor.

Lonsdale   From the Old English, meaning "Londe's valley." CONTEM-
PORARY EXAMPLE: Lonsdale Skinner, cricket player.

Lonzo   A variant form of Alphonso. *See* Alphonso.

Lorado   A variant spelling of Loredo. *See* Loredo. PLACE-NAME USAGE:
Lorado, West Virginia.

Loral   From the Old English *lar*, meaning "learning, teaching." Akin
to the Middle High German *luren*, meaning "to watch, see, learn." Akin
to the feminine Lorelei. CONTEMPORARY EXAMPLE: Loral Wyatt, football
player.

Lord   From the Old English name Hlafweard, a name compounded of
hlaf (bread, loaf) and *weard* (warden, guardian). Connoting a person of
great authority and power. CONTEMPORARY EXAMPLE: Lord Birkenhead,
biographer. SURNAME USAGE: Jack Lord, actor.

Loredo   From the place-name Loreto (Loretto), in Italy, famous for its
Catholic shrine. A variant form of Laurence. *See* Laurence. Lorado is a
variant spelling.

Loren, Lorence   Variant forms of Laurence. *See* Laurence.

Lorentz   A variant form of Laurence. *See* Laurence. CONTEMPORARY
EXAMPLES: Lorentz H. Adolfson, educator; Lorentz Melchior, singer.
SURNAME USAGE: Hendrik Antoon Lorentz (1853-1928), Dutch physicist.

Lorenzo   An Italian form of Laurence. *See* Laurence. CONTEMPORARY
EXAMPLE: Lorenzo Bandini, auto racer.

Lorimer   From the Latin, meaning "a harness maker."

Lorin   A variant spelling of Loren. *See* Loren. CONTEMPORARY EXAM-
PLE: Lorin Maazel, musical conductor.

Loring   A variant form of Laurence. *See* Laurence. CONTEMPORARY
EXAMPLE: Loring Black, U.S. congressman.

Loris   From the Dutch *loeres*, meaning "a clown." Or, a short form of
the feminine Cloris. CONTEMPORARY EXAMPLE: Loris Battis, editor.

Lorn, Lorne   Variant forms of Laurence. *See* Laurence. CONTEMPO-
RARY EXAMPLES: Lorne Green, actor; Lorne Worsley, hockey player.
PLACE-NAME USAGE: Lorne, Montana, named for the Marquis of Lorne,
a governor-general of Canada.

Lorry   A variant spelling of Laurie, a form of Laurence. *See* Laurence.

Lot   From the Hebrew, meaning "to envelop, cover." In the Bible,
Abraham's nephew. PLACE-NAME USAGE: a river in southern France.

Lotan   From the Hebrew, meaning "to envelop." Lot is the original
form. In the Bible, a son of Seir the Horite.

Lothar   A German form of Luther. *See* Luther. CONTEMPORARY EX-
AMPLE: Lothar Kahn, professor.

Lothario   An English form of Luther. *See* Luther.

Lother   A variant spelling of Luther. *See* Luther.

Lothur   A variant spelling of Luther. *See* Luther. Also, in Norse mythology, one of the creators of the first man and woman: Ask and Embla.
Lodur is a variant form.

Loual   A name invented by combining Louis and Albert. *See* Louis
and Albert.

Louis   From the Old French name Loeis, and the Old High German
name Hluodowig, meaning "famous in battle." VARIANT FORMS: Lewis
(English); Ludwig (German); Luigi (Italian); Luis (Spanish); Llewelyn
(Welsh); Clovis (French). *See also* Ludwig. Louise is a feminine form.
PET FORMS: Lou, Louie, Lew. Louis I (778-840), King of France and
emperor of the Holy Roman Empire. SURNAME USAGE: Joe Louis (Bar-
row), heavyweight champion. PLACE-NAME USAGE: Louisville, Kentucky; Louisburg, North Carolina; Louvain, Belgium; the state of
Louisiana.

Lovell   A variant form of Lowell. *See* Lowell. SURNAME USAGE: Sir
Bernard Lovell (born 1913), English astronomer.

Lowe   A variant form of the German name Loeb. *See* Loeb. Also, a
variant spelling of Louis. CONTEMPORARY EXAMPLE: Lowe Wren, football player.

Lowell   From the Old English, meaning "beloved." Or, from the Old
English *low*, meaning "a hill." CONTEMPORARY EXAMPLE: Lowell
Thomas, explorer and commentator. SURNAME USAGE: James Russell
Lowell (1819-1891), American poet. PLACE-NAME USAGE: Lowell,
Massachusetts.

Loy   A pet form of Loy. *See* Loy. CONTEMPORARY EXAMPLE: Loy Han-
ning, baseball player. SURNAME USAGE: Myrna Loy, actress.

Loyal   From the Old French *loial* and the Latin *legalis*, meaning "faithful, true." Loy is a pet form. CONTEMPORARY EXAMPLE: Loyal Robb,
football player. PLACE-NAME USAGE: Loyal, Oklahoma; Loyalton, California; Loyalsock, Pennsylvania.

Loyte   A variant form of Loyal. *See* Loyal. CONTEMPORARY EXAMPLE:
Loyte Humphrey, football player.

Lu   A pet form of Lucas or Lucius. *See* Lucius. CONTEMPORARY EXAM-
PLE: Lu Blue, baseball player.

Lubbock   From the city Lubeck, in northwest Germany. SURNAME
USAGE: T.S. Lubbock, a Confederate army officer. PLACE-NAME USAGE:
Lubbock, Texas, named for T.S. Lubbock.

Luby A pet form derived from the place-name Lubeck, a city in northwest Germany, or Lublin in southeast Poland. CONTEMPORARY EXAMPLE: Luby DiMelio, football player.

Luc A pet form of Lucas. See Lucas. Also a name derived from the Old English *loc*, meaning "an enclosure." CONTEMPORARY EXAMPLE: Luc H. Grollenberg, author.

Lucas A variant form of Lucius. See Lucius. Lu is a pet form.

Luce From the Old French *lus*, and the Latin *lucius*, a variety of fish similar to pike. Also, a form of Lucius. See Lucius. SURNAME USAGE: Claire Booth Luce, U.S. congressman.

Lucian, Lucien Variant forms of Lucius. CONTEMPORARY EXAMPLES: Lucian K. Truscott, novelist; Lucien Israel, scientist.

Luciano An Italian form of Lucius. See Lucius. CONTEMPORARY EXAMPLE: Luciano Pavaroti, opera singer. SURNAME USAGE: Felipe Luciano, television news reporter.

Lucio An Italian form of Lucius. See Lucius. CONTEMPORARY EXAMPLE: Lucio Amelio, actor.

Lucius From the Latin *lucere* and *lux*, meaning "light." VARIANT FORMS: Lucian (Latin); Luciano (Italian and Spanish); Luc, Luce, Lucien (French); Lucas (Spanish and Portuguese); Lukas (German). CONTEMPORARY EXAMPLE: Lucius Allen, basketball player. PET FORMS: Lu, Luke. Lucia is a feminine form.

Lucky Used primarily as a nickname. CONTEMPORARY EXAMPLE: Lucky Luciano, U.S. gangster. PLACE-NAME USAGE: Lucky Creek, Oregon; Luck Rock, Washington; Lucky Mound, North Dakota.

Ludek A variant form of Ludwig. See Ludwig. CONTEMPORARY EXAMPLE: Ludek Packman, chess master.

Ludlow An English variant form of Ludwig. See Ludwig. CONTEMPORARY EXAMPLE: Ludlow Wray, football player. PLACE-NAME USAGE: Ludlow, Massachusetts; Ludlow Creek, Ohio, named for Israel Ludlow, an early surveyor.

Ludwig From the Old German name Hluodowig, derived from the Germanic *hluda*, meaning "famous," and *wiga*, meaning "war." Akin to Louis. See Louis.

Lui The Hawaiian form of Lewis. See Lewis.

Luis A Spanish form of Louis. See Louis. CONTEMPORARY EXAMPLE: Luis Gomez, baseball player.

Luka The Hawaiian form of Luke. See Luke.

Luke The English form of Lucius. See Lucius. In the Bible, one of the four Evangelists, a companion of the apostle Paul.

Lupo, Lupus From the Latin, meaning "a wolf." SURNAME USAGE: Ida Lupino, actress. PLACE-NAME USAGE: Lupus, Missouri.

Luscious A variant spelling of Lucius. *See* Lucius. CONTEMPORARY EXAMPLE: Luscious Easter, baseball player.

Lute, Luter From the occupational surname, meaning "one who plays a flute." Flewitt is a variant form. CONTEMPORARY EXAMPLE: Lute Pease, Pulitzer Prize–winning cartoonist (1949).

Luther From the German, meaning "renowned soldier; famous fighter." VARIANT FORMS: Lothario (English); Lothaire (French); Lotario (Italian); Lothar (German). CONTEMPORARY EXAMPLE: Luther Bradley, football player. SURNAME USAGE: Martin Luther (1483–1546), German theologian.

Luvern A variant spelling of Lavern. *See* Lavern. CONTEMPORARY EXAMPLE: Luvern Fear, baseball player.

Luz A pet form of Luzerne. *See* Luzerne. CONTEMPORARY EXAMPLE: Luz Maldonado, Brooklyn, New York.

Luzerne From the French form, meaning "glowworm." Derived from the Latin *lucerna*, meaning "lamp." Lucerne is a variant spelling. CONTEMPORARY EXAMPLE: Luzerne Blue, baseball player. PLACE-NAME USAGE: Lucerne, Switzerland.

Lyall A variant form of Lyle. *See* Lyle. CONTEMPORARY EXAMPLE: Lyall Smith, publicist.

Lyam A variant form of Liam. *See* Liam.

Lycurgus A legendary (or possibly real) Spartan lawmaker who lived around the ninth century B.C.

Lyde, Lydell From the Old English *hlith*, meaning "hill," and the Middle English *lyth*, meaning "slope," referring to "hilly pastureland." CONTEMPORARY EXAMPLE: Lydell Mitchell, football player.

Lyell A variant form of Lyle. *See* Lyle. SURNAME USAGE: Sir Charles Lyell (1797-1875), British geologist.

Lyle A variant form of Lisle. *See* Lisle. Or, a Scottish form of Lytel. *See* Lytel. CONTEMPORARY EXAMPLES: Lyle Waggoner, actor; Lyle Alzado, football player. SURNAME USAGE: Richard Lyle, dancer.

Lyman An occupational name, meaning "one who works lime, a plasterer, a bricklayer." *See* Lyme. CONTEMPORARY EXAMPLE: Lyman Brooks, educator.

Lyme From the Old English *lim*, meaning "lime or mud."

Lyn From the Old English *hlynna*, meaning "a brook." VARIANT SPELLINGS: Lin, Linn.

Lynd, Lynde Variant spellings of Lind. *See* Lind. CONTEMPORARY

EXAMPLE: Lynd Ward, novelist. SURNAME USAGE: Paul Lynde, entertainer.

Lyndall   A variant form of Lynd and Lind. *See* Lind. CONTEMPORARY EXAMPLE: Lyndall Zal, musician.

Lynden   A variant spelling of Lyndon. *See* Lynd *and* Lind. CONTEMPORARY EXAMPLE: Lynden Chase, Pine Plains, New York.

Lyndon   A variant form of Lynd and Lind. *See* Lind. Lindon is a variant spelling. CONTEMPORARY EXAMPLE: Lyndon Baines Johnson (1908-1973), thirty-sixth president of the U.S.

Lynford   From the Old English, meaning "the crossing (ford) over the brook." CONTEMPORARY EXAMPLE: Lynford Larg, baseball player.

Lynley   From the Old English, meaning "the meadow (lea) near the brook." CONTEMPORARY EXAMPLE: Lynley Dodd, author. SURNAME USAGE: Carol Lynley, actress.

Lynn   A variant spelling of Lyn. *See* Lyn. CONTEMPORARY EXAMPLE: Lynn Swann, football player.

Lynton   From the Old English, meaning "a town near the brook." CONTEMPORARY EXAMPLE: Lynton K. Caldwell, author.

Lynwood, Lynwood   From the Old English, meaning "the forest near the brook." CONTEMPORARY EXAMPLES: Lynwood (Schoolboy) Rowe, baseball player.

Lyon   The French form of Lion. *See* Lion. SURNAME USAGE: Mary Lyon (1797-1849), American educator. PLACE-NAME USAGE: Lyon, France.

Lyons   The English form of Lyon. *See* Lyon.

Lyonel   A variant spelling of Lionel. *See* Lionel.

Lyron   A variant spelling of Liron. *See* Liron.

Lytel   From the Anglo-Saxon, meaning "little, less."

M

Maarten A variant spelling of Martin. *See* Martin. CONTEMPORARY
EXAMPLE: Maarten D. Hemsley, executive.

Mabry Probably a Cornish form of the feminine Mabel, meaning "to
love." *See* Mabel (feminine section). CONTEMPORARY EXAMPLE: Mabry
Harper, fishing expert.

Mac An Irish and Gaelic patronymic form prefixed to many personal
names, meaning "son of." Used also as an independent name. CONTEM-
PORARY EXAMPLES: Macdonald Harris, author; Mac Davis, singer.
PLACE-NAME USAGE: Maxton, North Carolina, so named because of the
many Scots who had names beginning with Mac.

Macabee From the Hebrew *makab*, meaning "a hammer." Also spelled
Maccabee. CONTEMPORARY EXAMPLE: Macabee Dean, journalist.

MacArthur A patronymic form, meaning "the son of Arthur." *See*
Arthur. CONTEMPORARY EXAMPLE: MacArthur Lane, football player.
SURNAME USAGE: Douglas MacArthur (1880-1964), U.S. Army general.

Macdonald A patronymic form, meaning "son of Donald." *See* Donald. CONTEMPORARY EXAMPLE: Macdonald Carey, actor.

Mace An English form of the Old French *masse*, meaning "a club,"
hence a symbol of authority. CONTEMPORARY EXAMPLE: Mace Roberts,
football player.

Maceo A Spanish form of Mace. *See* Mace. CONTEMPORARY EXAMPLE:
M. Maceo Nance, educator; Maceo Campbell, Hollywood, California.

Macey A variant form of Mace. *See* Mace. Also, a pet form of Matthew. *See* Matthew. Used also as an English form of the Hebrew Moshe
(Moses).

Mack A variant form of Mac. *See* Mac. Also, from the Middle English *maken*, akin to the German *machen*, meaning "to make." VARIANT
FORMS: Mackey, Mackinlay, Macon.

Mackey A variant form of Mack. *See* Mack. CONTEMPORARY EXAM-
PLE: Mackey Idome, football player.

MacKinlay From the Middle English *maken*, akin to the German
machen, meaning "to make." CONTEMPORARY EXAMPLE: MacKinlay
Kantor, novelist.

Maclean A patronymic form, meaning "the son of Leander." *See*
Leander. CONTEMPORARY EXAMPLE: Maclean Stevenson, actor.

Macon   From the Middle English *maken*, akin to the German *machen*, meaning "to make." CONTEMPORARY EXAMPLE: Macon McCalman, actor. SURNAME USAGE: Nathaniel Macon (1758-1837), a North Carolina leader. PLACE-NAME USAGE: Macon, Georgia, named for Nathaniel Macon.

Macy   A variant spelling of Macey. *See* Macey.

Madison   A patronymic form of Maude, meaning "son of Maude." Also, from the British *mad* and *made*, meaning "good." CONTEMPORARY EXAMPLE: Madison Jones, novelist. SURNAME USAGE: James Madison (1751-1836), fourth president of the U.S. PLACE-NAME USAGE: Madison, Wisconsin.

Madoc   An Old Welsh name, meaning "fortunate."

Magen   From the Hebrew, meaning "protector."

Magnus   From the Latin, meaning "great." Magnus I was king of Norway and Denmark (died 1047). Manus is an Irish form. CONTEMPORARY EXAMPLE: Magnus Magnuson, university rector.

Maguel   The Spanish form of Michael. CONTEMPORARY EXAMPLE: Maguel Valenzuelo, hockey player.

Magus   From the Latin, meaning "magician, sorcerer." In the Bible, Simon Magus is a Samaritan magician.

Mahir   From the Hebrew, meaning "industrious."

Mahlon   From the Hebrew, meaning "illness." In the Bible, the son of Naomi. CONTEMPORARY EXAMPLE: Mahlon Pitney, U.S. Supreme Court Justice (1912-1922).

Mailen   From the Middle English *maile*, meaning "a flexible, mesh body armor." CONTEMPORARY EXAMPLE: J. Mailen Kootsey, physicist.

Maimon, Maimun   From the Arabic, meaning "luck, good fortune." Moses ben Maimon [also called Maimonides] (1135-1204), a Spanish-Jewish philosopher. Maimun is a variant spelling.

Maitland   From the Old English, meaning "meadow land." SURNAME USAGE: Frederic William Maitland (1850-1906), English historian.

Major   From the Latin, meaning "great." Akin to Magnus. CONTEMPORARY EXAMPLE: Major Hazelton, football player. SURNAME USAGE: Lee Majors, actor.

Maks   A modern variant spelling of Max. *See* Max.

Malachai, Malachi   From the Hebrew, meaning "my messenger, my servant." In the Bible, the last of the Hebrew prophets (c. 450 B.C.). CONTEMPORARY EXAMPLE: Malachi Martin, actor.

Malachy   A variant spelling of Malachai. *See* Malachai.

Malcolm   From the Arabic, meaning "a dove." Or, from the Celtic name Maolcolm, meaning "servant of St. Columba." Until recently used primarily in Scotland. Mal is a common pet form of Malcolm.

Malden, Maldon   From the Old English, meaning "the meeting place in the pasture." SURNAME USAGE: Karl Malden, actor. PLACE-NAME USAGE: Malden, Massachusetts.

Malise   From the Gaelic name Mael-Iosa, meaning "servant of Jesus." Maoliosa is a current name in Ireland.

Malone   Probably from the French *malonique*, meaning "an acid," as in malonic acid. SURNAME USAGE: Edmund Malone (1741-1812), Irish literary editor.

Malory, Mallory   From the Old French *malart*, meaning "a wild duck," or from the Latin *malleare*, meaning "to beat with a hammer." Akin to Maccabee. SURNAME USAGE: Sir Thomas Malory, fifteenth–century English writer.

Malton   A variant form of Madon. *See* Maldon. CONTEMPORARY EXAMPLE: Malton Bullock, baseball player.

Malvern   From the British and Welsh, meaning "bare hill." PLACE-NAME USAGE: Malvern Hill, Virginia site of Civil War battle (1862).

Malvin   A variant spelling of Melvin. *See* Melvin.

Manasseh   A variant spelling of Menasseh. *See* Menasseh.

Mance   A short form of Manchester. *See* Manchester. CONTEMPORARY EXAMPLE: Mance Lipscomb, musician.

Manch   A pet form of Manchester. *See* Manchester. CONTEMPORARY EXAMPLE: Manch Wheeler, football player.

Manchester   From the Old English, meaning "a fortification, army camp." PET FORMS: Mance, Manch, Chester. SURNAME USAGE: William Manchester, author. PLACE-NAME USAGE: city in England; Manchester, Connecticut.

Mandel   From the Old French *amande*, and the Middle Latin *amandola*, meaning "an almond." Mandy is a pet form. SURNAME USAGE: Mandelbaum, Mandelcorn.

Mandy   A pet form of Manfred. *See* Manfred. CONTEMPORARY EXAMPLE: Mandy Pantinkin, actor.

Manford   From the Anglo-Saxon, meaning "a small crossing over a brook." CONTEMPORARY EXAMPLE: Manford A. Shaw, educator.

Manfred   From the German name Manifred, meaning "man of peace."

Manger   From the Old French *mangeure*, meaning "a feeding trough," hence "a stable." CONTEMPORARY EXAMPLE: Manger White, Pulitzer Prize winner in journalism (1924).

Manheim   From the German, meaning "the servant's home." CONTEM-

PORARY EXAMPLE: Manheim Shapiro, lecturer.

Mani   A pet form of Manuel. *See* Manuel. A third-century Persian prophet. CONTEMPORARY EXAMPLE: Mani Hernandez, soccer player.

Manley, Manly   From the Old English, meaning "protected field." Akin to Manning. CONTEMPORARY EXAMPLES: Manley Sarnowsky, football player; Manly Hall, author.

Mann, Mannes   Pet forms of Menachem. *See* Menachem. CONTEMPORARY EXAMPLE: Mann Rubin, scriptwriter.

Manning   From the Old English, meaning "to man, to garrison, to protect." CONTEMPORARY EXAMPLE: Manning Patillo, educator.

Manny   A pet form of Emanuel or Manfred. *See* Emanuel *and* Manfred.

Mannye   A variant spelling of Manny. *See* Manny. CONTEMPORARY EXAMPLE: Mannye London, civic leader.

Mano, Manolo   Spanish forms of Manuel and Emanuel. *See* Emanuel. CONTEMPORARY EXAMPLE: Manolo Villaverde, actor.

Mante   A variant form of Monte. *See* Monte. CONTEMPORARY EXAMPLE: Mante Fielding, author.

Manu   A pet form of Manuel. *See* Manuel. CONTEMPORARY EXAMPLE: Manu Topou, actor.

Manuel   A short form of Emanuel. *See* Emanuel. PET FORMS: Mani, Manny.

Manuela   The Hawaiian form of Manuel. *See* Manuel.

Manus   A form of Magnus popular in Ireland. *See* Magnus.

Manvel   A variant form of Manville. *See* Manville.

Manville   From the Old English, meaning "the village of the workers."

Marc   The French form of Marcus. *See* Marcus. CONTEMPORARY EXAMPLE: Marc Angel, clergyman. SURNAME USAGE: Franz Marc (1880-1916), German painter.

Marceau   A French form of Marc. *See* Marc.

Marcel   A French pet form of Marc and Marcus. *See* Marcus. Marcella is the feminine equivalent. CONTEMPORARY EXAMPLE: Marcel Grateau, French hairdresser.

Marcelino, Marcellino   Italian pet forms of the French Marcel. *See* Marcel. CONTEMPORARY EXAMPLE: Marcelino Lopez, baseball player.

Marcello   An Italian form of the French Marcel. *See* Marcel *and* Marcus.

Marcellus   The Latin pet form of Marcus. *See* Marcus. The name of a fourth-century pope. CONTEMPORARY EXAMPLE: Marcellus Pearson, baseball player. PLACE-NAME USAGE: Marcellus, New York.

March   A variant form of Marcus. *See* Marcus. The name of the first month in the Roman calendar, in honor of Mars, god of war. Also, possibly from the Old English *merc*, meaning "a boundary." SURNAME USAGE: Frederic March, actor.

Marchall   A variant spelling of Marshall. *See* Marshall. CONTEMPORARY EXAMPLE: Marchall Jones, football player.

Marcus   From the Latin name Mars, meaning "warlike." In Roman mythology, the god of war. Marcus Aurelius (121-180) was a Roman emperor and philosopher. VARIANT FORMS: Marcy, Mark (English); Marc (French); Marco (Italian); Markos (Greek); Marcos (Spanish and Portuguese); Marek (Polish); Markus (Hungarian). Marcia is the feminine equivalent. CONTEMPORARY EXAMPLE: Marcus Hurlbut, lacrosse player. PLACE-NAME USAGE: Marcus, Washington, named for Marcus Oppenheimer, town founder; Marcus Hook, Pennsylvania.

Marcy   A variant form of Marcus. *See* Marcus. Or, from the Old English *mar*, meaning "a pool, a lake." Used also as a feminine name.

Marden   From the British, meaning "the field near the water."

Mardyth   A variant form of Marden. *See* Marden. CONTEMPORARY EXAMPLE: Mardyth E. Pollard, U.S. city mayor (Lombard, Illinois).

Margene   Origin unknown. Probably an invented name combining Margery and Gene. *See* Margery *and* Gene (masculine section). CONTEMPORARY EXAMPLE: Margene Adkins, football player.

Mari   A pet form of Marius. *See* Marius.

Marian   A variant form of the feminine Mary once popular in England. *See* Mary (feminine section). Marion is a variant spelling. *See also* Marin.

Marilo   A Spanish form of Marcus. *See* Marcus. CONTEMPORARY EXAMPLE: Marilo Rubiao, Brazilian writer.

Marin, Marina, Marino   From the Latin *marinus*, meaning "a small harbor." CONTEMPORARY EXAMPLE: Marino Pieretti, baseball player. SURNAME USAGE: John Marin (1870-1953), American painter. PLACE-NAME USAGE: Marin County, California.

Mario, Marion   Variant forms of Marian or Marcus. *See* Marian *and* Marcus. CONTEMPORARY EXAMPLES: Mario Pei, linguist; Marion (John) Wayne, actor. SURNAME USAGE: Francis Marion, Revolutionary War hero.

Maris   From the Old English and French *mare*, meaning "sea, lake." SURNAME USAGE: Roger Maris, baseball player.

Marius   A variant form of Marc and Marcus. *See* Marcus.

Marjoe Probably an invented name, combining two elements (possibly Mary and Joseph). CONTEMPORARY EXAMPLE: Marjoe Gartner, evangelist and actor.

Mark A variant spelling of Marc. *See* Marc *and* Marcus. In the Bible, one of the four Evangelists to whom the second Gospel is ascribed.

Marlin From the Latin, Old English, and French *mare*, meaning "sea." A species of deep-sea fish. Also, from the Middle English and Old French *marle*, meaning "a sand pit." VARIANT FORMS: Marlon, Merlin, Marlis, Mario.

Marlis A variant form of Marlin. *See* Marlin. CONTEMPORARY EXAMPLES: Marlis G. Steinert, author; Marlis Schwieger, photographer.

Marlo A variant form of Marlin. *See* Marlin. Used also as a feminine form. CONTEMPORARY EXAMPLE: Marlo Clark, football player.

Marlon A variant spelling of Marlin. *See* Marlin. CONTEMPORARY EXAMPLE: Marlon Heck, golfer.

Marlow, Marlowe A variant form of Marlin. *See* Marlin. SURNAME USAGE: Christopher Marlowe (1564–1593), English poet–playwright.

Marne From the Latin, Old English, and French *mare*, meaning "sea." *See also* Marin. Or, from the Latin *maro*, meaning "master." CONTEMPORARY EXAMPLE: Marne Intrieri, football player. PLACE-NAME USAGE: a river in France.

Marnin From the Hebrew, meaning "one who creates joy" or "one who sings." Or, a variant form of Marne. *See* Marne.

Marques From the French *marquer*, meaning "a sign, a mark." Also, a variant form of Mark. *See* Mark. CONTEMPORARY EXAMPLE: Marques Johnson, basketball player.

Marquette A variant form of Marques. *See* Marques. CONTEMPORARY EXAMPLE: Marquette Christman, baseball player. SURNAME USAGE: Jacques Marquette (1637-1675), French explorer in North America, known also as Pere Marquette.

Marquis From the Old French, meaning "a nobleman." CONTEMPORARY EXAMPLE: Marquis James, Pulitzer Prize winner in biography (1930). SURNAME USAGE: Don Marquis (1878-1937), American journalist.

Marr From Spanish, meaning "a swine," and from the Arabic, meaning "a forbidden thing." Also, possibly a short form of Marin. *See* Marin. CONTEMPORARY EXAMPLE: Marr Phillips, baseball player. SURNAME USAGE: Richard Marr, actor.

Marriner An occupational surname derived from Marin, and meaning "a parlor." *See* Marin. CONTEMPORARY EXAMPLE: Marriner Eccles.

Mars Akin to Marcus. *See* Marcus. CONTEMPORARY EXAMPLE: Mars J. Fontana, professor.

Marsden　From the Old English, meaning "the pastureland near the sea."

Marshal, Marshall　From the Old English *mearh*, meaning "a horse," hence one who grooms a horse; later, one who masters a horse; and, finally, an officer in charge of military matters. CONTEMPORARY EXAMPLE: Marshall Mandell, physician and author. SURNAME USAGE: George Marshall (1880-1959), U.S. Army general and statesman. PLACE-NAME USAGE: Marshall, Texas; Marshalltown, Iowa.

Marshe　A variant of Marc or a form of Marshal. *See* Marc *and* Marshal. A popular feminine form is Marcia.

Marston　From the Anglo-Saxon, meaning "the town near the sea."

Martin　A French form of the Latin name Martinus. Akin to Marcus, meaning "warlike." *See* Marcus. Saint Martin of Tours was a fourth-century bishop. VARIANT FORMS: Martyn (English); Mertin (French); Marten (Dutch and Swedish); Martoni (Hungarian); Martino (Italian and Spanish); Mertil (German); Martinho (Portuguese). PET FORMS: Martie, Marty. SURNAME USAGE: Marten, Martens, Martins, Martinson, Martel, Martinet. PLACE-NAME USAGE: Martinique, West Indies; Martin's Ferry, Ohio, named for Ebenezer Martin (c. 1790); Martin, Washington.

Martine　A variant form of Martin. *See* Martin. CONTEMPORARY EXAMPLE: Martine Bercher, football player.

Marvel, Marvell　From the Latin *mirari*, meaning "to wonder, to marvel." SURNAME USAGE: Andrew Marvell (1621-1678), English poet.

Marvin　From the Old English *mar* plus *win* (vin), meaning "friend of the sea" or "friendly sea." SURNAME USAGE: Lee Marvin, actor.

Marwin　A variant form of Marvin. *See* Marvin. CONTEMPORARY EXAMPLE: Marwin Jonas, football player.

Maryland　A place named after Queen Henrietta Maria, wife of King Charles I. CONTEMPORARY EXAMPLE: Maryland Potter, baseball player. PLACE-NAME USAGE: one of the thirteen original States.

Maryse　A variant form of Maurice. *See* Maurice. CONTEMPORARY EXAMPLE: Maryse Chovel, editor.

Masefield　From the Spanish *maiz*, meaning "a field of ripe corn." SURNAME USAGE: John Masefield (1878-1967), English writer.

Maskil　From the Hebrew, meaning "enlightened, educated."

Mason　From the Old French macon, meaning "a mason, a worker in stone." CONTEMPORARY EXAMPLE: Mason W. Gross, educator. SURNAME USAGE: Jackie Mason, comedian. PLACE-NAME USAGE: Mason–Dixon line, boundary between Pennsylvania and Maryland.

Massey　A pet form of Massing. *See* Massing. CONTEMPORARY EXAMPLE: Massey H. Shepherd, physician and author. SURNAME USAGE: Raymond Massey, actor.

Massing From the Old English, compounded of *maes*, meaning "battle," and *incga*, meaning "children," hence "a home where the children of soldiers were housed."

Mat A pet form of Matthew. *See* Matthew.

Mateo A Spanish form of Matthew. *See* Matthew. CONTEMPORARY EXAMPLE: Mateo Alon, baseball player.

Mathern A British form of Matthew. *See* Matthew.

Mathias A variant form of Mattathias. *See* Mattathias.

Mati, Matia, Matiah Pet forms of Mattathias. *See* Mattathias.

Matomon From the Hebrew, meaning "treasure, wealth."

Matok From the Hebrew, meaning "sweet."

Matt A pet form of Matthew. *See* Matthew.

Mattathias The Greek form of the Hebrew name Matisyahu, meaning "gift of God." A Jewish patriot and priest who died about 167 B.C. The father of the five famous Hasmonean brothers, Judah the Maccabee being the most famous. VARIANT FORMS: Matthaeus and Mathieu (Latin). PET FORMS: Mati, Matti, Mattie, Matty.

Matteo An Italian form of Matthew. *See* Matthew.

Matthew From the Hebrew name Matisyahu, meaning "gift of God." In the Bible, one of the twelve apostles. VARIANT FORMS: Mattathias (Greek); Mathias, Matthias (English); Matheu, Mathieu (French); Mattia, Matteo (Italian); Mateo (Spanish); Mate, Matyas (Hungarian); Matthaus (German and Swedish). PET FORMS: Macey, Macy, Mat, Matt, Mati, Matti, Mattie. SURNAME USAGE: James Brander Matthews (1852-1929), author.

Matthias A variant form of Matthew. *See* Matthew. In the Bible, one of the apostles.

Mattie, Mattie Pet forms of Matthew. *See* Matthew. CONTEMPORARY EXAMPLE: Mattie Kilroy, baseball player.

Matty A popular short form of Mattathias and Matthew. Matti and Mattie are variant forms.

Maurey A pet form of Maurice. *See* Maurice.

Maurice From the Greek *mauros*, the Latin *maurius* and *maurus*, and the Middle English *morys*, meaning "a Moor," and generally associated with a dark-skinned person. Also, from the Old English *mor*, and the Middle English *mareis*, meaning "marshy, swampy wasteland." Maurice of Nassau (Prince of Orange, 1567-1625) was a Dutch statesman. VARIANT FORMS: Morris (English); Mauricio (Spanish); Maurizio (Italian); Moritz (German); Moriz (Russian);

Morets (Danish); Meuriz, Morus (Welsh). PET FORMS: Maurie, Morrie, Morrey, Morry, Maury, Morey. SURNAME USAGE: Mauer, Maur, Mohr, Moritz, Morris, Morrison, Morse.

Maurie   A pet form of Maurice. *See* Maurice..

Maury   A pet form of Maurice. *See* Maurice. CONTEMPORARY EXAMPLES: Maury Wills, baseball player; Maury Youmans, football player.

Max, Maxim, Maxime   Short forms of Maximilian. *See* Maximilian. Maxine is a feminine form. CONTEMPORARY EXAMPLES: Max Dimont, author; Maxim Surkont, baseball player; Maxime Rodison, professor. SURNAME USAGE: Max, North Dakota, named for Max Freitag, son of the first postmaster.

Maximilian   From the Latin *maximus*, meaning "great". Maxwell Maximilian I (1459-1519) was emperor of the Holy Roman Empire. PET FORMS: Max, Maxie, Maxey, Maxy. CONTEMPORARY EXAMPLE: Maximilian Schell, actor.

Maximino   The Spanish form of Maximilian. *See* Maximilian. CONTEMPORARY EXAMPLE: Maximino Leon, baseball player.

Maxwell   A variant form of Maximilian. *See* Maximilian. CONTEMPORARY EXAMPLE: Maxwell Anderson, playwright. SURNAME USAGE: James Clerk Maxwell (1831-1879), Scottish physician. PLACE-NAME USAGE: Maxwellton, Scotland.

Mayer   From the Latin *major*, meaning "great." Akin to Magnus. Also, a variant spelling of Meir. *See* Meir.

Mayes, Mays   From the British *maes* and *maise*, meaning "a field." CONTEMPORARY EXAMPLES: Mayes McCain, football player; Mays Copeland, baseball player. SURNAME USAGE: Willie Mays, baseball player.

Maynard   From the Old High German name Maganhard, compounded of *magan*, meaning "power," and *hardu*, meaning "hard, strong." CONTEMPORARY EXAMPLES: Maynard Reese, artist; Maynard Jackson, U.S. city mayor (Atlanta, Georgia).

Mayo   A variant form of Mayes or Matthew. *See* Mayes *and* Matthew. CONTEMPORARY EXAMPLE: Mayo Hohs, editor. SURNAME USAGE: William James Mayo (1861-1939), American physician.

Mazal-tov   From the Hebrew, meaning "good star, lucky star." Used by Jews in the Middle Ages, particularly among residents of Near East and Mediterranean countries.

McFerrin   A patronymic form, meaning "the son of Ferrin." *See* Ferrin. CONTEMPORARY EXAMPLE: W. McFerrin Stowe, clergyman.

McGeorge   A patronymic form, meaning "the son of George." *See* George. CONTEMPORARY EXAMPLE: McGeorge Bundy, executive.

McKinley A Scottish surname meaning "the son of Kinlay," a name meaning "fair herd." CONTEMPORARY EXAMPLE: McKinley Boston, football player. SURNAME USAGE: William McKinley, twenty-fifth president of the U.S. PLACE-NAME USAGE: Mount McKinley, Alaskan mountain range.

Medard From the Middle English *mede* and the Old English *maed*, meaning "a meadow." CONTEMPORARY EXAMPLE: Medard Gabel, author.

Medford From the Old English, meaning "the ford (brook crossing) in the meadow." Akin to Medard. CONTEMPORARY EXAMPLE: Medford Jones, educator. PLACE-NAME USAGE: a city in Massachusetts.

Medric From the Anglo-Saxon, meaning "rich meadow." CONTEMPORARY EXAMPLE: Medric Boucher, baseball player.

Meeno Possibly from the Italian *meno* and the Latin *minus*, meaning "less." CONTEMPORARY EXAMPLE: Meeno Peluce, actor.

Meged From the Hebrew, meaning "goodness, sweetness, excellence."

Meinhard From the German, meaning "my hart, my deer," a term of endearment. CONTEMPORARY EXAMPLE: Meinhard Pfyl, baseball player.

Meir, Meiri From the Hebrew, meaning "one who shines." SURNAME USAGE: Golda Meir (1898-1978), prime minister of Israel. Meira is the feminine equivalent.

Mel, Mell Pet forms of Melvin. *See* Melvin. CONTEMPORARY EXAMPLE: Mell Lazarus, author.

Melbourne From the Old English, meaning "the brook near the mill." PLACE-NAME USAGE: Melbourne, Australia.

Melchior From the Modern Latin name Melchita. Derived from the Hebrew *melech*, meaning "a king." SURNAME USAGE: Lauritz Melchior (1890-1973), opera singer.

Melchisadek, Melchizedek From the Hebrew, meaning "my king is righteousness." In the Bible, the king of Salem who blessed Abraham.

Meldon From the Old English *mill* and the Latin *dom* and *don*, meaning "the master of the mill." Or, from the German *melden*, meaning "to proclaim, to announce." CONTEMPORARY EXAMPLE: Meldon Wolfgang, football player.

Meldrim Origin unknown. CONTEMPORARY EXAMPLE: Meldrim Thomson, Jr., state governor (New Hampshire).

Melford From the Old English, meaning "the ford near the mill." CONTEMPORARY EXAMPLE: Melford E. Spiro, author.

Melton From the Old English, meaning "the town near the mill."

Milton is a variant spelling. CONTEMPORARY EXAMPLE: Melton Alonza McLauria, labor historian.

Melville   From the Old English, meaning "the village near the mill." Akin to Melton. SURNAME USAGE: Herman Melville (1819-1891), American novelist.

Melvin   From the Anglo-Saxon *mael*, meaning "council," plus *wine* (vin), meaning "friend." Or, from *mill* plus *win*, meaning "friend of the mill" or "mill worker." Melvyn is a variant spelling.

Melvyn   A variant spelling of Melvin. *See* Melvin. CONTEMPORARY EXAMPLE: Melvyn Leffler, historian.

Melwood   From the Old English, meaning "the mill near the woods." CONTEMPORARY EXAMPLE: Melwood Guy, football player.

Menachem, Menahem   From the Hebrew, meaning "comforter." In the Bible, a king of Israel (744-735 B.C.). CONTEMPORARY EXAMPLE: Menachem Begin, prime minister of Israel.

Menasseh   From the Hebrew, meaning "causing to forget." In the Bible, the elder son of Joseph. Manasseh is a variant spelling.

Mendel   From the Middle English *menden*, meaning "to repair, amend." Probably an occupational name for one who does general repairs. Also, a Yiddish name, a corrupt form of the Hebrew name Menachem. *See* Menachem. Or, a pet form of Emanuel. *See* Emanuel. CONTEMPORARY EXAMPLE: L. Mendel Rivers, U.S. congressman. SURNAME USAGE: Gregor Johann Mendel (1809-1884), Austrian monk; Felix Mendelssohn (1809-1847), German composer.

Mene   A pet form of Menelaus. *See* Menelaus.

Menelaus   In Greek legend, a king of Sparta, brother of Agamemnon.

Merald   From the Anglo-Saxon, meaning "old pool of water." CONTEMPORARY EXAMPLE: Merald Knight, musician.

Mercer   From the Old French *mercier* meaning "goods," hence "a dealer in textiles." CONTEMPORARY EXAMPLES: Mercer Mayer, author and illustrator; Mercer Ellington, author. SURNAME USAGE: Johnny Mercer, musician.

Meredith   From the Middle English and Welsh, meaning "defender of the sea." CONTEMPORARY EXAMPLE: Meredith Wilson, musician. SURNAME USAGE: George Meredith (1828-1909), English novelist.

Merle   From the Latin and French, meaning "blackbird." Used also as a feminine name. CONTEMPORARY EXAMPLES: Merle Goldman, professor; Merle Landerholm, educator.

Merlin   A variant form of Merlo. *See* Merlo. Or, from the Welsh, meaning "sea fort." In Arthurian legend, a magician and counsellor to

King Arthur. CONTEMPORARY EXAMPLES: Merlin J. Guilfoyle, clergyman; Merlin Olsen, actor.

Merlo   From the French and Italian, meaning "a parapet." CONTEMPORARY EXAMPLE: Merlo J. Pusey, Pulitzer Prize winner in letters (1952).

Merlon   A variant spelling of Merlin. *See* Merlin.

Meron   Origin uncertain. Possibly from the Hebrew, meaning "a flock."

Merrick   From the Old English *mer* plus *ric*, meaning "ruler of the sea." CONTEMPORARY EXAMPLE: Merrick Lewis, motor boat racer. SURNAME USAGE: David Merrick, theatrical producer.

Merrill   A compounded name, from the Old English *mer* and *mere*, meaning "a sea, a pool," and the British and Old English *il* and *iley*, meaning "a river, a body of water." SURNAME USAGE: Robert Merrill, singer.

Merrit, Merritt   From the Latin, meaning "valuable." CONTEMPORARY EXAMPLE: Merritt Roe Smith, historian.

Merton   From the Anglo-Saxon, meaning "from the town by the sea."

Mervin, Mervyn   Welsh forms of Marvin. *See* Marvin.

Merwin, Merwyn   Variant forms of Marvin. *See* Marvin.

Methuselah   From the Hebrew, meaning "a man who was sent, a messenger." In the Bible, the man who lived more years than anyone else (969 years).

Meyer   A variant spelling of Mayer. *See* Mayer.

Micah   From the Hebrew, meaning "Who is like God?" In the Bible, an eighth–century B.C. prophet. A short form of Michael.

Michael   From the Hebrew, meaning "Who is like God?" In the Bible, the archangel closest to God; i.e., the divine messenger who carries out God's judgments. Popular name in England in the twelfth century. VARIANT FORMS: Michel, Michon, Mitchel, Mitchell (French); Michele (Italian); Michiel (Dutch); Miguel (Spanish and Portuguese); Micha (German); Michail, Misha, Mikhail (Russian); Mikas, Mikel (Swedish); Mihal, Mihaly, Miska (Hungarian). PET FORMS: Mike, Mick, Mickey, Mitch. Occasionally used as a feminine form.

Michel   A French form of Michael. *See* Michael. CONTEMPORARY EXAMPLE: Michel Klein, French veterinarian.

Michelangelo   Compounded of Michel (Michael) and Angelo. *See* Michael *and* Angelo. CONTEMPORARY EXAMPLE: Justin Michelangelo Saccio, San Diego, California.

Mickey   A pet form of Michael. *See* Michael. CONTEMPORARY EXAMPLE: Mickey Mantle, baseball player.

Middleton   From the Old English, probably meaning "the town near the meadow."

Midgard   From the Old Norse, meaning "a midway house." In Norse mythology, the earth, encircled by a serpent, was considered to be midway between heaven and hell.

Midge   A variant form of Midgard. *See* Midgard. Also, a variant form of Mitch (from Michael) and Mitchell. *See* Michael *and* Mitchell. CONTEMPORARY EXAMPLE: Midge Didham, jockey.

Midrag   Possibly a variant form of Midgard. *See* Midgard.

Miguel   The Spanish and Portuguese forms of Michael. *See* Michael. CONTEMPORARY EXAMPLE: Miguel Lopez, soccer player.

Mike   A pet form of Michael. *See* Michael.

Mikel   A pet form of Michael. *See* Michael. CONTEMPORARY EXAMPLE: Mikel Ross Kennedy, Houston, Texas.

Mikhail   A Russian form of Michael. *See* Michael. CONTEMPORARY EXAMPLE: Mikhail Baryshnikov, ballet dancer.

Milan   From the Latin *militatus*, meaning "a warrior, a soldier." CONTEMPORARY EXAMPLE: Milan Zeleny, economics professor. PLACE-NAME USAGE: a city in northern Italy (Milano).

Milburn   From the Old English, meaning "the mill near the brook." CONTEMPORARY EXAMPLES: Milburn Calhoun, publisher; Milburn Stone, actor.

Miles   From the Latin *militatus*, meaning "a warrior, a soldier." Akin to Milan. In England, used as a short form of Michael. Myles is a variant spelling. SURNAME USAGE: Mills, Milson. PLACE-NAME USAGE: Miles City, Montana, named for General Nelson A. Miles.

Milfred   A name invented by changing the first "d" in Mildred to an "f".

Milford   From the Latin *militatus*, meaning "a warrior, a soldier." CONTEMPORARY EXAMPLE: Milford Berner, football player. PLACE-NAME USAGE: Milford, Connecticut.

Mili   A pet form of Milileilani. *See* Milileilani.

Milileilani   From the Hawaiian, meaning "to praise, to give thanks."

Millard   From the Latin *millium*, meaning "millet (a cereal grain grown in Europe)." CONTEMPORARY EXAMPLE: Millard Fillmore (1800-1874), thirteenth president of the U.S.; Millard Arnold, author.

Miller   An Old English occupational name, meaning "one who grinds or mills grain." *See also* Mills. CONTEMPORARY EXAMPLE: Miller Huggins, baseball manager. SURNAME USAGE: Arthur Miller, playwright.

Mills From the Old English *miln*, meaning "a mill." Akin to Miller. *See* Miller. CONTEMPORARY EXAMPLES: Mills E. Godwin, Jr., governor of Virginia; Mills Watson, actor.

Milo A variant form of Miles. *See* Miles. CONTEMPORARY EXAMPLE: Milo Rediger, educator.

Milton From the Old English, meaning "the town near the mill." Melton is a variant spelling. Akin to Mills and Miller.

Miner An occupational name from the Middle English and Old French, meaning "one who digs for coal."

Minor From the Middle English *mynor*, meaning "one of lesser rank." CONTEMPORARY EXAMPLE: Minor Heath, baseball player.

Minot From the Greek name Minos. In Greek mythology, a king of Crete, son of Zeus. One of the three judges of the netherworld. CONTEMPORARY EXAMPLE: Minot Crowell, baseball player. PLACE-NAME USAGE: Minot, North Dakota.

Minster From the Old English, meaning "a monastery, a church."

Minter A variant form of Minster. *See* Minster. Or, an occupational name from the Latin, meaning "a minter of coins." CONTEMPORARY EXAMPLE: Minter Hayes, baseball player.

Mircea From the Latin *mirari* and *mirus*, meaning "wonderful, marvelous," hence "to mirror." CONTEMPORARY EXAMPLE: Mircea Eliada, historian.

Miro Akin to Mircea. *See* Mircea. CONTEMPORARY EXAMPLE: Miro Todorovich, author.

Miroslav A Czechoslovak name derived from the Latin, meaning "beautiful slave." CONTEMPORARY EXAMPLE: Miroslav Ondricek, cinematographer.

Mirro From the Latin *mirari*, meaning "to mirror, to admire." CONTEMPORARY EXAMPLE: Mirro Roder, football player.

Misha A Russian form of Michael. *See* Michael.

Miska A Slovakian form of Michael. *See* Michael.

Mitchel, Mitchell Variant forms of Michael. *See* Michael. SURNAME USAGE: William Mitchell (1879–1936), U.S. Army general. PLACE-NAME USAGE: Mount Mitchell, North Carolina.

Mitford From the Middle English, meaning "a small river crossing." CONTEMPORARY EXAMPLE: Mitford Mathews, educator. SURNAME USAGE: Jessica Mitford, author.

Mizell From the Old High German *miza*, meaning "a tiny gnat." CONTEMPORARY EXAMPLE: Mizell Platt, baseball player.

Mo A pet form of Morris. *See* Morris.

Modred   From the Middle English *mourdant* and the Latin *mordere*, meaning "to bite." In Arthurian legend, the violent nephew of King Arthur. They killed each other in battle. Akin to Mordred.

Modris   Probably akin to Modred. *See* Modred. CONTEMPORARY EXAMPLE: Modris Ramans, artist.

Moe   The diminutive of Moses. *See* Moses.

Mohammad   A variant spelling of Mohammed. *See* Mohammed. CONTEMPORARY EXAMPLE: Mohammad Sadiq, cricket player.

Mohammed   From the Arabic *muhammed*, meaning "praised." An Arabian prophet (570-632), founder of the Moslem religion.

Moise   French and Italian variant forms of Moses. *See* Moses. CONTEMPORARY EXAMPLE: Moise Berger, attorney.

Moke   The Hawaiian form of Moses. *See* Moses.

Monford   From the British, meaning "a mountain ford (crossing)." CONTEMPORARY EXAMPLE: Monford Irvin, baseball player.

Monita   An Italian form of the Greek *monis*, meaning "single, alone." CONTEMPORARY EXAMPLE: Monita Kennedy, baseball player.

Monroe   An occupational name, from the Scottish *mon*, meaning "man", plus the French *rouer*, from the Latin *rota*, meaning "wheel," hence, "a wheeler, one who rolls objects on a wheel." In Ireland, Munroe is the mouth (mum) of the river Roe. CONTEMPORARY EXAMPLE: Monroe Stahr, movie producer. SURNAME USAGE: James Monroe (1758-1831), fifth president of the U.S. PLACE-NAME USAGE: Louisiana; Monrovia, capital of Liberia.

Montague   The French form of the Latin, meaning "a hill, a mountain." Montgomery is an English variant. Monte and Monty are diminutive forms. SURNAME USAGE: the family name of Romeo in Shakespeare's *Romeo and Juliet*.

Monte   A pet form of Montague and Montgomery. *See* Montague *and* Montgomery. Also, an independent name, from Montreal (Canada). CONTEMPORARY EXAMPLE: Monte Mathews, New York, New York.

Montgomery   The English form of Montague. *See* Montague. CONTEMPORARY EXAMPLE: Montgomery Clift, actor. SURNAME USAGE: Bernard Montgomery, English World War II general. PLACE-NAME USAGE: Montgomery, Alabama.

Monty   A variant spelling of Monte. *See* Monte.

Moon   From the Old English *mona*, meaning "a month." CONTEMPORARY EXAMPLE: Moon Landrieu, U.S. city mayor (New Orleans, Louisiana).

Mordecai   A Hebrew name derived from the Persian and Babylonian, meaning "warrior, warlike." A variant form of Marduk. In Babylonian mythology Marduk was the god of war. In the Bible, the cousin of Queen Esther, who saved the Jewish people of Persia from extermination by Haman, prime minister of King Ahasueros. The event was the origin of the Purim holiday in the Jewish calendar. In the Middle Ages, Jewish boys born on Purim were often named Mordecai. PET FORMS: Mordy, Morty.

Mordechai   The Hebrew form of Mordecai. *See* Mordecai. CONTEMPORARY EXAMPLE: Mordechai Tsanin, author.

Mordkhe   The Yiddish form of Mordecai. *See* Mordecai. CONTEMPORARY EXAMPLE: Mordkhe Schaechter, editor.

Mordred   A variant form of Modred. *See* Modred.

Mordy   A pet form of Mordecai. *See* Mordecai.

Moreton   A variant spelling of Morton. *See* Morton. CONTEMPORARY EXAMPLE: Moreton Marsh, author.

Morey   A pet form of Maurice. *See* Maurice. VARIANT SPELLINGS: Morie, Morrie, Morrey, Morry. CONTEMPORARY EXAMPLE: Morey Amsterdam, comedian.

Morgan   From the Celtic, meaning "one who lives near the sea." CONTEMPORARY EXAMPLE: Morgan Woodard, actor. SURNAME USAGE: J.P. Morgan, financier.

Morrey   A variant spelling of Morey. *See* Morey. CONTEMPORARY EXAMPLE: Morrie Kreiger, author.

Morrie   A variant spelling of Morey. *See* Morey. CONTEMPORARY EXAMPLE: Morrie Kreiger, author.

Morris   A variant form of Maurice. *See* Maurice. PET FORMS: Morie, Morrie, Morey, Morry. SURNAME USAGE: Gouverneur Morris (1752-1816), American statesman. PLACE-NAME USAGE: Cape Morris Jessup at the northern tip of Greenland.

Morrison   A patronymic form, meaning "the son of Morris." *See* Morris. CONTEMPORARY EXAMPLE: Morrison Warren, football player.

Morry   A variant form of Morey. *See* Morey.

Morse   A variant form of Maurice. *See* Maurice. Or, from Roman mythology, death personified as a god. Akin to Thanatos, the god of death in Greek mythology. CONTEMPORARY EXAMPLE: Morse Peckham, author. SURNAME USAGE: Samuel Morse (1791-1872), American inventor.

Mortimer   From the Anglo-French, meaning "one who lives near the sea." PET FORMS: Mort, Morty.

Morton   From the Old English, meaning "the town near the sea." A variant form of Moreton.

Morty   A pet form of Morton. *See* Morton.

Mose   A pet form of Moses. Also, the Hawaiian form of Moses. *See* Moses. CONTEMPORARY EXAMPLE: Mose Denson, football player.

Moses   From the Hebrew *mosheh*, meaning "drawn out of (the water)" or from the Egyptian *mes, mesu*, meaning "a son, a child." In the Bible, the leader who brought the Israelites out of their bondage in Egypt and led them to the Promised Land. A name rarely used in the post-biblical period. The eleventh-century Domesday Book in England records the form Moyses. President Grover Cleveland's first ancestor in America (1635) was named Moses. VARIANT FORMS: Moshe, Mosheh, Moss, Moy, Moyes, Moyse, Moyses. Morris and Maurice are often incorrectly regarded as equivalent forms of Moses. CONTEMPORARY EXAMPLE: Moses Malone, basketball player. SURNAME USAGE: Robert Moses, executive. Also: Moss, Moyce, Moys, Moyse, Moyses.

Mosha   From the Hebrew, meaning "salvation." Akin to Joshua.

Moshe   The exact Hebrew form of Moses. *See* Moses. PET FORMS: Mo, Mose, Moish, Moishe. CONTEMPORARY EXAMPLE: Moshe Dayan, Israeli general and statesman.

Moss   An English variant form of Moses. *See* Moses. CONTEMPORARY EXAMPLE: Moss Hart, playwright. PLACE-NAME USAGE: Moss Landing, California, named for Charles Moss, local builder.

Moy, Moyse   Variant forms of Moses. *See* Moses.

Mozart   From the Italian *mozzare*, meaning "to cut off." Probably an occupational name for "one who sells (and cuts off) cheese." Grew popular from the surname of the German composer Wolfgang Amadeus Mozart (1756-1791).

Muhammad   A variant spelling of Mohammed. *See* Mohammed. CONTEMPORARY EXAMPLE: Muhammad Ali, world boxing champion. He assumed this name after becoming a Muslim. His original name was Cassius Clay.

Muhammed   A variant spelling of Muhammad. *See* Muhammad.

Muhtar   From the Arabic, meaning "a village leader." CONTEMPORARY EXAMPLE: Muhtar Holland, translator.

Mull   From the Middle English *mullen*, meaning "to grind." Akin to Mills. *See* Mills. CONTEMPORARY EXAMPLE: Mull Dunfee, Guysville, Ohio. SURNAME USAGE: Martin Mull, actor.

Muller   An occupational name derived from Mull, meaning "a miller." *See* Mull.

Mungo   Probably a Yorkshire occupational name, meaning "one who makes shoddy cloth (from wool waste)." Or, from the Sanskrit, meaning "a bean."

Munro   A variant spelling of Monroe. *See* Monroe. CONTEMPORARY EXAMPLE: Munro Leaf, author and illustrator.

Murdoch, Murdock   From the Gaelic name Muireadhach, meaning "a sailor." Murtagh is an Irish variant form.

Murphy   From the Celtic and Irish *muir*, meaning "of the sea." An Irish slang word for a potato. CONTEMPORARY EXAMPLE: Murphy Currie, baseball player. SURNAME USAGE: Frank Murphy (1890-1949), U.S. Supreme Court Justice.

Murray   From the Celtic *muir*, and the Welsh *mor*, meaning "the sea." Akin to Maurice. *See* Maurice. CONTEMPORARY EXAMPLE: Murray Hamilton, actor.

Murry   A variant spelling of Murray. *See* Murray. CONTEMPORARY EXAMPLE: Murry Sidlin, musician.

Murtagh   An Irish variant spelling of Murtaug. *See* Murtaug.

Murtaug, Murtaugh   From the British *martawg*, meaning "the river of the border country." Also, an Irish form of Murdoch. *See* Murdoch. SURNAME USAGE: John Murtaugh, attorney.

Mychal   A variant spelling of Michael. *See* Michael. CONTEMPORARY EXAMPLE: Mychal Thompson, basketball player.

Myer   Variant spellings of Mayer. *See* Mayer.

Myles   A variant spelling of Miles. *See* Miles.

Myril, Myrl   Variant spellings of Merrill. *See* Merrill. CONTEMPORARY EXAMPLES: Myril Hoag, baseball player; Myrl Goodwin, football player.

Myron   From the Greek, meaning "fragrant, sweet, perfumed." A fifth-century B.C. sculptor. CONTEMPORARY EXAMPLE: Myron Cohen, comedian.

Myrton   A variant spelling of Morton. *See* Morton. CONTEMPORARY EXAMPLE: Myrton Basing, football player.

N

Naaman   From the Hebrew, meaning "sweet, beautiful, pleasant, good." In the Bible, the general who visited the prophet Elisha to be cured of his leprosy.

Naboth   From the Hebrew, possibly meaning "prophecy." Related to the Babylonian god Nebo. In the Bible, the owner of a vineyard coveted by Queen Jezebel.

Nadar, Nader   From the Arabic *nazir*, meaning "opposite the zenith." CONTEMPORARY EXAMPLE: Nadar Ardalan, Iranian architect. SURNAME USAGE: Ralph Nader, attorney.

Nadiv   From the Hebrew, meaning "prince, noble." Akin to Nagid.

Naftali, Naftalie   Variant spellings of Naphtali. *See* Naphtali. CONTEMPORARY EXAMPLE: Naftali Arbel, author.

Nagid   From the Hebrew, meaning "ruler, prince." Akin to Nadiv.

Nahir   From the Aramaic, meaning "light."

Nahum   From the Hebrew, meaning "comforted." In the Bible, a minor prophet who lived in the seventh–century B.C. and foretold the fall of Nineveh. CONTEMPORARY EXAMPLE: Nahum Sarna, author.

Namir   From the Hebrew, meaning "leopard."

Nansen   A Scandinavian matronymic form, meaning "son of Nancy."

Nap   A pet form of Napoleon. Also, from Danish *nappe*, meaning "to snatch." CONTEMPORARY EXAMPLE: Nap Lajoie, baseball player.

Naphtali, Naphthali   From the Hebrew, meaning "wrestle." In the Bible, the sixth son of Jacob, by his wife Bilhah.

Napoleon   From the Greek name Neapolis, meaning "new town." Napoli is the Italian form of Naples. Made famous through Napoleon I (Napoleon Bonaparte), 1769-1821, emperor of France. PLACE-NAME USAGE: Napoleon, North Dakota, named for Napoleon Goodsill, a local businessman; Napoleonville, Louisiana, named for J.L. Napoleon, plantation owner.

Nash, Nashe   From the Old English, meaning "a protruding cliff." VARIANT FORMS: Nase, Ness. CONTEMPORARY EXAMPLE: Nash Aussenbert, scholar. SURNAME USAGE: Thomas Nash (1567-1601), English writer; Ogden Nash, American author. PLACE-NAME USAGE: Nashua, New Hampshire; Nashville, Tennessee; Nash, North Carolina and Tennessee, named for General Francis Nash, Revolutionary War hero.

Nasser From the Arabic, meaning "the victorious one," a designation for God. Originally a surname made famous by Egyptian President Abdel Gamal Nasser.

Nat A pet form of Nathan. *See* Nathan. CONTEMPORARY EXAMPLE: Nat Turner (1800-1831), anti-slavery leader.

Nate A pet form of Nathan. *See* Nathan. CONTEMPORARY EXAMPLE: Nate Shaw, football player.

Nathan From the Hebrew, meaning "He gave," and implying a gift of God. In the Bible, the prophet who reprimanded King David because of his unfair treatment of Uriah the Hittite. Nate is a pet form.

Nathaniel From the Hebrew, meaning "gift of God." In the Bible, the fourth son of Jesse, a brother of David. PET FORMS: Nat, Nate, Nathan, Niel, Neal. CONTEMPORARY USAGE: Nathaniel Hawthorne (1804-1864), American author. PLACE-NAME USAGE: a suburb of Los Angeles, California.

Naylor From Nay, an Old English name derived from *cy*, meaning "water," hence "a sailor, one who makes a living from the sea."

Neal, Neale From the Middle English names Nel, Neel, Nele, and the Gaelic name Niall, meaning "a champion." Also, from the Norse name Niel, a variant form of Nicholas. *See* Nicholas.

Ned A pet form of Edward. *See* Edward. CONTEMPORARY EXAMPLE: Ned Williamson, baseball executive.

Neely A variant form of Neal. *See* Neal. CONTEMPORARY EXAMPLE: Neely Dixon McCarter, theologian.

Negev From the Hebrew, meaning "south, southerly." PLACE-NAME USAGE: the southern area of Israel.

Nehemiah From the Hebrew, meaning "comforted of the Lord." In the Bible, a contemporary of Ezra who served as governor of Judah. CONTEMPORARY EXAMPLE: Nehemiah Persoff, actor.

Neil A variant spelling of Neal. *See* Neal.

Neilson A patronymic form of Neil and Neal, meaning "the son of Neil." *See* Neal.

Nels A matronymic form used in England, meaning "the son of Nell." *See* Nell (feminine section). CONTEMPORARY EXAMPLE: Nels W. Hanson, educator.

Nelsi A variant form of Neal. *See* Neal. CONTEMPORARY EXAMPLE: Nelsi Morais, soccer player.

Nelson A patronymic form of Neal, meaning "the son of Neal." *See* Neal. CONTEMPORARY EXAMPLES: Nelson Rockefeller, U.S. vice president; Nelson DeMille, author. SURNAME USAGE: Horatio Nelson (1758-1805), English admiral. PLACE-NAME USAGE: a river in Manitoba.

Nemiah   A variant spelling of Nehemiah. *See* Nehemiah. CONTEMPO-RARY EXAMPLE: Nemiah Wilson, football player.

Nemo   Probably from the Old English *nym*, a contraction of Nehemiah. *See* Nehemiah. PLACE-NAME USAGE: a city in Texas.

Nestor   In Greek legend, a wise old man who fought with the Greeks at Troy, hence the meaning "wise old person." CONTEMPORARY EXAMPLE: Nestor Miller, boating champion.

Neven, Nevin, Nevins   From the Old English *nafa* or *navu*, meaning "the middle," hence "the hub of a wheel." CONTEMPORARY EXAMPLE: Nevin Cline, athlete. SURNAME USAGE: Ethelbert Woodbridge Nevin (1862-1901), American composer.

Nevil, Nevile   From the French, meaning "new village." VARIANT SPELLINGS: Nevill, Neville.

Nevill, Neville   Variant forms of Nevil. *See* Nevil. CONTEMPORARY EXAMPLES: Nevill F. Mott, English Nobel Prize winner in physics (1977); Neville Chamberlain (1869-1940), English statesman.

Newbold   From the Old English *bol* and *bold*, meaning "the bole, the trunk of a tree," hence "the new town beside the tree." CONTEMPORARY EXAMPLE: Newbold Morris, New York City borough president.

Newell   An English form of the Latin name Novellus, meaning "something new, unusual." Akin to Noel. CONTEMPORARY EXAMPLE: Newell Jenkins, musical conductor.

Newgate   Probably from the occupational name for one who guards a gate, hence "a watchman." CONTEMPORARY EXAMPLE: Newgate Callendar, literary critic.

Newland   From the Anglo-Saxon, meaning "a new land." SURNAME USAGE: Newlander.

Newman   From the Anglo-Saxon, meaning "a new man." Originally, an English surname. SURNAME USAGE: John Henry Newman (1801-1890), English theologian.

Newton   From the Anglo-Saxon, meaning "the new town." Originally an English place-name and surname. CONTEMPORARY EXAMPLE: Newton Thornberg, novelist. SURNAME USAGE: Isaac Newton (1642-1727), English mathematician.

Nic   A pet form of Nicholas. *See* Nicholas. Used also as an independent name. CONTEMPORARY EXAMPLE: Nic Rhoodie, sociologist.

Nicholas   From the Greek *nike*, meaning "victory," and *laos*, meaning "the people," hence "victory of the people." Akin to Nike. *See* Nike. St. Nicholas, a fourth-century bishop of Myra, was the patron saint of Russia, of Greece, and of young people. Nicholas I (1796-1855) was czar of Russia. Many popes and saints were named Nicholas. VARIANT FORMS: Colin, Nicole (French); Nicolas (French and

Spanish); Nicolaus (Latin); Niel (Norse); Nikolaos (Greek); Klaus, Nikolaus (German); Nikolai, Nikita (Russian); Nicol (Scotch); Cola, Niccolo, Nicolo (Italian); Nikola (Slavonic). PET FORMS: Nick, Nicol, Nilo, Cola, Claus, Klaus.

Nico   A pet form of Nicodemus. *See* Nicodemus. CONTEMPORARY EXAMPLE: Nico Castel, actor.

Nicodemus   From the Greek, meaning "the people's conqueror." Akin to Nicholas. *See* Nicholas.

Nicolas   A variant spelling of Nicholas. *See* Nicholas.

Niel   A variant Norse form of Nicholas. *See* Nicholas. Also, a variant spelling of Neal. *See* Neal.

Nig   A pet form of Nigel. *See* Nigel. CONTEMPORARY EXAMPLE: Nig Cuppy, baseball player.

Nigel   Probably from the Anglo-Saxon *nyht*, akin to the German *nacht*, meaning "night, dark." Also, possibly a short form of nightingale, meaning "to sing at night." CONTEMPORARY EXAMPLE: Nigel Calder, author.

Nike   From the Greek *nike*, meaning "victory." In Greek mythology, the winged goddess of victory, the equivalent of the Roman Victoria. Nike is the original form of Nicholas. *See* Nicholas.

Nikita   A Russian pet form of Nicholas. *See* Nicholas. CONTEMPORARY EXAMPLE: Nikita Khrushchev, Russian statesman.

Nikolai   The Russian form of Nicholas. *See* Nicholas.

Nikolaos   The Greek form of Nicholas. *See* Nicholas. CONTEMPORARY EXAMPLE: Nikolaos van Dam, political analyst.

Niland   A variant form of Newland. *See* Newland. CONTEMPORARY EXAMPLE: Niland Mortimer, publisher.

Niles   A patronymic form of Neal, meaning "son of Neal." *See* Neal. Popular in Denmark. CONTEMPORARY EXAMPLE: Niles Jordan, baseball player.

Nili   An acronym of the Hebrew words in I Samuel 15:29: "the eternity (victory) of Israel will not be denied." The name of a pro-British and anti-Turkish underground organization in Palestine during World War I. Used also as a feminine name.

Nils   A patronymic form of Neal, meaning "son of Neal." Popular among Scandinavians. *See* Neal. CONTEMPORARY EXAMPLES: Nils Lundgren, author; Nils E. Boe, governor of South Dakota.

Nir   From the Hebrew, meaning "a plow" or "a plowed field." VARIANT FORMS: Nirel, Niria, Niriel.

Nirel   From the Hebrew, meaning "the plowed field of the Lord."

Niria   A variant form of Nirel. *See* Nirel.

Niriel   A variant form of Nirel. *See* Nirel.

Nisi, Nissi   From the Hebrew, meaning "my sign, my emblem." Used in Israel. VARIANT FORMS: Nissan, Nissim. *See* Nissan.

Nissan   From the Hebrew *nais*, meaning "banner, emblem." The name of the Hebrew month in which the Passover holiday occurs. The first month of spring.

Nissim   From the Hebrew, meaning "signs, miracles." From the same Hebrew root as Nissan. *See* Nissan.

Niv   From the Aramaic and Arabic, meaning "speech."

Noah   From the Hebrew, meaning "rest, peace." In the Bible, the leading character in the story of the flood. CONTEMPORARY EXAMPLE: Noah Dale Jackson, football player; Noah N. Langdale, Jr., educator.

Noam   From the Hebrew, meaning "sweetness, friendship." Naomi is a feminine form. CONTEMPORARY EXAMPLE: Noam Chomsky, author.

Noble   From the Latin *nobilis*, meaning "well-known, famous." CONTEMPORARY EXAMPLE: Noble Doss, football player. PLACE-NAME USAGE: Noble, Oklahoma, named for J.W. Noble, secretary of the interior.

Noda   From the Hebrew, meaning "famous, well-known."

Noel   From the Old French name Nouel, derived form the Latin *natalis*, meaning "natal; to be born." An expression of joy used in Christmas carols. Natalie is the feminine form.

Noga   From the Hebrew, meaning "light, bright." In the Bible, a son of King David. Used also as a feminine name.

Nolan, Noland   Probably variant forms of the Anglo–Saxon Northland. Popular in Ireland. May also be from the Celtic, meaning "noble, famous." CONTEMPORARY EXAMPLE: Nolan Bushnell, inventor. PLACE-NAME USAGE: Noland, North Carolina, named for Andrew Noland, an early settler.

Nolen   A variant spelling of Noland. *See* Nolan. CONTEMPORARY EXAMPLE: Nolen Ellison, educator.

Nono   An American Indian name. Origin unknown. CONTEMPORARY EXAMPLE: Nono Minor, author. PLACE-NAME USAGE: Nono, Florida, named for a daughter of an early settler.

Norbert   From the German, meaning "divine brightness." CONTEMPORARY EXAMPLE: Norbert Wurtzel, educator.

Norman, Normann   From the Anglo-Saxon, meaning "a man from the North." Refers to any of the Northmen who conquered Normandy in the tenth century. Normand is a variant form. CONTEMPORARY EXAMPLE: Normann Burton, actor.

Normand A French form of Norman. *See* Norman. CONTEMPORARY EXAMPLE: Normand Dupont, hockey player. PLACE-NAME USAGE: Normandy, France.

Norris From the Anglo-Saxon, meaning "Norman's house" or "a house of a man from the North." CONTEMPORARY EXAMPLE: Norris McWhirter, author. SURNAME USAGE: Frank Norris (1870-1902), American novelist. PLACE-NAME USAGE: Norristown, New Jersey.

North From the Anglo-Saxon, meaning "a man from the North."

Northcote From the Anglo-Saxon and Middle English, meaning "cottage (*cote*) or shed in the North (field)." CONTEMPORARY EXAMPLE: Northcote C. Parkinson, author.

Norval From the Anglo-Saxon, meaning "northern valley." CONTEMPORARY EXAMPLE: Norval Morris, sociologist.

Norwood From the Old English, meaning "the woods in the North." CONTEMPORARY EXAMPLE: Norwood C. Thornton, editor. PLACE-NAME USAGE: cities in North Carolina, New Jersey, Illinois, and Kansas.

Nowell A variant form of Noel or Newell. *See* Noel *and* Newell.

Noy From the Hebrew, meaning "beauty."

Nugent Possibly from the Old English and Middle Low German, Meaning "to nudge, to shove." CONTEMPORARY EXAMPLE: Nugent Wininger, San Francisco, California.

Nuncio The Italian form of the Latin name Nuntius. *See* Nuntius.

Nuntius From the Latin, meaning "messenger." Nuncio is an Italian variant form.

Nur From the Hebrew and Aramaic, meaning "fire."

Nuri A variant form of *nur*, meaning "my fire."

Nuria From the Hebrew, meaning "the fire of the Lord."

Nye A pet form of Aneurin. *See* Aneurin.

Nyle A variant Irish form of Neal. *See* Neal. Also, from the Old English, meaning "island." CONTEMPORARY EXAMPLE: Nyle McFarlane, athlete.

O

Oak   A pet form of Oakley. *See* Oakley. PLACE-NAME USAGE: Oakland, Nebraska, named for John Oak, an early landowner; Oaks Lake, Montana.

Oakes   From the Old English, meaning "one who sells oak trees." CONTEMPORARY EXAMPLE: Oakes Ames, railroad executive.

Oakleigh   A variant spelling of Oakley. *See* Oakley. CONTEMPORARY EXAMPLE: Oakleigh Cookingham, Red Hook, New York.

Oakley   From the Old English, meaning "a field of oak trees." Oak is a pet form. Oakleigh is a variant spelling. CONTEMPORARY EXAMPLE: Oakley Hunter, financier.

Obadiah   From the Hebrew, meaning "servant of God." In the Bible, a sixth-century B.C. prophet, the fourth of the twelve minor prophets. Obe is a pet form. CONTEMPORARY EXAMPLE: Obadiah Starbuck, author.

Obe   A pet form of Obadiah. *See* Obadiah. CONTEMPORARY EXAMPLE: Obe Wenig, football player.

Obed   From the Hebrew *eved*, meaning "servant." CONTEMPORARY EXAMPLE: Obed Ashby, Amenia, New York. PLACE-NAME USAGE: Obed, Arizona.

Obert   A short form of Odbert. *See* Odbert. CONTEMPORARY EXAMPLE: Obert Logan, football player.

Octave   A variant form of Octavius. *See* Octavius. CONTEMPORARY EXAMPLE: Octave Chanute, aviator.

Octavio   The Italian form of Octavius. *See* Octavius. CONTEMPORARY EXAMPLES: Octavio Roja, baseball player; Octavio Paz, Mexican poet.

Octavius   From the Latin, meaning "eight." In some families, the eighth child, if a son, was named Octavius.

Odam   From the Middle English, meaning "son–in–law." Akin to the German name Eidam.

Odbert   From the Danish *od*, meaning "an otter," plus the German *bert*, meaning "bright." Obert is a variant form. CONTEMPORARY EXAMPLE: Odbert Hamric, baseball player.

Odd   From the Danish *od*, meaning "an otter." CONTEMPORARY EXAMPLE: Odd Hagen, clergyman.

Ode   A pet form of Odell or Odin. *See* Odell *and* Odin. CONTEMPORARY EXAMPLE: Ode Burrell, football player.

Odell An Irish form of the Danish *od*, meaning "an otter." Also, from the Greek, meaning "an ode, a melody." Used also as a patronymic form, meaning "son of Dale." *See* Dale. CONTEMPORARY EXAMPLE: Odell Shepard, Nobel Prize winner in letters.

Odie A pet form of Odin or Odell. *See* Odin *and* Odell. CONTEMPORARY EXAMPLE: Odie B. Faulk, Memphis, Tennessee.

Odin In Norse mythology, the chief god, creator of the world. CONTEMPORARY EXAMPLE: Odin Langen, U.S. congressman.

Odious From the Latin *odium*, meaning "hateful." CONTEMPORARY EXAMPLE: Odious Hickman, Cincinnati, Ohio.

Odis A variant form of Odin. *See* Odin. CONTEMPORARY EXAMPLE: Odis Crowell, football player.

Odo From the Old German *auda* and the Old English *ead*, meaning "rich." Otto is a variant form.

Ofer From the Hebrew, meaning "a young deer."

Og In the Bible, the King of Bashan. CONTEMPORARY EXAMPLE: Og Mandino, author.

Ogden From the Anglo-Saxon, meaning "from the oak valley." CONTEMPORARY EXAMPLE: Ogden Nash, author. PLACE-NAME USAGE: Ogden, Utah.

Ojars A Latvian name, meaning unknown. CONTEMPORARY EXAMPLE: Ojars Stikis, Weehawken, New Jersey.

Okapi A name used in Africa for a giraffe-like animal with a long neck.

Oke The Hawaiian form of Oscar. *See* Oscar. Also, a nickname for someone from Oklahoma. CONTEMPORARY EXAMPLE: Oke Carlson, football player.

Okie A nickname for a person from Oklahoma.

Olaf From the Norse and Danish, meaning "an ancestor." Olaf was an early royal saint name. Olaf I (969–1000) was a king of Norway.

Ole A pet form of Olaf and Oleg. *See* Olaf *and* Oleg. Also, the Hawaiian form of Ollie (Oliver). *See* Oliver. CONTEMPORARY EXAMPLE: Ole Risom, publisher.

Oleg From the Norse, meaning "holy." Helga and Olga are feminine forms. CONTEMPORARY EXAMPLE: Oleg Cassini, fashion designer.

Olin From the Old English *holegn* and the Middle English *holi*, meaning "the holly." *See also* Olney. CONTEMPORARY EXAMPLES: Olin Pinoyd, author; Olin Robinson, educator. PLACE-NAME USAGE: Olinda, California.

Oliver From the Latin and French, meaning "an olive tree," having the connotation of "peace." May also be from the Germanic *alf*, meaning elf, plus *hari*, meaning "a host, an army." Ollie is a pet form. Olive and Olivia are feminine forms. CONTEMPORARY EXAMPLE: Oliver Wendell Holmes (1841-1935), U.S. Supreme Court Justice.

Olivier   The French form of Oliver. *See* Oliver. SURNAME USAGE: Sir Laurence Olivier, actor.

Ollie   A pet form of Oliver. *See* Oliver. CONTEMPORARY EXAMPLE: Ollie Brown, baseball player.

Olney   A variant form of Olin. *See* Olin.

Olof   A variant form of Olaf. *See* Olaf. CONTEMPORARY EXAMPLE: Olof Idegren, fishing expert.

Omar   From the Arabic, meaning "long life." Omri is a variant form. Omar Khayyam, a twelfth–century Persian poet, author of *The Rubaiyat*. CONTEMPORARY EXAMPLES: Omar Bradley, U.S. Army general; Omar Sharif, actor.

Omri   From the Arabic, meaning "to live, to live long" or "to worship, worshiper." In the Bible, a king of Israel (887-876 B.C.). Akin to Omar.

Ona   From the British *onn*, meaning an "ash tree." CONTEMPORARY EXAMPLE: Ona Dodd, baseball player.

Onny   From the British, meaning "the water near the ash tree."

Oona   A variant form of Onny. *See* Onny. CONTEMPORARY EXAMPLE: Oona O'Neil, actress.

Opal   From the Sanskrit *upala*, meaning "a precious stone." The Latin form is *opalus*. Usually a feminine name.

Opher   A variant spelling of Ofer. *See* Ofer.

Oral   From the Latin *os* and *oris*, meaning "the mouth," hence "the spoken word, oral." CONTEMPORARY EXAMPLE: Oral Roberts, preacher.

Orban   From the French *orbe* and the Latin *orbis*, meaning "a circle, globe, sphere," hence "any of the heavenly spheres (sun, moon, etc.)." CONTEMPORARY EXAMPLE: Orban Sanders, football player.

Orde   From the Latin *ordo*, meaning "order," and the Old English *ord*, meaning "the beginning." CONTEMPORARY EXAMPLE: Orde Wingate, British soldier.

Ordell   A variant form of Orde. *See* Orde. CONTEMPORARY EXAMPLE: Ordell Braase, football player.

Oren   From the Hebrew, meaning "a tree (cedar or fir)." In the Bible, a descendant of Judah. VARIANT FORMS: Orin, Orrin, Oron. PLACE-NAME USAGE: Orenburg, a city in Russia.

Orenthal   Possibly from the Hebrew (*see* Oren) and Middle English *tal*, meaning "a tall tree." CONTEMPORARY EXAMPLE: Orenthal J. Simpson, football player.

Orest A variant form of Orestes. *See* Orestes. CONTEMPORARY EXAMPLE: Orest Kindrachuk, hockey player.

Orestes From the Greek *oros*, meaning "mountain." In Greek legend, son of Agamemnon.

Orge From the Old French, meaning "barley." CONTEMPORARY EXAMPLE: Orge Cooper, baseball player.

Orie A variant form of Orien. *See* Orien. CONTEMPORARY EXAMPLE: Orie Arntzen, baseball player.

Orien A French form of the Latin name Oriens, meaning "the Orient, the East (where the sun rises)." Akin to Orestes. *See* Orestes. Oria is a feminine form. Orion is a variant spelling. CONTEMPORARY EXAMPLE: Orien Crow, football player.

Orin, Orrin Variant forms of Orien. *See* Orien.

Orion A variant form of Orien. *See* Orien.

Oris A variant form of Orien. *See* Orien. CONTEMPORARY EXAMPLE: Oris Hockett, baseball player.

Orland, Orlando A variant form of Roland by metathesis. *See* Roland. Or, from the Latin *aurum*, meaning "golden, yellow," hence "the land of gold (sunshine)." Orlando, also known as Rolando, was the nephew of King Charles of England. CONTEMPORARY EXAMPLES: Orland Smith, football player; Orlando Cepeda, football player. SURNAME USAGE: Tony Orlando, singer. PLACE-NAME USAGE: Orlando, Florida, named for Orlando Reeves, a soldier killed on that site (1835).

Orleans From the Latin *aurum*, meaning "golden." Aurelius is a variant form. PLACE-NAME USAGE: New Orleans, Louisiana.

Orley A pet form of Orleans. *See* Orleans. CONTEMPORARY EXAMPLE: Orley M. Berg, theologian.

Orlin A variant form of Orleans. *See* Orleans. CONTEMPORARY EXAMPLE: Orlin Rogers, baseball player.

Orlo A variant form of Orleans. *See* Orleans. CONTEMPORARY EXAMPLE: Orlo E. Childs, educator.

Orman, Ormand From the Norse *ormr* and *orm*, meaning "a serpent, a worm." CONTEMPORARY EXAMPLE: Ormand West, Jr., television producer.

Ormond A variant form of Ormand. *See* Ormand. CONTEMPORARY EXAMPLE: Ormond Butler, baseball player. PLACE-NAME USAGE: Ormond, Ireland; Ormond Beach, Florida.

Oron, Orono   Variant spellings of Orin. *See* Orin. PLACE-NAME USAGE: Orono, Maine, named for Joseph Orono, an Indian chief.

Orrin   A variant spelling of Orin. *See* Orin. CONTEMPORARY EXAMPLE: Orrin Hatch, U.S. senator.

Orson   From the Latin *ursus*, meaning "a bear." Ursula is a feminine form. CONTEMPORARY EXAMPLE: Orson Welles, actor.

Orval   A variant form of Orville. *See* Orville. CONTEMPORARY EXAMPLES: Orval Faubus, U.S. state governor; Orval G. Johnson, author.

Orville   From the French, meaning "golden city." Orval is a variant form. CONTEMPORARY EXAMPLE: Orville Wright (1871–1948), airplane inventor. PLACE-NAME USAGE: a town in France.

Osbert   From the Anglo-Saxon *os*, meaning "a god," plus the German *beraht*, meaning "bright," hence "famous (bright) god." CONTEMPORARY EXAMPLE: Osbert Sitwell, author.

Osborn, Osborne   From the Anglo-Saxon, meaning "divinely strong." Akin to Osbert. *See* Osbert. CONTEMPORARY EXAMPLES: J. Osborn Fuller, educator; Osborne Lockhart, basketball player.

Oscar   From the Anglo-Saxon *os*, "a god," plus *gar*, "a spear," hence "divine strength." Oscar II (1829-1907) was king of Norway and Sweden. CONTEMPORARY EXAMPLE: Oscar Hammerstein, Jr., lyricist.

Osgood   From the Anglo-Saxon *os* and *good*, both meaning "a god." SURNAME USAGE: Charles Osgood, television news reporter.

Osias   A variant form of Hosea. *See* Hosea. CONTEMPORARY EXAMPLE: Osias Goren, community leader.

Osip   A Russian form of Joseph. *See* Joseph. CONTEMPORARY EXAMPLE: Osip Mandelstam, Russian poet.

Oskar   A variant spelling of Oscar. *See* Oscar. CONTEMPORARY EXAMPLE: Oskar Werner, actor.

Osman, Osmand   From the Anglo-Saxon, meaning "servant of God." Also, from the Middle Latin name Ottomanus, meaning "a member of the Osman (Othman) tribe, a Turk." CONTEMPORARY EXAMPLE: Osman France, baseball player.

Osmand   From the Anglo-Saxon, meaning "protected by God." Akin to Osman. *See* Osman. Osmund is a variant spelling.

Osmond   From the Anglo-Saxon, meaning "protected by God." Akin to Osman. *See* Osman. Osmund is a variant spelling.

Osmund   A variant spelling of Osmond. *See* Osmond.

Ossie   A pet form of Oswald or Oscar. *See* Oswald *and* Oscar. CONTEMPORARY EXAMPLE: Ossie Davis, actor.

Osvald   A variant spelling of Oswald. *See* Oswald. CONTEMPORARY EX-

AMPLE: Osvald Siren, author.

Oswald   From the Old English *os*, meaning "a god," and *weald*, meaning "forest," hence "god of the forest." PET FORMS: Oz, Ozzie, Ozzy. SURNAME USAGE: Oswall, Oswell.

Oswaldo   The Spanish form of Oswald. *See* Oswald. CONTEMPORARY EXAMPLE: Oswaldo Arnho, Brazilian statesman.

Oswin   From the Old English, meaning "friend of God."

Oswold   A variant spelling of Oswald. *See* Oswald.

Otavio   A short form of Octavio. *See* Octavio. CONTEMPORARY EXAMPLE: Otavio Reboucas, fishing expert.

Othello   Possibly, a variant form of Otto. *See* Otto. Or, from the Middle Latin name Ottomanus, meaning "a member of the Othman tribe, a Turk." The title character in Shakespeare's play. PLACE-NAME USAGE: a railroad name in Washington.

Othmar   A variant form of Osman. *See* Osman. CONTEMPORARY EXAMPLE: Othmar Keel, author.

Othniel   From the Hebrew, meaning "my strength is in God." In the Bible, a nephew of Joshua. CONTEMPORARY EXAMPLE: Darius Othniel Blaisdell, Auburn, Washington.

Otho   From the Old English, meaning "an otter." Akin to the Danish name Od. CONTEMPORARY EXAMPLE: Otho Nitcholas, baseball player.

Otis   From the Greek, meaning "one who hears well." CONTEMPORARY EXAMPLE: Otis Pike, political leader. SURNAME USAGE: James Otis (1725-1783), American statesman.

Ottmar   A variant form of Othmar. *See* Othmar. CONTEMPORARY EXAMPLE: Ottmar Mergenthaler, inventor.

Otto   From the Old High German *otho* and *odo*, meaning "prosperous, wealthy." Otto I (912-973), king of Germany and emperor of the Holy Roman Empire.

Overton   From the Old English, meaning "the upper town." CONTEMPORARY EXAMPLE: Overton Steven, physician and author.

Ovid   From the Latin *ovatus*, meaning "egg, egg-shaped," or *obediens*, meaning "to obey." Akin to the Arabic root *abd*, meaning "servant." Publius Ovidius Naso, a Roman poet of the first century B.C., generally called Ovid. CONTEMPORARY EXAMPLE: Ovid Nicholson, baseball player. PLACE-NAME USAGE: Ovid, New York; Ovid, Colorado, named for Newton Ovid, local resident.

Owen   Probably a variant Welsh form of the Latin name Eugenius, meaning "well born." *See* Eugene. CONTEMPORARY EXAMPLE: Owen Davis, Pulitzer Prize winner in drama (1923). SURNAME USAGE: Robert Owen (1771-1858), English industrialist.

Oxford   From the Anglo-Saxon, meaning "the place where the oxen cross the stream." PLACE-NAME USAGE: a city in England; cities in Maryland, Massachusetts, and Connecticut.

Oz   From the Hebrew, meaning "strength." *See also* Ozni. SURNAME USAGE: Amos Oz, author.

Ozay   Possibly a variant form of Jose and Joseph. *See* Joseph. CONTEMPORARY EXAMPLE: Ozay Mehmet, economist.

Ozni   From the Hebrew *ozen*, meaning "ear," hence "my hearing." In the Bible, a grandson of Jacob. Oz is a pet form.

Ozzie   A pet form of Oswald. *See* Oswald. CONTEMPORARY EXAMPLE: Ozzie Nelson, actor.

P

Pablo   A Spanish form of Paul. *See* Paul. CONTEMPORARY EXAMPLE: Pablo Casals, cellist.

Packard   From the Middle English *pakke*, meaning "to pack for carrying." An occupational name for peddlars who carried packs of goods for sale. CONTEMPORARY EXAMPLE: Packard Dillon, baseball player. SURNAME USAGE: Vance Packard, author.

Paco   Possibly from the Italian *pacco*, meaning "to pack." Akin to Packard. *See* Packard. CONTEMPORARY EXAMPLE: Paco Camino, bullfighter.

Paddy   An Irish pet form of Patrick. *See* Patrick. Because of its popularity in nineteenth-century Ireland, an Irishman in general was referred to as a Paddy. PLACE-NAME USAGE: Paddytown is a name given to Irish districts; Paddys Valley, Oregon.

Pagan   From the Latin *paganus*, meaning "a heathen," and its earlier form *pagus*, meaning "a country peasant." Introduced into England by the Normans, it evolved into popular surnames, including Pain, Paine, Payne, Paynel, Pannet. PLACE-NAME USAGE: Pagan Point, Maryland.

Page   An English form of the Italian *paggio*, meaning "a boy attendant, a servant." CONTEMPORARY EXAMPLES: Page Belcher, U.S. congressman; Page Smith, author. SURNAME USAGE: William Hines Page (1855-1918), American journalist.

Paine   A variant form of Pagan. *See* Pagan. SURNAME USAGE: Thomas Paine (1737-1809), American patriot.

Painton   From the Old English, meaning "Pain's town." A variant form of Pagan. *See* Pagan. CONTEMPORARY EXAMPLE: Painton Vowen, author.

Paley   A variant form of Paul. *See* Paul. SURNAME USAGE: William Paley (1743-1805), English philosopher.

Palmer   From the Middle English *palmere*, meaning "a pilgrim who carried a palm leaf," as a sign that he had been to the Holy Land. CONTEMPORARY EXAMPLE: Palmer Williams, television producer. SURNAME USAGE: Viscount Palmerston (1784-1864), English statesman. PLACE-NAME USAGE: Palmer Peninsula (formerly Antarctic Peninsula).

Paltai   A variant form of Palti. *See* Palti. In the Bible, a member of a priestly family.

Palti   From the Hebrew *palot*, meaning "my escape, my deliverance." In the Bible, the second husband of Michal, daughter of King Saul.

Paltiel   From the Hebrew, meaning "God is my savior." Akin to Palti. *See* Palti. In the Bible, a leader of the tribe of Issachar.

Panchito   A pet form of Pancho. *See* Pancho. CONTEMPORARY EXAMPLE: Panchito Gomez, actor.

Pancho   A Spanish form from the Old Italian *pennacchio*, meaning "a tuft, a plume," symbolic of a carefree spirit. CONTEMPORARY EXAMPLE: Pancho Gonzales, tennis player.

Paolo   The Italian form of Paul. *See* Paul.

Paris   In Greek legend, a king of Troy who precipitated the Trojan War. Used also as a feminine name. CONTEMPORARY EXAMPLE: Paris Seibold, horseshoe champion. PLACE-NAME USAGE: Paris, France.

Park, Parke   From the Middle English *parc*, meaning "an enclosed parcel of land." CONTEMPORARY EXAMPLE: Parke Coleman, baseball player. SURNAME USAGE: Mungo Park (1771-1806), Scottish explorer. PLACE-NAME USAGE: Park River, North Dakota.

Parker   An occupational name, meaning "one who tends a park." *See* Park. CONTEMPORARY EXAMPLE: Parker Stevenson, actor. SURNAME USAGE: Charlie Parker (1920-1955), American jazz musician. PLACE-NAME USAGE: Parkersburg, West Virginia.

Parkman   A variant form of Parker. *See* Parker. SURNAME USAGE: Francis Parkman (1823-1893), American historian.

Parlett   A variant form of Parley. *See* Parley. CONTEMPORARY EXAMPLE: Parlett L. Moore, educator.

Parley   From the Old French, meaning "to speak."

Parnell   The Anglicized form of Petronilla, a form of Peter. *See* Peter. CONTEMPORARY EXAMPLE: Parnell Dickinson, football player. SURNAME USAGE: Charles Stewart Parnell (1846-1891), Irish statesman.

Parren   A variant form of Parnell. *See* Parnell. Or, from parr, meaning "the young of certain fish." CONTEMPORARY EXAMPLE: Parren Mitchell, U.S. congressman.

Parrish   From the Greek *paroikia*, meaning "neighborhood, diocese." Akin to Parson. SURNAME USAGE: Maxfield Parrish, American artist.

Parry   A patronymic form from the Welsh apHarry, meaning "son of Harry." SURNAME USAGE: William Edward Parry (1790-1855), English explorer.

Parson   From the Middle English *persne*, meaning "a minister, a clergyman who heads a parish."

Partha   From the Greek *parthenos*, meaning "a maiden, a virgin."

Or, from the Latin *partis*, meaning "to part with, to sell, to divide." CONTEMPORARY EXAMPLE: Partha Mitter, author.

Pascal The Latin form of the Hebrew *pesach*, meaning "paschal lamb sacrifice," offered on Passover. Pasco is a variant form. SURNAME USAGE: Blaise Pascal (1623-1662), French philosopher.

Pasco, Pascoe From the Middle English *pask*, meaning "Easter." Akin to Pascal.

Pat A pet form of Patrick. *See* Patrick.

Patricio A variant Spanish form of Patrick. *See* Patrick. CONTEMPORARY EXAMPLE: Patricio Scantlebury, baseball player.

Patrick From the Latin, meaning "a patrician, a person of noble descent." VARIANT FORMS: Patricio, Paxton, Payton. PET FORMS: Pat, Patti, Patsy, Pad, Paddy, Packy. In Scotland, Peter was used as a pet form of Patrick. In Ireland, Padraig was the original form. Patricia is a feminine form. SURNAME USAGE: Patrickson, Pate, Pates, Patley, Paton, Patten, Pattison, Pattinson, Paterson, Patterson.

Pattison A patronymic form, meaning "the son of Patti (Patrick)." CONTEMPORARY EXAMPLE: Pattison Preston, football player.

Paul From the Latin *paulus* or the Greek *paulos*, meaning "small." In the Bible, Paul of Tarsus, an apostle of Christianity. His original name was Saul. VARIANT FORMS: Paulos (Greek); Paulus (Latin); Pawley (English); Pol, Paulot (French); Paolo (Italian); Pablo (Spanish); Pavel (Russian); Paulo (Portugese). FEMININE FORMS: Paula, Pauline. SURNAME USAGE: Paule, Pauli, Paulin, Pauling, Pauley, Paulet, Pawling, Powell, Pollit.

Paulinas A diminutive form of Paul. *See* Paul.

Paulos The Greek form of Paul. *See* Paul.

Pawley A variant form of Paul. *See* Paul.

Paxton From the Latin *pax*, meaning "peace," hence "town of peace." Or, a variant form of Patrick. *See* Patrick. CONTEMPORARY EXAMPLE: Paxton Price, librarian.

Payton The Scottish form of Patrick. *See* Patrick. Or, a variant form of Paxton. *See* Paxton.

Pedro A Spanish and Portuguese form of Peter. *See* Peter. CONTEMPORARY EXAMPLE: Pedro A. Noa, art critic.

Pelham From the Latin *pel* and *pellis*, meaning "the skin of a furbearing animal," hence "a town with a tannery." CONTEMPORARY EXAMPLE: Pelham Ballenger, baseball player.

Pembroke From the British *penn*, meaning "a hill," plus the Anglo-Saxon *brocen*, meaning "to break, weaken," hence "a broken hill." Or, possibly an occupational name, from the Old French *brokier*,

meaning "to broach, to tap," connoting "a wine dealer." CONTEM-
PORARY EXAMPLE: Pembroke Finlayson, baseball player. PLACE-NAME
USAGE: Pembrokeshire, Wales.

Penini   From the Hebrew, meaning "my pearl." Penina is the feminine form.

Penn   From the Latin *penna*, meaning "a pen, a quill." SURNAME US-
AGE: William Penn (1644-1718), a Quaker from England, founder of
Pennsylvania.

Pepe   Probably a variant form of Pip, a pet form of Philip. *See* Philip. CONTEMPORARY EXAMPLE: Pepe Serna, actor.

Pepper   From the Latin *piper*, meaning "a condiment derived from a
plant." Used also as a feminine name. CONTEMPORARY EXAMPLE: Pepper Martin, baseball player.

Per   A Swedish form of Peter. Akin to the English Piers. *See* Peter. CON-
TEMPORARY EXAMPLE: Per Dalin, educator.

Perceval, Percival   From the French *perce-val*, meaning "valley pier-
cer." Percival is a later spelling.

Percy   A pet form of Percival. *See* Percival. Used also as an independent name. Lord Percy Seymour (died 1721) was the son of Lady Elizabeth Percy. CONTEMPORARY EXAMPLE: Percy Forman, attorney.

Peregrine   From the Latin, meaning "a wanderer, a traveler."

Peretz, Perez   From the Hebrew, meaning "burst forth." In the Bible, a son of Judah.

Pernell   A variant form of Parnell. *See* Parnell. CONTEMPORARY EX-
AMPLE: Pernell Roberts, actor.

Perry   A pet form of Peter. *See* Peter.

Pervis   From the Latin *perius*, meaning "through the way." CONTEM-
PORARY EXAMPLE: Pervis Atkins, football player.

Pesach   From the Hebrew *pesach*, meaning "to pass over, to skip over."
In the Bible, a holiday commemorating the saving of the first-born son
of the Israelites, whose houses were skipped over when the last of the ten
plagues occurred. Also, the name of the Passover sacrificial animal.

Pete   A pet form of Peter. *See* Peter.

Peter   From the Greek *petra* and *petros* and the Latin *petrus*, meaning
"a rock." In the New Testament, Jesus gave Simon bar Jonah, one of the
twelve apostles, the nickname Cephas, meaning "rock" in Aramaic. Si-
mon Peter (Saint Peter) is considered the first pope. VARIANT FORMS:
Petros (Greek); Petrus (Latin); Piers (English); Pierre (French); Pier,
Pietro (Italian); Pieter (Dutch); Pedro (Spanish and Portuguese); Petur,
Petko (Bulgarian); Petr (Russian). PET FORMS: Pete, Perry. SURNAME
USAGE: Peterson, Petersham, Petersen, Petrarch, Petri, Petrie, Pierce,

Pearce, Pearse, Pearson, Pierson, Perrin, Perkins, Parkin, Parkinson, Perrot, Perrott. PLACE-NAME USAGE: St. Petersburg, Russia; Petersburg, Virginia; Petra, a city in south-west Jordan.

Petit From the French, meaning "small." Petite is a feminine form. PLACE-NAME USAGE: Petit Lake, Idaho, named for Tom Petit, a local resident.

Petits A variant form of Peter. *See* Peter.

Pettis, Pettus Variant forms of Peter. *See* Peter. CONTEMPORARY EXAMPLES: Pettis Norman and Pettus Farrar, football players.

Peyton A variant spelling of Payton. *See* Payton. Peyton Randolph was an eighteenth-century political leader in Virginia. PLACE-NAME USAGE: Peytona, West Virginia, named for Madison Peyton, coal-miner.

Phelim From the Irish *feiolin*, meaning "always good." Also considered akin to Felix. *See* Felix.

Phelps A variant form of Philip. *See* Philip.

Philadelphia From the Greek, meaning "brotherly love." Usually used as a feminine name. PLACE-NAME USAGE: a city in Pennsylvania.

Philander From the Greek, meaning "lover of man."

Philbert, Philibert From the Anglo-Saxon, meaning "bright" or "illustrious."

Philemon From the Greek, meaning "affectionate." In Greek mythology, the husband of Baucis. CONTEMPORARY EXAMPLE: Philemon Herbert, U.S. congressman.

Philip, Phillip From the Greek *philos*, meaning "loving." plus *hippos*, meaning "a horse," hence "a lover of horses." In the Bible, one of the twelve apostles. King Philip of Macedonia (382-336 B.C.), father of Alexander the Great. The name of many kings of France and Spain. Philippa is the feminine equivalent. VARIANT FORMS: Philippus (Latin); Phip (English); Philipot, Philippe (French); Lipp, Philipp (German); Filippo, Lippo, Pippo, (Italian); Phillipp (Scotch); Felipe (Spanish); Felippe (Portuguese). PET FORMS: Phil, Pip. SURNAME USAGE: Philips, Philipson, Phelps, Philpot, Philkin, Phipps, Philson. PLACE-NAME USAGE: Philippine Islands.

Phillipp A variant Scotch form of Philip. *See* Philip.

Philmore From the Greek *philos* plus the Welsh *mor*, meaning "lover of the sea."

Philo From the Greek *philos*, meaning "loving." The first Philo in history was Philo Judaeus, a first-century Jewish philosopher, born in Alexandria, Egypt.

Phineas From the Egyptian, meaning "Negro, dark-complexioned."

In the Bible, a priest, the grandson of Aaron. VARIANT FORMS: Pinchas, Pinchos, Pincus.

Phoebus   From the Latin *phoebus*, derived from the Greek *phoibos*, meaning "bright." Phoebe is the feminine form.

Pierce   A variant form of Peter. CONTEMPORARY EXAMPLE: Pierce Butler, U.S. Supreme Court Justice.

Pierre   A French form of Peter. *See* Peter. CONTEMPORARY EXAMPLE: Pierre Salinger, journalist.

Piers   An English variant form of Peter. *See* Peter. CONTEMPORARY EXAMPLE: Piers Paul Read, author.

Piltai   A variant form of Palti. *See* Palti. In the Bible, a priest in the days of Nehemiah.

Pinchas, Pinchos   Hebraic forms of Phineas. *See* Phineas. CONTEMPORARY EXAMPLES: Pinchas Lapide, author; Pinchos Chazin, clergyman.

Pincus   A variant form of Phineas. *See* Phineas. Pinkus is a variant spelling.

Ping   A nickname. Origin unknown. CONTEMPORARY EXAMPLE: Ping Bodies, the Americanized name of Francesco Pezzola, baseball player.

Pini   A pet form of Pincus. *See* Pincus.

Pink   A pet form of Pinkerton. *See* Pinkerton. CONTEMPORARY EXAMPLE: Pink May, baseball player.

Pinkerton   From the Old English *pynken*, meaning "to prick, to perforate." An occupational name for one who makes ornaments and decorations by piercing cloth or paper, hence "the town of the pinker." SURNAME USAGE: Allan Pinkerton (1819-1884), American private detective.

Pinkus   A variant spelling of Pincus. *See* Pincus.

Pinky   A pet form of Pinkerton or Pincus. *See* Pinkerton *and* Pincus. CONTEMPORARY EXAMPLE: Pinky Higgins, baseball player.

Pip   A pet form of Philip. *See* Philip. A character in Charles Dickens' *Great Expectations*.

Pitkin   From the Latin *pietas*, meaning "the little pious one." CONTEMPORARY EXAMPLE: Pitkin Gilman, baseball player.

Pius   From the Latin, meaning "pious, devoted." The name of twelve popes.

Placido   From the Latin *placare*, meaning "to appease, to quiet." CONTEMPORARY EXAMPLE: Placido Domingo, opera singer.

Plato   From the Greek *platys*, meaning "broad, flat." Perhaps an occupational name for one who made plates of metal armor. A fourth–century B.C. Greek philosopher. CONTEMPORARY EXAMPLE: Plato Andros, football player.

Poco   From the Italian, meaning "little; little by little." Originally a musical term. Primarily a nickname.

Poke   Possibly a form of pokeweed, a plant with purplish-white flowers; a nickname for a slow-poke; or, for one who has spent time in the pokey (slang for jail). CONTEMPORARY EXAMPLE: Poke Cobb, football player.

Pompey   From the Latin *pampinus*, meaning "a young shoot, a tendril." The popular name of Gnaeus Pompeius Magnus (106-148), Roman general. PLACE-NAME USAGE: Pompeii, an ancient city in southern Italy, named for Pompey; Pompey's Pillar, Montana.

Pompeyo   An Italian form of Pompey. *See* Pompey. CONTEMPORARY EXAMPLE: Pompeyo DavaLillo, baseball player.

Pope   From the Greek *papas*, meaning "a bishop" or "a father." The pope in Christendom is the Bishop of Rome and head of the Catholic Church. CONTEMPORARY EXAMPLE: Pope A. Duncan, educator. SURNAME USAGE: Alexander Pope (1688-1744), English poet.

Porter   From the Latin *portare*, meaning "to carry." An occupational name for "an attendant who carries luggage." CONTEMPORARY EXAMPLE: Porter Wagoner, singer. SURNAME USAGE: Cole Porter (1893-1964), composer.

Potter   From the Old English *pott*, meaning "to swell up." An occupational surname, meaning "one who makes pots." CONTEMPORARY EXAMPLE: Potter Stewart, American statesman.

Poul   A variant spelling of Paul. *See* Paul. CONTEMPORARY EXAMPLE: Poul Anderson, author.

Powell   A patronymic Welsh form from apHowell, meaning "son of Howell." *See* Howell. SURNAME USAGE: Lewis Franklin Powell, U.S. Supreme Court Justice.

Prentice   From the Middle English *prentis*, meaning "a beginner, a learner." Prentiss is a variant spelling. CONTEMPORARY EXAMPLE: Prentice Gantt, football player.

Prescott   From the Anglo-Saxon, meaning "the priest's house." SURNAME USAGE: William Hickling Prescott (1796-1859), American historian. PLACE-NAME USAGE: Prescott, Arizona, named for W.H. Prescott.

Preston   From the Old English, meaning "priest's town." SURNAME USAGE: Robert Preston, actor. PLACE-NAME USAGE: seaport in Lancashire, England; Preston, Connecticut.

Prezell   Origin unknown. CONTEMPORARY EXAMPLE: Prezell R. Robinson, educator.

Price   From the Middle English and Old French *pris*, meaning "price, value." SURNAME USAGE: Vincent Price, actor.

Priestley   From the Middle English *prest*, and the Anglo-Saxon *pro-est*, meaning "an elder," particularly of the church, hence "a clergyman." SURNAME USAGE: Joseph Priestley (1733-1804), English chemist.

Prime   From the Latin *primus*, meaning "first." CONTEMPORARY EXAMPLE: Prime F. Osborne, industrialist.

Primo   An Italian form of Prime. *See* Prime. CONTEMPORARY EXAMPLE: Primo Carnera, boxing champion.

Prince   From the Latin *primus*, meaning "first, chief." Akin to Prior. CONTEMPORARY EXAMPLE: Prince B. Woodward, educator. SURNAME USAGE: Hal Prince, theatrical producer–director. PLACE-NAME USAGE: Prince Edward County, Virginia; Princeton, New Jersey

Prior   From the Latin *primus*, meaning "first, a superior." Usually, the name of the leader of a religious house. Pryor is a variant spelling. SURNAME USAGE: Matthew Prior (1664-1721), English poet.

Procopio, Procopius   From the Latin, meaning "declared leader." Procopius was a sixth–century Byzantine historian. CONTEMPORARY EXAMPLE: Procopia Herrera, baseball player.

Proctor   A contracted Middle English form of the Latin *procurator*, meaning "a manager, a director."

Produs   From the British *pridd*, meaning "earth." Or, from the Middle English *prude*, meaning "pride, to be proud." CONTEMPORARY EXAMPLE: Produs Perkins, football player.

Prosper, Prospero   From the Latin *prosperus*, meaning "favorable, fortunate." Prospero is an Italian form. CONTEMPORARY EXAMPLE: Prosper Benlango, baseball player.

Proverb   From the Latin, meaning "a short, striking expression." CONTEMPORARY EXAMPLE: Proverb Jacobs, football player.

Pryor   A variant spelling of Prior. *See* Prior. CONTEMPORARY EXAMPLE: Pryor McBee, baseball player. SURNAME USAGE: Richard Pryor, comedian.

Purnal   From the Old English *pera*, meaning "a pear tree." CONTEMPORARY EXAMPLE: Purnal Goldy, baseball player.

Purvis   From the Anglo-French *purveir*, meaning "to provide food."

Putnam   From the Latin *putare*, meaning "to prune," hence "a gardener." Or, from the Anglo-Saxon, meaning "a pit-man, a miner." SURNAME USAGE: Israel Putnam (1718-1790), American general. PLACE-NAME USAGE: a county in upstate New York; Putnam, Connecticut.

Q

Quentin, Quenton   From the Latin name Quintus, meaning "the fifth." In Roman times, often given to the fifth son in a family, just as the seventh was called Septimus, and the eighth Octavius. Quintin is a variant spelling. Quint is a pet form. CONTEMPORARY EXAMPLES: Quentin Burdick, U.S. senator; Quentin Reynolds, journalist.

Quintin   A variant spelling of Quentin. *See* Quentin. An ancient Roman personal name.

Quincy   A variant form of Quentin. *See* Quentin. CONTEMPORARY EXAMPLE: Quincy Porter, Pulitzer Prize winner in music (1954). SURNAME USAGE: Josiah Quincy (1744-1775), American patriot. PLACE-NAME USAGE: Quincy, Massachusetts.

Quinn   A variant form of Quentin. *See* Quentin. Also, possibly from the Old English *cwen*, meaning "a queen" or "a companion." CONTEMPORARY EXAMPLES: Quinn Elson, jurist; Quinn Redeker, actor. SURNAME USAGE: Anthony Quinn, actor. PLACE-NAME USAGE: a river in Nevada.

R

Raanan From the Hebrew, meaning "fresh, luxuriant, beautiful." Ranan is a variant spelling.

Rabbit From the Middle English *rabette*, meaning "the young of the cony." Also, occasionally a form of Rob and Robert. *See* Robert. CONTEMPORARY EXAMPLE: Rabbit Maranville, baseball player. PLACE-NAME USAGE: Rabbit, Montana; Rabbithole Spring, Nevada; Rabbit Town, Kentucky.

Rachamim From the Hebrew, meaning "mercy, compassion." CONTEMPORARY EXAMPLE: Rachamim Alazar, Tel Aviv, Israel.

Rachmiel From the Hebrew, meaning "God is my comforter." CONTEMPORARY EXAMPLE: Rachmiel Fryland, author.

Radcliffe From the Anglo-Saxon, meaning "the red cliff."

Rafael A Spanish form of Raphael. *See* Raphael. CONTEMPORARY EXAMPLE: Rafael Campos, actor.

Raffaello An Italian form of Raphael. *See* Raphael. CONTEMPORARY EXAMPLE: Raffaello Santi, Italian painter (1483-1520).

Rafi A pet form of Raphael and its variant forms. *See* Raphael. CONTEMPORARY EXAMPLE: Rafi Jospe, Denver, Colorado.

Ragnar From the Old English, meaning "rugged, rocky." CONTEMPORARY EXAMPLE: Ragnar Hange, Scandinavian author.

Raimund A variant spelling of Raymond. *See* Raymond. CONTEMPORARY EXAMPLE: Raimund Wershing, football player.

Rain, Rainer, Raines, Rains Probably from the British *rhen*, meaning "a lord," or from *rhann*, meaning "a portion." Rain is a character in Colleen McCullough's *The Thorn Birds*. PLACE-NAME USAGE: Rains, Utah, named for F.L. Rains, engineer; Raintown, West Virginia, named for John Raine, local businessman.

Raleigh From the Old French *raale*, meaning "a field of wading birds" (similar to cranes). CONTEMPORARY EXAMPLE: Raleigh Owens, football player. SURNAME USAGE: Sir Walter Raleigh (1552-1618), English explorer. PLACE-NAME USAGE: Raleigh, North Carolina, named for Sir Walter Raleigh, English explorer.

Ralph From the Old Norse and Anglo-Saxon *rath*, meaning "counsel," and *ulfr*, meaning "a wolf," hence "courageous advice, fearless advisor." VARIANT FORMS: Raoul (French); Rolf, Rolphe (German); Randolph (English). *See also* Randolph.

Ralston From the Old English, meaning "Ralph's town." CONTEMPO-
RARY EXAMPLE: Ralston Hemsley, baseball player. PLACE-NAME USAGE:
Ralston, Oklahoma, named for J.H. Ralston, town founder; Ralston,
Washington.

Ramon A Spanish form of Raymond. *See* Raymond. CONTEMPORARY
EXAMPLE: Ramon Mifflin, soccer player.

Ramsay A variant spelling of Ramsey. *See* Ramsey. SURNAME USAGE:
Sir William Ramsay, Nobel Prize winner in chemistry (1904).

Ramsey From the Old English, meaning "ram's island." CONTEMPO-
RARY EXAMPLE: Ramsey Clark, U.S. attorney general.

Ran In Norse mythology, the goddess of the sea and people who are
drowning.

Ranald A variant spelling of Ronald. *See* Ronald. CONTEMPORARY EX-
AMPLE: Ranald P. Hobbs, publisher.

Ranan A variant spelling of Raanan. *See* Raanan. CONTEMPORARY
EXAMPLE: Ranan Lurie, Israeli correspondent.

Rance From the French, meaning a kind of marble found in Belgium.
CONTEMPORARY EXAMPLES: Rance Pless, baseball player; Rance Crain,
editor.

Randal, Randall From the Anglo-Saxon name Randwulf, derived
from *rand*, meaning "a shield," and *wulf*, meaning "a wolf," connoting
"superior protection." Akin to Ralph and Randolph. CONTEMPORARY
EXAMPLES: Randal Kleiser, movie director; Randall Jarrell, poet. SUR-
NAME USAGE: Tony Randall, actor.

Randell A variant spelling of Randall. CONTEMPORARY EXAMPLE:
Randell L. Tyree, city mayor, Knoxville, Tennessee.

Rander From the Middle English *rande*, meaning "a border, a
strip." Originally, an occupational name for shoemakers, derived
from the leather strip on which the heel of a shoe is fastened. CONTEM-
PORARY EXAMPLE: Rander Hollander, sportswriter.

Randi A variant spelling of Randy. *See* Randy.

Randl A pet form of Randal or Randolph. *See* Randal *and* Randolph.

Randle A variant spelling of Randal. *See* Randle. CONTEMPORARY
EXAMPLE: Randle Elliott, educator.

Randolph From the Anglo-Saxon name Randwulf. Akin to Ralph
and Randal. *See also* Ralph *and* Randal. CONTEMPORARY EXAMPLE:
Randolph Churchill, British statesman, father of Winston Churchill.
SURNAME USAGE: John Randolph (1773-1833), American statesman.
PLACE-NAME USAGE: Randolph, Massachusetts, named for Peyton Ran-
dolph (1721-1755), political leader; Randolph, Nebraska, named for

Lord Randolph Churchill (1849-1895).

Randy   A pet form of Randal or Randolph. *See* Randal *and* Randolph. Randi is a variant spelling. CONTEMPORARY EXAMPLE: Randy Newman, singer and songwriter.

Ranen   From the Hebrew, meaning "to sing, to be joyous." Ranon is a variant spelling.

Ranger   From the Middle English *raunger*, meaning "a wanderer." An occupational name for "one who guards the forest." PLACE-NAME USAGE: Ranger, Texas; Ranger Lake, Wyoming.

Rankin   A pet form of Ran or Randal. *See* Ran *and* Randal. Or, from the Middle English *renk*, meaning "a series, a row, a range." Akin to Ranger. CONTEMPORARY EXAMPLE: Rankin Britt, football player.

Ranon   A variant spelling of Ranen. *See* Ranen.

Ransom   From the Latin *redemptio*, meaning "to redeem." CONTEMPORARY EXAMPLE: Ransom Jackson, baseball player.

Raoul   A French form of Ralph and Randolph. *See* Randolph. CONTEMPORARY EXAMPLE: Raoul Birnbaum, author.

Raphael   From the Hebrew, meaning "God has healed." In the Bible, one of the Levites. In the Apocryphal books of Enoch and Tobit, the name of an archangel. Rafael is a variant spelling. PET FORMS: Rafe, Raff.

Rastus   From the Greek, meaning "not running away."

Raul   A variant spelling of Raoul. *See* Raoul. CONTEMPORARY EXAMPLE: Raul Julia, actor.

Raven   From the Old English *hraefn*, meaning "a raven, a large bird of the crow family." CONTEMPORARY EXAMPLE: Raven I. McDavid, Jr., professor of linguistics.

Ravi   From the Hindi, meaning "sun." CONTEMPORARY EXAMPLE: Ravi Mehra, publisher.

Ravid   From the Hebrew, meaning "ornament, jewelry."

Ravinder   From the Old French *ravine*, meaning "plundered, captured." CONTEMPORARY EXAMPLE: Ravinder Seng Hera, cricket player.

Raviv   From the Hebrew, meaning "rain, dew."

Rawly   A variant form of Ralph or Raleigh. *See* Ralph *and* Raleigh. CONTEMPORARY EXAMPLE: Rawly Eastwick, baseball player.

Ray   From the Old English *ree*, meaning "a stream." Rey is a variant spelling. Also, a pet form of Raymond. *See* Raymond.

Rayfield   From the Old English *ree* plus *field*, meaning "the stream in the field." CONTEMPORARY EXAMPLE: Rayfield Wright, football player.

Rayford From the Old English, meaning "the ford over the stream." *See also* Ray. CONTEMPORARY EXAMPLE: Rayford W. Logan, author.

Raymond A variant form of the Old French names Raimund and Raginmund, meaning "wise protection." VARIANT FORMS: Raimond (French); Ramon (Spanish); Raimondo (Italian).

Raymund A variant spelling of Raymond. *See* Raymond.

Raynard A variant spelling of Reynard. *See* Reynard.

Rayner An English form of Raynard. *See* Raynard. VARIANT FORMS: Rainer (English); Rene, Renier (French); Renato (Italian); Reiner (German).

Raz From the Aramaic, meaning "secret." Used also as a feminine form.

Razi From the Aramaic, meaning "my secret." Used also as a feminine form.

Raziel From the Aramaic, meaning "God is my secret."

Read, Reade From the Old English *hreod*, meaning "a reed." VARIANT SPELLINGS: Reed, Reid. SURNAME USAGE: Herbert Read (1893-1968), English poet; Charles Reade (1814-1884), English novelist. PLACE-NAME USAGE: Reading, Montana, named for H.H. Read, landowner.

Reamer From the Old English *reman*, meaning "to enlarge (a hole), to make roomy." Probably an occupational name. CONTEMPORARY EXAMPLE: Reamer Kline, educator.

Rebel From the Old French *rebelle* and the Latin *rebellis*, meaning "one who resists." CONTEMPORARY EXAMPLE: Rebel Oakes, baseball player.

Red A nickname for redheaded people. Also, a variant spelling of Reade and Redd. *See* Reade *and* Redd. CONTEMPORARY EXAMPLES: Red Holzman, basketball coach; Red Skelton, comedian.

Redd From the Old English *hreod*, meaning "a reed." CONTEMPORARY EXAMPLE: Redd Fox, comedian.

Redding From the Old English, meaning "a reed meadow." Akin to Reade. CONTEMPORARY EXAMPLE: Redding S. Sugg, professor. PLACE-NAME USAGE: Redding, California, named for B.B. Redding, a railroad official.

Redmond, Redmund From the Old English, meaning "a mound of reeds" or "protected by reeds."

Reece, Reese A Welsh form of the Old English *ree*, meaning "a stream." VARIANT FORMS: Race, Rase, Ray, Rey, Rhys, Rice, Royce. CONTEMPORARY EXAMPLE: Reese Diggs, baseball player.

Reed   A variant spelling of Read. *See* Read. SURNAME USAGE: Walter Reed (1851-1920), U.S. Army surgeon. PLACE-NAME USAGE: Reading, Connecticut, named for John Reed, an early settler.

Reeves   An Old English occupational name, meaning "a steward, one in charge of a manor." CONTEMPORARY EXAMPLE: Reeves McKay, baseball player.

Regan   From the Old High German *ragin*, meaning "wise." Also, possibly from the Latin *rex*, meaning "king." Akin to Regino.

Regem   From the Arabic, meaning "a friend." In the Bible, a descendant of the tribe of Judah.

Reggie   A pet form of Reginald. *See* Reginald. CONTEMPORARY EXAMPLE: Reggie Jackson, baseball player.

Reginald   From the Old High German name Raganald, derived from *ragin*, meaning "wise, judicious," plus *ald* (akin to the Old English *eald*), meaning "old." VARIANT FORMS: Rex, Reynold (English); Regnault, Renaud (French); Reinhold (German); Ronald, Ranald (Scotch); Renaldo, Rinaldo (Italian); Reynaldos (Spanish); Reinald (German). PET FORMS: Reg, Reggie.

Regino   An Italian form of the Latin *rex*, meaning "king." Regina is the feminine form. CONTEMPORARY EXAMPLE: Regino Otero, baseball player.

Regis   From the Latin *rex*, meaning "kingly, regal." CONTEMPORARY EXAMPLE: Regis Leheney, baseball player.

Reid   A variant spelling of Read. *See* Read. CONTEMPORARY EXAMPLE: Reid Boates, publicist.

Reidar   A variant form of Reid. *See* Reid.

Reigh   A variant form of Ray and Rey. *See* Ray.

Renfred   From the Old German name Raganfrid, meaning "peaceful counsel."

Reinhard, Reinhart   Variant German forms of Reynard. *See* Reynard. *See* Reynard. CONTEMPORARY EXAMPLE: Reinhard Bendix, author.

Reinhold   A German form of Reginald. *See* Reginald. CONTEMPORARY EXAMPLE: Reinhold Niebuhr, theologian.

Relman   Probably a variant form of the English Ralph and the French Raoul. *See* Ralph. CONTEMPORARY EXAMPLE: Relman Morrin, Pulitzer Prize–winning journalist (1955).

Remert   Origin uncertain. Probably related to Bertram. *See* Bertram. CONTEMPORARY EXAMPLE: Rembert E. Stokes, educator.

Remer An invented name, based on the mythological figure Remus. *See* Remus. CONTEMPORARY EXAMPLE: Remer Cox, Johnson City, Tennessee.

Remus Possibly a variant form of Roman. *See* Roman. In Roman mythology, the twin brother of Romulus.

Remy An English form of Remus. *See* Remus. CONTEMPORARY EXAMPLE: Remy Kremer, baseball player.

Ren A variant spelling of Ran. *See* Ran.

Renaldo An Italian form of Reginald. *See* Reginald. CONTEMPORARY EXAMPLE: Renaldo Victoria, boxer.

Renaud A French form of Reginald. *See* Reginald.

Rene A French name from the Latin *renatus* and *renovare*, meaning "to be reborn; to renew." St. Rene, also known as Renatus, was Bishop of Angers in the fifth century. CONTEMPORARY EXAMPLE: Rene L. Ash, publisher.

Renfred From the Old German name Raganfrid, meaning "peaceful counsel."

Reno Probably a variant form of Rene. *See* Rene. Or, a form of Renaud. *See* Renaud. CONTEMPORARY EXAMPLE: Reno Bertoia, baseball player. SURNAME USAGE: J.L. Reno, (1823-1862), U.S. Army general. PLACE-NAME USAGE: Reno, Nevada.

Reo A variant form of the Old English *rae*, meaning "a stream." Rio is a variant spelling. CONTEMPORARY EXAMPLE: Reo Fortune, psychologist.

Reuben From the Hebrew, meaning "behold – a son!" In the Bible, Jacob's first-born son from his wife Leah. VARIANT FORMS: Reuven, Ruvane, Ruven. VARIANT SPELLINGS: Reubin, Ruben, Rubin. CONTEMPORARY EXAMPLE: Reuben E. Alley, editor.

Reubin A variant spelling of Reuben. *See* Reuben. CONTEMPORARY EXAMPLE: Reubin Askew, governor of Florida.

Reuel From the Hebrew, meaning "a friend of God." CONTEMPORARY EXAMPLE: Reuel A. Stallones, educator.

Reuven The Hebraic form of Reuben. *See* Reuben. CONTEMPORARY EXAMPLE: Reuven Bar-Yotam, actor.

Revie A pet form of Reuven and Reuben. *See* Reuben. CONTEMPORARY EXAMPLE: Revie Sorey, football player.

Rex From the Latin, meaning "a king." CONTEMPORARY EXAMPLE: Rex Harrison, actor. PLACE-NAME USAGE: Rex Lake, Wyoming.

Rexer Probably akin to Rex. *See* Rex. Or, a British occupational name, from "rexine," a kind of imitation leather, hence "one who works with leather." CONTEMPORARY EXAMPLE: Rexer Bernat, educator.

Rexford   From the Latin *rex* and Old English *ford*, hence "a crossing on the king's estate." CONTEMPORARY EXAMPLE: Rexford G. Barry, U.S. congressman.

Rey   A variant spelling of Ray. *See* Ray. CONTEMPORARY EXAMPLE: Rey Comeau, hockey player.

Reynard   From the Old High German name Reginhart, compounded from the Germanic *ragin*, meaning "wise," and *hart*, meaning "hard, bold, courageous." In medieval legend, the title character in *Reynard the Fox* was noted for courage and cleverness. Akin to Reginald. VARIANT FORMS: Regnard, Renard, Renart, Renaud, Reynaud (French); Reinhard, Reinhart, Renke (German); Rainardo (Italian); Reinhard (Hungarian). SURNAME USAGE: Paul Reynaud (1878-1966), French statesman.

Reynaud   A variant French form of Reynard. *See* Reynard.

Reyner   A variant form of Reynard. *See* Reynard. CONTEMPORARY EXAMPLE: Reyner Banham, architect.

Reynold   A variant form of Reginald. *See* Reginald. Ronald is a popular Scottish form.

Reynolds   A patronymic form of Reynold, meaning "the son of Reynold." CONTEMPORARY EXAMPLE: Reynolds Kelly, baseball player. SURNAME USAGE: Joshua Reynolds (1723-1792), English portrait painter.

Rhett   A variant form of the Old English *ret*, from *rith*, meaning "a small stream." Akin to Redd. *See* Redd. Popularized as Rhett Butler, a character in Margaret Mitchell's *Gone With the Wind*. CONTEMPORARY EXAMPLE: Rhett Dawson, football player.

Rhodric   From the Greek *rhodon*, meaning "a rose," and the Middle English *riche*, meaning "rich, regal," hence "rich in roses," and also, possibly, "the royal rose-garden." CONTEMPORARY EXAMPLE: Rhodric Jeffreys–Jones, historian.

Rhoten   A variant Dutch form from the German *rot*, meaning "red, reddish." CONTEMPORARY EXAMPLE: Rhoten A. Smith, educator.

Rhys   A Welsh form of the Old English *ree*, meaning "a stream." *See also* Reece. CONTEMPORARY EXAMPLE: Rhys Davies, author.

Ribbans   A variant form of Rubens. *See* Rubens.

Ric   A pet form of Richard. *See* Richard.

Ricardo   A Spanish form of Richard. *See* Richard. CONTEMPORARY EXAMPLE: Ricardo Montalban, actor. SURNAME USAGE: David Ricardo (1772-1823), English economist.

Riccardo   An Italian form of Richard. *See* Richard.

Ricco   A pet form of Richard. *See* Richard.

Rice   A variant form of Reese. *See* Reese. SURNAME USAGE: Elmer Rice (born Elmer Reizenstein) (1892-1967), American playwright. PLACE-NAME USAGE: Rice Hope, South Carolina; Rice County, Montana, named for H.M. Rice, a U.S. senator.

Rich   A pet form of Richard. *See* Richard. CONTEMPORARY EXAMPLE: Rich Little, entertainer.

Richard   A French form of the Old High German name Richart, meaning "powerful, rich ruler." Popular name of the kings of England from the rule of Richard I, Richard the Lion-Hearted (1157-1199), onward. VARIANT FORMS: Diccon, Dick (English); Riccardo (Italian); Richardo (Spanish); Riik (Netherlands); Ricardo (Spanish and Portuguese); Ritchie (Scottish). PET FORMS: Dick, Dickie, Dicky, Ric, Rico, Rici, Ricci, Ricco, Rich, Richie, Rick, Ricki, Rickie, Ricky, Rocco. SURNAME USAGE: Richards, Richardson, Ritchie.

Richardo   A Spanish form of Richard. *See* Richard. Ricardo is a variant spelling.

Richardson   A patronymic form of Richard, meaning "the son of Richard." SURNAME USAGE: Samuel Richardson (1689-1761), English novelist.

Rici, Ricci   Pet forms of Richard. *See* Richard.

Rick, Ricki, Rickie   Pet forms of Richard. *See* Richard. CONTEMPORARY EXAMPLE: Rick Monday, baseball player.

Ricky   A pet form of Richard. *See* Richard.

Rico   A pet form of Richard. *See* Richard.

Rid   A variant form of Rider. *See* Rider.

Riddle   A variant form of Rider. *See* Rider. SURNAME USAGE: Nelson Riddle, conductor. PLACE-NAME USAGE: Riddle, Idaho.

Rider   From the Middle English *ridden* and *ruden*, akin to the Old English *rydden*, meaning "to clear land." An occupational name, meaning "one who clears land, a farmer." Ryder is a variant spelling. Rid and Riddle are Old English forms. CONTEMPORARY EXAMPLE: Rider Haggard, author.

Ridgley   From the Old English, meaning "the meadow near the ridge."

Ridley   From the Old English, meaning "the meadow near the farm." CONTEMPORARY EXAMPLES: Ridley Scott, English film director. SURNAME USAGE: Nicholas Ridley, sixteenth–century English bishop.

Rien   Akin to Rijn, the Dutch name for the river Rhine, meaning "clean, pure." CONTEMPORARY EXAMPLE: Rien Poortvliet, Dutch artist.

Rigo   A short form of the Italian name Arrigo, a pet form for Harry. *See* Harry.

Rigoberto   An Italian name compounded of Rigo and Bert. *See* Rigo *and* Bert. CONTEMPORARY EXAMPLE: Rigoberto (Tito) Fuentes, baseball player.

Rik   A short form of Hendrick or Heinrich. *See* Hendrick *or* Heinrich. CONTEMPORARY EXAMPLE: Rik Massengale, golfer.

Riley   From the Dutch *ril* and the Low German *rille*, akin to the Old English *rith*, meaning "a small stream, a rivulet." CONTEMPORARY EXAMPLE: Riley Odoms, football player. SURNAME USAGE: James Whitcomb Riley (1849-1916), American poet.

Rimon, Rimmon   From the Hebrew, meaning "pomegranate." In the Bible, a member of the tribe of Benjamin. Rimona is a feminine form. PLACE-NAME USAGE: Rock Rimmon, Connecticut.

Rinaldo   An Italian form of Reginald. *See* Reginald. CONTEMPORARY EXAMPLE: Rinaldo Padinelli, baseball player.

Ring   From the Greek *kirkos*, meaning "a ring," from which is derived "circus," which takes place in a circular enclosure. CONTEMPORARY EXAMPLE: Ring Lardner, sports reporter. SURNAME USAGE: the Ringling family of circus performers, consisting originally of five brothers.

Ringo   The Italian form of Ring. *See* Ring. CONTEMPORARY EXAMPLE: Ringo Starr, singer.

Rinold   A variant form of Renaldo. *See* Renaldo. CONTEMPORARY EXAMPLE: Rinold Duren Ryne, baseball player.

Rio   A variant spelling of Reo. *See* Reo. PLACE-NAME USAGE: Rio Grande; Rio de Janeiro, Brazil.

Riordan   Compounded from the Old English *ree*, meaning "a stream, a river," and the Latin *dominus*, meaning "lord, master," hence "master of the river."

Rip   From the Latin *ripa*, meaning "a river bank." Rip van Winkle is the title character in Washington Irving's classic story. CONTEMPORARY EXAMPLE: Rip Torn, actor.

Ripley   From the Latin and Old English, meaning "the meadow near the river's bank." *See also* Rip. SURNAME USAGE: Robert Ripley, creator of "Believe It Or Not." PLACE-NAME USAGE: a lake in Montana, named for F.N. Ripley, a local resident.

Ritt   A pet form of Ritter. *See* Ritter.

Ritter   The Low German form of *richter*, meaning "a judge." SURNAME USAGE: John Ritter, actor.

Rivers   From the Latin and French, meaning "a stream of water." Also a feminine name. CONTEMPORARY EXAMPLE: Rivers Lodge, educator. SURNAME USAGE: Mickey Rivers, baseball player. PLACE-NAME USAGE: localities in Kent and Sussex in England.

Rivington   From the Latin *rivus*, meaning "a brook," hence "the town (*ton*) near the brook." CONTEMPORARY EXAMPLE: Rivington Bisland, baseball player.

Roald   A short form of Ronald. *See* Ronald. CONTEMPORARY EXAMPLE: Roald Dahl, author.

Roarke   Possibly from the Old English *roche*, meaning "a rock."

Rob   A pet form of Robert. *See* Robert. PLACE-NAME USAGE: Rob Roy, Arkansas.

Roban   A variant spelling of Robin. *See* Robin.

Robard, Robart   Variant French forms of Robert. *See* Robert. PLACE-NAME USAGE: Robertsville, Ohio, named for Joseph Robard (Robert), a Frenchman who was the town founder.

Robben   A variant spelling of Robin. *See* Robin. Also, possibly a form of Reuben. *See* Reuben. CONTEMPORARY EXAMPLE: Robben W. Flemings, educator.

Robert   From the Old High German, meaning "bright fame" or "famous counsel." Roberta is a feminine form. VARIANT FORMS: Hob, Robin (English); Rab, Robbie (Scotch); Rupert (English, French, German); Roberto (Spanish and Italian); Ruberto, Ruperto (Italian); Robard, Robart (French). PET FORMS: Bob, Bobbi, Bobby, Dob, Hob, Rob, Robbie, Robin, Robby. SURNAME USAGE: Dobb, Dobbs, Hobson, Hopson, Roberts, Robertson. PLACE-NAME USAGE: Robert Lee, Texas, named for General Robert E. Lee.

Roberto   The Spanish and Italian form of Robert. *See* Robert. CONTEMPORARY EXAMPLE: Roberto Clemente, baseball player.

Robin   A form of Robert. *See* Robert. Used also as a feminine form. CONTEMPORARY EXAMPLE: Robin Cook, author.

Robinson   A patronymic form, meaning "the son of Robin." *See* Robin. Popularized by the novel *Robinson Crusoe*, by Daniel DeFoe. CONTEMPORARY EXAMPLE: Robinson Jeffers, poet. SURNAME USAGE: Mames Harvey Robinson (1863-1936), American historian.

Robson   A patronymic form, meaning "the son of Rob (Robert)." *See* Robert. PLACE-NAME USAGE: Mount Robson, British Columbia.

Robyn   A variant spelling of Robin. *See* Robin.

Rocco   A pet form of Richard or Rockne. *See* Richard *and* Rockne. CONTEMPORARY EXAMPLE: Rocco Krsnich, baseball player.

Rock   From the Old English *roche*, meaning "a rock." CONTEMPORARY

EXAMPLE: Rock Hudson, actor.

Rocker   An occupational name, meaning "one who shapes rocks, a mason." VARIANT FORMS: Rock, Rockne. CONTEMPORARY EXAMPLE: Rocker Robinson, cricket player.

Rockne   From the Old English *roche*, meaning "a rock." CONTEMPORARY EXAMPLE: Rockne Freitas, football player. SURNAME USAGE: Knute Rockne, football coach.

Rockwell   From the Old English, meaning "the well near the rock." CONTEMPORARY EXAMPLE: Rockwell Kent, artist. SURNAME USAGE: Norman Rockwell, artist.

Rocky   A pet form of Rockne and Rockwell. *See* Rockne *and* Rockwell. Used also as a nickname for the surname Rockefeller. CONTEMPORARY EXAMPLE: Rocky Marciano, boxer.

Rod, Rodd   From the British, meaning "open or cleared land." VARIANT FORMS: Rodney, Roderick. Used also as independent names. CONTEMPORARY EXAMPLE: Rod Steiger, actor.

Roddy   A pet form of Rodman. *See* Rodman. CONTEMPORARY EXAMPLE: Roddy McDowell, actor.

Roderic, Roderick   From the Old German, meaning "famous ruler." VARIANT FORMS: Rory (Irish); Rodrigo (Spanish and Italian); Rodrique (French); Roderich (German). CONTEMPORARY EXAMPLES: Roderic Jeffries, author; Roderick Grant, journalist.

Rodger, Rodgers   Variant forms of Roger. *See* Roger. CONTEMPORARY EXAMPLE: Rodger van Allen, theologian. SURNAME USAGE: Richard Rodgers, composer.

Rodman   An occupational name. From the Old English, meaning "one who clears the land, a farmer." PET FORMS: Rod, Roddy.

Rodney   From the Old English, meaning "the cleared land near the water." CONTEMPORARY EXAMPLE: Rodney Dangerfield, comedian. SURNAME USAGE: George Brydges Rodney (1718-1792), British admiral. PLACE-NAME USAGE: Rodney Stoke, England.

Rodolph   A variant spelling of Rudolph. *See* Rudolph.

Rodolpho   An Italian form of Rudolph. *See* Rudolph. CONTEMPORARY EXAMPLE: Rodolpho Hernandez, baseball player.

Rodrigo   A Spanish and Italian form of Roderic. *See* Roderic. CONTEMPORARY EXAMPLE: Rodrigo Barnes, football player.

Rogelio   Origin uncertain. An Italian and Spanish form of Roger. *See* Roger. CONTEMPORARY EXAMPLE: Rogelio Martinez, baseball player.

Roger   An Old French form of the German name Ruodiger or Hrodger, akin to the Old English name Hrothgar. Hrothgar is from the Anglo–Saxon *hruod*, meaning "fame," plus *ger*, meaning "spear," hence "famous, noble warrior." VARIANT FORMS: Hodge (English); Ruggiero, Rugero (Italian); Rogerio (Spanish); Rutger (Dutch); Rozer (Russian). PET FORMS: Dodge, Hodge, Roj. SURNAME USAGE: Dodge, Hodges, Hodgkins, Hodgkiss, Hotchkiss, Hodgkinson.

Rohn A variant form of the Greek *rhodon*, meaning "a rose." CONTEMPORARY EXAMPLES: Rohn Enagh, photographer; Rohn Wesley Heidgerd, Wallingford, Connecticut.

Roland A French form of the Old High German, meaning "fame of the land." A legendary medieval figure famous for his strength. VARIANT FORMS: Rowland (English); Orlanda (Italian); Rolando (Italian and Portuguese).

Rolando An Italian and Portuguese form of Roland. *See* Roland.

Rolf, Rolfe Pet forms of Rudolph. *See* Rudolph.

Rolla A variant form of Rolland. *See* Rolland. CONTEMPORARY EXAMPLE: Rolla Mapel, baseball player.

Rollan A variant form of Rolland. *See* Rolland.

Rolland A variant spelling of Roland. *See* Roland. CONTEMPORARY EXAMPLE: Rolland Smith, television newscaster.

Rollen A variant form of Rolland. *See* Rolland. CONTEMPORARY EXAMPLE: Rollen Toby Smith, football player.

Rollin A variant form of Rolland. *See* Rolland. CONTEMPORARY EXAMPLE: Rollin Kirby, Pulitzer Prize–winning cartoonist (1922).

Rollo A variant form of Rolland. *See* Rolland. Introduced into France by the early Normans. The name of a Norse Viking chieftain. CONTEMPORARY EXAMPLE: Rollo May, psychologist.

Romain A variant French form of Roman. *See* Roman. Romaine is a feminine form. CONTEMPORARY EXAMPLE: Romain Rolland, Nobel Prize winner in literature (1915). PLACE-NAME USAGE: Cape Romain, South Carolina.

Romallus A variant spelling of Romulus. *See* Romulus. CONTEMPORARY EXAMPLE: Romallus Murphy, educator.

Roman From the Latin name Romanus, meaning "a person from Rome." Akin to Romain. CONTEMPORARY EXAMPLE: Roman Gabriel, football player; Roman Polanski, film director. PLACE-NAME USAGE: Roman, Virginia.

Romanus From the Latin, meaning "a person from Rome." CONTEMPORARY EXAMPLE: Romanus Basgall, baseball player.

Romeo A variant form of the Italian name Romolo, meaning "a Roman." The hero of Shakespeare's *Romeo and Juliet*. CONTEMPORARY EXAMPLE: Romeo Adrera, karate expert.

Romi   From the Hebrew, meaning "heights, noble." CONTEMPORARY
EXAMPLE: Romi Yovel, Beer Sheba, Israel.

Rommie   A pet form of Romney. *See* Romney. CONTEMPORARY EXAM-
PLE: Rommie Loudd, football player.

Romney   A variant form of Romulus. *See* Romulus. CONTEMPORARY
EXAMPLE: Romney Hunter, football player. SURNAME USAGE: George
Romney, American statesman. PLACE-NAME USAGE: Romney, West
Virginia.

Romolo   From the Italian, meaning "a Roman." Akin to Romulus.
See Romulus.

Romulus   A variant form of Romolo. *See* Romolo. In Roman mythology, one of the sons of Mars; founder and first king of Rome. The
twin brother of Remus, whom he later killed. VARIANT FORMS: Romain, Roman, Romney, Romolo.

Ron   A pet form of Ronald. *See* Ronald. Also, from the Hebrew,
meaning "joy." CONTEMPORARY EXAMPLE: Ron Eliran, singer.

Ronald   The Scottish form of Reginald. *See* Reginald.

Ronel   A pet form of Ronald. *See* Ronald. Or, from the Hebrew *ron
el*, meaning "the song of the Lord."

Ronello   A pet form of Ronald. *See* Ronald. CONTEMPORARY EXAM-
PLE: Ronello M. Davis, agricultural expert.

Roni   From the Hebrew, meaning "joy is mine."

Ronnie, Ronny   Pet forms of Ronald. *See* Ronald.

Roone   From the Old English *rune*, meaning "counsel." Or, a variant
form of Ronald. *See* Ronald. CONTEMPORARY EXAMPLE: Roone Arl-
edge, television executive.

Roosevelt   From the Dutch, meaning "field of roses." PET FORMS:
Rosey, Rosie. CONTEMPORARY EXAMPLE: Roosevelt Brown, football
player. SURNAME USAGE: Franklin Delano Roosevelt, thirty–second
president of the U.S. PLACE-NAME USAGE: Mount Roosevelt, South
Dakota; Roosevelttown, New York.

Rori, Rory   Irish forms of Roderick and Robert. *See* Roderick *and*
Robert. Also, from the Celtic, meaning "the ruddy one."

Roric   A pet form of Rory. *See* Rory. CONTEMPORARY EXAMPLE: Roric
Harrison, baseball player.

Roscoe   A variant form of Ross. *See* Ross. A Celtic place-name. CON-
TEMPORARY EXAMPLE: Roscoe C. Brown, educator.

Rosey   A pet form of Roosevelt. *See* Roosevelt. Rosie is a variant spelling.

Rosie   A pet form of Roosevelt. *See* Roosevelt. CONTEMPORARY EXAM-

PLE: Rosie Greer, football player.

Ross   From the British *rhos*, meaning "woods, meadow," or from the Norse *ross*, meaning "a headland," or from the Latin, meaning "a rose." CONTEMPORARY EXAMPLES: Ross Martin, actor; Ross Firestone, author. SURNAME USAGE: Martin Ross, actor. PLACE-NAME USAGE: Fort Ross, California.

Rossano   The Italian form of Ross. CONTEMPORARY EXAMPLE: Rossano Brazzi, actor.

Roswald   From the Old English, meaning "a field of roses." Akin to Ross. *See* ROSS. CONTEMPORARY EXAMPLE: Roswell S. Danielson, physician.

Roul   A variant French form of Rudolph. *See* Rudolph. Akin to Raoul.

Rowby   From the Old English *ruh*, meaning "rugged land," and the Danish *by*, meaning "a town," hence "the town near the rugged land." CONTEMPORARY EXAMPLE: Rowby Goren, television scriptwriter.

Rowe   From the Old English *ruh*, meaning "rugged land."

Rowland   From the Old English *ruh*, meaning "rugged land." Also, a variant form of Roland. *See* Roland. CONTEMPORARY EXAMPLE: Rowland Grant, basketball player.

Roy   From the Old French, meaning "king." Also, from the Gaelic *rhu*, meaning "red." Also, possibly from the Old English *hry*, meaning "a thorn." CONTEMPORARY EXAMPLE: Roy Campanella, baseball player.

Royal   From the Middle English *roial* and the Latin *rex*, meaning "king." CONTEMPORARY EXAMPLE: Royal Cathcart, football player. PLACE-NAME USAGE: cities in North Carolina and Nebraska.

Royce   A variant form of Reece. *See* Reece. Also, a variant form of Rose introduced into England by the Normans. *See* Rose (feminine section). CONTEMPORARY EXAMPLE: Royce Lint, baseball player. SURNAME USAGE: Josiah Royce (1855-1916), American philosopher.

Royden   From the Middle English, meaning "the king's land." CONTEMPORARY EXAMPLE: Royden C. Braithwaite, educator.

Roye   A variant spelling of Roy. *See* Roy.

Royle   A variant form of Royal. *See* Royal.

Royston   From the Middle English, meaning "the king's town." CONTEMPORARY EXAMPLE: Royston C. Hughes, administrator.

Rube   A pet form of Reuben. *See* Reuben. CONTEMPORARY EXAMPLE: Rube Bressler, baseball player.

Ruben   A variant spelling of Reuben. *See* Reuben.

Rubens   A patronymic form of Reuben, meaning "son of Reuben."

See Reuben. SURNAME USAGE: Peter Paul Rubens (1577-1640), Flemish painter.

Rubin A variant spelling of Reuben. *See* Reuben.

Ruby A pet form of Reuben. *See* Reuben. Or, a French name from the Latin *rubeus*, meaning "red," and usually referring to the precious stone. Used also as a feminine name. PLACE-NAME USAGE: Ruby Mountains, Nevada; Ruby Creek, South Dakota.

Rudd From the Anglo-Saxon *rudu*, meaning "red." SURNAME USAGE: Paul Rudd, actor.

Rudel From the Anglo-Saxon *rudu* and *rude*, meaning "red." Akin to Rudd. CONTEMPORARY EXAMPLE: Rudel Miller, baseball player.

Rudolph From the Old High German name Hrodulf, derived from *hruod*, meaning "fame," plus *wolf*, meaning "a wolf." Rudolph I (1218-1291) was a German king and emperor of the Holy Roman Empire. VARIANT FORMS: Raoul, Rodolphe, Raul, Roul (French); Rudolf (German and Hungarian); Rodolfo (Italian and Spanish); Rodulfo (Spanish); Rolf (Swedish). PET FORMS: Rolf, Rolfe, Rollo, Rudi, Rudy.

Rudulph A variant spelling of Rudolph. *See* Rudolph.

Rudyard From the Anglo–Saxon *rudu*, meaning "red," and *gyrd*, meaning "rod, pole." CONTEMPORARY EXAMPLE: Rudyard Kipling, Nobel Prize winner in literature (1907). PLACE-NAME USAGE: Rudyard, Minnesota.

Ruel A variant spelling of Reuel. *See* Reuel. CONTEMPORARY EXAMPLE: Ruel V. Churchill, mathematician.

Rufus From the Latin, meaning "red, red-haired." CONTEMPORARY EXAMPLE: Rufus King, U.S. vice–presidential candidate (1808).

Rupert A variant English, French, and German form of Robert, from the German Ruprecht and Rupprecht. *See* Robert. CONTEMPORARY EXAMPLE: Rupert Murdoch, publisher.

Ruperto An Italian variant form of Robert. *See* Robert.

Rush From the Old English, meaning "a grassy plant with a hollow stem," which grows in marshy places. SURNAME USAGE: Benjamin Rush (1745-1813), signer of the Declaration of Independence.

Rusk From the Spanish *rosca*, meaning "a twisted roll, bread; a cake." SURNAME USAGE: Dean Rusk, U.S. secretary of state; John Ruskin (1819-1900), English writer.

Russ A pet form of Russell. *See* Russell.

Russel, Russell From the French *roux*, meaning "red." Akin to the Latin name Rufus. *See* Rufus. Also, from the Old English name Rut, derived from *rot*, meaning "red," usually referring to the color of rocks. Among Anglo-Saxons, Rut took on the meaning of "a horse." PET

FORMS: Russ, Rusty. CONTEMPORARY EXAMPLES: Russel Blaine Nye, Pulitzer Prize winner in literature (1945); Russell Long, U.S. senator. PLACE-NAME USAGE: Mount Russel, Alaska, named for I.C. Russel, geologist.

Rusty   A nickname for a redheaded person. Akin to Russel. *See* Russel. CONTEMPORARY EXAMPLE: Rusty Staub, baseball player.

Rutherford   From the Old English, meaning "the river crossing made of red stones." CONTEMPORARY EXAMPLES: Rutherford B. (Birchard) Hayes, nineteenth president of the U.S.; Rutherford Adkins, educator. SURNAME USAGE: Ernest Rutherford, British Noble Prize winner in chemistry (1908).

Ruvane   The Hebrew form of Reuben. *See* Reuben. Reuven is a variant form.

Ryan   A short form of Bryan. *See* Bryan. Popular in Ireland. CONTEMPORARY EXAMPLE: Ryan O'Neal, actor.

Ryder   A variant spelling of Rider. *See* Rider. SURNAME USAGE: Albert Pinkham Ryder (1847-1917), American painter.

Ryen   A variant spelling of Ryan. *See* Ryan. CONTEMPORARY EXAMPLE: Ryen Durin, author.

Ryerson   A patronymic Dutch form, meaning "son of Ryder (Rider)." *See* Rider. CONTEMPORARY EXAMPLE: Ryerson Jones, baseball player.

S

Saadia, Saadiah   From the Hebrew and Aramaic, meaning "the help of God." Saadya is a variant spelling. Saadiah ben Joseph (882-942) was an Egyptian–born Jewish scholar.

Saadya   A variant spelling of Saadia. *See* Saadia.

Sabath   From the Hebrew *shabbat*, meaning "rest." Sabbath is a variant spelling. CONTEMPORARY EXAMPLE: Sabath Mele, baseball player.

Sabin   From the Old French *savine* and the Latin *sabina*, meaning "a juniper tree." The Sabines were an ancient Italian tribe. St. Sabinus was a fourth–century bishop of Spoleto. Savin is a variant form. Sabina is the feminine form. SURNAME USAGE: Albert B. Sabin, American physician and bacteriologist.

Sacha   A Russian pet form of Alexander. *See* Alexander.

Saer   A variant spelling of Sayer. *See* Sayer.

Sagi   From the Hebrew and Aramaic, meaning "strong, mighty."

Sahm   Probably a variant spelling of Sam. *See* Sam. CONTEMPORARY EXAMPLE: Sahm Doherty, photographer.

Saint   From the Latin *sanctus*, meaning "holy." CONTEMPORARY EXAMPLE: Saint Saffold, football player. SURNAME USAGE: Charles Camille Saint-Saens, (1835-1921), French composer.

Sal, Sale   From the Latin *sal*, meaning "salt." Or, from the Old English *salh*, meaning "a willow." Sal is also a common pet form of Salvador. CONTEMPORARY EXAMPLE: Sal Bando, baseball player.

Salem   The English form of the Hebrew *shalom*, meaning "peace." In the Bible, a place over which Melchizedek ruled. PLACE-NAME USAGE: cities in Massachusetts and Ohio.

Salim   From the Arabic, meaning "flawless, whole." Akin to Salem. CONTEMPORARY EXAMPLE: Salim Lewis, stockbroker.

Salmon   A variant form of Solomon. *See* Solomon. Also, from the Middle English Salmoun, referring to the fish of the Salmonidae family.

Salo   A pet form of Salomon. *See* Salomon. Used also as an independent form. CONTEMPORARY EXAMPLE: Salo Baron, historian.

Saloman, Salomon   Variant forms of Solomon. *See* Solomon.

Salvador   From the Latin *salvare*, meaning "to be saved." Sal is a pet form. CONTEMPORARY EXAMPLE: Salvador Dali, painter. PLACE-NAME

USAGE: a seaport in Brazil; El Salvador, a South American country.

Salvadore　A variant spelling of Salvador. *See* Salvador.

Salvatore　A variant spelling of Salvador. *See* Salvador.

Sam　A pet form of Samuel. *See* Samuel.

Sami　From the Arabic, meaning "high, lofty, exalted." CONTEMPORA-RY EXAMPLE: Sami Khalil Mari, author.

Samir　From the Arabic, meaning "entertainer." CONTEMPORARY EX-AMPLE: Samir Amin, author.

Samm　A variant spelling of Sam. *See* Sam. CONTEMPORARY EXAMPLE: Samm Sinclair Baker, author.

Sammy　A pet form of Samuel. *See* Samuel.

Sampson　A variant spelling of Samson. *See* Samson.

Samson　From the Hebrew *shemesh*, meaning "sun." In the Bible, one of the judges, a member of the tribe of Dan, noted for his great strength. SURNAME USAGE: Samm, Sams, Sampson, Samson, Sansom, Sansome, Sansum.

Samuel　From the Hebrew, meaning "His name is God" or "God has heard." In the Bible, an eleventh–century B.C. prophet and judge who anointed Saul as first king of Israel. PET FORMS: Sam, Sami, Sammy. SURNAME USAGE: Samuels, Samuelson, Samwell.

Samy　A pet form of Samuel. *See* Samuel. CONTEMPORARY EXAMPLE: Samy ben Youb, actor.

Sanche, Sanchez　Spanish forms of the Latin *sanctus*, meaning "saint." VARIANT FORMS: Saint, Sancho. CONTEMPORARY EXAMPLE: Sanche de Gramont, Pulitzer Prize winner for journalism (1961).

Sancho　A Spanish form of the Latin *sanctus*, meaning "saint." VARI-ANT FORMS: Saint, Sanche, Sanchez. Sancho Panza is the simple, prac-tical young man who serves Cervantes' fictional character Don Quixo-te.

Sandalio　The Italian form of the Latin *sandalium*, meaning "foot-wear, sandals." CONTEMPORARY EXAMPLE: Sandalio Consuegra, base-ball player.

Sander　A pet form of Alexander. *See* Alexander.

Sanders　A patronymic form, meaning "son of Sander." *See* Sander.

Sandol　From the Latin *sandalium*, meaning "sandals, footwear." Also, from the Old English *sond*, meaning "the sand of the sea." CON-TEMPORARY EXAMPLE: Sandol Stoddard, author.

Sandor　A variant spelling of Sander, a pet form of Alexander. *See* Alexander. CONTEMPORARY EXAMPLE: Sandor Frankel, author.

Sandy   A pet form of Alexander or Sanford. *See* Alexander *and* Sanford.

Sanford   From the Old English *sond*, meaning "sand," plus *ford*, meaning "a crossing," hence "the sandy river crossing." PLACE-NAME USAGE: Mount Sanford, Alaska, named for Reuben Sanford, an early resident.

Santiago   A variant form of Saint Diego (James). *See* James. CONTEMPORARY EXAMPLE: Santiago Formoso, soccer player. PLACE-NAME USAGE: Santiago, Minnesota.

Santo, Santos   Spanish forms of the Latin *sanctus*, meaning "saint." CONTEMPORARY EXAMPLE: Santo Alcala and Santos Alomar, baseball players. PLACE-NAME USAGE: Santo, Texas.

Saphir   From the Greek *sappheiros* and the Hebrew *sappir*, meaning "sapphire," a blue-colored precious stone.

Sapir   A variant form of Saphir. *See* Saphir. SURNAME USAGE: Edward Sapir, linguist.

Sardis   From the Latin *sarda*, meaning "a hard, precious stone." CONTEMPORARY EXAMPLE: Sardis Birchard, an uncle of U.S. President Rutherford Birchard Hayes. PLACE-NAME USAGE: cities in Mississippi and Oklahoma; Sardis Creek, Georgia.

Sargent   From the Latin, meaning "a military man." Seargent is a variant spelling. CONTEMPORARY EXAMPLE: Sargent Shriver, business executive. SURNAME USAGE: John Singer Sargent (1856-1925), American painter. PLACE-NAME USAGE: Sargent, Nebraska.

Sarto   The Italian form of the Latin *sartus*, meaning "to patch (material)." An occupational name for tailors. SURNAME USAGE: Sartre, Sartori.

Sasha   A Russian pet form of Alexander. *See* Alexander.

Saturnino   The Italian name for the Latin Saturnus. In Roman mythology, the god of agriculture, akin to the Greek god Cronus. Also, the name of the second largest planet in the solar system. CONTEMPORARY EXAMPLE: Saturnino Escalera, baseball player.

Saul   From the Hebrew, meaning "borrowed." In the Bible, the first king to rule over Israel. He was the son of Kish, from the tribe of Benjamin. Saul of Tarsus, in the New Testament, adopted the name Paul after his conversion to Christianity.

Saulo   A Spanish form of Saul. *See* Saul. CONTEMPORARY EXAMPLE: Saulo Klahr, physician.

Saunders   A variant spelling of Sanders. *See* Sanders.

Saverio An Italian form of the Middle English *saven* and the Old French *sauver*, meaning "to save."

Saville A masculine form of Sevilla. *See* Sevilla (feminine section). CONTEMPORARY EXAMPLE: Saville Crother, football player.

Savin A variant form of Sabin. *See* Sabin.

Sawney A Scottish pet name for Alexander. *See* Alexander.

Sawyer From the Middle English *sawier*, meaning "one who works with a saw." An occupational name used by woodcutters and cabinet makers.

Saxon From the Old High German *sahs*, meaning "a sword, a knife." The Saxons carried short swords (seax).

Sayer From the Old German *sigiheri*, compounded of *sigu*, meaning "victory," and "harja," meaning "army, people," hence "victory of the people." Saer is a variant spelling.

Scatman Meaning uncertain. Possibly a jazz term, meaning "one who sings scat, or makes sounds in imitation of music." CONTEMPORARY EXAMPLE: Scatman Crothers, actor.

Schubert From the German meaning "bright protector." CONTEMPORARY EXAMPLE: Schubert M. Ogden, editor. SURNAME USAGE: Franz Schubert (1797-1828), Austrian composer.

Schuyler From the Dutch *schuilen*, meaning "to hide, to skulk." Or, from the Old English *scola*, meaning "a shoal, a school of fish." CONTEMPORARY EXAMPLE: Schuyler Chapin, musicologist. SURNAME USAGE: Philip John Schuyler (1733-1804), American statesman. PLACE-NAME USAGE: Schuylkill River, Pennsylvania.

Scipio A Roman general who defeated Hannibal in 202 B.C. in the Second Punic War. CONTEMPORARY EXAMPLE: Scipio Spinks, baseball player.

Scoey Possibly a pet form of Roscoe. *See* Roscoe. CONTEMPORARY EXAMPLE: Scoey Mitchill, actor.

Scoop A nickname. U.S. Senator Henry Jackson of Washington was so named during his years as a newspaper reporter.

Scot, Scott From Scoti, a Late Latin name for a tribe of people in North Britain. PET FORMS: Scottie, Scotty. CONTEMPORARY EXAMPLE: F. Scott Fitzgerald, author. SURNAME USAGE: Dred Scott, nineteenth-century Negro slave.

Seabern From the Anglo-Saxon *beorn*, meaning "sea warrior." Or, from the Norse, meaning "sea bear." CONTEMPORARY EXAMPLE: Seabern Hill, football player.

Seabrook From the Old English, meaning "a brook running into the sea."

Seaman   From the Old English, meaning "a sailor." CONTEMPORARY EXAMPLE: Seaman Squyres, football player.

Seamus   A variant form of the Erse name Seumuis, derived from Jacob and James. *See* Jacob *and* James. Or, a contracted form of "sea mouse," a type of large, flat-bodied sea worm. CONTEMPORARY EXAMPLE: Seamus Ennis, translator.

Sean   An Irish form of John. *See* John. The original Irish spelling was Eoin. CONTEMPORARY EXAMPLE: Sean Connery, actor.

Sear   From the Old English *saer*, meaning "a battle." Sears is a patronymic form.

Seargent   A variant spelling of Sargent. *See* Sargent.

Searle   A variant form of Sear. *See* Sear.

Sears   A patronymic form, meaning "son of Sear." *See* Sear.

Sebastian   From the Greek, meaning "venerable." VARIANT FORMS: Bastien, Sebastien (French); Bastiano, Sebastian (Italian). PLACE-NAME USAGE: Cape Sebastian, Oregon, named in honor of Sebastian Viscaino, a seventeenth-century Spanish explorer.

Sebert   From the Anglo-Saxon, meaning "bright victory."

Sebold   From the Anglo-Saxon, meaning "bold victory."

Sedgewick, Sedgwick   From the Middle English *segge*, meaning "saw-shaped" (leaves of a tree), and *wicke*, meaning "village," hence, "the village with the trees that have leaves with saw-shaped edges."

Seef, Seff   Variant spellings of Zev and Zeev. *See* Zev *and* Zeev. Commonly used as surnames.

Segel   From the Hebrew *segula*, meaning "treasure." In the Bible, Israel is referred to as "a treasured people." Commonly used as a surname in the forms Segal and Siegal.

Segev   From the Hebrew, meaning "majestic, exalted."

Selby   A variant form of Shelby. *See* Shelby.

Selden, Seldon   From the Middle English, meaning "rare, strange." SURNAME USAGE: John Selden (1584-1654), English historian.

Selig   From the German and Old English *saelig*, meaning "blessed, holy." A common name among Jews of the eighteenth and nineteenth centuries. Zelig is a variant spelling.

Selman, Sellman   An Old English occupational name used by peddlers.

Selva   The Spanish and Portuguese form of the Latin *silva*, meaning "a forest." Sylvan is a variant form. CONTEMPORARY EXAMPLE: Selva Burdette, baseball player.

Selwyn   From the Old English *sel* (*saelig*), meaning "holy," plus *wyn*, meaning "friend," hence "holy friend." A common name in Wales. CONTEMPORARY EXAMPLE: Selwyn K. Troen, educator.

Sender   A variant spelling of Sander, a pet form of Alexander. *See* Alexander.

Seneca   An early American Indian word, meaning "people of the standing rock." The name of North American Indians who lived in the northern parts of New York State. Seneca was a first-century A.D. Roman philosopher and statesman. CONTEMPORARY EXAMPLE: Seneca Sampson, football player. PLACE-NAME USAGE: Seneca Lake, New York.

Senior   From the Latin, meaning "the elder."

Sep   A short form of Septimus. *See* Septimus. CONTEMPORARY EXAMPLE: Sep Palin, trotters driver.

Septimus   From the Latin, meaning "seventh." Often given to the seventh child (if a male) in a family, and also to the seventh son in a family.

Seraf, Serafino   From the Hebrew *sarof*, meaning "to burn." In the Bible, the serafim were fiery angels guarding the throne of God. Serafina is a feminine form.

Seraph   A variant spelling of Seraf. *See* Seraf.

Serge, Sergei   From the Old French *sergant* and the Latin *servire*, meaning "to serve." CONTEMPORARY EXAMPLE: Sergei Starikov, author.

Sergi, Sergio   Variant Italian forms of Serge. *See* Serge. CONTEMPORARY EXAMPLE: Sergio Perosa, professor.

Sergiu   A Roumanian form of Serge. *See* Serge. CONTEMPORARY EXAMPLE: Sergiu Comissiona, musical conductor.

Serle, Serlo   Variant forms of Sear. *See* Sear. Or, forms of the Old English name Serlo and the Old German name Sarilo, derived from *sarva*, meaning "armor."

Seth   From the Hebrew, meaning either "garment" or "appointed," or from the Syriac, meaning "appearance." In the Bible, a son of Adam who was born after the death of Abel. CONTEMPORARY EXAMPLE: Seth Kantor, author.

Seton   From the Anglo-Saxon, meaning "a town near the sea." CONTEMPORARY EXAMPLE: Seton Lloyd, archeologist.

Seumas, Seumus   Variant forms of Shamus, the Irish form of James. *See* James.

Seusmas   A variant form of Seumas. *See* Seumas. CONTEMPORARY EXAMPLE: Seusmas Stewart, bibliophile.

Sewal, Sewall   From the Old English, meaning "the wall near the sea."

Also, from the Old English *sige*, meaning "victory," and *weald*, meaning "strength." SURNAME USAGE: Samuel Sewall (1652-1730), American jurist.

Seward From the Anglo-Saxon, meaning "defender of the sea coast." SURNAME USAGE: Henry William Seward (1801-1869), American statesman.

Sewell From the Old English, meaning "the well near the sea." Or, a variant form of Sewal. *See* Sewal.

Sextus From the Latin, meaning "sixth." Usually given to the sixth child (if male) in a family, and also to the sixth son in a family.

Seymore A variant spelling of Seymour. *See* Seymour.

Seymour From the Old English *sae*, meaning "sea," and *mor*, meaning "marsh, marshy, wild land," hence "marshy land near the sea." Akin to Maurice. *See* Maurice. SURNAME USAGE: Maurice Seymour, photographer.

Shaanan From the Hebrew, meaning "peaceful." VARIANT FORMS: Shanan, Shanon.

Shabbetai From the Hebrew *shabbat*, meaning "to rest; the Sabbath." CONTEMPORARY EXAMPLE: Shabbetai Tzevi, seventeenth–century Jewish mystic.

Shadrach A Babylonian name of uncertain meaning. In the Bible, one of the three captive friends of Daniel (Shadrach, Meshach, and Abednego) who emerged alive from the fiery furnace. His original Hebrew name was Hananiah. It was changed to Shadrach by Nebuchadnezzar's (king of Babylonia) chief officer.

Shafer From the Aramaic *shapir*, meaning "good, beautiful." CONTEMPORARY EXAMPLE: Shafer Suggs, football player. SURNAME USAGE: Shaffer, Schaffer, Shapira, Shapiro.

Shalom From the Hebrew, meaning "peace." VARIANT FORMS: Sholom, Shlomo, Solomon. CONTEMPORARY EXAMPLE: Shalom Spiegel, author.

Shamir From the Hebrew, meaning "a diamond," capable of cutting through metal. According to talmudic legend, the Shamir is a worm-like creature that could cut like a diamond. It was used to cut the stones of which Solomon's temple was built.

Shammai From the Hebrew and Aramaic, meaning "name." A first–century Palestinian Jewish scholar.

Shamus, Shammus Irish forms of James. *See* James.

Shanan A variant spelling of Shaanan. *See* Shaanan.

Shane A variant form of the Gaelic Sean. *See* Sean. VARIANT FORMS: Shaun, Shawn. CONTEMPORARY EXAMPLE: Shane Sinutko, actor; Shane Stevens, author.

Shanen A variant spelling of Shanon. *See* Shanon. CONTEMPORARY EXAMPLE: Shanen A. Hovanessian, scientist.

Shannon, Shanon Variant forms of Sean. *See* Sean. Or, variant forms of Shaanan. *See* Shaanan. PLACE-NAME USAGE: Shannon, Texas, named for Luke Shannon, an early settler.

Shap From the Old English *sceap,* meaning "sheep." VARIANT FORMS: Shep, Ship, Shipper, Skip, Skipper.

Shapir From the Aramaic, meaning "good, beautiful." Shafer is a variant form. SURNAME USAGE: Shafer, Shapira, Shapiro.

Shapley A variant form of Shepley. *See* Shepley.

Sharon A masculine as well as feminine form. *See* Sharon (feminine section). In the Bible, a place–name. CONTEMPORARY EXAMPLE: Sharon Turner (1768-1847), historian.

Sharvy Origin unknown. CONTEMPORARY EXAMPLE: Sharvy G. Umbeck, educator.

Shaul The Hebrew name for Saul. *See* Saul. CONTEMPORARY EXAMPLE: Shaul Mishal, author.

Shaun A variant spelling of Shawn and Sean. *See* Sean. CONTEMPORARY EXAMPLE: Shaun Cassidy, singer.

Shaw From the Old English *scaega,* meaning "a thicket, a grove." SURNAME USAGE: George Bernard Shaw (1856-1950), English author.

Shawn A variant spelling of Sean. *See* Sean.

Shearman An occupational name. From the Old English, meaning "one who shears sheep."

Shefer From the Hebrew, meaning "pleasant, beautiful." Akin to Shapir. *See* Shapir.

Shel A pet form of Shelley or Shelby. *See* Shelley *and* Shelby. CONTEMPORARY EXAMPLE: Shel Silverstein, author.

Shelby From the Anglo-Saxon, meaning "a sheltered town." CONTEMPORARY EXAMPLE: Shelby Jordan, football player. Used also as a feminine name. SURNAME USAGE: Isaac Shelby (1750-1826) Revolutionary War commander, first governor of Kentucky for whom many counties and towns were named.

Sheldon From the Old English *scyld,* meaning "a hill," hence "protected hill." Also, possibly akin to Skelton. *See* Skelton.

Shelley, Shelly From the Old English, meaning "island of shells." CONTEMPORARY EXAMPLE: Shelley Berman, comedian. SURNAME USAGE: Percy Bysshe Shelley (1792-1822), English poet.

Shelomi A variant spelling of Shlomi. *See* Shlomi.

Shelomo   A variant spelling of Shlomo. *See* Shlomo.

Shelton   From the Old English, meaning "protected town." Akin to Sheldon. CONTEMPORARY EXAMPLE: Shelton Hale, author.

Shem   From the Hebrew, meaning "name." In the Bible, the oldest of Noah's sons. Shammai is a variant form.

Shep   A variant form of Shap. *See* Shap.

Shepard   A variant form of Shepherd. *See* Shepherd.

Shepherd   An occupational name. From the Old English *shap*, meaning "sheep," and *heord*, meaning "a group, a row," hence "one who tends sheep."

Shepley   From the Old English *sceap*, meaning "a sheep meadow." VARIANT FORMS: Shapley, Shipley.

Sheppard   A variant spelling of Shepherd. *See* Shepherd. CONTEMPORARY EXAMPLE: Sheppard Strudwick, actor.

Sheraga, Sheragal   From the Aramaic, meaning "light." In Yiddish, the hybrid name Shraga–Feivel is commonly used, Feivel being a variant from of Phoebus, the goddess of light in Greek mythology.

Sheridan   From the Old English, meaning "master of the shire, head of the district." Akin to Sherwood. CONTEMPORARY EXAMPLE: Sheridan Snyder, builder. SURNAME USAGE: Philip Henry Sheridan (1831-1888), Civil War general. PLACE-NAME USAGE: Sheridan, Wyoming; Sheridan, New York, named for R.B. Sheridan, nineteenth-century English dramatist.

Sherill   From the Old English *scire*, meaning "a shire," plus *hyl*, meaning "a hill," hence "the hill in the district (shire)" or "the hilly shire." Akin to Sherwood. Sherrill is a variant spelling. CONTEMPORARY EXAMPLE: Sherill Headrick, football player.

Sherira   From the Aramaic, meaning "strong." A tenth-century Jewish scholar, head of an academy in Pumbedita.

Sherlock   From the Old English *scire*, meaning "a shire, a district," plus *loc*, meaning "a lock, an enclosure," hence "a protected area." Popularized by Sir Arthur Conan Doyle in his *Sherlock Holmes* mystery novels.

Sherman   From the Old English, meaning "a servant (or resident) of the shire (district)." Akin to Sherwood. Also, an occupational name, meaning "one who shears sheep." CONTEMPORARY EXAMPLE: Sherman Billingsley. SURNAME USAGE: William Tecumseh Sherman (1820-1891), Civil War general. PLACE-NAME USAGE: counties in Nebraska, Oregon, and Kansas; Sherman, Maine, named for Senator John Sherman.

Sherps   Origin unknown. CONTEMPORARY EXAMPLE: Sherps Wiemers, bowling champion.

Sherrill A variant spelling of Sherill. *See* Sherill. CONTEMPORARY EXAMPLE: Sherrill Milnes, opera singer. Commonly used as a surname.

Sherry A pet form of Sherman or Sherwood. *See* Sherman *and* Sherwood. CONTEMPORARY EXAMPLE: Sherry Magee, baseball player.

Sherwin From the Old English, meaning "a friend, a member of the shire." Akin to Sherwood. *See* Sherwood.

Sherwood From the Old English *scyre, scir, scire,* meaning "a shire, a county, an official district," plus *wood,* meaning "a wooded area, a forest." CONTEMPORARY EXAMPLE: Sherwood Anderson, author. PLACE-NAME USAGE: Sherwood Forest, Nottinghamshire, England.

Shimon The Hebraic form of Simon. *See* Simon. In the Bible, the second son of Jacob. CONTEMPORARY EXAMPLE: Shimon Peres, Israeli political leader.

Ship A pet form of Shipley. *See* Shipley.

Shipley A variant form of Shepley. *See* Shepley. CONTEMPORARY EXAMPLE: Shipley Farroh, football player.

Shirley Used occasionally as a masculine name. *See* Shirley (feminine section). CONTEMPORARY EXAMPLE: Shirley Wentworth, football player. SURNAME USAGE: James Shirley (1596-1666), English dramatist. PLACE-NAME USAGE: Shirley, Massachusetts, named for William Shirley, colonial governor.

Shlomi From the Hebrew, meaning "my place." Akin to Shalom. *See* Shalom.

Shlomo From the Hebrew, meaning "his peace." The Hebrew name of King Solomon. *See* Solomon.

Shneur A Yiddish name derived from the Latin name Senior, meaning "the elder." *See* Senior.

Sholom A variant spelling of Shalom. *See* Shalom. CONTEMPORARY EXAMPLE: Sholom J. Kahn, author.

Shoon A variant Irish form of Sean. *See* Sean.

Shraga, Shragal Variant forms of Sheraga. *See* Sheraga.

Shug Probably a nickname. Origin unknown. CONTEMPORARY EXAMPLE: Shug Fisher, actor.

Shushan From the Hebrew, meaning "a rose, a lily." In the Bible, the name of the capital city of Persia.

Si A pet form of Simon and Simeon. *See* Simon *and* Simeon.

Sidney A contracted form of Saint Denys. Derived from Dionysius, the Greek god of wine, drama, and fruitfulness. Sydney is a variant spelling. Used also as a feminine form. SURNAME USAGE: Sir Philip Sidney (1554-1586), English poet and statesman. PLACE-NAME USAGE: Sidney, Australia.

Siegfried   From the German *sieg,* meaning "victory," and *fridu,* meaning "freedom, peace." In Germanic legend, a hero who kills a dragon.

Siegmond   A variant spelling of Siegmund. *See* Siegmund.

Siegmund   From the German *sieg,* meaning "victory," and *mund,* meaning "hard, protection."

Sif   A variant form of Seff. *See* Seff. CONTEMPORARY EXAMPLE: Sif Rund, Swedish actor.

Sigismund   A German and English form of Siegmund. *See* Siegmund. A Holy Roman emperor (1411-1437).

Sigmund   A variant German form of Siegmund. *See* Siegmund.

Signe   From the Latin *signum,* meaning "a sign, a mark, a seal," CONTEMPORARY EXAMPLE: Signe Anderson, rock musician.

Sigurd   In Norse legend, the hero of the Volsunga Saga. Akin to the German Siegfried. CONTEMPORARY EXAMPLE: Sigurd Sandberg, football player.

Silas   A Latin form of the Aramaic and Hebrew *sha-ol,* meaning "to ask, to borrow." Also, a short form of Silvanus. *See* Silvanus. CONTEMPORARY EXAMPLE: Silas Dean, U.S. statesman.

Silvan, Silvano   Variant forms of Silvanus. *See* Silvanus.

Silvanus   From the Latin, meaning "a forest." In Roman mythology, the god of woods and fields. VARIANT FORMS: Silvan, Silvano, Silvio, Sylvan, Sylvia (the feminine form).

Silver   From the German *silber,* meaning "silver." Used originally as an occupational name, meaning "one who works with silver." CONTEMPORARY EXAMPLE: Silver King, baseball player. SURNAME USAGE: Abba Hillel Silver (1893-1963), clergyman. PLACE-NAME USAGE: Silver Creek, West Virginia; Silver Butte, Arizona; Silver Valley, Texas.

Silvester   A variant spelling of Sylvester. *See* Sylvester.

Silvio   An Italian form of Silvan and Silvanus. *See* Silvanus. CONTEMPORARY EXAMPLE: Silvio Conte, U.S. congressman.

Sim   A pet form of Simon and Simeon. *See* Simon *and* Simeon.

Simcha   From the Hebrew, meaning "joy." CONTEMPORARY EXAMPLE: Simcha Dinitz, Israeli ambassador to the U.S.

Simeon   A Greek and Latin form of the Hebrew Shimon, from *shama,* meaning "he heard." In the Bible, the second son of Jacob and Leah. Simon is a variant form used in the New Testament. *See* Simon. Simeon Stylites was a fifth-century Syrian monk.

Simha   A variant spelling of Simcha. *See* Simcha. CONTEMPORARY EXAMPLE: Simha Erlich, Israeli finance minister.

Simi, Simie, Simmie Pet forms of Simeon and Simon. *See* Simeon *and* Simon.

Simon A variant spelling of Simeon. *See* Simeon. In the New Testament, one of the twelve apostles was called Peter or Simon Peter; also, a brother or relative of Jesus. Simon Legree is a cruel slave overseer in Harriet B. Stowe's *Uncle Tom's Cabin*. PET FORMS: Si, Sy, Sim, Simi, Simmie. SURNAME USAGE: Paul Simon, singer; also Simes, Simons, Sims, Simpson, Simmonds.

Simp A pet form of Simpson. *See* Simpson.

Simpson A patronymic form, meaning "son of Simon." *See* Simon. PLACE-NAME USAGE: sites in Nevada and Utah, named for nineteenth-century explorer J.H. Simpson.

Sims A patronymic form, meaning "son of Simon." *See* Simon. CONTEMPORARY EXAMPLE: Sims Stokes, football player.

Sinclair From the Latin, meaning "a clear sign." Also, may be a contracted form of Saint Claire. CONTEMPORARY EXAMPLE: Sinclair Lewis, Pulitzer Prize winner in letters (1926). SURNAME USAGE: Upton Sinclair (1878-1968), American novelist.

Sisi, Sissi From the Hebrew, meaning "my joy."

Siv A short form of Siva. *See* Siva. CONTEMPORARY EXAMPLE: Siv Cedering Fix, poet.

Siva A member of the Hindu trinity: the god of destruction and reproduction. Siv is a short form.

Sivan An Assyrian-Babylonian word of uncertain meaning. The ninth month in the Jewish calendar, corresponding to May-June. In the Zodiac, its sign is Gemini ("twins").

Siward From the Old English name Sigeweard, compounded of *size*, meaning "victory," and *weard*, meaning "protection." SURNAME USAGE: Seaward, Seward.

Skee From the Old Norse *skeyti*, meaning "a projectile." CONTEMPORARY EXAMPLE: Skee Foremsky, bowling champion.

Skelton From the Greek *skeletos*, meaning "dried up." Akin to the Modern Dutch *schelle*, "a shell," hence "the town where the shells are." Also, possibly a variant form of Sheldon. *See* Sheldon. SURNAME USAGE: John Skelton (died 1529), English poet; Red Skelton, comedian.

Skip A pet form of Skipper. *See* Skipper. CONTEMPORARY EXAMPLE: Skip Homeier, actor.

Skipper From the Middle Dutch *schipper*, meaning "one who captains a ship."

Sky A variant form of Skee. *See* Skee. CONTEMPORARY EXAMPLE: Sky

Saxon, rock musician.

Skylab   An invented name, adopted from the name of the first U.S. space station that crash-landed in 1979. CONTEMPORARY EXAMPLE: Skylab Singh, born in Northern India a few hours before the vehicle fell to earth.

Slim   From the Old English, meaning "slime, mud." Also, a nickname for a tall, thin person. CONTEMPORARY EXAMPLE: Slim Summerville, actor; Slim Randles, editor and publisher. PLACE-NAME USAGE: Slim Butte, South Dakota.

Sloan   From the Celtic, meaning "warrior." CONTEMPORARY EXAMPLE: Sloan Wilson, novelist. SURNAME USAGE: John Sloan (1871-1951), American painter.

Sly   A pet form of Sylvester. *See* Sylvester.

Snowy   A nickname for a white-complexioned person. CONTEMPORARY EXAMPLE: Snowy Fleet, rock musician.

Sol   A pet form of Solomon. *See* Solomon. Also, from the Latin *sol,* meaning "sun." Often identified with Apollo, who was identified with Helios, the sun-god in Greek and Roman mythology.

Solomon   From the Hebrew *shalom,* meaning "peace." In the Bible, the son of David, king of Israel. VARIANT FORMS: Salamon, Salman, Salmen, Salome, Saloman, Salomon, Solmon, Selman, Suleiman, Zalman, Zelman. SURNAME USAGE: Salmon, Sammon, Sammond. PLACE-NAME USAGE: Solomon Islands in the Pacific; Solomonville, Arizona, named for I.E. Solomon, an early resident.

Solon   From the Latin *sol,* meaning "the sun." *See* Sol. An Athenian statesman and lawgiver (638-559 B.C.). PLACE-NAME USAGE: Solon Springs, Wisconsin, named for Thomas Solon, of the site.

Somerby   From *sombre,* a Middle English form of the Latin *supra,* meaning "over," plus *by,* meaning "town," hence "the town over there." CONTEMPORARY EXAMPLE: Somerby R. Dowst, author.

Sonny   A popular nickname, meaning "son" or "boy." CONTEMPORARY EXAMPLES: Sonny Werblin, sports executive; Sonny Bono, actor. PLACE-NAME USAGE: Sonny, Oregon.

Soren   Origin uncertain. Possibly from Thor, the Norse god of war. CONTEMPORARY EXAMPLE: Soren Kierkegaard, Danish philosopher.

Sorrell   From the Old French *sore, sorel,* meaning "light brown," often referring to a horse because of its color. CONTEMPORARY EXAMPLE: Sorrell Brooke, actor.

Soule   From the Old English *salh,* meaning "a willow." CONTEMPORARY EXAMPLE: Soule McLeod, baseball player.

Soup, Soupy   An invented name. From the slang expression "to soup up," meaning "to increase power, energy." CONTEMPORARY EXAMPLE: Soupy Sales, comedian.

Spark   From the Old English *spearca,* meaning "a flash of light." Also, from the Old Norse *sparkr,* meaning "a gay, dashing young man." Also, from the Dutch, meaning "a spruce stream." CONTEMPORARY EXAMPLE: Spark M. Matsunaga, U.S. congressman. PLACE-NAME USAGE: Sparkill, New York.

Sparky   A pet form of Spark. *See* Spark. CONTEMPORARY EXAMPLE: Sparky Lyle, baseball player.

Speed   From the Old English *spaed,* meaning "wealth, power, success." CONTEMPORARY EXAMPLE: Speed Lees, author.

Speer   From the Middle English and Old English *spere,* akin to the German *speer,* "a spearlike weapon." CONTEMPORARY EXAMPLE: Speer Morgan, author.

Spencer   From the Middle English *spenser,* meaning "steward, administrator, butler." CONTEMPORARY EXAMPLE: Spencer Tracy, actor. SURNAME USAGE: Herbert Spencer (1820-1903), English philosopher. PLACE-NAME USAGE: Spencer, Iowa, named for Senator G.E. Spencer.

Spessard   A form of the French *Spessart,* a mountain range in Bavaria. CONTEMPORARY EXAMPLE: Spessard L. Holland, U.S. senator.

Spider   From the Middle English *spithre,* referring to a variety of insects. CONTEMPORARY EXAMPLE: Spider Robinson, author. PLACE-NAME USAGE: Spider, Kentucky; Spider Lake, Minnesota.

Spike   From the Middle English *spik* and the Latin *spica,* meaning "an ear of grain." CONTEMPORARY EXAMPLE: Spike Mulligan, author.

Spiro   From the Latin *spirate,* meaning "to breathe." CONTEMPORARY EXAMPLE: Spiro Agnew, a U.S. vice-president.

Spruille   Meaning uncertain. May be related to the Dutch *spruw,* meaning "anemic." CONTEMPORARY EXAMPLE: Spruille Braden, author.

Spud   From the Middle English *spudde,* meaning "a spade, a trowel," used to dig up weeds, potatoes, etc. CONTEMPORARY EXAMPLE: Spud Chandler, baseball player.

Spurgeon   From the Middle English and Middle French *espurge,* referring to a family of plants. CONTEMPORARY EXAMPLE: Spurgeon B. Eure, educator.

Squire   From the Old French *esquier,* meaning "a young man of high birth serving as an attendant to nobility." CONTEMPORARY EXAMPLE: Squire Fridell, actor.

Srully   A pet form of Israel. *See* Israel. CONTEMPORARY EXAMPLE: Srully Blotnick, publicist.

Stacey, Stacy   From the Latin, meaning "firmly established." CON-TEMPORARY EXAMPLE: Stacy Keach, actor.

Stafford   From the Old English *staef* plus *ford,* meaning "a pole with which to ford (cross) a river." CONTEMPORARY EXAMPLE: Stafford Connors, football player. PLACE-NAME USAGE: a county in Virginia, named in 1661 for Viscount Stafford; a town in Connecticut, named in 1718 for the city in England; Stafford, Texas, named for W.M. Stafford, landowner.

Stahrl   Origin unknown. CONTEMPORARY EXAMPLE: Stahrl W. Edmunds, author.

Stan   A pet form of many names, but primarily Stanley. *See* Stanley.

Stancil   Probably a form of the Middle English *stanchon*, meaning "an upright bar, a beam." CONTEMPORARY EXAMPLE: Stancil Powell, football player.

Stanford   From the Old English, meaning "a stone river crossing." CONTEMPORARY EXAMPLE: Stanford Friedman, professor of medicine.

Stanhope   From the Old English *stan* plus *hopa*, meaning "hope stone," on which one stood to see afar. SURNAME USAGE: Fitzroy Stanhope (1787-1864), English clergyman.

Stanislao   The Italian form of Stanislav. *See* Stanislav.

Stanislas   The French form of Stanislav. *See* Stanislav.

Stanislaus   A variant English form of Stanislav. *See* Stanislav. PLACE-NAME USAGE: Stanislaus, California.

Stanislav   From the Slavic, meaning "glory of the camp." A popular Polish name. VARIANT FORMS: Stanislaus, Stanislaw, Stanislus (English); Estanislau (Portuguese); Stanislao (Italian); Stanislas (French).

Stanislaw   A variant form of Stanislav. *See* Stanislav. CONTEMPORARY EXAMPLE: Stanislaw Kuczek, baseball player.

Stanislus   A variant form of Stanislav. *See* Stanislav.

Stanley   From the Old English *stan* plus *lea*, meaning "a stony meadow." Akin to Stansfield. Stan is a pet form. CONTEMPORARY EXAMPLE: Stanley Baldwin (1867-1947), British prime minister. SURNAME USAGE: Henry Morton Stanley (1841-1904), English explorer. PLACE-NAME USAGE: Mount Stanley, in Africa.

Stansfield   From the Old English *stans* plus *feld*, meaning "a field of stone." Akin to Stanley. *See* Stanley. CONTEMPORARY EXAMPLE: Stansfield Turner, director of the U.S. Central Intelligence Agency.

Stanton   From the Old English, meaning "the town near the stony field." Akin to Stanley and Stansfield. CONTEMPORARY EXAMPLE: Stanton Altgelt, golfer. SURNAME USAGE: Elizabeth Cady Stanton (1815-1902), U.S. suffragist leader.

Stanwood   From the Old English, meaning "a stony wooded area." Akin to Stanley and Stansfield. CONTEMPORARY EXAMPLE: Stanwood Baumgartner, baseball player.

Stefan   A variant spelling of the German Stephan. *See* Stephan.

Stefano   The Italian form of Stephen. *See* Stephen.

Stemsy   A nickname. Origin unknown. CONTEMPORARY EXAMPLE: Stemsy Hunter, rock musician.

Stephan   The German form of Stephen. *See* Stephen.

Stephen   From the Greek *stephanos,* meaning "a crown." In the Bible, one of the seven chosen to assist the apostles. A popular saint name. VARIANT FORMS: Stephanas (Greek); Stephanus (Latin); Etienne (French); Stephan (German); Stefano (Italian); Esteban (Spanish); Stepan (Russian); Stepka (Slavic); Stevan, Steven (English). Stephanie is the feminine form. PET FORMS: Steve, Stevie. SURNAME USAGE: Stephens, Stephenson, Steffens, Stevenson, Steverson, Stevens, Stinson, Stimpson, Stenson, Steenson.

Sterling   From the Middle English *sterlinge,* meaning "a silver penny." Also, possibly from the Old English *staerlinc,* meaning "a starling (bird)." CONTEMPORARY EXAMPLE: Sterling Hayden, actor. PLACE-NAME USAGE: Sterling, Connecticut, named for Dr. John Sterling, a local resident; Sterling, Idaho.

Stevan   An English variant form of Stephen. *See* Stephen. CONTEMPORARY EXAMPLE: Stevan Harnad, editor.

Steven   An English variant form of Stephen. *See* Stephen.

Stew   A pet form of Stewart. *See* Steward and Stuart.

Stewart   A variant form of Stuart. *See* Stuart. PLACE-NAME USAGE: Mount George Stewart, California, named for George W. Stewart, a founder of the Sequoia National Park.

Stillman   From the Old English *stael,* meaning "a stall, a station," hence "a man (servant) who cares for a station." CONTEMPORARY EXAMPLE: Stillman Drake, author and professor.

Stirling   A variant spelling of Sterling. *See* Sterling. CONTEMPORARY EXAMPLE: Stirling Cooper, educator. PLACE-NAME USAGE: a city in Scotland; Stirling, New Jersey, named for Lord Stirling, a Revolutionary War general.

Stobe   Origin unknown. CONTEMPORARY EXAMPLE: Stobe Talbott, diplomatic correspondent.

Stockton   From the Old English *stoc, stocc,* akin to the German *stock,* meaning "the trunk of a tree," hence "the town (*ton*) near the tree trunk." PLACE-NAME USAGE: a city in California, named for R.F. Stockton (1795-1866), a U.S. naval officer.

Storm   From the Old English, meaning "a storm." CONTEMPORARY EXAMPLE: Storm Field, television weather reporter. PLACE-NAME USAGE: Storm Canyon, Arizona.

Stover   From the Middle English, meaning "cured stalks of grain." CONTEMPORARY EXAMPLE: Stover Hire, motor boat racer.

Stringfellow   An occupational name used by persons engaged in stringing musical instruments. CONTEMPORARY EXAMPLE: Stringfellow Barr, author.

Strobe   From the Greek *strobos*, meaning "to twist around." CONTEMPORARY EXAMPLE: Strobe Talbott, journalist.

Strom   From the Greek *stroma*, meaning "a bed, a mattress." CONTEMPORARY EXAMPLE: J. Strom Thurmond, U.S. senator.

Struther   From the Latin *struthio*, meaning "an ostrich." CONTEMPORARY EXAMPLE: Struther Martin, film director.

Stu   A pet form of Stuart. *See* Stuart.

Stuart   From the Old English, meaning "a steward, a keeper of an estate." Used by the ruling family of Scotland and England from the fourteenth to the eighteenth century. Stewart is a variant spelling. Stu is a pet form.

Studs   From the Old English *studu*, meaning "a post, a pillar," and later, "a house." CONTEMPORARY EXAMPLE: Studs Terkel, author.

Styles   From the Latin name Stilus, meaning "a pointed instrument for writing," hence "one who writes." Probably an occupational name. CONTEMPORARY EXAMPLE: Styles Bridges, U.S. senator.

Sullivan   From the Old English *sul* or *syl*, meaning "a plough," plus the British *ban*, meaning "high, a high place," hence "a plowed plot on the hill." CONTEMPORARY EXAMPLE: Sullivan Mills, football player. SURNAME USAGE: John Sullivan (1858-1918), American prizefighter.

Sully   From the Old French, meaning "stain, tarnish." CONTEMPORARY EXAMPLE: Sully Boger, actor.

Sumner   From the Latin, meaning "one who summons or calls." CONTEMPORARY EXAMPLE: Sumner Welles, U.S. statesman. SURNAME USAGE: William Graham Sumner (1840)1910), American economist.

Sunny   A nickname which has become an independent name. Or, from the Old English *sunna*, meaning "the sun." CONTEMPORARY EXAMPLE: Sunny J. Levy, columnist.

Sutton   From the Old English *suth*, meaning "the town to the south." SURNAME USAGE: Percy Sutton, New York City politician.

Svarne   From Svear, the name of an ancient Swedish tribe. CONTEMPORARY EXAMPLE: Svarne Jenyns, author.

Sven   From Svealand, the earliest name of the area in which Sweden is located, named for the Swedish tribe called Svear. CONTEMPORARY EXAMPLE: Sven Anderson, badminton champion.

Svend   A variant form of Sven. *See* Sven. CONTEMPORARY EXAMPLE: Svend Otto, author.

Swen   A variant form of Sven. *See* Sven. CONTEMPORARY EXAMPLE: Swen Nater, basketball player.

Swithin, Swithun   From the Old English *swip*, meaning "strong."

Sy   A pet form of Seymour and Sylvan. *See* Seymour *and* Sylvan.

Sydney   A variant spelling of Sidney. *See* Sidney.

Sylvan   A variant form of Silvanus, meaning "forest, woods." *See also* Silvanus. VARIANT FORMS: Silvan, Sylvester, Sylvia. Sylvia is a feminine form.

Sylveanus   A variant form of Silvanus. *See* Silvanus. CONTEMPORARY EXAMPLE: Sylveanus Gregg, baseball player.

Sylvester   A variant form of Silvanus. *See* Silvanus. Akin to Sylvan. CONTEMPORARY EXAMPLE: Sylvester Stallone, actor.

Syshe   A Yiddish form of the German *suss*, meaning "street." VARIANT FORMS: Zisya, Zushe, Zusye.

T

Tab   A pet form of David. *See* David. Taffy is a variant form. CONTEMPORARY EXAMPLES: Tab Hunter, actor; Tab Brooke, author.

Tabbai   From the Aramaic, meaning "good."

Tabor   From the Persian *tabirah,* meaning "a drum." CONTEMPORARY EXAMPLE: Tabor McMoride, screenwriter. PLACE-NAME USAGE: a mountain in northern Israel.

Tad   A pet form of Thaddeus. *See* Thaddeus. Also, a nickname for Talmadge. Tod is a variant spelling. CONTEMPORARY EXAMPLE: Tad Mosel, author. PLACE-NAME USAGE: Tad, West Virginia, named for Talmadge (Tad) Dunlap, first postmaster.

Taffy   From the British *taf,* meaning "a river." Also, the Welsh nickname for David. (Davy pronounced Taffy). Tab is a variant form.

Taft   From the British *taf,* meaning "a river." Akin to Taffy. *See* Taffy. CONTEMPORARY EXAMPLE: Taft Reed, football player. SURNAME USAGE: William Howard Taft, twenty-seventh president of the U.S. (1857-1930). PLACE-NAME USAGE: cities in California, Oklahoma, and Texas.

Tal   From the Hebrew, meaning "dew" or "rain." Used as a masculine and feminine form in Israel. Also, from the British, meaning "the end of a lake."

Talbot   From the Old English, meaning "Botolph's River." Used by Chaucer as a nickname for a dog. CONTEMPORARY EXAMPLE: Talbot F. Hamlin, Pulitzer Prize winner in letters (1956).

Talcott   From the Old English, meaning "one who lives in a cottage near the lake." *See also* Tal.

Taldon   From the Celtic and the Old English, meaning "the lake near the hill (don). CONTEMPORARY EXAMPLE: Taldon Manton, football player.

Talia   From the Aramaic, meaning "a young lamb." Used also as a feminine name in Israel.

Talmadge   From the British, possibly meaning "the lake midway between two towns." Tad is a pet form. CONTEMPORARY EXAMPLE: Talmadge Maples, football player. SURNAME USAGE: Herman Talmadge, U.S. senator.

Talmai   From the Hebrew, meaning either "a furrow" or "a mound." In the Bible, father-in-law of King David.

Talman From the Aramaic, meaning "oppress, injure." Talmon is a variant spelling.

Talmi From the Hebrew, meaning "my mound, hill." Akin to Talmai.

Talmon A variant spelling of Talman. *See* Talman.

Talor From the Hebrew, meaning "dew of the morning."

Tamir From the Hebrew, meaning either "a hidden (sacred) vessel" or "tall, stately," as the palm tree.

Tamsen A Scandinavian patronymic form of Thomas, meaning "son of Thomas." *See* Thomas.

Tamson A patronymic form of Thomas, meaning "son of Thomas." *See* Thomas.

Tarky A nickname. Origin uncertain. CONTEMPORARY EXAMPLE: Tarky Lombardi, Jr., New York state senator.

Tarver From the Old English *tor*, meaning "a tower, a hill." Or, from the Old English *tawer*, meaning "a leader." CONTEMPORARY EXAMPLE: Tarver Hagen, university administrator.

Tate From the Old English *teotha*, meaning "a tenth, a tithing." Used also as a feminine name. CONTEMPORARY EXAMPLE: Tate Armstrong, basketball player.

Tavi From the Aramaic, meaning "good." Akin to Tobiah. *See* Tobiah.

Taylor An Old English occupational name, meaning "tailor." CONTEMPORARY EXAMPLE: Taylor Stoehr, historian. SURNAME USAGE: Zachary Taylor (1784-1850), twelfth president of the U.S.

Taz From the Arabic *tassa*, meaning "a shallow, ornamental cup." CONTEMPORARY EXAMPLE: Taz William Kinney, physician.

Tazwell A variant form of Taz. *See* Taz. CONTEMPORARY EXAMPLE: Tazwell Anderson, football player.

Teague From the Celtic, meaning "a poet." Also, an Irish form of Thadeus. Teige is a variant spelling. SURNAME USAGE: Bob Teague, television news reporter.

Ted, Teddy Pet forms of Theodore. *See* Theodore.

Teige A variant spelling of Teague. *See* Teague.

Telem From the Hebrew, meaning "a mound." Akin to Talmai. *See* Talmai.

Telford From the Latin *tellus*, meaning "earth," plus *ford*, meaning "a shallow stream." CONTEMPORARY EXAMPLE: Telford Taylor, law professor.

Telly   A pet form of Theodosios (Theodore), used among Greek–speaking people. CONTEMPORARY EXAMPLE: Telly Savalas, actor.

Telmo   Possibly from the Old English *tillan*, meaning "to till, cultivate." CONTEMPORARY EXAMPLE: Telmo Pires, soccer player.

Teman, Temani   From the Hebrew *yamin*, meaning "right side," denoting the south. (The south is to the right of a person as he faces east, towards Jerusalem.) The form Temani, meaning "a man from Teman," is used in Israel, and refers primarily to new settlers who came from Yemen (*Teman*).

Temple   From the Latin *templum*, meaning "a sanctuary." CONTEMPORARY EXAMPLE: Temple Fielding, author. PLACE-NAME USAGE: Temple, Pennsylvania.

Templeton   From the Old English, meaning "a town in which a sanctuary is situated." CONTEMPORARY EXAMPLE: Templeton Parcely, rock musician.

Tennessee   From Tanasi, a Cherokee Indian village name. Meaning unknown. CONTEMPORARY EXAMPLE: Tennessee Williams, playwright. PLACE-NAME USAGE: a southern U.S. state; Tennessee, California.

Tennis   A patronymic form, meaning "son of Tenny (Dennis)." *See* Dennis.

Tennyson   A patronymic form, meaning "son of Tenny (Dennis)." *See* Dennis. Tennis is a variant form. SURNAME USAGE: Alfred Tennyson, poet.

Teodoro   A Spanish form of Theodore. *See* Theodore. CONTEMPORARY EXAMPLE: Teodoro Martinez, baseball player.

Terence, Terrence   From the Latin, meaning "tender, good, gracious." Terentius was an early Roman family name. Terry is a pet form. CONTEMPORARY EXAMPLE: Terence Cardinal Cooke, clergyman; Terrence McNally, playwright.

Terrance   A variant spelling of Terrence. *See* Terrence. CONTEMPORARY EXAMPLE: Terrance Dill, golfer.

Terrel   Probably a variant form of Terrence. *See* Terrence. CONTEMPORARY EXAMPLE: Terrel H. Bell, educator.

Terris   Probably a patronymic form of Terry, meaning "son of Terry." *See* Terry. CONTEMPORARY EXAMPLE: Terris Temple, Maui, Hawaii.

Terry   A pet form of Terrence. *See* Terrence.

Terryal   A variant form of Terry. *See* Terry. CONTEMPORARY EXAMPLE: Terryal Humphrey, baseball player.

Tex   A nickname for a Texan. CONTEMPORARY EXAMPLE: Tex Hughson, baseball player.

Thad   A pet form of Thadeus. *See* Thadeus. CONTEMPORARY EXAMPLE: Thad Cochran, U.S. senator.

Thadeus, Thaddeus   From the Greek, meaning "gift of God." Variant Latin forms of the Greek Theodosius. Akin to Theodore. Thad is a pet form. CONTEMPORARY EXAMPLE: Thaddeus Kwalick, football player.

Thadford   From the Old English, meaning "Thad's (Thadeus's) crossing (ford)." CONTEMPORARY EXAMPLE: Thadford Treadway, baseball player.

Thady   A pet form of Thadeus. *See* Thadeus.

Thalmus   From the Greek *thallos*, meaning "a young shoot, a sprout." CONTEMPORARY EXAMPLE: Thalmus Rasulala, actor.

Than   From the Greek, meaning "death." A pet form of Thanatos.

Thanatos   In Greek mythology, death personified.

Thane   From the Middle English *thayne*, meaning "to engender, to beget," hence "a freeborn man." CONTEMPORARY EXAMPLE: Thane Baker, Olympic track star.

Thann   A variant spelling of Than. *See* Than. CONTEMPORARY EXAMPLE: Thann Wyenn, actor.

Tharon   A variant spelling of Theron. CONTEMPORARY EXAMPLE: Tharon Collins, baseball player.

Thatcher   An occupational name. From the Old English *thac*, meaning "one who fixes roofs."

Thayer   A name meaning "of the nation's army." CONTEMPORARY EXAMPLE: Thayer David, actor.

Thel   From the Old English *thel*, meaning "an upper story." CONTEMPORARY EXAMPLE: Thel Fisher, football player.

Theo   A pet form of Theobald and Theodore. *See* Theobald *and* Theodore. CONTEMPORARY EXAMPLE: Theo Arinson, author.

Theobald, Theobold   From the Old German name Theudobald, compounded of *theuda*, meaning "people, folk," and *bald*, meaning "bold." VARIANT FORMS: Tebald, Tibald, Tibbald. Theo is a pet form.

Theodor, Theodore   From the Greek *theos*, meaning "God," plus *doron*, meaning "gift," hence "divine gift." Theodore was a seventh-century Archbishop of Canterbury. VARIANT FORMS: Teodoro

(Spanish); Theodoro (Portuguese); Fedor, Feodor, Fyoder (Russian); Tudor (Welsh); Feodore (Polish). Theodora is a feminine form. PET FORMS: Ted, Teddy, Theo.

Theodoric   A variant form of Theodric. *See* Theodric.

Theodosius   From the Greek, meaning "gift of God." Akin to Theodore.

Theodric   From the Old German name Thiudoricus. Compounded of *theuda*, meaning "folk, people," and *ric*, meaning "ruler," hence "ruler of the people." VARIANT FORMS: Theodore (English); Thierry (French). PET FORMS: Derek, Terry.

Theophillus, Theophilus   From the Greek, meaning "beloved of God." In the Bible, the person to whom St. Luke's Gospel was addressed. CONTEMPORARY EXAMPLE: Theophillus Neal, baseball player.

Theorus   A name invented by combining Theodore and Russell. *See* Theodore *and* Russell. CONTEMPORARY EXAMPLE: Theorus Stoner, Hilo, Hawaii.

Theron   From the Greek, meaning "a hunter." Tharon is a variant spelling. CONTEMPORARY EXAMPLE: Theron B. Maxson, educator.

Thom   A pet form of Thomas. *See* Thomas. CONTEMPORARY EXAMPLE: Thom Mooney, rock musician.

Thomas   From the Hebrew and Aramaic *t'ome*, meaning "a twin." Also, from the Phonecian, meaning "sun god." In the Bible, one of the twelve apostles is Didymus, a Greek name, meaning "twin." VARIANT FORMS: Tam, Tamlane (Scotch); Tomas, Tome (Spanish); Maso, Tomaso (Italian); Foma (Russian); Thoma (German); Tamas (Hungarian). PET FORMS: Thom, Tom, Tommie, Tommy. FEMININE FORMS: Tami, Tammy, Thomasine.

Thompson   A patronymic form, meaning "son of Thomas." Commonly as a surname. CONTEMPORARY EXAMPLE: Thompson Clayton, author.

Thor   In Norse mythology, the god of thunder and war. Thor was the eldest son of Odin, creator of the world. CONTEMPORARY EXAMPLE: Thor Heyerdahl, explorer.

Thork   A Gaelic form of Thor. *See* Thor.

Thorndike   From the Old English, meaning "the hedge thorn," hence "a dike near the hawthorne tree." CONTEMPORARY EXAMPLE: Thorndike Hawkes, baseball player.

Thornton   From the Anglo-Saxon, meaning "from the thorny place (town)." CONTEMPORARY EXAMPLE: Thornton Wilder, playwright.

Thorold   A variant form of Thor. *See* Thor. VARIANT FORMS: Turrell, Terrell, Tirrell, Tirrell, Tyrell.

Thorpe   From the Old English, meaning "a farm house." SURNAME USAGE: Jim Thorpe, athlete.

Thorwald   From the Old English, meaning "Thor's forest." *See* Thor. CONTEMPORARY EXAMPLE: Thorwald Salverson, football player.

Thron   From the Greek *thronos*, meaning "a seat of royalty, a throne." CONTEMPORARY EXAMPLE: Thron Riggs, football player.

Thruston   A variant form of Thurston. *See* Thurston. CONTEMPORARY EXAMPLE: Thruston Morton, statesman.

Thunderbird   From the Old English, meaning "the bird of Thor." *See* Thor. CONTEMPORARY EXAMPLE: Thunderbird Hawkins, Indian mystic.

Thurgood   From the Old English, meaning "Thor is good." *See* Thor. CONTEMPORARY EXAMPLE: Thurgood Marshall, U.S. Supreme Court Justice.

Thurlow   From Thor plus *loe*, meaning "a hill," hence "Thor's sanctuary." *See* Thor. CONTEMPORARY EXAMPLE: Thurlow Cooper, football player.

Thurman   From the Norse and Old English, meaning "servant of Thor." *See* Thor. CONTEMPORARY EXAMPLE: Thurman Munson, baseball player.

Thurmon   A variant spelling of Thurman. *See* Thurman. CONTEMPORARY EXAMPLE: Thurmon M. Spencer, football player.

Thurstan, Thurston   From the Scandinavian, compounded of Thor and *stan* (*stein*), meaning "stone," hence "Thor's stone or jewel." SURNAME USAGE: Ted Thurston, actor.

Tibon   From the Hebrew, meaning "a naturalist, a student of nature." Tivon is a variant form.

Tibor   From the Old English *tiber*, meaning "holy, a holy place, an altar." CONTEMPORARY EXAMPLE: Tibor Molnar, soccer player.

Tige   Possibly a nickname for Tiger. *See* Tiger. CONTEMPORARY EXAMPLE: Tige Andrews, actor.

Tiger   From the Iranian *tigra*, meaning "sharp." An animal name used occasionally in the U.S. CONTEMPORARY EXAMPLE: Tiger Haynes, musician. PLACE-NAME USAGE: Tiger, Oklahoma.

Tilden   From the Anglo-Saxon, meaning "a tilled or fertile valley." CONTEMPORARY EXAMPLE: Tilden Edwards, author. SURNAME USAGE: Bill Tilden, tennis player. PLACE-NAME USAGE: Tilden, Pennsylvania, named for Samuel H. Tilden, presidential candidate (1876).

Tilghman   From the Old English *tille*, meaning "a station," hence "one who works at or guards a station." CONTEMPORARY EXAMPLE: Tilghman Aley, educator.

Tilly A pet form of Tilden or Tilghman. *See* Tilden *and* Tilghman. CONTEMPORARY EXAMPLE: Tilly Shafer, baseball player.

Tim A pet form of Timothy. *See* Timothy.

Timmy A pet form of Timothy. *See* Timothy.

Timothy From the Greek, meaning "to honor God." In the Bible, a companion of St. Paul. Thaddeus is an Old Greek variant. PET FORMS: Tad, Tim, Timmy. PLACE-NAME USAGE: Timothy, Minnesota.

Timur From the Hebrew, meaning "tall, stately." A variant form of Tamar, meaning "a stately palm tree."

Tino An Italian suffix meaning "small." Also, a pet form of Tony. *See* Tony. CONTEMPORARY EXAMPLE: Tino Sabuco, baseball player.

Tinsley From the Old English *din*, meaning "fortification," plus *lea*, meaning "meadow," hence "the fortification in or near the meadow." CONTEMPORARY EXAMPLE: Tinsley Ginn, baseball player. PLACE-NAME USAGE: a locality in Yorkshire, England.

Tip A nickname for Thomas. CONTEMPORARY EXAMPLE: Thomas (Tip) O'Neill, U.S. congressman.

Tito A variant form of Titos. *See* Titos. The name adopted by Yugoslav President Marshal Tito (1892-), born Josip Broz. CONTEMPORARY EXAMPLE: Tito Francona, baseball player.

Titos From the Greek name Titan, meaning "a person or thing of great size and power." CONTEMPORARY EXAMPLE: Titos Vandis, actor.

Titus The Latin form of Titos. *See* Titos. Titus Vespasianus was a first–century Roman general, son of Vespasian. In the Bible, a disciple of St. Paul. CONTEMPORARY EXAMPLE: Titus Sheard, U.S. political leader.

Tivon A variant form of Tibon. *See* Tibon.

Tobiah From the Hebrew, meaning "the Lord is my good." Tobias is a Greek form. PET FORMS: Tobey, Tobin, Tobyn. Tobit is a feminine form.

Tobias The Greek form of Tobiah. *See* Tobiah.

Tobey A variant spelling of Toby. *See* Toby.

Tobin A pet form of Tobiah. *See* Tobiah. CONTEMPORARY EXAMPLE: Tobin Rote, football player.

Toby A pet form of Tobiah. *See* Tobiah.

Tobyn A pet form of Tobiah. *See* Tobiah.

Tod, Todd From the Old English *tod*, meaning "fox." Also, a pet form of Robert, and a variant spelling of Tad. *See* Robert *and* Tad.

Tolbert A variant form of Talbot. *See* Talbot. CONTEMPORARY EXAM-

PLE: Tolbert Lanston, inventor.

Tolia   Origin unknown. CONTEMPORARY EXAMPLE: Tolia Solaito, baseball player.

Toller   From the Old English *toll*, meaning "one who levies or collects taxes." CONTEMPORARY EXAMPLE: Toller Cranston, figure skater.

Tom   A pet form of Thomas. *See* Thomas.

Tomas   A variant form of Thomas. *See* Thomas. CONTEMPORARY EXAMPLE: Tomas Blanco, author.

Tomie, Tommie   Pet forms of Thomas. *See* Thomas. The pet name of President (Thomas) Woodrow Wilson was Tommie. CONTEMPORARY EXAMPLE: Tomie de Pada, author.

Tommy   A pet form of Thomas. *See* Thomas.

Toney   A variant spelling of Tony. *See* Tony. CONTEMPORARY EXAMPLE: Toney P. Brown, educator.

Toni, Tony   Pet forms of Anthony. *See* Anthony. Toni is also a feminine form. PLACE-NAME USAGE: Tony Creek, Oregon.

Topo   From the Spanish, meaning "a mole, a gopher."

Topper   From the British *top*, meaning "a hill." CONTEMPORARY EXAMPLE: Topper Rigney, baseball player.

Torbert   From the Anglo-Saxon *tor*, meaning "hill," and *bert*, meaning "bright." CONTEMPORARY EXAMPLE: Torbert H. MacDonald, U.S. congressman.

Torn   A pet form of Torrance. *See* Torrance. Also, from the Dutch *toren*, meaning "a tower." SURNAME USAGE: Rip Torn, entertainer. PLACE-NAME USAGE: Torn, New Jersey.

Torrance, Torrence   An Irish form of Terence. *See* Terence. CONTEMPORARY EXAMPLE: Torrance Russell, football player.

Torrey   A pet form of Torrance. *See* Torrance. CONTEMPORARY EXAMPLE: Torrey Sun, figure skater.

Tory   A variant spelling of Torrey. *See* Torrey.

Tov   From the Hebrew, meaning "good." Tovi is a variant form. Akin to Tobiah and Tobias.

Tovi   From the Hebrew, meaning "my good." *See also* Tov.

Townsend   From the Anglo-Saxon, meaning "the end of town." CONTEMPORARY EXAMPLE: Townsend Hoopes, publisher.

Toxey   Origin unknown. CONTEMPORARY EXAMPLE: Toxey French, rock musician.

Tracey, Tracy   From the Old French, meaning "path" or "road." Also, a pet form of Christina. *See* Christina in feminine section. A popular name in England for both boys and girls.

Trader   From the Middle English *trede*, meaning "a tread, a path," hence "a skilled worker." CONTEMPORARY EXAMPLE: Trader Faulkner, actor.

Traphes   Meaning uncertain. Possibly, from the Greek *trephein*, meaning "to nourish." CONTEMPORARY EXAMPLE: Traphes Bryant, author.

Travers   A variant form of Travis. *See* Travis.

Travis   From the Latin and French, meaning "crossroads." CONTEMPORARY EXAMPLE: Travis White, educator.

Trenton   From the French *trente*, meaning "thirty." CONTEMPORARY EXAMPLE: Trenton Jackson, football player; Trenton E. Williams, Lincoln, Nebraska. PLACE-NAME USAGE: Trenton, New Jersey, named for William Trent (1655-1725), early colonist; a city in Italy where the Council of Trent was held (1545-63).

Treva   A variant form of the French *trier*, meaning "to assign priorities." Akin to Trevor. *See* Trevor. CONTEMPORARY EXAMPLE: Treva Bolin, football player.

Trevor   From the Celtic, meaning "prudent." Akin to Treva. *See* Treva. CONTEMPORARY EXAMPLE: Trevor Wallace, film producer.

Trini   From the Latin *trinitas*, meaning "three, trinity." CONTEMPORARY EXAMPLE: Trini Lopez, musician.

Tristam   A variant form of the Celtic Drystan, meaning "tumult, noise." Also, a variant form of Tristram. *See* Tristram. CONTEMPORARY EXAMPLE: Tristam Potter Coffin, author.

Tristan   An Old French form of Tristram. *See* Tristram. CONTEMPORARY EXAMPLE: Tristan Jones, author.

Tristram   A variant form of the Old French name Tristran and Tristan. Derived from the Latin *tristis*, meaning "sad." In medieval legend, a knight sent to Ireland by King Mark of Cornwall to bring back the princess Isolde to be his bride.

Trot   From the British *trothy*, meaning "a trickling stream."

Troy   From the Greek name Troia, a form of Tros, father of Ilos in Homer's *The Illiad*. Also, from the British *wye*, meaning "water." CONTEMPORARY EXAMPLE: Troy Howell, artist. PLACE-NAME USAGE: Troy, New York; Troyes, France.

Trubo   From the British, meaning "the town near the hilly path." SURNAME USAGE: Richard Trubo, author.

Truby   A variant form of Trubo. *See* Trubo.

Truett From the Middle English *treue*, meaning "true." CONTEMPO-RARY EXAMPLE: Truett Sewell, baseball player.

Truman From the Anglo-Saxon, meaning "a true, loyal man." CON-TEMPORARY EXAMPLE: Truman Capote, author. SURNAME USAGE: Harry S. Truman (1884-1972), thirty-third president of the U.S.

Trygve From the British, meaning "the town (*tre*) by the water (*vy*)." CONTEMPORARY EXAMPLE: Trygve Lie, United Nations director.

Tucker An English occupational name, meaning "one who cleans and thickens cloth." CONTEMPORARY EXAMPLE: Tucker P. Smith, U.S. vice-presidential candidate (1948). SURNAME USAGE: Richard Tucker, opera singer.

Tug From the Old Norse *toga*, meaning "to draw, to pull." CONTEM-PORARY EXAMPLE: Tug McGraw, baseball player. PLACE-NAME USAGE: Tug Fork, West Virginia.

Tullis, Tullos From the Latin *titulus*, meaning "a title, a rank." Variant forms of Tullius (Marcus Tullius Cicero). CONTEMPORARY EX-AMPLE: Tullis McGowan and Tullos (Tully) Hartsel, baseball players.

Tully A pet form of Tullis and Tullos. *See* Tullis. Used in Scotland and Ireland. PLACE-NAME USAGE: a town in Scotland.

Turk A nickname usually for a person from Turkey. CONTEMPORARY EXAMPLE: Turk Edwards, football player.

Turner From the Latin, meaning "a worker with a lathe."

Tuvia From the Hebrew, meaning "God is good" or "goodness of God." Tobias is the Anglicized form.

Twy A variant form of Ty. *See* Ty.

Ty From the British, meaning "a house." Twy is a variant form. *See also* Tyrus. CONTEMPORARY EXAMPLE: (Tyrus) Ty Cobb, baseball player. PLACE-NAME USAGE: Ty, Georgia.

Tydeus In Greek legend, the father of Diomedes, and one of the seven heroes who helped one of their number recover his share of the throne of Thebes.

Tyger A variant spelling of Tiger. *See* Tiger. PLACE-NAME USAGE: Tyger River, South Carolina.

Tyler From the British, possibly meaning "a house builder." Ty is a pet form. CONTEMPORARY EXAMPLE: Tyler Wasson, film producer. SUR-NAME USAGE: John Tyler (1790-1862), tenth president of the U.S. PLACE-NAME USAGE: Tyler, Texas.

Tyron, Tyrone From the Latin *tiro*, meaning "a young soldier." Also, an Old English form of Thor. *See* Thor. CONTEMPORARY EXAM-PLE: Tyrone Power, actor. PLACE-NAME USAGE: Tyrone, a former county of Northern Ireland.

Tyrus From the Latin Tyrus, meaning "a person from Tyre," a seaport in southwestern Lebanon. Ty is a pet form. CONTEMPORARY EXAMPLE: Tyrus (Ty) Cobb, baseball player.

Tyson A patronymic form, meaning "the son of Ty." *See* Ty.

Tzevi, Tzvi From the Hebrew, meaning "a deer." VARIANT SPELLINGS: Zevi, Zvi.

U

Udo A Japanese plant of the Ginseng family. CONTEMPORARY EXAMPLE: Udo Kultermann, art critic.

Uel A short form of Samuel. *See* Samuel. CONTEMPORARY EXAMPLE: Uel Wade, musician.

Uku From the Hawaiian, meaning "a flea, an insect," hence "to jump." A nickname for one adept at the ukulele, a musical instrument introduced into Hawaii from Portugal. CONTEMPORARY EXAMPLE: Uku Meri.

Ulf, Ulfa Variant forms of Ull. *See* Ull.

Ulises A variant spelling of Ulysses. *See* Ulysses. CONTEMPORARY EXAMPLE: Ulises Wensell, artist.

Ull A variant form of Ulrich. *See* Ulrich. In Norse mythology, the son of Sif, stepson of Thor. VARIANT FORMS: Ulf, Ulfa, Ulric, Ulrich, Ulrick, Ulu.

Ulmo From Ulm, a city in Baden-Wurttemberg in southwest Germany, on the Danube. Akin to Ull. CONTEMPORARY EXAMPLE: Ulmo Randle, football player.

Ulric, Ulrich, Ulrick From the Danish, meaning "a wolf." *See also* Ull. CONTEMPORARY EXAMPLE: Ulrich Schaeffer, author.

Ulu A variant form of Ull. *See* Ull. CONTEMPORARY EXAMPLE: Ulu Grossbard, theatrical producer.

Ulysses The Latin name of Odysseus, the hero of Homer's *The Odyssey*, a king of Ithaca and one of the Greek heroes of the Trojan War. CONTEMPORARY EXAMPLE: Ulysses Simpson Grant (1822-1885), eighteenth president of the U.S. PLACE-NAME USAGE: cities in New York, Nebraska, and Kansas.

Umberto From the Italian *terra d'ombre*, meaning "shade (color) of the earth." Also, a variant Italian form of Humbert. Humbert I was a king of Italy (1878-1900). CONTEMPORARY EXAMPLE: Umberto Saba, poet.

Upshaw From the Old English, meaning "the upper wooded area." CONTEMPORARY EXAMPLE: Upshaw Bentley, U.S. city mayor.

Upton From the Anglo-Saxon, meaning "the upper town." CONTEMPORARY EXAMPLE: Upton Sinclair, Pulitzer Prize winner in letters (1943). PLACE-NAME USAGE: cities in Massachusetts, North Carolina, and Utah.

Urban From the Latin *urbanus*, meaning "a city." Urban II was an eleventh–century pope (1088-1099). Urbane is a variant form. CONTEMPORARY EXAMPLE: Urban T. Holmes, theologian.

Urbane A variant form of Urban. *See* Urban. CONTEMPORARY EXAMPLE: Urbane Pickering, baseball player.

Uri From the Hebrew, meaning "my light." CONTEMPORARY EXAMPLE: Uri Almago, sociologist.

Uriah From the Hebrew, meaning "God is my light." In the Bible, the husband of Bathsheba, before she became King David's wife.

Urie A variant spelling of Uri. *See* Uri.

Uriel From the Hebrew, meaning "God is my light." Akin to Uriah. In Jewish legend, one of four angels who ministers in God's presence.

Ursel From the Latin *ursus*, meaning "a bear." Ursula is the feminine form. CONTEMPORARY EXAMPLE: Ursel Norman, author.

Urshell A variant form of Ursel. *See* Ursel. CONTEMPORARY EXAMPLE: Urshell Whitlenton, football player.

Uwe Probably a variant form of the British *uch*, meaning "higher, above." CONTEMPORARY EXAMPLE: Uwe George, author.

Uzi From the Hebrew, meaning "my strength." CONTEMPORARY EXAMPLE: Uzi Arad, scientist.

V

Vachel A French occupational name, meaning "one who raises cows." Also, possibly from the British *vaches*, a variant form of *machen*, meaning "a little ash tree." CONTEMPORARY EXAMPLE: (Nicholas) Vachel Lindsay, poet.

Vada From the Latin *vadum*, meaning "a shallow place, a ford." CONTEMPORARY EXAMPLE: Vada Pinson, baseball player.

Vail From the Latin *vallis*, meaning "the valley." Val is a French form. VARIANT SPELLINGS: Vale, Valle.

Val The French form of Vail. *See* Vail. Also a pet form of Valentine. *See* Valentine. CONTEMPORARY EXAMPLE: Val de Vargas, actor.

Vale A variant spelling of Vail. *See* Vail.

Valentine From the Latin *valere*, meaning "strong, valorous." Akin to Valerius. A third-century saint. Val is a pet form. CONTEMPORARY EXAMPLE: Valentine Healy, educator. PLACE-NAME USAGE: Valentine, Nebraska, named for E.K. Valentine, a local resident.

Valentinian A variant form of the Latin name Valentinianus, an early form of Valentine. *See* Valentine. Valentinian was the name of three Roman emperors.

Valentino An Italian form of Valentine. *See* Valentine. SURNAME USAGE: Rudolph Valentino.

Valerian An Anglo–Saxon form of the Latin Valerianus, a third–century Roman emperor. A variant form of Valerius. *See* Valerius.

Valerio A Spanish form of Valerius. *See* Valerius. CONTEMPORARY EXAMPLE: Valerio Jansante.

Valerius From the Latin *valere*, meaning "to be strong." Akin to Valentine. A Roman family name. VARIANT FORMS: Valerian, Valery, Valerio.

Valery The French form of Valerius. *See* Valerius. CONTEMPORARY EXAMPLE: Valery Giscard d'Estang, president of France.

Vali In Norse mythology, a son of Odin, creator of the world. Also, a variant form of Valentine. *See* Valentine.

Valle A variant French form of Vali. *See* Vali.

Vallie A pet form of Valery and Valentine. *See* Valery *and* Valentine. CONTEMPORARY EXAMPLE: Vallie Eaves, baseball player.

269

Vamer   Origin uncertain. Possibly related to the Old English, French, and Latin *mer, mere*, meaning "sea."

Van   The Dutch form of the German *von*, meaning "from" a particular city. Akin to the French *de*. Possibly derived from the British *faen*, meaning "a rock, a boundary," hence "a locality, a region." CONTEMPORARY EXAMPLE: Van Cliburn, pianist.

Vance   A form of the British name Vans, from *fannau*, meaning "high, high places." CONTEMPORARY EXAMPLE: Vance Brand, astronaut. SURNAME USAGE: Cyrus Vance, U.S. statesman.

Vander   Probably from the Dutch, meaning "of the" or "from the," a prefix to many place-names. CONTEMPORARY EXAMPLE: Vander Beatty, New York state senator.

Van Dyke   From the Dutch, meaning "a person living in the region of the dike." *See also* Van. CONTEMPORARY EXAMPLE: Van Dyke Parks. SURNAME USAGE: Van Dyck (Sir Anthony), seventeenth–century Flemish painter; Dick van Dyke, actor.

Vane   A variant form of Van. *See* Van. CONTEMPORARY EXAMPLE: Vane Vest, ballet dancer. SURNAME USAGE: Henry Vane, seventeenth–century colonial governor of Massachusetts.

Vanne   A variant spelling of Van. *See* Van.

Varner   Probably a variant form of Werner. *See* Werner. Also, a variant form of Vernon. *See* Vernon. CONTEMPORARY EXAMPLE: Varner L. Paddack, U.S. city mayor.

Varney   A variant form of Varner or Vernon. *See* Varner *and* Vernon. SURNAME USAGE: Carlton Varney, home decorator.

Vaughan, Vaughn   From the Celtic, meaning "small." CONTEMPORARY EXAMPLE: Vaughn Monroe, singer. SURNAME USAGE: Robert Vaughn, actor.

Vean   Probably a variant form of Venice. *See* Venice. CONTEMPORARY EXAMPLE: Vean Gregg, baseball player.

Vedie   Probably from the Latin *vidi*, meaning "to see." CONTEMPORARY EXAMPLE: Vedie Himsl, baseball player.

Venice   From the Latin *venia*, meaning "a grace, a favor." Akin to Venus, the goddess of love in Roman mythology. The Veneti were an ancient Italian people (now extinct) who lived in the area that became known as Venice. CONTEMPORARY EXAMPLE: Venice Farrar, football player. PLACE-NAME USAGE: a city in Italy; cities in California and Ohio.

Venn   From the British *wen* or *gwen*, meaning "fair, beautiful." SURNAME USAGE: John Venn (1834-1923), English logician.

Ventan   A variant form of Venice. *See* Venice. CONTEMPORARY EXAM-

PLE: Ventan Yablonski, football player.

Verda   From the Old French *verd*, meaning "green." CONTEMPORARY EXAMPLE: Verda Carpenter, football player.

Verdi   From the Old French *verd*, meaning "green, springlike." Used also as a feminine form. SURNAME USAGE: Giuseppe Verdi (1813-1901),

Verdo   A variant form of Verda. *See* Verda. CONTEMPORARY EXAMPLE: Verdo Elmore, baseball player.

Vere   A French form of the Latin *verus*, meaning "true." Vera is the feminine form. A rare eighteenth-century name used in England.

Vered   From the Hebrew, meaning "a rose."

Vergit   A variant spelling of Virgil. *See* Virgil.

Verion   From the Latin *ver*, meaning "spring," hence "flourishing."

Verle   A variant form of Verlin. *See* Verlin. CONTEMPORARY EXAMPLE: Verle N. Vevan, U.S. city mayor.

Verlin   From the Latin *ver*, meaning "spring," hence "flourishing." CONTEMPORARY EXAMPLE: Verlin Adams, football player.

Verlon   A variant spelling of Verlin. *See* Verlin. CONTEMPORARY EXAMPLE: Verlon Biggs, football player.

Vern   From the British *gwern*, meaning "an alder tree." Or, a pet form of Vernon. *See* Vernon. CONTEMPORARY EXAMPLE: Vern G. Williamsen, professor.

Vernal   From the Latin *vernalis*, meaning "belonging to spring." CONTEMPORARY EXAMPLE: Vernal Jones, baseball player.

Verne   A variant spelling of Vern. *See* Vern. SURNAME USAGE: Jules Verne (1828-1905), French novelist. PLACE-NAME USAGE: LaVerne, California.

Vernice   A variant form of Vern. *See* Vern. CONTEMPORARY EXAMPLE: Vernice Herod, Sallis, Mississippi.

Vernon   From the Latin *vernalis* and *vernus*, meaning "belonging to spring," hence "flourishing." Also from the British *gwern*, meaning "an alder tree." PET FORMS: Vern, Verne. CONTEMPORARY EXAMPLE: Vernon Cheadle, educator. SURNAME USAGE: Jackie Vernon, comedian. PLACE-NAME USAGE: Mt. Vernon, New York.

Verrier   From the Latin *ver*, meaning "spring," hence "flourishing." CONTEMPORARY EXAMPLE: Verrier Elwin, author.

Versil   From the Latin *versus*, meaning "a verse, a line, a row." CONTEMPORARY EXAMPLE: Versil Deskin, football player.

Vester   A pet form of Sylvester. *See* Sylvester. Also, the masculine form of Vesta, who in Roman mythology is the goddess of the hearth;

akin to Hestia in Greek mythology. CONTEMPORARY EXAMPLE: Vester Presley, uncle of singer Elvis Presley.

Veston   From the Latin *vestis*, meaning "a garment," generally applied to the vestments of the clergy, hence "a town of churches." CONTEMPORARY EXAMPLE: Veston Stewart, baseball player.

Vibert   From the French *vie*, meaning "life," plus the Old English *beort*, meaning "bright," hence "full of good cheer, vivacious." CONTEMPORARY EXAMPLE: Vibert Clarke, baseball player.

Vic   A pet form of Victor. *See* Victor. CONTEMPORARY EXAMPLE: Vic Miles, television newscaster.

Vicente   From the Latin *viceni*, meaning "twenty." Derived from Vicenza, a town in Italy. CONTEMPORARY EXAMPLE: Vicente Amor, baseball player.

Vickie   A pet form of Victor. *See* Victor.

Victor   From the Latin *vincere*, meaning "victor, conqueror." Three kings of Sardinia and Italy were named Victor Emmanuel, between 1759 and 1947. PET FORMS: Vic, Vickie. Victoria is the feminine form. PLACE-NAME USAGE: Victorville, California, named for J.N. Victor, a railroad official.

Vida   A variant form of Vitas. *See* Vitas. Used also as a form of Davida. *See* Davida (feminine section). CONTEMPORARY EXAMPLE: Vida Blue, baseball player.

Vidal   A variant form of Vida. *See* Vida. CONTEMPORARY EXAMPLE: Vidal Sassoon, hair stylist. PLACE-NAME USAGE: Vidal Bayou, Louisiana, named for Jose Vidal, an eighteenth-century Spanish officer.

Viktor   A Russian form of Victor. *See* Victor. CONTEMPORARY EXAMPLE: Viktor Korchnoi, chessmaster.

Vin   A pet form of Vincent. *See* Vincent.

Vince   A pet form of Vincent. *See* Vincent. CONTEMPORARY EXAMPLE: Vince Lombardi, football coach.

Vincent   From the Latin *vincere*, meaning "victor, conqueror." Akin to Victor. PET FORMS: Vin, Vince, Vine, Vinnie. Vincent van Gogh (1853-1890) was a Dutch painter.

Vincente   A variant form of Vincent. *See* Vincent. CONTEMPORARY EXAMPLE: Vincente Minnelli, film director.

Vine   A pet form of Vincent. *See* Vincent. CONTEMPORARY EXAMPLE: Vine Deloria, Jr., author.

Vinicent   A variant spelling of Vincent. *See* Vincent.

Vinicio   A Spanish form of Venice. *See* Venice. Also, a variant form of Vincent. *See* Vincent. CONTEMPORARY EXAMPLE: Vincio Garcia, baseball player.

Vinson   A patronymic form, meaning "the son of Vincent." *See* Vincent. SURNAME USAGE: Fred M. Vinson, U.S. Supreme Court Justice.

Virgil   From the Latin, meaning "strong, flourishing." Vergil is a variant spelling. Vergilius is the Roman family to which the poet Virgil belonged. CONTEMPORARY EXAMPLE: Virgil I. Grissom, astronaut.

Virgilio   The Spanish form of Virgil. *See* Virgil. CONTEMPORARY EXAMPLE: Virgilio P. Elizondo, theologian.

Virginius   From the Latin *virgo*, meaning "untouched, pure." An ancient Roman family name. Virginia is the feminine form. CONTEMPORARY EXAMPLE: Virginius Dabney, Pulitzer Prize winner in journalism (1948).

Virl   A variant spelling of Verle. *See* Verle. CONTEMPORARY EXAMPLE: Virl Doolin, airplane pilot.

Virle   A variant spelling of Verle. *See* Verle. CONTEMPORARY EXAMPLE: Virle Rounsaville, baseball player.

Viron   From the Latin *ver*, meaning "spring," hence "flourishing."

Vitalis   From the Latin *vitalis*, meaning "alive, vital." The name of several early saints.

Vitas   From the Latin *vita*, meaning "life." CONTEMPORARY EXAMPLE: Vitas Gerulaitis, tennis player.

Vito   A pet form of Vittorio. *See* Vittorio.

Vittorio   The Italian form of Victor. Vittoria is the feminine form. CONTEMPORARY EXAMPLE: Vittorio Orlando (1860-1952), Italian statesman.

Vivian, Vivien, Vyvyan   Used primarily as feminine names. *See* Vivian (feminine section). CONTEMPORARY EXAMPLE: Vivian Holtman, football player.

Vladimir, Vladmir   From the Slavic, meaning "world prince." Vladimir I was a ruler of Russia (980-1015). CONTEMPORARY EXAMPLE: Vladimir Horowitz, concert pianist. PLACE-NAME USAGE: a city in Russia.

Volley   From the Latin *volare*, meaning "to fly." CONTEMPORARY EXAMPLE: Volley Murphy, football player.

Vollon   A variant form of Volley. *See* Volley. CONTEMPORARY EXAMPLE: Vollon Dixon, football player.

Volney   A variant form of Volley. *See* Volley. CONTEMPORARY EXAMPLE: Volney Croswell, Jr., book designer.

Von   The German form of Van. *See* Van. Akin to Vander. CONTEMPORARY EXAMPLE: Von Joshua, baseball player.

W

Wade From the Old English *waden*, meaning "to wade." Also, associated with Waddy, son of Woden, a mythical hero. CONTEMPORARY EXAMPLE: Wade H. McGree, Jr., American statesman. SURNAME USAGE: Carlson Wade, author.

Wadell A variant form of Wade. *See* Wade. CONTEMPORARY EXAMPLE: Wadell Smith, football player.

Wadsworth From the Old English *waden*, "to wade," plus *wyrth*, meaning "a manor, an estate," hence "a homestead with a wading pool."

Wagner From the Old English *waeg*, meaning "a way," hence "one who makes wagons. SURNAME USAGE: Robert Wagner, actor.

Waights From the Old English *waad*, meaning "a road." Waith is an old variant form. CONTEMPORARY EXAMPLE: Waights Henry, Jr., educator.

Waite From the Old English *waad*, meaning "a road." Akin to Waights. CONTEMPORARY EXAMPLE: Waite Hoyt, baseball player. SURNAME USAGE: Ralph Waite, actor.

Wal A short form of Walter or Wallace. *See* Walter *and* Wallace.

Walbert From the Old English *gwal*, meaning "wall, fortification," plus *beorht*, meaning "bright, respected," hence "secure fortification." CONTEMPORARY EXAMPLE: Walbert Buhlman, author.

Walcott From the Old English *wealcere*, meaning "a fuller of cloth."

Waldemar From the Old English *walda*, meaning "a ruler," plus *mar*, meaning "sea," hence "ruler of the sea." CONTEMPORARY EXAMPLE: Waldemar F.A. Wendt, U.S. admiral.

Walden From the Old English *waeald*, meaning "woods." CONTEMPORARY EXAMPLE: Walden Erickson, football player. SURNAME USAGE: Robert Walden, actor. PLACE-NAME USAGE: Walden, Colorado, named for M.A. Walden, an early settler; Walden Pond, New York.

Waldo, Waldron From the Old English *walda*, meaning "a ruler." CONTEMPORARY EXAMPLE: Waldo Hage, iceboating champion.

Walena The Hawaiian form of Warren. *See* Warren.

Walerian The Polish form of the masculine Valerius and the feminine Valerie. From the Latin *valere*, meaning "to be strong." CONTEMPORARY EXAMPLE: Walerian Borowczyk, Polish film director.

Walker   From the Old English occupational name for "one who cleans and thickens cloth." CONTEMPORARY EXAMPLE: Walker Cooper, baseball player. SURNAME USAGE: Robert Walker, actor. PLACE-NAME USAGE: Walker, California, named for J.R. Walker, frontiersman.

Wallace   From the Anglo-French name Waleis and the Middle English Walisc, meaning "a foreigner, stranger." Akin to the name Welsh. Walsh is a variant form. Originally an English surname. CONTEMPORARY EXAMPLE: Wallace Beery, actor. SURNAME USAGE: Henry A. Wallace (1888-1965), U.S. vice-president.

Wallie   A pet form of Walter or Wallace. *See* Walter *and* Wallace. Wally is a variant spelling.

Wallis   A variant spelling of Wallace. *See* Wallace.

Wally   A pet form of Walter or Wallace. *See* Walter *and* Wallace. Wallie is a variant spelling. CONTEMPORARY EXAMPLE: Wally Pipp, baseball player.

Walsh   A variant form of Wallace. *See* Wallace.

Walt   A pet form of Walter. *See* Walter. CONTEMPORARY EXAMPLE: Walt (Walter) Whitman (1819-1912), U.S. poet.

Walter   From the Old English *weald*, meaning "woods." Also, from the Old French *waldan*, meaning "to wield, to rule," plus *heri, hari*, meaning "army," hence "a general." PET FORMS: Wallie, Wally, Walt, Wat. CONTEMPORARY EXAMPLE: Walter Cronkite, television news reporter. SURNAME USAGE: Bruno Walter (1876-1962), musical conductor.

Walther   A variant spelling of Walter. *See* Walter. CONTEMPORARY EXAMPLE: Walther Gebhardt, editor.

Walton   From the Old English *gwal*, meaning "a wall, a fortification," plus *ton*, meaning "town," hence the fortified town." CONTEMPORARY EXAMPLE: Walton Cruise, baseball player.

Wanqualin   Origin unknown. CONTEMPORARY EXAMPLE: Wanqualin Williams, football player.

Ward   From the Old English *weardian*, meaning "to guard; a guardian." CONTEMPORARY EXAMPLE: Ward Just, novelist.

Warner   A variant form of Warren. *See* Warren. Werner is a variant spelling. CONTEMPORARY EXAMPLE: Warner Miller, New York political leader. SURNAME USAGE: John Warner, U.S. senator.

Warren   From the Middle English *wareine* and the Old French *warir*, meaning "to preserve." Also, "an enclosure (for rabbits)." VARIANT FORMS: Warner, Werner. CONTEMPORARY EXAMPLE: Warren G. Harding (1865-1923), twenty-ninth president of the U.S. PLACE-NAME USAGE: Warren, Michigan, named for Moses Warren, nineteenth–century U.S. surveyor.

Warrick   A variant form of Warwick. *See* Warwick.

Warwick   From the British *gwawr*, meaning "a hero," and the Norse *wic*, meaning "a village." PLACE-NAME USAGE: a town and county in England; Warwick, Massachusetts.

Washington   From the Old English *waes*, meaning "water, a damp site." Washington Irving (1783-1859) was a U.S. writer. SURNAME USAGE: George Washington (1732-1799), first president of the U.S. PLACE-NAME USAGE: the capital of the United States; a Western State; the name of many cities and sites in the U.S.

Wat   A pet form of Walter. *See* Walter.

Watkins   From the Celtic *wath*, meaning "a ford." Also, a patronymic form, meaning "the son of Wat (Walter)." *See* Walter. CONTEMPORARY EXAMPLE: Watkins M. Abbitt, U.S. congressman.

Watly   From the Old English *watel*, meaning "a fortification made from tree trunks joined by mud and lime." Also, from the Old English, meaning "Wat's (Walter's) lea or field." *See* Walter. CONTEMPORARY EXAMPLE: Watly Piper, author.

Watson   A patronymic form, meaning "son of Wat (Walter)." *See* Walter. SURNAME USAGE: James Dewey Watson, biochemist.

Waud   A variant form of Wauld, from the Old English *waeald*, meaning "woods." CONTEMPORARY EXAMPLE: Waud H. Kracke, anthropologist.

Wayland   From the Old English *waeg*, meaning "way, road," hence "the land near the highway." CONTEMPORARY EXAMPLE: Wayland Dean, baseball player.

Wayman   A variant form of Wyman. *See* Wyman. CONTEMPORARY EXAMPLE: Wayman Kerksieck, baseball player.

Wayne   From the British *waun*, meaning "a meadow." Or, from the Old English *waeg*, meaning "a way." VARIANT FORMS: Duane, Dwayne. CONTEMPORARY EXAMPLE: Wayne Newton, singer. SURNAME USAGE: General Anthony Wayne (1745-1797). PLACE-NAME USAGE: Fort Wayne, Indiana.

Weaver   From the Old English *waeg-faru*, meaning "a path by the water." SURNAME USAGE: Dennis Weaver, actor.

Webb   A pet form of Webster. *See* Webster. CONTEMPORARY EXAMPLE: Webb Garrison, author. SURNAME USAGE: Jack Webb, actor.

Webster   From the Old English *wiba*, meaning "a weaver." Webb is a pet form. CONTEMPORARY EXAMPLE: Webster Mews, author. SURNAME USAGE: Daniel Webster, nineteenth-century U.S. statesman. PLACE-NAME USAGE: cities in Massachusetts, Pennsylvania, and South Dakota.

Weeb   A variant form of Webb. *See* Webb. CONTEMPORARY EXAMPLE:

Weeb Ewbank, football coach.

Welby From the Old English, meaning "the village near the willow trees." CONTEMPORARY EXAMPLE: Welby Frantz, business executive.

Welcome From the Old English *willa*, meaning "pleasure," plus *cuma*, meaning "guest," hence "a welcome or invited guest." Used also as a feminine name. CONTEMPORARY EXAMPLE: Welcome Gaston, baseball player. PLACE-NAME USAGE: Welcome, Minnesota, named for A.M. Welcome, an early resident.

Weldon From the Old English *wel*, meaning "a willow," plus *dun*, from the Latin *dunum*, meaning "a hill," hence "the willow trees on the hill." Also, an invented name from the words "well done," as in the name of Joe Weldon Bailey, a Texas senator of the early 1900s. CONTEMPORARY EXAMPLE: Weldon Edwards, football player.

Wellesley A variant spelling of Wesley. *See* Wesley.

Wellington From the Old English, meaning "the town near the water" or "the town near the willow trees." CONTEMPORARY EXAMPLE: Wellington Quinn, baseball player. PLACE-NAME USAGE: Wellington, Utah, named for J. Wellington Seeley, a local judge.

Wells From the Old English *wel*, meaning "a well" or "a willow tree." CONTEMPORARY EXAMPLE: Wells Drorbaugh, Jr., publisher. PLACE-NAME USAGE: Wells, Nevada; Wellsville, Ohio, named for William Wells, a town founder.

Wellwood From the Old English, meaning "the willows in the woods." CONTEMPORARY EXAMPLE: Wellwood E. Beall, airplane designer.

Welsh From the Old English *wealas*, meaning "strangers."

Welthy From the Old English, meaning "the house near the willow tree." CONTEMPORARY EXAMPLE: Welthy Fisher, author.

Welton From the Old English *wel*, meaning "a willow," plus *ton*, meaning "town," hence "a town near the willow trees." CONTEMPORARY EXAMPLE: Welton Ebrhardt, baseball player. PLACE-NAME USAGE: Welton, Iowa.

Wendayne From the British *gwen*, meaning "fair," plus *daene*, meaning "a Dane." CONTEMPORARY EXAMPLE: Wendayne Ackerman, translator.

Wendel, Wendell From the British and Old English, meaning "a good dale or valley." CONTEMPORARY EXAMPLE: Wendell Wilkie, U.S. politician.

Wendelin From the British *gwen*, meaning "fair." CONTEMPORARY EXAMPLE: Wendelin J. Nold, clergyman.

Wene The Hawaiian form of Wayne. *See* Wayne.

Wentford From the British *gwent*, meaning "bright, fair (good)

land," plus *ford*, hence "the land near the ford." CONTEMPORARY EX-
AMPLE: Wentford Gaines, football player.

Werner   A variant form of Warren. *See* Warren. Warner is a variant
spelling. CONTEMPORARY EXAMPLE: Werner Klemperer, musical conductor.

Wernher   A German form of Werner. *See* Werner. CONTEMPORARY
EXAMPLE: Wernher von Braun, scientist.

Wesley   From the Old English, meaning "the west meadow." Wellesley is a variant spelling. CONTEMPORARY EXAMPLE: Wesley Branch
Rickey, baseball executive. PLACE-NAME USAGE: Wesley, Maine and
Wesley, Idaho, both named for John Wesley, founder of the Method-
ist Church.

Westbrook   From the Old English, meaning "the brook in the western
field." CONTEMPORARY EXAMPLE: Westbrook Pegler, Pulitzer Prize-win-
ning reporter.

Westcott   From the Old English, meaning "the cottage in the western
field." CONTEMPORARY EXAMPLE: Westcott Kingdon, baseball player.

Weston   From the Old English *waest-town*, meaning "house built on
waste land," or from "west town," the town to the west. CONTEM-
PORARY EXAMPLE: Weston LaBarre, anthropologist. SURNAME USAGE:
Jack Weston, actor. PLACE-NAME USAGE: Weston, Colorado, named for
Bert Weston, first postmaster; also, cities in Idaho, Massachusetts,
and West Virginia; a common place-name in England.

Wharton   From the Old English *waeg-faru*, meaning "a way by the
water." CONTEMPORARY EXAMPLE: Wharton R. Shober, educator.

Wheeler   An English occupational name for "one who drives a vehicle, a driver." CONTEMPORARY EXAMPLE: Wheeler Johnston, baseball
player. PLACE-NAME USAGE: a mountain in Nevada, named for Captain
G.M. Wheeler, explorer.

Whitcomb   From the Early Modern English *wiht*, meaning "small,"
plus *cwm*, the British form of *combe*, meaning "a dingle, a valley,"
hence "small valley."

Whitfield   From the Early Modern English *wiht*, meaning "small," plus
field. CONTEMPORARY EXAMPLE: Whitfield Foy, editor.

Whitelaw   From the Early Modern English *wiht*, meaning "small,"
plus the Old English *hlaew*, meaning "hill," hence "small hill." CON-
TEMPORARY EXAMPLE: Whitelaw Reid, U.S. vice-presidential candidate (1892). SURNAME USAGE: Arthur Whitelaw, theatrical producer.

Whitey   A nickname for a light-complexioned person. CONTEMPO-
RARY EXAMPLE: Whitey Ford, baseball player.

Whitley   From the Early Modern English *wiht*, meaning "small," plus
lea, meaning "meadow," hence "a small field." CONTEMPORARY EXAM-

PLE: Whitley Strieber, author.

Whitney   From the Old English, meaning "a small piece of land near the water (*ey*)." Akin to Whitley and Whittaker. CONTEMPORARY EXAMPLE: Whitney North Seymour, author. SURNAME USAGE: Eli Whitney (1765-1825), U.S. inventor. PLACE-NAME USAGE: Mount Whitney, California, named for J.D. Whitney (1819-1896), U.S. geologist.

Whittaker   From the Early Modern English *wiht*, meaning "small," plus the Old English *acer*, meaning "acre," hence "a small amount of land." CONTEMPORARY EXAMPLE: Whittaker Chambers, editor.

Wid   From the Old English, meaning "wide." CONTEMPORARY EXAMPLE: Wid Matthews, baseball player.

Wilber, Wilbert   Variant forms of Walbert. *See* Walbert. Also, from the Old English *wel* and *wil*, meaning "willow," plus *beohrt*, meaning "bright," hence "bright willows." CONTEMPORARY EXAMPLE: Wilbert Greenfield, educator.

Wilbur, Wilburn   Variant forms of Wilber. *See* Wilber. Also, from the Old English forms Wilburh and Wilgburh, meaning "willow town." CONTEMPORARY EXAMPLES: Wilbur Wright, (1867-1912), inventor; Wilburn Butland, baseball player.

Wilce   From the Old English *wil* and *wigle*, meaning "magic," and *wicce*, meaning "witch." CONTEMPORARY EXAMPLE: Wilce Carnes, football player.

Wilder   From the Old English, meaning "a person from the wilds, wilderness." SURNAME USAGE: Thornton Wilder, playwright.

Wile   The Hawaiian form of Willie (William). *See* William.

Wilem   A variant form of Willem. *See* Willem. CONTEMPORARY EXAMPLE: Wilem Daems, pharmacologist.

Wiley, Wylie   From the Old English, meaning "willow field; a meadow of willows." CONTEMPORARY EXAMPLE: Wiley B. Rutledge, U.S. Supreme Court Associate Justice.

Wilf   A variant form of Wolf. *See* Wolf. CONTEMPORARY EXAMPLE: Wilf Paiement, hockey player.

Wilford   From the Old English, meaning "the willow tree near the ford." CONTEMPORARY EXAMPLE: Wilford White, football player.

Wilfred, Wilfrid, Wilfried   From the Old English name Wilfrith, derived from *willa*, meaning "wish, desire," plus *frith*, meaning "peace," hence "hope for peace." CONTEMPORARY EXAMPLE: Wilfred W. Westerfield, educator; Wilfrid Sheed, novelist; Wilfried Fest, professor.

Wilfredo   An Italian form of Wilfred. *See* Wilfred. CONTEMPORARY EXAMPLE: Wilfredo Benito, boxer.

Wilhelm   The German form of William. *See* William. CONTEM-PORARY EXAMPLE: Wilhelm Rapp, fishing champion.

Will   A pet form of William. *See* William. CONTEMPORARY EXAMPLE: Will Rogers, humorist and actor.

Willard   From the Old English, meaning "a yard full of willows." Also, a variant form of William. *See* William. CONTEMPORARY EXAMPLE: Willard Deurveall, football player. SURNAME USAGE: Frances Willard (1839-1898), U.S. temperance leader.

Wille   A variant spelling of Will. *See* Will.

Willem   A Dutch form of William. *See* William. CONTEMPORARY EXAMPLE: Willem de Koonig, artist.

Willi   A pet form of William. *See* William. CONTEMPORARY EXAMPLE: Willi Fischauer, author.

William   A variant form of the Old French name Willaume and the Old High German Willehelm. From the Old High German *willeo*, meaning "will, desire," and *helm*, meaning "protection," hence "resolute protector." A popular name for kings of England. VARIANT FORMS: Guglielmo (Italian); Willem (Dutch); Guillim (Welsh); Guillaume, Guillemot (French); Willard, Wilmot (English); Wilhelm (German); Guillermo (Spanish). PET FORMS: Bill, Billie, Billy, Will, Willi, Willie, Willy. SURNAME USAGE: Williams, Williamson, Willis, Wilson. PLACE-NAME USAGE: Williams, Arizona; Williamsburg, Virginia, named for King William III; Williamstown, Massachusetts, named for Colonel Ephraim Williams, founder of Williams College.

Williamson   A patronymic form, meaning "son of William." *See* William. Popular as a Welsh surname. PLACE-NAME USAGE: Williamson, West Virginia, named for W.J. Williamson, an early landowner.

Willie   A pet form of William. *See* William.

Willis   A patronymic form, meaning "son of William." *See* William. Akin to Wilson. CONTEMPORARY EXAMPLE: Willis Reed, basketball player. PLACE-NAME USAGE: Williston, North Dakota, named for S. Willis James, a railroad stockholder.

Willoughby   From the Dutch *wilg*, meaning "willow," plus the Old Danish *bye*, meaning "a house," hence "a house near (or amidst) the willow trees."

Willy   A pet form of William. Willie is a variant spelling. CONTEMPORARY EXAMPLE: Willy Brandt, German statesman.

Wilmar, Wilmer, Willmer   From the Old English *wil* plus *mar*, meaning "the willows near the sea." Or, names meaning "William's sea." CONTEMPORARY EXAMPLES: Wilmar Levels, football player; Wilmer Mizell, baseball player.

Wilmot   A variant form of William. *See* William.

Wilson A patronymic form, meaning "the son of William." *See* William. CONTEMPORARY EXAMPLE: Wilson G. Pong, professor. SURNAME USAGE: (Thomas) Woodrow Wilson (1856-1924), twenty-eighth president of the U.S. PLACE-NAME USAGE: Mount Wilson, California; Wilson Peak, Colorado.

Wilt A variant form of Walt (Walter). *See* Walter. Or, a pet form of Wilton. *See* Wilton. Also, possibly from the tribe (also called Wylte) that settled in Germany in the sixth and seventh centuries, some of whose members moved to England. CONTEMPORARY EXAMPLE: Wilt Chamberlain, basketball player.

Wilton From the Old English, meaning "the town near the well, or near the willow trees." CONTEMPORARY EXAMPLE: Wilton Wynn, news correspondent. PLACE-NAME USAGE: Wilton, England; Wilton, Connecticut.

Wilver Possibly a variant form of Wilber. *See* Wilber. CONTEMPORARY EXAMPLE: Wilver Stargell, baseball player.

Win From the Old English, meaning "victory." CONTEMPORARY EXAMPLE: Win Pendleton, journalist.

Windell From the Old English *wendel*, meaning "a tree from which baskets are woven (the osier)." CONTEMPORARY EXAMPLE: Windell Williams, football player.

Windlan A variant form of Windell. *See* Windell. CONTEMPORARY EXAMPLE: Windlan Hall, football player.

Winfield From the Old English *win*, meaning "victory," hence "successful, productive field." CONTEMPORARY EXAMPLE: Winfield Scott, U.S. Army general.

Winford A variant spelling of Winfred. *See* Winfred. CONTEMPORARY EXAMPLE: Winford Vaughan–Thomas, television executive.

Winfred, Winfrid From the Old English name Winfrith, derived from *wine*, meaning "friend," plus *frithu*, meaning "peace," hence "friend of peace" or "peaceful friend." Winifred is the feminine form.

Wingate From the Old English *win*, meaning "victory," plus *gate*, hence "victory gate." CONTEMPORARY EXAMPLE: Wingate Froscher, novelist. SURNAME USAGE: Orde Wingate, British soldier.

Winslow From the Old English *win*, meaning "victory," plus *loe*, meaning "hill," hence "victory hill." CONTEMPORARY EXAMPLE: Winslow Homer (1836-1910), American painter.

Winston From the Old English *win*, meaning "victory," plus *ton*, meaning "town," hence "victory town." CONTEMPORARY EXAMPLE: Sir Winston Churchill (1874-1965), English statesman. PLACE-NAME USAGE: Winston-Salem, North Carolina, named for Revolutionary War General Joseph Winston.

Winthrop   From the Old English *win*, meaning "victory," plus *throp*, meaning "crossroads," hence "victory at the crossroads." CONTEMPORARY EXAMPLE: Winthrop Rockefeller, Arkansas governor. SURNAME USAGE: John Winthrop (1588-1649), first governor of Massachusetts. PLACE-NAME USAGE: Winthrop, Massachusetts.

Winton   A variant form of Winston. *See* Winston. CONTEMPORARY EXAMPLE: Winton George Wilks III, Gainesville, Florida.

Wirt   From the Old English *wyrth*, meaning "an estate, a manor." CONTEMPORARY EXAMPLE: Wirt Cannell, baseball player.

Witt   From the Old English *hwit*, meaning "white, fair." CONTEMPORARY EXAMPLE: Witt Gube, baseball player.

Witter   A variant form of Witt. *See* Witt. CONTEMPORARY EXAMPLE: Witter Brynner, poet.

Wolcott   From the Old English, meaning "cottage in the field (*wald*)."

Wolf, Wolfe   From the Old English *wulf*, meaning "a wolf." SURNAME USAGE: Thomas Wolfe, author. PLACE-NAME USAGE: Wolf Trap, Virginia; Wolf Creek, Iowa.

Wolfgang   A variant form of Wolf, meaning "wolf path." CONTEMPORARY EXAMPLE: Wolfgang Amadeus Mozart (1756-1791), Austrian composer.

Wolfhart   A variant form of Wolf. *See* Wolf. CONTEMPORARY EXAMPLE: Wolfhart Pannenberg, author.

Wolli, Wolly   Pet forms of Walter. *See* Walter.

Wood   From the Anglo-Saxon, meaning "from the wooded area (forest)." PLACE-NAME USAGE: Wood River, Oregon; Woodyard, West Virginia.

Woodie   A pet form of Woodrow. *See* Woodrow. Woody is a variant spelling. CONTEMPORARY EXAMPLE: Woodie Jensen, baseball player.

Woodrow   From the Old English, meaning "wooded hedge." CONTEMPORARY EXAMPLE: Woodrow Wilson (1856-1924), twenty–eighth president of the U.S.

Woodruff   One of a genus of plants in the coffee family. CONTEMPORARY EXAMPLE: Woodruff Bruder, football player.

Woodson   A patronymic form, meaning "son of Wood." *See* Wood. CONTEMPORARY EXAMPLE: Woodson Held, baseball player.

Woody   A pet form of Woodrow. *See* Woodrow. Woodie is a variant spelling. CONTEMPORARY EXAMPLE: Woody Allen, comedian.

Worley   From the Old English, meaning "a piece of uncultivated land." CONTEMPORARY EXAMPLE: Worley Thorne, author.

Worthy   From the Old English *wyrth*, meaning "an estate, a manor."

CONTEMPORARY EXAMPLE: Worthy McClure, football player.

Wray Possibly from the Old English *awry*, meaning "crooked." CONTEMPORARY EXAMPLE: Wray Carlton, football player.

Wright From the Old English, meaning "an artisan, a worker." CONTEMPORARY EXAMPLE: Wright Morris, author.

Wyatt, Wyatte From the British *gwy*, meaning "water." CONTEMPORARY EXAMPLE: Wyatt Blassingame, author. SURNAME USAGE: Thomas Wyatt, sixteenth-century English poet.

Wyche A variant form of Wyck. *See* Wyck. CONTEMPORARY EXAMPLE: Wyche Fowler, U.S. congressman.

Wyck From the Old Norse *wic*, meaning "a village." CONTEMPORARY EXAMPLE: Wyck Neeley, football player.

Wycliffe A variant form of Wyck, meaning "village near the cliff." CONTEMPORARY EXAMPLE: Wycliffe Morton, baseball player. SURNAME USAGE: John Wycliffe, fourteenth-century English religious reformer.

Wyeth A variant form of Wyatt. *See* Wyatt. CONTEMPORARY EXAMPLE: Wyeth Chandler, U.S. city mayor. SURNAME USAGE: Andrew Wyeth, painter. PLACE-NAME USAGE: Wye, a river in Southeast Wales.

Wylie From the Old English *wil* and *wigle*, meaning "deceitful, beguiling, coquettish."

Wyman From the British *gwy*, meaning "water," hence "a person who works on the water, a sailor."

Wyndham From the Scotch *wynde*, meaning "a winding road," plus *hamlet*, hence "the village near the winding road." CONTEMPORARY EXAMPLE: Wyndham D. Miled, editor.

Wynn From the British *gwyn*, meaning "white, fair." CONTEMPORARY EXAMPLE: Wynn Rogers, badminton champion.

Wystan A variant spelling of Winston. *See* Winston. CONTEMPORARY EXAMPLE: Wystan Hugh Auden (1907-1973), American poet.

X

Xanthus   From the Greek *xanthos*, meaning "yellow."

Xavier   From the Arabic, meaning "bright." A favorite name throughout the Christian world, popularized by Saint Francis Xavier (1506-1552), Spanish Jesuit missionary. Used also as a feminine name. CONTEMPORARY EXAMPLE: Xavier Cugat, band leader. PLACE-NAME USAGE: Xavier, Kansas.

Xerxes   From the Persian, meaning "king." Xerxes I, a fifth-century B.C. king of Persia, son of King Darius, was called The Great. PLACE-NAME USAGE: Xerxes, Kentucky.

Y

Yaacov, Yaakov, Yaaqov   Hebraic forms of Jacob. *See* Jacob. CONTEMPORARY EXAMPLE: Yaacov R'oi, author.

Yadid   From the Hebrew, meaning "beloved" or "friend." Yedid is a variant form.

Yadin   From the Hebrew, meaning "He [God] will judge." SURNAME USAGE: Yigael Yadin, archaeologist.

Yadon   A variant form of Yadin. *See* Yadin.

Yafet   A variant form of Japhet. *See* Japhet.

Yagel   From the Hegrew, meaning "to reveal, to uncover" or "to rejoice." Akin to Yigal.

Yagil   From the Hebrew, meaning "to rejoice." Yagel is a variant form.

Yakir   From the Hebrew, meaning "dear, beloved, honorable."

Yale   From the German, meaning "one who pays or produces." Also, from the Old English *eald*, meaning "old." SURNAME USAGE: Linus Yale (1821-1868), inventor of Yale cylinder lock. PLACE-NAME USAGE: cities in Oklahoma and South Dakota; Lake Yale, Florida (originally called Lake Yulee) named for Senator D.L. Yulee.

Yalin   A name invented by joining the license plate letters Yal to Lin of Linda. CONTEMPORARY EXAMPLE: Yalin Krause, Mattawan, Michigan.

Yan, Yana   Variant forms of John. *See* John.

Yancy   A corruption of the French word for "Englishman," which evolved into Yankee. Also, a variant form of the Danish name Jan (John). *See* John.

Yank   A variant form of Yancy. *See* Yancy. CONTEMPORARY EXAMPLE: Yank Robinson, baseball player. PLACE-NAME USAGE: Yank's Canyon, Arizona.

Yanni   A variant form of Yan. *See* Yan. CONTEMPORARY EXAMPLE: Yanni Ritsos, Greek poet.

Yaphet   The Hebraic form of Japhet. *See* Japhet. CONTEMPORARY EXAMPLE: Yaphet Kotto, actor.

Yarden   The Hebrew name for Jordan. *See* Jordan.

Yardley   From the Old English *geard*, meaning "an enclosure, a yard."

Yarkon   From the Hebrew *yarok*, meaning "green." The name of a bird of greenish-yellow color that inhabits Israel in the summertime and migrates to Egypt in the fall. PLACE-NAME USAGE: a river in Israel.

Yaron From the Hebrew, meaning "He will sing." CONTEMPORARY EXAMPLE: Yaron Brecker, musician.

Yashar, Yesher From the Hebrew, meaning "upright, honest." In the Bible, the son of Caleb. CONTEMPORARY EXAMPLE: Yashar Kemal, novelist.

Yates From the British *iat*, meaning "a gate."

Yavin From the Hebrew, meaning "He will understand." In the Bible, a Canaanite king in the days of Deborah. Jabin is the Anglicized spelling.

Yavniel From the Hebrew, meaning "God will build." Jabniel is a variant spelling.

Yedid A variant form of Yadid. *See* Yadid.

Yedidia, Yedidiah From the Hebrew, meaning "friend of God." Jedidiah is the Anglicized form.

Yediel From the Hebrew, meaning "knowledge of the Lord." In the Bible, a son of Benjamin. VARIANT FORMS: Jediel, Jediael.

Yehezkel The Hebraic form of Ezekiel. *See* Ezekiel. Yehezekel is a variant spelling. A sixth-century B.C. prophet. CONTEMPORARY EXAMPLE: Yehezkel Kaufmann, author.

Yehiel From the Hebrew, meaning "May God live!" In the Bible, one of King Daivd's chief musicians. Jehiel is a variant spelling.

Yehoram From the Hebrew, meaning "God will exalt." CONTEMPORARY EXAMPLE: Yehoram Gaon, Israeli singer.

Yehoshafat From the Hebrew, meaning "God will judge." Jehoshafat is the Anglicized spelling. CONTEMPORARY EXAMPLE: Yehoshafat Harkabi, author.

Yehuda, Yehudah From the Hebrew, meaning "praise." Hebraic forms of Judah. *See* Judah. King Solomon's Jewish empire was split after his death. The southern and smaller part was called Yehuda (Judah), and an inhabitant of that sector was called Yehudi, from which evolved the name Jew. CONTEMPORARY EXAMPLE: Yehuda Blum, Israeli ambassador to the United Nations.

Yehudi From the Hebrew, meaning "a Jew, a man who comes from Judah." Akin to Yehuda. *See* Yehuda. CONTEMPORARY EXAMPLE: Yehudi Menuhin, violinist.

Yekutiel From the Hebrew, meaning "God will nourish." Jekuthiel is a variant form. Kuti is a pet form. In the Bible, a son of Ezra. CONTEMPORARY EXAMPLE: Yekutiel Gershoni, Israeli military officer.

Yelberton   From the Old English *yeldo*, meaning "a crane," hence "a town inhabited by cranes." CONTEMPORARY EXAMPLE: Yelberton Tittlelya, football player.

Yemin   From the Hebrew, meaning "right handed." Akin to Benjamin. *See* Benjamin.

Yeshaia, Yeshaiah, Yeshayahu   Hebraic forms of Isaiah. *See* Isaiah.

Yeshurun   From the Hebrew, meaning "upright." A poetic appellation used in the Bible to designate the Hebrew nation.

Yigael   From the Hebrew, meaning "God will redeem." Akin to Yigal. CONTEMPORARY EXAMPLE: Yigael Yadin, archaeologist.

Yigal   From the Hebrew, meaning "He will redeem." In the Bible, a son of Shemaiah. Akin to Yigael and Yagel. Igal is a variant form. CONTEMPORARY EXAMPLE: Yigal Allon, Israeli statesman.

Yigdal   From the Hebrew, meaning "He will grow, He will be exalted."

Yitzchak, Yitzhak   Hebraic forms of Isaac. *See* Isaac. CONTEMPORARY EXAMPLE: Yitzhak Rabin, Israeli statesman.

Yivchar   From the Hebrew, meaning "He will choose." In the Bible, a son of David.

Yoav   The Hebraic form of Joab, meaning "God is father." In the Bible, King David's nephew, captain of his army.

Yochanan   A variant spelling of Yohanan. *See* Yohanan.

Yoel   The Hebraic form of Joel. *See* Joel.

Yogi   A nickname. Also, from the Sanskrit *yogin*, meaning "a person who practices yoga." CONTEMPORARY EXAMPLE: Yogi Berra, baseball player.

Yohanan   From the Hebrew, meaning "God is gracious." John is the English form. In the Bible, a son of King Josiah. VARIANT SPELLINGS: Johanan, Yochanan. CONTEMPORARY EXAMPLE: Yohanan Aharoni, archeologist.

Yona, Yonah   The Hebraic forms of Jonah. *See* Jonah. Also, an American Indian name, meaning "a bear." CONTEMPORARY EXAMPLE: Yona Fisher, museum curator. PLACE-NAME USAGE: Yonah Mountain, Georgia.

Yonatan   The modern Hebraic form of Jonathan. *See* Jonathan.

Yora   From the Hebrew, meaning "to teach." Jorah is the Anglicized spelling.

Yoram   From the Hebrew, meaning "God is exalted." Joram and Jehoram are Anglicized spellings. In the Bible, a king of Judah. CON-

TEMPORARY EXAMPLE: Yoram Golan, songwriter.

Yorick   Probably a Danish variant form of George. *See* George. A character in Shakespeare's *Hamlet*.

York   A variant form of Yorick. *See* Yorick. SURNAME USAGE: Michael York, actor. PLACE-NAME USAGE: an ancient Roman city; Yorkshire, England; New York.

Yosef, Yoseph   Hebraic forms of Joseph. *See* Joseph. CONTEMPORARY EXAMPLE: Yosef Criden, author.

Yosel, Yossel, Yossele   Yiddish forms of Joseph. *See* Joseph. Yossele is a pet form. CONTEMPORARY EXAMPLE: Yossele Rosenblatt, cantor.

Yosi   A pet form of Yosef (Joseph). *See* Joseph. CONTEMPORARY EXAMPLE: Yosi Piamenta, musician.

Yudan   From the Hebrew *din*, meaning "law, judgment."

Yuki   A pet form of Jacob. *See* Jacob. CONTEMPORARY EXAMPLE: Yuki Hartman, editor.

Yul   From the Old English *geol* and *iul*, akin to the Old Norse *jol*, meaning "jolly; the Christmas season." The origin of yuletide. CONTEMPORARY EXAMPLE: Yul Brynner, actor.

Yuma   An American Indian name, meaning "the chief's son." PLACE-NAME USAGE: Yuma, Arizona.

Yuri   A pet form of Uriah. *See* Uriah. CONTEMPORARY EXAMPLE: Yuri Suhl, author.

Yvan   A variant spelling of Ivan. *See* Ivan. CONTEMPORARY EXAMPLE: Yvan Vautour, hockey player.

Yves   From the Scandinavian, meaning "an archer." Ives is a variant spelling. Ive is a feminine form. CONTEMPORARY EXAMPLE: Yves Saint-Laurent, French fashion designer.

Yvon   A variant form of Ivan. *See* Ivan. CONTEMPORARY EXAMPLE: Yvon Lambert, hockey player.

Z

Zabdi From the Hebrew, meaning "my gift." In the Bible, a member of the tribe of Benjamin.

Zabdiel From the Hebrew, meaning "God is my gift." In the Bible, the father of an officer of King David. Zavdiel is a variant spelling.

Zachariah, Zacharias Variant forms of Zechariah. *See* Zechariah. Zacharias is a Greek form. CONTEMPORARY EXAMPLE: Zacharias Janssen, inventor. SURNAME USAGE: Sachar, Zach.

Zachary A variant form of Zechariah. *See* Zechariah. Zachary Taylor (1784-1858) was the twelfth president of the U.S.

Zaida From the Yiddish, meaning "grandfather" or "old man."

Zak A pet form of Isaac and Zachary. *See* Isaac *and* Zachary.

Zakkai From the Hebrew, meaning "pure, clean, innocent." In the Bible, the head of a family during the Babylonian Exile. Johanan ben Zakkai was a second–century leading Jewish scholar.

Zales From the Old English *sala*, meaning "to sell" or "salary." Derived from the Latin *sal*, meaning "salt," originally used as currency. CONTEMPORARY EXAMPLE: Zales Ecton, politician.

Zalman, Zalmen, Zalmon Variant Yiddish forms of Solomon. *See* Solomon. CONTEMPORARY EXAMPLE: Zalman King, actor.

Zamir From the Hebrew, meaning "a song" or "a bird (nightingale)." Currently used in Israel.

Zan From the Italian *zanni*, meaning "a clown." Derived from Giovanni, the Italian form of John. *See also* John.

Zander A variant form of Sander (Alexander). *See* Alexander. CONTEMPORARY EXAMPLE: Zander Matthews, New York, New York.

Zane A variant form of Zan. *See* Zan. CONTEMPORARY EXAMPLE:

Zavdi, Zavdiel Variant spellings of Zabdi and Zabdiel. *See* Zabdi *and* Zabdiel.

Zeb A pet form of Zebulun. *See* Zebulun. CONTEMPORARY EXAMPLE: Zeb Terry, baseball player.

Zebedee From the Hebrew, meaning "gift of God." In the Bible, the father of James and John.

Zebulon A variant spelling of Zebulun. *See* Zebulun. CONTEMPORARY

EXAMPLE: Zebulon Pike, baseball player. PLACE-NAME USAGE: Zebulon, Georgia; Zebulon, North Carolina, named for Zebulon B. Vance, state governor (1862-65 and 1877-79).

Zebulun   From the Hebrew, meaning "to exalt, to honor" or "a lofty house." In the Bible, the sixth son of Jacob and Leah. Zevulun is the Hebrew spelling. Zubin is a variant form. PET FORMS: Zeb, Zev.

Zecharia   A variant spelling of Zechariah. See Zechariah. CONTEMPORARY EXAMPLE: Zecharia Stichin, author.

Zechariah   From the Hebrew, meaning "the remembrance of the Lord." In the Bible, a sixth-century B.C. prophet who lived during the return of the Jewish captives from Babylonia to Israel. Also, a king of Israel, son of Jeroboam II, in the eighth century B.C. VARIANT FORMS: Zachariah, Zacharias, Zecharias, Zachary. Zecharia is a variant spelling. Zeke is a pet form.

Zecharias   A Greek form of Zechariah. See Zechariah. Zacharias is a variant spelling.

Zed   A pet form of Zedekiah. See Zedekiah.

Zedekiah   From the Hebrew, meaning "God is righteousness." In the Bible, king of Judah from 597 to 586 B.C. His original name was Mattaniah. He adopted the name Zedekiah when he was appointed king by Nebuchadnezzar of Babylonia to succeed the exiled Jehoiakin.

Zeeb   A variant spelling of Zev. In the Bible, a prince of Midian. See Zev.

Zeev   A variant spelling of Zev. See Zev. CONTEMPORARY EXAMPLE: Zeev Schiff, military analyst.

Zehavi   From the Hebrew zahav, meaning "gold." Used also as a feminine name.

Zeira   From the Aramaic, meaning "small."

Zeke   A pet form of Zechariah. See Zechariah. Also, from the Aramaic, meaning "a spark." Or, from the Arabic, meaning "a shooting star."

Zelig   A variant spelling of Selig. See Selig. A popular Yiddish name.

Zelman   A variant form of Zalman. See Zalman.

Zelmo   Possibly a variant form of Zelman, a form of Solomon. See Solomon. CONTEMPORARY EXAMPLE: Zelmo Beatty, basketball player.

Zemaria, Zemariah   From the Hebrew zemer, meaning "song of God."

Zemer   From the Hebrew, meaning "a song." Akin to Zemaria.

Zemira, Zemirah   From the Hebrew, meaning "choice products." Also, akin to Zemer. See Zemer. In the Bible, a descendant of the tribe of Benjamin.

Zeno   From the Greek *sema*, meaning "a sign, a symbol," and the Latin *semita*, meaning "a path, a way." A fifth–century B.C. Greek philosopher. CONTEMPORARY EXAMPLE: Zeno Rawley, golfer. PLACE-NAME USAGE: a town in Italy.

Zenon   A variant form of Zeno. *See* Zeno. CONTEMPORARY EXAMPLE: Zenon Andrushyshyn, football player.

Zephaniah   From the Hebrew, meaning "God has treasured." In the Bible, a seventh–century B.C. prophet, a member of an aristocratic Judean family.

Zephyr   From the Greek *zephyros*, meaning "the west wind," hence "a gentle breeze." In Greek mythology, the god of the west wind. CONTEMPORARY EXAMPLE: Zephyr Cohen, author.

Zeppo   A nickname. CONTEMPORARY EXAMPLE: Zeppo Marx, comedian.

Zenas   A variant form of Zeno. *See* Zeno. In the Bible, a lawyer who became a Christian follower of Jesus.

Zera   From the Hebrew, meaning "a seed."

Zerah, Zerach   From the Hebrew, meaning "shining, dawning." In the Bible, a son of Judah and Tamar.

Zeri   From the Hebrew, meaning "balsam." In the Bible, a musician.

Zerian   Meaning unknown. CONTEMPORARY EXAMPLE: Zerian Hagerman, baseball player.

Zero   From the French and Italian *zero*, derived from the Arabic *tzifr*, meaning "cipher." CONTEMPORARY EXAMPLE: Zero Mostel, actor.

Zetan   From the Hebrew, meaning "olive tree." In the Bible, a member of the tribe of Benjamin.

Zev   From the Hebrew *z'ayv*, meaning "a wolf." In the Bible, Benjamin, when blessed by his father, Jacob, is compared to a wolf. As a result, among Jews, Zev and Wolf are used as first and middle names. Zev is sometimes used as a pet form of Zevulun (Zebulun). Zeev is a variant spelling. CONTEMPORARY EXAMPLE: Zev Wanderer, psychologist.

Zevadia   From the Hebrew, meaning "God has bestowed." In the Bible, a member of the tribe of Benjamin.

Zevi   From the Hebrew *tz'vee*, meaning "a deer, a gazelle." VARIANT SPELLINGS: Tzevi, Tzvi, Zvi.

Zeviel   From the Hebrew, meaning "gazelle of the Lord."

Zevulun   The original Hebrew spelling of Zebulun. *See* Zebulun. Zev is a pet form.

Zia   From the Hebrew, meaning "to tremble." In the Bible, a member of the tribe of Gad. PLACE-NAME USAGE: Zia, New Mexico.

Zimran A variant form of Zimri. *See* Zimri. In the Bible, the son of Abraham and Keturah.

Zimri From the Hebrew, meaning either "mountain-sheep, goat" or "protected, sacred thing" or "my vine, my branch." In the Bible, a member of the tribe of Simeon.

Zinn Probably a short form of Zinnia, a plant named for botanist J.G. Zinn (died 1759). CONTEMPORARY EXAMPLE: Zinn Bertram, baseball player.

Zion From the Hebrew, meaning "excellent" or "a sign." In the Bible, used as an appellation for the Hebrew people. PLACE-NAME USAGE: Mt. Zion, in Jerusalem; Zion Canyon, Utah.

Ziv, Zivi From the Hebrew, meaning "to shine, brilliance." Ziv is also a biblical synonym for the Hebrew spring-month Iyar.

Zohar From the Hebrew, meaning "light, brilliance." Used frequently as a feminine name. Also, the name of a mystical commentary on the Bible.

Zoie From the Greek, meaning "life." Spelled Zoe, it is used as a feminine form. *See* Zoe (feminine section).

Zoilo A variant form of Zola. *See* Zola. CONTEMPORARY EXAMPLE: Zoilo Versales, baseball player.

Zola From the German *zoll*, meaning "toll, duty, cost." SURNAME USAGE: Emile Zola (1840-1902), French novelist.

Zollie A variant form of Zola. *See* Zola. CONTEMPORARY EXAMPLE: Zollie Toth, football player.

Zoltan A variant form of the Arabic *sultan*, meaning "a ruler, a prince." CONTEMPORARY EXAMPLE: Zoltan Kenessey, author.

Zonar From the Latin *sonor*, meaning "a sound." CONTEMPORARY EXAMPLE: Zonar Wissinger, football player.

Zoran Meaning unknown. CONTEMPORARY EXAMPLE: Zoran Perisic, photographer.

Zubin A variant form of Zebulun. *See* Zebulun. Also, a Hindi name. CONTEMPORARY EXAMPLE: Zubin Mehta, musical conductor.

Zvi A variant spelling of Zevi. *See* Zevi.

FEMININE
NAMES

A

Abbe, Abbey   Variant forms of Abigail. *See* Abigail. Used also as masculine names. *See* Abba (masculine section).

Abbie   A variant form of Abbe. *See* Abbe. Used also as a masculine name. *See* Abbie (masculine section).

Abby   A variant form of Abbey. *See* Abbey. CONTEMPORARY EXAMPLE: Abby Lane, singer. PLACE-NAME USAGE: Abbyville, Kansas, named for Abby McLean, first child born in that town.

Abela   A feminine form of Abel. *See* Abel. Also, a Latin and French form, meaning "beautiful, good."

Abibi, Abibit   From the Hebrew *aviv*, meaning "springlike, youthful." VARIANT FORMS: Avivi, Avivit.

Abiela, Abiella   From the Hebrew, meaning "God is my father." The masculine form is Abiel.

Abigail   The anglicized form of the Hebrew name Avigayil, meaning "father of joy." In the Bible, a wife of King David. David manipulated her first husband's death. In the 1616 play by Beaumont and Fletcher, *The Scornful Lady*, Abigail was a maid, which gave the name its lowly connotation. PET FORMS: Abbey, Abby, Gail.

Abital   A Hebrew name compounded of *abi* (or *avi*), meaning "my father," and *tal*, meaning "dew." In the Bible, one of the wives of King David. In Israel, Abital (pronounced Avee-tal) is also a masculine name.

Abra   A short form of Abraham. In seventeenth–century England, it achieved a degree of popularity. *See* Abraham (masculine section).

Acenith   The name of the African goddess of love. CONTEMPORARY EXAMPLE: Acenith Maloy, Bakersfield, California.

Acquanetta   Meaning uncertain. Probably derived from the Latin *aqua*, meaning "water." CONTEMPORARY EXAMPLE: Acquanetta Spencen, Tampa, Florida.

Acton   Primarily a masculine name. *See* Acton (masculine section). CONTEMPORARY EXAMPLE: Acton Bell, author (pseudonym of Anne Bronte).

Ada, Adah   From the Hebrew, meaning "adorned, beautiful." Also, from the Latin and German, meaning "of noble birth." In the Bible, Ada was the wife of Lamech. A popular name in nineteenth–century England. Lord Byron's daughter was Augusta Ada. Ada is often a pet form of Adelaide. VARIANT FORMS: Aeda, Eda, Etta.

Adabelle   A compounded name of Ada and Belle. *See* Ada *and* Belle.

Adalee   A compounded name of Ada and Lee. *See* Ada *and* Lee. CON-
TEMPORARY EXAMPLE: Adalee Winter, needlework designer.

Adalia   A variant form of Adelaide. *See* Adelaide.

Adaline   A pet form of Adelaide. *See* Adelaide.

Adamina   Coined in the nineteenth century as a feminine pet form of
Adam. *See* Adam (masculine section).

Adamma   Used by the Ibo of Nigeria, meaning "child of beauty."

Adda, Addie   Pet forms of Adelaide. *See* Adelaide.

Addison   A patronymic form of the pet form of Adelaide, meaning "Addie's son." *See* Adelaide. Used frequently as a masculine name. CONTEM-
PORARY EXAMPLE: Addison Steele, author.

Adel   A variant spelling of Adele and Adelaide. *See* Adelaide. CONTEM-
PORARY EXAMPLE: Adel, Oregon, named by the founder in honor of his
sweetheart.

Adela, Adella   Variant forms of Adelaide. *See* Adelaide. CONTEM-
PORARY EXAMPLE: Adela Turin, author.

Adelaide   A French form of the German name Adelheid, meaning "of
noble birth." Became popular in tenth-century Germany when Queen
Adelaide ruled the country. In the nineteenth century, the popularity of
King William IV's Good Queen Adelaide led to its general use in
England. Adelais, Aaliz, and Aliz, all Norman-French forms, evolved in-
to Alice, the English form of the name. VARIANT FORMS: Adeline, Adeliza,
Adela, Alice, Alicia, Elsie (English); Adeline, Adelaise, Adele, Alix,
Aline (French); Alisa (Italian); Adele, Else, Ilse (German); Adelheid
(Dutch).

Adele, Adelle   Variant forms of Adelaide. *See* Adelaide.

Adelia   A variant form of Adelaide. *See* Adelaide.

Adelina, Adeline   Variant pet forms of Adelaide. *See* Adelaide.
Adelina is the name of a twelfth-century saint. VARIANT FORMS: Adelin,
Adlin, Aline, Edelin, Edlin.

Adena   From the Hebrew and Greek, meaning "noble" or "adorned."
PLACE-NAME USAGE: a town in Colorado, named in 1910 for Edna Adena.

Adene   A variant spelling of Adena. *See* Adena. CONTEMPORARY EXAM-
PLE: Adene Corns, sales representative.

Aderes, Aderet   From the Hebrew, meaning "a cape, a covering, a crown."

Adie   From the Hebrew, meaning "ornament." A pet form of Adele,
Adelaide, and Adeline.

Adiella   From the Hebrew, meaning "ornament of the Lord." Akin to
Adie.

Adin   From the Hebrew, meaning "delicate." Adena and Adina are variant forms. Used also as a masculine name.

Adina   A variant spelling of Adena. *See* Adena.

Adine   A variant spelling of Adin. *See* Adin.

Adira   From the Hebrew, meaning "mighty, strong."

Adiva   From the Arabic, meaning "gracious, pleasant."

Adonia   The feminine form of the masculine Adonis, meaning "beautiful lady." *See* Adonis (masculine section).

Adora   From the Latin and French, meaning "one who is adored or loved."

Adorna   From the Anglo-Saxon, meaning "to adorn."

Adrea, Adria   Variant spellings of Adrienne. *See* Adrienne. CONTEMPORARY EXAMPLE: Adrea Carter, civic leader.

Adrian   Basically a masculine name, derived from Hadrian. *See* Adrian *and* Hadrian (masculine section). CONTEMPORARY EXAMPLE: Adrian Arpel, author.

Adriana   A form of Adrian. *See* Adrian. A character in Shakespeare's *Comedy of Errors*.

Adriane, Adrianne   Forms of Adrian. *See* Adrian.

Adrie   Probably a variant pet form of Adrien. *See* Adrien. CONTEMPORARY EXAMPLE: Adrie Hospes, author.

Adrien, Adrienne   French forms derived from the Greek, meaning "a girl from Adria." VARIANT FORMS: Adria, Adrian.

Adva   From the Aramaic, meaning "a wave, a ripple."

Aelfreda   The feminine form of Alfred. *See* Alfred (masculine section).

Affrica   From the Celtic, meaning "pleasant." Affrica was a twelfth–century princess who married the Lord of the Isles, Semerled, and thereafter ruled over the Isle of Man as his queen.

Afra   From the Hebrew, meaning "a young female deer." VARIANT FORMS: Aphra, Aphrah.

Agate   From the Old French, meaning "a hard, semi-precious stone." In legend, a magical name believed to confer independence and eloquence, and to make one favored by princes.

Agatha   From the Greek and Latin, meaning "good." A third–century Sicilian martyr was named Agatha, as were daughters of Emperor Henry II and William the Conqueror. VARIANT FORMS: Ageia (Latin); Agace (French); Agafia (Russian); Agathe (German and French). Aggie was a pet form in use in the seventeenth century. CONTEMPORARY EXAMPLE: Agatha Christie, author.

Aggie A pet form of Agatha. *See* Agatha. Agg is a variant form.

Aggy, Agy Pet forms of Agatha. *See* Agatha. CONTEMPORARY EXAMPLE: Agy Reid, communal worker.

Agnes From the Greek and Latin, meaning "lamb," symbolizing purity and chastity. Saint Agnes was a popular third-century saint. Five churches in England are named after her. From the twelfth to the sixteenth century, Agnes was one of the three most commonly used names in England. (Joan and Elizabeth led the list). Because of its common usage, it was often mispronounced and misspelled, and appeared as Anis, Annis, Annys, Annice, and Annes. VARIANT FORMS: Agnese, Agnete, Agnesa (Italian); Inez (Portuguese); Tagget (Old English); Neza, Nezika (Slavonic); Ines, Inesila (Spanish). PET FORMS: Aggie, Aggy, Agnette, Agy, Taggy.

Agostina The Italian form of Augusta. *See* Augusta.

Aharona, Aharonit Hebrew feminine forms of the masculine Aharon or Aaron. *See* Aaron (masculine section). VARIANT FORMS: Arni, Arnina, Arninit, Arona.

Ahava From the Hebrew, meaning "love." Ahuva is a variant form.

Ahuda From the Hebrew, meaning "beloved."

Ahulani From the Hawaiian, meaning "a heavenly shrine."

Ahuva From the Hebrew, meaning "beloved." Ahava is a variant form.

Aida From the Latin and Old French, meaning "to help." An Ethiopian princess enslaved in Egypt. The principal character in the Italian opera by Giuseppe Verdi (1871). CONTEMPORARY EXAMPLE: Aida Alvarez, television news reporter.

Aidan A variant form of Aida. *See* Aida.

Aileen, Ailene From the Greek, meaning "light." Akin to Helen. VARIANT FORMS: Alene, Aline, Eileen, Ilene, Illine, Illene, Illona.

Aili, Ailie Scotch forms of Alice. *See* Alice. CONTEMPORARY EXAMPLE: Aili Tabock, publisher's representative.

Ailina The Hawaiian form of Aileen. *See* Aileen.

Ailith A variant form of Aldith. *See* Aldith.

Aimee The French form of the Latin *amor*, meaning "love." Amy is a variant spelling.

Ainslee From the Scottish, meaning "one's own meadow or land." Used also as a masculine name. CONTEMPORARY EXAMPLE: Ainslee Newton, Ruston, Louisiana.

Aintre A name created by the mother of Aintre Bairn Keliner, of St.

Louis, Missouri. Derived by dropping the first and last letter of Raintree, from the book *Raintree County*.

Alaina, Alaine   Feminine forms of Alan. *See* Alan (masculine section). May also be a variant form of Helen. *See* Helen. CONTEMPORARY EXAMPLE: Alaina Reed, actress.

Alameda   A North American Indian name, meaning "cottonwood grove." Also, from the Spanish *alamo*, meaning "a grove of poplar trees." PLACE-NAME USAGE: Alameda, California.

Alana, Alanna   A feminine form of Alan. *See* Alan (masculine section). VARIANT FORMS: Allana, Alina, Lana, Lane. CONTEMPORARY EXAMPLES: Alana Collins, model; Alanna Nash, author.

Alayne   A variant spelling of Alaine. *See* Alaine. CONTEMPORARY EXAMPLE: Alayne Yates, physician.

Alba   A pet form of Alberta. *See* Alberta. CONTEMPORARY EXAMPLE: Alba Francesa, actress.

Alberta   A feminine form of Albert. *See* Albert (masculine section). Alberta became popular in the nineteenth century when King Albert was king of England. Albertha is a variant spelling. PET FORMS: Albertina, Albertine. PLACE-NAME USAGE: Alberta, Canada, a province named for Princess Louise Alberta, fourth daughter of Queen Victoria.

Albertha   A variant spelling of Albert. *See* Albert.

Albertina, Albertine   Feminine pet forms of Alberta. *See* Alberta. CONTEMPORARY EXAMPLE: Albertina Noyes, figure skater.

Albina, Albinia   From the Latin *albus*, meaning "white." *See also* Albin *and* Alben (masculine section). Albina was a third–century saint. Through the eighteenth century, Albina was the more common form; thereafter, Albinia, the Italian form, became popular. VARIANT FORMS: Albigna, Alvinia. CONTEMPORARY EXAMPLES: Albina H. Gautreau, Gardner, Massachusetts; Albina Tomsha, LaSalle, Illinois.

Albirda   A variant spelling of Alverta or Albreda. *See* Alverta *and* Albreda.

Albreda   An Old German, thirteenth century feminine equivalent of Albert. *See* Albert (masculine section). Albirda is a variant form.

Alcestis   In Greek mythology, the wife of Admetus, king of Thessaly. A name connoting "a hero" because Alcestis risked her life to save her husband.

Alcina   Probably a feminine form of the Greek Alcindor and Alcander, meaning "manly." In Greek mythology, the name of the enchantress in *Astolpho and the Enchantress*. PET FORMS: Alcie, Elsie. CONTEMPORARY EXAMPLES: Alcina Morais, Pawtucket, Rhode Island; Alcina Rathert, Long Beach, California.

Alda   From the Old German, meaning "old." Aude is a variant form used in twelfth–century England. VARIANT FORMS: Aldona, Aldina, Aldine, Aldyne, Aleda. Aldo and Aldous are masculine forms. SURNAME USAGE: Frances Alda (1885-1952), American opera singer.

Aldine, Aldyne   Variant forms of Alda. *See* Alda. CONTEMPORARY EXAMPLE: Aldyne Dilling, Eureka, California.

Aldis   The Latin form of the Old English name Aldith. *See* Aldith.

Aldith, Alditha   From the Old English, meaning "old in battle." Popular in the eleventh and twelfth centuries. VARIANT FORMS: Aldis (Latin), Ailith.

Aldona   From the Old German, meaning "old one."

Aldora   From the Anglo-Saxon, meaning "noble gift."

Aleda   A variant form of Alda. *See* Alda. CONTEMPORARY EXAMPLE: Aleda Renken, author.

Aleen, Aleene   From the Dutch, meaning "alone." Or, variant forms of Helen. *See* Helen.

Aleeza   From the Hebrew, meaning "joy" or "happy one." Aliza and Alizah are variant spellings.

Aleka   A variant spelling of Alika. *See* Alika.

Alena   A Russian form of Helen. *See* Helen.

Alene   A variant form of Arlene or Eileen. *See* Arlene *and* Eileen.

Aleph   The first letter of the Hebrew alphabet, meaning "a prince." Alupha is a variant form. CONTEMPORARY EXAMPLE: Inza Aleph Beasley, Nederland, Texas.

Alessandra   An Italian variant form of Alexandra. *See* Alexandra. Alessandria, a city in northwestern Italy. CONTEMPORARY EXAMPLE: Alessandra Comini, art historian.

Alethea, Alethia, Alithea   From the Greek, meaning "truth." A seventeenth–century name that came to England through Spain. In her writings, Jane Austen uses the spellings Alethea and Alithea.

Aletta   From the Latin, meaning "the winged one."

Alevia   Probably a variant form of Alva. *See* Alva. CONTEMPORARY EXAMPLE: Alevia van Pelt Ballard, St. Albans, West Virginia.

Alexa   A variant form of Alexandra. *See* Alexandra.

Alexandra, Alexandria, Alexandrina   Feminine forms of the Greek name Alexander, meaning "protector of man." Queen Salome-Alexandra, ruler of Judea from 76-67 B.C., was one of the earliest to use this name. In the thirteenth century, Alexandra and Alexandria were used in England, probably in honor of a fourth-century Christian martyr.

Alexandra and Alexandrina are Russian usages which became popular in England in the fourteenth century after the marriage of Edward II to Princess Alexandra of Denmark. VARIANT FORMS: Alexa, Alexia, Alexis (English); Aleixo (Portuguese); Alejo (Spanish); Alexe, Alexis (French); Alexscha, Alexei (Russian); Allesanda, Alessio (Italian); Elek (Hungarian). PET FORMS: Alexina, Alexine, Sandra, Sandy.

Alexina, Alexine   Pet form of Alexandra. *See* Alexandra.

Alexis   A variant form of Alexandra. *See* Alexandra. Used also as a masculine name. Aliki is an Hawaiian form. CONTEMPORARY EXAMPLE: Alexis Smith, actress.

Alfreda   The feminine form of Alfred. *See* Alfred (masculine section).

Ali   A pet form of Alice or Alison. *See* Alice *and* Alison. CONTEMPORARY EXAMPLE: Ali McGraw, actress.

Alice   From the Middle English names Alys and Aeleis, which evolved from the Old French Aliz and Aaliz. Originally the Old High German name Adelheidis, akin to Adelaide, meaning "of noble birth." Alice evolved as a popular English form probably as a result of the publication, in 1865, of *Alice in Wonderland* by Lewis Carroll. VARIANT FORMS: Alie, Alix, Alyse, Alyce, Alyse, Alissa, Alecia, Alison. Alison and Allison have become surnames. PLACE-NAME USAGE: a city in Texas named after Alice Kleberg (1886); Alicel, Oregon, named after Alice Ladd (the L of Ladd was added to Alice.)

Alicen   An early form of Alison. *See* Allison.

Alicia   A variant form of Alice. *See* Alice. CONTEMPORARY EXAMPLES: Alicia Ostriker, editor; Alicia Meadowes, author.

Alida, Alidia   From the Greek, meaning "beautifully dressed." Derived from a city in ancient Asia-Minor, well-known for its finely-dressed citizens. CONTEMPORARY EXAMPLE: Alidia Becker, editor.

Alika   An Hawaiian form of Alice. *See* Alice.

Aliki   A variant form of Alexis. *See* Alexis. CONTEMPORARY EXAMPLE: Aliki Barnstone, poet.

Alina   A short form of Adeline, which is a derivative of Adelaide. *See* Adelaide. Commonly used in the twelfth to fifteenth centuries.

Aline   A short form of Adeline, which is a variant form of Adelaide. *See* Adelaide.

Alinor   The heroine of the novel *Alinor*, by Roberta Gellis. A variant form of Eleanor. *See* Eleanor.

Alisa, Alissa   Variant forms of Alice. *See* Alice.

Alison   A matronymic form, meaning "the son of Alice." Popular as a surname. In the northern portion of England, Alicen was the form of Alison.

Alistair   More commonly used as a masculine name. *See* Alistair (masculine section).

Alitza, Alitzah   Variant spelling of Aliza. *See* Aliza.

Alix   A French form of Alice. *See* Alice. CONTEMPORARY EXAMPLE: Alix Kate Shulman, novelist.

Aliya, Aliyah   From the Hebrew, meaning "to ascend, to go up."

Aliza, Alizah   From the Hebrew, meaning "joy, joyous one." VARIANT FORMS: Aleeza, Aleezah, Alitza, Alitzah. CONTEMPORARY EXAMPLE: Aliza Begin, wife of Israeli Prime Minister Menachem Begin.

Alla   A feminine form of Allah. *See* Allah (masculine section). CONTEMPORARY EXAMPLE: Alla Bozarth-Campbell, ordained minister. PLACE-NAME USAGE: Allamore, Texas, named for Alla Moore, wife of an early settler.

Allana   A feminine form of Alan. *See* Alan (masculine section).

Allegra   From the Latin *alacer*, meaning "brisk, cheerful." CONTEMPORARY EXAMPLE: Allegra Kent, dancer.

Allen   Primarily a masculine name. *See* Allen (masculine section).

Alley   A pet form of Alice. *See* Alice.

Allianora   An invented name probably compounded of Alice or Allison and Nora. CONTEMPORARY EXAMPLE: Allianora Ruder, editor.

Allie   A pet form of Alice or Allison. *See* Alice *and* Allison. CONTEMPORARY EXAMPLE: Allie Beth Martin, librarian.

Allison   A matronymic form, meaning "son of Alice." *See* Alice. A common surname. VARIANT SPELLINGS: Alison, Alyson.

Allissa   A variant form of Alice. *See* Alice. CONTEMPORARY EXAMPLE: Allissa Dietmeyer, Madison, Wisconsin.

Allonia   A variant form of Allon. From the Hebrew, meaning "oak tree." CONTEMPORARY EXAMPLE: Allonia Gadsden, educator.

Allyn   A variant spelling of Allen. Primarily a masculine name. *See* Allen (masculine section). CONTEMPORARY EXAMPLE: Allyn Ann McLerie, actress.

Alma   From the Hebrew, meaning "maiden." May also be derived from the Latin, meaning "nourishing" or "bountiful," as in *alma mater* ("nourishing mother"). In Italian and Spanish, *alma* means "soul." After the battle of the Alma River, in 1854, during the Crimean War, the name became popular. CONTEMPORARY EXAMPLE: Alma Larson, secretary of state of South Dakota.

Almarine   A pet form of Almeria. *See* Almeria. CONTEMPORARY EXAMPLE: Almarine Wininger, San Jose, California.

Almeria   Probably a feminine form of Almeric. *See* Almeric (masculine section). PLACE-NAME USAGE: a seaport in southeastern Spain, on the Mediterranean; Almeria, Nebraska, named for Almeria Strohl, wife of the founder.

Almira   From the Arabic, meaning "princess" or "exalted one." May also be from the Spanish, meaning "a woman from Almeria." *See* Almeria. Mira is a pet form.

Almodine   A form of the Latin name Alabandina, meaning "precious gem" (of the garnet variety).

Aloha   An Hawaiian name, connoting love, mercy, kindness, greetings, and farewell.

Alola   The Hawaiian form of Aurora. *See* Aurora.

Alona   From the Hebrew, meaning "oak tree." The feminine form of Alon. *See* Alon (masculine section).

Alouise   From the German, meaning "famous in battle." A feminine form of Louis. *See* Louis (masculine section).

Alpha   From the Greek, meaning "the first," being the first letter of the Greek alphabet. PLACE-NAME USAGE: Alpha, Oregon, named for Alpha Lundey, a resident; Alpha Lake, Montana.

Alsace   A region in the northeastern part of France, once under the control of Germany. CONTEMPORARY EXAMPLE: Alsace Lorraine Stewart, Conroe, Texas.

Alta   A Spanish form of the Latin *alta*, meaning "tall." Used also as a masculine name. *See* also Altai. CONTEMPORARY EXAMPLE: Alta B. Atkinson, food expert. PLACE-NAME USAGE: Alta, Iowa, named after Altair Blair, daughter of a railroad official.

Altai   A variant form of Alta. *See* Alta.

Altair   From the Arabic, meaning "a bird." The name of the brightest star in the constellation Aquila. Used also as a masculine name. CONTEMPORARY EXAMPLE: Altair Blair. *See* Alta. PLACE-NAME USAGE: Altair, Texas.

Althea   From the Greek and Latin, meaning "to heal" or "healer." CONTEMPORARY EXAMPLE: Althea Gibson, tennis player.

Alto   A Spanish form of Alta. *See* Alta. PLACE-NAME USAGE: Alto, West Virginia.

Alufa   A variant spelling of Alupha. *See* Alupha.

Aluma, Alumit   From the Hebrew *alma*, meaning "a girl, a maiden." VARIANT FORMS: Alma, Alumit.

Alupha   From the Hebrew, meaning "leader" or "princess." The feminine form of Aluph. *See* Aluph (masculine section). Akin to Aleph. *See* Aleph. Alufa is a variant spelling.

Alva, Alvan   From the Latin, meaning "white" or "fair." Akin to the masculine Alvan. *See* Alvan (masculine section).

Alvagene   An invented name, combining Alva and the masculine Eugene. CONTEMPORARY EXAMPLE: Alvagene Wininger, Madill, Oklahoma.

Alvania   A variant form of Alva. *See* Alva.

Alyce   A variant spelling of Alice. *See* Alice. CONTEMPORARY EXAMPLE: Alyce Caufield, actress.

Alyna   A Latin form of Aline. Commonly used from the twelfth to the fifteenth century. *See* Aline.

Alys, Alyse   Original forms of Alice, in use in England before the seventeenth century. *See* Alice. Alyce is a variant spelling.

Alyson   A variant spelling of Alison. *See* Alison. CONTEMPORARY EXAMPLE: Alyson Huxley, horticulturist.

Alyss, Alyssa   Variant spellings of Alice. *See* Alice. CONTEMPORARY EXAMPLE: Alyss Barlow Dorese, editor.

Alzina   A variant spelling of Alcina. *See* Alcina. CONTEMPORARY EXAMPLE: Alzina Stone Dale, author.

Amabel   Compounded from the Latin *amador*, meaning "love," and the French *belle*, meaning "beautiful." Popular in England in the twelfth and the thirteenth centuries. VARIANT FORMS: Annabel, Arabel, Mabel.

Amadis   From the Spanish, meaning "love of God."

Amalia, Amaliah   From the Hebrew, meaning "the work of the Lord." CONTEMPORARY EXAMPLE: Amalia Fleming, Greek political leader.

Amalie   A German form of Amelia. *See* Amelia.

Amalthea   A variant form of Amalia. *See* Amalia. In Greek and Latin mythology, the goat that nursed Zeus (Jupiter), one of its horns being called *cornucopia*, or Horn of Plenty.

Amana   From the Hebrew, meaning "faithful." A place-name in the Bible.

Amanda   From the Latin, meaning "worthy of love." Mandy is a pet form. CONTEMPORARY EXAMPLE: Amanda Hope Wolfe, Savannah, Tennessee.

Amarinda   From the Greek and Latin, meaning "long–lived." In poetry, an imaginary flower that never fades or dies.

Amaryllis   A shepherdess in the poems of the Greek poets Virgil and Theocritus, and since then a synonym for a shepherd. Also, a name of a flower in the lily family.

Amber   From the Arabic and French, meaning "yellowish-brown resin," found on some seashores. PLACE-NAME USAGE: Amber, Iowa.

Amberlie   A variant form of Amber. *See* Amber. CONTEMPORARY EXAM-

PLE: Amberlie Harris, Sacramento, California, named for her mother's birthstone, Amber (November).

Ambrosia From the Greek and Latin, *ambrosios* and *ambrosius* respectively, meaning "immortal." In Greek and Roman mythology, the food of the gods and the immortal beings, hence anything that has a delicious taste. Used as a first name since the sixteenth century. VARIANT FORMS: Ambrosina, Ambrosine. Ambrose is a masculine form.

Ambrosina, Ambrosine From the Greek, meaning "immortal." Ambrosina occurs in the writings of Charles Dickens. Ambrosia is a variant form. Ambrose is the masculine equivalent.

Amby A pet form of Amber and Ambrosia. *See* Amber *and* Ambrosia.

Amelia From the Hebrew and Latin *amal*, meaning "work." Princess Amelia, youngest daughter of King George III, was often called Princess Emily. VARIANT FORMS: Amalie (German); Emily (English). PET FORMS: Millie, Milly. PLACE-NAME USAGE: Amelia County, Virginia.

Amelinda An invented name. Created by combining Amelia and Linda. *See* Amelia and Linda.

Amera A short form of America. Mera is a pet form. CONTEMPORARY EXAMPLE: Amera Dame, Concord, New Hampshire.

America Mrs. Orma Weil, of Dallas, Texas, reports that her paternal grandmother's name was America. Used primarily as a masculine name. *See* America (masculine section).

Amethyst The name of a violet-blue jewel worn by ancient Greeks to prevent intoxication.

Ami, Amie Variant spellings of Amy. *See* Amy.

Amia From the Latin *amor*, meaning "love." Also from the Hebrew *ami*, meaning "my people." CONTEMPORARY EXAMPLE: Amia Lieblich, Israeli psychotherapist.

Amice From the Latin and Old French, meaning "a cloak" or "a hood" usually worn by priests at mass.

Amina, Amine From the Hebrew and Arabic *amin*, meaning "trusted, faithful." Feminine forms of Amin. PLACE-NAME USAGE: Amine Peak, Oregon, named for Harriet Amine Salzman, an early settler.

Aminta From the Latin, meaning "to protect." Coined in England in the seventeenth century.

Amira From the Hebrew, meaning "speech, utterance."

Amiret, Amiretta Possibly forms of Amira. *See* Amira. PLACE-NAME USAGE: Amiret, Montana, named for Amiretta Sykes, wife of a railroad official.

Amisa, Amissa From the Hebrew, meaning "friend."

Amita   From the Hebrew, meaning "truth."

Amity   From the Latin *amor*, meaning "love, friendship." PLACE-NAME USAGE: cities in Pennsylvania, Oregon, and Colorado.

Amitza   A variant form of Amiza. *See* Amiza.

Amiza   From the Hebrew, meaning "strong." Amitza is a variant spelling.

Amma   From the Hebrew and Arabic, meaning "servant." PLACE-NAME USAGE: Amma, West Virginia.

Amy   The French form of the Latin *amor*, meaning "love." VARIANT FORMS: Amata, Amia.

Ana   The Spanish and Hawaiian forms of Anna. *See* Anna. Anita is a pet form. CONTEMPORARY EXAMPLE: Ana Margarita Menendez, actress.

Anabela   A variant spelling of Annabella. *See* Annabella.

Anabeth   Compounded of Anna and Elizabeth. *See* Anna *and* Elizabeth. CONTEMPORARY EXAMPLE: Anabeth Judy Dollins, Pittsburgh, Pennsylvania.

Anais   A variant English form of Anne. *See* Anne. CONTEMPORARY EXAMPLE: Anais Nin, author.

Ana-Maria   A hybrid name. *See* Ana *and* Maria. CONTEMPORARY EXAMPLE: Ana-Maria Rizzuto, psychiatrist.

Anastasia   From the Greek, meaning "resurrection." Anastasius is the masculine form. In Ireland, two Christian martyrs were so named. VARIANT FORMS: Anstace (English); Anty, Stacy (Irish); Anastasie (French); Nastassja, Nastenka (Russian). PLACE-NAME USAGE: Anastatia Island, Florida, probably named after Saint Anastasia.

Anat   From the Hebrew, meaning "to sing." In the Bible, a masculine name, the father of Shamgar, an Israelite judge.

Anatola   From the Greek, meaning "from the East." Anatole is the masculine form.

Anatone   A variant form of Antonia. *See* Antonia. Also an Indian name. PLACE-NAME USAGE: Anatone, Washington.

Anchoret, Anchoretta   The original form was probably Ancret, an English variant of the Welsh name Angahard. *See* Angahard.

Ancilla   From the Latin, meaning "handmaid." It first appears in the seventeenth century, possibly as a feminine form of Ancel.

Andra   From the Old Norse, meaning "a breath." It may also be a short form of Andrea. *See* Andrea. CONTEMPORARY EXAMPLE: Anda Amir, author.

Andrea   From the Greek, meaning "valiant, strong, courageous." Andreas is the masculine form.

Ane   The Hawaiian form of Nancy. *See* Nancy.

Anemone   From the Greek, meaning "a breath." In Greek legend, Anemone was a nymph pursued by the wind and changed into a delicate flower. CONTEMPORARY EXAMPLE: Anemone Morgan, Edmond, Oklahoma.

Anett   A variant spelling of Annette. *See* Annette.

Angahard, Angharad   From the Welsh, meaning "loved one." VARIANT FORMS: Anchoret, Anchoretta. CONTEMPORARY EXAMPLE: Angharad Rees, actress.

Angela   From the Middle Latin name Angelica and the Latin *angelicus*, meaning "angelic." St. Angela was a sixteenth-century nun who founded the Ursuline Order of teaching nuns. Angel is the masculine form. VARIANT FORMS: Angele, Angeline (French); Engel (German); Angiola, Angelica (Italian); Anjela, Anjelika (Slavonic). PET FORMS: Angeletta, Angelina, Angie.

Angele   A variant form of Angela. *See* Angela. CONTEMPORARY EXAMPLE: Angele Coggin, Goodlettsville, Tennessee.

Angeles   A variant form of Angela and Angele. *See* Angela. CONTEMPORARY EXAMPLE: Angeles Knebel, Marina del Ray, California. PLACE-NAME USAGE: Los Angeles, California.

Angeleta   A pet form of Angela. *See* Angela. CONTEMPORARY EXAMPLE: Lassie Angeleta Martin, Clarksville, Tennessee.

Angelica   The Latin form of Angela. *See* Angela.

Angelina, Angeline   Pet forms of Angela. *See* Angela. PLACE-NAME USAGE: a river and county in Texas, named for an Indian girl.

Anina   A pet form of Anna. *See* Anna. CONTEMPORARY EXAMPLE: Anina Yaron, Israeli scientist.

Anita   The Spanish form of Anna. *See* Anna.

Anjean   Compounded of Ann and Jean. PLACE-NAME USAGE: Anjean, West Virginia, named for Ann and Jean, the mother and daughter of a local mine owner.

Anka   A Slavic pet form of Anna. *See* Anna. CONTEMPORARY EXAMPLE: Anka Ostajic, resident of Montreal, Canada.

Anmore   Compound of Ann and the surname Moore. PLACE-NAME USAGE: Anmore, West Virginia, named for Ann Moore Run, a local resident.

Ann   A variant spelling of Anne. *See* Anne. Popular as a middle name, e.g., Sue Ann, Barbara Ann, etc.

Anna   The Greek form of the Hebrew name Hannah, meaning "gracious." An early name popular among German-speaking peoples, and in Italy. It was later carried to Russia, where it became popular after the appearance of Leo Tolstoy's nineteenth-century novel *Anna Karenina.* VARIANT FORMS: Hannah (Hebrew); Anne, Nan, Nancy, Nanny (English); Annot (Scotch); Naatja (Dutch); Panna, Panni (Hungarian); Anusia (Polish); Ana, Anita (Spanish); Anne, Annette, Nannette (French); Anca, Anica (Slavonic). PET FORMS: Nan, Nance, Nancy, Nanette, Nannie, Nana, Nanita.

Annabel   A variant form of Annabella. *See* Annabella. Its first usage was in England. In 1367, Robert III of Scotland married Annabel Drummond, who became the mother of James I of Scotland. Edgar Allen Poe's poem *Annabel Lee* popularized the name.

Annabella, Annabelle   Compounded of Anna and Bella, meaning "gracious and beautiful." *See* Anna *and* Bella. PLACE-NAME USAGE: Annabella, Utah, named for Ann Roberts and Isabella Dalton, the first two female residents.

Annada   Compounded of Ann and Ada. *See* Ann *and* Ada. PLACE-NAME USAGE: Annada, Missouri, named for the daughters of Carson Jamison, Ann and Ada.

Annalyn, Annalynn   Compounded of Anna and Lyn. CONTEMPORARY EXAMPLE: Annalyn Swan, journalist.

Annarose   Compounded of Anna and Rose. PLACE-NAME USAGE: Annarose, Texas, named for Anna Rose Scott, a local resident.

Annazette   An invented name. Created by combining Anna and Suzette (Susan). *See* Anna *and* Susan. CONTEMPORARY EXAMPLE: Annazette Chase, actress.

Anncar   An invented name, from Ann plus the first syllable of Carroll. PLACE-NAME USAGE: Anncar, Nebraska, named for Ann Carroll O'Neill.

Anne   A French form of the Hebrew name Hannah, meaning "gracious." *See* Anna *and* Hannah. Queen Anne ruled over Great Britain and Ireland (1665–1714). PET FORMS: Annette, Nanette, Hanon, Ninon, Ninette.

Annell   Compounded of Ann and Nell. *See* Ann *and* Nell.

Annelle   A variant spelling of Annell. *See* Annell.

Annemarie   A compound of Anne and Marie. *See* Ann *and* Marie. CONTEMPORARY EXAMPLE: Annemarie Moser Proel, skier.

Annette   A French form of Anna. *See* Anna.

Annfred   Compounded of Ann and Fred. *See* Ann; *see also* Fred (masculine section). PLACE-NAME USAGE: Annfred, West Virginia, named for a railroad official and his wife.

Annice   An Old English variant form of Ann. *See* Ann. Annis is a variant spelling. *See* Annis.

Annie   Usually a pet form of Ann, Anna, or Hannah. *See* Anna. CON-

TEMPORARY EXAMPLE: Annie Oakley (1860—1926), a rifle expert.

Annimae   Compounded of Annie and Mae. *See* Annie and Mae.

Annis   A form of Agnes used in the Middle Ages. *See* Agnes. Also, an Old English variant form of Ann. *See* Ann. Annais and Annys are variant spellings. PLACE-NAME USAGE: Annis, Idaho, named for Ann Kearney, first postmistress.

Annona   An Indian name possibly compounded of Ann and Nona. *See* Ann *and* Nona. PLACE-NAME USAGE: Annona, Texas, named for an Indian girl (1884).

Annrae   A hybrid name of Ann and Rae. *See* Ann *and* Rae. CONTEMPORARY EXAMPLE: Annrae Walterhouse, actress.

Anouk   Origin unknown. CONTEMPORARY EXAMPLE: Anouk Aimee, actress.

Anthea   From the Greek, meaning "flowery." Popular among poets who wrote about nature. CONTEMPORARY EXAMPLE: Anthea Goddard, author.

Antoinette   The feminine French form of Antony. *See* Antony (masculine section). St. Antonia was a third-century Portuguese saint. Queen Marie Antoinette (1755-1793) was the wife of King Louis XVI. VARIANT FORMS: Antonia, Antonietta, Antonica (Italian); Toinette (French); Tonneli (Old German); Antonma (Swedish). PET FORMS: Nettie, Netty, Toni, Tonia, Tonya, Tanya.

Antonette   A variant form of Antoinette. CONTEMPORARY EXAMPLE: Antonette Parish, Dallas, Texas.

Antonia   The Italian and Swedish form of Antoinette. *See* Antoinette.

Anya   A Russian form of Ann. *See* Ann. CONTEMPORARY EXAMPLE: Anya Seton, author.

Aolani   An Hawaiian name, meaning "heavenly cloud."

Aphra   From the Hebrew, meaning "a young, female deer." VARIANT FORMS: Afra, Aphrah, Ayfara. CONTEMPORARY EXAMPLE: Aphra Behn (1640-1689), dramatist.

Aphrodite   From the Greek *aphros*, meaning "foam." In Greek mythology, the goddess of love and beauty who is supposed to have sprung from the foam of the sea. CONTEMPORARY EXAMPLE: Aphrodite Polemis, author.

Aprial   A name created by Vivian D. Fulk of Mt. Pleasant, Michigan. Both her mother and father served in the Army Air Force (AAF) during World War II. To match the letters AAF, the name Aprial Augusta Fulk was selected.

April   From the Latin, meaning "to open," symbolic of springtime. April was used by the early Romans as the name of the second month of the year.

Arabel, Arabela, Arabella, Arabelle   From the German *ara*, meaning "eagle," plus the Latin *bella*, meaning "beautiful." First used as Scottish names in the thirteenth century. Lady Arabella Stuart (1575-1615) was called Arbell by her friends. VARIANT FORMS: Arbel, Arbela, Arbell, Orable, Orabell.

Arachne   From the Greek, meaning "a spider." In Greek mythology, a girl turned into a spider by Athena.

Araminta   A compounded form of Arabel and Aminta. *See* Arabel *and* Aminta. Coined in the seventeenth century, and used by Araminta Lundy and Araminta Roberts, both members of the aristocracy of England. CONTEMPORARY EXAMPLE: Araminta Sybil Gruenenfelder, Woonsocket, Rhode Island. The name Arminta has been in her family for four generations.

Arbel, Arbela, Arbell   Variant forms of Arabel. *See* Arabel. PLACE-NAME USAGE: an ancient Persian city (in northern Iran) now called Erbil.

Arda, Ardah   From the Hebrew, meaning "bronze, bronzed." Also, a variant form of the Hebrew month Adar.

Ardath   A variant spelling of Arda. *See* Arda.

Ardelia   From the Latin, meaning "zealous." Ardis is a variant form.

Arden   From the Old French *ardour* and the Latin *ardor*, meaning "a flame" or "passionate." CONTEMPORARY EXAMPLE: Arden Shelton, art critic. PLACE-NAME USAGE: a forest and several villages in England.

Ardis   A variant form of Ardelia. *See* Ardelia.

Ardith   An Anglo-Saxon form of Edith. *See* Edith.

Ardra   From the Celtic, meaning "high, the high one."

Areal   A name invented by Reba Swicegood, Rockwood, Tennessee. When a healthy baby arrived screaming, the father shouted, "that's *a real* baby," hence the name.

Arela, Arella   From the Hebrew, meaning an "angel, a messenger."

Aretha   A variant form of Arethusa. *See* Arethusa. Oretha is a variant spelling. CONTEMPORARY EXAMPLE: Aretha Franklin, singer.

Arethusa   In Greek mythology, a woodland nymph who was changed into a stream by Artemis. Also, a variety of orchid.

Aria   From the Latin, meaning "a melody in an opera." Or, the feminine form of the Hebrew name Ari, meaning "a lion." CONTEMPORARY EXAMPLE: Aria Eliav, author.

Ariadne   In Greek legend, the name of the daughter of King Midas. In Greek mythology, the daughter of the sun god. VARIANT FORMS: Arianna, Ariane.

Ariane, Arianna   Variant forms of Ariadne. *See* Ariadne. CONTEM-PORARY EXAMPLE: Arianna Stassinopoulos, author.

Ariel, Ariela, Ariella, Arielle   From the Hebrew, meaning "lioness of God." CONTEMPORARY EXAMPLE: Ariel Durant, author.

Arilita   A pet form of Arlene. *See* Arlene. CONTEMPORARY EXAMPLE: Arilita Wandling, California resident.

Arista   From the Latin, meaning "a beard," referring to the beardlike part of grain or grasses. May also be related to the Greek name Aristos, meaning "the best."

Aritha   A variant form of Arethusa. *See* Arethusa. CONTEMPORARY EXAMPLE: Aritha van Herk, novelist.

Ariza   From the Hebrew, meaning "cedar panels."

Arla   A variant form of Arlene. Or, a short form of Carla. *See* Arlene *and* Carla. CONTEMPORARY EXAMPLES: Arla H. Gibbs, Greensboro, North Carolina; Arla Nickols, Sacramento, California.

Arlana   A pet form of Arlene. *See* Arlene.

Arleen   A variant spelling of Arlene. *See* Arleen. CONTEMPORARY EXAMPLE: Arleen Keylin, editor.

Arlene   A variant spelling of Arline. *See* Arline. Or, from the Celtic, meaning "a pledge, an oath."

Arleta, Arlette   Pet forms of Arlene or Arline. *See* Arlene *and* Arline.

Arleyne   A variant spelling of Arlene. *See* Arlene.

Arline, Arlyne   From the German, meaning "girl." Or, a form of Adeline. *See* Adeline.

Arlise   A variant spelling of Arlyss. *See* Arlyss.

Arlynn   A name compounded of Arlene and Lynn. Also, a variant form of Arlene. *See* Arlene, *and* Lynn. CONTEMPORARY EXAMPLE: Arlynn Greenbaum, publicity director.

Arlyss   A variant form of the masculine names Arliss and Arles. *See* Arles (masculine section). CONTEMPORARY EXAMPLE: Arlyss Stump, educator.

Arminta   Probably a corrupt form of Aminta. *See* Aminta. CONTEM-PORARY EXAMPLE: Arminta Ray, Kansas.

Armona, Armonit   From the Hebrew, meaning "a castle, a palace." Also, a tree in the oak family.

Arna   From the Hebrew, meaning "a cedar tree." CONTEMPORARY EX-AMPLE: Arna Wendell Bontemps, author.

Arnit   A variant form of Arna. *See* Arna.

Arni, Arnina, Arninit   Forms of Arona and Aharona, currently used is Israel. *See* Arona *and* Aharona.

Arnit A variant form of Arna. *See* Arna.

Arnoldine A French variant of the Old German masculine name Arnold, meaning "eagle rule" and signifying power. The French name Arnolde is a variant form.

Arolyn Created by dropping the C of Carolyn. CONTEMPORARY EXAMPLE: Arolyn Sargent, Concord, New Hampshire.

Arona A variant spelling of Aharona. *See* Aharona.

Arone A name invented by combining *Ar*lene and I*o*ne.

Arta Probably a variant form of Artema or Artemis. *See* Artema *and* Artemis. May also derive from the Latin name Artis, and the Old French name Arte, meaning "to join together." CONTEMPORARY EXAMPLE: Arta Saunders, for whom Artic, Washington, was named in 1880.

Artema, Artemas Variant forms of Artemis. *See* Artemis. In the Bible, a companion of Paul.

Artemis In Greek mythology, the goddess of the moon, wild animals, and hunting. Identified with the Roman goddess Diana. Artemis is mentioned in the Bible in the Book of Acts. Used also as a masculine name.

Artemisa, Artemisia Variant forms of Artemis. *See* Artemis. CONTEMPORARY EXAMPLE: Artemisa Hicks, Albuquerque, New Mexico.

Arue Origin uncertain, but may come from Tahitian, meaning "to dance." CONTEMPORARY EXAMPLE: Arue Szura, free–lance writer.

Arva From the Latin, meaning "from the coast." Or, from the Danish, meaning "the eagle," signifying strength. Used also as a masculine name.

Arvelle A variant form of Arva. *See* Arva. CONTEMPORARY EXAMPLE: Arvelle Carey, Memphis, Tennessee.

Arvilla A variant form of Arva. *See* Arva. PLACE-NAME USAGE: Arvilla, North Dakota, named for Arvilla Hersey, wife of a local landowner.

Arza From the Hebrew, meaning "cedar wood." Originally a masculine name. In the Bible, a steward of Elah.

Arzit A variant form of Arza. *See* Arza.

Asenath From the Egyptian, probably meaning "belonging to." In the Bible, the wife of Joseph, the mother of Ephraim and Manasseh. CONTEMPORARY EXAMPLE: Asenath Petrie, author.

Ashira From the Hebrew, meaning "wealthy."

Asisa From the Hebrew, meaning "juicy, ripe."

Aspasia A fifth-century B.C. wise Athenian woman, mistress of Pericles. CONTEMPORARY EXAMPLE: Aspasia Sabot, teacher.

Asphodel From the Greek name Asphodelos. Any of a number of related plants in the lily family.

Assia From the Hebrew, meaning "action, performance." CONTEMPORARY EXAMPLE: Assia Neuberg, Israeli editor.

Asta A variant form of Astera. *See* Astera.

Astera, Asteria From the Greek *aster*, meaning "a star." Because of its star-shaped leaves, the aster flower has been called the"starflower." VARIANT FORMS: Asta, Astra, Astrea, Esther (Persian); Hester, Hadassah (Hebrew).

Astra, Astraea Variant forms of Astera. *See* Astera. In Greek mythology, Astraea was a goddess of justice and innocence.

Astrid, Astred A form of Astra. *See* Astra. Or, from the Old Norse, meaning "divine strength." CONTEMPORARY EXAMPLE: Astrid Lindgren, author.

Atalanta In Greek legend, a beautiful and swift-footed huntress.

Atalia The Hawaiian form of Athalia. *See* Athalia.

Atara From the Hebrew, meaning "a crown." Ateret is a variant form.

Ateret From the Hebrew, meaning "a crown, a covering." Atara is a variant form.

Athalee Probably a variant form of Athalia. *See* Athalia. CONTEMPORARY EXAMPLE: Athalee Ada Stearns, a resident of Chicago, Illinois.

Athalia From the Hebrew, meaning "God is exalted." In the Bible, Queen of Judah (842-836 B.C.), the daughter of Ahab and Jezebel. PLACE-NAME USAGE: Athalia, Ohio, named for the daughter of the founder.

Athena From the Greek, meaning "wisdom." In Greek mythology, the goddess of wisdom and warfare. Minerva is its equivalent in Roman mythology. CONTEMPORARY EXAMPLE: Athena V. Lord, author. PLACE-NAME USAGE: Athena, Oregon, named for the Greek goddess.

Athol Probably a variant form of atoll, a ring-shaped island. CONTEMPORARY EXAMPLE: Athol Wininger, Bowie, Texas.

Atira From the Hebrew, meaning "a prayer."

Atura From the Hebrew, meaning "adorned" or "crowned."

Audlice An invented name combining *Aud*rey and *Alice*. CONTEMPORARY EXAMPLE: Charlinda Audlice Nance, resident of San Antonio, Texas.

Audra A variant form of Audrey. *See* Audrey. CONTEMPORARY EXAM-

PLE: Audra Lindley, actress.

Audre A modern spelling of Audrey. *See* Audrey. CONTEMPORARY EX-
AMPLE: Audre Lorde, author.

Audrey From the Old English, meaning "noble strength." Audrey
was a pet name until the seventeenth century, when it became an independent name. Shakespeare uses Audrey in *As You Like It*, for the
name of the poor country wench.

Audris From the Old German, meaning "fortunate" or wealthy."

Augusta From the Latin, meaning "revered, sacred." The feminine
form of Augustus. *See* Augustus (masculine section). Augusta, the
Princess of Wales, was the daughter-in-law of King George II. VARIANT
FORMS: Auguste, Aste, Guste, Gustel (German); Gusta (Slavonic). PET
FORMS: Gus, Gussie. PLACE-NAME USAGE: Augusta, Georgia, Augusta
County, Virginia.

Auguste A German form of Augusta. *See* Augusta.

Augusteen The Irish form of Augusta. *See* Augusta.

Augustina A German form of Augusta. *See* Augusta.

Aura, Aural From the Greek, meaning "air, breeze." May also be a
variant form of Aurelia. *See* Aurelia.

Aurea A variant form of Aurelia. *See* Aurelia.

Aurelia The feminine form of the Latin name Aurelius, meaning
"gold." VARIANT FORMS: Aurelie (French); Arelia (Old English).

Aurora From the Latin, meaning "dawn." In Roman mythology, the
goddess Eos. VARIANT FORMS: Zora, Zorica (Slavic); Aurore (French).
PLACE-NAME USAGE: cities in Colorado, New York, and Ohio.

Autumn Named for the season of the year. CONTEMPORARY EXAMPLE:
Autumn Burke, daughter of Yvonne Braithwaite Burke, U.S. con-
gresswoman.

Ava From the Latin name Avis, meaning "bird." Or, a short form of
Avalon or Aveline. *See* Avalon *and* Aveline. Used as a pet form of
Aveline. PLACE-NAME USAGE: a town in Missouri.

Avalon, Avallon French forms of the Middle Latin name Avallonis,
meaning "island." In Celtic mythology, the Isle of the Dead, an island
in paradise where King Arthur and other heroes went after death.
Popularized by Lord Tennyson in his *Idylls of the King*. Avilion is a
French form. CONTEMPORARY EXAMPLE: Avalon Zann, Detroit, Michigan. SURNAME USAGE: Frankie Avalon, singer. PLACE-NAME USAGE:
Avalon, California; Avalon, Pennsylvania.

Avella A pet form of Aveline. *See* Aveline. CONTEMPORARY EXAMPLE:

Avella Schuller, wife of evangelist Robert Schuller.

Aveline From the French, meaning "hazel nut." Akin to Hazel. VAR-IANT FORMS: Ava, Avella, Evaline.

Averi From the Old French *averrer*, meaning "to confirm." CONTEM-PORARY EXAMPLE: Averi Torres, salesperson.

Avi From the Hebrew, meaning "my father." Used also as a masculine name.

Avice A variant spelling of Avis. *See* Avis.

Aviella A variant spelling of Abiela. *See* Abiela.

Avima Origin uncertain. Possibly a hybrid name from the Hebrew *av*, meaning "father," and *ima*, meaning "mother". CONTEMPORARY EXAMPLE: Avima Ruder, editor.

Avirit From the Hebrew, meaning "air, atmosphere."

Avis From the Latin, meaning "a bird." Avice is a variant spelling. SURNAME USAGE: Aves, Avison.

Avital A variant spelling of Abital. *See* Abital. CONTEMPORARY EXAMPLE: Avital Sharansky, wife of a Soviet dissident scientist.

Aviva, Avivah From the Hebrew, meaning "springtime," connoting youthfulness, freshness.

Avivi, Avivit From the Hebrew, meaning "springlike." Aviva is a variant form. Avivi is a masculine form.

Avodal Probably related to the Arabic and Hebrew, meaning "father." Possibly related to Avital. *See* Avital. CONTEMPORARY EXAMPLE: Avodal K. Offit, physician.

Avuka, Avukah From the Hebrew, meaning "torch, flame."

Ayala, Ayalah From the Hebrew, meaning "a deer, a gazelle." Akin to Ayelet.

Ayelet From the Hebrew, meaning "a deer, a gazelle." A variant form of Ayala.

Ayla From the Hebrew, meaning "a terebinth tree" or "an oak tree."

Aza From the Hebrew, meaning "strong."

Azalea, Azalee, Azalia From the Greek, meaning "dry." The name of a flower, so called because it thrives in dry, sun-baked soil. PLACE-NAME USAGE: a town in Oregon where azaleas grow in abundance.

Aziaz, Azizah From the Hebrew, meaning "strong."

Azora A variant form of Azura. *See* Azura. CONTEMPORARY EXAMPLE: Azora P. Blair, Bridgeport, Connecticut.

Azura From the Persian, meaning "sky-blue."

B

Bab, Babette   Pet forms of Elizabeth and Barbara. *See* Elizabeth *and* Barbara. CONTEMPORARY EXAMPLE: Babette Rosmand, novelist.

Babs, Babson   Matronymic forms of Barbara, meaning "Barbara's son." *See* Barbara. Babs, a short form of Barbara, has been in use since the seventeenth century.

Baila   A Yiddish form of the Hebrew name Bilhah. *See* Bilhah. Also, from the Slavic, meaning "white." VARIANT SPELLINGS: Bayle, Beylah.

Bain   A variant spelling of Bayn. *See* Bayn. SURNAME USAGE: Barbara Bain, actress.

Bairn   From the Scottish, meaning "a child." CONTEMPORARY EXAMPLE: Aintre Bairn Keliner.

Balfouria   A feminine form of Balfour. *See* Balfour (masculine section). Used primarily in Israel.

Bambalina   The diminutive form of the Italian *bambo*, meaning "child, childish." Bambi is a variant form. Bambino is a masculine form.

Bambi   A pet form of Bambalina. *See* Bambalina.

Bara, Barra   From the Hebrew, meaning "to choose." Or, from the Old English *bar*, meaning "a gate, a fence." PLACE-NAME USAGE: Great Barrington, Massachusetts.

Barbara   From the Roman name Barbari, derived from the Latin *barbarus*, meaning "strange, foreign." The ancient Greeks applied the term "barbaros" to all foreigners. In the ancient world, anyone who was not Greek, Roman, or Christian was a stranger, hence a barbarian. A third-century Syrian saint was named St. Barbara. In the twelfth century, St. Barbara became the patron saint of architects and engineers, and was invoked against thunder and lightning. VARIANT FORMS: Barbe (French); Bara, Vara, Varvara, Varinka (Russian); Babie (Scotch); Bab, Barbraa (Danish); Barbica, Barica (Slavonic); Babola, Boris (Hungarian); Barbary (Old English). PET FORMS: Bab, Babs, Barb, Barbo, Bobs, Bobbi, Bobby, Barbi, Barbo. SURNAME USAGE: Barbarita, Barbarossa, Barber. PLACE-NAME USAGE: Barbary, a region of North Africa; Barber, Ohio, named for O.C. Barber, town founder; Barbara, Alaska.

Barbaralee   An invented name, compounded of Barbara and Lee. *See* Barbara *and* Lee. CONTEMPORARY EXAMPLE: Barbaralee Diamonstein, author.

Barbi, Barbo   Pet forms of Barbara. *See* Barbara.

Bari, Barrie   Feminine forms of Barrie. *See* Barrie (masculine section).

Barra   A short form of Barbara. *See* Barbara. CONTEMPORARY EXAMPLE: Barra Grant, writer.

Basilia, Basilie   Feminine forms of Basil. *See* Basil (masculine section). Popular in England and France in the twelfth and thirteenth centuries. SURNAME USAGE: Bassil, Bazel, Basley, Basely.

Basya   A variant spelling of Batya. *See* Batya.

Bathsheba   From the Hebrew, meaning "daughter of an oath." In the Bible, the wife of Uriah the Hittite, and later the wife of King David; the mother of King Solomon. In the Middle Ages, it appears as a Christian name in the form of Barsabe. VARIANT FORMS: Bathshua, Batsheva, Batshua.

Bathshua, Bathsua   From the Hebrew, meaning "daughter of misfortune." Variant forms of Batsheva and Bathsheba. In the Bible, the wife of King David, the mother of King Solomon. In the Book of Chronicles (1:3), the name Batsheva appears as Batshua.

Batsheva   A modern Israeli form of Bathsheba. *See* Bathsheba.

Batya   From the Hebrew, meaning "daughter of God." In the Bible, Bitya (English spelling: Bithia) was a daughter of Pharaoh who married Mered, a member of the tribe of Judah. Basya is a variant spelling.

Bayle   A variant form of Baila and Bilhah. *See* Baila *and* Bilhah.

Bayn   From the Latin *paganus*, meaning "a pagan, a heathen" or "a man of the land." A modified form of the Old English name Payn or Paine. Bain is a variant spelling. CONTEMPORARY EXAMPLE: Bayn Johnson, actress.

Bea, Beah   Pet forms of Beatrice. *See* Beatrice. CONTEMPORARY EXAMPLE: Beah Richards, actress.

Beata   From the Latin, meaning "blessed." Derived from *Beata Virgo Maria*, Blessed Virgin Mary. CONTEMPORARY EXAMPLE: Beata Bishop, author.

Beate   A variant form of Beatrice. *See* Beatrice. CONTEMPORARY EXAMPLE: Beate Gordon, art director.

Beatrice   From the Latin *beatrix*, meaning "one who brings happiness, a blessing." Beatrix is the original Latin form. Beatrice is the English and Italian spelling. Beatrice Portinari (1266-1290) was a woman from Florence, Italy, immortalized by Dante in his *Divine Comedy*. Made famous by the witty heroine of Shakespeare's *Much Ado*

About Nothing. VARIANT FORMS: Beatrice, Bice (Italian); Beatriz (Spanish); Bettrys (Welsh); Beatrix (French, Portuguese, and English); Beatriks (Russian); Beatrica (Salvonic). Beathy and Beton were popular in the Middle Ages. PET FORMS: Bea, Beatie, Beatty, Trix, Trixie.

Beatrix   The original form of Beatrice. *See* Beatrice.

Beckie, Becky   Popular pet forms of Rebecca. *See* Rebecca.

Bedelia   A nickname for girls christened Bridget. Used in Ireland. Delia is a pet form. SURNAME USAGE: Bonnie Bedelia, actress.

Behira   From the Hebrew, meaning "light, clear."

Bela   A short form of Isabella, meaning "God's oath," being the Spanish form of Elizabeth. *See* Isabella *and* Elizabeth. May also be from the Hungarian, meaning "nobly bright," or from the Latin, meaning "beautiful one." Belle is a popular French form. Bella is a variant spelling.

Belinda   From the Latin *bel* and *bellus*, meaning "beautiful," and the Old Norse *linnr*, meaning "snake." Serpents were once regarded as sacred animals. In Babylonian mythology, Baal (*bel*) was the god of heaven and earth. Linda is a pet form. CONTEMPORARY EXAMPLE: Belinda Montgomery, actress.

Bell   A pet form of Isabel used since the thirteenth century. *See* Isabel.

Bella, Belle   Short forms of Isabella. *See* Bela *and* Isabella. CONTEMPORARY EXAMPLE: Bella Abzug, U.S. politician.

Belva   From the Latin, meaning "beautiful view." CONTEMPORARY EXAMPLES: Belva Plain, novelist; Belva Parsons, Webster, New York.

Bena   From the Hebrew, meaning "wise." Bina is a variant spelling.

Bendetta   The Italian form of Benedicta. *See* Benedicta.

Benedicta   A feminine form of Benedict, meaning "blessed." *See* Benedict (masculine section). VARIANT FORMS: Benoite (French); Benedetta, Betta, Bettina (Italian); Benita (Spanish); Benedictine (German). In seventeenth-century England, Benet, Bennet, and Bennitt were commonly used forms.

Benedictine   A German form of Benedicta. *See* Benedicta.

Benet   A short form of Benedicta. *See* Benedicta.

Benita   The Spanish form of Benedicta. *See* Benedicta. CONTEMPORARY EXAMPLE: Benita Valente, singer.

Benjamina   A feminized form of Benjamin. *See* Benjamin (masculine section).

Bennet, Bennitt   Variant forms of Benedicta. *See* Benedicta.

Benoite   The French form of Benedicta. *See* Benedicta.

Beracha   A variant spelling of Bracha. *See* Bracha.

Berenice   From the Greek, meaning "bringer of victory." In the Bible, a daughter of Agrippa. Also spelled Bernice. The name of a fourth–century martyr, but not used afterwards for more than a thousand years.

Bernadette   From the French and German, meaning "bold as a bear." Bernard is the masculine form. VARIANT FORMS: Bernadot, Bernadotte, Bernadina, Bernadine, Bernela, Bernetta, Bernette. CONTEMPORARY EXAMPLE: Bernadette Peters, actress.

Bernadina, Bernadine   Pet forms of Bernadette. *See* Bernadette.

Bernadot, Bernadotte   Swedish and Norwegian forms of Bernadette. *See* Bernadette. CONTEMPORARY EXAMPLE: Bernadotte E. Schmitt, historian.

Berneta, Bernetta, Bernette   Variant forms of Bernadette. *See* Bernadette. CONTEMPORARY EXAMPLE: Berneta Metcalf, Christianburg, Virginia.

Bernice, Berniece   Variant forms of Berenice. *See* Berenice. CONTEMPORARY EXAMPLE: Berniece Freschet, author.

Bernine, Bernita   Pet forms of Bernice and Bernadette. *See* Bernice *and* Bernadette.

BernNadette   A unique spelling of Bernadette. *See* Bernadette. CONTEMPORARY EXAMPLE: BernNadette Stanis, actress.

Berta   An Italian form of Bertha. *See* Bertha.

Bertha   From the Old High German name Berahta, meaning "bright one." Akin to the Old English *beorht* and *bryht*, meaning "bright." Bertram is a masculine equivalent. VARIANT FORMS: Berthe (French); Berta (Italian). PET FORMS: Birdie, Bert, Bertie.

Bertrice   Probably a hybrid name of Bertha and Beatrice. *See* Bertha *and* Beatrice. CONTEMPORARY EXAMPLE: Bertrice Small, author.

Berura, Beruria   From the Hebrew and Assyrian, meaning "pure, clean, shining." Also, from the Aramaic, meaning "pious, kind, honest." Beruria was the learned wife of the second- century talmudic scholar Rabbi Meir.

Beryl   From the Greek and Sanskrit, meaning "a precious stone." Also, from the Persian and Arabic, meaning "crystal, crystal clear." Commonly used as a masculine name. Berylla is a variant spelling. CONTEMPORARY EXAMPLE: Beryl Bainbridge, novelist.

Berylla   A variant spelling of Beryl. *See* Beryl.

Bess, Bessie   Pet forms of Elizabeth. *See* Elizabeth.

Beta   A Greek form of the Hebrew *beth*, meaning "a house." The second letter of the Greek alphabet.

Beth   A short form of Elizabeth. *See* Elizabeth.

Bethany   A Greek and Latin form of the Hebrew, meaning "house of figs (or dates)." In the Bible, a town in Palestine near Jerusalem.

Bethel   From the Hebrew, meaning "house of God." In the Bible, a town near Jerusalem. CONTEMPORARY EXAMPLE: Bethel Leslie, actress.

Bethesda   From the Greek and Aramaic, meaning "house of mercy." In the Bible, a pool near Jerusalem possessing healing powers.

Bethia   The Latin form of the Hebrew name Batya. *See* Batya.

Betsey, Betsy   Pet forms of Elizabeth. *See* Elizabeth.

Bette   A pet form of Elizabeth. *See* Elizabeth. CONTEMPORARY EXAMPLE: Bette Midler, entertainer.

Bettina   A pet form of Elizabeth. *See* Elizabeth.

Betty   A popular pet form of Elizabeth. *See* Elizabeth.

Bettylou   A hybrid name of Betty and Lou (from Louise). *See* Betty *and* Louise. CONTEMPORARY EXAMPLE: Bettylou Valentine, anthropologist.

Beulah   From the Hebrew, meaning "married" or "ruled over." In the Bible, an allegorical reference to the land of Israel. In Bunyan's *Pilgrim's Progress*, a peaceful country near the end of man's journey. CONTEMPORARY EXAMPLE: Beulah Tannenbaum, author. PLACE-NAME USAGE: Beulah, North Dakota, named for Beulah Stinchcombe, local resident.

Beverley, Beverly   From the Old English, meaning "a beaver's meadow." Beverley is the spelling common in England. Used also as masculine forms (*see* masculine section). PLACE-NAME USAGE: Beverly Hills, California, named for Beverly Farms in Massachusetts.

Beylah   A variant spelling of Baila. *See* Baila.

Bianca   The Italian of the Spanish *blanc*, meaning "white." In Shakespeare's *Taming of the Shrew*, Bianca is the sweet, docile daughter of the wild Katherine. CONTEMPORARY EXAMPLE: Bianca Jagger, ex-wife of singer Mick Jagger.

Bibi   From the French *beubelot*, hence the English *bibelot*, meaning "a bauble, a toy." Akin to Bubbles. CONTEMPORARY EXAMPLE: Bibi Anderson, Swedish actress.

Biddie   A variant form of Bridget. *See* Bridget. Or, from *chickabiddy*, meaning "a chicken," particularly a hen.

Biddy   A pet form of Bridget. *See* Bridget. CONTEMPORARY EXAMPLE: Biddy Baxter, author.

Bidu   A variant form of Biddie. CONTEMPORARY EXAMPLE: Bidu Sayao, concert singer. *See* Bid (masculine section).

Bijou   The French form of the British *bizou*, meaning "a ring."

Bilhah   From the Hebrew, meaning "weak, old." In the Bible, Jacob's wife, the servant of Rachel, and mother of Dan and Naphtali.

Billie   A feminine form of William. *See* William (masculine section). CONTEMPORARY EXAMPLE: Billie Burke, actress.

Billie Jean   A compounded name of Billie and Jean. *See* Billie *and* Jean. CONTEMPORARY EXAMPLE: Billie Jean King, tennis player.

Bina   From the Hebrew, meaning "wisdom, understanding." Buna is a variant form.

Binnie   From the Celtic and Anglo-Saxon, meaning "a bin, a receptacle." Bin is a masculine form. CONTEMPORARY EXAMPLE: Binnie Barnes, actress.

Bira   From the Hebrew, meaning "fortress, capital."

Bird, Birdie   From the Anglo-Saxon and Middle English *brid* and *bridd*, meaning "a bird." Used also as diminutive forms of Bertha. Byrd and Byrdie are variant spellings.

Birgit, Birgitta   Variant forms of Bridget. *See* Bridget. Birgitta is a Swedish form. CONTEMPORARY EXAMPLE: Birgit Nilsson, concert soprano; Birgitta Valberg, Actress.

Blair   From the Gaelic, meaning "field" or "battle." Used also as a masculine name. CONTEMPORARY EXAMPLE: Blair Brown, actress.

Blanca   The Spanish form of the French *blanc*, meaning "white." In Old English, *blanca* means "a white steed." VARIANT FORMS: Blanche (French); Blanca (German and Spanish); Bianca (Italian). CONTEMPORARY EXAMPLE: Blanca Florido, singer. PLACE-NAME USAGE: Blanca Peak, the highest peak of the Sangre de Cristo in Colorado.

Blanch   An English form of Blanche. *See* Blanche.

Blanche   From the Old French *blanc*, meaning "white." VARIANT FORMS: Bianca (Italian); Blanca (Spanish); Branca (Portuguese); Blanch (English). *See also* Blanca.

Blandina   A pet form of Blanche. *See* Blanche. CONTEMPORARY EXAMPLE: Blandina F. Badger, Folsom, California.

Blasia   A feminine form of Blase. *See* Blase (masculine section).

Blaze   From the Old English, meaning "a flame" or "a mark made on a tree" to mark a trail in a forest. Also, from the Middle English, meaning "to blow, to announce, to proclaim." Used occasionally as a masculine name. *See* Blase *and* Blaze (masculine section). CONTEMPORARY EXAMPLE: Blaze Starr, actress. PLACE-NAME USAGE: Blaze

Mountain, Montana.

Blenda   A short form of Belinda. *See* Belinda. Or, from the Old English, *blendan*, and the Old Norse, *blanda*, meaning "to mix, to blend."

Bliss   From the Anglo-Saxon, meaning "perfect joy." CONTEMPORARY EXAMPLE: Bliss Holland, television news reporter. PLACE-NAME USAGE: Blissville, New York, named for Neziah Bliss (1841), town planner.

Blodwen   From the Welsh *gwen*, meaning "white," and *blod-yu*, meaning "flower."

Blossom   From the Old English, meaning "a blooming flower." CONTEMPORARY EXAMPLE: Blossom Elfman, author. PLACE-NAME USAGE: Cape Blossom, Alaska, named in 1826 by Captain Bleechey for his exploring ship *Blossom*.

Bluma   From the German, meaning "flower." A popular Yiddish name.

Blythe   From the Anglo-Saxon, meaning "happy." Used also as a masculine name. VARIANT FORMS: Bliss, Blisse. CONTEMPORARY EXAMPLES: Blythe Danner, actress; Blythe Bowne, Columbia, Mississippi.

Bob   A pet form of Barbara and Roberta. *See* Barbara *and* Roberta.

Bobbe   A pet form of Barbara and Roberta. *See* Barbara *and* Roberta. CONTEMPORARY EXAMPLE: Bobbe Siegel, publicity director.

Bobette   A pet form of Barbara and Roberta. Also, an invented name, created by combining Bob (Robert) and Bette. *See* Robert (masculine section), *and* Bette. CONTEMPORARY EXAMPLE: Bobette Seymour, Bellevue, Ohio.

Bobbie, Bobby   Pet forms of Barbara and Roberta. *See* Barbara *and* Roberta.

Bona   From the Hebrew, meaning "a builder."   •

Bonita   A Spanish form of Bonnie. *See* Bonnie. CONTEMPORARY EXAMPLE: Bonita Granville, actress.

Bonnie, Bonny   From the Latin *bonus* and the French *bon*, meaning "good" or "pretty." CONTEMPORARY EXAMPLE: Bonnie Franklin, actress.

Bracha   From the Hebrew, meaning "a blessing." Beracha is a variant spelling. CONTEMPORARY EXAMPLE: Bracha Habas, author.

Braunette   From the Middle English *braun*, meaning "fleshy" or "muscular."

Bree   From the Middle English *bre*, meaning "a broth; a thin, watery soup." Akin to the Germanic *brei*. Used in Scotland.

Brenda   A feminine form of Brand and Brendan. *See* Brand *and*

Brendan (masculine section). The name of the heroine in Sir Walter Scott's novel *The Pirate*. CONTEMPORARY EXAMPLE: Brenda Vaccaro, actress.

Brenna Probably a variant form of Brenda. *See* Brenda.

Breyette A pet form of Bree. *See* Bree.

Brian From the Celtic and Gaelic, meaning "strong." Used also as a masculine form. Bryan is a variant spelling. Brina is a Slavic form.

Brianne A variant form of Brian. *See* Brian. CONTEMPORARY EXAMPLE: Brianne Leary, actress.

Brick A variant form of the masculine Brice. *See* Brice (masculine section). CONTEMPORARY EXAMPLE: Brick Autry, a librarian in Dimmitt, Texas.

Bridget A variant form of Brighid. From the Celtic, meaning "strong, lofty." In medieval folklore, Brighid was a Celtic fire goddess. The cult of St. Brighid was popular in England and Ireland, and use of the name spread to other countries. VARIANT FORMS: Brigitta (French, German, and Swedish); Biddy (Irish); Brigitte (French and German); Brighid (Irish); Bride (Scotch and English); Bryde (English); Birte, Britte (Slavonic). PET FORMS: Biddy, Bridie, Brit, Brita. CONTEMPORARY EXAMPLE: Bridget Reston, Haverhill, Massachusetts.

Bridgit A variant spelling of Bridget. *See* Bridget.

Briget A variant spelling of Bridget. *See* Bridget.

Brigid, Brigit, Brigitte Variant forms of Bridget. *See* Bridget. CONTEMPORARY EXAMPLES: Brigid Keenan, journalist; Brigitte Fossey, actress.

Brilane A hybrid name from *Brig*ham and *Lane*. CONTEMPORARY EXAMPLE: Brilane K. Bowman, Burke, Virginia.

Brilliant From the French *brillant* and the Italian *brillare*, meaning "sparkle, whirl." CONTEMPORARY EXAMPLE: Brilliant Laurie, Finleyville, Pennsylvania. SURNAME USAGE: N.E. Brill (1860-1925), U.S. physician.

Brina From the Slavic, meaning "protector." Akin to Brian.

Brine, Briny Variant forms of Brian. *See* Brian.

Brit, Brita Slavonic pet forms of Bridget. *See* Bridget. CONTEMPORARY EXAMPLE: Brit Lind, actress.

Britain A short form of Britannia. *See* Britannia. SURNAME USAGE: Barbara Britain, actress.

Britannia An Old Latin name for Great Britain. Used as a feminine name in the eighteenth century.

Bronwen, Bronwyn   From the Welsh, meaning "white breast." Also, from the Anglo-Saxon *braun*, meaning "fleshy," and *wyn*, *wen*, or *win*, meaning "friend." CONTEMPORARY EXAMPLES: Bronwyn M. Flanagan, Boulder Creek, California; Bronwyn Anne Kelly, Export, Pennsylvania.

Brook, Brooke   From the Old English *broc* and the Middle English *brok*, meaning "to break out," as a stream of water. May also be a form of Brock. *See* Brock (masculine section). CONTEMPORARY EXAMPLES: Brook Neal, sales representative; Brooke Shields, actress.

Brown   From the Middle English *broun*, meaning "brown-colored." A popular surname. CONTEMPORARY EXAMPLE: Brown Meggs, author.

Brunhild, Brunhilda, Brunhilde   From the Old High German *brunna*, meaning "armor," plus *hilti*, meaning "fight," hence "a fighter in armor." In the *Nibelungenlied*, Brunhild is a queen in Iceland. VARIANT FORMS: Brynhild, Brynhilda, Brynhilde.

Brunnhilde   A variant spelling of Brunhilde. *See* Brunhilde. A Valkyrie in Wagner's *Die Walkure*.

Bryn, Bryna   A variant form of Brian. *See* Brian. CONTEMPORARY EXAMPLES: Bryn Burns, Buffalo, New York; Bryna Stevens, author.

Brynhild, Brynhilda, Brynhilde   Variant spellings of Brunhild. *See* Brunhild.

Brynie   A pet form of Bryn. *See* Bryn. CONTEMPORARY EXAMPLE: Brynie Weinstock, Israeli singer.

Brynja   An Icelandic (Old Norse) form of Bryna. *See* Bryna. CONTEMPORARY EXAMPLE: Brynja Brown, Toledo, Ohio.

Brynn   A variant spelling of Bryn. *See* Bryn. CONTEMPORARY EXAMPLE: Jennifer Brynn Shoppell, Carmel, Indiana.

Bubbles   From the Middle Dutch *bubbel*, meaning "a thin spherical film of liquid." Or, from the Old French *beubelot*, meaning "a toy, a bauble." Bibi is a pet form. CONTEMPORARY EXAMPLE: Linda Lee (Bubbles) Wiley, Arlington, Texas.

Buna   A variant form of Bina. *See* Bina.

Bunie   A variant form of Bina. *See* Bina.

Bunny   A nickname for Roberta or Barbara. *See* Roberta *and* Barbara.

Burlene   The feminine form of Burl. *See* Burl (masculine section).

Burma   From the name of the country in Southeast Asia. CONTEMPORARY EXAMPLE: Burma G. Orton, Tucson, Arizona.

Butterfly   An Old English name derived from the colorful insect with the large wing-span seen fluttering in the fields. CONTEMPORARY EXAMPLE: Butterfly McQueen, actress.

Byrd From the Anglo-Saxon, meaning "a bird." Used also as a masculine name. CONTEMPORARY EXAMPLE: Byrd Baylor, author.

Byrdie A variant spelling of Birdie. *See* Bird.

C

Caasi A variant form of Catherine or Cassandra. *See* Catherine *and* Cassandra.

Cadence From the Latin, meaning "to fall," with particular reference to the rhythm of speaking. Cadenza (Italian) is a variant form.

Cadette A pet form of the French name Cadice, meaning "little chief." *See* Cadice.

Cadice From the French *cad*, meaning "a chief." Cadette is a pet form. CONTEMPORARY EXAMPLE: Cadice Aglor, figure skater.

Caitlin A variant Welsh form of Catherine. *See* Catherine. CONTEMPORARY EXAMPLE: Caitlin Thomas, wife of poet Dylan Thomas.

Calandra From the Greek, meaning "a park."

Caledonia From Calydon, a place-name in ancient Greece. Later, it was the Latin name for Scotland, used mostly in poetry.

California Of Spanish origin, but meaning uncertain. Possibly related to the Old French *calife*, meaning "caliph, successor." First appeared in a novel by the Spaniard Montalvo in which California is a fabled island.

Calista From the Greek, meaning "the most beautiful."

Callan From the Middle English *callen* and the Old Norse *kalla*, meaning "to scream, to shriek."

Calliope From the Greek, meaning "one with a beautiful voice." In Greek mythology, Calliope was the Muse of eloquence and epic poetry.

Calpurnia From the Greek *kallos* and *porne*, meaning "beautiful prostitute." Caesar's wife in Shakespeare's *Julius Caesar*.

Calypso A Greek flower name for a family of orchids. In Homer's *The Odyssey*, a sea nymph who held Odysseus captive on her island for seven years.

Cameo The Italian form of the Latin, meaning "a carving." A two-layered gem with a figure carved into one layer.

Camilla A variant form of Camille. *See* Camille.

Camille From the Latin, meaning "a virgin of unblemished character." Camilla is a variant form. Popularized after the appearance of Mme. D'Arblay's novel *Camilla* (1796). *See also* Camillus (masculine section). CONTEMPORARY EXAMPLE: Camille Motta, librarian.

Candace   From the Greek, meaning "fire-white" or "incandescent." Also, from the Latin, meaning "pure, unsullied." In the Bible, the dynastic title of the Queen of Ethiopia. Candy is a pet form. Candide is a French form. VARIANT FORMS: Candance, Candase, Candice, Candida, Candide. CONTEMPORARY EXAMPLE: Candace Caruthers, television news reporter.

Candance   A variant form of Candace. *See* Candace. CONTEMPORARY EXAMPLE: Candance Shoppell, Carmel, Indiana.

Candia   The former name of Crete, now called Heraklion. Popular among Quaker families.

Candice   A variant spelling of Candace. *See* Candace. CONTEMPORARY EXAMPLE: Candice Bergen, actress.

Candida, Candide   Variant forms of Candace. *See* Candace. Became popular after the appearance of George Bernard Shaw's play *Candida* (1898). CONTEMPORARY EXAMPLE: Candida Donadio, literary agent.

Candy   A pet form of Candace. *See* Candace. CONTEMPORARY EXAMPLE: Candy Clark, actress.

Candyce   A pet form of Candace. *See* Candace. CONTEMPORARY EXAMPLE: Candyce Goldstein, publisher.

Canli   A name invented by combining the zodiac signs Cancer and Libra. CONTEMPORARY EXAMPLE: Canli Seibert, Santa Ana, California.

Caprice   From the Latin, meaning "a head with bristling hair; a hedgehog." Or, from the French, meaning "erratic." CONTEMPORARY EXAMPLE: Caprice Blasingame, Carencro, Louisiana.

Cara   A short form of Charlotte and Caroline. *See* Charlotte *and* Caroline. CONTEMPORARY EXAMPLE: Cara Williams, actress.

Carabelle, Carrabelle   Names invented by combining Cara and Belle. *See* Cara *and* Belle. PLACE-NAME USAGE: Carrabelle, Florida, named for Carrie Hall (1897), a local beauty.

Caren   A variant form of Catherine. *See* Catherine. Also spelled Karin.

Caretta   A name invented by combining Cara (or Car) and Etta. PLACE-NAME USAGE: Caretta, West Virginia, named for Etta Carter.

Carey   A pet form of Caroline. *See* Caroline. A variant spelling of Carrie. Used also as a masculine name. PLACE-NAME USAGE: Carey, Ohio, named for Judge John Carey.

Carin   A variant spelling of Caren. *See* Caren. Also spelled Karin.

Carina   From the Latin, meaning "a keel." One of the five stars in the constellation Orion, each of which bears the name of a part of a ship.

Carita   From the Latin *caritas*, meaning "charity." Also spelled Karita.

Carla   The feminine form of Carl or Charles; a short form of Caroline. *See* Caroline. Also spelled Karla.

Carlana   A variant form of Charlene. *See* Charlene. CONTEMPORARY EXAMPLE: Indi Carlana Curreri, Dover, New Hampshire.

Carleen   A variant form of Caroline. *See* Caroline.

Carlen   A pet form of Caroline. *See* Caroline.

Carlene   A variant spelling of Carleen. *See* Carleen. Also spelled Karlene. CONTEMPORARY EXAMPLE: Carleen Carter, singer.

Carley   A variant form of Carla and Caroline. *See* Caroline. Carly is a variant spelling. CONTEMPORARY EXAMPLE: Carley Janice Rice, Spokane, Washington.

Carlia   A pet form of Carla and Caroline. *See* Caroline. CONTEMPORARY EXAMPLE: Carlia Foster, Opelika, Florida.

Carlin   A variant form of Caroline. *See* Caroline.

Carlita   An Italian pet form of Carla and Caroline. *See* Caroline.

Carlotta   The Italian form of Charlotte. *See* Charlotte.

Carly   A pet form of Carla and Caroline. *See* Caroline. Carley is a variant spelling. CONTEMPORARY EXAMPLE: Carly Simon, singer.

Carlyn   A variant spelling of Carlin. *See* Carlin.

Carma   From the Hebrew *kerom*, meaning "a vineyard." Or, from the Arabic, meaning "a field of fruit." VARIANT FORMS: Carmen (Spanish); Carmine (Italian); Carmia, Carmiya, Carmit (Hebrew).

Carmania   A variant form of Carmen and Carmel. *See* Carmel.

Carmel, Carmela, Carmelit   From the Hebrew, meaning "a vineyard." Carmen is a Spanish form. VARIANT SPELLINGS: Karmel, Karmela, Karmelit. PLACE-NAME USAGE: Carmel, New York, Carmel, California; a mountain in the northern part of Israel.

Carmen   The Spanish form of Carma or Carmel. *See* Carma and Carmel. CONTEMPORARY EXAMPLE: Carmen Diaz, wife of the president of Mexico (1980). PLACE-NAME USAGE: Carmen, Oklahoma, named for Carmen Diaz (1910); cities in Idaho and New Mexico.

Carmia   From the Hebrew, meaning "vineyard of the Lord." Carmiela is a variant form.

Carmiela   A variant form of Carmia. *See* Carmia.

Carmine   The Italian form of Carmen. *See* Carmen.

Carmit   A variant Hebrew form of Carmel. *See* Carmel.

Carmiya   A variant spelling of Carmia. *See* Carmia.

Carnell   A name invented by combining *Car*men and *Nell*ie. CON-
TEMPORARY EXAMPLE: Carnell Zaccaro, Reseda, California.

Carna   From the Hebrew, meaning "a horn." Karna is a variant spelling. VARIANT FORMS: Carnit, Karnit.

Carniela, Carniella   From the Hebrew, meaning "the horn of the
Lord." VARIANT SPELLINGS: Karniela, Karniella.

Carnit   From the Hebrew, meaning "a horn." Used in Israel. Carna is
a variant form.

Caro   A pet form of Caroline. *See* Caroline.

Carol, Carola, Carole   From the Gaelic, meaning "melody, song."
Also, short forms of Caroline. See Caroline.

Caroleen   A variant form of Caroline. *See* Caroline. PLACE-NAME US-
AGE: Caroleen, North Carolina, named for the mother of the founder,
S.B. Tanner.

Carolina   An Italian form of Caroline. *See* Caroline. PLACE-NAME US-
AGE: North Carolina and South Carolina, for King Charles I and King
Charles II.

Caroline   A French form of the Middle Latin name Carolus and the
English name Charles, meaning "strong, virile." *See* Charles (mascu-
line section). Introduced into England when King George II married
Caroline of Brandenburgh-Anspach. Became popular in the eigh-
teenth-century. *See also* Charlotte. VARIANT FORMS: Carolina (Italian);
Charo (Spanish); Carleen, Carlene, Carley, Carlin, Carlyn, Carol, Ca-
rola, Carole, Caroleen, Caroly, Carolly, Charlena, Charlene. Carolyn is
a variant spelling. PET FORMS: Carey, Carlen, Carlia, Carlita, Carley,
Carly, Caro, Carrie, Carry, Cassie, Charlet, Charlot, Lina. PLACE-NAME
USAGE: Caroline Islands, a group of islands in the West Pacific; Caroline
County, Virginia, named for Queen Caroline, wife of King George II.

Carolyn   A variant spelling of Caroline. *See* Caroline.

Caron, Carona   Variant spellings of Caren. *See* Caren. SURNAME US-
AGE: Leslie Caron, actress. PLACE-NAME USAGE: Carona, Kansas.

Caronia   A variant form of Caron. *See* Caron.

Caroly, Carolly   Variant forms of Caroline. *See* Caroline. CONTEMPO-
RARY EXAMPLE: Carolly Erikson, author.

Carpathia   From the Greek *karpos*, meaning "fruit." PLACE-NAME US-
AGE: mountain ranges extending from Poland and Czechoslovakia into
Romania.

Carrie   A pet form of Caroline. *See* Caroline. Cary is a variant spelling. CONTEMPORARY EXAMPLE: Carrie Nye, actress.

Carroll   A variant spelling of Carol. *See* Carol. Used also as a masculine name.

Carry   A pet form of Caroline. *See* Caroline. CONTEMPORARY EXAMPLE: Carry Fisher, actress.

Caryl   A variant spelling of Carol. *See* Carol.

Caryn   A variant spelling of Caren. *See* Caren. CONTEMPORARY EXAMPLE: Caryn Tens, West Patterson, New Jersey.

Cass   A pet form of Cassandra. *See* Cassandra. Used also as a masculine name. *See* Cass (masculine section).

Cassandra   From the Greek, referring to "one whose warnings are ignored." In Greek legend, the daughter of Priam and Hecuba, to whom Apollo gave prophetic power in order to win her love, but later regretted having done so. First used in the thirteenth century. VARIANT FORMS: Caasi, Case, Cash, Caso.

Cassia   From the Greek *kasia*, meaning "a type of cinnamon." A feminine form of Cassius. *See* Cassius (masculine section). PLACE-NAME USAGE: Cassia, Idaho.

Cassie   A pet form of Catherine. *See* Catherine. CONTEMPORARY EXAMPLE: Cassie Yates, actress.

Casy   A variant spelling of Cassie. *See* Cassie.

Cathee   A variant spelling of Cathy. *See* Cathy. CONTEMPORARY EXAMPLE: Cathee Shirriff, actress.

Catherine   From the Greek *katharos*, meaning "pure, unsullied." VARIANT SPELLINGS: Katherine, Katharine, Kathryn, Catharine, Cathryn. VARIANT FORMS: Caterina and Katerina (Italian); Cassie, Casy, Cathleen, Cathlin, Kathleen, Katty (Irish); Ekaterina, Katinka, Katja (Russian); Kasia (Polish); Katalin, Kati (Hungarian); Katrina, Katrine, Katrinka (Slavic); Caren and Karen (Scandinavian); Catalina and Catarina (Spanish); Caton, Gaton, Trinette (French); Kathchen, Kathe, Thrine, Treinel (German); Caitlin (Welsh). PET FORMS: Cathy, Cattie, Kate, Kat, Kit, Kitty, Trinette, Trini.

Cathleen   An Irish form of Catherine. *See* Catherine.

Cathlin   An Irish form of Catherine. *See* Catherine.

Cathryn   A variant spelling of Catherine. *See* Catherine.

Cathy   A pet form of Catherine and Cathleen. *See* Catherine *and* Cathleen.

Cattie   A pet form of Catherine. *See* Catherine.

Cecelia   From the Latin name Caecilia, the feminine form of the Roman family name Caecilius, meaning "a member of the (legless) lizard family." Also, from the Latin *caecus*, meaning "blind." In ancient Rome, the founder of the famous Caecilius family was blind. The third–century St. Cecilia was the patron saint of music. VARIANT FORMS: Cecil, Cecily, Cecile, Cecille, Cecely, Cicely, Cicily, Sheila, Sisley, Sissot (English); Cecile (French); Cacilia, Cile (German); Cecylia (Polish). PET FORMS: Ceil, Cele, Celia, Cis, Cissie, Sis, Siss, Sissot, Sissy. Cecil is the masculine equivalent.

Cecely   A variant form of Cecelia. *See* Cecilia.

Cecil, Cecile, Cecille   Variant forms of Cecilia. *See* Cecilia.

Cecily   A variant form of Cecilia. *See* Cecilia.

Ceil   A pet form of Cecelia. *See* Cecelia.

Cele   A pet form of Cecilia. *See* Cecilia.

Celeste   From the Latin, meaning "heavenly." VARIANT FORMS: Celestine, Celia, Celina. CONTEMPORARY EXAMPLE: Celeste Holm, actress.

Celia   A variant form of Cecilia *and* Celest. *See* Cecilia. A character in Shakespeare's *As You Like It.* CONTEMPORARY EXAMPLE: Celia Johnson, actress.

Celina   A variant form of Celeste. *See* Celeste. Also, a variant spelling of Salina. CONTEMPORARY EXAMPLE: Celina Wieniewska, translator. PLACE-NAME USAGE: cities in Ohio and New York.

Celosia   From the Greek, meaning "a flame." Celo is a masculine form.

Cena   Probably a variant form of Xena. *See* Xena. CONTEMPORARY EXAMPLE: Cena C. Draper, author.

Cezanne   From the French *zani*, derived from the Italian *zanni*, meaning "a clown." Originally an abbreviated form of Giovanni, a variant form of John. *See* John (masculine section). CONTEMPORARY EXAMPLE: Cezanne Green, Ann Arbor, Michigan, named for Paul Cezanne (1839-1906), the French painter.

Chana, Chanah   Variant Hebrew forms of Hana and Hannah. *See* Hannah.

Chanda   In Hindu mythology, one of the names assumed by Devi, "The Great Goddess."

Chandelle   From the French, meaning "candle."

Chandra   From the Sanskrit, meaning "illustrious" or "eminent." The name given to the moon, because it outshines the stars.

Chani   A pet form of Chana. *See* Chana.

Chantal   A French form of the Latin *cantus*, meaning "a song." *See* Chanticleer (masculine section). CONTEMPORARY EXAMPLE: Chantal Alvesleben, daughter of the Baron of Switzerland, Bodo von Alvesleben.

Char   Probably a pet form of Charlotte or Charlene. *See* Charlotte *and* Charlene. CONTEMPORARY EXAMPLE: Char Fontane, actress.

Charel   A name invented by combining *Char*les and *El*eanor. CONTEMPORARY EXAMPLE: Charel McCulley, Ogden, Utah.

Charis, Charissa   From the Greek, meaning "grace, beauty, kindness." Charissa is a character in Spencer's *Faerie Queen.*

Charito   An Italian form of Charis. *See* Charis. CONTEMPORARY EXAMPLE: Charito Luna, actress.

Charity   From the Latin *caritas*, meaning "esteem, affection." Used as a Christian name after the Reformation. Popular in the seventeenth century. Triplets were often named Faith, Hope, and Charity. Cherry is a pet form. PLACE-NAME USAGE: Charity Branch, Kentucky.

Charla   A feminine form of Charles. *See* Charles (masculine section). Akin to Carla. VARIANT FORMS: Carla, Caroline, Charlene, Charlotte, Charlayne, Charlen. CONTEMPORARY EXAMPLE: Charla McIntosh, Castro Valley, California.

Charlayne   A variant form of Charlene. *See* Charlene. VARIANT FORMS: Charla, Charlene, Caroline, Charlotte. CONTEMPORARY EXAMPLE: Charlayne Hunter-Gault, television interviewer.

Charleen   A variant spelling of Charlene. *See* Charlene.

Charlen   A variant spelling of Charlene. *See* Charlene. Also, a name invented by combining *Char*lotte and H*elen*. CONTEMPORARY EXAMPLE: Charlen Goodenough, Honolulu, Hawaii.

Charlena, Charlene   Variant forms of Caroline and Charlotte. *See* Caroline *and* Charlotte. Akin to Charles. *See* Charles (masculine section). CONTEMPORARY EXAMPLE: Charlene Haddock Seigfried, professor.

Charlet   A pet form of Caroline and Charlotte. *See* Caroline *and* Charlotte.

Charlinda   A name invented by combining *Char*les and *Linda*. CONTEMPORARY EXAMPLE: Charlinda Audlice Nance, San Antonio, Texas.

Charlot   A variant spelling of Charlotte. *See* Charlotte.

Charlotta   The Italian form of Charlotte. *See* Charlotte. Carlotta is a variant spelling. CONTEMPORARY EXAMPLE: Charlotta A. Bass, U.S. vice-presidential candidate (1952).

Charlotte   The French pet form of Charlot, a feminine form of Charles. *See* Charles (masculine section). Akin to Caroline. *See* Caroline. The heroine in Goethe's *Sorrows of Werther* (1774). VARIANT FORMS: Charlotta, Carlotta (Italian); Caroline (French, English, and German); Lotta (Swedish); Carlota, Lola (Spanish); Charla, Charlena, Charlene, Charlotta. PET FORMS: Charlet, Charlie, Charlot, Lottie, Lot-ty, Totly. PLACE-NAME USAGE: Charlotte, North Carolina; Charlotte County, Virginia, named for Charlotte Sophia, wife of King George III, whom he married in 1761.

Charmain, Charmaine From the Latin *carmen*, meaning "to sing." CONTEMPORARY EXAMPLE: Charmaine Carr, actress.

Charmian From the Greek, meaning "a bit of joy." One of Cleopatra's slaves in Shakespeare's *Antony and Cleopatra*.

Charo A variant form of Caroline. *See* Caroline. CONTEMPORARY EXAMPLE: Charo Cugat, entertainer.

Chasya From the Hebrew, meaning "protected by God." CONTEMPORARY EXAMPLE: Chasya Pincus, author.

Chaya From the Hebrew, meaning "life, living." CONTEMPORARY EXAMPLE: Chaya Burstein, author and illustrator.

Cheera An invented name, meaning "cheer, cheerfulness." CONTEMPORARY EXAMPLE: Cheera Lona Roadarmel, Warner Robins, Georgia.

Chelsea From the Anglo-Saxon, meaning "a port of ships." CONTEMPORARY EXAMPLE: Chelsea Quinn Yarbro, novelist. PLACE-NAME USAGE: a city in Massachusetts.

Chenetta From the Greek *chen*, meaning "a goose." Or, from the French *chene*, meaning "an oak."

Chenoa An American Indian name, meaning "white dove." PLACE-NAME USAGE: Chenoa, Illinois.

Cher A pet form of Cheryl. *See* Cheryl.

Cher Ami From the French surname Cherami, meaning "dear friend." PLACE-NAME USAGE: a bayou in Louisiana.

Chere A variant spelling of Cher. *See* Cher *and* Cheryl.

Cheri, Cherie Pet forms of Cheryl. *See* Cheryl.

Cherlene A variant form of Charlene. *See* Charlene.

Cherrie A pet form of Cheryl. *See* Cheryl.

Cherry A pet form of Cheryl. *See* Cheryl. PLACE-NAME USAGE: Cherry, California.

Cheryl, Cheryle From the French, meaning "beloved." VARIANT FORMS: Sherelle, Sheryl. PET FORMS: Cher, Cheri, Cherie, Cherrie, Cherry. CONTEMPORARY EXAMPLE: Cheryl Ladd, actress.

Cherylie A variant form of Cheryl. CONTEMPORARY EXAMPLE: Cherylie Becke, figure skater.

Chesna From the Slavic, meaning "peaceful." Chessy is a pet form.

Chessy A pet form of Chesna. *See* Chesna.

Cheven   A name invented by combining *Cheryle* and St*even*. CON-TEMPORARY EXAMPLE: Cheven Meyncke, Windfall, Indiana.

Chita   From the Middle English *chitte*, a variation of *kitte*, meaning "kitten." CONTEMPORARY EXAMPLE: Chita Rivera, actress.

Chloe   From the Greek, meaning "blooming, verdant." In the Bible (First Corinthians), a family name. Cloe is a variant spelling.

Chlorine   From the Greek *chloe*, meaning "blooming, verdant." CON-TEMPORARY EXAMPLES: Chlorine Wininger Chappell and Chlorine Bowen, San Jose, California.

Chloris   From the Greek, meaning "blooming, verdant." Akin to Chloe. In Greek mythology, the goddess of flowers. Chloris turned white after being pursued by Apollo. Cloris is a variant spelling.

Chriselda   A variant form of Griselda. *See* Griselda.

Chrisman   From the Latin, meaning "one who is anointed." CONTEM-PORARY EXAMPLE: Chrisman Delane, singer.

Chrissie   A pet form of Christine. *See* Christine.

Christa   A pet form of Christabel. *See* Christabel. CONTEMPORARY EX-AMPLE: Christa Ludwig, opera singer.

Christabel, Christabell   Compounded of *Christ* and *bella*, meaning "handsome Christ." PET FORMS: Chris, Chrissy, Christy.

Christal   A Scotch form of Christian or Christopher. *See* Christian *and* Christopher (masculine section). Akin to Christina.

Christeena   A variant spelling of Christina. *See* Christina. CONTEMPO-RARY EXAMPLE: Christeena McNatt, Ashland, Alabama.

Christel   A variant spelling of Christal. *See* Christal.

Christiana   The feminine form of Christianus, meaning "a Christian." VARIANT FORMS: Christiania, Christina (English); Christina (Swedish); Christine (French); Kristel (German); Cristine (Spanish); Cristina (Italian); Karstin (Danish); Kina, Kirsto, Kirsten, Kristina (Slavonic). PET FORMS: Chrissie, Christie, Tina, Xena, Xina. PLACE-NAME USAGE: Christiana, Delaware.

Christie   A pet form of Christiana. *See* Christiana.

Christina   A variant form of Christiana. *See* Christiana.

Christine   A variant form of Christiana, the feminine form of Christianus, meaning "a Christian, a believer in Jesus as the anointed one." VARIANT FORMS: Christiana, Christina. *See* Christiana. PET FORMS: Chris, Chrissy, Christie, Christy, Crissie.

Christmas   From the Greek, meaning "Christ's mass." Used also as a masculine form. Since the thirteenth century, often given to children born on Christmas Day. In the last century, it was replaced by Noel, normally a masculine form. PLACE-NAME USAGE: Christmas Creek, Oregon; Christmas Lake, Oregon; Christmas, Arizona; Christmas, Florida.

Christy   A pet form of Christine. *See* Christine.

Chrysanthemum   From the Greek, meaning "golden flower." A family of plants with colorful flowers. Crisann is a variant form.

Chryseis   A variant form of Chrysanthemum. *See* Chrysanthemum. In Homer's *Iliad*, the daughter of a priest of Apollo.

Chrystal   A variant spelling of Crystal. *See* Crystal. CONTEMPORARY EXAMPLE: Chrystal Eileen Palmer, Dover Plains, New York.

Cicely, Cicily   Variant forms of Cecilia. *See* Cecilia. CONTEMPORARY EXAMPLE: Cicely Tyson, actress.

Cinderella   A diminutive form of the French *cendre*, meaning "ashes." The heroine of a popular fairy tale. PLACE-NAME USAGE: Cinderella, West Virginia.

Cindy   A pet form of Cynthia. *See* Cynthia.

Cipora   A variant form of Zippora. *See* Zippora. CONTEMPORARY EXAMPLE: Cipora Kronen, teacher.

Cis, Ciss, Cissy   Pet forms of Cecilia. *See* Cecilia. CONTEMPORARY EXAMPLE: Cissy Spacek, actress.

Civia   The form of the Hebrew *tzevi* (*tzvi*), meaning "a deer."

Claira   A variant form of Clara. *See* Clara.

Claire   The French form of Clara. *See* Clara. VARIANT FORMS: Clare, Claret, Clarisse.

Clairene   A pet form of Claire. *See* Claire.

Clara   From the Latin *clarus*, meaning "clear, bright." VARIANT FORMS: Claira, Claire, Clare, Clarice, Clarinda, Clarissa, Clarita, Claretha, Clarette.

Clarabella, Clarabelle   A name compounded of the Latin *clarus*, meaning "bright," and *bella*, meaning "beautiful."

Clare   A variant form of Clara. *See* Clara. Clare of Assisi (1194-1253), Italian nun who became a saint. Used also as a masculine form. PLACE-NAME USAGE: a county in Ireland.

Claretha   A variant form of Clara. *See* Clara.

Clarette   A variant form of Clara. *See* Clara. Also, from the Old French *claret*, meaning "clear (wine)," and referring to a dry red wine.

Claribel   A variant form of Clarabella. *See* Clarabella. The name of the Queen of Tunis in *The Tempest*.

Clarice   A variant spelling of Clarisse. *See* Clarisse. VARIANT FORMS: Clarette, Clarus, Clarissa, Clares.

Clarimond, Clarimonde   Names compounded of the Latin *clarus*, meaning "clear, bright," and the Old German *munt* (Old English *mund*), meaning "protection."

Clarinda   A variant form of Clara. *See* Clara. Used by Spencer in the *Faerie Queen.*

Clarine   A pet form of Clara. *See* Clara.

Clarissa   An Italian form of Clara. *See* Clara. VARIANT FORMS: Clarice, Clarisse, Clarita. The eighteenth–century novel *Clarissa Harlowe*, by Samuel Richardson, made the name fashionable.

Clarisse   The French form of Clarissa. *See* Clarissa.

Clarita   The Spanish form of Clara. *See* Clara.

Clarnie   A name invented by combining Clara and Jennie. PLACE-NAME USAGE: Clarnie, Oregon, named for Clara and Jennie, daughters of two railroad pioneers.

Clatie   A pet form of Clara (from Clarita). *See* Clara.

Claude   A feminine name used as a masculine form primarily in France. *See* Claude (masculine section). Claudia is the more common feminine form.

Claudella   A pet form of Claudia. *See* Claudia. Claudel is the masculine form.

Claudette   A French pet form of Claudia. *See* Claudia. CONTEMPO-RARY EXAMPLE: Claudette Colbert, actress.

Claudia   From the Latin, meaning "lame." Gladys is the Welsh form. *See also* Claude. PET FORMS: Claudette, Claudine.

Claudine   A French pet form of Claudia, popular in Switzerland. *See* Claudia.

Claylene   A feminine pet form of Clay. *See* Clay (masculine section).

Clea   A variant form of Chloe. *See* Chloe.

Cleantha   From the Greek, meaning "in praise of flowers." Akin to Clio.

Clematis   From the Greek, meaning "a vine" or "a twig."

Clemence, Clemency   Feminine forms of Clement. *See* Clement (masculine section).

Clementina   A variant form of Clementine. *See* Clementine.

Clementine   A French form of the Latin *clemens*, meaning "merciful." The feminine form of Clement. *See* Clement (masculine section). Clementina is a variant form.

Cleo A variant spelling of Clio. *See* Clio. Also, a masculine name. *See* Cleo (masculine section).

Cleona, Cleone Feminine forms of Cleon. *See* Cleon (masculine section).

Cleopatra From the Greek, meaning "fame of her father." Queen of Egypt (51-30 B.C.).

Cleora Probably a variant form of Clio. *See* Clio. PLACE-NAME USAGE: Cleora, Oklahoma, named for Cleora Sunday, a member of the family of the first postmaster.

Cleta A short French form of Cleopatra. *See* Cleopatra. CONTEMPORARY EXAMPLE: Cleta Cohen, Artesia, California.

Clio From the Greek, meaning "to celebrate, to glorify." In Greek mythology, the Muse of history. Cleo is a variant spelling. Used also as a masculine name. *See* Clio (masculine section).

Clodia A variant spelling of Claudia. *See* Claudia. CONTEMPORARY EXAMPLE: Clodia Taylor.

Cloe A variant spelling of Chloe. *See* Chloe.

Clorinda A variant form of Clara. *See* Clara. The name of the heroine in *Jerusalem Delivered*, by the Italian poet Tasso.

Cloris A variant spelling of Chloris. *See* Chloris. CONTEMPORARY EXAMPLE: Cloris Leachman, actress.

Clotilda From the Old German name Chlotichilda, meaning "famous in battle." The wife of Clovis, King of the Franks (465-511).

Clotilde A variant form of Clotilda. *See* Clotilda.

Clove From the Latin *clavus*, meaning "a nail." Also, a dried flower bud of a tree of the myrtle family. A name current in the southern United States.

Clover From the Anglo-Saxon, meaning "to adhere." Also, the name of a species of low-growing herbs. Akin to Clove. *See* Clove.

Colena Probably a variant form of Colleen. *See* Colleen. CONTEMPORARY EXAMPLE: Colena M. Andersen, author.

Colette From the Latin, meaning "victorious." The French pet form of Nicole.

Colleen From the Irish *cailun*, meaning "girl." VARIANT SPELLINGS: Coleen, Colene. CONTEMPORARY EXAMPLE: Colleen Dewhurst, actress.

Collice Probably a variant form of Colleen. *See* Colleen. CONTEMPORARY EXAMPLE: Collice Portnoff, translator.

Columbia From the Latin *columba*, meaning "a dove." PLACE-NAME USAGE: the capital of South Carolina; a city in Missouri; a river that flows from British Columbia through Washington and Oregon.

Columbine   The name of flower in the buttercup family, so named because it resembles a flock of doves. Akin to Columbia. *See* Columbia.

Comfort   From the Middle English *comforten*, derived from the Latin, meaning "to strengthen greatly." Used after the Reformation as a masculine and feminine name. PLACE-NAME USAGE: Lake Comfort, Montana, named for J.W. Comfort, a local physician.

Concha   From the Greek and Latin, meaning "a shell."

Conchata   A variant form of Concha. *See* Concha. CONTEMPORARY EXAMPLE: Conchata Ferrel, actress.

Conetta   Possibly a form of Connie. *See* Connie. CONTEMPORARY EXAMPLE: Lucia Conetta Vidal, Stamford, Connecticut.

Connie   A pet form of Constance. *See* Constance. PLACE-NAME USAGE: Connie Knob, Kentucky.

Constance   From the Latin *constantia*, meaning "constant, faithful." Connie is a pet form. The name of the daughter of Constantine the Great.

Constancy   A variant form of Constance. *See* Constance.

Constantia   Akin to Constance. *See* Constance.

Consuela   Used among Puritans in the sixteenth and seventeenth centuries. A variant form of Consuelo. *See* Consuelo.

Consuelo   From the Latin, meaning "consolation." Used also as a masculine name. *Consuelo*, the novel by George Sand, popularized the name. Connie is a pet form. CONTEMPORARY EXAMPLE: Consuelo Joerns, artist.

Conte   Probably a pet form of Constance. *See* Constance.

Content   From the Latin *contentus*, meaning "satisfied." A Puritan virtue name. PLACE-NAME USAGE: Content, Montana; Content Key, Florida.

Cora   From the Greek *kore*, meaning "maiden." VARIANT FORMS: Corinna (English); Corinne (French). PET FORMS: Coretta, Corette, Cori, Corie.

Coral   From the Greek *korallion*, meaning "a small stone," usually red in color. PLACE-NAME USAGE: Coral Gables, Florida.

Coralie   A variant form of Cora. *See* Cora.

Cordelia   From the Celtic, meaning "daughter of the sea." Used by Shakespeare in *King Lear* for the youngest of the king's daughters, the only one faithful to him.

Cordelle   The French diminutive form of *corde*, meaning "a rope."

Coretta, Corette   Pet forms of Cora. *See* Cora. CONTEMPORARY EXAM-

PLE: Coretta Scott King, wife of Martin Luther King, Jr.

Corey   From the Gaelic, meaning "a ravine, a deep hollow."

Cori, Corie   Pet forms of Cora. *See* Cora.

Corinna   A pet form of Cora. *See* Cora. The name of a Greek lyric poetess. Popular in eighteenth–century England.

Corinne   A French form of Cora. *See* Cora. CONTEMPORARY EXAMPLE: Corinne Freeman, a U.S. city mayor.

Corisande   From the Greek, meaning "one who sings in a chorus." A heroine in Disraeli's play *Lothair*.

Corita   A pet form of Cora. *See* Cora. CONTEMPORARY EXAMPLE: Corita Kent, illustrator.

Cornelia   From the Latin *cornus*, meaning "a cornell tree." The feminine form of Cornelius. *See* Cornelius (masculine section). In second–century Rome, the mother of Tiberius and Gaius, leaders of the democratic party.

Correy, Corrie, Corry, Cory   Variant forms of Corey. *See* Corey.

Cosima   From the Greek *kosmos*, meaning "universe, harmony." CONTEMPORARY EXAMPLE: Cosima Wagner, wife of composer Richard Wagner.

Courtney   From the Old French, meaning "one who frequents the king's court." Also a masculine form when spelled Courtnay. CONTEMPORARY EXAMPLE: Courtney Kennedy, daughter of Robert F. Kennedy.

Creola   From the French and Spanish, meaning "a native," hence the connotation "a dark-skinned person." The feminine form of Creole. PLACE-NAME USAGE: Creola, Alabama.

Crescent   From the Latin *crescere*, meaning "to increase or grow," a reference to the moon in its first or last quarter. PLACE-NAME USAGE: La Crescent, Montana.

Cressida   Used in various forms from early Greek times. In medieval legend, a Trojan woman who was unfaithful to her lover. Popularized through Shakespeare's *Troilus and Cressida*. VARIANT FORMS: Cressid, Criseyde.

Crete   A variant form of Christiana. Also, a pet form of Lucretia. CONTEMPORARY EXAMPLE: Crete Stanley Hill, so named because her father was in Crete, Nebraska, when she was born. PLACE-NAME USAGE: a Greek island in the Mediterranean; Crete, North Dakota, named for Lucretia Steele, daughter of a local landowner.

Crisann   A name invented by combining Christine and Ann. *See* Christine *and* Ann. Also, a short form of Chrysanthemum. CONTEMPORARY EXAMPLE: Crisann Rhodes, whose parents named her after the chrysanthemum flower.

Crissie A pet form of Christine. *See* Christine. CONTEMPORARY EXAMPLE: Crissie Sossing, actress.

Crystal From the Greek, meaning "a clear, brilliant glass." In Scotland, a pet form of the masculine Christopher. CONTEMPORARY EXAMPLE: Crystal Gayle, singer. PLACE-NAME USAGE: Crystal Bay, Montana; Crystal Falls, Minnesota.

Cuba From the Spanish, meaning "a tank, a trough." CONTEMPORARY EXAMPLE: Cuba Fay Yetman, Houston, Texas. PLACE-NAME USAGE: a country in the West Indies; cities in New Mexico, Kansas, and Wisconsin.

Cybil, Cybill From the Latin, meaning "soothsayer." Sibyl is a variant spelling. CONTEMPORARY EXAMPLE: Cybil Shepherd, actress.

Cyd From the Old English, meaning "a public hill." CONTEMPORARY EXAMPLE: Cyd Charisse, dancer.

Cyma From the Greek and Latin, meaning "to sprout, grow, flourish." Syma is a variant spelling. CONTEMPORARY EXAMPLE: Cyma Rubin, theatrical producer.

Cymbaline, Cymbeline Either from the Celtic, meaning "lord of the sun," or from the Greek *kyme*, meaning "a hollow vessel," which later became the name of the cymbal, a musical percussion instrument. *Cymbeline* is one of Shakespeare's dramas.

Cyndi Lu A nickname for Lucinda.

Cyndy A pet form of Cynthia. *See* Cynthia. CONTEMPORARY EXAMPLE: Cyndy Szekeres, author and illustrator.

Cynthia From the Greek *kynthos*, meaning "from the cynthus." In Greek mythology, a mountain on which Artemis, goddess of the moon, was born. Hence, it took on the meaning of "the moon personified." Diana is the goddess of the moon in Roman mythology. Cindy is a popular pet form.

Cynthiana A name invented by combining Cynthia and Anna. *See* Cynthia *and* Anna. PLACE-NAME USAGE: Cynthiana, Kentucky.

Cypris From the Greek, meaning "from Cyprus," an ancient Greek city. In Greek legend, Aphrodite was called The Cyprian, after Cyprus, the place of her birth. The city was known for its frivolity.

Cyr From the Old English *cyrnel*, meaning "a corn kernel." Or, a form of Cyril. *See* Cyril (masculine section). CONTEMPORARY EXAMPLE: Cyr Copertini, San Francisco, California.

Cyrilla From the Greek, meaning "lordly." Cyril is the masculine form. CONTEMPORARY EXAMPLE: Cyrilla McDowell, International Falls, Montana.

D

Dafna, Dafne   Variant forms of the Greek name Daphne. *See* Daphne.

Dafnit   The Hebrew form of Daphne. *See* Daphne. Daphnit is a variant spelling.

Dagania, Daganya   From the Hebrew *dagan*, meaning "corn: the seed or grain of cereals." Akin to Dagon, the chief god of the ancient Philistines, and later of the Phoenicians, represented as half man and half fish. VARIANT SPELLINGS: Degania, Deganya. *See also* Dagan (masculine section).

Dagmar   From the Danish and German *dag* and *tag*, meaning "day, brightness," plus *mar*, akin to the Old English *maere*, meaning "splendid."

Dahlia   A perennial plant with large flower heads named for eighteenth-century Swedish botanist A. Dahl.

Dahtee   A variant spelling of Dotty, a pet form of Dorothy. *See* Dorothy. CONTEMPORARY EXAMPLE: Dahtee Maree West, Boston, Massachusetts.

Daien   A name invented by the parents of Daien Knight because when first and last names are said together it sounds like "day and night." Her sisters are named Windy Knight and Gay Knight.

Daisy   From the Middle English *daies ie*, meaning "day's eye." A popular plant with white rays surrounding a yellow center. A common nickname for Margaret. Derived from St. Margherita of Italy, who took the daisy (flower) as her symbol. CONTEMPORARY EXAMPLE: Daisy Lion-Goldschmidt, curator.

Dale   From the Anglo-Saxon, meaning "a dweller in a vale between hills." More commonly used as a masculine name.

Dalia   From the Hebrew, meaning either "a branch, a bough" or "to draw water." CONTEMPORARY EXAMPLE: Dalia Friedland, Israeli entertainer.

Dalit   A variant Hebrew form of Dalia. *See* Dalia.

Dallas   From the Old English *dael*, meaning "a valley." PLACE-NAME USAGE: Dallas, Texas, named for G.M. Dallas (1792-1864), a U.S. vice-president.

Dalores   A variant spelling of Dolores. *See* Dolores. CONTEMPORARY EXAMPLE: Dalores Broome Wingate, writer.

Dama   From the Latin *domina*, meaning "a lady." Damita is a pet form.

Damaris   From *damar*, a variety of evergreen tree indigenous to Malaya and Indonesia. In the Bible, an Athenian woman converted by St. Paul. CONTEMPORARY EXAMPLE: Damaris Rowland, editor.

Dame   From the Latin *domina*, meaning "a lady." CONTEMPORARY EXAMPLE: Dame Robson, actress.

Damita   A pet form of Dama and Dame. *See* Dama *and* Dame.

Dana   From the Latin, meaning "bright, pure as day," or from the Hebrew, meaning "to judge." In Israel, Dana is used as the feminine form of Dan. CONTEMPORARY EXAMPLE: Dana McCorkle, reporter. SURNAME USAGE: Charles Anderson Dana (1819-1897), newspaper editor.

Danae   A variant form of Dana. *See* Dana.

Dandylyon   A variant spelling of the common flower usually spelled dandelion, from the Old French and Latin, meaning "tooth of the lion," so called because of the shape of the leaves. CONTEMPORARY EXAMPLE: Dandylyon Rosebud Shannon, Pacifica, California.

Danelle   An invented name consisting of the syllables of Nelda. *See* Nelda.

Dania   A feminine form of Dan and Daniel. *See* Dan *and* Daniel (masculine section). Danya is a variant spelling.

Danice   A feminine form of Dan and Daniel. *See* Dan *and* Daniel (masculine section). CONTEMPORARY EXAMPLE: Danice Chisholm, Plymouth, Massachusetts.

Daniela, Daniella, Daniele, Danielle   Feminine forms of Daniel, meaning "God is my judge." *See* Daniel (masculine section). CONTEMPORARY EXAMPLE: Danielle Spencer, actress.

Danit   A feminine form of Dan and Daniel. *See* Dan *and* Daniel (masculine section).

Dantel   A feminine form of Dante. *See* Dante (masculine section).

Dantia   A feminine form of Dante. *See* Dante (masculine section). CONTEMPORARY EXAMPLE: Dantia Quirk, editor.

Daoma   Origin unknown. CONTEMPORARY EXAMPLE: Daoma Winston, author.

Daomi   An invented name. Originally Naomi, it was changed to Daomi so all daughters in the family would have the same initials. CONTEMPORARY EXAMPLE: Daomi Jackson Williams, Coats, North Carolina.

Daphna   A variant spelling of Daphne. *See* Daphne.

Daphne From the Greek, meaning "the laurel or bay tree." In Greek mythology, a nymph who escaped from Apollo by turning into a laurel tree. As a consequence, laurel leaves were worn by victors. VARIANT FORMS: Dafna, Dafne, Daphna, Daphnit.

Daphnit A variant form of Daphne. *See* Daphne. Dafnit is a variant spelling.

Dara From the Middle English *dar* and the Old English *dear*, meaning "to dare," hence "a courageous person." Dare is a variant form.

Darcie, Darcy From the Celtic, meaning "dark." Darcy is also a masculine form.

Dare A variant form of Dara. *See* Dara. CONTEMPORARY EXAMPLE: Dare Wright, author and illustrator.

Dareth A variant form of Dara. *See* Dara. CONTEMPORARY EXAMPLE: Dareth Newley, wife of actor Anthony Newley.

Daria The feminine form of the Persian name Darius. *See* Darius (masculine section). Or, a variant form of Dara. *See* Dara.

Darla From the Middle English *sereling*, meaning "dear, a loved one." CONTEMPORARY EXAMPLE: Darla Baio, Garden Grove, California.

Darleen, Darlene, Darline From the Anglo-Saxon, meaning "dearly beloved." Pet forms of Darla. *See* Darla. CONTEMPORARY EXAMPLE: Darlene Geis, editor.

Daryl From the Old English *deorling*, meaning "dear, beloved." Akin to Dara and Darlene.

Darlyn A variant form of Daryl. *See* Daryl. CONTEMPORARY EXAMPLE: Sandra Darlyn Evans, Corpus Christi, Texas.

Darragh A variant spelling of Dara. *See* Dara. CONTEMPORARY EXAMPLE: Darragh Park, author.

Dasi, Dassi Pet forms of Hadassah. *See* Hadassah.

Dasia, Datia From the Hebrew, meaning "the law of the Lord."

Davalyn An invented name, compounded of David and Lyn. CONTEMPORARY EXAMPLE: Davalyn Ruggles, San Bernadino, California.

Davene A variant form of David. *See* David (masculine section).

Davi, Davida Variant forms of the masculine form David. *See* David (masculine section).

Davina A Scottish form of David used in the seventeenth century. *See* David (masculine section).

Davita A Spanish form of David. *See* David (masculine section).

Dawn From the Old Norse *dagan*, meaning "dawn." Akin to the Old

English *daeg*, meaning "day." In Greek mythology, Aurora was the goddess of dawn, consequently Orrie and Rora have become pet forms of Dawn. CONTEMPORARY EXAMPLE: Dawn Lindsay, novelist.

Daya, Dayah   From the Hebrew, meaning "a bird."

Dean, Deane   More commonly used as masculine names. *See* Dean (masculine section).

Deanna, Deanne   Variant spellings of Diane or Dinah. *See* Diane *and* Dinah. CONTEMPORARY EXAMPLES: Deanna Durbin, actress; Deanne Barkley, television programmer.

Deannie   A pet form of Deanna. *See* Deanna. CONTEMPORARY EXAMPLE: Deannie Salerno, editor.

Dearaine   A name invented for a baby born at Christmas time. The syllables of Reindeer are reversed, and the spelling modified. CONTEMPORARY EXAMPLE: Dearaine Joy Gubbins, Burt, Minnesota.

Debbe   A variant form of Deborah. *See* Deborah.

Debbi, Debbie   Pet forms of Deborah. *See* Deborah.

Debby   A pet form of Deborah. *See* Deborah. VARIANT FORMS: Debbe, Debbi, Debbie, Debi.

Debera   A variant spelling of Debra, a form of Deborah. *See* Deborah. CONTEMPORARY EXAMPLE: Debera Schesinger, Wilmette, Illinois.

Debi   A variant form of Debby. *See* Debby. CONTEMPORARY EXAMPLE: Debi Holliday, book club director.

Debora   A variant spelling of Deborah. *See* Deborah.

Deborah   From the Hebrew, meaning "a bee," or "to speak kind words." In the Bible, a prophet and judge of Israel, wife of Lapidos who led the revolt against the Canaanites. VARIANT FORMS: Debra, Devora, Devra, Dobra, Dovra. PET FORMS: Debbi, Debby.

Debra   A variant form of Deborah. *See* Deborah. Devra is a variant form. Debera is a variant spelling.

Decima   From the Latin *decimus*, meaning "the tenth." Used as the name of the tenth child in a family.

Dee   From the British *du-wy*, meaning "dark water." Also, a popular pet name for Dorothy and Doris.

Deena   A variant Hebrew form of Dinah. *See* Dinah. CONTEMPORARY EXAMPLE: Deena Rosenberg, author.

Degania, Deganya   Variant spellings of Dagania. *See* Dagania. PLACE-NAME USAGE: a kibbutz in Israel.

Degula   From the Hebrew, meaning "excellent, outstanding."

Deirdre   From the Middle Irish *der*, meaning "a young girl." In Irish legend, a princess of Ulster who eloped to Scotland with her young lover. A popular name among the poets and playwrights of Ireland. CONTEMPORARY EXAMPLE: Deirdre Lenihan, actress.

Deka From the Greek *deka*, meaning "ten." CONTEMPORARY EXAMPLE: Deka Beaudine, actress.

Delia The Latin feminine form of Delius, meaning "an inhabitant of Delos" (a small island in the Aegean, the legendary birthplace of Artemis and Apollo). CONTEMPORARY EXAMPLE: Delia Ephron, author. Bedelia is a variant form.

Delila, Delilah From the Hebrew, meaning either "poor" or "hair." In the Bible, a Philistine woman, the mistress of Samson, who betrayed him. The connotation: a treacherous seductive woman. CONTEMPORARY EXAMPLE: Delilah Beasely, author.

Deliz A name invented by combining parts of *Dean* and *Eliza*beth. CONTEMPORARY EXAMPLE: Renise Deliz Bentley, Capistrano Beach, California.

Dell, Della, Delle Pet forms of Adele and Adeline. *See* Adele *and* Adeline. CONTEMPORARY EXAMPLES: Lou Dell Ann Printz, Canton, Ohio; Della Reese, singer; Hazelle Delle Kimberlin, Santa Ana, California.

Dellene A name invented, created by adding the diminutive suffix *ene* to a hybrid of Della (feminine) and Odell (masculine). CONTEMPORARY EXAMPLE: Dellene Ellis Hornsby, Austin, Texas.

Delores A variant Spanish spelling of Dolores. *See* Dolores.

Delpha From the Greek *delphis*, meaning "a dolphin." Akin to Delphinia. CONTEMPORARY EXAMPLE: Delpha Brasseur, Milford, Michigan.

Delphinia From the Greek *delphis*, meaning "a dolphin." Akin to Delphinus, a northern constellation. In Greek mythology, the dolphin was symbolic of the calm sea.

Delta From the Greek *delta* and the Hebrew *daled* (*dalet*), the fourth letter of both alphabets, meaning "a door."

Demelda Probably from the Greek *melden*, meaning "to announce, to proclaim." CONTEMPORARY EXAMPLE: Demelda Southward, Ventura, California.

Dena A variant Hebrew form of Dinah. *See* Dinah. Also a variant spelling of Denna. *See* Denna.

Denette A name invented by substituting a D for the J of Jenette (Jeanette) so all six children in the family would have D as the initial of the first name.

Deney A pet form of Denise. *See* Denise. CONTEMPORARY EXAMPLE: Deney Terrio, dancer.

Deniece, Deniese A variant spelling of Denise. *See* Denise. CONTEMPORARY EXAMPLE: Yvonne Deniese Abner, Blanchester, Ohio; Deniece Williams, actress.

Denis Basically, a masculine name. Used as a masculine form since the twelfth century. *See* Denis (masculine section).

Denise A feminine form of Denis, derived from Dionysius, the Greek god of wine and drama. *See* Denis (masculine section). VARIANT FORMS: Denis, Dennet, Dionis, Dionysia, Diot.

Denna From the Anglo-Saxon, meaning "glen, valley." Also, a variant spelling of Dena. *See* Dena.

Dennet A variant form of Denise. *See* Denise.

Denyse A variant spelling of Denise. *See* Denise.

Derede A German form of Dorothea. *See* Dorothea.

Derora, Derorit From the Hebrew, meaning "a flowing stream" or a "bird (a swallow)," connoting freedom.

Desdemona From the Latin, meaning "of the devil; evil, cruel." In Shakespeare's *Othello*, the wife of Othello, whom he murders.

Desire, Desiree From the Old French *desirer* and the Latin *desiderare*, *meaning "to look to the stars, to crave."*

Desta From the Old French, meaning "destiny."

Detta A short form of Odetta, a variant form of Ottilia. *See* Ottilia. CONTEMPORARY EXAMPLE: Detta Penna, book designer.

Deva Probably a variant form of Devorah. *See* Devorah.

Devaki From the Sanskrit *deva*, meaning "a god." CONTEMPORARY EXAMPLE: Devaki Berkson, nutritionist.

De Vee An invented name. Probably from the initials D.V. CONTEMPORARY EXAMPLE: De Vee Lange, San Diego, California.

Devera A variant form of Devorah. *See* Devorah.

Devlynn An invented name in which a D was added to Evelyn, and the second "e" dropped and an "n" added. CONTEMPORARY EXAMPLE: Devlynn L. Tanner, Xenia, Ohio.

Devon A first name derived from the place-name on the English Channel. Also referred to as Devonshire. CONTEMPORARY EXAMPLE: Devon Ericson, actress.

Devora, Devorah Variant Hebraic forms of Deborah. *See* Deborah.

Devorit A variant spelling of Devora. *See* Devora.

Devra A variant form of Deborah. *See* Deborah.

Di   A pet form of Diana. *See* Diana. CONTEMPORARY EXAMPLE: Lady Di Beauclerk (1734-1808.)

Diahann   A variant form of Diane. *See* Diane. CONTEMPORARY EXAMPLE: Diahann Carroll, actress.

Diana   From the Latin *dius*, meaning "divine." In Roman mythology, the virgin goddess of the moon and of hunting. VARIANT FORMS: Diane (French); Dione, Dionne (Greek); Dyan, Dyana. Di is a pet form. CONTEMPORARY EXAMPLE: Diana Rigg, actress.

Diandra   From the Greek, meaning "a flower with two stamens." CONTEMPORARY EXAMPLE: Diandra Biship, San Francisco, California.

Diane   The French form of Diana. *See* Diana.

Diantha, Dianthe   From the Modern Latin *dianthus*, derived from the Greek *dios*, meaning "divine," plus *anthos*, meaning "a flower." In Greek mythology, the flower of Zeus. CONTEMPORARY EXAMPLE: Diantha Warfel, author.

Dicey   A variant spelling of Dicie. *See* Dicie.

Dicia   A variant form of Dicie. *See* Dicie.

Dicie   From the British, meaning "risky, hazardous." Dicia is a variant form. CONTEMPORARY EXAMPLE: Dicie H. Utsey, Red Level, Alabama.

Dickla   The Aramaic form of the Hebrew and Arabic, meaning "a palm or date tree." In the Bible, used as a masculine and feminine form. VARIANT FORMS: Dikla, Diklit.

Dido   In Greek mythology, the founder and queen of Carthage, who stabbed herself when she was deserted by Aeneas.

Diedra   A variant form of Dierdra. *See* Dierdra.

Dierdra   A variant spelling of Deirdre. *See* Deirdre.

Dierdre   A variant spelling of Deirdre. *See* Deirdre.

Dikla, Diklit   Variant forms of Dickla. *See* Dickla.

Dilli   A variant form of Dillian. *See* Dillian.

Dillian   From the British *delw*, meaning "an idol." VARIANT FORMS: Dilli, Dillo (Old High German); Dilliana (Dutch).

Dilliana   A variant form of Dillian. *See* Dillian.

Dillo   A variant form of Dillian. *See* Dillian.

Dilys   From the Welsh, meaning "genuine." CONTEMPORARY EXAMPLE: Dilys Winn, editor.

Dimitra   The feminine form of Demetrius. *See* Demetrius (masculine section). CONTEMPORARY EXAMPLE: Dimitra Arliss, actress.

Dimity   Possibly a corrupt feminine form of Dimitry. *See* Dimitry (masculine section). CONTEMPORARY EXAMPLE: Dimity S. Berkner, librarian.

Dinah   From the Hebrew, meaning "judgement." In the Bible, the daughter of Jacob and Leah. VARIANT FORMS: Deena, Deanna, Deanne, Dena, Dina, not to be confused with Diana. CONTEMPORARY EXAMPLE: Dinah Shore, entertainer.

Diona   A variant form of Dione. *See* Dione. CONTEMPORARY EXAMPLE: Diona Ryon, Kentwood, Michigan.

Dione, Dionne   The Greek form of the Latin name Diana. *See* Diana. CONTEMPORARY EXAMPLE: Dione Pattullo, cooking authority; Dionne Warwick, singer.

Dionetta   A variant form of Dione. *See* Dione.

Ditza, Ditzah   From the Hebrew, meaning "joy." Diza is a variant spelling.

Dixie   From the Old English *dix*, meaning "a dike (dyke), a wall." CONTEMPORARY EXAMPLE: Dixie Carter, actress. PLACE-NAME USAGE: Dixton, Connecticut.

Diza   A variant spelling of Ditza. *See* Ditza.

Dobra   A variant form of Deborah. *See* Deborah.

Doda   From the Hebrew, meaning "an aunt."

Dodi, Dodie   From the Hebrew, meaning "my friend, my beloved." Also, a pet form of Dorothy. CONTEMPORARY EXAMPLE: Dodie Edmonds, author.

Dodo   A variant form of Dorothy. *See* Dorothy.

Dody   A variant spelling of Dodi. *See* Dodi. CONTEMPORARY EXAMPLE: Dody Goodman, actress.

Doe   A pet form of Dorothy. *See* Dorothy.

Doirean   An Irish form of Doreen. *See* Doreen.

Dolley   A variant spelling of Dolly. *See* Dolly.

Dollie   A variant spelling of Dolly. *See* Dolly.

Dolly   A variant form of Dorothy. *See* Dorothy. Dolly (also spelled Dolley) Madison, wife of the fourth president of the U.S., was christened Dorothea. Dolly Vardin was a character in *Barnaby Rudge*, a novel by Charles Dickens.

Dolores   From the Latin and Spanish, meaning "lady of sorrows." Derived from *Maria de los Dolores*, the name by which the Blessed Virgin was called, especially in Spanish–speaking countries. Delores is a variant Spanish spelling.

Domenica   A variant spelling of Dominica. *See* Dominica.

Dominica   The feminine form of Dominic, meaning "belonging to the Lord." PLACE-NAME USAGE: an island in the West Indies.

Dominique   The French form of Dominica. *See* Dominica. CONTEMPORARY EXAMPLE: Dominique Sanda, actress.

Donalie   A pet form of Donna. *See* Donna. Also, a name invented by combining Donna and Lee (Lea). *See* Donna *and* Lee. CONTEMPORARY EXAMPLE: Donalie Fitzgerald, author.

Donella   A pet form of Donna. *See* Donna.

Donita   A Spanish pet form of Donna. *See* Donna.

Donna   An Italian form of the Latin *domina*, meaning "lady, madam," a title of respect. VARIANT FORMS: Donni, Donnis. PET FORMS: Donella, Donita.

Donnarae   An invented name, compounded of Donna and Rae. *See* Donna *and* Rae. CONTEMPORARY EXAMPLE: Donnarae MacCann, author.

Donnelle   A name invented by combining the masculine Donn and the feminine Nelle.

Donni, Donnis   Variant forms of Donna. *See* Donna. CONTEMPORARY EXAMPLE: Donni Betts, author.

Dora   A variant form of Dorothea. *See* Dorothea. VARIANT FORMS: Doreen, Dorene, Doraleen, Doralene, Doretta.

Doraleen, Doralene   Variant forms of Dora. *See* Dora.

Doralice   A French form of Dorothea. *See* Dorothea.

Doralyn   An invented name compounded of Dora and Lyn. *See* Dora *and* Lyn. CONTEMPORARY EXAMPLE: Doralyn Harris, community leader.

Dorann   An invented name compounded of Dora and Ann. *See* Dora *and* Ann. CONTEMPORARY EXAMPLE: Dorann Pohmurski, Warren, Ohio.

Dorcas   From the Greek *dorkas*, meaning "a gazelle." In the Bible, a woman who spent her life sewing clothes for poor people.

Dorcia   A variant form of Dorcas. *See* Dorcas.

Dore   A German form of Dorothea. *See* Dorothea. CONTEMPORARY EXAMPLE: Dore Ashtow, art critic.

Dorea   A variant form of Doris. *See* Doris.

Doreen, Dorene   Variant pet forms of Dorothy and its diminutive Dora. *See* Dorothy. Doirean is an Irish variant form. CONTEMPORARY EXAMPLE: Doreen Yarwood, costume designer.

Dorelle   A name borrowed from a cosmetic product advertised in the 1930s. CONTEMPORARY EXAMPLE: Dorelle Bishop, Sallis, Mississippi.

Dorenda   A variant spelling of Dorinda. *See* Dorinda.

Doretta   A diminutive form of Dora. Also, a name invented by combining Dora and Etta. *See* Dora *and* Etta. CONTEMPORARY EXAMPLE: Doretta Durnil, Knightstown, Indiana.

Dorette   A French form of Dorothea. *See* Dorothea.

Doria   A variant form of Doris. *See* Doris.

Dorie   A variant form of Doris. *See* Doris.

Dorinda   An eighteenth-century invented name styled after Belinda and Melinda. Rinda is a pet form. Also, a variant form of Dorothea. *See* Dorothea. CONTEMPORARY EXAMPLE: Dorinda Bishop, San Francisco, California.

Doris   From the Greek, meaning "a sacrificial knife." In Greek mythology, a sea nymph, the wife of Nereus, mother of sea gods. Some authorities believe it is akin to Dorothy. *See* Dorothy. VARIANT FORMS: Dorea, Doria, Dorie, Dorit, Dorrit. CONTEMPORARY EXAMPLE: Doris Day, actress. PLACE-NAME USAGE: a mountainous region in Greece.

Dorit   From the Hebrew *dor*, meaning "a generation." Or, a pet form of Doris. *See* Doris.

Dorita   A pet form of Dorothy. *See* Dorothy.

Dorith   A variant spelling of Dorit. *See* Dorit.

Doritt   A variant spelling of Dorit. *See* Dorit. CONTEMPORARY EXAMPLE: Doritt A. Kirk, Newport Beach, California.

Dorma   From the Latin *dormire*, meaning "to sleep," and the Old French *dormeour*, meaning "a window in a sloping roof." CONTEMPORARY EXAMPLE: Dorma B. Smith, Three Rivers, Michigan.

Doronit   From the Aramaic, meaning "a gift."

Dorotea   The Spanish form of Dorothea. *See* Dorothea.

Dorothea   The original form of Dorothy. From the Greek *doron*, meaning "gift," plus *theos*, meaning "God," hence "gift of God." *See also* Dorothy. Theodora is an inverted form. VARIANT FORMS: Dolly, Dora, Dorinda (English); Dorothee, Dorette, Doralice (French); Derede, Dore, Dorlisa (German); Dorotea (Spanish); Dorka (Russian); Dorosia, Dorota (Polish); Tiga, Tigo, Tio (Slavonic). PET FORMS: Dodi, Dodo, Doll, Dolley, Dollie, Dora, Dorat, Dot, Dottie, Dotty.

Dorothee   A variant form of Dorothy. *See* Dorothy. CONTEMPORARY EXAMPLE: Dorothee Soell, a French painter.

Dorothy   From the Greek *doron*, meaning "gift of God." Dorothea is the original form. *See* Dorothea.

Dorri, Dorrie   Pet forms of Dorothy. *See* Dorothy. CONTEMPORARY EXAMPLE: Dorrie Kavanaugh, actress.

Dorris   A variant spelling of Doris. *See* Doris.

Dorrit   A variant spelling of Dorit. *See* Dorit.

Dot, Dottie, Dotty   Pet forms of Dorothy. *See* Dorothy.

Dova, Dove   From the Middle English *douve*, meaning "a dove."

Dreama   From the Middle English and Old English *dream*, meaning "joy, music." CONTEMPORARY EXAMPLE: Dreama Riley, Sonoma, California.

Dreane   Possibly from the Slavonic name Drenka, a variant form of Cornelia. *See* Cornelia. CONTEMPORARY EXAMPLE: Dreane Swanson, New London, Connecticut.

Drucilla   A variant spelling of Drusilla. *See* Drusilla.

Drusilla   A form of the Roman family name Drausus and its diminutive form Drusus. In the Bible, the daughter of Herod Agrippa I. CONTEMPORARY EXAMPLE: Drusilla Webster, wife of F.B.I. director.

Duba   From the Hebrew, meaning "a bear."

Dulce, Dulcea   Variant forms of Dulcie. *See* Dulcie.

Dulcee   A variant spelling of Dulcie. *See* Dulcie.

Dulcie   From the Latin, meaning "charming, sweet." CONTEMPORARY EXAMPLE: Dulcie Jordan, actress.

Dulcy   A variant spelling of Dulcie. *See* Dulcie.

Dumont   From the French, meaning "from the mountain." Dusty is a pet form. CONTEMPORARY EXAMPLE: Dumont "Dusty" Deane, New York City.

Durene   From the Latin *durare*, meaning "enduring, lasting."

Dusty   A nickname. Dusty Deane was born in Texas during a raging dust storm. *See* Dumont. Also, a masculine pet form.

Dvera   A variant form of Devorah. *See* Devorah. CONTEMPORARY EXAMPLE: Dvera Berson, author.

Dvorit   A variant spelling of Devorit. *See* Devorit.

Dyan   A variant form of Diana. *See* Diana. CONTEMPORARY EXAMPLE: Dyan Cannon, actress.

Dyana   A variant form of Diana. Used since the seventeenth century. *See* Diana.

Dysis   From the Greek, meaning "sunset." Often given to children born to older parents.

E

Earla A feminine form of Earl. *See* Earl (masculine section). CONTEMPORARY EXAMPLE: Earla Silva, Long Beach, California.

Earlene A feminine form of Earl. *See* Earl (masculine section). CONTEMPORARY EXAMPLE: Earlene B. Cunningham, biochemist.

Eartha From the Old English, meaning "ground." CONTEMPORARY EXAMPLE: Eartha Kitt, actress.

Easter Originally, a pagan festival in honor of the dawn goddess, Eastre. In Middle English, *ester* was akin to the German *Ostern*, eastern (where the sun rises). Used as a masculine as well as feminine form. Sometimes confused with Esther. Eacy is a pet form.

Ebony From the Greek, meaning "a hard, dark wood."

Echo From the Greek, meaning "sound." In Greek mythology, Echo was a nymph who, because her love for Narcissus was not reciprocated, pined away until only her voice remained.

Eda A variant Italian form of Edda or Edith. *See* Edda *and* Edith. CONTEMPORARY EXAMPLES: Eda LeShan, author; Eda Sagarra, author.

Edda From the Old Norse, meaning "poetry."

Eddy A masculine diminutive spelling of Eddie; a pet form of Edward. Also, from the Old Norse, meaning "a whirlpool." CONTEMPORARY EXAMPLE: Eddy Dalton, wife of a former governor of Virginia. SURNAME USAGE: Mary Baker Eddy (1821-1910), religious leader.

Ede A pet form of Edith. *See* Edith.

Eden From the Hebrew, meaning "delight" or "adornment." In the Bible, the garden where Adam and Eve lived, called Paradise. CONTEMPORARY EXAMPLE: Eden Phillpotts, novelist. SURNAME USAGE: Sir Robert Anthony Eden, British prime minister; Barbara Eden, actress.

Edessa An ancient city in Mesopotamia, present-day Turkey.

Edga The feminine form of Edgar. *See* Edgar (masculine section).

Edia A variant form of Edga and Edya. From the Hebrew, meaning "adornment of the Lord."

Edie A popular Scottish diminutive form of Edith. *See* Edith. CONTEMPORARY EXAMPLES: Edie Adams and Edie Gorme, entertainers.

Edina From the Anglo-Saxon, meaning "rich friend." A feminine form of Edwin. PLACE-NAME USAGE: a suburb of Minneapolis, Minnesota, named by Scottish settlers after Edinburgh, capital of Scotland.

Edita   A Spanish pet form of Edith. *See* Edith. CONTEMPORARY EXAMPLE: Edita Morris, author.

Edith, Edythe   A compounded Anglo-Saxon name from *ead*, meaning "rich, happy, prosperous," and *gyth* or *guth*, meaning "battle, war." Edythe is the modern variant spelling. VARIANT FORMS: Eda, Edda, Edie, Editha. CONTEMPORARY EXAMPLE: Edythe S. Clark, editor.

Editha   A variant form of Edith. *See* Edith.

Edlyn   From the Old English, meaning "happy (bubbling) brook." Also, a name created by combining *Edw*ard and Mari*lyn*, the names of the parents of Edlyn Vancina, a resident of Los Angeles, California.

Edna, Ednah   From the Hebrew, meaning "delight, desired, adorned, voluptuous." May also be a contracted form of Edwina. Edna occurs in the Apocrypha, in the Book of Tobit, and in the Book of Jubilees. VARIANT FORMS: Adena, Adina.

Edwarda   The feminine form of Edward. *See* Edward (masculine section).

Edwina   The feminine form of Edwin. *See* Edwin (masculine section).

Edya, Edyah   From the Hebrew, meaning "adornment of the Lord." Edia is a variant spelling.

Edythe   A variant spelling of Edith. *See* Edith.

Eeva   A Finnish variant spelling of Eva. *See* Eva.

Effie   A pet form of Euphemia. *See* Euphemia. CONTEMPORARY EXAMPLE: Effie Lee Morris, librarian.

Efrat   A variant form of Efrata. *See* Efrata.

Efrata   From the Hebrew, meaning "honored, distinguished." In the Bible, the name of the wife of Caleb who was also called Efrat. PLACE-NAME USAGE: a site near Bethel (between Jerusalem and Bethlehem) where Rachel, the wife of Jacob, died and was buried.

Efrona   From the Hebrew, meaning "a bird" (of a species that sings well).

Egelina   A form of the Old German name Agilina, popular in thirteenth and fourteenth–century England. SURNAME USAGE: Eglon, Eglin, Eagling, Eggling.

Egla, Eglah   From the Hebrew, meaning "a heifer." In the Bible, the name of one of David's wives. CONTEMPORARY EXAMPLE: Eglah McGuire Lambert, LaMesa, California.

Eila   A variant form of Eileen. *See* Eileen. CONTEMPORARY EXAMPLE: Eila Watanen, nurse.

Eileen   An Irish form of Helen and Elaine. *See* Helen *and* Elaine. Also, perhaps a variant form of Evelyn. *See* Evelyn. Aileen is a variant spelling. PET FORMS: Eily, Elie.

Elain, Elaine   French forms of Helen, meaning "light" in the Greek. Eileen is an Irish variant. Elane, Elain, and Elayne are variant spellings. Some authorities claim that Elain and its various forms are derived from the Welsh, meaning "a fawn, a young hind." Elaine was made popular by Tennyson in *Idylls of the King*. In Arthurian legend, Elaine was the mother of Sir Galahad.

Elana   From the Hebrew, meaning "a tree." Ilana is a variant spelling.

Elane   A variant spelling of Elaine. *See* Elaine.

Elayne   A variant spelling of Elaine. *See* Elaine.

Elba   A variant form of Elbert and Albert. *See* Elbert and Albert (masculine section). CONTEMPORARY EXAMPLE: Elba Torres, Jersey City, New Jersey. PLACE-NAME USAGE: an Italian island, site of Napoleon's first exile.

Elberta   The feminine form of Elbert. *See* Elbert (masculine section).

Elda   From the Middle English *elde*, meaning "old." Akin to Alda. CONTEMPORARY EXAMPLE: Elda-Jo Klanrud, Kansas City, Missouri.

Eldora   From the Spanish *dorado*, meaning "the gilded." Eldorado was an imaginary country in South America fabled to be rich in gold.

Ele   A pet form of Eleanor. *See* Eleanor. CONTEMPORARY EXAMPLE: Ele M. Quinn, public relations.

Eleanor, Eleanore   Variant German forms of Helen. From the Greek, meaning "light." VARIANT FORMS: Eleonora and Leonora (Italian); Lenore (German); Elien (French). PET FORMS: Ellie, Nell, Nellie, Ella, Nora.

Electra   From the Greek, meaning "the shining one." In Greek mythology, the daughter of Agamemnon.

Elen   A variant spelling of Ellen. Also, a short form of Eleanor. *See* Eleanor.

Elena   From the Greek, meaning "light." The Italian form of Helen. Also, the Hawaiian form of Ellen.

Elenor   A variant spelling of Eleanor. *See* Eleanor.

Elese   The Hawaiian form of Elsie. *See* Elsie.

Elfreda, Elfride, Elfrieda   Variant spellings of Alfreda. The masculine Alfred is the original form. *See* Alfred.

Eli   A pet form of Eleanor. *See* Eleanor. Used also as a masculine name. VARIANT FORMS: Ele, Elie, Ellie.

Eliana, Eliane, Elianna   From the Hebrew, meaning "God has answered me." Akin to the masculine Elias and Elihu. CONTEMPORARY EXAMPLE: Eliane Benisti, literary agent.

Elie   A pet form of Eleanor. *See* Eleanor. Used also as a masculine name. *See* Elie (masculine section).

Elin   A variant spelling of Ellen. Also, a short form of Eleanor. *See* Eleanor.

Elinoar   From the Hebrew, meaning "God is my youth," or "God of my youth."

Elinor, Elinore, Elinorr   Variant spellings of Eleanor. *See* Eleanor.

Eliora, Eleora   From the Hebrew, meaning "God is my light."

Elisa   A pet form of Elisabeth. *See* Elisabeth.

Elisabeta   The Hawaiian form of Elisabeth. *See* Elisabeth.

Elisabeth   A variant spelling of Elizabeth commonly used in England. *See* Elizabeth.

Elise   A pet form of Elisabeth. *See* Elisabeth. CONTEMPORARY EXAMPLE: Elise Boulding, professor.

Elisheva   From the Hebrew, meaning "God is my oath." The original form of Elizabeth. *See* Elizabeth.

Elissa   A pet form of Elisabeth. Also, a hybrid name from *Emma* and *Melissa*. CONTEMPORARY EXAMPLE: Elissa Lewis Pe Ries, Wilmington, North Carolina.

Eliza   A pet form of Elizabeth. *See* Elizabeth.

Elizabeth   From the Hebrew, meaning "God's oath." The original Hebrew form is Elisheva. In the Bible, Elisheva (also spelled Elisheba) was the wife of Aaron, the brother of Moses. Also, the mother of John the Baptist. Elisabeth (with an "s") is the way the Greek translation of the Bible rendered Elisheva. It is the preferred spelling in Europe. Elizabeth, spelled with a "z", is the more common spelling. VARIANT FORMS: Eliza (English); Elspeth, Elspie (Scotch); Elise, Lise, Elsbet, Bettine, Ilse (German); Elsebin, Helsa (Danish); Babet, Babette, Babichon (French); Elisabetta, Lisettina (Italian); Lisa, Lisenka (Russian); Erzebet, Orse (Hungarian). PET FORMS: Babette, Bess, Bessie, Bessy, Bet, Beth, Bettina, Betsie, Betsey, Betta, Bette, Betty, Eliza, Elsie, Elize, Elspeth, Elspie, Isabel, Ilse, Libbie, Libby, Lilibet, Lilla, Lillah, Lisa, Lisbeth, Liz, Liza, Lizzie, Lizzy, Tetsy, Tetty. A popular nursery rhyme indicates the proliferation of names used as variant forms of Elizabeth:

> Elizabeth, Elspeth, Betsy, and Bess,
> They all went together to seek a bird's nest,
> They found a bird's nest with five eggs in,
> They all took one and left four in.

Elize   A pet form of Elizabeth. *See* Elizabeth.

Elke   A pet form of Alice or Alexandra. *See* Alice *and* Alexandra. CONTEMPORARY EXAMPLE: Elke Sommer, actress.

Ella   A pet form of Eleanor. *See* Eleanor. CONTEMPORARY EXAMPLE: Ella Fitzgerald, singer.

Ellen   A short form of Eleanor. *See* Eleanor.

Ellendea   Compounded of Ellen, a pet form of Helen, meaning "light" in Greek, and *dea*, from the Latin *dro*, meaning "God," hence "God's light." CONTEMPORARY EXAMPLE: Ellendea Proffer, editor.

Ellette   A pet form of Ella. *See* Ella.

Ellice   Originally a place–name. Ellice Blazan, of Concord, New Hampshire, was so named after the Ellice Islands, in the Pacific, which her father found particularly beautiful when he was stationed there during World War II.

Ellie   A pet form of Eleanor. *See* Eleanor.

Ellin   A variant spelling of Ellen. *See* Ellen.

Ellyn, Elyn   Variant spellings of Ellen and short forms of Eleanor. *See* Eleanor. CONTEMPORARY EXAMPLE: Ellyn Burstyn, actress.

Elma   From the Greek and Latin, meaning "pleasant, fair, kind." Alma is a variant spelling. *See* Alma. May also be a short form of Guglielma, the Italian feminine form of William.

Elmira   The feminine form of Elmer, from Anglo-Saxon, meaning "noble and famous." A city in New York State.

Elnora   A variant form of Eleanor. *See* Eleanor.

Elodie   From the Greek. A flower name.

Eloise   A variant form of the French Heloise and Louise. *See* Louise.

Eloren   A name invented by rearranging the letters in the name Roneel. *See* Roneel.

Elsa   A German diminutive form of Elizabeth. Or, from the Anglo-Saxon, meaning "a swan." The name of the heroine of Richard Wagner's opera *Lohengrin*. CONTEMPORARY EXAMPLE: Elsa Lanchester, actress.

Else   A variant spelling of Elsa. *See* Elsa.

Elsena   A name invented by combining the sounds of Elnora and Cynthia. *See* Elnora *and* Cynthia. CONTEMPORARY EXAMPLE: Elsena Felker, Princeton, Kentucky.

Elsie   A variant form of Elisabeth. *See* Elisabeth. A pet form of Alice, Elizabeth, or Elsa.

Elspeth   A Scottish form of Elizabeth. *See* Elizabeth. CONTEMPORARY

EXAMPLE: Elspeth Huxley, author.

Elula Possibly a variant form of Elul. *See* Elul (masculine section).
CONTEMPORARY EXAMPLE: Elula Perrin, French author.

Elva From the Anglo-Saxon, meaning "elf."

Elverta A variant form of Alberta. *See* Alberta. PLACE-NAME USAGE:
Elverta, California, named for the wife of a local benefactor.

Elvina From the Anglo-Saxon, meaning "a friend of elves."

Elvira A Spanish form from the Germanic *ala* and *wer*, meaning "to
close up completely."

Elyn, Elynn Variant spellings of Ellen. Also, short forms of Eleanor.
See Ellen *and* Eleanor.

Elysa, Elyse, Elyssa Variant forms of Elisabeth. *See* Elisabeth. CON-
TEMPORARY EXAMPLE: Elyssa Davalos, actress.

Elza From the Hebrew, meaning "God is my joy." Aliza is a variant
form.

Em A pet form of Emma. *See* Emma. CONTEMPORARY EXAMPLE: Em
Riggs, author.

Ema The Hawaiian form of Emma. *See* Emma.

Emaline A variant form of Emily. *See* Emily. Emiline is a variant
spelling.

Emanuela, Emanuella The feminine forms of Emanuel, meaning
"God is with us."

Emele The Hawaiian form of Emily. *See* Emily.

Emelin, Emelina, Emeline Variant forms of Emily. *See* Emily.

Emerald, Emeralda, Emeraldine From the Middle English and the
Old French *smaragde*, meaning "a bright green precious stone." Used
also as a masculine form.

Emerlin, Emerline A variant form of Emeraldine. *See* Emeraldine.

Emilia A variant form of Emily. *See* Emily. A section of northern
Italy.

Emilie A variant form of Emily. *See* Emily.

Emily The feminine form of the Latin name Aemilius, meaning
"ambitious, industrious." VARIANT FORMS: Amelia (English); Emilia
(Italian); Emilie (French). PET FORMS: Emaline, Emeline. Princess
Amelia, King George II's daughter, was usually called Princess Emily.

Emma From the Greek name Erma, meaning "the big one" or
"grandmother." VARIANT FORMS: Ymma, Imma, Irma, Ema. In the
twelfth century, it appeared as Em. Emmie is a popular pet form.

Emmaline   A French form of Emily. Also, a name invented by combining Emma and a form of Lynn. CONTEMPORARY EXAMPLE: Emmaline Henry, actress.

Emmeleia   A variant form of Emily. *See* Emily. CONTEMPORARY EXAMPLE: Irene Emmeleia Craig, Temple City, California.

Emmie, Emmy   Pet forms of Emily or Emma. *See* Emily *and* Emma.

Emmylou   A hybrid name, compounded of Emmy and Lou. CONTEMPORARY EXAMPLE: Emmylou Harris, rock singer.

Emrick   A variant form of Americus. *See* Americus. Used also as a surname in the family of Harold G. Emrick, of Indianapolis, Indiana, since 1777.

Emuna, Emunah   From the Hebrew, meaning "faith."

Ena   A variant spelling of Ina. Or, a pet form of Eugenia. *See* Eugenia.

Enid   Either from the Anglo-Saxon, meaning "fair," or from the Celtic, meaning "purity." In Arthurian legend, the wife of Geraint, a model of loyalty and patience. PLACE-NAME USAGE: a city in Oklahoma.

Eolande   From the Greek *eos*, meaning "dawn," hence "the land (in the East) where dawn first appears." In Greek mythology Eos was the goddess of dawn. Akin to the Roman Aurora. Yolande is a variant form.

E'O'lini   A variant form of Eolande. *See* Eolande. CONTEMPORARY EXAMPLE: E'O'lini Barrett, Palo Alto, California.

Erda   From the German *erde*, meaning "earth." Eartha is a variant form.

Erga   From the Hebrew *arog*, meaning "yearning, longing."

Erica, Erika   The feminine form of Eric. From the German, meaning "honorable ruler." CONTEMPORARY EXAMPLE: Erica Jong, author.

Erin   A poetic name for Ireland. CONTEMPORARY EXAMPLES: Erin Gray, model; Erin Mahony, Stanfordsville, New York.

Eris   In Greek mythology, the goddess of strife and contention.

Erlinia   A variant form of the masculine Earl. *See* Earl (masculine section).

Erma   A variant spelling of Irma. *See* Irma. CONTEMPORARY EXAMPLE: Erma Bombeck, author.

Erna   A feminine form of Ernest. *See* Ernest (masculine section).

Ernesta   A feminine form of Ernest. *See* Ernest (masculine section).

Ernestine   A feminine form of Ernest. *See* Ernest (masculine section).

Errin   A variant spelling of Erin. *See* Erin. CONTEMPORARY EXAMPLE:

Errin Pizzey, author.

Esme   From the Old French, meaning "esteemed."

Esmeralda   From the Spanish, meaning "emerald." Since its use by Victor Hugo in his *Hunchback of Notre Dame*, it has been used in England and France. VARIANT FORMS: Emerald, Emeralda, Emeraldine.

Essie   A pet form of Esther. *See* Esther.

Esta, Estee, Estella, Estelle   Variant forms of Esther. *See* Esther. Estella is a Spanish form.

Ester   A modern spelling of Esther. *See* Esther.

Esther   From the Persian, meaning "a star." Also identified with Ishtar, the Babylonian and Assyrian goddess of love and fertility. In Phonecian mythology, the goddess of the moon. In the Bible, the Jewish heroine who became the queen of the Persian king Ahasueros, and saved her people from the plot of Haman. VARIANT FORMS: Esta, Essie, Ettie, Etty, Estella, Estelle, Hester, Hesther, Hetty.

Estralita   From the Spanish, meaning "little star."

Etana   From the Hebrew, meaning "strong." Etan and Ethan are masculine forms.

Ethel   From the Anglo-Saxon *aethel*, meaning "noble." Akin to the German Adelaide. *See* Adelaide. VARIANT FORMS: Adal, Edel, Adele, Alice.

Ethelyn   A hybrid name of Ethel and Lyn (Lynn). *See* Ethel *and* Lyn. CONTEMPORARY EXAMPLE: Ethelyn M. Parkinson, author.

Etta   A short form of Henrietta. Or, a variant spelling of Edda. *See* Henrietta *and* Edda.

Eudice   A modern variant spelling of Judith. *See* Judith.

Eudora   From the Greek, meaning "good gift." CONTEMPORARY EXAMPLE: Eudora Welty, author.

Eugenia   From the Greek, meaning "well born." Eugenie is a variant form. PET FORMS: Ina, Ena, Genie. CONTEMPORARY EXAMPLES: Eugenia Price, author; Eugenia Lanzetta, Vineland, New Jersey.

Eugenie   The French form of Eugenia. *See* Eugenia. Became popular in France during the reign of Empress Eugenia (1826-1920), wife of Louis Napoleon.

Eulalia, Eulalie   From the Greek, meaning "sweet talk." Eulalie is a Spanish and French form. CONTEMPORARY EXAMPLE: Eulalia Fagan, Hollidaysburg, Pennsylvania.

Eunice   From the Greek, meaning "good victory." In the Bible, the mother of Timothy. Unice is a variant spelling. PET FORMS: Niki, Nikki.

Euphemia   From the Greek, meaning "good speech" or "well spoken." PET FORMS: Effie, Phemie.

Euradean   A name invented by combining Eura (from Europe) and the last syllable of Na*dine* (with spelling altered, but sound retained). CONTEMPORARY EXAMPLE: Euradean Dowler, Escondido, California.

Euridice, Eurydice   From the Greek *eury*, meaning "wide, broad," and *dike*, meaning "justice." In Greek legend, the wife of Orpheus. Eurydice is the original spelling.

Eustacia   The feminine form of Eustace. *See* Eustace (masculine section).

Eva, Eve   Eva is the Latin and German form of Eve. Derived from the Hebrew, meaning "life." In the Bible, Eve, the wife of Adam, was the first woman. Eva gained popularity after the appearance of Harriet Beecher Stowe's *Uncle Tom's Cabin* in 1852. PET FORMS: Ev, Evie, Evita (Spanish).

Evadne   A variant form of Eva and Eve. *See* Eva.

Evalina, Evaline   Pet forms of Eva and Evelyn. Evalina is also the Hawaiian form of Evelyn. *See* Eva *and* Evelyn. CONTEMPORARY EXAMPLE: Evaline Ness, author.

Evangeline   From the Greek, meaning "bearer of glad tidings, a messenger." A name created by Henry Wadsworth Longfellow. The heroine of his 1847 narrative poem *Evangeline*. Eva is a pet form. CONTEMPORARY EXAMPLE: Evangeline Rupert, Branchard, Pennsylvania.

Evanne   An invented name. Pronounced Eve-Anne, it is the middle name of Ruth Evanne DeAmicis, Bellefontaine, Ohio. A combination of her grandmothers' first names: Eva and Anne.

Eveleen   An Irish pet form of Eva. *See* Eva.

Evelina, Eveline   A form of the Old German name Avelina. Also, a pet form of Eva. *See* Eva. CONTEMPORARY EXAMPLE: Eveline Craddock, educator.

Evelyn   A variant spelling of the Celtic name Eveline, meaning "pleasant." VARIANT FORMS: Avi, Avila, Avelina, Evalina, Evelina, Eve, Evie. Since the seventennth century, Evelyn has been used as a masculine name as well. One of the earliest examples is Evelyn Pierrepont (1665-1726), first Duke of Kingston. SURNAME USAGE: John Evelyn (1620-1706), English author.

Evette   A pet form of Evelyn. *See* Evelyn.

Evie   A pet form of Eve or Evelyn. *See* Eve *and* Evelyn.

Eviene   A pet form of Eve or Evelyn. *See* Eve *and* Evelyn. CONTEMPORARY EXAMPLE: Eviene C. Fulginti, Cupertino, California.

Evita   A Spanish pet form of Eve. *See* Eve. CONTEMPORARY EXAMPLE:

Eva (Evita) Peron, Argentinian political leader.

Evona   A variant form of Yvonne. *See* Yvonne. CONTEMPORARY EXAM-
PLE: Evona Allensworth, Midwest City, Oklahoma.

Evonne   A pet form of Eva and Evelyn. *See* Eva *and* Evelyn. Or, a
variant form of Yvonne. *See* Yvonne. CONTEMPORARY EXAMPLE: Evonne
Goolagong, tennis player.

Evy   A variant spelling of Evie. *See* Evie.

Ewa   The Hawaiian form of Eva. *See* Eva.

Exie   A name invented from the word "exit" because Exie Copps was to
be the last child in the family. CONTEMPORARY EXAMPLE: Exie Copps,
Bowie, Texas.

Ezra   Primarily a masculine name. *See* Ezra (masculine section).

Ezraela, Ezraella, Ezrela   Feminine forms of Ezra. *See* Ezra (masculine section).

F

Fabia   From the Greek and Latin, meaning "bean farmer." The feminine form of Fabian. *See* Fabian (masculine section).

Fabrice   From the French *fabrique*, meaning "a trade, a product, a fabric." CONTEMPORARY EXAMPLES: Fabrice Wilfong, Matawan, New Jersey; Fabrice Florin, author.

Faga, Faiga   Variant forms of Faigel. *See* Faigel.

Faigel   From the Yiddish, meaning "a bird," a form of the German *vogel*. VARIANT FORMS: Faga, Faiga. Feigel is a variant spelling.

Faith   From the Middle English name Feith, and the earlier Latin *fidere*, meaning "to trust." Faith, along with Hope and Charity, came to be used as a personal feminine name after the Reformation. After the seventeenth century it was used for both sexes. CONTEMPORARY EXAMPLE: Faith Baldwin, author. PLACE-NAME USAGE: Faith, North Carolina; Faith, South Dakota, probably named for Faith Rockefeller, a stockholder in the local railroad.

Falba   From the French *falbala*, meaning "a useless article." CONTEMPORARY EXAMPLE: Falba Patrick, Corpus Christi, Texas.

Falda   From the Spanish, meaning "a skirt" or "a slope skirting an area." PLACE-NAME USAGE: Falda, California.

Falice, Falicia   Variant spellings of Felice. *See* Felice.

Fania   A Slavic equivalent of the German Fannie and Fanny, pet forms of Frances. *See* Frances.

Fanya   A variant spelling of Fania. *See* Fania.

Farina   From the Latin, meaning "flour, ground corn." PLACE-NAME USAGE: Farina, Illinois.

Farista   A pet Spanish form of Farina. *See* Farina. PLACE-NAME USAGE: Farista, Colorado, named for the daughter of A.S. Faris, the local postmaster.

Farrah   From the Arabic, meaning "a wild ass." CONTEMPORARY EXAMPLE: Farrah Fawcett Majors, actress.

Fauna   The wife or sister of Faunus, who in Roman mythology is a god of nature, a patron of farming and animals. *See* Faunus (masculine section).

Fauniel   A variant form of Fauna. *See* Fauna.

Fawn, Fawna, Fawne Either from the Middle English *faunen*, meaning "to be friendly," or from the Latin, meaning "a young deer." May also be a variant form of Fauna. *See* Fauna. CONTEMPORARY EXAMPLES: Fawn M. Brodie, author; Fawne Harriman, actress. PLACE-NAME USAGE: Fawnskin Meadows, California.

Fawnia A French form of Fawn. *See* Fawn.

Fay, Faye From the Old French, meaning "fidelity." and often a short form of Faith. Also, from the Latin *fata*, meaning "a fairy." *See* Faye (masculine section). CONTEMPORARY EXAMPLE: Fay Compton, actress. SURNAME USAGE: Alice Faye, entertainer.

Fayette A pet form of Fay. *See* Fay. SURNAME USAGE: The Marquis de La Fayette, a popular soldier who served under George Washington, and after whom many places were named.

Faylena A name invented by combining Fay and Lena. *See* Fay *and* Lena. CONTEMPORARY EXAMPLE: Faylena C. Flint, Miami, Florida.

Fayme From the Old English, meaning "fame."

Fedora From the Greek, meaning "divine gift." Theodora is a Russian form. Or, from the French *fedora*, a soft felt hat, with curved brim. Popularized in 1882 when Sardon's play *Fedora* was staged.

Fee From the Middle English, meaning "a fief, an estate." Also, a pet form of Fiona. *See* Fiona.

Feenie Origin uncertain. Possibly, a pet form of the masculine Phineas. *See* Phineas (masculine section). Or, a form of Fee. *See* Fee. CONTEMPORARY EXAMPLE: Feenie Ziner, author.

Feiga A variant spelling of Faigel. *See* Faigel.

Felecia A variant spelling of Felicia. *See* Felicia.

Felice, Felicia From the Latin *felicitas*, meaning "happiness." Felicitas was the Roman goddess of good luck. Felicia was common in twelfth–century England, where it was used as a feminine form of Felix. Akin to Felicity. Felicia has been erroneously confused with Phyllis. VARIANT SPELLINGS: Felecia, Felisse.

Feliciana The Spanish form of Felicity. *See* Felicity. Akin to Felicite. PLACE-NAME USAGE: Feliciana, Louisiana.

Felicite A French and Spanish form of Felicity. *See* Felicity.

Felicity A variant spelling of Felice. *See* Felice. PLACE-NAME USAGE: a lake in Louisiana, named for Felicite, wife of Governor Bernardo de Galvez.

Feline From the Latin, meaning "a cat."

Felisse A variant spelling of Felice. *See* Felice.

Felta From the Dutch, meaning "a field, a forest." Also, probably a feminine form of Felton or a variant form of Velda. CONTEMPORARY EXAMPLE: Felta Lanpher, Newport, Maine.

Fenella   From the Gaelic, meaning "white shoulder." In Ireland, it emerged as Penelope. The more common Irish form is Finola. Fiona is a variant form. SURNAME USAGE: Francois Fenelon (1651-1715), French clergyman.

Fern   The feminine form of Ferdinand. *See* Ferdinand (masculine section). Also, from the Old English *fearn*, "a non-flowering variety of leafy plants."

Fernandina   A feminine form of Ferdinand. *See* Ferdinand (masculine section). PLACE-NAME USAGE: Fernandina, Florida.

Fidella   From the Latin *fidelis*, meaning "faithful." Fidel is the masculine form.

Filomena   From the Middle English name Philomene, a form of the Latin Philomela, meaning "lover of songs." In Greek mythology, Philomela was changed by the gods into a nightingale. CONTEMPORARY EXAMPLE: Filomena Simora, editor.

Finola   A variant form of Fenella. *See* Fenella.

Fiona, Fione   From the Celtic, meaning "white." Akin to Fenella. A character in Colleen McCullough's *The Thorn Birds*. Fee is a pet form. CONTEMPORARY EXAMPLE: Fiona Hill, author.

Fionnula   A variant Irish form of Fiona. *See* Fiona. CONTEMPORARY EXAMPLE: Fionnula Flanagan, actress.

Fiorella   Used most often as a masculine name. A variant form of Florence. *See* Florence. CONTEMPORARY EXAMPLE: Fiorella Ljunggren, author.

Flannery   From the Old French *flaon*, meaning "a flat piece of metal." Used also as a masculine form. *See* Flannery (masculine section). CONTEMPORARY EXAMPLE: Flannery O'Connor, author.

Flavia, Flavus   From the Latin, meaning "yellow–haired, blond." Flavius is the masculine form.

Fleta   From the Old English *fleot*, meaning "an inlet, a creek."

Fleur   A French form of the Latin *flos*, meaning "flower." *See* Flora. Popularized by John Galsworthy in his novel *Forsyte Saga*. CONTEMPORARY EXAMPLES: Fleur Cowles, editor; Fleur H. Sullivan, Augusta, Georgia. SURNAME USAGE: Andre H. Fleury (1653-1743), French statesman.

Flora   From the Latin *flos* and *floris*, meaning "a flower." In Roman mythology, the goddess of flowers. Popularized by Swedish botanist Carolus Linnaeus in the eighteenth century. Akin to Florence. *See* Florence. VARIANT FORMS: Florence, Flonda, Floris, Fleur (French); Flower (English). PET FORMS: Flo, Flossie, Floren, Florrie, Floryn. PLACE-NAME

USAGE: Flora, Illinois; Flora, Oregon, named for Flora Buzzard, daughter of the first postmaster.

Floreen A variant form of Florence. *See* Florence.

Florella A diminutive form of Flora. *See* Flora. Used also as an independent name, formed by combining Flora and Ella.

Floren A short form of Florence. *See* Florence.

Florence From the Latin name Florentia, meaning "blooming." VARIANT FORMS: Florenz (German); Fiorenza (Italian); Florencia (Spanish); Florentia (Latin). In the Middle Ages, used equally for men and women. Became predominantly a female name after its use by Charles Dickens as Florence Dombey in his novel *Dombey and Son* (c. 1846), and by Florence Nightingale (1820-1912), who was so named because she was born in Florence, Italy. Akin to Flora. *See* Flora. PET FORMS: Flo, Floris, Florrie, Flory, Floryn, Flossie. PLACE-NAME USAGE: a city in Italy (Firenze); Florence, Oregon, probably named for State Senator A.B. Florence.

Florenz A German form of Florence. *See* Florence.

Floria A variant form of Flora. *See* Flora. Used in the thirteenth and fourteenth centuries.

Florida A Spanish form of the Latin name Flora. *See* Flora. The State of Florida was so named by Ponce de Leon because he landed there in 1513 on Easter Day, the feast of flowers. CONTEMPORARY EXAMPLE: Florida Friebus, actress.

Floris A variant form of Flora. *See* Flora.

Florrie A pet form of Flora. *See* Flora.

Floryn A pet form of Flora. *See* Flora.

Flower A rare form of Flora and Florence first used in the seventeenth century. Fleur is a French form. *See* Flora *and* Florence. PLACE-NAME USAGE: Flower Dieu Hundred, Virginia.

Fonda From the French *fondre*, meaning "to melt." Used loosely by the French in America to mean "bottom, lower end." Originally applied to a soft, creamy candy-filling made of sugar. CONTEMPORARY EXAMPLE: Traba Fonda Parks, a resident of Colorado. SURNAME USAGE: Jane Fonda, actress. PLACE-NAME USAGE: Fond du Lac, Minnesota and Wisconsin.

Fondea A variant form of Fonda. *See* Fonda. Used by Gypsies. CONTEMPORARY EXAMPLE: Fondea Loftus, Kansas City, Missouri.

Foneda A variant form of Fonda. *See* Fonda. CONTEMPORARY EXAMPLE: Foneda Loftus (daughter of Fondea), Kansas City, Missouri.

Forsythia A flower named for English botanist William Forsythe

(1737-1804), who introduced the yellow bell-shaped flower to England.

Fortuna   In Roman mythology, the goddess of fortune. CONTEMPORARY EXAMPLE: Fortuna Sarton, Dover Plains, New York. Akin to Fortunata. *See* Fortunata. PLACE-NAME USAGE: Fortuna, California.

Fortunata   From the Latin *fortuna,* meaning "chance, good luck." Fortuna is a variant form. CONTEMPORARY EXAMPLE: Fortunata Dota, Holiday, Florida.

Fran   A pet form of Frances. *See* Frances. Used also as a masculine name.

France   A variant form of Frances. *See* Frances. CONTEMPORARY EXAMPLE: France Nuyen, actress. SURNAME USAGE: Anatole France (1844-1924), pseudonym of Jacques Anatole Francois Thibault, French novelist. PLACE-NAME USAGE: a country in western Europe.

Frances   The Old French feminine form of Franceis. From the French *franc,* meaning "free." *See* Francis (masculine section). VARIANT FORMS: Francesca (Italian); Fracoise, Fanchette, Fanchon (French); Francina (Dutch); Franika, Franja (Slavonic); Franziske, Franconia (German); Francisca (Spanish and Portuguese). PET FORMS: Fania, Fannie, Fanny, Fannye, Fanya, Fran, Francie, Francine, Frania, Frankie, Franny. PLACE-NAME USAGE: Francestown, New Hampshire, named for Lady Frances Wentworth, wife of the governor (1772).

Francesca   An Italian form of Frances. *See* Frances.

Francine   A pet form of Frances. *See* Frances.

Francoise   A variant French form of Frances. *See* Frances. Francois is the masculine form. CONTEMPORARY EXAMPLE: Francoise Sagan, author.

Franconia   A variant form of Frances. *See* Frances. The name of one of the medieval German duchies. PLACE-NAME USAGE: Franconia, New Hampshire, named for Sir Francis Bernard; Franconia, Arizona, named for Frank Smith, name of a railroad official.

Frania   A variant form of Frances. *See* Frances. CONTEMPORARY EXAMPLE: Frania Tye Lee, wife of industrialist H.L. Hunt.

Frankie   A pet form of Frances. *See* Frances. More commonly used as a form of the masculine Francis.

Frayda, Frayde   From the Yiddish, meaning "joy." VARIANT SPELLINGS: Freida, Freide. Fraydyne is a variant form.

Freda   A variant form of Frieda. *See* Frieda.

Fredannette   A name invented by combining Fred and Annette. *See* Fred *and* Annett. CONTEMPORARY EXAMPLE: Fredannette Hackler, Carrollton, Texas.

Fredda, Freddie   Pet forms of Frederica. *See* Frederica. Also, pet forms of Frieda. *See* Frieda.

Frederica   The feminine form of Frederic, meaning "peaceful ruler." *See* Frederic (masculine section). Coined in Germany, it was first used in England in the nineteenth century. VARIANT FORMS: Federica, Feriga (Italian); Fritze, Rike (German); Frydryka (Polish); Frederica (English and Portuguese). Freddie is a pet form.

Frederika   A variant spelling of Frederica. *See* Frederica. PLACE-NAME USAGE: Frederika, Iowa.

Freida, Freide   Variant forms of Frieda. *See* Frieda. Also, variant spellings of Frayda. *See* Frayda.

Frenelle   A name invented by combining *Fre*derick and Don*nelle*. CONTEMPORARY EXAMPLE: Frenelle Mappus, Richardson, Texas.

Freya   In Norse mythology, the goddess of love and beauty. Freyja is a variant spelling. CONTEMPORARY EXAMPLE: Freya Manston, literary agent.

Frieda   From the Old High German, meaning "peace." VARIANT FORMS: Freda, Freida, Freide, Friede, Fredyne. PET FORMS: Fredda, Freddie, Fritzi.

Friede   A variant spelling of Frieda. *See* Frieda.

Fritzi   A pet form of Frieda. *See* Frieda. Also, a pet form of Frederica. *See* Frederica.

Fronde   From the Latin *frons*, meaning "a leafy branch."

Fronia   A variant spelling of Frania, a form of Frances. *See* Frances.

Fruma   From the Yiddish, meaning "pious one." CONTEMPORARY EXAMPLE: Fruma Rosenberg, marriage counselor.

G

Gabi   A pet form of Gabriela. *See* Gabriela.

Gabriela, Gabriella   From the Hebrew, meaning "God is my strength." Feminine forms of Gabriel. *See* Gabriel (masculine section). VARIANT FORMS: Gabriele (German); Gavrila (Hebrew and Slavonic); Gavra (Slavonic). PET FORMS: Gabi, Gavi. CONTEMPORARY EXAMPLE: Gabriela Mistral, Nobel Prize winner in literature (1945).

Gabrielle   The French form of the Hebrew, meaning "God is my strength." A feminine form of Gabriel. VARIANT FORMS: Gabriela, Gabriella.

Gada   The feminine form of Gad. *See* Gad (masculine section). In Israel, used also as a plant name.

Gae   A variant spelling of Gay. *See* Gay.

Gafna   From the Hebrew, meaning "a vine."

Gail   A pet form of Abigail. *See* Abigail. Gale is a variant spelling.

Gailard   From the Old French *gaillard*, meaning "strong, brave."

Gainell   From the Middle English *gainen*, meaning "to profit." CONTEMPORARY EXAMPLE: Gainell Sorrow, publisher's representative. SURNAME USAGE: locality in early England. Athelred, father-in-law of Alfred, was the Earl of Gaini.

Gal   From the Hebrew, meaning either "a mound, a hill" or "a fountain, a spring." Also, from the Irish, meaning "courageous."

Gale   A variant spelling of Gail. *See* Gail.

Gali   From the Hebrew, meaning "my spring, my fountain" or "my hill." Akin to Gal. CONTEMPORARY EXAMPLE: Gali Atari, Israeli singer.

Galia   From the Hebrew *gaal*, meaning "God has redeemed."

Galit   A variant form of Gali. *See* Gali.

Galya   A variant spelling of Galia.

Gana, Ganit   From the Hebrew, meaning "a garden."

Ganit   From the Hebrew, meaning "defender." Also, a variant form of Gana. *See* Gana.

Ganya   From the Hebrew, meaning "the garden of the Lord."

Gardenia   Subtropical Old World plants with glossy leaves and white or yellow fragrant flowers. Named for Alexander Garden (1730-1791), American botanist.

Garland From the Old French *garlande*, meaning "a wreath of flowers." SURNAME USAGE: A.H. Garland, U.S. attorney general; Judy Garland, actress.

Garldina A variant pet form of Garland. *See* Garland.

Garnet From the Middle English *gernet* and the Latin *granatum*, meaning "a pomegrante," hence "a red variety of rocks used as gems."

Garniata From the French *garnir*, meaning "to garnish, to adorn." CONTEMPORARY EXAMPLE: Garniata Hiss, Tarzana, California.

Garnit From the Hebrew, meaning "a granary."

Gavi A pet form of Gabi. *See* Gabi.

Gavrila, Gavrilla From the Hebrew, meaning "a heroine, strong." Akin to Gabriela. Feminine forms of Gabriel.

Gay From the Middle English *gai*, meaning "gay, merry." SURNAME USAGE: John Gay (1685-1732), English playwright.

Gayle A variant spelling of Gail. *See* Gail.

Gaynell A variant spelling of Gainell. *See* Gainell. CONTEMPORARY EXAMPLE: Gaynell Bordes Cronin, author.

Gayora From the Hebrew, meaning "valley of light."

Gazella From the Latin, meaning "a gazelle, a deer."

Gazit From the Hebrew, meaning "hewn stone."

Gedda From the Old English *gaed* and *gad*, meaning "a goad, a javelin."

Gedula, Gedulah From the Hebrew, meaning "big, great, greatness."

Geela, Geelan From the Hebrew, meaning "joy." VARIANT SPELLINGS: Gila, Gilah.

Geene A variant spelling of Jean. CONTEMPORARY EXAMPLE: Geene Schultz, Pompano Beach, Florida.

Gelsey Probably related to the Italian *gelsomino*, meaning "gelsemium," akin to the jasmine flowering shrub family. CONTEMPORARY EXAMPLE: Gelsey Kirkland, dancer.

Gemma From the Latin *gemma*, meaning "a swelling, a bud, a precious stone." CONTEMPORARY EXAMPLE: Gemma Jones, actress.

Gena A variant spelling of Gina. *See* Gina.

Gene A pet form of Genevieve and Jean. *See* Genevieve *and* Jean. More commonly used as a masculine pet form of Eugene.

Geneva, Genevia   From the Old French *genevre* and the Latin *juniperus*, meaning "juniper berry." CONTEMPORARY EXAMPLE: Geneva Long, Frankfort, Kentucky. PLACE-NAME USAGE: Geneva, Switzerland.

Genevieve   From the Celtic, meaning "white wave." Or, a variant form of Geneva. *See* Geneva.

Genie   A pet form of Genevieve. *See* Genevieve. Also a variant pet form of Jeanette. *See* Jeanette. CONTEMPORARY EXAMPLE: Genie Iverson, journalist.

Genna   A variant spelling of Jenna, a form of Jeanette. *See* Jeanette. Or, a variant form of Geneva. *See* Geneva.

Georgea   A variant spelling of Georgia. *See* Georgia.

Georgeanne   A name invented by combining George and Anne. *See* George (masculine section) *and* Anne.

Georgeen   A variant spelling of Georgeene. *See* Georgeene.

Georgeene   A name invented by combining George and Geene. *See* George (masculine section) *and* Geene.

Georgess   A variant form of Georgia. *See* Georgia. CONTEMPORARY EXAMPLE: Georgess McHargue, editor.

Georgette   A pet form of Georgia. *See* Georgia.

Georgia   From the Greek, meaning "husbandman, farmer." The feminine form of George. VARIANT FORMS: Georgiana, Georgina (English); Georgette, Georgine (French). PET FORMS: Georgett, Georgiana, Georgina. PLACE-NAME USAGE: a southern U.S. state, named for King George II of England.

Georgiana, Georgianna   Pet forms of Georgia. *See* Georgia.

Georgina, Georgine   Pet forms of Georgia. *See* Georgia.

Georie   A name invented by combining *Geo*rgea and M*arie*. *See* Georgea *and* Marie.

Georja   A variant spelling of Georgia. *See* Georgia.

Geraldene, Geraldine   From the Old High German *ger*, meaning "spear," plus *hart*, meaning "hard." Feminine forms of Gerard. PET FORMS: Geri, Gerrie, Gerry.

Geralynne   A name invented by combining Geraldine and Lynne. *See* Geraldine *and* Lynne. CONTEMPORARY EXAMPLE: Geralynne Hobbs, secretary.

Gerardene, Gerardine   From the Old High German *ger*, meaning "spear," plus *hart*, meaning "hard." Feminine forms of Gerard. PET FORMS: Geri, Gerrie, Gerry.

Gerda   From the Old High German, meaning "the protected one."

Akin to Gertrude. *See* Gertrude.

Geri A pet form of Geraldine and Gerardine. *See* Geraldine *and* Gerardine.

Geremi A feminine form of Jeremy. *See* Jeremy (masculine section).

Gererdine A variant spelling of Gerardine. *See* Gerardine.

Germaine From the Middle English *germain* and the Latin *germanus*, meaning "a sprout, a bud." CONTEMPORARY EXAMPLE: Germaine Greer, author.

Gerrie, Gerry Pet forms of Geraldine and Gerardine. *See* Geraldine *and* Gerardine.

Gertrude From the Old High German *ger*, meaning "spear," plus *trut*, meaning "dear," hence "adored warrior." VARIANT FORMS: Trudel (Dutch); Gerte, Truta, Trude (German); Jera, Jerica (Slavonic). PET FORMS: Gert, Gertie, Trudi, Trudy.

Geula, Geulah From the Hebrew, meaning "redemption." CONTEMPORARY EXAMPLE: Geula Gill, singer.

Gevira From the Hebrew, meaning "lady, queen."

Gevura, Gevurah From the Hebrew, meaning "strength."

Ghila From the Hebrew, meaning "joy." A variant spelling of Gila. CONTEMPORARY EXAMPLE: Beth Ghila Sherman, Mill Valley, California.

Gia A pet form of Regina. *See* Regina. CONTEMPORARY EXAMPLE: Gia Houck, Houston, Texas.

Gibora, Giborah From the Hebrew, meaning "strong, heroine."

Gila, Gilah From the Hebrew, meaning "joy."

Gilada From the Hebrew, meaning "my hill is my witness." The feminine form of Gilead. *See* Gilead (masculine section).

Gilana From the Hebrew, meaning "joy, exultation."

Gilat From the Hebrew, meaning "age" or "a stage of life."

Gilberta The feminine form of Gilbert. *See* Gilbert (masculine section).

Gilda From the Celtic, meaning "servant of God." Or, from the Old English *gyldar*, meaning "gold, coated with gold." CONTEMPORARY EXAMPLE: Gilda Radner, comedienne.

Gili From the Hebrew, meaning "my joy."

Gilia, Giliah From the Hebrew, meaning "my joy is in the Lord."

Gilit A variant form of Gilat. *See* Gilat.

Gill   A short form of Gillian. *See* Gillian. Or, from the Middle English *gille* and the Old Norse *gil*, meaning "a wooded ravine, a glen" or "a brook."

Gillian   A variant form of the Latin name Juliana, the feminine form of Julianus (Julian). *See* Julian (masculine section). CONTEMPORARY EXAMPLE: Gillian Jolis, editor.

Gimone   Origin unknown. CONTEMPORARY EXAMPLE: Gimone Hall, novelist.

Gimra   From the Hebrew, meaning "to ripen, to complete."

Gina   A pet form of Regina. *See* Regina. Also, from the Hebrew, meaning "garden."

Ginat   From the Hebrew, meaning "garden." Akin to Gina. Used also as a masculine name.

Ginette   A pet form of Virginia. *See* Virginia. Also, a variant form of Jeanette. *See* Jeanette. CONTEMPORARY EXAMPLE: Ginette Reno, singer.

Ginger   A pet form of Virginia. *See* Virginia.

Ginnie, Ginny   Pet forms of Virginia. *See* Virginia. CONTEMPORARY EXAMPLE: Ginnie Newhart, wife of comedian Bob Newhart.

Gipsy   A variant spelling of Gypsy. *See* Gypsy.

Gisa   A variant spelling of Giza. *See* Giza.

Gisela, Giselle   From the Anglo-Saxon, meaning "a bright pledge" or "a sword."

Gita, Gitel, Gittel   From the Yiddish, meaning "good." CONTEMPORARY EXAMPLE: Gita May, author.

Gitit   From the Hebrew, meaning "cut off." In the Bible, the name of a musical instrument.

Giza   From the Hebrew, meaning "hewn stone." Gisa is a variant spelling. PLACE-NAME USAGE: a city in Egypt, site of the Sphinx and three pyramids.

Gizela   A variant spelling of Gisela. *See* Gisela.

Giva   From the Hebrew, meaning "a hill, a high place."

Givona   A variant form of Giva. *See* Giva.

Gladys   From the Welsh name Gwladys. A variant form of the Latin Claudia and the French Claude, meaning "lame."

Glamma   From the Latin *glann*, meaning "a bank of a river."

Gleanus   From the Old English *gleann*, meaning "a narrow valley, a glen." CONTEMPORARY EXAMPLE: Gleanus Serepta Gilliain, Henderson, North Carolina.

Glenna The feminine form of Glenn. *See* Glenn (masculine section).

Glora A variant form of Gloria. *See* Gloria.

Gloria From the Latin, meaning "glory."

Gloriana, Glorianne Invented names combining Gloria and Anne. *See* Gloria *and* Anne.

Glory A variant form of Gloria. *See* Gloria.

Glynis From the British *glynn*, meaning "a glen, a narrow valley." CONTEMPORARY EXAMPLE: Glynis Johns, actress.

Gnosha From the Greek *gnosis*, meaning "knowledge." CONTEMPORARY EXAMPLE: Gnosha Buk, Napa, California.

Golda From the Old English and German, meaning "gold." Akin to Gilda. CONTEMPORARY EXAMPLE: Golda Meir, prime minister of Israel.

Goldarina A variant form of Golda. *See* Golda.

Goldie, Goldy Pet forms of Golda. *See* Golda.

Gomer From the Hebrew, meaning "to finish, complete." In the Bible, the wife of Hosea, the prophet. Used also as a masculine name.

Gozala From the Hebrew, meaning "a young bird."

Grace From the Latin, meaning "grace." Gracie is a pet form. Grazia and Grazina are Italian forms. CONTEMPORARY EXAMPLE: Grace Kelly, actress (and later Princess Grace of Monaco).

Gracie A pet form of Grace. *See* Grace. CONTEMPORARY EXAMPLE: Gracie Allen (Burns), comedienne.

Grania From the Latin *granum*, meaning "grain" or "granary." CONTEMPORARY EXAMPLE: Grania Beckford, author.

Graylen A name invented by combining the names of both parents: *Gray*don and He*len*. CONTEMPORARY EXAMPLE: Graylen Milligan, Webster, New York.

Grazia, Grazina Italian forms of the Latin, meaning "grace." CONTEMPORARY EXAMPLE: Grazina Babrisis, librarian.

Greer From the Greek and Latin, meaning "guard, guardian, watchful." CONTEMPORARY EXAMPLE: Greer Garson, actress.

Greta A pet form of Margaret. *See* Margaret. Popular in Sweden.

Gretchen The German form of Margaret. *See* Margaret.

Gretel A variant form of Gretchen. *See* Gretchen. Also, from the Old English name Gret, meaning "great." CONTEMPORARY EXAMPLE: Gretel H. Pelto, editor.

Griselda From the French *gris*, meaning "gray." In German medieval tales, a heroine famous for her patience. CONTEMPORARY EXAMPLE: Griselda Barton, author.

Gudrid   A variant form of Gudrun. *See* Gudrun.

Gudrun   From the Old Norse *guthr*, meaning "war," plus *runa*, meaning "close friend." In Norse legend, the daughter of the Nibelung king. VARIANT FORMS: Gudrid, Guthrun.

Guenevere, Guinevere   From the Celtic *gwen*, meaning "white wave" or "white phantom." In Arthurian legend, the wife of King Arthur.

Gula   A variant spelling of Geula. *See* Geula.

Gulnare   From Norwegian, meaning "war hero." VARIANT FORMS: Gudmund, Gulmuna (Norwegian); Gutman (German); Gondomar (Spanish). CONTEMPORARY EXAMPLE: Gulnare Kergel, Woodland, California.

Gunhilda   From the Middle English *gunne*, meaning "war."

Gunna   A pet form of Gunhilda. *See* Gunhilda.

Gunnel   A variant form of Gunhilda. *See* Gunhilda. CONTEMPORARY EXAMPLE: Gunnel Lindblom, Swedish actress.

Gurit   From the Hebrew, meaning "the young of an animal," most often referring to the lion.

Gussie, Gussy   Pet forms of Augusta. *See* Augusta.

Guthrun   A variant form of Gudrun. *See* Gudrun.

Guylynn   A hybrid of Guy and Lynn. CONTEMPORARY EXAMPLE: Guylynn Remmenga, Miss Nebraska of 1979.

Gwen   From the Celtic *gwen*, meaning "white."

Gwendaline   A pet form of Gwen. *See* Gwen.

Gwendolen   A pet form of Gwen. *See* Gwen.

Gwendoline   A pet form of Gwen. *See* Gwen. CONTEMPORARY EXAMPLE: Gwendoline Butler, author.

Gwendolyn   A pet form of Gwen. *See* Gwen. CONTEMPORARY EXAMPLE: Gwendolyn Brooks, poet.

Gwenn, Gwenne   Variant forms of Gwen. *See* Gwen.

Gwenth, Gwenith   Variant forms of Gwen. *See* Gwen.

Gwyn   A variant form of Gwen. *See* Gwen.

Gwynne   A variant spelling of Gwyn. *See* Gwyn.

Gypsy   The name signifies "a bohemian" or "rover." Gipsy is a variant spelling. CONTEMPORARY EXAMPLE: Gypsy Rose Lee, entertainer.

H

Hadara   From the Hebrew, meaning "beautiful, ornamented, honored."

Hadassa   A variant spelling of Hadassah. *See* Hadassah.

Hadassah   From the Hebrew, meaning "a myrtle tree," the symbol of victory. In the Bible, the Hebrew name of Esther, cousin of Mordecai. Hadassa is a modern variant spelling. PET FORMS: Dasa, Dasi.

Hadura   A variant form of Hadara. *See* Hadara.

Hagar   From the Hebrew, meaning "forsaken, stranger." In the Bible, the concubine of Abraham, the mother of Ishmael.

Hagia   From the Hebrew, meaning "festive, joyous." Originally, a biblical masculine name. Currently used as a masculine form in Israel.

Hagit   From the Hebrew, meaning "festive, joyous." Hagia is a variant form. In the Bible, the wife of David.

Haile   A variant spelling of Haley. *See* Haley.

Haley   From the Norse *haela*, meaning "a hero." VARIANT FORMS: Haile, Halie, Hallie, Hally.

Haliaka   The Hawaiian form of Harriet. *See* Harriet.

Halie, Hallie, Hally   Variant forms of Haley. *See* Haley.

Halina   From the Hawaiian, meaning "resemblance." CONTEMPORARY EXAMPLE: Halina Meldy, Santa Monica, California.

Hamuda   From the Hebrew, meaning "desirable, precious."

Hana   A variant spelling of Hannah. *See* Hannah.

Hania, Haniya   From the Hebrew, meaning "a rest place, an encampment." Hanniah is a variant spelling.

Hanit   From the Hebrew, meaning "a spear."

Hanita   A pet form of Hannah and Hanit. *See* Hannah *and* Hanit.

Hannah   From the Hebrew, meaning "gracious, merciful." In the Bible, the mother of Samuel. The New Testament records Hannah as Anna. Hana is a variant spelling.

Hannia   A variant spellng of Hania. *See* Hania.

Hanniah   A variant spelling of Hania. *See* Hania.

Happy   A nickname for a person with a happy disposition. CONTEM-PORARY EXAMPLE: Happy Rockefeller, wife of U.S. Vice-President Nelson Rockefeller

Hardie   From the Middle English and Old French, meaning "bold, robust."

Harmony   From the Greek *harmonia*, meaning "a fitting, a blending into the whole."

Harriet, Harriette   Feminine forms of Harry, a variant form of Henry, an Old High German form of Heimerich, meaning "home ruler." VARIANT FORMS: Etta, Hetta, Harriot, Harriott, Henrietta. PET FORMS: Harri, Hattie, Hatty, Hetty.

Harva   An invented name derived from Harvey. *See* Harvey. CON-TEMPORARY EXAMPLE: Harva George Thomas, Kodak, Mississippi, named for her two grandfathers: Harvey and George.

Harviena   A name invented by combining *Harv* (Harvey) and *Viena*. CONTEMPORARY EXAMPLE: Harviena Redd, Arcadia, Indiana.

Hasia   From the Hebrew, meaning "protected by the Lord." Hasya is a variant spelling.

Hasida   From the Hebrew, meaning "a stork" or "pious one."

Hasina   From the Hebrew, meaning "strong."

Hasse   Possibly from the Old English *haesl*, meaning "a hazel tree." CONTEMPORARY EXAMPLE: Hasse Bunnelle, author.

Hasya   A variant spelling of Hasia. *See* Hasia. CONTEMPORARY EXAMPLE: Hasya Milo, Israeli teacher.

Hattie, Hatty   Pet forms of Harriet. *See* Harriet.

Hava   From the Hebrew, meaning "life, alive." In the Bible, the Hebrew name of Eve, the first woman, so called because she was "the mother of all human life."

Haviva   From the Hebrew, meaning "beloved."

Haya   From the Hebrew, meaning "life." A variant spelling of Chaya. Akin to Hava.

Hayley   A variant spelling of Haley. *See* Haley. CONTEMPORARY EXAMPLE: Hayley Mills, actress.

Hazel   From the Old English *haesl*, meaning "a hazel tree." Some authorities relate Hazel to Aveline, which is French for hazel nut. Among the ancients of northwestern Europe, the wand formed from the hazel tree was a symbol of protection and authority.

Hazelbelle   A combination of Hazel and Belle. *See* Hazel *and* Belle.

Hazelle   A pet form of Hazel. *See* Hazel. CONTEMPORARY EXAMPLE:

Hazelle Kimberlin, Santa Ana, California.

Healani   From the Hawaiian, meaning "message from heaven."

Heather   From the Middle English *haddyr*, meaning "a heath, a shrub, a plant." CONTEMPORARY EXAMPLE: Heather Bernard, television news reporter.

Hedda   From the German, meaning "strife, warfare." CONTEMPORARY EXAMPLE: Hedda Hopper, costume designer.

Hedia   From the Hebrew, meaning "the voice, the echo of the Lord."

Hedley   From the Old English *heder*, meaning "a hiding place," plus *ley*, meaning "meadow land." CONTEMPORARY EXAMPLE: Hedley Hemingway, wife of Ernest Hemingway.

Hedva   From the Hebrew, meaning "joy."

Hedwig   From the Old English *heder*, meaning "a hiding place," plus *wig*, meaning "to fight," hence "a munitions depot." VARIANT FORMS: Avice, Avicia, Avis, Havoise (English); Hedvige (French); Edde, Eddo, Edo (Slavonic); Hedda (German). CONTEMPORARY EXAMPLE: Hedwig Rappolt, translator.

Hedy, Heddy   Pet forms of Hedda or Hester. *See* Hedda *and* Hester.

Hedya   A variant spelling of Hedia. *See* Hedia.

Heidi   Probably a variant form of Hester and its pet form Hettie, both derivatives of Esther. *See* Esther.

Heiki   The Hawaiian form of Heidi. *See* Heidi.

Hel   In Norse mythology, Loki's daughter, goddess of death. *See also* Helgi in masculine section.

Helaine   A variant form of Helen, meaning "light" in the Greek.

Helayne   A variant form of Helen. *See* Helen.

Helen   From the Greek, meaning "a torch," hence "light." VARIANT FORMS: Helena (Latin); Elaine, Eleanor, Elinor, Leonora, Lina, Lino (English); Helene (French); Eileen, Nelly (Irish); Elena, Elene (Italian); Helena (Greek, Spanish, Polish); Jelena, Jelika (Slavonic).

Helena   A variant form of Helen. *See* Helen.

Helene   The French form of Helen. *See* Helen.

Helenmae   A name invented by combining Helen and Mae. *See* Helen *and* Mae.

Helga   From the Anglo-Saxon, meaning "holy." CONTEMPORARY EXAMPLE: Helga Halaki, editor.

Helina   The Hawaiian form of Helen. *See* Helen.

Hella   A variant form of Helen. *See* Helen. CONTEMPORARY EXAMPLE:

Hella Freud Bernays, editor.

Hemda   From the Hebrew, meaning "desirable, precious." Akin to Hamuda.

Henrietta   The feminine form of Henry. From the Old High German, meaning "home ruler." *See* Henry. VARIANT FORMS: Harriet, Harriot, Hatty, Hetty (English); Henriette (French and German); Enriqueta (Spanish); Enrichetta (Italian); Henriqueta (Portuguese); Enrica, Henrinka (Slavonic); Hendrike (Dutch).

Henriette   The French form of Henrietta. *See* Henrietta.

Hephziba, Hephzibah   From the Hebrew, meaning "my desire is in her." In the Bible, the wife of King Hezekiah. CONTEMPORARY EXAMPLE: Hephzibah Menuhin, violinist.

Hepzi   From the Hebrew, meaning "my desire."

Hepziba, Hepzibah   Variant spellings of Hephziba and Hephzibah. *See* Hephziba *and* Hephzibah.

Herma   From the Latin *herma*, meaning "a square pillar of stone" used as a milestone or signpost. Or, a feminine form of Herman. *See* Herman (masculine section).

Hermine   A variant form of Hermione. *See* Hermione. CONTEMPORARY EXAMPLE: Hermine Weinberg, Los Angeles, California.

Hermione   In Greek legend, the daughter of Menelaus and Helen of Troy. Akin to Hermes, who in Greek mythology was the messenger and servant of the other gods. CONTEMPORARY EXAMPLE: Hermione Gingold, actress.

Herodias   The feminine form of Herod. *See* Herod (masculine section). In the Bible, the second wife of Herod Antipas and mother of Salome.

Herzlia, Herzliah   The feminine form of Herzl. *See* Herzl (masculine section). PLACE-NAME USAGE: a city in Israel.

Hesba   Probably a short form of Hephziba. *See* Hephziba. CONTEMPORARY EXAMPLES: Hesba Brinsmead, author; Hesba Ghormley, Cochran, Georgia.

Hester, Hesther   The Latin form of Esther. *See* Esther. PET FORMS: Hedy, Heddy, Heidi, Hettie, Hetty.

Hestia   In Greek mythology, the goddess of the hearth. Akin to the Roman name Vesta.

Hetta   A variant form of Harriet. *See* Harriet.

Hetty   A form of Harriet. *See* Harriet.

Hila   From the Hebrew *hallel*, meaning "praise." Feminine forms of

Hillel. See Hillel (masculine section). PET FORMS: Hili, Hilly. Also, a pet form of Hilary. *See* Hilary. CONTEMPORARY EXAMPLES: Hila Colman, author; Hila Blair, California, Pennsylvania.

Hilaire   The French form of Hilary. *See* Hilary.

Hilary, Hillary   From the Latin *hilarius*, meaning "cheerful." Hilaire is a French form. CONTEMPORARY EXAMPLE: Hilary Rubinstein, literary agent.

Hilda, Hilde   Variant forms of Hildegarde. *See* Hildegarde.

Hildegard, Hildegarde   From the German, meaning "battle protector, warrior." VARIANT FORMS: Hilda, Hilde, Hildy.

Hildy   A variant form of Hildegarde. *See* Hildegarde. CONTEMPORARY EXAMPLE: Hildy Parks, writer.

Hilla, Hillah   Variant spellings of Hila. *See* Hila.

Hillela   The feminine form of Hillel. *See* Hillel (masculine section).

Hilma   Probably a variant form of Wilhelmina. *See* Wilhelmina. CONTEMPORARY EXAMPLE: Hilma Wolitzer, author.

Hina   In Tahitian legend, the goddess of the moon.

Hinda   From the German *hinde*, meaning "a deer." A popular Yiddish name.

Holiday   From the Middle English *holidei*, meaning "festive day."

Hollace   A variant form of Haley. *See* Haley.

Holli   A variant spelling of Holly. *See* Holly. CONTEMPORARY EXAMPLE: Holli Morton, social worker.

Hollis   A variant form of Haley. *See* Haley. CONTEMPORARY EXAMPLE: Hollis Hodges, author.

Holly, Hollye   From the Old English *holegn*, a variety of shrub with red berries, hung on the doors of ancient English homes to bring luck. CONTEMPORARY EXAMPLE: Holly Holmes, actress.

Holt   From the German *holz*, meaning "wood." CONTEMPORARY EXAMPLE: Holt T. Aaron, Laurel Bay, South Carolina.

Honeah   A variant form of Honey. *See* Honey. CONTEMPORARY EXAMPLE: Honeah Berry, Nacaville, California.

Honey   From the German *honig*, meaning "honey." CONTEMPORARY EXAMPLE: Honey Lamb, Dallas, Texas.

Honor, Honora   From the Latin, meaning "honorable." VARIANT FORMS: Honoria, Nora, Norah, Noreen, Norine, Norrie. A popular Puritan name and a favorite in Ireland where it gave rise to Nora. CONTEMPORARY EXAMPLE: Honor Blackman, actress.

Honorine   A variant form of Honora. *See* Honora.

Hope   From the Old English *hopa*, meaning "trust, faith." First used as a Christian name by the Puritans, who delighted in adopting abstract virtues for names, among them: Hope, Faith, Charity, Prudence, and Honor. Used also as a masculine name. Nadezhda is a Russian variant form from which the French created the name Nadine. CONTEMPORARY EXAMPLE: Hope Lange, actress. SURNAME USAGE: Bob Hope, actor.

Hortense   From the Latin *hortus*, meaning "gardener."

Huela   A feminine form of Hugh. *See* Hugh (masculine section). CONTEMPORARY EXAMPLE: Huela Winifred Webber, Phoenix, Arizona.

Hula   From the Hebrew, meaning "to play (an instrument)." Also a Hawaiian dance.

Hulda   From the Hebrew, meaning "a weasel."

Hyacinth   From the Greek *hyakinthos*, meaning "a blue gem, a sapphire." CONTEMPORARY EXAMPLE: Hyacinth Thrash, Guyana, South America.

I

Ianna   The feminine form of Ian. *See* Ian (masculine section).

Ianthe   From the Greek, possibly meaning "flower." In Greek mythology, a sea-nymph, daughter of Oceanus and Tethys.

Icyl   Origin uncertain. Possibly from the Old English Ic, Icken, and Hicks, surnames derived from Hugh. CONTEMPORARY EXAMPLE: Icyl DiBerg, Marietta, Ohio.

Ida   From the Old English *ead* and *id*, meaning "a possession" and "protection," hence "a fortunate warrior." Also, from the Old Norse *id* and *idh*, meaning "labor." Used in Ireland as the equivalent of Ita. PLACE-NAME USAGE: Mount Ida, Crete.

Idalee   A name invented by combining Ida and Lee. *See* Ida *and* Lee.

Idalou   A name invented by combining Ida and Lou. *See* Ida *and* Lou. PLACE-NAME USAGE: Idalous, Texas, named for Ida Basset and Lou Bacon, the wives of the founders.

Idamay   A name invented by combining Ida and May. *See* Ida *and* May. PLACE-NAME USAGE: Idamay, West Virginia, named for Ida May Watson, a local resident.

Idana   A name invented by combining Ida and Anna. PLACE-NAME USAGE: Idana, Kansas, named for Ida Howland and Anna Broughton, the wives of the men who founded the town in 1879.

Idane   From the Old German *id* and the Old Norse *idh*, meaning "labor." The name was brought to England by the Normans and used in the Middle Ages. Used also as a masculine name. VARIANT FORMS: Idonea, Idonia, Ideny, Idony, Idena, Ita. May also be an invented name, a hybrid of Ida and Jane. *See* Ida *and* Jane. Akin to the place-name Idana. *See* Idana. CONTEMPORARY EXAMPLE: Idane Hamlyn, Seattle, Washington.

Idande   From the Old English *ead*, meaning "protection, prosperity." VARIANT FORMS: Iddes, Idena.

Idel, Idelle   Pet forms of Ida. *See* Ida.

Idena   A name invented by combining *Ida* and *Dena* (Dinah). *See* Ida *and* Dena. Also, a variant form of Idane, Idande, and Idonea. *See* Idane, Idande, *and* Idonea. CONTEMPORARY EXAMPLE: Idena Williams, New York, New York.

Idette   A pet form of Ida. *See* Ida.

Idit   A Yiddish form of the Hebrew name Yehudit (Judith). *See* Judith. Also, from the Arabic, meaning "the best, choicest."

Idonea   From the Old Norse *id* and *idh*, meaning "labor." Akin to Ida. In Norse mythology, Idhuna was a goddess of spring. Idena is a variant form.

Idra   From the Aramaic, meaning "a flag" or "a fig tree." The fig tree was symbolic of the scholar in ancient Hebrew culture.

Ignacia, Ignatia   Feminine forms of Ignatius. *See* Ignatius (masculine section).

Ila   A variant form of Ilit. *See* Ilit. Also, a pet form of Ilsa. *See* Ilsa. CONTEMPORARY EXAMPLE: Ila P. Walker, Farrell, Pennsylvania.

Ilajean   A name invented by combining Ila and Jean. *See* Ila *and* Jean. CONTEMPORARY EXAMPLE: Ilajean Feldmiller, professor.

Ilana, Ilanit   From the Hebrew *ilan*, meaning "a tree." Ilan is a masculine form.

Ilene   A variant form of Eileen. *See* Eileen. VARIANT SPELLINGS: Ilean, Ileane, Illene.

Ilisa, Ilise   Variant forms of Elisabeth. *See* Elisabeth.

Ilit   From the Aramaic, meaning "the best, superlative." Ila is a variant form.

Ilka   A Scottish form of the Middle English *ilke*, meaning "of the same class."

Ilsa   A variant form of Elisabeth. *See* Elisabeth.

Ilse   A variant form of Elisabeth. *See* Elisabeth.

Ilyse   A variant form of Elisabeth. *See* Elisabeth.

Ima   A variant spelling of Imma. *See* Imma.

Imma   From the Hebrew, meaning "mother." Also, a variant form of Emma. *See* Emma.

Imogen, Imogene   From the Latin, meaning "image, likeness." CONTEMPORARY EXAMPLE: Imogene Coca, comedienne.

Ina   From the Latin, meaning "mother." CONTEMPORARY EXAMPLE: Ina Balin, actress.

Indi, Indy   From the Hindi, meaning "Indian" or "from India." CONTEMPORARY EXAMPLES: Indi Carlana Curreri, Dover, New Hampshire; Indy Shriner, daughter of comedian Herb Shriner.

Indiana   Adopted from the name of the state.

Indra   The chief god of the early Hindu religion, in control of rain and thunder.

Inez   The Spanish form of Agnes. *See* Agnes.

Inga, Inge   From the Old English *ing*, meaning "a meadow." Also, a contraction of the Old English *incga*, meaning "children, descendants." CONTEMPORARY EXAMPLE: Inga Swenson, actress.

Ingeborg   From the Old English, meaning "Borg's children."

Inger   A variant form of Inga. *See* Inga. CONTEMPORARY EXAMPLE: Inger Stevens, actress.

Inglath   From the British *engylion*, meaning "angels."

Ingrid   A variant Scandinavian form of Inga. *See* Inga. In Norse mythology, Ing was the god of fertility and peace.

Inza   An invented name. A heroine in one of Frank Merriweather's novels. CONTEMPORARY EXAMPLE: Inza Aleph Beasley, Nederland, Texas.

Iolana   The Hawaiian form of Yolanda. *See* Yolanda.

Iolani   From the Hawaiian, meaning "royal hawk."

Iona   From the Greek, meaning "a purple-colored jewel." VARIANT FORMS: Ione, Ionia.

Iora   From the Latin *aurum*, meaning "gold." Also, possibly of Indian origin, meaning "sunshine." CONTEMPORARY EXAMPLE: Iora Alexander, Andover, Massachusetts.

Iphigenia   In Greek mythology, a beautiful young girl snatched from the altar, where she was to be sacrificed by Artemis and carried to heaven.

Ipo   From the Hawaiian, meaning "darling."

Irena   A Polish form of Irene. *See* Irene. VARIANT FORMS: Irenka, Irina. CONTEMPORARY EXAMPLE: Irena Narell, author.

Irene   From the Greek, meaning "peace." Renie is a pet form.

Irenee   A variant form of Irene. *See* Irene. CONTEMPORARY EXAMPLE: Irenee Hausherr, author.

Irenka   A variant form of Irena. *See* Irena.

Irina   A variant form of Irena. *See* Irena.

Iris   From the Greek, meaning "a play of colors." In Greek mythology, the goddess of the rainbow. In Homer's *The Iliad*, she is the messenger of the gods. CONTEMPORARY EXAMPLE: Iris V. Cully, editor.

Irma   From the Old High German Irmin, the name associated with Tiu, the god of war. A contracted form of Irmonberta and Irmgard.

Iryl   Origin uncertain. Possibly a variant form of Iris. *See* Iris. CONTEMPORARY EXAMPLE: Iryl McClintock, Elizabeth, Pennsylvania.

Isa   A pet form of Isabel used chiefly in Scotland. *See* Isabel.

Isaaca   The feminine form of Isaac. *See* Isaac (masculine section).

Isabeau   A French form of Isabel. *See* Isabel.

Isabel   A variant form of Elisabeth. *See* Elisabeth. In the Middle Ages, the name of queens of England and France. VARIANT FORMS: Nib (English); Isobel, Tibbi (Scotch); Isabeau, Isabelle (French); Bela, Isabella (Spanish). SURNAME USAGE: Ibb, Ibbs, Ibsen, Ibson, Nibbs, Tibbs.

Isabele   A variant spelling of Isabel. *See* Isabel.

Isabella   The Spanish form of Isabel. *See* Isabel. Queen of Castille (1474-1504) who helped finance the expedition of Columbus.

Isabelle   A variant form of Isabel. *See* Isabel.

Isadora, Isidora   Variant forms of the masculine Isadore. *See* Isadore (masculine section). CONTEMPORARY EXAMPLE: Isadora Duncan, dancer.

Isobel   A variant Scottish spelling of Isabel. *See* Isabel. Tibby is a pet form. CONTEMPORARY EXAMPLE: Isobel S. Sainsbury, physician.

Isolda   A variant spelling of Isolde. *See* Isolde.

Isolde   Probably, from the Old High German, meaning "to rule." Also, possibly from the Celtic, meaning "the fair one." Isolda is a variant spelling. In medieval legend, an Irish princess loved by Tristram.

Ita, Itta   Yiddish forms of the Hebrew name Yehudit (Judith). Also, an Irish name, akin to Ida.

Italia   The Latin form of Italy, earlier called Vitalia, meaning "life."

Iti, Itti   From the Hebrew, meaning "with me."

Ivana, Ivanna   Feminine forms of Ivan, the Russian form of John. *See* John (masculine section). CONTEMPORARY EXAMPLE: Ivana Griffin Hays, Norfolk, Virginia.

Iverna   From the Old English *ofer*, meaning "a bank, a shore." CONTEMPORARY EXAMPLE: Melvene Iverna Wilson, Glen St. Mary, Florida.

Ivette   A variant form of Yvette. *See* Yvette. CONTEMPORARY EXAMPLE: Ivette Pacheco, Perth Amboy, New Jersey.

Ivria, Ivriah   The feminine form of Ivri is the original name by which Jews are known in the Bible. Ivri means "from the other side (of the river Euphrates)," from which Abraham came.

Ivrit   A Hebrew word, meaning "the Hebrew language."

Ivy   From the Middle English *ivi*, meaning "a vine (of the ginseng family)." CONTEMPORARY EXAMPLE: Ivy Priest Baker, treasurer of the U.S. Used also as a masculine name.

Izellah   Probably from the Arabic *dil*, meaning "a part." Or, an Austro-Hungarian name, meaning "little princess." CONTEMPORARY EXAMPLE: Izellah Bristow, Brea, California.

Izetta   Probably a pet form of Isabel. *See* Isabel.

J

Jacinta From the Middle English *jacinte*, the Latin *hyacinthus*, and the Greek *hyacinth*, meaning "a reddish-orange precious stone." VARIANT FORMS: Jacinth, Jacinthe.

Jacinth An English variant form of Jacinta. *See* Jacinta.

Jacinthe A French form of Jacinta. *See* Jacinta.

Jackie A pet form of Jacoba and Jacqueline. *See* Jacoba *and* Jacqueline.

Jacklyn A variant form of Jacqueline. *See* Jacqueline. CONTEMPORARY EXAMPLE: Jacklyn O'Hanlon, author.

Jaclyn A variant form of Jacqueline. *See* Jacqueline. CONTEMPORARY EXAMPLE: Jaclyn Smith, actress.

Jacoba From the Hebrew, meaning "to supplant" or "protect." The feminine form of Jacob. *See* Jacob (masculine section). Jacobina is a pet form.

Jacobina A Scottish pet form of Jacoba. *See* Jacoba.

Jacqueline, Jacquelyn, Jacquelynne Variant French forms of Jacoba. *See* Jacoba.

Jacquetta A French pet form of Jacques (James). *See* Jacques and James (masculine section). Jaquetta is a variant spelling.

Jacqui A pet form of Jacqueline. *See* Jacqueline. CONTEMPORARY EXAMPLE: Jacqui Moore, Vacaville, California.

Jacquie A pet form of Jacqueline. *See* Jacqueline. CONTEMPORARY EXAMPLE: Jacquie Hann, author and illustrator.

Jada From the Middle English and Old Norse *jalda*, meaning "a horse," especially an old, worn-out (jaded) one. Also, from the French and Spanish, meaning "a hard stone," generally green in color.

Ja Donne From the Latin *domina*, meaning "a lady." Akin to Donna. CONTEMPORARY EXAMPLE: Ja Donne Lulla, Fort Worth, Texas.

Jael From the Hebrew, meaning "mountain goat" or "to ascend." Also, from the Arabic, meaning "prominent." In the Bible, a Kenite woman who slew Sisera with a tent-pin, in the days of Deborah. A favorite Puritan name. Used also as a masculine name.

Jaen From the Hebrew *yaen*, meaning "an ostrich."

Jaffa, Jafit From the Hebrew *yaffa*, meaning "beautiful, comely." PLACE-NAME USAGE: Jaffa, Israel.

Jaime, Jaimee Feminine forms of James. *See* James (masculine section).

Jaimie A feminine pet form of James. *See* James (masculine section).

Jalene A name invented by combining the masculine James and a variant form of Lenore (Eleanor). *See* James *and* Eleanor. CONTEMPORARY EXAMPLE: Jalene Kalbaugh, Redding, California.

Jamese A French feminine form of James. *See* James (masculine section). CONTEMPORARY EXAMPLE: Jamese Ann Gucciardi, Detroit, Michigan.

Jamesena, Jamesina A feminine pet form of James. *See* James (masculine section). CONTEMPORARY EXAMPLE: Jamesena Faulk, librarian; Jamesina Marshall, Fishkill, New York.

Jamie A feminine pet form of James. *See* James (masculine section). CONTEMPORARY EXAMPLE: Jamie Gobb, author.

Jan A pet form of Jeanette. *See* Jeanette. CONTEMPORARY EXAMPLE: Jan Clayton, actress.

Jane From the Hebrew, meaning "gracious, merciful." Akin to Hannah and a feminine form of John. Probably evolved from the Old French name Jehane. VARIANT FORMS: Janet, Johanna, Joan, Jenny (English); Jean, Jeanie, Joanna (Scotch); Jessie, Sine, Sheena, Shena (Gaelic); Hanne, Johanna (German); Jantina (Dutch); Jeanne, Jeannette, Jehane, Jehanne (French); Juana, Juanita (Spanish); Jovanna (Portuguese); Giovanna (Italian); Zaneta (Russian).

Janee A pet form of Jane. *See* Jane.

Janel, Janella, Janelle Pet forms of Jane. *See* Jane. CONTEMPORARY EXAMPLE: Janelle Price, actress.

Janerette A pet form of Jane. *See* Jane. CONTEMPORARY EXAMPLE: Janerette Chamberlain, Somerset, New Jersey.

Janet, Janette Pet forms of Jane. *See* Jane. CONTEMPORARY EXAMPLE: Janette Zavattero, author.

Janey A pet form of Jane. *See* Jane.

Jani A pet form of Jane. *See* Jane. CONTEMPORARY EXAMPLE: Jani Franco, Brooklyn, New York.

Janice A variant form of Jane. *See* Jane. CONTEMPORARY EXAMPLE: Janice Marie Ginn, Grass Valley, California.

Janie A pet form of Jane. *See* Jane.

Janina A pet form of Jane. *See* Jane.

Janine   A pet form of Jane. CONTEMPORARY EXAMPLE: Janine Parker, dancer.

Janis   A variant form of Johanna. *See* Johanna. CONTEMPORARY EXAMPLE: Janis Joplin, singer.

Janita   A variant form of the Spanish name Juanita, a pet form of Jane. *See* Jane. Jan is a pet form. CONTEMPORARY EXAMPLE: Janita (Jan) Stewart, Amherst, Ohio.

Janna   A variant form of Johanna. *See* Johanna.

Jaonne   A variant form of Joan. *See* Joan. CONTEMPORARY EXAMPLE: Jaonne Carson, Beaumont, Texas.

Jaqualine   A variant spelling of Jacqueline. *See* Jacqueline. CONTEMPORARY EXAMPLE: Jaqualine Sue Broome, librarian.

Jaquetta   A variant spelling of Jacquetta. *See* Jacquetta. A character in Shakespeare's *Love's Labour's Lost*.

Jara   A Slavonic form of Gertrude. *See* Gertrude.

Jardena   From the Hebrew, meaning "to descend, to flow downward." Jordan is the masculine form.

Jaredene   A feminine form of Jared. From the Hebrew, meaning "to descend." CONTEMPORARY EXAMPLE: Jaredene Lee Johnston, Fullerton, California.

Jarietta   Probably from the Arabic *jarrah*, meaning "an earthen water jug."·

Jarita   A Spanish form of Jarietta. *See* Jarietta.

Jasa   A name invented by combining *Ja*mes and *Sa*ra. *See* James *and* Sara.

Jasmin   From the Arabic and Persian *yasamin*, "a flower" in the olive family. Yasmin is the Persian form.

Jasmina, Jasmine   Pet forms of Jasmin. *See* Jasmin.

Jean, Jeane   Scottish forms of Jane. *See* Jane. Also, short forms of Jeannette. *See* Jeannette.

Jeanette   A French form of Jane. *See* Jane.

Jeanice   A variant form of Jean. *See* Jean. CONTEMPORARY EXAMPLE: Jeanice Mary Ginn, Grass Valley, California.

Jeanine   A pet form of Jane. *See* Jane.

Jeanne   A variant form of Jane. *See* Jane.

Jeannette   A French form of Jane. *See* Jane. PET FORMS: Jeanie, Jenni, Jenny, Nettie, Netty.

Jeannine   A pet form of Jane. *See* Jane.

Jehane   A French form of Jane. See Jane. CONTEMPORARY EXAMPLE: Jehane Benoit, author.

Jemima   From the Arabic, meaning "a dove." In the Bible, one of the three daughters of Job. Yonina and Jonina are Hebrew equivalents.

Jemina   From the Hebrew, meaning "right-handed."

Jen   A pet form of Jeannette. *See* Jeannette.

Jenale Joed   A double name created from *Jennie, Leota, Joseph,* and Mildr*ed*. CONTEMPORARY EXAMPLE: Jenale Joed Harris, Glendale, California.

Jenalyn   A name created from Jeannette and Lynn. *See* Jeannette *and* Lynn.

Jenat   A variant form of Jeanette. *See* Jeanette. CONTEMPORARY EXAMPLE: Jenat L. Feldman, Atlanta, Georgia.

Jene   A variant spelling of Jean. *See* Jean. CONTEMPORARY EXAMPLES: Jene Eckenfelder, Westport, Connecticut; Jene Barr, author.

Jenine   A pet form of Jane. *See* Jane.

Jenise   A variant form of Janis. *See* Janis. CONTEMPORARY EXAMPLE: Jenise S. Trammell, Woodstock, Georgia.

Jennelle   An invented name. A combination of Jenny and Nell. CONTEMPORARY EXAMPLE: Jennelle Smart, Versailles, Kentucky.

Jennie, Jenny   Pet forms of Jane. *See* Jane. Jinny is a variant form.

Jennifer   From the Welsh name Guinevere which later became Winifred. *See* Winifred. Jen and Jenny are pet forms.

Jennilee   A name created by combining Jennifer and Lee. *See* Jenifer *and* Lee. CONTEMPORARY EXAMPLE: Jennilee Barnhart, Neapolis, Ohio.

Jereva   A combination of the names Junior (masculine) and Reva (feminine). CONTEMPORARY EXAMPLE: Jereva Kae Williams, Ann Arbor, Michigan.

Jeri, Jerri   A diminutive form of Geraldene. *See* Geraldene.

Jerriann   A name created by combining Jerri and Ann. *See* Jerry (masculine section) *and* Ann. CONTEMPORARY EXAMPLE: Jerriann Feola, Santa Ana, California.

Jerrilyn   A name created by combining Jerri and Lyn. *See* Jerry (masculine section) *and* Lyn. CONTEMPORARY EXAMPLE: Jerrilyn Szelle, editor.

Jerusha   From the Hebrew, meaning "taken possession of, inheritance." In the Bible, the mother of King Jotham. Used by nine-teenth-century Puritans. The heroine of James Michener's novel *Hawaii*.

Jessamine   From the Middle French *jessemin* and *jasmin*, referring to a variety of plant with fragrant flowers used in scenting perfumes and teas. CONTEMPORARY EXAMPLE: Jessamine Middleton, Holden, Massachu-setts.

Jessica   A variant form of Jessie. *See* Jessie. Popularized by Shake-speare's heroine in the *Merchant of Venice*.

Jessie   From the Hebrew, meaning "God's grace," akin to Hannah. Or, if taken from the same root as the masculine Jesse, the meaning is "riches." VARIANT FORMS: Jesse, Jessica.

Jethra   A feminine form of Jethro, meaning "abundance, riches," in the Hebrew.

Jetta   From the Old French *jaiet* and the Latin *gagates*, meaning "a hard variety of black coal which takes a high polish," hence the expres-sion "black like jet." CONTEMPORARY EXAMPLE: Jetta Eng Katowitz, New Port Richey, Florida.

Jewel, Jewell   From the Old French, meaning "joy." CONTEMPORARY EXAMPLES: Jewel Brodsky, teacher; Jewell Jacobs, publisher; Jewell W. Jordan, Arizona state auditor, 1960s.

Jezebel   From the Hebrew, meaning "unexalted" or "impure." In the Bible, Jezebel was the wife of King Ahab.

Jill   A variant form of Gill (Gillian), meaning "girl." *See* Gill.

Jindalee   An Australian tribal name. Origin unknown. Jindy is a pet form. CONTEMPORARY EXAMPLE: Rebecca Jindalee Grayson, Culver City, California.

Jinny   A Scottish form of Jenny. *See* Jenny.

Jinx   An invented name. Mrs. Jinx Heaton of Carmel, Indiana, was born on Friday the 13th, in December 1946, and was called Jinx ever since. CONTEMPORARY EXAMPLE: Jinx Falkenberg, actress.

Jo   A pet form of Josephine. *See* Josephine.

Joan, Joann   Variant forms of Jane *and* Johanna. *See* Jane *and* Johanna.

Joanna, Joanne   From the Hebrew, meaning "God is gracious." Akin to the Hebrew name Johanan (John). VARIANT FORMS: Jane, Jean, Joan, Johanna, Johanne.

Jo-Ann, Jo-Anne   A hybrid name of Jo (Josephine) and Ann(e). *See* Josephine *and* Ann(e). Also, variant forms of Joanna and Joanne.

Jobina   A feminine form of Job. *See* Job (masculine section).

Jobyna Possibly the feminine form of Job. *See* Job (masculine section). CONTEMPORARY EXAMPLE: Jobyna Davis, San Gabriel, California. Named after Jobyna Ralston, wife of Richard Arlen, actor.

Jocelin, Joceline A variant Germanic form of the Hebrew name Jacoba, the feminine form of Jacob, meaning "supplanted, substituted." Akin to Jacqueline. SURNAME USAGE: Gosling, Joslin.

Jocelyn A variant form of Jocelin. *See* Jocelin.

Jocelynd A variant form of Jocelyn. *See* Jocelyn.

Jocelyne A variant form of Jocelin. *See* Jocelin. CONTEMPORARY EXAMPLE: Jocelyne LaGarde, actress.

Jochebed, Jocheved From the Hebrew, meaning "God is glorious" or "God is honorable." In the Bible, the wife of Amram; mother of Moses, Aaron, and Miriam. Yocheved is a variant spelling.

Jodette A French form of Jodi. *See* Jodi.

Jodi, Jodie Feminine pet forms of Judah. *See* Judah (masculine section). Also, pet forms of Josephine. *See* Josephine. CONTEMPORARY EXAMPLE: Jodie Foster, actress.

Jody A variant spelling of Jodi. *See* Jodi. CONTEMPORARY EXAMPLE: Jody Paonessa, editor.

Joel A feminine form adopted from the masculine form. *See* Joel (masculine section). Also, a name created by combining Joseph and Ellen. CONTEMPORARY EXAMPLE: Sister Joel Read, Milwaukee, Wisconsin, college president.

Joela A feminine form of Joel. *See* Joel (masculine section).

Joella A name created by combining Joan and Eleanore. CONTEMPORARY EXAMPLE: Joella Ruth Girardin, Auburn, Maine.

Joelle A feminine form of Joel. *See* Joel (masculine section). CONTEMPORARY EXAMPLE: Joelle Moone, Vacaville, California.

Joelynn A name created by combining Joseph or Josephine and Ellen. *See* Josephine *and* Ellen. CONTEMPORARY EXAMPLE: Joelynn Snyder–Ott, author.

Johanna From the Hebrew, meaning "God is gracious." Akin to Hannah and the masculine Johanan (John). Jane is the more popular English form. VARIANT FORMS: Jane, Janet, Jenny, Janice, Janis, Joan, Joanna (English); Jean, Jeanie (Scotch); Hanne (German); Jeanne, Jeannette, Jehane (French); Juana, Juanita (Spanish); Jovana, Jovanna (Portuguese and Slavonic); Ivanna (Russian); Giovanna, Giovannina (Italian).

Johanne A variant form of Johanna. *See* Johanna.

Johnath An invented name. Akin to the masculine Jonathan. *See*

Jonathan (masculine section). Johny is a pet form. CONTEMPORARY EXAMPLE: Johnath Lynn Beckman, Phippsburg, Colorado.

Johnna   A variant spelling of Johanna or a feminine form of John. *See* Johanna *and* John (masculine section).

Johnnie   A pet form of Johanna. *See* Johanna.

Joia   An early form of Joy and Joyce (thirteenth century). *See* Joyce.

Joice   A variant spelling of Joyce. *See* Joyce.

Jolaine   An invented name. A combination of Joseph and Elaine. See Joseph (masculine section) *and* Elaine. CONTEMPORARY EXAMPLE: Jolaine Munck, Camarillo, California.

Jolande   A variant spelling of Yolande. *See* Yolande. CONTEMPORARY EXAMPLE: Jolande Gumz, journalist.

Jolea   A name invented by combining Joseph and Lea. *See* Joseph (masculine section) *and* Lea. CONTEMPORARY EXAMPLE: Jolea Noel Rucker, Huntington Beach, California.

Jolene   A pet form of Jolie. *See* Jolie.

Joletta   A pet form of Jolie. *See* Jolie.

Jolie   A French form of the Middle English *joli*, meaning "high spirits, good humor, pleasant."

Joliet   A variant form of Juliet or Jolie. *See* Juliet *and* Jolie. SURNAME USAGE: Louis Joliet (1645–1700), Canadian explorer. PLACE-NAME USAGE: a city in Illinois.

Jona   A feminine form of Jonah. *See* Jonah (masculine section).

Jonati   From the Hebrew *yona*, meaning "my dove." Akin to Jona.

Joneda   A name created by combining the masculine Jon and the feminine Foneda. CONTEMPORARY EXAMPLE: Joneda Loftus, Kansas City, Missouri.

Jonina   From the Hebrew *yona*, meaning "a dove." Jemima is the Arabic equivalent.

Jonit   A variant spelling of Jona. *See* Jona. Akin to Jonina.

Jonnie   A pet form of Johanna. *See* Johanna.

Jordana   The feminine form of Jordan. *See* Jordan in masculine section.

Jordie   A pet form of Jordana. *See* Jordana. CONTEMPORARY EXAMPLE: Jordie Brown, daughter of model Nancy Brown.

Jorel   A name invented by combining Joyce and the masculine Reuel. *See* Joyce *and* Reuel. CONTEMPORARY EXAMPLE: Jorel Stallones, Woodside, California.

Joscelin An Old French form of Jocelin. *See* Jocelin.

Joscelind A variant form of Jocelin. *See* Jocelin.

Josceline An Old French form of Joceline. *See* Joceline.

Joscelyn A variant spelling of Josceline. *See* Josceline.

Josefa A variant spelling of Josepha. *See* Josepha.

Josepha From the Hebrew, meaning "He (God) will add." A feminine form of Joseph. Josephine is a pet form.

Josephine A feminine French form of Joseph. *See* Joseph (masculine section). Josepha is a variant form. The wife of Napoleon (1796-1809) and empress of France (1804-1809). PET FORMS: Jo, Josette, Josie.

Josette A pet form of Josephine or Jocelyn. *See* Josephine *and* Jocelyn.

Josie A pet form of Josephine or Joceline. *See* Josephine *and* Joceline.

Joslyn A variant spelling of Jocelin. *See* Jocelin. CONTEMPORARY EXAMPLE: Joslyn Ginn, Palm Beach Gardens, Florida.

Jovita From the Latin, meaning "jovial."

Joy A pet form of Joyce. *See* Joyce.

Joya A variant form of Joy. *See* Joy. CONTEMPORARY EXAMPLE: Joya Utermohlen, figure skater.

Joyce From the Latin *jocosa*, meaning "merry." VARIANT FORMS: Joia, Joy, Jocosa. Used also as a masculine name. SURNAME USAGE: James Joyce (1882-1941), Irish novelist and poet.

Joycelyn A name created by combining Joyce and Lynne. CONTEMPORARY EXAMPLE: Joycelyn R. Donway, Mapple Valley, Washington.

Juana The Spanish form of Johanna and Jane. *See* Johanna *and* Jane.

Juanita A Spanish pet form of Juana (Jane). *See* Jane.

Judith From the Hebrew, meaning "praise." The feminine form of Judah. In the Bible, Esau's wife, and the beautiful heroine in the Book of Judith (in the Apocrypha.) VARIANT FORMS: Eudice, Yehudit, Yudit, Yuta. PET FORMS: Judi, Judy.

Judi, Judie Pet forms of Judith. *See* Judith.

Judy A pet form of Judith. *See* Judith.

Judyann A name invented by combining Judy and Ann. *See* Judy *and* Ann. CONTEMPORARY EXAMPLE: Judyann Elder, actress.

Jule, Jules Variant forms of Julia. *See* Julia.

Julia, Julian, Juliana From the Greek, meaning "soft-haired," symbolizing youth. Feminine forms of Julius. The Roman family Julii was noted for having long hair. Julian and Juliana may be derived from Gillian, meaning "girl" (*see* Gill). CONTEMPORARY EXAMPLE: Juliana, daughter of Wilhelmina, Queen of the Netherlands (1948-   ). VARIANT FORMS: Giula, Giulia, Giulietta (Italian); Ujli (Hungarian); Julie (French and German); Julka (Polish); Gill, Gillian (English); Sheila (Irish). PET FORMS: Gill, Jill, Juliet, Juliette. SURNAME USAGE: Gillet, Gillot, Gilson, Jewett, Jowett.

Julie   A variant form of Julia. *See* Julia.

Julieanne   A name invented by combining Julie and Anne. *See* Julie *and* Anne. CONTEMPORARY EXAMPLE: Julieanne Newbould, actress.

Julienne   The French form of Julia and Juliana. *See* Julia.

Juliet, Juliette   French pet forms of Julia. *See* Julia. The heroine of Shakespeare's *Romeo and Juliet*. VARIANT PET FORMS: Juet, Juetta.

Julinda   A name invented by combining Julie and Linda. *See* Julie *and* Linda. CONTEMPORARY EXAMPLE: Julinda G. Sanders, Shoals, Indiana.

June   From the Latin name Junius, meaning "the sixth month of the year." Akin to the masculine Junius.

Junez   An invented name. A combination of June and Inez. CONTEMPORARY EXAMPLE: Junez Whitehill, Morro Bay, California.

Jussy   A pet form of Justine. *See* Justine. A character in Colleen McCullough's *The Thorn Birds*.

Justina, Justine   From the Latin, meaning "just, honest." Justin is the masculine form. St. Justina was the fourth-century patron saint of Padua.

Jymie   A variant form of Jamie. *See* Jamie. CONTEMPORARY EXAMPLE: Jymie Kelly, Butler, Pennsylvania.

Jynx   A variant spelling of Jinx. *See* Jinx. Also, the name of a small bird similar to the woodpecker.

K

Kaaren   A variant spelling of Karen. *See* Karen. CONTEMPORARY EXAMPLE: Kaaren Kurtzman, executive.

Kacy   A name invented from the initials K.C. CONTEMPORARY EXAMPLE: Kacy Soper, Dearborn, Michigan.

Kaela   An invented name. Formed from Kathy (Katherine) and Ella. *See* Katherine and Ella. CONTEMPORARY EXAMPLE: Kaela Janelle Blagrove, Maybrook, New York.

Kaimana   An Hawaiian name meaning "a diamond."

Kaile, Kayle   Variant forms of Kelila. *See* Kelila.

Kaki   A nickname derived from Kathryn. CONTEMPORARY EXAMPLES: Kaki Hunter, actress; Kaki Kozelek, Bexley, Ohio.

Kalanit   A Hebrew name for plants with cup-shaped, colorful flowers.

Kaley   A variant form of Kelly. *See* Kelly. Akin to Kelton. *See* Kelton. CONTEMPORARY EXAMPLE: Kayley Abato, Branchville, New Jersey.

Kami   In Shintoism, a divine power or aura associated with deities or ancestors. CONTEMPORARY EXAMPLE: Kami Cotter, actress.

Kamillen   An invented name. Adopted from the name of a tea sold in Germany called *kamillen tee*. CONTEMPORARY EXAMPLE: Kamillen Eads, Twain Harte, California.

Kandi   A variant spelling of Candy. *See* Candy. CONTEMPORARY EXAMPLE: Kandi Keith, actress.

Kara   A pet form of Katherine. *See* Katherine.

Kareen   A variant spelling of Karen. *See* Karen. CONTEMPORARY EXAMPLE: Kareen Zebraff, yoga instructor.

Karen   A Danish form of Katherine. *See* Katherine. Caren is a variant spelling.

Karin   A variant form of Karen. *See* Karen. Also spelled Carin. CONTEMPORARY EXAMPLE: Karin Jorgensen, badminton champion.

Karina   A variant spelling of Carina. *See* Carina. CONTEMPORARY EXAMPLE: Karina Agosta, book club director.

Karita   A variant spelling of Carita. *See* Carita.

Karla   A feminine form of Karl. *See* Karl (masculine section). Also spelled Carla.

Karleen   A pet form of Karla. *See* Karla. Carleen is a variant spelling.

Karlene   A pet form of Karla. *See* Karla. Carlene is a variant spelling. CONTEMPORARY EXAMPLE: Karlene H. Roberts, researcher.

Karma   A variant spelling of Carma. *See* Carma.

Karmel, Karmela, Karmelit   From the Hebrew, meaning "vineyard." Karmel is also used as a masculine name. VARIANT SPELLINGS: Carmel, Carmela, Carmelit.

Karmia   From the Hebrew, meaning "vineyard of the Lord." Carmia is a variant spelling.

Karmit   A variant form of Karmel. *See* Karmel.

Karna, Karnit   From the Hebrew *keren*, meaning "horn (of an animal)." VARIANT SPELLINGS: Carna, Carnit.

Karniela, Karniella   From the Hebrew, meaning "the horn of the Lord." Akin to Karna. VARIANT SPELLINGS: Carniela, Carniella.

Karole   A variant spelling of Carole. *See* Carole. CONTEMPORARY EXAMPLE: Karole Hope, author.

Karolina   The Polish form of Caroline. *See* Caroline.

Karolyn   A variant spelling of Carolyn (Caroline). *See* Caroline.

Karon   A variant spelling of Karen. *See* Karen. CONTEMPORARY EXAMPLE: Karon Shanor, author.

Karyl   A variant spelling of Carol. *See* Carol. CONTEMPORARY EXAMPLE: Karyl Aronoff, Dallas, Texas.

Karyn   A variant spelling of Karen. *See* Karen. CONTEMPORARY EXAMPLE: Karyn Pfarr, author.

Kasia, Kassia   Variant Polish forms of Katherine. *See* Katherine.

Kasimira   A Slavic name, meaning "command for peace."

Kate   A pet form of Katherine. *See* Katherine.

Kath   A pet form of Katherine. *See* Katherine.

Katha   A pet form of Katherine. *See* Katherine. CONTEMPORARY EXAMPLE: Katha Pollitt, poet.

Katharina, Katharine   Variants of Catherine. *See* Catherine. CONTEMPORARY EXAMPLES: Katharina Havekamp, author; Katharine Ross, actress.

Kathe   A pet form of Katherine. *See* Katherine. VARIANT SPELLINGS: Kathie, Kathy.

Katherine   From the Greek *katharos*, meaning "pure, unsullied." Catherine is the more popular spelling. *See* Catherine. VARIANT FORMS:

Caterina (Italian); Catlin (Middle English); Catalina (Spanish); Katarina (Swedish); Karen, Kathrina (Danish); Thrine (German); Katya, Katinka (Russian); Caitlin, Cathleen, Kathleen (Irish). PET FORMS: Kate, Katty, Kerry, Ketty, Kitty.

Kathie, Kathy Pet forms of Katherine. *See* Katherine.

Kathleen An Irish form of Catherine. *See* Catherine (Katherine).

Kathrene A variant spelling of Katherine. *See* Katherine.

Kathryn A variant spelling of Katherine. *See* Katherine.

Kati, Katie Pet forms of Katherine. *See* Katherine. CONTEMPORARY EXAMPLE: Kati Breckenridge, psychologist.

Katina A Slavic pet form of Katherine. *See* Katherine. CONTEMPORARY EXAMPLE: Katina Paxinou, actress.

Katrina, Katrine, Katrinka Variant forms of Katherine popular in Slavic countries. *See* Katherine. CONTEMPORARY EXAMPLE: Katrina Blickle, novelist. PLACE-NAME USAGE: Katrine, a lake in Scotland, setting of Sir Walter Scott's *Lady of the Lake*.

Katy A pet form of Katherine. *See* Katherine.

Katya A Russian pet form of Katherine. *See* Katherine.

Kay From the Greek, meaning "rejoice." Also, a form of Katherine. *See* Katherine.

Kaygey An invented name from the initials K.G. CONTEMPORARY EXAMPLE: Kaygey Cash, community leader.

Kayla A variant spelling of Kaile. *See* Kaile. CONTEMPORARY EXAMPLE: Kayla F. Bernheim, psychologist.

Kayle A variant spelling of Kaile. *See* Kaile.

Kaylee A variant form of Kaile. *See* Kaile. CONTEMPORARY EXAMPLE: Kaylee Laskowitz, teacher.

Kayley A variant spelling of Kaley. *See* Kaley. CONTEMPORARY EXAMPLE: Kayley Abato, Branchville, New Jersey.

Kayo An invented name. Derived from the initials K.O., or from the abbreviated form of the word knockout. CONTEMPORARY EXAMPLE: Kayo Boles Nash, a resident of Ladysmith, Wisconsin.

Kayreen An invented name. Origin unknown. CONTEMPORARY EXAMPLE: Kayreen Francksen, Salt Lake City, Utah.

Kedma From the Hebrew *kedem*, meaning "towards the East."

Keely A variant form of Kelly. *See* Kelly. CONTEMPORARY EXAMPLE: Keely Smith, singer.

Kefira From the Hebrew, meaning "a young lioness." Also, a form of *kefir*, a mildly alcoholic Russian drink made from cow's milk.

Kelda   An Old Norse name, meaning "a fountain or spring."

Kelila, Kelula   From the Hebrew, meaning "a crown, a laurel." VARIANT FORMS: Kaile, Kayle, Kyla, Kyle.

Kellee   A variant spelling of Kelly. *See* Kelly. CONTEMPORARY EXAMPLE: Kellee Patterson, actress.

Kelli   A variant spelling of Kelly. *See* Kelly. CONTEMPORARY EXAMPLE: Kelli Krull, Miss New York of 1979.

Kelly   A variant form of Kelt (also spelled Celt). The Kelts were antecedents of the Gaelic families of Europe. CONTEMPORARY EXAMPLES: Kelly Patterson, librarian; Kelly Lange, television news reporter.

Kelton   From Celtic, meaning "a town inhabited by Celts." Akin to Kelly. Also, from the Old English *ceol*, meaning "keel town, a town where ships are built." CONTEMPORARY EXAMPLE: Kelton Valentine, Newton, Mississippi. Used also as a masculine name.

Kemba   From the Old English name Cymaere, meaning "a Saxon lord." Kem is a pet form. VARIANT FORMS: Kemp, Kemps. CONTEMPORARY EXAMPLE: Kemba Lowen, Phoenix, Arizona.

Ken   A pet form of Kenna. *See* Kenna.

Kendai   An invented name designed to sound like the German *kinder*, meaning "children." CONTEMPORARY EXAMPLE: Kendai Kay Kehrer, Louisville, Kentucky.

Kendis   A variant form of Kenna. *See* Kenna.

Kendra   A variant form of Kenna. *See* Kenna. CONTEMPORARY EXAMPLE: Kendra Brown, daughter of model Nancy Brown.

Kendy   An invented name. The feminine form of Kenneth. *See* Kenneth (masculine section). CONTEMPORARY EXAMPLE: Kendy M. Parent, Fontana, California.

Kenna   From the Old English *cen*, meaning "head," or from *cyn*, meaning "children." Also, from the Old Norse *kenna*, meaning "to know, knowledge." CONTEMPORARY EXAMPLE: Kenna Berendsen, Strongsville, Ohio.

Keren, Keryn   From the Hebrew, meaning "horn (of an animal)." CONTEMPORARY EXAMPLE: Keren Shaw, editor.

Keret   From the Hebrew, meaning "city or settlement."

Kerrie, Kerry   From the British name Ceri, one of the early kings of Britain. Kerry is a variant spelling. CONTEMPORARY EXAMPLES: Kerrie Serepta Gilliam, Hendersonville, North Carolina; Kerry Tucker, salesman.

Keshet   From the Hebrew, meaning "a bow, a rainbow."

Keshisha From the Aramaic, meaning "old, an elder."

Ketifa From the Arabic, meaning "to pluck (usually ripened fruit)."

Ketty A pet form of Katherine. *See* Katherine. CONTEMPORARY EXAMPLE: Ketty Lester, actress.

Ketura, Keturah From the Hebrew, meaning "a burnt offering." In the Bible, the wife of Abraham.

Ketzia From the Hebrew, meaning "a powdered cinnamon-like bark," hence, the secondary meaning of "fragrant." In the Bible, one of the daughters of Job. PET FORMS: Kessie, Kezzie, Kezzy.

Kezia A variant spelling of Ketzia. *See* Ketzia.

Kezzie, Kezzy Pet forms of Ketzia. *See* Ketzia.

Kim An invented name made up of the first letters of Kansas, Illinois, and Missouri; these states meet at one point. CONTEMPORARY EXAMPLE: Kim Hunter, actress. PLACE-NAME USAGE: a town in Colorado, named for the character in Rudyard Kipling's novel *Kim*.

Kimberly A name adopted from kimberlite, a type of rock formation often containing diamonds. The name of the diamond-mining center in South Africa. CONTEMPORARY EXAMPLES: Kimberly Beck, actress; Kimberly Worthington, Chattanooga, Tennessee; Kimberly Ann Brown, Toledo, Ohio.

Kimet An invented name inspired by the British World War II airplane *Kimet*. CONTEMPORARY EXAMPLE: Kimet M. Laidlaw, Stratton Mountain, Vermont.

Kin From the Old English *cynn* and the Old Norse *kyn*, meaning "to produce," hence "offspring, relatives." CONTEMPORARY EXAMPLE: Kin Platt, author.

Kinbarra A variant form of Kinborough. *See* Kinborough.

Kinborough From the Old English, meaning "royal fortress." Kinbarra is a variant form.

Kinchen A pet form of Kin. *See* Kin.

Kineta From the Greek, meaning "to move."

Kinsey Probably a variant form of Kin. *See* Kin. SURNAME USAGE: Alfred Charles Kinsey, zoologist.

Kiny A pet form of Katherine. *See* Katherine.

Kiona Probably an Indian name, meaning "brown hills." PLACE-NAME USAGE: Kiona, Washington.

Kirby From the Old English *ciric*, meaning "a church." Used also as a masculine name.

Kireen From the Old English *ciric*, meaning "a church." CONTEMPO-

RARY EXAMPLE: Kireen Potter, Vista, California.

Kirsten From the Old English *ciric*, meaning "church," plus *stan*, meaning "stone," hence "stone church." Also, a Scandinavian form of Christine. *See* Christine. CONTEMPORARY EXAMPLE: Kirsten Flagstad, opera singer.

Kirsti, Kirstie Norwegian pet forms of Kirsten. *See* Kirsten. CONTEMPORARY EXAMPLE: Kirsti Cates, Minot AFB, North Dakota.

Kirsty A pet form of Kirsten. *See* Kirsten.

Kismet From the Arabic *quismah*, meaning "fate, destiny." PLACE-NAME USAGE: Kismet, Kansas.

Kit, Kitty Pet forms of Katherine. *See* Katherine. Kit is also used as a masculine name. CONTEMPORARY EXAMPLE: Kitty Carlisle, actress.

Kitra Possibly a variant form of the Hebrew name Ketara. Derived from the Hebrew *keter*, meaning "a crown." An Arabian girl in Lloyd C. Douglas's novel *The Big Fisherman.* CONTEMPORARY EXAMPLE: Kitra K. Diehl, LaPorte, Texas.

Kolleen A variant spelling of Colleen. *See* Colleen. CONTEMPORARY EXAMPLE: Kolleen Casey, athlete.

Korenet From the Hebrew, meaning "to shine, to emit rays."

Kriss A pet form of Christine. *See* Christine.

Krist, Krista Short forms of Kristin. *See* Kristin. CONTEMPORARY EXAMPLE: Krista Bradford, television news reporter.

Kristian A variant form of Christine. *See* Christine.

Kristie A pet form of Christine. *See* Christine. CONTEMPORARY EXAMPLE: Kristie L. Montgomery, Pekin, Illinois.

Kristien A variant form of Christine. *See* Christine.

Kristin A variant form of Christine. *See* Christine.

Kristy A pet form of Kristin. *See* Kristin. CONTEMPORARY EXAMPLE: Kristy McNichol, actress.

Kyla Variant form of Kelila. *See* Kelila. Also, from the Greek *kylix*, an ancient two-handled drinking cup.

Kyle A variant form of Kyla. *See* Kyla. Used also as a masculine name. CONTEMPORARY EXAMPLE: Kyle Meriwether, daughter of actress Lee Meriwether.

Kylene A pet form of Kyle. *See* Kyle. CONTEMPORARY EXAMPLE: Kylene Barker, Miss America of the year 1979.

Kylia A variant form of Kyla. *See* Kyla.

Kyna   The Welsh form of Kin. *See* Kin.

Kyrene   From the Greek *kyrios*, meaning "a lord" or "god." PLACE-NAME USAGE: Kyrene, Arizona.

L

LaBelle   From the French, meaning "the beautiful one." CONTEMPO-
RARY EXAMPLE: LaBelle Lance, wife of Georgia banker Bert Lance.

LaDean   From the French, meaning "the dean." *See* Dean. CONTEM-
PORARY EXAMPLE: LaDean McMahon, Van Nuys, California.

Lady   From the Old English *hlaefdige*, meaning "lady, mistress."
CONTEMPORARY EXAMPLE: Lady Annan, author.

Lahela   The Hawaiian form of Rachel. *See* Rachel.

Lahoma   An abbreviated form of Oklahoma. A name used by American Indians.

Laila   From the Hebrew, meaning "night."

Laili, Lailie   From the Hebrew, meaning "my night." Akin to Laila.
to Laila.

LaJuan   A variant Spanish form of Joanna. *See* Joanna. Used by
American Indians. CONTEMPORARY EXAMPLE: LaJuan Slaton, Idalow,
Texas.

Laleh   A variant form of Leila. *See* Leila. CONTEMPORARY EXAMPLE:
Laleh Bakhtiar, Iranian architect.

LaMarilys   Probably derived from the Greek and Latin *amarylis*,
meaning "a shepherdess." Also a plant name. CONTEMPORARY EXAM-
PLE: LaMarilys Doering, El Cajon, California.

Lamorna   From the Middle English *morne*, meaning "morning."
CONTEMPORARY EXAMPLE: Lamorna Heath, author.

Lana   From the Latin *lanatus*, meaning "wooly." Also, a pet form of
Alana. *See* Alana. Or, from the British *llan*, meaning "an enclosure,"
and *hena*, "a church." CONTEMPORARY EXAMPLE: Lana Turner, actress.

Lanai   From the Hawaiian, meaning "a veranda, a terrace." PLACE-
NAME USAGE: an island of Hawaii.

Lancey   A feminine form of Lance. *See* Lance (masculine section).
CONTEMPORARY EXAMPLE: Lancey Lynn Holly Wilson, Escondido,
California.

Lani   From the Hawaiian, meaning "sky."

LaNora   A variant form of Nora. *See* Nora.

402

Laqueta   An Indian name, possibly meaning "the quiet one." CONTEMPORARY EXAMPLE: Laqueta Sinclair, Norwalk, California.

Lara   A variant spelling of Laura. *See* Laura. In Roman mythology, a nymph punished by Jove because of her talkativeness.

Laraine   From the Latin, meaning "sea-bird." Also, a variant spelling of Lorraine. *See* Lorraine.

Larinda   Probably a pet form of Laura. *See* Laura.

Laris   A variant form of Larisa. *See* Larisa. Also, an invented name: a combination of *L*uke and *A*llen, plus *ris*. CONTEMPORARY EXAMPLE: Laris Nichols, Rockingham, North Carolina.

Larisa, Larissa   From the Latin, meaning "cheerful." Also, a short form of Clarissa. *See* Clarissa. PLACE-NAME USAGE: Larissa, a city in Greece.

Lark   From the Middle English *larke*, meaning "a bird of the family of old-world songbirds," the most common being the meadowlark.

LaSara   A name invented by combining Laura and Sara. PLACE-NAME USAGE: LaSara, Texas, named after two residents: Laura Harding and Sara Gill.

Lasca   A variant form of the Arabic *al-askar*, meaning "army," hence "soldier." The heroine of Frank Desprez's poem *Lasca*. CONTEMPORARY EXAMPLE: Lasca Lynne Stucki, Holyoke, Massachusetts.

Lassie   A Socttish form of the Middle English *lasce*, meaning "a young girl, a maiden." Made popular by the television series *Lassie*. CONTEMPORARY EXAMPLE: Lassie A. Martin, Clarksville, Tennessee.

Laulani   From the Hawaiian, meaning "heavenly branch."

Laura   From the Latin *laurus*, meaning "laurel." Akin to Laurel. PET FORMS: Laure, Laurie, Lolly, Loretta.

Lauraine, Laurane   Variant forms of Laura. *See* Laura.

Laure   A pet form of Laura. *See* Laura.

Laurel   From the Latin *laurus*, meaning "a laurel (tree)," symbol of victory. Laura is a variant form. CONTEMPORARY EXAMPLE: Laurel H. Rabin, scholar. PLACE-NAME USAGE: Laurel Ridge, Pennsylvania.

Laurelen   A name invented by combining Laura and Helen. CONTEMPORARY EXAMPLE: Laurelen J. Pratts, Avon, New York.

Lauren, Laurene   Variant forms of Laura. *See* Laura.

Laurestine   A pet form of Laura, from the Modern Latin *laurustinus*, meaning "laurel." CONTEMPORARY EXAMPLE: Laurestine Beeghley, Jane Lew, West Virginia.

Laurette, Lauretta   Pet forms of Laura. *See* Laura.

Lauri   A pet form of Laura. *See* Laura.

Laurice   A variant form of Laurel. *See* Laurel. CONTEMPORARY EXAMPLE: Laurice Prewett, Taft, California.

Laurie   A pet form of Laura. *See* Laura.

Lauve   From the Old English *hlaford*, meaning "a lord." Also, from the Old French *laveoir*, meaning "to wash." CONTEMPORARY EXAMPLE: Lauve Metcalfe, Tallahassee, Florida.

Laverne   From the Latin and French, meaning "spring, springlike; to be verdant." VARIANT FORMS: Verne, Verna, Verne, Vern.

Lavinia   From the Latin, meaning "woman of Rome." PET FORMS: Vina, Vinia. CONTEMPORARY EXAMPLE: Lavinia M. Henryes, Cuero, Texas. PLACE-NAME USAGE: Lavinium, an Italian city.

LaWanda   Probably a variant form of LaJuan. *See* LaJuan. CONTEMPORARY EXAMPLE: LaWanda Page, actress.

Lawrie   A feminine form of Lawrence. Akin to Laura. *See* Laura. CONTEMPORARY EXAMPLE: Lawrie Mifflin, sports reporter.

Laylie   A variant spelling of Laili. *See* Laili.

Lea   A variant French form of Leah. *See* Leah. Also, from the Old English *lege*, meaning "a meadow."

Leabel   A name invented by combining Leah and Belle. CONTEMPORARY EXAMPLE: Leabel C. Lees, San Diego, California.

Leah   From the Hebrew, meaning "to be weary." Also, from the Assyrian, meaning "mistress, ruler." In the Bible, daughter of Laban and the first of Jacob's wives. VARIANT FORMS: Lea (French); Lia (Italian). Lee is a pet form.

Leala   From the Middle English *lele* and the Latin *legalis*, meaning "legal, loyal."

Leana, Leanne   Variant forms of Liana. *See* Liana.

Leandra   A name invented by combining Lea and Ann. *See* Lea *and* Ann. Also, the feminine form of Leander, from the Greek, meaning "the lion-man." CONTEMPORARY EXAMPLE: Leandra Lynae Pierce, Hermosa Beach, California.

Leanor, Leanore   Variant forms of Eleanor. *See* Eleanor.

Leather   From the Old English *hleothor*, meaning "an oracle."

Leatrice   Probably a combination of Leah and Beatrice. *See* Leah *and* Beatrice.

Leavonia   Probably a variant form of Levona. *See* Levona. Lee is a pet form. CONTEMPORARY EXAMPLE: Ova Leavonia Jordan, Long Beach, California.

Leda   In Greek mythology, a Spartan queen, the mother of Helen of Troy. Lida is a variant spelling. CONTEMPORARY EXAMPLE: Leda Thompson, Bethlehem, Pennsylvania.

Lee   From the Old English *lege*, meaning "meadowland." Also, a pet form of Leah.

Leeanna   A name invented by combining Lee and Anna. *See* Lee *and* Anna.

Leeba   From the Yiddish, meaning "beloved." Also, from the Hebrew *lev*, meaning "heart."

Leesha   Possibly a variant form of the masculine Elisha. *See* Elisha (masculine section). CONTEMPORARY EXAMPLE: Leesha Rose, author.

Lei   A pet form of Leilani. *See* Leilani. Also, from the Hawaiian, meaning "wreath, garland."

Leigh   From the Old English *lege*, meaning "meadowland." Akin to Lee. CONTEMPORARY EXAMPLE: Leigh French, actress. SURNAME USAGE: Vivian Leigh, actress.

Leihina   From the Hawaiian, meaning "wreath of the moon."

Leila   From the Arabic and Hebrew, meaning "dark, oriental beauty" or "night." Also, from the Persian, meaning "dark-haired." VARIANT FORMS: Laila, Laili, Lailie, Laleh, Laylie. CONTEMPORARY EXAMPLE: Leila Martin, actress.

Leilani   From the Hawaiian, meaning "heavenly flower." Lelani is a variant spelling.

Leimomi   From the Hawaiian, meaning "wreath of pearls."

Lei-Shell   An Hawaiian name. Created by combining *lei* ("wreath") and *shell* ("seashell"). CONTEMPORARY EXAMPLE: Lei-Shell Ho, Ewa Beach, Hawaii.

Lela   A variant spelling of Leala. *See* Leala. CONTEMPORARY EXAMPLE: Lela Rolontz, publicist.

Leland   From the Old English *lege*, meaning "meadowland." Lea is a variant form. CONTEMPORARY EXAMPLE: Leland Palmer, actress.

Lelani   A variant spelling of Leilani. *See* Leilani. CONTEMPORARY EXAMPLE: Lelani Livermore, El Cajon, California.

Lelia   A variant form of Lela. *See* Lela.

LeMyra   A variant form of Myra. *See* Myra.

Lena   A pet form of Eleanor, Helen, and Magadalene. *See* Eleanor, Helen, *and* Magdalene. Also, from the Hebrew, meaning "to sleep, to dwell," and the Old English, meaning "a farm." CONTEMPORARY EXAMPLE: Lena Horne, singer. PLACE-NAME USAGE: a river in Russia.

LeNann   A name invented by combining Lena and Ann. *See* Lena *and* Ann. CONTEMPORARY EXAMPLE: LeNann Avinger, Harlingen, Texas.

Lenea   Probably a variant form of Lena. *See* Lena.

Lenis   From the Latin *lenitus*, meaning "gentle, mild."

Lennie   A pet form of Eleanor. *See* Eleanor.

Lenora, Lenore   Pet forms of Eleanor. *See* Eleanor. PLACE-NAME USAGE: Lenora, Oklahoma, coined from the names of two early settlers: Lee Moore and Nora Stovall.

Leola   A variant form of Leona. *See* Leona.

Leoma   A variant form of Leona. *See* Leona.

Leona   From the Greek, meaning "lion-like." Akin to the masculine Leo. *See* Leo (masculine section). PLACE-NAME USAGE: Leona, Texas.

Leonarda   The feminine form of Leonard. *See* Leonard (masculine section). Akin to Leona.

Leonia   A variant form of Leona. *See* Leona. CONTEMPORARY EXAMPLE: Leonia Bronnell, Amenia, New York.

Leonie   A pet form of Leona. *See* Leona.

Leonora, Leonore   Variant forms of Eleanor. *See* Eleanor.

Leontine, Leontyne   From the Latin, meaning "lion–like." Akin to Leona. CONTEMPORARY EXAMPLE: Leontyne Price, opera singer.

Leora, Leorit   From the Hebrew, meaning "light, my light."

Leota   A variant form of Leona. *See* Leona. PLACE-NAME USAGE: Leota, Minnesota.

Lera   Possibly a variant form of the French *le roi*, meaning "the king." CONTEMPORARY EXAMPLE: Lera Nell England, Garland, Texas.

Leron, Lerone   From the Hebrew *lee rone*, meaning "song is mine." Used as feminine and masculine names in Israel.

Lesley, Leslie   From the Old English *lege*, meaning "meadowlands." Lea is a variant form. CONTEMPORARY EXAMPLES: Lesley Hazleton, author; Leslie Uggams, singer.

Leta   A pet form of Elizabeth. *See* Elizabeth. Also, a pet form of Letitia. *See* Letitia. CONTEMPORARY EXAMPLE: Leta W. Clark, author.

Letha   A pet form of Elizabeth. *See* Elizabeth. CONTEMPORARY EXAMPLE: Letha Scanzoni, author. PLACE-NAME USAGE: Letha, Idaho, named for Letha Wilson, an early resident.

Letifa, Letipha   From the Hebrew, meaning "to pat, caress."

Letitia   From the Latin *laetita*, meaning "joy." PET FORMS: Leta, Letty,

Lettie, Tisha, Titia. CONTEMPORARY EXAMPLE: Letitia Baldrige, author.

Letty A pet form of Elizabeth. *See* Elizabeth. Also, a pet form of Letitia. *See* Letitia. CONTEMPORARY EXAMPLE: Letty M. Russell, theologian.

Levana From the Hebrew, meaning "the moon" or "white." Akin to Levona. Livana is a variant form.

Levani From the Fijian, meaning "anointed with oil." CONTEMPORARY EXAMPLE: Levani Lipton, Honolulu, Hawaii.

Levia From the Hebrew, meaning "to join." The feminine form of Levi. Also, from the Hebrew, meaning "lioness."

Levina From the Middle English *levene*, meaning "to shine."

Levona From the Hebrew, meaning "spice, incense," usually white in color. Akin to Levana. *See* Levana. Livona is a variant spelling.

Lexi A pet form of Alexandra. *See* Alexandra.

Leyla A variant spelling of Leila. *See* Leila.

Lia The Italian form of Leah. *See* Leah.

Liala Origin unknown. CONTEMPORARY EXAMPLE: Liala Caroline Matthews, Oakmont, Pennsylvania.

Liana From the French *lierne* and *liorne*, meaning "to bind, to wrap around." Akin to the Latin *viorne*, meaning "a tree with creeping vines."

Lianne A variant form of Liana. *See* Liana.

Liba A variant spelling of Leeba. *See* Leeba.

Libbie, Libby Pet forms of Elizabeth. *See* Elizabeth.

Liberty From the Latin *libertas*, meaning "free." CONTEMPORARY EXAMPLE: Liberty Godshall, actress.

Licia A pet form of Alicia (Alice). *See* Alice. CONTEMPORARY EXAMPLE: Licia Albanese, singer.

Lida, Lidia Variant spellings of Leda. *See* Leda. CONTEMPORARY EXAMPLES: Lida Levine, Boston, Massachusetts; Lidia Postma, artist.

Lila A variant form of Lilac. *See* Lilac. CONTEMPORARY EXAMPLE: Lila Cockrell, U.S. city mayor (San Antonio, Texas).

Lilac From the Arabic and Persian *lilak*, meaning "bluish." Relating to the hardy shrubs or trees of the olive family with their bluish and lavender flowers. VARIANT FORMS: Lila, Lilah, Lilas, Lilias.

Lilah A variant form of Lilac. *See* Lilac.

Lili A variant form of Lilian. *See* Lilian.

Lilia   A variant form of Lilian. *See* Lilian.

Lilian   From the Latin *lilium*, meaning "a lily." Or, from the Hebrew Elizabeth, meaning "God's oath." Lillian is a variant spelling. VARIANT FORMS: Lili, Lilia, Liliane, Lilias. PET FORMS: Lil, Lilibet (the popular pet name of Queen Elizabeth).

Liliana   The Hawaiian form of Lilian. *See* Lilian. CONTEMPORARY EXAMPLE: Liliana Betti, author.

Liliane   A variant form of Lilian. *See* Lilian. CONTEMPORARY EXAMPLE: Liliane Winn, Los Angeles, California.

Lilias   A variant form of Lilian. *See* Lilian. CONTEMPORARY EXAMPLE: Lilias Folan, physical education instructor.

Lilibet   A pet form of Lilian and Elizabeth. *See* Lilian *and* Elizabeth.

Lilis   A variant form of Lilith. *See* Lilith.

Lilita   A pet form of Lilian. *See* Lilian. PLACE-NAME USAGE: Lilita, Alabama, named for Lilita Bizelle, daughter of the postmaster.

Lilith   From the Assyrian and Babylonian, meaning "of the night." In ancient Semitic folklore, "a female demon"; the first wife of Adam before the creation of Eve.

Lilli   A pet form of Lillian. *See* Lillian. CONTEMPORARY EXAMPLE: Lilli Palmer, actress.

Lillian   A variant spelling of Lilian. *See* Lilian.

Lillis   A variant spelling of Lilis. *See* Lilis.

Lillith   A variant spelling of Lilith. *See* Lilith.

Lillus   A variant form of Lillith. *See* Lillith. CONTEMPORARY EXAMPLE: Lillus Black, Laguna Beach, California.

Lilo   From the Hawaiian, meaning "to be generous." CONTEMPORARY EXAMPLE: Lilo Lorentz, Brooklyn, New York.

Lily, Lilly   Pet forms of Lilian. *See* Lilian.

Lilyan   A variant spelling of Lilian. *See* Lilian.

Lilybeth   A hybrid name of Lily (Lilian) and Beth (Elizabeth). *See* Lilian *and* Elizabeth. CONTEMPORARY EXAMPLE: Lilybeth K. Teske, Bay Village, Ohio.

Lin   A variant spelling of Lyn. *See* Lyn. CONTEMPORARY EXAMPLE: Lin Farley, author.

Lina   A pet form of Carolina or Adeline. *See* Carolina *and* Adeline. CONTEMPORARY EXAMPLE: Lina Wertmuller, movie director.

Linda   A pet form of Belinda. *See* Belinda. Also, from the Spanish, meaning "handsome."

Linde   A variant spelling of Linda. *See* Linda. Also, a pet form of Linden. *See* Linden.

Linden   Derived from the Old English *lind* and the German *linde*, meaning "a linden tree." PLACE-NAME USAGE: Linden, New Jersey.

Lindi   A pet form of Linden or Linda. *See* Linden *and* Linda.

Lindsay, Lindsey   From the Old English, meaning "the camp near the stream." Used also as a masculine name. CONTEMPORARY EXAMPLE: Lindsay Wagner, actress. SURNAME USAGE: (Nicholas) Vachel Lindsay (1879-1931), U.S. poet.

Lindy   A pet form of Linden or Linda. *See* Linden *and* Linda.

Linita   A Spanish pet form of Belinda. *See* Belinda. CONTEMPORARY EXAMPLE: Linita Brumfield, Jackson, Mississippi.

Linn, Linne   Variant forms of Lyn. *See* Lyn.

Linnea   Derived from the name of the national flower of Sweden, a small blue flower with a yellow center, named for Karl Linnaeus, Swedish botanist. CONTEMPORARY EXAMPLE: Linnea Leedham, editor.

Linnet, Linnette   From the Old French *lin*, meaning "flax." The name of a bird that feeds on flaxseed. Also, pet forms of the Welsh name Lyn. *See* Lyn.

Liora   A variant spelling of Leora. *See* Leora.

Lirit   A Hebrew form of the Greek *lyrikos*, meaning "lyrical, musical, poetic."

Liron, Lirone   From the Hebrew, meaning "song is mine." Used also as masculine names. VARIANT SPELLINGS: Leron, Lerone.

Lisa, Lise   Pet forms of Elisabeth. *See* Elisabeth. CONTEMPORARY EXAMPLE: Lisa Kirk, actress.

Liselotte   A name invented by combining Lise (Elisabeth) and Lotte (Charlotte). CONTEMPORARY EXAMPLE: Liselotte L. Schloss, translator.

Lisette   A pet form of Elisabeth. *See* Elisabeth. Also, a variant form of Louise. *See* Louise. CONTEMPORARY EXAMPLE: Lisette S. Smith, author.

Lisl   A variant form of Elisabeth. *See* Elisabeth. CONTEMPORARY EXAMPLE: Lisl Cade, editor.

Lita   A short form of Lolita. *See* Lolita. CONTEMPORARY EXAMPLE: Lita Milan, actress.

Lital   From the Hebrew, meaning "dew (rain) is mine."

Livana   A variant form of Levana. *See* Levana.

Livia, Liviya   A pet form of Olivia. *See* Olivia. Also, from the Hebrew, meaning "a lioness." Akin to Levia.

Livona   A variant spelling of Levona. *See* Levona.

Liza   A pet form of Elizabeth. *See* Elizabeth. CONTEMPORARY EXAMPLE: Liza Minelli, entertainer.

Lizbeth   A short form of Elizabeth. *See* Elizabeth. CONTEMPORARY EXAMPLE: Lizbeth Perrone, author.

Lize   A variant spelling of Liza. *See* Liza.

Lizette   A pet form of Elizabeth. *See* Elizabeth. CONTEMPORARY EXAMPLE: Lizette Santos, New York, New York.

Lizzie, Lizzy   Pet forms of Elizabeth. *See* Elizabeth.

Llda   A variant form of the British name Llwyd, meaning "grey" or "brown." CONTEMPORARY EXAMPLE: Llda Jean Myers, Pitcairn, Pennsylvania.

Lloyd   Commonly used as a masculine name. *See* Lloyd (masculine section).

Lodema   A variant form of Lodemia. *See* Lodemia. CONTEMPORARY EXAMPLE: Lodema Simpkins, Fremont, Ohio.

Lodemia   From the Old English *loddan*, meaning "a canal, a stream." CONTEMPORARY EXAMPLE: Lodemia Burroughs, Randolph, Massachusetts.

Lois   From the Greek, meaning "good, desirable."

Lola   A pet form of the Spanish Carlota (Caroline). *See* Caroline. Also, the Hawaiian form of Laura. CONTEMPORARY EXAMPLE: Lola Falana, entertainer.

Loleta, Lolita   Pet forms of Lola. *See* Lola.

Lolly   A pet form of Laura. *See* Laura.

Lona   From the Middle English, meaning "alone." Akin to Lorna. CONTEMPORARY EXAMPLE: Cheera Lona Roadarmel, Warner Robins, Georgia.

Look   A personal name inspired by *Look* magazine. CONTEMPORARY EXAMPLE: Look Kathleen Freeland, Halleston, Massachusetts.

Lora   From the Latin, meaning "she who weeps; sorrowful." Or, from Old High German, meaning "famous warrior."

Loraine   A variant form of Lora. *See* Lora. Lorraine is a variant spelling. PLACE-NAME USAGE: Loraine, Texas, named for Loraine Crandall, wife of a local resident.

Loral   A variant form of Laurel. *See* Laurel.

Loran, Lorann   A hybrid of Lora or Laura and Ann. *See* Lora, Laura, *and* Ann. Also, an invented name based on the words Long Range Navigation. CONTEMPORARY EXAMPLE: Lorann Stallones, Woodside, California.

Loree   A variant spelling of Laurie. *See* Laurie.

Lorelei, Lorelie   From the German, meaning "melody, song." Derived from Lurlei in German legend, a rock or cliff on the Rhine from which a siren was sounded to lure sailors who were shipwrecked on the reefs.

Lorell   A name adopted from the laurel plant. CONTEMPORARY EXAMPLE: Lorell Tutt, Southampton, New York.

Loren   From the Latin, meaning "crowned with laurel." Akin to Laura.

Lorene   A variant form of Laura. *See* Laura. CONTEMPORARY EXAMPLE: Lorene Cohen, editor.

Loretah   A variant spelling of Loretta. *See* Loretta. Also, the name of an Indian princess. CONTEMPORARY EXAMPLE: Loretah Darlene Emrick, Indianapolis, Indiana.

Loretta   A pet form of Laura. *See* Laura. Lorette is a variant form. CONTEMPORARY EXAMPLE: Loretta Young, actress.

Lorette   A pet form of Laura. *See* Laura. Loretta is a variant form.

Lori   A pet form of Laura. *See* Laura.

Lorice   From the Latin *lorum*, meaning "a thong." In ancient Rome, the leather corselet worn by a Roman soldier. Also, a short form of Chloris. *See* Chloris. CONTEMPORARY EXAMPLE: Lorice F. Mulhern, Brooklyn, New York.

Lorinda   A variant form of Laura. *See* Laura. CONTEMPORARY EXAMPLE: Lorinda Bryan Cauley, artist.

Lorine   A pet form of Laura. *See* Laura.

Loris   From the Dutch *loeres*, meaning "a clown." Also, a variant spelling of Lorice. *See* Lorice. CONTEMPORARY EXAMPLE: Shirley Loris Cooper, Los Angeles, California.

Lorna   From the Middle English, meaning "alone." Created by R.C. Blackmore for his novel *Lorna Doone*, in 1869. CONTEMPORARY EXAMPLE: Lorna Luft, singer.

Lorraine   A variant form of Lora. *See* Lora. Also, adopted from Alsace-Lorraine, a former province of France. Loraine and Laraine are variant spellings. CONTEMPORARY EXAMPLE: Alsace Lorraine Stewart, Conroe, Texas.

Lotta   A pet form of Charlotte. *See* Charlotte.

Lotte   A pet form of Charlotte. *See* Charlotte. CONTEMPORARY EXAMPLE: Lotte Lenya, singer.

Lottie   A pet form of Charlotte. *See* Charlotte.

Lotus   From the Greek *lotos,* one of the varieties of African and Asian water lilies. In Greek legend, the fruit of a plant that induced languor and forgetfulness.

Loudella   A name invented by combining Lou (Louise) and Della. *See* Louise *and* Della.

Loudonna   A name invented by combining Loudon (masculine) and Anna, or Loudon and Donna. CONTEMPORARY EXAMPLE: Loudonna Jo Watkins, Lancaster, Ohio.

Louella   A hybrid name created by combining Lou (Louise) and Ella. *See* Louise *and* Ella. CONTEMPORARY EXAMPLE: Louella V. Wetherbee, librarian.

Louisa   An English form of Louise. *See* Louise.

Louise   A feminine French form of Louis. *See* Louis (masculine section). VARIANT FORMS: Louisa, Eloise (English); Luisa (Italian and Spanish); Heloise, Lisette (French); Lova (Swedish); Luiza (Portuguese). PET FORMS: Lou, Lulu. CONTEMPORARY EXAMPLE: Louise Lasser, actress. SURNAME USAGE: Tina Louise, actress. PLACE-NAME USAGE: Lake Louise, Canada.

Loura   A variant spelling of Laura. *See* Laura.

Lourana   A hybrid name created by combining Loura (Laura) and Anna. *See* Laura *and* Anna.

Louvenia   A name invented by combining the masculine Louis and a form of Lavinia. *See* Louis *and* Lavinia. CONTEMPORARY EXAMPLE: Louvenia A. Spalding, music publisher.

L'Pree   Adapted from the French *grand prix,* meaning "great prize." CONTEMPORARY EXAMPLE: L'Pree Evette Corum, Henderson, Kentucky.

Luana   From the Hawaiian, meaning "to be at leisure."

Luba   A variant form of Leeba. *See* Leeba. Also, the name of a group in the southern Congo that speaks the Bantu language. CONTEMPORARY EXAMPLE: Luba Krugman Gurdus, author.

Lucania   From the Latin *lucius,* meaning "a fish." PLACE-NAME USAGE: an ancient district in southern Italy, presently called Basilicata.

Lucette   A pet form of Lucille. *See* Lucille.

Luci   A pet form of Lucille. *See* Lucille. CONTEMPORARY EXAMPLE: Luci Arnaz, actress.

Lucia, Luciana   From the Latin *lucere,* meaning "to shine." A feminine form of Lucian. CONTEMPORARY EXAMPLE: Lucia Vidal, Stamford, Connecticut.

Lucile, Lucille   From the Latin *lucere,* meaning "to shine, to bring light." Akin to Lucia. CONTEMPORARY EXAMPLE: Lucille Ball, actress.

Lucina   A pet form of Lucia. *See* Lucia.

Lucinda   An English form of Lucia. *See* Lucia. CONTEMPORARY EXAMPLE: Lucinda Baker, novelist.

Lucinda Lee   A double name combining Lucinda and Lee. *See* Lucinda *and* Lee. CONTEMPORARY EXAMPLE: Lucinda Lee Deweese, Cincinnati, Ohio.

Lucine   A pet form of Lucia and Lucille. *See* Lucia *and* Lucille.

Lucy   An English form of Lucia. *See* Lucia. VARIANT FORMS: Lucie (French); Luzia (Italian); Lleulu (Welsh).

Luedella   A variant spelling of Loudella. *See* Loudella.

Luella   A name invented by combining Lu (Louise) and Ella. *See* Louise *and* Ella. Louella is a variant spelling.

Luisa   An Italian and Spanish form of Louise. *See* Louise.

Luise   A variant French form of Louise. *See* Louise. CONTEMPORARY EXAMPLE: Luise Rainer, actress.

Lula   A pet form of Louise. *See* Louise.

Lulie   From the Middle English *lullen*, meaning "to lull, to soothe."

Lulu   A pet form of Louise. *See* Louise.

Luna   From the Latin *lunaris* and *luna*, meaning "the moon." CONTEMPORARY EXAMPLE: Luna I. Mishoe, educator.

Lunamae   A name invented by combining Luna and Mae. *See* Luna *and* Mae.

Lunette   A pet form of Luna. *See* Luna.

Lupe   From the Latin *lupus*, meaning "a wolf."

Lupita   A pet form of Lupe. *See* Lupe. CONTEMPORARY EXAMPLE: Lupita Ferrer, actress.

Lurchel   From the Old Norse *lur*, meaning "a war horn," used in prehistoric times especially in Scandinavia. May also be a form of Lorelei. *See* Lorelei. CONTEMPORARY EXAMPLE: Lurchel F. Wittler, Lake Charles, Louisiana.

Lurleen   From the Old Norse *lur*, meaning "a war horn." Akin to Lurchel. Also, from the Middle French *leurre*, meaning "to lure, to invite." May also be a form of Lorelei. *See* Lorelei.

Lurline   A variant spelling of Lurleen. *See* Lurleen.

Lusitania   The name of a British steamship that was sunk, in 1915, by a German submarine off Ireland. PLACE-NAME USAGE: an ancient Roman province in the Iberian Peninsula.

Luwana   An invented name. Possibly a combination of Lu (Louise) and Anna. *See* Louise *and* Anna.

Luzine   A variant pet form of Lucinda or Lucile. *See* Lucinda *and* Lucile.

Lycoris   From the Greek *lychnos*, meaning "a lamp, light."

Lyda, Lydda, Lydia   From the Greek place-name, meaning "a maiden from Lydia," an ancient kingdom in Asia Minor.

Lynda, Lynde   Variant spellings of Linda. *See* Linda.

Lynell   A pet form of Lyn. *See* Lyn. CONTEMPORARY EXAMPLE: Lynell Tobler, Pleasant Hill, California.

Lynette   A pet form of Lyn. *See* Lyn. CONTEMPORARY EXAMPLE: Lynette De Denne, author.

Lynlee   A name invented by combining Lynda and Lee. *See* Lynda *and* Lee. CONTEMPORARY EXAMPLE: Lynlee Ann Smith, Lewisburg, Pennsylvania.

Lynn, Lynne   Variant spellings of Lyn. *See* Lyn. Used also as masculine names. PLACE-NAME USAGE: cities in North Carolina and Massachusetts.

Lynwood   From the Old English, meaning "a lake in the woods." CONTEMPORARY EXAMPLE: Lynwood Jenkins, Wayne, Illinois.

Lynx   From the Old English *lox* and the German *lucks*, meaning "to shine." An animal with shining eyes. PLACE-NAME USAGE: Lynx, Alaska; Lynx Creek, Arizona.

Lyris   From the Greek *lyricos*, meaning "a lyre, a harp."

Lysandra   From the Greek *lysis*, meaning "to free, to liberate." The feminine form of Lysander, a fourth-century B.C. Spartan military commander. Also, a variant form of Alesandra (Alexandra). *See* Alexandra.

Lytle   From the Greek *lytikos*, meaning "to loosen, to free." Akin to Lysandra. CONTEMPORARY EXAMPLE: Lytle G. Blaisdell, Auburn, Washington.

M

Mabel   From the Latin *amabilis*, meaning "my beautiful one; amiable." Amabel is an early English form. CONTEMPORARY EXAMPLE: Mabel Mercer, singer. SURNAME USAGE: Mabley, Mabb, Mabbs, Mapp, Mapps, Mabbit, Mabbot, Mapson, Mappin.

Mabella, Mabelle   Variant forms of Mabel. *See* Mabel.

Mable   A variant spelling of Mabel. *See* Mabel.

Mackenzie   A Gaelic patronymic form, meaning "a son (descendant) of Kenneth." *See* Kenneth (masculine section). Used basically as a surname. CONTEMPORARY EXAMPLE: Mackenzie Phillips, actress.

Madalynne   A variant form of Magdalene. *See* Magdalene. CONTEMPORARY EXAMPLE: Madalynne Reuter, editor.

Madeena   A variant form of Magdalene. *See* Magdalene. CONTEMPORARY EXAMPLE: Madeena Spary Nolan, author.

Madelaine   A variant form of Magdalene. *See* Magdalene. PET FORMS: Maddie, Maddy.

Madeleine   A French form of Magdalene. *See* Magdalene. Madlin and Maudlin are short forms. Madeleine Paulnier, a nineteenth-century French cook. PLACE-NAME USAGE: La Madeleine, a region in southwest France.

Madelia   A variant form of Madeline. *See* Madeline. PLACE-NAME USAGE: Madelia, Montana, named after Madelia Hartshorn, daughter of one of the founders.

Madeline   A variant form of Magdalene. *See* Magdalene. PLACE-NAME USAGE: Madeline, California.

Madelon   A variant form of Magdalene. *See* Magdalene.

Madelyn   A variant form of Magdalene. *See* Magdalene.

Madge   A pet form of Margaret. *See* Margaret.

Madra, Madre   From the Latin, meaning "mother." Madre is a Spanish form.

Madrona   A variant form of Madra. *See* Madra.

Mady   A pet form of Madge or Magdalene. *See* Madge *and* Magdalene. CONTEMPORARY EXAMPLE: Mady Mesple, French singer.

Mae   A variant spelling of May. *See* May. CONTEMPORARY EXAMPLE:

Mae West, entertainer.

Maergrethe   A variant Welsh form of Margaret. *See* Margaret.

Maeve   The Irish form of Mauve. *See* Mauve. CONTEMPORARY EXAMPLE: Maeve McGuire, actress.

Mag   A pet form of Margaret or Magdalene. *See* Margaret *and* Magdalene.

Magda   A German pet form of Magdalene. *See* Magdalene.

Magdalen   A variant spelling of Magdalene. *See* Magdalene.

Magdalena   A variant form of Magdalene. *See* Magdalene. PLACE-NAME USAGE: Magdalena, New Mexico.

Magdalene, Magdaline   From the Hebrew *migdal*, meaning "a high tower." In the Bible, Mary Magdalene, identified with a repentant woman in the Book of Luke. VARIANT FORMS: Madeline, Maudlin (French); Magli, Mali, Malin (Dutch); Madelaine, Madeleine, Madelon (French); Maddalena (Italian); Madalena, Magdalena (Spanish); Madli, Mai, Marleen, Marlena (Slavic). PET FORMS: Leli, Lena, Magda, Manda. PLACE-NAME USAGE: Magdala (Migdala), a town on the Sea of Galilee in Israel.

Maggie   A pet form of Margaret. *See* Margaret. CONTEMPORARY EXAMPLE: Maggie Lane, designer.

Magna   From the Latin, meaning "great." Magnus is the masculine form.

Magnolia   Any trees or shrubs of the magnolia family, named for French botanist Pierre Magnol (1638-1705).

Mago   A pet form of Margo. *See* Margo.

Mahala, Mahalah   From the Aramaic and Arabic, meaning "fat (fattings)" or "marrow, brain." In the Bible, a daughter of Zelophehad.

Mahalia   A variant form of Mahala or Mahola. *See* Mahala *and* Mahola. CONTEMPORARY EXAMPLE: Mahalia Jackson, singer.

Mahina   From the Hawaiian, meaning "the moon."

Mahira   From the Hebrew, meaning "speedy, energetic."

Mahola   From the Hebrew *mahol* (*machol*), meaning "dance."

Mai   A Slavonic form of Maria. *See* Maria.

Maia   In Greek mythology, the daughter of Atlas, the mother of Hermes. In Roman mythology, goddess of the earth and growth. Romans offered sacrifices on the first day of May. *See also* May. Maya is a variant spelling.

Maida   From the Middle English *maide*, a contracted form of *maiden*, meaning "a young unmarried girl." Maidie is a variant form.

Maidie   A variant form of Maida. *See* Maida. Occassionally used as a pet form of Mary.

Maie   A Slavonic form of Maria. *See* Maria.

Maire   An Irish form of Mary. *See* Mary.

Mairead   An Irish form of the Old French *maire*, meaning "a magistrate." CONTEMPORARY EXAMPLE: Mairead Corrigan, Nobel Peace Prize winner (1976).

Mairin   An Irish form of Mary. *See* Mary.

Maisie   From the British name Maise, meaning "a field." Also, a Scottish pet form of Margaret. *See* Margaret. Mysie is a variant form.

Maite   From the Spanish *matar*, meaning "to kill," and *mate*, meaning "to checkmate." CONTEMPORARY EXAMPLE: Maite Manjon, author.

Majesta   From the Latin *majestas*, meaning "dignity, sovereign power."

Makala   From the Hawaiian, meaning "myrtle."

Mala   From the Norman-French, meaning "bad, evil." Or, from the Old English *mal*, meaning "a meeting place." CONTEMPORARY EXAMPLE: Mala Powers, actress.

Malia   The Hawaiian form of Mary. *See* Mary.

Malinda   A short form of Marcelinda. *See* Marcelinda. Lindy is a pet form.

Malka, Malkah   From the Hebrew, meaning "a queen." CONTEMPORARY EXAMPLE: Malka Drucker, author.

Malvina   The feminine form of Melvin. *See* Melvin (masculine section).

Malvinda   A variant feminine form of Melvin. *See* Melvin (masculine section). CONTEMPORARY EXAMPLE: Malvinda Kinard, author.

Mamie   A pet form of Mary or Margaret. *See* Mary *and* Margaret. May also be a form of the French *m'aimie*, meaning "my (girl) friend." CONTEMPORARY EXAMPLE: Mamie van Doren, actress.

Manda   A pet form of Amanda. *See* Amanda. Mandy is a variant form. Also, a pet form of Magdalene. *See* Magdalene.

Mandy   A pet form of Amanda. *See* Amanda. Manda is a variant form.

Manetta   Adapted from the place-name Manatee Pocket at Salerno, Florida. Also, a variant form of Manette. *See* Manette. CONTEMPORARY EXAMPLE: Manetta Summerlin Gould, Elsegundo, California.

Manette   The pet form of the French name Marion. *See* Marion.

Mangena, Mangina   From the Hebrew, meaning "song, melody."

Manila   From the place-name Manila Bay, in the Philippines, captured by Admiral George Dewey in 1898. CONTEMPORARY EXAMPLE: Manila D. Stead, Santa Cruz, California.

Manuela   A Spanish feminine form of Manuel. *See* Manuel (masculine section). CONTEMPORARY EXAMPLE: Manuela Soares, editor.

Mara, Marah   From the Hebrew, meaning "bitter." Akin to Mary and Miriam. *See* Mary *and* Miriam.

Maralee   A name invented by combining parts of Marguerite and Lee. *See* Marguerite *and* Lee. CONTEMPORARY EXAMPLE: Maralee Baker, Raleigh, North Carolina.

Maralou   A name invented by combining part of Mary and Lou. *See* Mary *and* Lou. CONTEMPORARY EXAMPLE: Maralou Taylor, Littleton, Colorado.

Maralyn   A variant spelling of Marilyn. *See* Marilyn. CONTEMPORARY EXAMPLE: Maralyn Bailey, author.

Marcelinda   A variant form of Marcella. *See* Marcella.

Marcella   From the Latin, meaning "brave, martial" or "a hammer." VARIANT FORMS: Malinda, Melinda, Marcelinda, Marcelyn, Marcia, Marcilen. Akin to the masculine form Mark. *See* Mark (masculine section).

Marcelyn   A variant form of Marcella. *See* Marcella. Marcie is a pet form. CONTEMPORARY EXAMPLE: Marcelyn (Marcie) Louie, tennis player.

Marcha   A variant spelling of Marsha. *See* Marsha.

Marcia   A variant form of Marcella. *See* Marcella. PET FORMS: Marcie, Marcy. CONTEMPORARY EXAMPLE: Marcia Lewis, comedienne.

Marcie   A variant form of Marcella and Marcia. *See* Marcella *and* Marcia.

Marcilen   A variant form of Marcella. *See* Marcella.

Marcy   A pet form of Marcia. *See* Marcia.

Mardell   From the Old English, meaning "the meadow near the sea (or lake)." CONTEMPORARY EXAMPLE: Mardell W. Stansberry, Los Angeles, California.

Mardeth   A variant form of Martha. *See* Martha.

Mardi   A pet form of Martha. Used also as an independent name. CONTEMPORARY EXAMPLE: Mardi W. Lewis, Pueblo, Colorado.

Mare From the Latin, meaning "sea." CONTEMPORARY EXAMPLE: Mare Winningham, actress.

Maree A variant spelling of Marie. *See* Marie. CONTEMPORARY EXAMPLE: Dahtee Maree West, Boston, Massachusetts.

Mareea A variant spelling of Maria. *See* Maria.

Maren, Marena From the Latin, meaning "sea." Akin to Marina. CONTEMPORARY EXAMPLE: Maren Jensen, actress.

Marenda A variant form of Miranda. *See* Miranda. CONTEMPORARY EXAMPLE: Marenda Perry, singer.

Maretta A name invented by combining Martel and Izetta. *See* Martel *and* Izetta. CONTEMPORARY EXAMPLE: Maretta M. Grego, Moore, Montana.

Margalit, Margalith Hebrew variant forms of the Greek Margaret. *See* Margaret.

Marganit A plant with blue, gold, and red flowers, indigenous to Israel.

Margaret From the Greek name Margaron, meaning "a pearl." *See also* Marguerite. VARIANT FORMS: Gogo, Margo, Margot, Marguerite (French); Gretle, Gretchen, Margarete (German); Maergrethe (Welsh); Ghita, Margherita (Italian); Margarida (Portuguese); Reta (Finland); Margarita (Spanish); Margery, Marjorie (English and Scotch). PET FORMS: Daisy, Greta, Madge, Mae, Mago, Margaretta, Marge, Marget, Margita, Meta, Meg, Mittie, Mog, Peg, Peggy, Rita. In Scotland Maggie, Maisie, and Mysie have been pet form favorites.

Margarete A German form of Margaret. *See* Margaret.

Margaretta A Spanish pet form of Margaret. *See* Margaret. CONTEMPORARY EXAMPLE: Margaretta (Happy) Rockefeller, wife of Nelson Rockefeller, U.S. vice-president.

Margarita A Spanish form of Margaret. *See* Margaret.

Marge A pet form of Margaret. *See* Margaret.

Margene A variant form of Margaret. *See* Margaret. Or, a name invented by combining Marge and Gene. *See* Marge *and* Gene (masculine section). CONTEMPORARY EXAMPLE: Margene Libertino, Long Branch, New Jersey.

Margerie A variant spelling of Margery. *See* Margery.

Margery A variant form of Margaret. *See* Margaret.

Marget A pet form of Margaret. *See* Margaret.

Margherita An Italian form of Margaret. *See* Margaret.

Margiad The Welsh form of Margaret. *See* Margaret. Megan is a variant form.

Margita   A short form of Margarita. *See* Margarita. CONTEMPORARY EXAMPLE: Margita White, U.S. government official.

Margo, Margot   Variant forms of Margaret. *See* Margaret. Mago is a pet form.

Marguerita   A Spanish form of Margarite. *See* Margarite. CONTEMPORARY EXAMPLE: Marguerita Rudolph, author.

Marguerite   From the French, meaning "a pearl, a daisy." *See* also Margaret. Daisy is a pet form.

Margy   A pet form of Margaret. *See* Margaret.

Mari   A variant spelling of Mary. *See* Mary. CONTEMPORARY EXAMPLE: Mari Brady, author.

Maria   The Latin, French, Italian, Spanish, and Swedish form of Mary. *See* Mary. Maria Theresa (1717-1780) was queen of Bohemia and Hungary, mother of Marie Antoinette. PLACE-NAME USAGE: Marias (Maria's) River, Montana, named by Captain Lewis (of Lewis and Clark fame) for his cousin Maria Woods (1804).

Mariabella   A hybrid name of Maria and Bella. *See* Maria *and* Bella.

Mariah   A variant form of Maria. *See* Maria. Or, a variant spelling of Moriah. *See* Moriah. CONTEMPORARY EXAMPLE: Mariah Brooke Martin, Mannington, West Virginia.

Mariamne   An early form of Mary. Used by Josephus, a first–century historian.

Marian, Mariane, Marianne   Variant forms compounded of Mary and Ann. *See* Mary *and* Ann. Marion is a variant form.

Maribel   A variant form of Mary, meaning "beautiful Mary."

Maribeth   A name invented by combining Mary and Beth. *See* Mary *and* Beth.

Marie   The French and Old German form of Mary. *See* Mary. Marie Antoinette (1755-1793), wife of Louis XVI, queen of France (1774-1792). PLACE-NAME USAGE: Marie, Texas, named for Marie Gentry, wife of a local landowner.

Mariel, Mariele   Dutch forms of Mary. *See* Mary. CONTEMPORARY EXAMPLE: Mariel Arayon, actress.

Mariene   A variant form of Marian. *See* Marian.

Mariesa, Mariessa   Pet forms of Marie (Mary). *See* Mary.

Marietta   An Italian pet form of Mary. *See* Mary. CONTEMPORARY EXAMPLE: Marietta Lynch, author. PLACE-NAME USAGE: Marietta, Ohio.

Mariette   A French pet form of Mary. *See* Mary. CONTEMPORARY EX-

AMPLE: Mariette Hartley, actress.

Marigold   From the Middle English *marigolde*, a variety of annual plant with yellow, red, and orange flowers. Compounded of Marie plus "gold," hence "Marie's (Mary's) gold" flower, referring to the Virgin Mary.

Marijon   A name invented by combining Mari (Mary) and John. *See* Mary *and* John.

Marijune   A name invented by combining Marie (Mary) and June. *See* Mary *and* June. CONTEMPORARY EXAMPLE: Marijune Belt, Wilmington, North Carolina.

Marika   A Slavonic pet form of Mary. *See* Mary. CONTEMPORARY EXAMPLE: Marika Hanbury-Tenison, cookbook editor.

Marilee   A name invented by combining a form of Mary and Lee. *See* Mary *and* Lee. CONTEMPORARY EXAMPLE: Marilee Brand, Huntington Beach, California.

Marilu   A variant spelling of Marylu. *See* Mary *and* Lou (Louise). CONTEMPORARY EXAMPLE: Marilu Henner, actress.

Marilyn, Marilynn   Names derived from Mary and meaning "Mary's line" or "descendants of Mary." *See* Mary. Maralyn is a variant. CONTEMPORARY EXAMPLE: Marilyn Monroe, actress.

Marina, Marinna   From the Latin *marinus* and *mare*, meaning "the sea." Rina is a pet form. CONTEMPORARY EXAMPLES: Marina Adams, landscape artist; Marina Kay Lomas, New Albany, Indiana.

Marion   A pet form of the French name Marie. Also, a variant form of Mary. *See* Mary. Often used as a nickname for Molly. Used also as a masculine name. PLACE-NAME USAGE: a city in Indiana named after Francis Marion, Revolutionary War hero.

Maris   From the Latin *mare*, meaning "the sea." SURNAME USAGE: Roger Maris, baseball player.

Marisa   A variant form of Maris. *See* Maris. CONTEMPORARY EXAMPLE: Marisa Berenson, actress.

Marise   A name invented by adding an "e" to Maris. *See* Maris. CONTEMPORARY EXAMPLE: Marise Meier, Seaticket, Massachusetts.

Marisela   A Spanish form of Maris and Marcella. *See* Maris *and* Marcella.

Marissa   A variant form of Maris. *See* Maris. Marisa is a variant spelling. CONTEMPORARY EXAMPLE: Marissa Pavan, actress. PLACE-NAME USAGE: Marissa, Illinois.

Mariwin   A name invented by combining Mari (a form of Mary) and Winifred. *See* Mary *and* Winifred.

Marjabelle A name invented by combining Marjarie and Belle. *See* Marjarie *and* Belle. CONTEMPORARY EXAMPLE: Marjabelle Young, author.

Marjarie, Marjary Variant spellings of Marjorie. *See* Marjorie.

Marjorie In Scotland, the popular spelling of Margery. *See* Margery.

Marjory A variant spelling of Marjorie. *See* Marjorie.

Markay A name invented by combining Mary and Kay. *See* Mary *and* Kay. CONTEMPORARY EXAMPLE: Markay Schroeder, Escondido, California.

Marla A variant form of Marlene. *See* Marlene.

Marlea, Marleah Invented names. Created by combining Margaret and Lea(h). *See* Margaret *and* Leah. CONTEMPORARY EXAMPLE: Marlea M. Dutt, Webster, New York.

Marleen A Slavic form of Magdalene. *See* Magdalene.

Marlena, Marlene Variant forms of Magdalene. *See* Magdalene. CONTEMPORARY EXAMPLE: Marlene Dietrich, actress, whose original name was Maria Magdalena.

Marles A name invented by combining Margaret and the masculine Leslie. *See* Margaret *and* Leslie (masculine section). CONTEMPORARY EXAMPLE: Marles Burrel, Dyer, Indiana.

Marlie A pet form of Marlena. *See* Marlena. CONTEMPORARY EXAMPLE: Marlie Wasserman, editor.

Marlo A variant form of Marlene. *See* Marlene. Marla is a variant form. CONTEMPORARY EXAMPLE: Marlo Thomas, actress.

Marlowe A variant form of Marlene. *See* Marlene. CONTEMPORARY EXAMPLE: Marlowe Duval, Moline, Illinois. SURNAME USAGE: Julia Marlowe, actress.

Marlyn A short spelling of Marilyn. *See* Marilyn.

Marlys A variant form of Marlene. *See* Marlene. CONTEMPORARY EXAMPLE: Marlys Millhiser, author.

Marna A variant form of Marina. *See* Marina. CONTEMPORARY EXAMPLE: Marna Elyea Kern, author.

Marne A variant form of Marna. *See* Marna. Also, an independent name derived from the Marne River, in France. CONTEMPORARY EXAMPLE: Marne Caporizzo, Pittsburgh, Pennsylvania.

Marni A pet form of Marnina. *See* Marnina.

Marnina From the Hebrew, meaning "rejoice." Also, a variant form of Marne. *See* Marne.

Marquita, Marquite From the French *marquise*, meaning "an awning, a canopy" to protect an official.

Marsha, Marshe   Variant forms of Marcia. *See* Marcia. CONTEMPORARY EXAMPLE: Marsha Mason, actress.

Marta   A variant form of Martha. *See* Martha. CONTEMPORARY EXAMPLE: Marta Randall, author.

Martelle   A feminine French form of Martin. *See* Martin (masculine section).

Martha   From the Aramaic, meaning either "sorrowful" or "a lady." In the Bible, a sister of Lazarus and Mary. VARIANT FORMS: Marthe (French); Marta (Italian and Spanish). Martita is a pet form. CONTEMPORARY EXAMPLE: Martha Raye, actress. PLACE-NAME USAGE: Martha's Vineyard, Massachusetts.

Marthe   A French form of Martha. *See* Martha. CONTEMPORARY EXAMPLE: Marthe Keller, actress.

Marthellen   A name invented by combining Martha and Ellen. *See* Martha *and* Ellen. CONTEMPORARY EXAMPLE: Tameron Marthellen Wade, Coronado, California.

Martina   A feminine form of Martin. *See* Martin (masculine section). CONTEMPORARY EXAMPLE: Martina D'Alton, author.

Martine   A feminine form of Martin. *See* Martin (masculine section). CONTEMPORARY EXAMPLE: Martine Beswicke, actress.

Martita   A pet form of Martha. *See* Martha.

Martylu   A name invented by combining Marty and Lou (Louise). *See* Marty (masculine section) *and* Louise. CONTEMPORARY EXAMPLE: Martylu Estrada, Venice, California.

Marva   From the Hebrew plant-name for sage, a plant in the Salvia mint family. CONTEMPORARY EXAMPLE: Marva Schoen, Annapolis, Maryland.

Marvel, Marvella   From the Middle English *mervaile* and the Latin *mirari*, meaning "to wonder, admire." CONTEMPORARY EXAMPLES: Marvel Jochinsen, Lolo, Montana; Marvella Bayh, wife of U.S. Senator Birch Bayh.

Mary   The English form of the Greek names Mariam and Mariamne, derived from the Hebrew name Miriam, meaning "sea of bitterness, sorrow." Also from the Chaldaic, meaning "mistress of the sea." In the Bible, the mother of Jesus; sister of Martha and Lazarus. Also known as Mary Magdalene. VARIANT FORMS: Marie (Middle English, Old German, French); Marion, Manette, Manon, Mariette (French); Maria (Greek, Latin, Italian, and Spanish); Mariamne (Greek); Miriam, Miryam (Hebrew); Masha (Russian); Marya (Russian and Polish); Marita, Mariquita (Spanish); Mair (Welsh); Mari, Maire, Mairin, Maureen, Maura, Moira, Moya, Muire (Irish); Minnie (Scotch); Mariele (Dutch). PET FORMS: Mae, Marietta, Mariette, Min, Minnie, May, Moll, Molly, Polly.

PLACE-NAME USAGE: the state of Maryland, named for Henrietta Maria, queen of Charles I. (In early years the spelling was Marieland and Mary-Land); Marysville, Ohio, named for Mary Culbertson, daughter of the founder (1820); Maryhill, Washington, named for Samuel Hill, a local landowner whose mother and wife were both named Mary.

Marya   A Russian and Polish form of Mary. *See* Mary. CONTEMPORARY EXAMPLE: Marya Zaturemska, Pulitzer Prize winner in poetry (1938).

Maryalice   A hybrid name of Mary and Alice. *See* Mary *and* Alice. CONTEMPORARY EXAMPLE: Maryalice Rooke, editor.

Maryalls   An invented name. Probably a combination of Mary and Alice. *See* Mary *and* Alice. CONTEMPORARY EXAMPLE: Maryalls G. Strom, editor.

Maryanne   A compounded name. *See* Mary *and* Anne. CONTEMPORARY EXAMPLE: Maryanne VanderVelde, author.

Marybeth   A hybrid form of Mary and Beth. *See* Mary *and* Beth.

Marygold   A variant form of Marigold. *See* Marigold.

Maryhelen   A hybrid name of Mary and Helen. *See* Mary *and* Helen. CONTEMPORARY EXAMPLE: Maryhelen Clague, novelist.

Marylin, Maryline   Variant forms of Mary, meaning "from Mary's line" or "descendants of Mary." *See* Mary.

Marylois   A hybrid name of Mary and Lois. *See* Mary *and* Lois. CONTEMPORARY EXAMPLE: Marylois Purdy Vega, editor.

Marylu   A hybrid name of Mary and Lu (Louise). *See* Mary *and* Louise. CONTEMPORARY EXAMPLE: Marylu Antonelli, potter.

Masada   From the Hebrew, meaning "foundation, support." Used in Israel. PLACE-NAME USAGE: an ancient Jewish mountain fortress in Israel, near the Dead Sea.

Matana   From the Hebrew, meaning "gift."

Mathilda, Mathilde   From the Old High German *macht*, meaning "might, power," plus *hiltia*, meaning "battle," hence "powerful in battle." VARIANT FORMS: Matilda (English); Matilda (Italian). PET FORMS: Matti, Matty, Matya, Mattye, Maud, Maude, Patty, Tilda, Tillie, Tilly. SURNAME USAGE: Tilson, Tillison, Tillotson.

Matilda   A variant form of Mathilda. *See* Mathilda.

Matti, Mattie   Pet forms of Mathilda. *See* Mathilda.

Matty, Mattye   Pet forms of Mathilda. *See* Mathilda.

Matya   A pet form of Mathilda. *See* Mathilda.

Maud, Maude   Pet forms of Mathilda. *See* Mathilda. Popular in

France. CONTEMPORARY EXAMPLE: Maud Adams, model. SURNAME USAGE: Madison (Maud's son) Maudson.

Maudene   A pet form of Maude. *See* Maude. CONTEMPORARY EXAMPLE: Maudene Nelson, nutritionist.

Maura   A variant form of Mary used predominately in Ireland. *See* Mary. Also, from the Celtic, meaning "dark." VARIANT FORMS: Maureen, Maurella, Morena.

Mauraine   A name invented by combining Maureen and Lorraine. *See* Maureen *and* Lorraine. CONTEMPORARY EXAMPLE: Mauraine Mitchell, Sodus, New York.

Maureen   A variant form of Mary. From the Irish Mairin, a pet form of Maire. *See* Mary. Akin to Maura.

Mauretania   Derived from Mauritania, a country in West Africa.

Maurine   A variant spelling of Maureen. *See* Maureen.

Mauve   The French form of the Latin *malva*, a plant of the purple-colored mallow family. Maeve is a variant form.

Mavis   From the Old French *mauvis*, meaning "song thrush."

Maxa   The feminine form of Maximilian, meaning "great." *See* Maximilian (masculine section).

Maxima   From the Hebrew, meaning "enchanter, diviner, miracle worker."

Maxime, Maxine   Variant feminine forms of Maximilian. *See* Maximilian (masculine section).

May   A pet form of Mary and Margaret. *See* Mary *and* Margaret. Also, from the Old English, meaning "a flower" (daisy). Mae is a variant spelling. PLACE-NAME USAGE: Maywood, Nebraska, named for a local girl, May Wood; Maytown, Pennsylvania.

Maya   A variant spelling of Maia. *See* Maia. CONTEMPORARY EXAMPLE: Maya Angelou, author.

Mayan   A language spoken by Central American Indians. CONTEMPORARY EXAMPLE: Mayan Wilcox, publicist.

Maybelle   A name invented by combining May and Belle. *See* May *and* Belle. CONTEMPORARY EXAMPLE: Maybelle Carter, country singer. PLACE-NAME USAGE: Maybell, Colorado, named for May Bell, wife of a local rancher.

Mayleiday   An invented name. Derived from Hawaiian May Day (May 1), when everyone wears a fragrant flower *lei*. Mili is a pet form. CONTEMPORARY EXAMPLE: Mayleiday van Ostrand, Kailua, Hawaii.

Mayo   Derived from the county in northwestern Ireland. CONTEMPO-

RARY EXAMPLE: Mayo Loiseau Gray, author. SURNAME USAGE: Charles Horace Mayo, physician.

Mayphine   Origin unknown. CONTEMPORARY EXAMPLE: Mayphine van Zant, dancer.

Mazal   From the Hebrew, meaning "a star."

Mazana   An invented name. A modification of the word "amazing." Also, from the Old French *masere,* meaning "maple wood."

Mea   A variant form of Mia. *See* Mia. Used also as a masculine form. CONTEMPORARY EXAMPLE: Mea Allan, journalist.

Meave   A variant Irish form of Mavis. *See* Mavis.

Meg   A pet form of Margaret. *See* Margaret.

Megan   A variant form of Margiad, the Welsh form of Margaret. *See* Margaret. CONTEMPORARY EXAMPLE: Megan Marshack, journalist.

Mehalia   A variant spelling of Mahalia. *See* Mahalia.

Mehira   From the Hebrew *mahir,* meaning "speedy, energetic."

Mei   The Hawaiian form of May. *See* May.

Meira   From the Hebrew *ohr,* meaning "light." Meir is a masculine form.

Melane   A name invented by combining the masculine Mel and a form of the feminine Annis. CONTEMPORARY EXAMPLE: Melane Zoe Grayson, Culver City, California.

Melanie   From the Greek *melas,* meaning "black, dark in appearance." In Greek mythology, Melania was the earth goddess. St. Melania the Elder and St. Melania the Younger were grandmother and granddaughter Roman ladies devoted to St. Jerome. PET FORMS: Mel, Melly. PLACE-NAME USAGE: The Melanesia Islands of the Pacific.

Melantha   A variant form of Melanie. *See* Melanie.

Melba   A variant spelling of Melva. *See* Melva. CONTEMPORARY EXAMPLE: Melba Moore, singer.

Mele   The Hawaiian form of Mary. *See* Mary.

Melesina   A pet form of Millicent. *See* Millicent.

Melevine   A feminine form of Melvin. *See* Melvin (masculine section). VARIANT FORMS: Melva, Melvina.

Melicent   A variant form of Millicent. *See* Millicent.

Melina   From the Greek *melos,* meaning "a song." Melody is a variant form. CONTEMPORARY EXAMPLE: Melina Mercouri, actress.

Melinda   A variant spelling of Malinda. *See* Malinda. CONTEMPORARY EXAMPLE: Melinda Kemp, teacher; Melinda Dillon, actress.

Melissa From the Greek, meaning "a bee," derived from *meli*, meaning "honey." Millicent is a variant form. PET FORMS: Melita, Melleta, Millie, Missie, Lissa, Lisse.

Melita, Melleta Italian pet forms of Melissa. *See* Melissa.

Melloney A variant form of Melanie. *See* Melanie.

Melody, Melodye From the Greek *melos*, meaning "a melody, a song." VARIANT FORMS: Melina, Melosa. CONTEMPORARY EXAMPLE: Melody Childs, Springfield, Illinois.

Melon From the Greek *melopepon*, meaning "an apple-shaped melon."

Melora From the Greek *melon*, meaning "apple," plus *ora*, meaning "gold," hence "golden apple," which is in some languages a reference to an orange. CONTEMPORARY EXAMPLE: Melora Harden.

Melosa From the Greek *melos*, meaning "melody." VARIANT FORMS: Melina, Melody.

Meltha An invented name. The name of a character in a novel by Mary J. Holmes. CONTEMPORARY EXAMPLE: Meltha E. Higgins, Yale, Michigan.

Melva A feminine form of Melvin. *See* Melvin (masculine section).

Melveen A feminine form of Melvin. *See* Melvin (masculine section).

Melvene A feminine form of Melvin. *See* Melvin (masculine section). CONTEMPORARY EXAMPLE: Melvene Wilson, Glen St. Mary, Florida.

Melvina A feminine form of Melvin. *See* Melvin (masculine section). VARIANT FORMS: Melva, Melevine.

Menora, Menorah From the Hebrew, meaning "a candelabrum." A modern Israeli name.

Mercedes "A variant form of Mercy." *See* Mercy. Used also as a masculine name. CONTEMPORARY EXAMPLE: Mercedes M. Bowen, San Jose, California.

Mercia A variant form of Mercy. *See* Mercy. CONTEMPORARY EXAMPLE: Mercia Tinker, Pawling, New York. PLACE-NAME USAGE: a former Anglo-Saxon kingdom in England.

Mercille A French form of Mercy. *See* Mercy. CONTEMPORARY EXAMPLE: Mercille Gray Williams, author.

Mercy From the Latin *merces*, meaning "reward, payment," and in Late Latin "pity, favor." Adopted as a Christian name in the seventeenth century along with Faith, Hope, and Charity.

Meredith From the Welsh *mor*, meaning "sea," hence "protector of the sea." Used also as a masculine name. CONTEMPORARY EXAMPLES: Meredith MacRae, singer; Meredith Baxter Birney, actress.

Meri   From the Hebrew, meaning "rebellious."

Merie   A variant spelling of Merrie. *See* Merrie. CONTEMPORARY EX-AMPLE: Merie Earle, actress.

Meris   A variant spelling of Maris. *See* Maris.

Merit, Merritt   From the Latin *meritus*, meaning "deserve, having value."

Merla   A variant form of Merle. *See* Merle. CONTEMPORARY EXAMPLE: Merla Zellerbach, San Francisco, California.

Merle   From the Latin and French, meaning "a bird" (blackbird). CONTEMPORARY EXAMPLE: Merle Park, ballet dancer.

Merlin   From the Old High German *smirl*, meaning "a falcon." PLACE-NAME USAGE: Merlin, Oregon.

Merlon   From the Italian *merlo*, meaning "a battlement, a parapet."

Merloyd   Origin uncertain. Probably an invented name. CONTEMPORARY EXAMPLE: Merloyd L. Lawrence, editor.

Mernie   A name invented by combining forms of Marion and Marie. *See* Marion *and* Marie. CONTEMPORARY EXAMPLE: Mernie Bochoff, Sandpoint, Idaho.

Merridee   A name invented by combining Merri and Dee. *See* Merri *and* Dee. CONTEMPORARY EXAMPLE: Merridee Jo Lee, Nacaville, California.

Merrie, Merrielle   From the Anglo-Saxon, meaning "joyous, pleasant." Merry is a variant spelling.

Merril, Merrill   Variant spellings of Meryl. *See* Meryl. CONTEMPORARY EXAMPLE: Merrill Ashley, ballerina.

Merris   A variant form of Merrie. *See* Merrie.

Merrita   A pet form of Merrie. *See* Merrie. CONTEMPORARY EXAMPLE: Merrita Jackson, Huntsville, Alabama.

Merry   From the Anglo-Saxon, meaning "joyous, pleasant." Merrie is a variant spelling. PLACE-NAME USAGE: Merry Point, Virginia, named for Thomas Merry; Merry Oaks, North Carolina.

Merryl   A variant spelling of Meryl. *See* Meryl.

Merta   A variant form of Marta (Martha). *See* Martha. CONTEMPORARY EXAMPLE: Merta Cota, Bend, Oregon.

Meryl, Meryle   Variant forms of Muriel or Merle. *See* Muriel *and* Merle. CONTEMPORARY EXAMPLE: Meryl Streep, actress; Meryle Secrest, author.

Meta   A pet form of Margaret used in the nineteenth century. *See*

Margaret. CONTEMPORARY EXAMPLE: Meta Rosenberg, television producer.

Metuka   From the Hebrew *matok*, meaning "sweet."

Mia   A short form of the Hebrew name Michaela, meaning "Who is like God?" Akin to Michal. CONTEMPORARY EXAMPLE: Mia Farrow, actress.

Mica   A short form of Michal. *See* Michal.

Michael   Although basically a masculine name, it is used occasionally for women. *See* Michael (masculine section). CONTEMPORARY EXAMPLE: Michael Learned, actress.

Michaela   The feminine form of Michael, meaning "Who is like God?" *See* Michael (masculine section). CONTEMPORARY EXAMPLE: Michaela Hamilton, editor.

Michaelann   A hybrid name of Michael and Ann. *See* Michael *and* Ann.

Michal   A contracted form of the masculine Michael. From the Hebrew, meaning "Who is like God?" In the Bible, the daughter of King Saul; the wife of King David. *See also* Michael (masculine section). Mica is a pet form.

Michel, Michele, Michelle   French forms of Michal. *See* Michal. VARIANT FORMS: Micheline, Mikelina (Russian); Miguella (Portuguese).

Michona   A name invented by combining the names of two states: Michigan and Arizona. CONTEMPORARY EXAMPLE: Michona E. Hummel, Phoenix, Arizona.

Mickey   A pet form of Michal. *See* Michal.

Midgard   From the Norse, meaning "mid-yard, mid-point." Midge is a variant form. In Norse mythology, the earth was a "mid-point yard" between heaven and hell.

Midge   A variant form of Madge. *See* Madge. Also a form of Midgard. CONTEMPORARY EXAMPLE: Midge Constanza, political activist.

Miette   From the French, meaning "small sweet things." CONTEMPORARY EXAMPLE: Miette Linnea Jeannette, Mission Viejo, California. PLACE-NAME USAGE: a rock strata in Canada.

Migdala   From the Hebrew, meaning "fortress, tower." Magdalene is a variant form. *See* Magdalene. In the Bible, a town on the Sea of Galilee. Also called Magdala.

Migdana   From the Hebrew, meaning "gift."

Mignon   From the Old French *mignot*, meaning "delicate, graceful, petite." CONTEMPORARY EXAMPLE: Mignon Warner, novelist.

Mil   A pet form of Mildred. *See* Mildred.

Mila, Milah   Variant forms of Milan. *See* Milan. CONTEMPORARY EX-AMPLE: Milah Faith Lynn, Santa Ana, California.

Milan   From the Italian *milano*, meaning "a fine type of straw from Milan," from which hats are made. PLACE-NAME USAGE: a city in Italy.

Milda   From the Middle English *milde*, meaning "mild." Akin to Milena.

Mildred   From the Old English *milde*, meaning "mild," plus *thryth*, meaning "power, strength." PET FORMS: Mil, Millie, Milly.

Milena   From the Old High German *milo*, meaning "mild, peaceful." Akin to Milda. CONTEMPORARY EXAMPLE: Milena Lukesove, author.

Mili   A modern Israeli name compounded of *mi* and *li*, meaning "Who is for me?" Also, a variant spelling of Millie, the pet form of Millicent and Mildred. *See* Millicent *and* Mildred.

Miliama   The Hawaiian form of Miriam. *See* Miriam.

Millicent   From the Old French name Melisent and the Old High German name Amalswind, a form of *amal*, meaning "work," and *swind*, meaning "strong." Melisande was a popular tenth-century French form. PET FORMS: Mandy, Millie, Milly, Molly. CONTEMPORARY EXAMPLE: Millicent Martin, singer-actress.

Millie, Milly   Pet forms of Millicent and Mildred. *See* Millicent and Mildred.

Mim, Mimi   Pet forms of Miriam. *See* Miriam. CONTEMPORARY EX-AMPLE: Mim Dixon, author.

Mina   A pet form of Wilhelmina. *See* Wilhelmina. PLACE-NAME USAGE: Mina, South Dakota, named for Mina Earling, daughter of the railroad president.

Mindy   A pet form of Melinda and Mildred. *See* Melinda *and* Mildred.

Minerva   The Roman goddess of wisdom. Akin to Athena in Greek mythology. Minerva sprang fully armed from the head of Zeus. PLACE-NAME USAGE: Minerva, Ohio, named for Minerva Whiteacre, daughter of one of the town's founders.

Minette   A French pet form of Mary. *See* Mary.

Minna   A pet form of Wilhelmina. *See* Wilhelmina.

Minnie   A pet form of Miriam. *See* Miriam. Also, from the Scottish, meaning "mother." CONTEMPORARY EXAMPLE: Minnie Pearl, enter-tainer.

Mira   A short form of Miriam and Miranda. *See* Miriam *and* Miranda. CONTEMPORARY EXAMPLE: Mira Schackne, editor.

Mirabel, Mirabell, Mirabella, Mirabelle   From the Latin, meaning "of great beauty." Also from the Latin *mirabilis*, meaning "wonderful, glorious." Marabel is a variant English form.

Miranda   From the Latin *mirandus*, meaning "strange, wonderful." Probably an invention of Shakespeare for the heroine of *The Tempest*. CONTEMPORARY EXAMPLE: Miranda Seymour, author.

Mirella   A short form of Mirabella. *See* Mirabella. CONTEMPORARY EXAMPLE: Mirella Freni, opera singer.

Miri, Mirit   Pet forms of Miriam used in Israel. *See* Miriam.

Miriam   From the Hebrew *mar yam*, meaning "sea of bitterness, sorrow." Or, from the Chaldaic, meaning "mistress of the sea." In the Bible, the sister of Moses and Aaron. Mary is the English form.

Mirjana   A Slavonic pet form of Miriam. *See* Miriam. CONTEMPORARY EXAMPLE: Mirjana Vujnovich, indexer.

Mirra   A variant spelling of Mira. *See* Mira. CONTEMPORARY EXAMPLE: Mirra Ginsburg, author.

Misalyn   A name invented by combining Missy and Alyn. *See* Missy *and* Alyn. CONTEMPORARY EXAMPLE: Misalyn Young, San Diego, California.

Missie   A modern American name, meaning "young girl."

Misty   From the Old English *mistig*, meaning "obscure, covered with mist."

Mittie   A pet form of Margaret. *See* Margaret. CONTEMPORARY EXAMPLE: Mittie Lawrence, actress.

Mitzi   A pet form of Mary. *See* Mary. CONTEMPORARY EXAMPLE: Mitzi Gaynor, actress.

Mitzpa, Mitzpah   From the Hebrew, meaning "a tower" or "observation post."

Mizpa, Mizpah   Variant spellings of Mitzpa. *See* Mitzpa.

Mo   A pet form of Maureen. *See* Maureen.

Moana   From the Hawaiian, meaning "ocean, open sea."

Modesta, Modeste, Modestine   From the Latin *modestus*, meaning "shy, modest." PET FORMS: Desta, Deste.

Mog   A pet form of Margaret. *See* Margaret.

Moina   From the Celtic, meaning "gentle, soft."

Moira, Moirae   In Greek mythology, the goddess of destiny and fate. Also, variant forms of Maire, the Irish form of Mary. *See* Mary. CONTEMPORARY EXAMPLE: Moira Timms, author.

Mollie, Molly, Mollye   Pet forms of Miriam and Mary. *See* Miriam *and* Mary. Also, pet forms of Millicent. *See* Millicent.

Momi   From the Hawaiian, meaning "pearl."

Mona   From the Irish *muadhnait*, meaning "noble." Also, a variant form of Monday. *See* Monday.

Monday   From the Old English *monandaeg*, meaning "moon's day." Used in the Middle Ages for children born on a Monday. VARIANT FORMS: Mona, Mundy.

Monete   A French pet form of Monday. *See* Monday.

Monette   A French pet form of Monday. *See* Monday.

Monica   A variant form of Mona. *See* Mona. St. Monica was the mother of St. Augustine. CONTEMPORARY EXAMPLE: Monica Dickens, author.

Moniece   An invented name designed to sound like Denise, but to begin with an "m" so as to match the names of the other members of the family. CONTEMPORARY EXAMPLE: Moniece Charlton Smiley, Sunnyvale, California.

Monique   A French form of Monica. *See* Monica. CONTEMPORARY EXAMPLE: Monique van Vooren, actress.

Monna   A variant spelling of Mona. *See* Mona.

Montina   From the Latin, meaning "of the mountain."

Morasha   From the Hebrew, meaning "inheritance."

Morgan   From the Welsh, meaning "sea dweller." Most often used as a masculine name. Very popular as a surname.

Moria   A variant spelling of Moriah. *See* Moriah. Also, a variant of Maura. *See* Maura.

Moriah, Moriel   From the Hebrew, meaning "God is my teacher." In the Bible, Moriah is the mountain where Abraham prepared to sacrifice his son, Isaac. CONTEMPORARY EXAMPLE: Moriah Blum, wife of Israeli ambassador to the U.N.

Morine   A variant spelling of Maureen. *See* Maureen. CONTEMPORARY EXAMPLE: Morine Krissdottier, author.

Morit   From the Hebrew, meaning "teacher."

Morna   From the Middle English *morne*, a form of the German *morgen*, meaning "morning." Also, from the Celtic and Gaelic *muirne*, meaning "gentle, beloved." Myrna is a variant form.

Morrell   Probably a variant form of Merril. *See* Merril. CONTEMPORARY EXAMPLE: Morrell Gipson, editor.

Morrigan   A variant spelling of Morgan. *See* Morgan.

Morrisa   The feminine form of Morris. *See* Morris (masculine section).

Morrow   From the Old English and German *morgen*, meaning "morning." Akin to Morna. CONTEMPORARY EXAMPLE: Morrow Coffey Graham, mother of evangelist Billy Graham. SURNAME USAGE: Karen Morrow, actress.

Morwenna   A variant Cornish form of Maureen. *See* Maureen. Also, from the Welsh, meaning "wave of the sea."

Moyna   From the Celtic, meaning "gentle, soft."

Moyra   A variant spelling of Moira. *See* Moira. CONTEMPORARY EXAMPLE: Moyra Caldecott, author.

Murial   A variant form of Muriel. CONTEMPORARY EXAMPLE: Murial Breckenridge, author.

Muriel   From the Irish *muir*, meaning "sea," plus *geal*, meaning "bright." VARIANT FORMS: Meriel, Miriel, Murial. SURNAME USAGE: Merrill, Murrel.

Murle   A variant spelling of Merle. *See* Merle. CONTEMPORARY EXAMPLE: Murle Lindstrom, golfer.

Musette   From the Old French *muser*, meaning "to play music." CONTEMPORARY EXAMPLE: Mercedes Musette Bowen, San Jose, California.

Myra   A variant form of the Irish name Moira. *See* Moira. PLACE-NAME USAGE: a seaport in ancient Lycia, in Asia Minor.

Myrna   From the Greek and Arabic, meaning "myrrh," hence the connotation of bitter and sorrowful. Also, a variant form of Miranda and Morna. *See* Miranda *and* Morna.

Myrtilla   From the Middle Latin *myrtillus*, meaning "a myrtle." *See* Myrtle.

Myrtle   From the Greek *myrtos*, meaning "tree, shrub." The myrtle tree was the symbol of victory. PLACE-NAME USAGE: Myrtle Creek, Oregon.

N

Naama, Naamah   From the Hebrew, meaning "pleasant, beautiful."
CONTEMPORARY EXAMPLE: Naama Kitov, artist.

Naamana   From the Hebrew, meaning "pleasant."

Naamit   The Hebrew name of an ostrich-like bird.

Naava   From the Hebrew, meaning "beautiful, pleasant." Nava is a
variant spelling.

Nada, Nadia   From the Slavic, meaning "hope," or from the Spanish,
meaning "nothing." VARIANT FORMS: Nadie, Nadine. CONTEMPORARY
EXAMPLE: Nadia Comaneci, Olympic gymnast champion. PLACE-NAME
USAGE: Nada, Texas.

Nadie   A variant form of Nada. *See* Nada. CONTEMPORARY EXAMPLE:
Nadie T. Kaufman, Tustin, California.

Nadine   A French form of the Russian *nadezhda*, meaning "hope."
Akin to Nada and Nadia.

Nado   A variant form of Nadine. *See* Nadine. CONTEMPORARY EXAM-
PLE: Nado Beth Glick, editor.

Nagida   From the Hebrew, meaning "a member of the nobility."

Naia, Naiad   From the Greek *naein*, meaning "to flow." In Greek
and Roman mythology, Naiad was one of the nymphs giving life to
and nourishing springs, rivers, and lakes. VARIANT FORMS: Naida,
Naiia. CONTEMPORARY EXAMPLE: Naia Dawn Wright, Lincolnton,
North Carolina.

Naida   The Russian form of the Greek *naiad*. *See* Naiad. Also, an invented name. Created by combining Nell and Aida. CONTEMPORARY
EXAMPLE: Naida Hearn, Huntington Beach, California.

Naiia   A variant form of Naia. *See* Naia. CONTEMPORARY EXAMPLE:
Naiia Ardsley, editor.

Nairne   From the Scottish, meaning "from the river narrows." PLACE-
NAME USAGE: Nairn County, in northeastern Scotland.

Nalani   From the Hawaiian, meaning "calmness of the heavens."

Nalene   An invented name. A variant form of Nellene. CONTEMPO-
RARY EXAMPLE: Regina Nalene Hill, Mountain City, Indiana; Nalene
Placentino, artist.

Nama   A variant spelling of Naama. *See* Naama. CONTEMPORARY EX-

AMPLE: Nama Frankel, sociologist.

Nan, Nana Pet forms of Nancy, Ann, Anna, and Hannah. *See* Hannah.

Nancy A variant form of Hannah, derived from the Hebrew, meaning "gracious." Or, a pet form of Annis and Agnes. *See* Annis *and* Agnes. PLACE-NAME USAGE: a city in northeastern France.

Nanella A name invented by combining Nancy and Ella. CONTEMPORARY EXAMPLE: Nanella L. Jones, Little Rock, Arkansas,

Nanette A pet form of Anna and Hannah. *See* Anna *and* Hannah.

Nani From the Hawaiian, meaning "glory, splendor."

Nanine A variant pet form of Nanette. *See* Nanette. CONTEMPORARY EXAMPLE: Nanine Valen, author.

Nanna A pet form of Hannah. *See* Hannah.

Naoma A variant form of Naomi. *See* Naomi. PLACE-NAME USAGE: Naoma, West Virginia, named for Naoma Pettry.

Naomi From the Hebrew, meaning "beautiful, pleasant, delightful." In the Bible, the mother-in-law of Ruth, a Moabitess who converted to Judaism.

Napea From the Latin *napus*, meaning "a turnip, turnip–shaped."

Nara From the Celtic, meaning "happy." Also, from the Old English *nar*, meaning "north."

Narcissa, Narcisse From the Greek *narziss*, meaning "self-love." In Greek mythology, a beautiful youth who falls in love with his own reflection in a spring and then changes into a narcissus plant. CONTEMPORARY EXAMPLE: Narcisse Chamberlain, editor.

Narda From the Greek *nardos*, meaning "a spikenard, an Asiatic plant that yields an ointment." CONTEMPORARY EXAMPLE: Narda Onyx, actress.

Nardi A personal name derived from an Italian sports car. Also, an Italian surname. CONTEMPORARY EXAMPLE: Nardi Ferge, Rawlins, New York.

Nasia From the Hebrew *nes*, meaning "miracle," plus *yah*, meaning "God," hence "miracle of the Lord."

Nastasya A Russian form of Anastasia. *See* Anastasia.

Nasya A variant spelling of Nasia. *See* Nasia.

Nata From the Latin *natare*, meaning "to swim." Also, from the Sanskrit, meaning "a dancer."

Natala, Natalia Variant Russian forms of Natalie. *See* Natalie.

Natasha is a pet form. CONTEMPORARY EXAMPLE: Natalia Makarova, Russian ballet dancer.

Natalie   A French and German form of the Latin *natalis*, meaning to be born." A name often given to children born on Christmas Day. VARIANT FORMS: Natalya, Nathalie. CONTEMPORARY EXAMPLE: Natalie Savage, author.

Natalya   A variant form of Natalie. *See* Natalie. CONTEMPORARY EXAMPLE: Natalya Babiak, Boulder, Colorado.

Natania, Nathania   Feminine forms of Nathan. *See* Nathan (masculine section).

Nataniella, Natanielle   Feminine forms of Nathan. *See* Nathan (masculine section). Nathaniella and Nathanielle are variant forms.

Natasha   A Russian pet form of Natalia (Natalie). *See* Natalie. CONTEMPORARY EXAMPLE: Natasha Peters, author.

Nathalie   A variant form of Natalie. *See* Natalie.

Nathaniella, Nathanielle   Feminine forms of Nathan. *See* Nathan (masculine section) *and* Nataniella.

Natividad   From the Latin, meaning "of the Nativity."

Nava, Navit   From the Hebrew, meaning "beautiful, pleasant." CONTEMPORARY EXAMPLE: Nava Arad, Israeli executive.

Nayer   From the Persian, meaning "sunshine." Also, from the Old English *ey*, meaning "water," hence "one who works on water, a sailor."

Neala   An Irish feminine form of Neal. *See* Neal (masculine section).

Nebraska   The Sioux Indian name of the Platte River, meaning "flat water." PLACE-NAME USAGE: a mid-western state admitted to the Union in 1867.

Nebula   From the Latin, meaning "vapor, cloud, mist."

Nechama   From the Hebrew, meaning "comfort." Nehama is a variant spelling. Nahum is the masculine form.

Neda, Nedda   From the British *naid*, meaning "a sanctuary, a retreat." Also, pet forms of Edward. *See* Edward.

Nediva   From the Hebrew, meaning "noble, generous."

Nedra   From the Old English *neothera*, meaning "lower, below the surface of the earth." CONTEMPORARY EXAMPLE: Nedra Volz, actress. PLACE-NAME USAGE: The Netherlands.

Neena   A variant spelling of Nina. *See* Nina.

Neeta   The name of an Indian princess. Possibly from the French *ne* and *naître*, meaning "born, to be born." CONTEMPORARY EXAMPLE: Neeta Webb, Mount Airy, North Carolina.

Negina   From the Hebrew, meaning "song, melody, tune."

Nehama   A variant spelling of Nechama. *See* Nechama.

Nehora   From the Aramaic, meaning "light." Akin to Ora. *See* Ora.

Neigy   A corrupt form of Nicia. *See* Nicia. CONTEMPORARY EXAMPLE: Neigy P. Cupoli, Newton, Massachusetts.

Neila, Neilla   Feminine forms of Neil. *See* Neil (masculine section). Neala is a variant spelling. CONTEMPORARY EXAMPLE: Neila Smith, television producer; Neilla Warren, author.

Nelda   An invented name. Meaning unknown. CONTEMPORARY EXAMPLE: Nelda M. Faust, Fairborn, Ohio.

Nelia   A feminine form of Neil. *See* Neil (masculine section). Or, a variant form of Nell. *See* Nell. CONTEMPORARY EXAMPLE: Nelia P. Salazar, scientist.

Nell, Nella, Nellie   Pet forms of Helen and Eleanor. *See* Helen *and* Eleanor. CONTEMPORARY EXAMPLE: Nella Boshia, illustrator.

Nellene   A variant form of Nell. *See* Nell.

Nellwyn   From the Old English, meaning "friend (*wyn*) of Nell." *See* Nell.

Nelly   A pet form of Eleanor. *See* Eleanor. CONTEMPORARY EXAMPLE: Nelly Sachs, Nobel Prize winner in literature (1966).

Nema   From the Hebrew, meaning "a thread, a hair."

Nena   A variant spelling of Nina. *See* Nina. CONTEMPORARY EXAMPLE: Nena O'Neil, author.

Neola   From the Greek *neos*, meaning "new." PLACE-NAME USAGE: Neola, Oklahoma, named for Neola Schooling, daughter of the first postmaster.

Neoma   Possibly from the Greek *nemos*, meaning "a wooded pasture."

Nerine   From the Greek name Nereid. In Greek mythology, one of fifty sea nymphs, daughters of Neurus, a kindly sea god.

Nerissa   A variant form of Nerita. *See* Nerita.

Nerita   From the Greek *nerites*, meaning "a sea snail." Nerissa is a variant form.

Nerolia   From the Italian *neroli*, named after the Princess of Nerole (seventeenth century), reputed to have discovered an oil (neroli) distilled from orange flowers, used in perfumery.

Nesha   A variant form of Nessa. *See* Nessa. CONTEMPORARY EXAMPLE: Nesha Springer, author.

Nessa   From the Old Norse *nes*, meaning "a promontory, a headland." CONTEMPORARY EXAMPLE: Nessa Rapoport, free-lance writer.

Nessie   A Welsh pet form of Agnes. *See* Agnes.

Nest, Nesta   Welsh pet forms of Agnes. *See* Agnes. Nest was an eleventh-century princess, the mistress of Henry I.

Neta, Netta   From the Hebrew, meaning "a plant, a shrub." Or, pet forms of Antoinette. *See* Antoinette. Also, a Scottish pet form of Janet. *See* Janet.

Netania, Netanya, Nethania   From the Hebrew, meaning "gift of God." Akin to the masculine Nathaniel. VARIANT SPELLINGS: Natania, Nathania.

Netia   A variant form of Neta. *See* Neta.

Nettie, Netty   Pet forms of Antoinette. *See* Antoinette.

Neva   From the Spanish, meaning "snow." Or, from the Old English *niwe*, meaning "new." CONTEMPORARY EXAMPLE: Neva Sly, San Francisco, California.

Nevada   From the Latin *nix*, meaning "snow." The state of Nevada was so named because of its snow–capped mountains.

Nicci   The Italian form of the Latin *nike*, meaning "victory." Akin to the masculine Nicholas. CONTEMPORARY EXAMPLE: Nicci Bertomen, Millerton, New York.

Nichelle   A variant form of Nicci. *See* Nicci. CONTEMPORARY EXAMPLE: Nichelle Nichols, actress.

Nicia   A pet form of Berenice. *See* Berenice. Nicias was a fifth–century B.C. Athenian general.

Nicola   Italian and French feminine forms of Nicholas. *See* Nicholas (masculine section). Akin to Nicole. CONTEMPORARY EXAMPLE: Nicola Pagett, actress.

Nicole, Nicolle, Nicolette   Feminine French forms of Nicholas. *See* Nicholas (masculine section). VARIANT FORMS: Bernice, Berenice, Colette.

Nijole   A Slavic form of Nicole. *See* Nicole.

Nika   A Russian feminine form of Nicholas. *See* Nicholas (masculine section). CONTEMPORARY EXAMPLE: Nika Hazleton, author.

Nila   A name adopted from the river Nile. Nyla is a variant spelling. *See* Nyla.

Nima   A variant spelling of Nema. *See* Nema.

Nina   A French and Russian pet form of Anne (from Nanine). *See* Anne. Also, from the Spanish, meaning "young girl." Also, of Babylonian origin, meaning "goddess of the deep waters." Because her daughter was born on the nineteenth day of the ninth month (September) at nine A.M. in the year 1919, Joyce Pagan, of Gilroy, California, named her daughter Nina.

Ninon, Ninette   French forms of Anne. *See* Anne.

Nira   An invented name adopted from the acronym of National Industrial Recovery Act, which became law in the 1930s. CONTEMPORARY EXAMPLE: Nira Lynn Dolan, Livonia, Michigan.

Nirel   From the Hebrew, meaning either "a cultivated field" or "light of God." Used also as a masculine name.

Nirit   A yellow–flowering annual plant found in Israel.

Nissa   From the Hebrew *nes*, meaning "a sign, an emblem." Also, from the Scandinavian, meaning "an elf."

Nita   A pet form of Anita. *See* Anita. Also, a short form of the Spanish Juanita. *See* Juanita.

Nitza, Nitzana, Nizana   From the Hebrew, meaning the "bud (of a flower)." CONTEMPORARY EXAMPLE: Nitza Hanon, Brooklyn, New York.

Nixie   From the Old High German *nihhus*, meaning "a water sprite." In German mythology, a half–girl and half–fish form. Also, a pet form of Berenice. Used also as a masculine name.

Noel, Noelle   More commonly used as masculine names. From the French, meaning "to be born." Akin to Natalie. *See* Natalie.

Noelani   The name of an Hawaiian princess, meaning "beautiful one from heaven." Akin to Noel. CONTEMPORARY EXAMPLE: Noelani Kay Auwae, Hartselle, Alabama.

Nofia   From the Hebrew, *nof*, meaning "panorama," hence "God's beautiful landscape."

Noga   From the Hebrew, meaning "morning light, shining." Used also as a masculine name.

Nokomis   An American Indian name, meaning "moon daughter."

Nola   From the Celtic, meaning "famous." Nolan and Noland are masculine forms.

Nolina   The Hawaiian form of Noreen. *See* Noreen.

Noma   The Hawaiian form of Norma. *See* Norma.

Nona   From the Laine *nonus*, meaning "the ninth." CONTEMPORARY EXAMPLE: Nona Coxhead, novelist.

Noni, Nonie Variant forms of Nona. *See* Nona. CONTEMPORARY EX-
AMPLE: Noni Caroll Murphy, novelist.

Nophia A variant spelling of Nofia. *See* Nofia.

Nora, Norah Irish pet forms of Honora, Eleanor, and Leonora. *See*
Eleanor. From the Latin, meaning "honor, respect." Noreen is a variant form.

Norberta The feminine form of Norbert. *See* Norbert (masculine
section).

Nordica From the Modern Latin *nordicus*, meaning "a Nordic, one
from the northern lands."

Noreen A variant Irish form of Nora. *See* Nora. CONTEMPORARY EX-
AMPLE: Noreen McNatt, Ashland, California.

Norella The name of Norella J. Scarborough, of Virginia Beach,
Virginia, coined by her mother, from Nora and Ella.

Norene A variant spelling of Noreen. *See* Noreen. CONTEMPORARY
EXAMPLE: Norene Durham, Columbus, Ohio.

Norina A variant form of Noreen. *See* Noreen.

Norine A variant spelling of Noreen. *See* Noreen.

Norma From the Latin, meaning "exact to the pattern; normal,
peaceful." A character in the popular opera *Norma* by Vincenzo
Bellini (1831). Also, the name of a constellation in the Milky Way.

Norna From Norn, in Norse mythology. Any of three goddesses, repre-
senting the past, present, and future.

Nova, Novia From the Latin *nova*, meaning "new." A type of star
that increases and decreases in brightness with the passage of time.

Novenda A name invented to sound like November, the month in
which Novenda Watkins of Newark, Ohio was born.

Noya From the Hebrew, meaning "beautiful, ornamented."

Nubye Probably from the Latin *nubere*, meaning "to veil oneself, to
marry." CONTEMPORARY EXAMPLE: Nubye Fraser Lane, Glendale, Arizona. PLACE-NAME USAGE: Nubian Desert, Sudan.

Numida From Numidia, an ancient kingdom in North Africa, once
part of the province of Rome.

Nunciata From the Latin *nuntius*, meaning "a messenger."

Nureen Possibly from the Hebrew *nur*, meaning "light." Also, a variant form of Noreen. *See* Noreen.

Nurit, Nurita Names of a plant, common in Israel, having red and
yellow flowers. CONTEMPORARY EXAMPLE: Nurit Hirsh, songwriter.

Nydia   From the Latin, meaning "a haven of refuge."

Nyla   A variant spelling of Nila, the name of an ancient Egyptian princess. Also, a variant form of *nyala*, an East African species of antelope. CONTEMPORARY EXAMPLE: Nyla J. Witmore, Acton, Massachusetts.

Nylora   A name created for her daughter by Arolyn Sargent, of Concord, New Hampshire. Nylora is Arolyn spelled backwards. Arolyn is Carolyn without the C.

Nysa, Nyssa   From the Greek, meaning "the goal." PLACE-NAME USAGE: Nyssa, Oregon; Nyssa, Missouri.

Nyx   In Greek mythology, the goddess of light.

O

O'Beda   A short form of Obedience. *See* Obedience.

Obedience   From the Latin, meaning "to obey." Popular among the Puritans in England and America. PET FORMS: Beta, O'Beda.

Obelia   From the Greek *obelos*, meaning "a needle, a pointer."

Obsidian   From the Latin *obsidere*, meaning "a siege, to besiege."

Octavia   From the Latin *octava*, meaning "the eighth." The eighth girl (or child, if a female) in a Roman family was often named Octavia. Octavius is the masculine form. PET FORMS: Tavi, Tavia.

Odeda   From the Hebrew, meaning "strong, courageous." The feminine form of Oded.

Odele   From the Greek, meaning "an ode, a melody." Also, from the Danish *od*, meaning "an otter."

Odelet   A variant form of Odele. *See* Odele.

Odelia   A variant form of Odele. *See* Odele. Also, from the Hebrew, meaning "I will praise God."

Odell   A variant spelling of Odele. *See* Odele.

Odera   From the Hebrew, meaning "plough."

Odessa   From the Greek, meaning "of *The Odyssey*," referring to the ancient Greek epic ascribed to Homer. PLACE-NAME USAGE: a Russian seaport on the Black Sea.

Odetta, Odette   Pet forms of Odele. *See* Odele. Detla is a pet form.

Ofira   A variant spelling of Ophira. *See* Ophira. CONTEMPORARY EXAMPLE: Ofira Navon, wife of Israeli President Yitzhak Navon.

Ofra   From the Hebrew, meaning "a kid, a young goat." PLACE-NAME USAGE: a biblical city of the tribe of Manasseh.

Ohio   An Iroquoian name, meaning "fine (or large) river." PLACE-NAME USAGE: a midwestern U.S. state.

Ola   From the Old Norse, meaning "an ancestor." PLACE-NAME USAGE: Ola, Alabama.

Olga   A Russian name, derived from Old Norse Helga, meaning "holy." Popular in Russia and the Scandinavian countries.

Olinda   Possibly a variant form of Yolanda. *See* Yolanda.

Olive, Olivia   From the Latin *oliva*, meaning "olive, olive tree," the symbol of peace. PET FORMS: Livia, Nola, Nollie, Livy, Olivette, Ollye. Oliver is the masculine form. CONTEMPORARY EXAMPLE: Olivia Newton-John, singer.

Ollye   A pet form of Olive. *See* Olive.

Olympia   From the Greek, meaning "of Olympus," the mountain that was the residence of the gods. CONTEMPORARY EXAMPLE: Olympia Dukakis, actress.

Oma   A Sioux Indian tribal name, meaning "river people." CONTEMPORARY EXAMPLE: Zoe Oma Hunter, Amarillo, Texas. PLACE-NAME USAGE: Omaha, Nebraska.

Omega   From the Greek, meaning "great."

Ona   Probably from the British *oni*, meaning "from the river." Or, a variant form of Oona. *See* Oona. CONTEMPORARY EXAMPLE: Ona Munson, actress.

Oneida   From the Iroquois tribal language, meaning "standing rock." CONTEMPORARY EXAMPLE: Oneida R. Ortiz, educator. PLACE-NAME USAGE: Oneida, Idaho; Oneida, New York.

Onetha   A variant form of Oneida. *See* Oneida. CONTEMPORARY EXAMPLE: Onetha Smith, Alungdon, Virginia.

Oona   An Irish form of the Latin *una*, meaning "one." VARIANT FORMS: Ona, Onnie, Unity. CONTEMPORARY EXAMPLE: Oona O'Neil Chapman, actress.

Opal   From the Sanskrit *upala*, meaning "a jewel."

Ophelia   From the Greek, meaning "to help." Polonius's daughter in Shakespeare's *Hamlet*.

Ophira   From the Hebrew, meaning "gold." Ofira is a variant spelling.

Ora   From the Hebrew, meaning "light." Also, from the Latin *aurum*, meaning "gold, bright yellow." CONTEMPORARY EXAMPLE: Ora Eitan, illustrator.

Orabel   A combination of the Latin and French, meaning "golden beauty." *See* Ora and Bella.

Orah   A variant spelling of Ora. *See* Ora.

Oralee   From the Hebrew, meaning "my light" or "I have light." VARIANT FORMS: Orlee, Orly.

Oralia   From the Latin *ora*, meaning "a margin, a border."

Oretha   A variant form of Aretha. *See* Aretha.

Oria, Oriana   From the Latin *oriens*, meaning "Orient, the East."

CONTEMPORARY EXAMPLES: Oria Douglas-Hamilton, Scottish zoologist; Oriana Fallaci, Italian author.

Oriel   From the Old French *oriol* and the Latin *aurum*, meaning "gold."

Oriente   From the Latin *oriens*, meaning "the direction of the sunrise." CONTEMPORARY EXAMPLE: Oriente Tegla Dunskis, Vandergrift, Pennsylvania.

Oriole   A variant form of Oriel. *See* Oriel. A species of American bird with bright plumage.

Orion   In Greek and Roman mythology, a hunter whom Diana loved, but accidentally killed, and was placed by her in heaven as a constellation. CONTEMPORARY EXAMPLE: Orion Smith Gosnell, Barnwell, South Carolina.

Orit   A variant form of Ora. *See* Ora.

Orlean, Orleans   A French form of the Latin *aurum*, meaning "gold." Orleans, the city in France, was named for the Roman emperor Aurelian. CONTEMPORARY EXAMPLE: Orlean Richards, Magna, Utah.

Orlee   A variant form of Oralee. *See* Oralee.

Orlena, Orlene   Variant spellings of Orlean. *See* Orlean.

Orli   From the Hebrew, meaning "light is mine."

Orlit   From the Hebrew, meaning "light."

Orly   A variant form of Oralee and Orlean. *See* Oralee *and* Orlean.

Orma   A pet form of Ormanda. *See* Ormanda. CONTEMPORARY EXAMPLE: Orma Jane Weil, Dallas, Texas.

Ormanda   A variant feminine form of Armand. *See* Armand (masculine section). CONTEMPORARY EXAMPLE: Ormanda Brun, actress.

Orna   From the Hebrew *or*, meaning "let there be light," or *oren*, meaning "a cedar tree."

Ornette   A pet form of Orna. *See* Orna. CONTEMPORARY EXAMPLE: Ornette Coleman, musician.

Ornit   From the Hebrew, meaning "a cedar tree." Orna is a variant form.

Orpah   From the Hebrew, meaning "to flee, to turn one's back." In the Bible, a Moabite woman.

Osma   From the Old English *os*, meaning "hero," plus *mund*, meaning "protection." A variant form of the masculine Osmund. CONTEMPORARY EXAMPLE: Osma Foster, Hollywood, Florida.

Ottalie, Ottilie   Variant Swedish forms of Otto. *See* Otto (masculine section). CONTEMPORARY EXAMPLE: Ottalie Foster, Lake Montezuma, Arizona.

Ottilia   A variant form of Odele. *See* Odele. Detta is a pet form.

Ova   From the Latin *ovum*, meaning "egg." CONTEMPORARY EXAMPLE: Ova Lee Jordan, Long Beach, California.

Ozma   Adapted from the name of the little fairy princess of the Land of Oz. Also, a variant spelling of Osma. *See* Osma. CONTEMPORARY EXAMPLE: Ozma Maloy, Bakersfield, California.

Ozora   Probably a variant form of Azora. *See* Azora.

P

Page   From the Italian *paggio*, meaning "a boy attendant." CONTEM-
PORARY EXAMPLE: Page Cuddy, publisher. SURNAME USAGE: Geraldine
Page, actress.

Pallas   From the Greek name Pallas, meaning "goddess." In Greek
mythology, a name for Athena, the goddess of wisdom.

Palma   From the Latin, meaning "a palm tree," so named because its
leaves resemble the palm of the hand. CONTEMPORARY EXAMPLE: Palma
Harcourt, author. PLACE-NAME USAGE: a seaport on Majorca; Palma
Sola, Florida.

Palmeda   A variant form of Palma. *See* Palma.

Palmer   A variant form of Palma. *See* Palma. The name of the hero-
ine in the movie *The Champion*. Polly is a pet form. CONTEMPORARY
EXAMPLE: Palmer A. Schneider, Evart, Michigan. SURNAME USAGE:
Betsy Palmer, actress.

Palmira, Palmyra   A variant form of Palma. *See* Palma. PLACE-
NAME USAGE: an ancient Syrian city, now a village in Syria; Palmstown,
Pennsylvania.

Paloma   From the Spanish and Latin, meaning "dove." CONTEMPO-
RARY EXAMPLE: Paloma Picasso, costume designer. PLACE-NAME USAGE:
Palomas Canyon, California.

Pama   An invented name. CONTEMPORARY EXAMPLE: Pama Lynn
Tavernier, San Diego, California.

Pamela   A name coined by Sir Philip Sidney for a character in his novel
Arcadi (1590). Also, possibly a variant form of Palma. *See* Palma.

Pamelia   A variant form of Pamela. *See* Pamela. PLACE-NAME USAGE:
Pamelia, New York, named for the wife of the founder, General Jacob
Brown, hero of the War of 1812.

Pamelyn   A name invented by combining Pamela and Lyn. *See* Pamela *and* Lyn. CONTEMPORARY EXAMPLE: Pamelyn Ferdin, actress.

Pandora   From the Greek *pan*, meaning "all, totally," plus *doron*,
meaning "gift," hence "very gifted." In Greek mythology, Pandora was
the first woman who, out of curiosity, opened a sealed box and permit-
ted human ills to escape into the world. PLACE-NAME USAGE: Pandora
Reef, Washington.

Panfila, Panphila   From the Greek, meaning "loved by all."

Pansy   From the French *penser*, meaning "to think." Shakespeare uses the phrase "pansies for thought." Also, a small garden plant of the violet family. PLACE-NAME USAGE: Pansy Mountain, Oregon.

Parilee   Probably a variant form of Parrilla, a Spanish family name. CONTEMPORARY EXAMPLE: Parilee Elaine Brinkerhoff, Gainesville, Florida.

Paris, Parris   A variant spelling of Paris, the capital of France. In Greek legend, a son of Priam, king of Troy. CONTEMPORARY EXAMPLE: Parris Afton Bonds, author. PLACE-NAME USAGE: Paris, Oregon, named for G.G. Parris, the first postmaster.

Pascha   From the Greek, derived form the Hebrew *pesach*, meaning "the paschal lamb" and "to pass over."

Pashell   Probably a variant form of Pascha. *See* Pascha.

Pat   A pet form of Patricia. *See* Patricia.

Patch   An Old English form of Peter. *See* Peter (masculine section). CONTEMPORARY EXAMPLE: Patch Mackenzie, actress.

Patia   A variant form of Patricia. *See* Patricia. Or, a variant form of Patience. *See* Patience. CONTEMPORARY EXAMPLE: Patia Waggoner, Indianapolis, Indiana.

Patience   From the Latin *pati*, meaning "to suffer." CONTEMPORARY EXAMPLE: Patience Gatling, U.S. city mayor.

Patrice   A variant form of Patricia. *See* Patricia. CONTEMPORARY EXAMPLE: Patrice Munsel, opera singer.

Patricia   From the Latin *patricius*, meaning "a patrician" or "one of noble descent." Patrick is the masculine form. PET FORMS: Pat, Patsy, Pattie, Patty.

Patsy   A pet form of Patricia. *See* Patricia. CONTEMPORARY EXAMPLE: Patsy Kelly, actress.

Patti, Patty   Pet forms of Patricia. *See* Patricia. CONTEMPORARY EXAMPLE: Patti Page, entertainer.

Paula   From the Latin *paulus*, meaning "small." Paul is the masculine form. PET FORMS: Paulette, Pauline.

Paulette   A pet form of Paula. Popular in France. *See* Paula.

Paulina, Pauline   Paulina is the Spanish form of the French Pauline. Both are pet forms of Paula. *See* Paula. PLACE-NAME USAGE: cities in Oregon and Louisiana.

Paz, Pazia, Pazit   From the Hebrew *paz*, meaning "gold." Paz is also used as a masculine name.

Peale   From the Latin *pax*, meaning "peace."

Pearl   From the Middle English *perle*, meaning "pearl." Used as a pet form for Margaret, the Greek form of Pearl.

Pearlie   A pet form of Pearl. *See* Pearl.

Pearliemae   A name invented by combining Pearlie and Mae. *See* Pearlie *and* Mae. CONTEMPORARY EXAMPLE: Pearliemae, actress Pearl Bailey's pet name.

Peg, Peggie, Peggy   Pet forms of Margaret and Pearl. *See* Margaret *and* Pearl.

Pegi   A variant spelling of Peggy. *See* Peggy.

Pegeen   An Irish form of Peggy. *See* Peggy. CONTEMPORARY EXAMPLE: Pegeen Fitzgerald, radio hostess.

Peig   An Irish form of Peg, a pet form of Margaret. *See* Margaret. CONTEMPORARY EXAMPLE: Peig Sayers, author.

Pelagia   From the Greek *pelagos*, meaning "the sea." Pelagia is the feminine form of Pelagious, a fourth–century British monk.

Penelope   From the Greek, meaning "a worker in cloth, a weaver" or "silent worker." The wife of Ulysses, who waited loyally for his return from war. PET FORMS: Penney, Pennie, Penny. CONTEMPORARY EXAMPLE: Penelope Milford, actress.

Penina, Peninah, Peninit   From the Hebrew, meaning "coral, pearl." Penny is a pet form. CONTEMPORARY EXAMPLE: Peninah Petruck, photographer.

Penney, Pennie   Pet forms of Penelope. *See* Penelope.

Pennoky   A name invented by using letters from Pennsylvania, Ohio, and Kentucky Railroad. CONTEMPORARY EXAMPLE: Pennoky E. Wood, Columbus, Ohio.

Penny   A pet form of Penelope. *See* Penelope. CONTEMPORARY EXAMPLE: Penny Stallings, author. PLACE-NAME USAGE: Penny Pot, New Jersey.

Penthea   From the Greek *penta*, meaning "the fifth." Often given to the fifth child in a family.

Peony   From the Greek Paion, an epithet of Apollo, physician of the gods. A flower of the buttercup family with medicinal properties.

Pepita   A Spanish pet form of Josephine. *See* Josephine.

Pepper   From the Latin *piper*, meaning "a condiment derived from a plant." Used also as a masculine name. CONTEMPORARY EXAMPLE: Pepper Ann Salter, Pope Air Force Base, North Carolina. PLACE-NAME USAGE: Pepper, Texas, a creek named for W.W. Pepper, local landowner.

Peppy   A variant form of Pepita. *See* Pepita.

Perdita   From the Latin *perditus*, meaning "lost." Invented by Shakespeare for his heroine in *A Winter's Tale*.

Perfecta   A Spanish form of the Latin *perfectus*, meaning "perfect."

Perla   A variant form of Pearl. *See* Pearl. CONTEMPORARY EXAMPLE: Perla Meyers, author.

Perle   A variant spelling of Pearl. *See* Pearl. CONTEMPORARY EXAMPLE: Perle Mesta, socialite.

Perpetua   From the Latin *perpetualis*, meaning "constant, everlasting." PLACE-NAME USAGE: Cape Perpetua, named for St. Perpetua (1778) by Captain James Cook.

Perri, Perry   Variant pet forms of Perrin. *See* Perrin.

Perrin, Perrine   Variant forms of the masculine Peter. *See* Peter (masculine section). CONTEMPORARY EXAMPLE: Perrin Paige Hays, Norfolk, Virginia. SURNAME USAGE: Valerie Perrine, actress.

Perryn   A variant spelling of Perrin. *See* Perrin.

Persephone   From the Greek, meaning "the prosperous one." In Greek mythology, the daughter of Zeus.

Persia   Probably from the Assyrian, meaning "to divide, to hinder." PLACE-NAME USAGE: the Asian country now called Iran; Persian Creek, California, named for John Persian, an early rancher.

Persis   From the Greek, meaning "of Persia" or "Persian woman." *See* Persia.

Pert   From the Latin *apertus*, meaning "open, bold, impudent." Also, a variant form of Perth, a city in Scotland.

Peta   From the Hebrew and Arabic, meaning "bread." Also, a pet form of Petra. *See* Petra.

Petie   A feminine form of Peter. *See* Peter. Petty is a variant spelling. CONTEMPORARY EXAMPLE: Petie Walters, Winston–Salem, North Carolina.

Petite   From the French, meaning "small." Petit is the masculine form. CONTEMPORARY EXAMPLE: Petite J. Proutsos, Sparks, Nevada.

Petra   From the Greek, meaning "a rock." Peter is the masculine form. CONTEMPORARY EXAMPLE: Petra Perk, Goldwater, Michigan; Petra Leigh, author. PLACE-NAME USAGE: an ancient city in Jordan.

Petrina   A Russian form of the Greek Petra. *See* Petra.

Petronella, Petronilla   A variant form of Petra. *See* Petra.

Petty   A variant spelling of Petie. *See* Petie. PLACE-NAME USAGE: Petty, Texas, named for J.M. Petty, an early settler.

Petula   From the Latin, meaning "impatient." CONTEMPORARY EXAMPLE: Petula Clark, singer.

Petunia   From the French *petun*, referring to plants of the nightshade variety, with flowers of various colors and patterns.

Phe   A pet form of Phemia. *See* Phemia.

Phebe   A variant spelling of Phoebe. *See* Phoebe.

Phedre   From the Greek, meaning "the shining one." A variant form of Phaedra, daughter of Minos, in Greek mythology.

Phemia   From the Greek *pheme*, meaning "voice, speech." Phe is a pet form.

Phemie   A pet form of Euphemia. *See* Euphemia *and* Phemia.

Phenice   An Egyptian form of Phoenix, the beautiful bird in Egyptian mythology that was able to revive itself from its own ashes. Symbol of immortality.

Phila   From the Greek, meaning "love." CONTEMPORARY EXAMPLE: Phila Chackerian, Downey, California.

Philadelphia   From the Greek, meaning "brotherly love." Phila is a short form. *See* Phila. A favorite Puritan name. The settlers in Philadelphia named the first girl born to each family Philadelphia, meaning "lover of people (brethren)." Used also as a masculine name. PLACE-NAME USAGE: Philadelphia, Pennsylvania.

Philana   From the Greek, meaning "lover of mankind."

Philantha   From the Greek, meaning "lover of flowers."

Philberta   From the Greek *philos*, meaning "loving" and the Anglo-Saxon *beorht*, meaning "bright."

Philena   From the Greek, meaning "lover of mankind." CONTEMPORARY EXAMPLE: Philena Trompeter, Lakeside, California.

Philina   From the Greek, meaning "lover of mankind."

Philippa   From the Greek, meaning "lover of horses." Philip is the masculine form. VARIANT FORMS: Philippine (French); Felipa (Portuguese); Pine (Dutch); Flippa, Pippa (Italian). CONTEMPORARY EXAMPLE: Philippa Carr, author.

Phillina   A variant spelling of Philina. *See* Philina.

Phillippa   A variant spelling of Philippa. *See* Philippa.

Philomela   From the Greek *philein*, meaning "to love," and *melos*, meaning "song." In Greek mythology, a princess of Athens changed by the gods into a nightingale.

Philopena   A feminine form of the German name Philippchan, meaning "little Philip." *See* Philip (masculine section).

Philyra   From the Greek *philein*, meaning "to love," and *lyra*, "the lyre," hence "musical."

Phoebe   From the Greek, meaning "bright, shining one." In Greek mythology, the moon goddess. Akin to Diana in Roman mythology. Phebe is a variant spelling.

Phyl   A pet form of Phyllis. *See* Phyllis.

Phylliss   A variant spelling of Phyllis. *See* Phyllis.

Phyllie   A pet form of Phyllis. *See* Phyllis.

Phyliss   A variant spelling of Phyllis. *See* Phyllis.

Phyllis   From the Greek *phyllon*, meaning "a leaf." The name of a country girl in Virgil's *Eclogues*. VARIANT SPELLINGS: Philis, Phillis, Phylis, Phyliss. PET FORMS: Phyl, Phyllie.

Pia   From the Latin, meaning "pious." Also, an invented name created by combining the initials of names of the parents of news reporter Pia Lindstrom: *P*eter *A*aron Lindstrom and *I*ngrid Bergman. PLACE-NAME USAGE: Pia Oik, Arizona.

Pier   Probably a feminine form of Pierre, the French form of Peter. *See* Peter (masculine section). CONTEMPORARY EXAMPLE: Pier Angeli, actress.

Pilar   From the Latin *pilare*, meaning "a pillar, a column." Also, from the Spanish, meaning "a water basin." Used as an appellation for the Virgin Mary. CONTEMPORARY EXAMPLE: Pilar Lorengar, opera singer. PLACE-NAME USAGE: Pilares, Texas.

Pippa   An Italian pet form of Philippa. *See* Philippa.

Piuta   From the Greek and Hebrew, meaning "poetry."

Placida, Placidia   From the Latin *placidus*, meaning "to please, to placate."

Pleasance, Pleasant   From the Middle French *plaisant*, meaning "agreeable, delightful." Pleasant is occasionally used as a masculine name.

Plennie   From the Latin *plenus*, meaning "full, complete." CONTEMPORARY EXAMPLE: Plennie Elizabeth Hefner, Cattawba, North Carolina.

Pocahantas, Pocahontas   Origin unknown. An American Indian princess reputed to have saved Captain John Smith from execution. CON-

TEMPORARY EXAMPLE: Pocahantas Lee Watkins, Illinois Station, Oklahoma.

Polly   A variant form of Molly, which was often used as a pet name for Mary. Also, a pet form of Palmer. *See* Palmer.

Pomona   From the Latin *pomum*, meaning "apple, fruit." In Roman mythology, the goddess of fruit trees and their products. PLACE-NAME USAGE: cities in California, Missouri, and North Carolina.

Poppy   From the Latin *papaver*, "a plant that yields a juice from which opium is made." CONTEMPORARY EXAMPLE: Poppy Kepford, New Canaan, Connecticut.

Pora, Poria   From the Hebrew, meaning "fruitful."

Portia   From the Latin *porcus*, meaning "a hog." Derived from Porcii, an ancient Roman clan. Made famous by Shakespeare in *The Merchant of Venice.*

Prescovia   Origin unknown. CONTEMPORARY EXAMPLE: Prescovia Robinette, Alderson, West Virginia.

Prima   From the Latin *primus*, meaning "first, the best."

Primavera   From the Latin, meaning "springtime."

Primrose   From the French and Latin, meaning "the first rose." Used most often in Scotland.

Priscilla   From the Latin *priscus*, meaning "ancient, old." PET FORMS: Pris, Prissie, Prissy. CONTEMPORARY EXAMPLE: Priscilla Pointer, actress.

Procopia   From the Latin, meaning "the progressive." The feminine form of Procopius, a seventh-century historian.

Prudence   From the Latin *prudentia*, meaning "prudent, cautious." PET FORMS: Pru, Prud, Prudi, Prudie, Prudy.

Prudwen   Probably from the Old French *prous*, meaning "excellent," plus the Anglo-Saxon *win*, meaning "joy," hence "great happiness."

Prue   A pet form of Prudence. *See* Prudence. CONTEMPORARY EXAMPLE: Prue Napier, author.

Psyche   From the Greek, meaning "soul."

Pua   From the Hawaiian, meaning "a flower, a blossom." Also, from the Hebrew and Aramaic, meaning "to bleat, to groan."

Pulcheria   From the Latin *pulchritudo*, meaning "physically beautiful."

Pyralis   From the Greek *pyr*, meaning "fire." Also, a flying insect of the moth family that lives in or near fire.

Pyrene   From the Greek *pyr*, meaning "of the fire."

Q

Quanda From the Old English *cwen*, meaning "a companion" or "a queen."

Queena A variant form of Queenie. *See* Queenie.

Queenie From the Old English *cwen*, meaning "a queen." A nickname for Regina. Used in England as an independent name. Queena is a variant form.

Quella From the Old English *cwellan*, meaning "to kill."

Quenby From the Old English *cwen*, meaning "queen," plus the Danish *bye*, meaning "abode," hence "the queen's castle."

Querida A Spanish form of the Latin *quaere*, meaning "to ask, to inquire," hence "one who is sympathetic."

Quilla From the Middle English *quil*, meaning "a quill."

Quinn From the Old English *cwen*, meaning "a queen." CONTEMPO- RARY EXAMPLE: Quinn Cummings, actress. PLACE-NAME USAGE: a river in Nevada, a variant form of Queen, so called because of its proximity to King River.

Quinta, Quintilla, Quintina From the Latin, meaning "the fifth." A name usually given to the fifth child in a family, if a girl, or to the fifth girl in a family.

R

Rachel   From the Hebrew, meaning "a ewe, a female sheep." In the Bible, the wife of Jacob, mother of Joseph and Benjamin. Not used as a Christian name until after the Reformation. Raquel is a Spanish variant form. VARIANT SPELLINGS: Rachael, Rachelle, Rahel. CONTEMPORARY EXAMPLE: Rachel Carson, author.

Racheli   A variant form of Rachel. *See* Rachel. CONTEMPORARY EXAMPLE: Racheli Edelman, editor.

Rachelle   A variant spelling of Rachel. *See* Rachel.

Radella   A French form of the German *radi*, meaning "counsel."

Radinka   A Russian form of Radella. *See* Radella.

Rae   A pet form of Rachel. *See* Rachel. VARIANT SPELLINGS: Ray, Raye. CONTEMPORARY EXAMPLE: Rae Allen, actress. SURNAME USAGE: Charlotte Rae, actress.

Raelaine   A name invented by combining Ray and Elaine. *See* Ray *and* Elaine. CONTEMPORARY EXAMPLE: Raelaine Peterson, Riverside, California.

Rafaela, Rafaele   Variant spellings of Raphaela. *See* Raphaela.

Rahel   A variant Hebraic spelling of Rachel. *See* Rachel.

Raina   From the Latin *regnum*, meaning "to rule." Akin to Regina. *See also* Rayna.

Raine   A variant form of Raina. *See* Raina.

Raisa, Raissa   From the Yiddish, meaning "a rose." PET FORMS: Raizel, Rayzel, Razel.

Raizel, Rayzel, Razil   Pet forms of Raisa. *See* Raisa.

Ralna   A feminine form of Roland. *See* Roland (masculine section).

Rama   From the Hebrew, meaning "lofty, exalted." Also, from the Sanskrit, one of the three incarnations of the Hindu god Vishnu.

Ramona   A short form of the masculine Raymond. *See* Raymond (masculine section). Raymonda is a variant form. CONTEMPORARY EXAMPLE: Ramona Stewart, novelist. PLACE-NAME USAGE: Ramona, California.

Ran   In Norse mythology, a sea goddess who reigns over destruction; wife of Aegir.

Rana   A variant form of Raina. *See* Raina. CONTEMPORARY EXAMPLE: Rana Dobbagh, art historian.

Randa   A feminine form of Randall. *See* Randall (masculine section). CONTEMPORARY EXAMPLE: Randa Harris, Saffard, Arizona.

Randi   A pet form of Randa. *See* Randa.

Rane   A variant form of Raina. *See* Raina.

Rani   From the Hebrew, meaning "my joy."

Ranit, Ranita   From the Hebrew, meaning "joy" or "song."

Ranny   A pet form of Frances. CONTEMPORARY EXAMPLE: Ranny Sinclair, singer.

Raona   A name invented by scrambling the letters of Aaron. *See* Aaron (masculine section). CONTEMPORARY EXAMPLE: Raona Pearl, Ridgecrest, California.

Raoul   A variant form of the masculine Randolph and Ralph. *See* Randolph *and* Ralph (masculine section). Used primarily as a masculine name.

Rapa   From the Hawaiian, meaning "moon beam."

Raphaela   The femine form of Raphael. *See* Raphael. (masculine section).

Raquel   A variant Spanish form of Rachel. *See* Rachel. CONTEMPORARY EXAMPLE: Raquel Welsh, actress.

Ravital   From the Hebrew, meaning "my Master is my dew," hence "God provides for me." CONTEMPORARY EXAMPLE: Ravital Silver, Jerusalem, Israel.

Ray, Raye   Variant spellings of Rae. *See* Rae. SURNAME USAGE: Martha Raye, actress.

Raya   From the Hebrew, meaning "friend."

Raymonda   The feminine form of Raymond. *See* Raymond (masculine section). Akin to Ramona.

Rayna, Reyna   From the Yiddish, meaning "pure, clean." *See also* Raina.

Raz   From the Aramaic, meaning "secret." Used also as a masculine form.

Razi   From the Aramaic, meaning "my secret." Used also as a masculine form.

Razia, Raziah, Raziela   From the Aramaic, meaning "secret of the Lord."

Razilee, Razili   From the Aramaic and Hebrew, meaning "the secret is mine."

Reade   From the Old English *raedan*, meaning "to counsel, advise." CONTEMPORARY EXAMPLE: Reade Johnson, publicist.

Reatha   A variant form of Marguerita. *See* Marguerita. Akin to Retha and Rita.

Reba   A pet form of Rebecca. *See* Rebecca.

Rebecca   From the Hebrew and Arabic, meaning "to tie, to bind." In the Bible, the wife of Isaac, mother of Jacob and Esau. Rebekah is a variant spelling. PET FORMS: Beck, Beckie, Becky, Reba. Not used as a Christian name until after the Reformation.

Rebekah   A variant spelling of Rebecca. *See* Rebecca.

Reda   A variant form of Rita. *See* Rita.

Reeta   A variant spelling of Rita. *See* Rita. CONTEMPORARY EXAMPLE: Reeta B. Wolfsohn, author.

Regan   A variant form of Regina. *See* Regina.

Regina   From the Latin *regnum*, meaning "to rule," hence "queen." VARIANT FORMS: Raina, Rani, Rayna, Regan, Reina. PET FORMS: Gina, Rene, Reena.

Reida   A variant form of Rita. *See* Rita. Also, a name invented by combining Reid and Anna. *See* Reid (masculine section) *and* Anna. CONTEMPORARY EXAMPLE: Reida Buehler, Las Vegas, Nevada.

Reina, Reine   Variant forms of Raina. *See* Raina.

Reitha   A variant spelling of Reatha. *See* Reatha.

Reja   An invented name. An acronym of Ronnie, Elbert, John, and Alan, four brothers.

Remigilia   From the Latin, pertaining to "the removal of the large quill feathers of a bird's wing."

Rena, Reena   Pet forms of Regina or Serena. *See* Regina *and* Serena. Also, from the Hebrew, meaning "joy." Rina is a variant spelling.

Renana, Renanit   From the Hebrew, meaning "joy, song." Akin to Rina.

Renata   From the Latin *renatus*, meaning "to be born again." VARIANT FORMS: Rene, Renee, Rennie.

Rene, Renee   French forms of Renata. *See* Renata. May also be variant forms of Irene. *See* Irene.

Renette   A French pet form of Rene. *See* Rene. CONTEMPORARY EXAMPLE: Renette Ezralow, civic leader.

Renise   A name invented by combining Ray and Denise. *See* Ray *and* Denise. CONTEMPORARY EXAMPLE: Renise DeLiz Bentley, Capistrano

Beach, California.

Renita   A Spanish pet form of Rene. *See* Rene.

Retha   A short form of Marguerita. *See* Marguerita. Rita is a variant form. CONTEMPORARY EXAMPLES: Rita Alarid, Carmichael, California; Retha F. Hollenbeck, Brea, California.

Reubena, Reuvena   Feminine form of Reuben. *See* Reuben (masculine section).

Reva   A variant spelling of Reba. *See* Reba.

Rexana   The feminine form of the Latin *rex*, meaning "king." Akin to Regina. *See* Regina.

Rexella   A feminine pet form of Rex. *See* Rex (masculine section). CONTEMPORARY EXAMPLE: Rexella van Impe, evangelist singer.

Reyna   A variant form of Raina. *See* Raina.

Rhea   From the Greek, meaning "protector of cities" or "a poppy" (flower). CONTEMPORARY EXAMPLE: Rhea Seddon, astronaut.

Rheta   A variant spelling of Rita. *See* Rita. Also, from the Greek, meaning "one who speaks well."

Rhoda, Rhode   From the Greek, meaning "a flower" (rose). VARIANT FORMS: Rosa, Rose. *See also* Rose.

Rhodeia   A variant form of Rhoda. *See* Rhoda.

Rhodope   A variant form of Rhoda. *See* Rhoda.

Rhona   A hybrid of Rose and Anna. *See* Rose *and* Anna. Also, a variant form of the masculine Ronald. *See* Ronald (masculine section).

Rhonda, Rhondda   From the Celtic, meaning "powerful river." PLACE-NAME USAGE: a river in Wales. CONTEMPORARY EXAMPLE: Rhonda Fleming, actress.

Rhonnie   A pet form of Rhonda. *See* Rhonda.

Ria   From the Spanish, meaning "a small river."

Riane   An invented name. Origin unknown. Possibly a variant form of the masculine Ryan. *See* Ryan (masculine section). CONTEMPORARY EXAMPLE: Riane Tennenhauseisler, author.

Rica   A pet form of Ricarda. *See* Ricarda.

Ricarda   A feminine Italian form of Richard. *See* Richard (masculine section). Rica is a pet form.

Richanda   A feminine form of Richard. *See* Richard (masculine section). CONTEMPORARY EXAMPLE: Richanda Conley, Duncansville, Pennsylvania.

Richarda   A variant spelling of Ricarda. *See* Ricarda.

Richardyne   A sixteenth–century pet form of Richarda. *See* Richarda.

Richela   A pet form of Richarda. *See* Richarda.

Richenda   A feminine form of Richard. *See* Richard (masculine section). VARIANT FORMS: Richanda, Richarda, Richenza.

Richenza   A feminine form of Richard. *See* Richard (masculine section).

Richia   A feminine form of Richard. *See* Richard (masculine section). CONTEMPORARY EXAMPLE: Richia Eliza Atkinson, Palm Beach, Florida.

Ricka   A pet form of Ricarda. *See* Ricarda.

Rickell   A name invented by combining Rick and Ellen. *See* Rick (masculine section) *and* Ellen. CONTEMPORARY EXAMPLE: Rickell Eddleman, Portsmouth, Virginia.

Ricki   A pet form of Ricarda. *See* Ricarda. Also, a nickname for Roseanne. CONTEMPORARY EXAMPLE: Ricki Stofsky, television programmer.

Rickma   From the Hebrew, meaning "woven, a woven product."

Ricky   A variant spelling of Ricki. *See* Ricki.

Riesa   A pet form of Theresa. *See* Theresa. CONTEMPORARY EXAMPLE: Riesa Howard, civic leader.

Riki   A variant spelling of Ricki. *See* Ricki. Also, a pet form of Rebecca. *See* Rebecca. CONTEMPORARY EXAMPLE: Riki E. Kosut, publicist.

Rikma   A variant spelling of Rickma. *See* Rickma.

Rilla   From the Dutch *ril* and Low German *rille*, meaning "a little stream." CONTEMPORARY EXAMPLE: Rilla–Luretta Peck Hight, Grand Haven, Michigan.

Rimona   From the Hebrew, meaning "a pomegranate."

Rina   A variant spelling of Rena. *See* Rena.

Rinda   A pet form of Dorinda. *See* Dorinda.

Rishona   From the Hebrew, meaning "first."

Rita   From the Sanskrit, meaning "brave" or "honest." Also, a short form of Marguerita. *See* Marguerita. Rheta is a variant spelling.

Riva   From the Old French *rive* and the Latin *ripa*, meaning "a bank, coast, shore."

Rivana   A variant form of River. *See* River.

Rivca A variant spelling of Rivka. *See* Rivka.

River From the Old French *riviere* and the Latin *riparia*, meaning "a stream of water." Akin to Riva.

Rivers A variant form of River. *See* River. CONTEMPORARY EXAMPLE: Rivers Ann Hatchett, North Jackson, Ohio. SURNAME USAGE: Joan Rivers, comedienne.

Rivka The Hebrew form of Rebecca. *See* Rebecca. CONTEMPORARY EXAMPLE: Rivka Ben-Yitzhak, editor.

Roanna A hybrid of Rose and Anna. *See* Rose *and* Anna. Rhona is a variant form.

Roanne A hybrid of Rose and Anne. *See* Rose *and* Anne. CONTEMPORARY EXAMPLE: Roanne Stradcutter Butier, Oakland, California.

Robann A hybrid of Rob (Robert) and Ann. *See* Robert (masculine section) *and* Ann. CONTEMPORARY EXAMPLE: Robann Dishongh, Lawrence, Tennessee.

Robbie A pet form of Roberta. *See* Roberta. CONTEMPORARY EXAMPLE: Robbie Fanning, author.

Roberta The feminine form of Robert. *See* Robert (masculine section). Robina is a variant form.

Robin A pet form of Roberta. *See* Roberta. Robyn is a variant spelling. CONTEMPORARY EXAMPLE: Robin Mattson, actress.

Robina A variant form of Robin. *See* Robin. VARIANT FORMS: Rebinah, Robin, Robyn, Rubinah. CONTEMPORARY EXAMPLE: Robina Cromwell, sister of Oliver Cromwell.

Robyn A variant spelling of Robin. *See* Robin.

Rochella A variant form of Rochelle. *See* Rochelle.

Rochelle From the Old French *roche*, meaning "a large stone." Rochella is a variant English form. Rochette is a pet form.

Rochette A French pet form of Rochelle. *See* Rochelle.

Roderica A feminine form of Roderick. *See* Roderick (masculine section).

Rohana A hybrid of Rose and Hannah. *See* Rose *and* Hannah. Or, from the Sanskrit, meaning "the sandalwood tree."

Rohn A name invented to rhyme with John. CONTEMPORARY EXAMPLE: Rohn Wesley Heidgerd, Wallingford, Connecticut.

Rolaine Probably a variant form of the masculine Roland. *See* Roland (masculine section). CONTEMPORARY EXAMPLE: Rolaine Hochstein, novelist.

Rolanda A feminine form of Roland. *See* Roland (masculine section).

Rolene   A feminine form of Roland. *See* Roland (masculine section). CONTEMPORARY EXAMPLE: Rolene Wehr, Waterloo, Iowa.

Rolleen   A name invented by combining Roland and a form of Pauline. *See* Roland *and* Pauline. CONTEMPORARY EXAMPLE: Roleen Cord, Watefield, Rhode Island.

Roma   The Italian form of Rome, named for Romulus. In Roman mythology, Romulus was one of the sons of Mars. *See* Romulus (masculine section). Also, from the Hebrew, meaning "heights, lofty, exalted."

Romaine   A variant form of Roma. *See* Roma. Romayne is a variant spelling. Romain is a masculine form. CONTEMPORARY EXAMPLE: Romaine Forsythe, Jacksonville, Florida.

Romana   A variant form of Roma. *See* Roma. CONTEMPORARY EXAMPLE: Romana de Vries, cosmetician.

Romayne   A variant spelling of Romaine. *See* Romaine.

Romelda, Romilda   From the German, meaning "Roman warrior."

Romia, Romit   From the Hebrew, meaning "lofty, exalted." Roma is a variant form.

Romola   The Italian feminine form of Romulus. *See* Romulus (masculine section). The heroine of George Eliot's novel *Romola.*

Romy   A variant form of Roma. *See* Roma. CONTEMPORARY EXAMPLE: Romy Schneider, actress.

Rona   From the Gaelic *roman,* meaning "a seal." Also, a feminine form of Ronald. *See* Ronald (masculine section). Akin to Roni. CONTEMPORARY EXAMPLE: Rona Barrett, newspaper columnist.

Ronaele   A name invented by spelling Eleanor backwards. CONTEMPORARY EXAMPLE: Ronaele Kelly Gaynor, Philadelphia, Pennsylvania.

Ronalda   The feminine form of Ronald. *See* Ronald (masculine section).

Ronalee   A name invented by combining Rona and Lee. *See* Rona *and* Lee.

Ronda   A variant spelling of Rhonda. *See* Rhonda. PLACE-NAME USAGE: Ronda, North Carolina.

Ronee   A feminine pet form of the masculine Ronald. *See* Ronald (masculine section).

Roneel   A name invented by scrambling the letters of the name Lorene. CONTEMPORARY EXAMPLE: Roneel G. Bowden, Linden, Texas. (Roneel Bowden scrambled her name to arrive at Lorene, a name for her daughter. Lorene later scrambled her own name, Lorene, to arrive at Eloren, a name for her daughter.)

Roni   From the Hebrew, meaning "my joy."

Ronia   From the Hebrew, meaning "my joy is in the Lord."

Ronit   From the Hebrew, meaning "joy."

Ronl   A feminine pet form of Ronald. *See* Ronald (masculine section).

Ronli   From the Hebrew, meaning "joy is mine."

Ronna   A feminine variant form of Ronald. *See* Ronald (masculine section). CONTEMPORARY EXAMPLE: Ronna Wilson, Garden Grove, California.

Ronne   A feminine pet form of Ronald. *See* Ronald (masculine section).

Ronnie   A feminine pet form of Ronald. *See* Ronald (masculine section).

Ronnit   From the Hebrew, meaning "joy, song."

Ronsy   Probably a pet form of one of the many pet forms of the masculine Ronald. CONTEMPORARY EXAMPLE: Ronsy Reaner, Toronto, Canada.

Rori, Rory   Irish feminine forms of Roderick and Robert. *See* Roderick *and* Robert (masculine section). Often used as masculine names. CONTEMPORARY EXAMPLE: Rory Rosenberg, Roslindale, Massachusetts.

Rosa   The Italian form of Rose. *See* Rose. PLACE-NAME USAGE: a mountain on the Swiss-Italian border.

Rosabel   From the Latin and French, meaning "beautiful rose." *See also* Rose.

Rosabeth   A hybrid of Rosa and Beth. *See* Rosa *and* Beth. CONTEMPORARY EXAMPLE: Rosabeth Moss Kanter, author.

Rosalba   From the Latin, meaning "white rose." PLACE-NAME USAGE: Rosalba Lake, Mississippi.

Rosaleen   A variant form of Rosalind. *See* Rosalind.

Rosalia, Rozalia   From the Latin *rosalia*, pertaining to the ceremony of hanging garlands of roses on tombs. St. Rosalia was a twelfth–century Sicilian patron saint of Salerno.

Rosalie   A French form of the Latin *rosalia,* annual ceremony of hanging garlands of roses on tombs.

Rosalind   From the Latin, meaning "beautiful rose." Rosalinda is a Spanish form. Also, from the Old High German Roslindis, derived from *hros,* meaning "horse," plus *lind,* meaning "a shield made of linden wood." Popularized in England by Shakespeare's heroine in *As You Like It.* CONTEMPORARY EXAMPLE: Rosalind Russell, actress.

Rosalinda   A Spanish form of Rosalind. *See* Rosalind.

Rosaline   A variant form of Rosalind. *See* Rosalind. A character in Shakespeare's *Romeo and Juliet.*

Rosalyn   A variant form of Rosalind. *See* Rosalind.

Rosamond   From the Latin, meaning "rose of the world." *See also* Rose. Also, from the Old High German Hrosmund, derived from *hros*, meaning "horse," plus *mund*, meaning "protection," hence "protector of the horse."

Rosamund, Rosamunde   Variant forms of Rosamond. *See* Rosamund. CONTEMPORARY EXAMPLE: Rosamunde Pilcher, author.

Rose   The English form of the Latin *rosa*, meaning "any genus of shrub of the rose family." Also, from the Old High German *hros*, meaning "horse." *See* Rosamond. PET FORMS: Rosena, Rosette, Rosina, Rosita, Rosella, Rosie, Rozina, Rozy. PLACE-NAME USAGE: Rose Creek, Arizona; Rose Point, Alaska.

Roseanna   A hybrid of Rose and Anna. *See* Rose *and* Anna.

Roseanne   A hybrid of Rose and Anne. *See* Rose *and* Anne. CONTEMPORARY EXAMPLE: Roseanne Colleti, television news reporter.

Rosebud   A variant form of Rose, meaning "the bud of a rose." CONTEMPORARY EXAMPLES: Dandylyon Rosebud Shannon, Pacifica, California; Rosebud Merrick, New York, New York.

Rosedale   From the Old English, meaning "a valley of roses."

Rosel, Roselle   Pet forms of Rose used in Switzerland. *See* Rose.

Roseleen   A variant form of Rosalind. *See* Rosalind. CONTEMPORARY EXAMPLE: Roseleen Milne, author.

Rosellen   A hybrid of Rose and Ellen. *See* Rose *and* Ellen. CONTEMPORARY EXAMPLE: Rosellen Brown, author.

Roselotte   A hybrid of Rose and Lotte. *See* Rose *and* Lotte.

Roseltha   An invented name. Akin to Rose and Althea. *See* Rose *and* Althea. CONTEMPORARY EXAMPLE: Roseltha Mathews, North Branch, Michigan.

Roselyn   A variant form of Rosalind. *See* Rosalind. CONTEMPORARY EXAMPLE: Roselyn Carter, San Bernardino, California.

Roselynde   A hybrid of Rose and Lynde. *See* Rose *and* Lynde.

Rosemary   A hybrid of Rose and Mary. *See* Rose *and* Mary. Also, a plant-name, derived from the Latin, meaning "dew of the sea." Medicine made from the plant was believed to refresh the memory.

Rosetta   An Italian pet form of Rose. *See* Rose. CONTEMPORARY EXAMPLE: Rosetta Stone, author.

Rosette   A French pet form of Rose. *See* Rose.

Rosi, Rosie   Pet forms of Rose. *See* Rose.

Rosina   A pet form of Rose. *See* Rose.

Rosine   A pet form of Rose. *See* Rose.

Rosita   A pet form of Rose. *See* Rose. PLACE-NAME USAGE: Rosita, Colorado.

Roslyn   A variant spelling of Rosalyn. *See* Rosalyn.

Rowan   From the Old English *ruh*, meaning "rugged land." Akin to the masculine Rowe. CONTEMPORARY EXAMPLE: Rowan L. Wolnik, Van Nuys, California.

Rowena   A variant form of Rowan. *See* Rowan. Also, from the Celtic, meaning "flowering white hair." Ro is a pet form. CONTEMPORARY EXAMPLE: Rowena Reed, author. PLACE-NAME USAGE: Rowena, South Dakota; Rowena, Oregon, named in honor of H.S. Rowe, a railroad official.

Roxane, Roxanna, Roxanne   From the Persian, meaning "dawn, brilliant light." PET FORMS: Roxie, Roxy. CONTEMPORARY EXAMPLE: Roxanne Hart, actress.

Roxie, Roxy   Pet forms of Roxanne. *See* Roxanne.

Royal, Royale   From the Middle English *roial* and the Latin *rex*, meaning "king, royal." CONTEMPORARY EXAMPLE: Royal Kennedy, television reporter. Used also as a masculine name. PLACE-NAME USAGE: Royal, North Carolina; Royal Arch, California.

Royce   More commonly used as a masculine name. *See* Royce (masculine section). CONTEMPORARY EXAMPLE: Royce Wallace, actress.

Roz   A pet form of Roslyn. *See* Roslyn.

Rozanne   A variant spelling of Roseanne. *See* Roseanne. CONTEMPORARY EXAMPLE: Rozanne Elder, editor.

Rozina   A variant spelling of Rosina. *See* Rosina.

Rubetta, Rubette   Pet forms of Ruby. *See* Ruby.

Ruby   From the Latin *rubeus*, meaning "red, reddish." A clear, deep-red precious stone. Used also as a masculine name. In England and Scotland, Ruby is used as a nickname for Roberta and Robina. CONTEMPORARY EXAMPLE: Ruby Dee, actress. PLACE-NAME USAGE: Ruby, Arizona, name for Lille B. Ruby, maiden name.

Rudelle   From the Old High German *hruod*, meaning "fame." Akin to Rue.

Rue   From the Old High German *hruod*, meaning "fame." Also, a family of strong-scented plants. Akin to Rudelle. CONTEMPORARY EXAMPLE: Rue McClanahan, actress.

Ruel   Probably a feminine form of the masculine Reuel. *See* Reuel (masculine section).

Ruey   A variant form of Rue. *See* Rue. Or, a pet form of Ruel. *See* Ruel. CONTEMPORARY EXAMPLE: Wyome Ruey Smith, Sioux City, Iowa.

Rula   From the Middle English *reule* and the Latin *regula*, meaning "ruler." CONTEMPORARY EXAMPLE: Rula Lenska, actress.

Rumer   Possibly a variant form of Romany (Roman), originally meaning "a gypsy." CONTEMPORARY EXAMPLE: Rumer Godden, English author.

Runa   From the Old Norse *rinna*, meaning "to flow, to cause to run." CONTEMPORARY EXAMPLE: Runa Zurbel, author.

Ruperta   The feminine form of Rupert. *See* Rupert (masculine section). First used for a daughter of Prince Rupert.

Ruth   From the Hebrew and Syriac, meaning "a companion; friendship." In the Bible, the ever-loyal daughter-in-law of Naomi. Ruthie is a pet form. PLACE-NAME USAGE: Ruth, Nevada, named for Ruth MacDonald, wife of an early landowner.

Ruthanna   A hybrid of Ruth and Anna. *See* Ruth *and* Anna. CONTEMPORARY EXAMPLE: Ruthanna Long, author.

Ruthven   Probably an invented name. CONTEMPORARY EXAMPLE: Ruthven Tremain, author.

S

Saada   From the Hebrew, meaning "support, help." Saadia is the masculine form. *See* Saadia (masculine section).

Saba   From the Hebrew and Aramaic, meaning "old, aged."

Sabina   A variant form of Sabine. *See* Sabine.

Sabine   A feminine form of Sabin. *See* Sabin (masculine section). From the Latin, meaning "of the Sabines." The Sabines were an ancient Italian people who conquered Rome in 290 B.C. CONTEMPORARY EXAMPLE: Sabine D. Jordan, author.

Sabra   From the Hebrew, meaning "thorny cactus." Native-born Israelis are referred to as Sabras because of their outer toughness and inner softness. CONTEMPORARY EXAMPLE: Sabra Jones, actress.

Sabrina   A pet form of Sabra. *See* Sabra.

Sacha   A pet form of Alexandra. *See* Alexandra. Used also as a masculine name.

Sada   A variant form of Sadie. *See* Sadie. Also, possibly from the Old English *saed*, meaning "a seed." CONTEMPORARY EXAMPLE: Sada Thompson, actress.

Sadella, Sadelle   Pet forms of Sadie. *See* Sadie.

Sadi   A variant spelling of Sadie. *See* Sadie.

Sadie   A pet form of Sarah. *See* Sarah. The form Sadie was once popular among Roman Catholics, having been used as a pet form of Mercedes, meaning "Mary of the Mercies." VARIANT FORMS: Sada, Sadella, Sadelle. VARIANT SPELLINGS: Sadi, Sady, Sadye.

Sadira   From the Arabic, meaning an "ostrich returning from water." Also, the Arabic name of a constellation.

Sady, Sadye   Variant spellings of Sadie. *See* Sadie.

Sadybeth   A name invented by combining Sady (Sadie) and Beth. *See* Sadie *and* Beth. CONTEMPORARY EXAMPLE: Sadybeth Lowitz, author.

Saffron   From the Arabic, meaning "the crocus," a plant with purple flowers.

Sahara   From the Arabic, meaning "moon." PLACE-NAME USAGE: Sahara Desert, North Africa.

Salene   A name invented by combining Salvatore and Irene. *See* Salvatore (masculine section) and Irene. CONTEMPORARY EXAMPLE: S. Selene Williams, Pittsburgh, Pennsylvania.

Saliee   A variant spelling of Sally. *See* Sally. CONTEMPORARY EXAMPLE: Saliee O'Brian, author.

Salena, Salina   From the Latin *sal*, meaning "salt."

Sallie, Sally   Variant forms of Sarah. *See* Sarah.

Salome   From the Hebrew *shalom*, meaning "peace." Salome Alexandra was the ruler of Judea from 76–67 B.C. A sister of King Herod was also named Salome. Shulamit is the Hebrew form. *See* Shulamit. PLACE-NAME USAGE: Salome, Arizona, named for Grace Salome Pratt, wife of town founder.

Samantha   From the Aramaic, meaning "the listener." A biblical name, revived in the latter part of the nineteenth century by the book *Samantha Among the Brethren*. CONTEMPORARY EXAMPLE: Samantha Eggar, actress.

Samara   From the Latin *samara* and *samera*, meaning "the seed of the elm."

Samira   From the Arabic, meaning "entertainer." Samir is a masculine form.

Samuela   The feminine form of Samuel. *See* Samuel (masculine section).

Sande, Sandi   Pet forms of Sandra. *See* Sandra. CONTEMPORARY EXAMPLE: Sandi Gelles–Cole, editor.

Sandra   A pet form of Alexandra. *See* Alexandra.

Sandy   A pet form of Sandra. *See* Sandra. VARIANT SPELLINGS: Sande, Sandi.

Santina   From the Latin *sancta*, meaning "little saint." CONTEMPORARY EXAMPLE: Santina Santoro, Hewet, California.

Sapir, Sapira   From the Hebrew, meaning "a sapphire, a precious stone." Sapir is also a masculine name.

Sapphira, Sapphire   From the Hebrew, meaning "sapphire." Akin to Sapir and Sapira.

Sara   A modern spelling of Sarah. Popular in Israel. CONTEMPORARY EXAMPLE: Sara Davidson, author. PLACE-NAME USAGE: Saranap, California, named for Sara Naphthaly, mother of a railroad official.

Sarah   From the Hebrew, meaning "princess, noble." In the Bible, Sarah was originally Sarai. The name was later changed to Sarah. She and Abraham were the parents of Isaac. Among Jews the name was always popular, but among Christians it was rarely used before the Reformation. Sara is a variant spelling. VARIANT FORMS: Sallie, Sally,

Sarene, Sarice, Sarina, Sarine. PET FORMS: Sadie, Saretta, Sarette, Sarita.

Sarai The original biblical form of Sarah. *See* Sarah. Sari is a variant spelling.

Saran, Sarann, Saranne Hybrid forms of Sarah and Ann (Anne). *See* Sarah *and* Ann.

Sarayn A name coined by Sarayn Micel of New York City. Created by modifying the spelling of Sarah Ann. *See* Sarah *and* Ann.

Sarene A variant form of Sarah. *See* Sarah.

Saretta A pet form of Sarah. *See* Sarah. CONTEMPORARY EXAMPLE: Saretta Berlin, editor.

Sarette A pet form of Sarah. *See* Sarah.

Sari From the Hindi and Sanskrit, meaning "an outer garment worn by Hindu women." Also a variant spelling of Sarai. *See* Sarai. CONTEMPORARY EXAMPLE: Sari Grayson, Culver City, California.

Sarice From the Hebrew, meaning "a ruler, a princess." A variant form of Sarah. *See* Sarah.

Sarina, Sarine Variant forms of Sarah. *See* Sarah.

Sarita A Spanish form of Sarah. *See* Sarah.

Sass A short form of the Irish name Sasanach and the Gaelic name Sasunn, meaning "a Saxon." SURNAME USAGE: Siegfried Sassoon, English poet.

Saturnia The feminine form of Saturn. From the Latin *satus*, meaning "sowed, planted." In Roman mythology, Saturn is the god of agriculture.

Saundra A variant spelling of Sandra. *See* Sandra.

Savanna, Savannah From the Spanish *sabana*, meaning "a treeless plain." PLACE-NAME USAGE: a seaport in Georgia; a river in South Carolina and Georgia.

Savina A variant form of Sabina. *See* Sabina.

Saxon A Germanic name, from the Latin *saxum*, meaning "a sword, knife, stone."

Scarlet, Scarlett From the Middle English, meaning "a deep red color." Scarlett O'Hara, a character in Margaret Mitchell's *Gone With the Wind*.

Schifra A variant spelling of Shifra. CONTEMPORARY EXAMPLE: Schifra Strizower, author.

Scientia From the Latin *scientia*, meaning "to know, discern, distinguish."

Season   From the Latin *satio*, meaning "sowing, planting." CONTEMPORARY EXAMPLE: Season Hubley, actress.

Season Music   A name created for a child "so she shall have music wherever she goes." CONTEMPORARY EXAMPLE: Season Music Terrill, Deadwood, South Dakota.

Secunda   From the Latin, meaning "the second." SURNAME USAGE: Sholom Secunda, musician.

Seema, Sema   From the Greek, meaning "a sign, a symbol."

Sela   From the Hebrew, meaning "a rock." Used also as a masculine name.

Selda   From the Old English *seldan*, meaning "strange, rare, precious."

Selena   A variant form of Selene. *See* Selene.

Selene   From the Greek, meaning "the moon." In Greek mythology, the goddess of the moon. Akin to Diana in Roman mythology.

Selima, Selimah   Feminine Arabic forms of Solomon, meaning "peace." *See* Solomon (masculine section).

Selina   A variant spelling of Selene. *See* Selene.

Selma   From the Celtic, meaning "fair." Also, from the Greek, meaning "a ship."

Semele   From the French *semer*, meaning "to sow." In Greek mythology, the mother of Dionysius.

Semiramis   The legendary queen of Assyria noted for her beauty.

Senalda   From the Spanish, meaning "a sign, a symbol." Akin to Seema.

Septima   The feminine form of Septimus. From the Latin, meaning "the seventh." Often given to the seventh child in a family (if a female) or to a girl born in September. *See* Septimus (masculine section).

Serafina   A variant spelling of Seraphina. *See* Seraphina.

Seraphina, Seraphine   From the Hebrew *sarof*, meaning "to burn." In the Bible, Serafim (also spelled Seraphim) were heavenly, winged beings (angels) that surrounded the throne of God.

Serena   From the Latin *serenus*, meaning "peaceful." *See also* Sirena.

Serepta   An Old English form of Serena. *See* Serena. CONTEMPORARY EXAMPLE: Gleanus Serepta Gilliam, Hendersonville, North Carolina.

Seven   A Middle English form of the Latin *septem*, meaning the cardinal number "seven." Akin to Septima. *See* Septima. CONTEMPORARY EXAMPLE: Seven Anne McDonald, actress.

Sevilla   A variant form of Sibyl. *See* Sibyl. PLACE-NAME USAGE: a city in Spain.

Shaaron   A variant spelling of Sharon. *See* Sharon. CONTEMPORARY EXAMPLE: Shaaron Cosner, author.

Shaina, Shaine   From the Yiddish, meaning "beautiful." Also, variant Irish forms of Sean, meaning "gracious." *See* Sean (masculine section).

Shalgia   From the Hebrew, meaning "snow, snow-white." In Israel, the name of a plant with white flowers.

Shana   A variant spelling of Shaina. *See* Shaina. CONTEMPORARY EXAMPLE: Shana Alexander, journalist.

Shane, Shanie   Variant spellings of Shaina. *See* Shaina. CONTEMPORARY EXAMPLE: Shanie Jacobs, fashion designer.

Shannon   A feminine variant form of Sean. *See* Sean (masculine section). CONTEMPORARY EXAMPLE: Shannon Lucid, astronaut.

Shareen   A variant form of Sharon. *See* Sharon. CONTEMPORARY EXAMPLE: Shareen Blair Brysac, editor.

Shari   A pet form of Sharon. *See* Sharon. CONTEMPORARY EXAMPLE: Shari Lewis, entertainer. PLACE-NAME USAGE: a river in Central Africa.

Sharlea   An invented name. A feminine form of Charles. *See* Charles (masculine section). CONTEMPORARY EXAMPLE: Sharlea S. Gilcrease, Pineville, Louisiana.

Sharleen   A variant spelling of Charlene. *See* Charlene. CONTEMPORARY EXAMPLE: Sharleen Cooper Cohen, author.

Sharlene   A variant spelling of Charlene. *See* Charlene.

Sharma   Possibly a variant form of Sharon. *See* Sharon.

Sharman   From the Middle English *schar*, meaning "a plowshare," hence "one who uses a plowshare, a farmer." CONTEMPORARY EXAMPLE: Sharman Lee Key Martin, Lubbock, Texas.

Sharol   A variant form of Cheryl. *See* Cheryl. CONTEMPORARY EXAMPLE: Sharol Clark, Groveport, Ohio.

Sharon   From the Hebrew *yashar*, meaning "a plain, a flat area." In the Bible, an area of ancient Palestine where roses grew in abundance. Occasionally used as a masculine name. VARIANT SPELLINGS: Shaaron, Sharyn. PLACE-NAME USAGE: cities in South Carolina and Connecticut.

Sharyn   A variant spelling of Sharon. *See* Sharon.

Shasta   Origin uncertain. Probably derived from a tribal name. CONTEMPORARY EXAMPLE: Shasta Lynn Powers, Murells Inlet, South Carolina. PLACE-NAME USAGE: a mountain in northern California.

Shayna, Shayne   Variant spellings of Shaina and Shaine. *See* Shaina *and* Shaine.

Sheba   A pet form of Bathsheba. *See* Bathsheba.

Sheena, Shena   Gaelic forms of Jane. *See* Jane. Akin to Shaina. *See also* Shaina. CONTEMPORARY EXAMPLE: Sheena Porter, author.

Sheila, Sheilah, Sheilla   Variant forms of Cecelia and Celia introduced into Ireland by early settlers. *See* Cecelia. In Australia, a slang word, meaning "girl, maiden."

Shelagh   An Irish form of Sheilah. *See* Sheilah. CONTEMPORARY EXAMPLE: Shelagh McGee, illustrator.

Shelby   Used primarily as a masculine name. *See* Shelby (masculine section). CONTEMPORARY EXAMPLE: Shelby Hiatt, actress.

Shelia   A variant form of Sheila. *See* Sheila. CONTEMPORARY EXAMPLE: Shelia Hailey, author.

Shelley, Shelly   Irish pet forms of Cecelia. *See* Cecelia. Used also as a masculine name. CONTEMPORARY EXAMPLE: Shelley Winters, actress. SURNAME USAGE: Mary W. Shelley (1797-1851), English novelist.

Shelli   A variant spelling of Shelley. *See* Shelley. CONTEMPORARY EXAMPLE: Shelli Wolis, publisher.

Sher   A variant form of Cher. *See* Cher. Sher Lynette Patrick, Miss Ohio of 1979.

Shera   A name invented by combining the words "she" and "her." Also, a variant spelling of Shira. *See* Shira. CONTEMPORARY EXAMPLE: Shera Ann Hube, Jr., university administrator; Shera Denise, actress.

Sheral   A variant form of Cheryl. *See* Cheryl.

Shere   A pet form of Cheryl. *See* Cheryl. CONTEMPORARY EXAMPLE: Shere Hite, author.

Sheree   A variant form of Cheryl. *See* Cheryl. CONTEMPORARY EXAMPLE: Sheree North, actress.

Sherelle, Sherrelle   Variant spellings of Cheryl. *See* Cheryl.

Sheri   A variant form of Cheri. *See* Cheri. Sherrie is a variant spelling. CONTEMPORARY EXAMPLE: Sheri Lucter Hand, Chicago, Illinois.

Sherran   A variant form of Sharon. *See* Sharon. CONTEMPORARY EXAMPLE: Sherran M. Denkler, Key West, Florida.

Sherrie   A variant spelling of Sheri. *See* Sheri. CONTEMPORARY EXAMPLE: Sherrie Wills, actress.

Sherrie–Dee   A compound of Sherrie and Dee. *See* Sherrie *and* Dee. CONTEMPORARY EXAMPLE: Sherrie-Dee Schubert Wagner, Methuen, Massachusetts.

Sherry   A variant pet form of Cheryl. *See* Cheryl.

Sheryl, Sheryle   Variant forms of Cheryl. *See* Cheryl. CONTEMPORARY EXAMPLE: Sheryle Leekley, photographer.

Sheva   A pet form of Batsheva. *See* Batsheva.

Shevon   A name invented to sound like the Old Irish name Siobhan. CONTEMPORARY EXAMPLE: Shevon Sherod, Honolulu, Hawaii.

Sheyanne   An invented name. A modified spelling of Cheyenne, the river in Wyoming and in South Dakota. CONTEMPORARY EXAMPLE: Sheyanne Koenigseker, Toledo, Ohio.

Shiela, Shielah   Variant spellings of Sheila. *See* Sheila.

Shifra   From the Hebrew *shefer*, meaning "beautiful." Schifra is a variant spelling.

Shimra, Shimria, Shimrit   From the Hebrew, meaning "to guard, conserve."

Shira, Shirah   From the Hebrew, meaning "song."

Shiri   From the Hebrew, meaning "my song."

Shirlee   A variant form of Shirley. *See* Shirley. Also, from the Hebrew, meaning "song is mine." CONTEMPORARY EXAMPLE: Shirlee Newman, author.

Sherleigh   A variant spelling of Shirley. *See* Shirley.

Shi Sunshine   A name invented to represent hope for a life of light and sunshine, meaning "may she be sunshine." CONTEMPORARY EXAMPLE: Shi Sunshine Terrell, Deadwood, South Dakota.

Shirley   From the Old English *scire*, meaning "a shire, a district," plus *lea*, meaning "a meadow," hence "the meadow where the district meetings were held." Shirl is a pet form. Occasionally used as a masculine form. CONTEMPORARY EXAMPLE: Shirley Jones, actress. PLACE-NAME USAGE: a city in England.

Shona   A variant form of Shaina. *See* Shaina. CONTEMPORARY EXAMPLE: Shona DeSilva, Oak Bluffs, Massachusetts.

Shoni, Shonie   A variant form of Shaina. *See* Shaina. CONTEMPORARY EXAMPLE: Shoni Levi, author.

Shoshan   A variant form of Shoshana. *See* Shoshana. Used also as a masculine form.

Shoshana, Shoshanah   From the Hebrew, meaning "a lily" or "a rose." Shoshan is a variant form. CONTEMPORARY EXAMPLE: Shoshana Damari, Israeli singer.

Shulamit, Shulamith   From the Hebrew, meaning "peaceful." Salome is the Greek form. *See* Salome. CONTEMPORARY EXAMPLE: Shulamit

Volkon, author.

Shuly   A pet form of Shulamit. *See* Shulamit.

Sibil, Sibilla   Variant forms of Sibyl. *See* Sibyl.

Sibley   From the Old English *sibling*, meaning "having one parent in common."

Sibyl   From the Greek *sibylla*, meaning "sorceress, fortune teller," women considered prophets by ancient Greeks and Romans. Also, from the Old Italian *sabius*, meaning "wise old woman." VARIANT SPELLINGS: Sibel, Sibil. Sevilla is a variant form.

Sid   A pet form of Sidney. *See* Sidney.

Sidi   Possibly a pet form of Sydel. *See* Sydel. CONTEMPORARY EXAMPLE: Sidi Hessel, author.

Sidne   A variant spelling of Sidney. *See* Sidney. CONTEMPORARY EXAMPLE: Sidne Scheinbaum, Encino, California.

Sidney   A contracted form of Saint Denys. Commonly used as a masculine name. *See* Sidney (masculine section).

Sidonia   From the Hebrew *tzidon*, meaning "to ensnare, to entice." PLACE-NAME USAGE: an ancient Phoenician seaport, now in Lebanon; Sidonia, Tennessee.

Sidonie   A variant form of Sidonia. *See* Sidonia.

Sidra   From the Latin, meaning "starlike."

Signa   From the Latin *signum*, meaning "a signal, a sign."

Sigrid   A feminine form of Siegfried. *See* Siegfried (masculine section). CONTEMPORARY EXAMPLE: Sigrid Stottrup, Decatur, Illinois.

Silva, Silvana   Variant forms of Sylvia. *See* Sylvia.

Silvano   A feminine form of Silvanus. *See* Silvanus (masculine section). CONTEMPORARY EXAMPLE: Silvano Mangano, actress.

Silver   From the German *silber*, meaning "silver." Usually a masculine form. *See* Silver (masculine section). CONTEMPORARY EXAMPLE: Silver A. Kim, Pleasanton, California.

Silvia   A variant spelling of Sylvia. *See* Sylvia.

Sima   From the Aramaic, meaning "a treasure."

Simajean   A hybrid name of Sima and Jean. *See* Sima *and* Jean.

Simeona   A feminine form of Simeon. *See* Simeon (masculine section).

Simone   A French form of Simon. *See* Simon (masculine section). CONTEMPORARY EXAMPLE: Simone Signoret, actress.

Sindy A variant spelling of Cindy. *See* Cindy (Cynthia).

Sirena A variant spelling of Serena. *See* Serena. Or, from the Greek *seiren*, meaning "a rope," hence "one who ensnares." In Greek and Roman mythology, a sea nymph, part bird and part woman, who entices sailors.

Sirius From the Greek *seirios*, meaning "a scorcher," hence the name of the brightest star (Dog Star) in the constellation Canis Major.

Sisley A variant spelling of Cicely. *See* Cicely.

Siss A pet form of Cecelia. *See* Cecelia.

Sissela A pet form of Cecelia. *See* Cecelia. CONTEMPORARY EXAMPLE: Sissela Bok, author.

Sissie, Sissy Pet forms of Cecelia. *See* Cecelia. CONTEMPORARY EXAMPLE: Sissy Spacek, actress.

Sivana The feminine form of Sivan. *See* Sivan (masculine section).

Sivia, Sivya From the Hebrew *tzvi*, meaning "a deer." VARIANT SPELLINGS: Civia, Tzivya. Also, feminine forms of Siva. *See* Siva (masculine section).

Sloan, Sloane From the Celtic, meaning "warrior." Used also as masculine names.

Sofia An Italian form of Sophia. *See* Sophia.

Solace From the Latin *solacium* and *solari*, meaning "to comfort." CONTEMPORARY EXAMPLE: Solace Connors, Redford, Minnesota.

Solange An Italian form of the Latin *solitarius* and *solus*, meaning "alone," connoting " a special diamond or gem."

Soma From the Greek, meaning "body." Also, the name of an intoxicating plant juice.

Sona From the Latin *sonare*, meaning "to sound."

Sondra A variant spelling of Sandra. *See* Sandra.

Sonia, Sonja, Sonya Variant Slavic and Russian forms of Sophia. *See* Sophia. CONTEMPORARY EXAMPLE: Sonja Bullaty, author.

Soozie A variant spelling of Suzy. *See* Suzy. CONTEMPORARY EXAMPLE: Soozie de Leon, author

Sophia An English and German name from the Greek *sophos* and *sophia*, meaning "wisdom, skill." VARIANT FORMS: Sophy (English); Sophie (French); Sofia (Italian); Sonia, Sonja, Sonya (Russian); Saffi (Danish); Zofia, Zosia (Polish). CONTEMPORARY EXAMPLE: Sophia Loren, actress.

Sophie The French form of Sophia. *See* Sophia. CONTEMPORARY EX-

AMPLE: Sophie Tucker, singer.

Sophy An English variant form of Sophie. *See* Sophie. CONTEMPORARY EXAMPLE: Sophy Barnham, author.

Sorale, Soralie, Sorolie Yiddish pet forms of Sarah. *See* Sarah.

Sparkle From the Middle English *sparklen,* meaning "to throw off sparks, brighten."

Spring From the German *springen,* meaning "to leap." CONTEMPORARY EXAMPLE: Spring Byington, actress. PLACE-NAME USAGE: Spring Valley, New York; Spring Hope, North Carolina; Springs, a city in South Africa.

Stacey, Stacy Irish forms of Anastasia. *See* Anastasia. Used also as masculine names.

Stacia, Stacie Pet forms of Anastasia. *See* Anastasia.

Stana Lee An invented name. Adapted from the masculine Stanley. *See* Stanley. CONTEMPORARY EXAMPLE: Stana Lee Dennis, Walla Walla, Washington.

Star From the Old English *steorra,* meaning "a star." CONTEMPORARY EXAMPLE: Star Helmer, editor.

Starene An invented name. Probably adapted from Star. *See* Star. CONTEMPORARY EXAMPLE: Starene Power, Santa Rosa, California.

Starla A name invented to commemorate Texas, the Lone Star State, and the star of Christmas. CONTEMPORARY EXAMPLE: Starla Doreen Coogan, Blanchester, Ohio.

Starlit A name invented for a child born on a starlit night. CONTEMPORARY EXAMPLE: Starlit June Grazulis, Aliquippa, Pennsylvania.

Starr A variant spelling of Star. *See* Star.

Stefana, Stefania Variant forms of Stephanie. *See* Stephanie.

Stefanie, Stefenie Variant spellings of Stephanie. *See* Stephanie.

Stella From the Latin, meaning "star." Esther is the Persian form of Stella. Estella is a variant form. CONTEMPORARY EXAMPLE: Stella Adler, actress.

Stellise A name invented by combining Stella and Louise. *See* Stella *and* Louise. CONTEMPORARY EXAMPLE: Stellise Kiek, Beverley, Massachusetts.

Stephanie, Stephenie Feminine forms of Stephen. From the Greek *stephanos,* meaning "a crown." *See* Stephen (masculine section). VARIANT FORMS: Etienette, Stefanie (French); Estephania (Portuguese); Stefanida, Stepanida, Stevana, Stevena (Russian); Stephanine (German). VARIANT SPELLINGS: Stefanie, Stefenie.

Stevana, Stevena Variant forms of Stephanie. *See* Stephanie.

Stockard From the Middle English *stocke*, meaning "a stump of a tree" or "blocks of woods to make an enclosure." Also, possibly a short form of stockyard. CONTEMPORARY EXAMPLE: Stockard Channing, actress.

Storm, Stormie, Stormy From the Anglo-Saxon, meaning "a tempest." Usually a masculine nickname.

Su A pet form of Susan. *See* Susan.

Suanne A hybrid name of Sue (Susan) and Anne. *See* Susan *and* Anne.

Sudy From the Old English *suth*, meaning "south, from the south." CONTEMPORARY EXAMPLE: Sudy Hurst, Tucson, Arizona.

Sue A pet form of Susan. *See* Susan.

Suella A hybrid of Sue (Susan) and Ella. *See* Susan *and* Ella. CONTEMPORARY EXAMPLE: Suella G. Hart, Roanoke, Virginia.

Sue Zann A variant spelling of Suzanne. *See* Suzanne. CONTEMPORARY EXAMPLE: Temperance Sue Zann Cullum, Marlow, Oklahoma.

Sugar From the Sanskrit *sarkara*, meaning "a pebble, a sweet crystal." CONTEMPORARY EXAMPLE: Sugar Blymer, hair stylist.

Sukey A pet name for Susan popular in the mid–nineteenth century. *See* Susan.

Sulu A name invented by combining parts of Sue (Susan) and Lu (Louis or Louise.) *See* Susan *and* Louise. CONTEMPORARY EXAMPLE: Sulu Lubin, songwriter.

Sunny Usually a nickname. Also, an independent name. CONTEMPORARY EXAMPLE: Sunny Jean Bond, Red Bluff, California (so named because she was born on a sunny day).

Susan From the Hebrew *shoshana*, meaning "a rose" or "a lily." VARIANT FORMS: Susanna, Susannah (English); Susanne, Suzette (French). PET FORMS: Su, Sue, Sukie, Sukey, Suzette, Suzie, Suzy.

Susanna, Susannah Variant forms of Susan. *See* Susan. CONTEMPORARY EXAMPLE: Susannah York, actress.

Susanne A variant form of Susan. *See* Susan. Akin to Susanna. Suzanne is a variant spelling.

Susi, Susie, Susy Pet forms of Susan. *See* Susan. CONTEMPORARY EXAMPLE: Susy Smith, author.

Suzanne A variant spelling of Susanne. *See* Susanne. CONTEMPORARY EXAMPLE: Suzanne Newton, author.

Suzette A French form of Susan. *See* Susan.

Suzy A pet form of Susan. *See* Susan. Soozie is a variant spelling.

Svea   From the Swedish and Finnish, meaning "south." CONTEMPORA-
RY EXAMPLE: Svea Ingrid Furnish, Spokane, Washington. PLACE-NAME
USAGE: a town in Finland.

Swana   From the German *schwan*, meaning "a swan."

Swoosie   Origin unknown. Probably a nickname. CONTEMPORARY EX-
AMPLE: Swoosie Kurtz, actress.

Sybella   A variant form of Sibyl. *See* Sibyl. CONTEMPORARY EXAMPLE:
Sybella Snyder, author.

Sybil   A variant spelling of Sibyl. *See* Sybil.

Sybille   A variant form of Sibyl. *See* Sibyl. CONTEMPORARY EXAMPLE:
Sybille Bedford, author.

Sybyl, Sybylla   Variant forms of Sibyl. *See* Sibyl.

Syd   A pet form of Sydney. *See* Sydney.

Sydel, Sydelle   Variant forms of Sydney. *See* Sydney. Also, a variant
form of Sadie. *See* Sadie.

Sydney   A variant spelling of Sidney. *See* Sidney. PET FORMS: Sid, Syd.
CONTEMPORARY EXAMPLE: Sydney Callahan, professor. PLACE-NAME
USAGE: Sydney, Australia.

Syke   From the Greek *sykaminos* and the Hebrew *shikma*, meaning "a
mulberry" or "a sycamore tree." CONTEMPORARY EXAMPLE: Syke Anbrey,
actress.

Sylva, Sylvana   Variant forms of the Latin *silvanus*, meaning "forest."
Akin to Sylvia. *See* Sylvia. CONTEMPORARY EXAMPLE: Sylva Koseina, actress.

Sylverta   A variant form of Sylva. *See* Sylva. CONTEMPORARY EXAM-
PLE: Silverta Blaugher, Fort Wayne, Indiana.

Sylvi   A Norwegian form of Sylvia. *See* Sylvia.

Sylvia   From the Latin *silvanus*, meaning "forest." In Roman mythology, Silvanus is the god of the woods and fields. Silvia is a variant
spelling. Sylvan is a masculine form. In ancient times, Sylvia was a
favorite name for a shepherdess as Sylvan was for a shepherd. VARIANT
FORMS: Silvi, Silvie, Silva, Silvana, Sylva, Sylvana.

Sylvie   A variant form of Sylvia. *See* Sylvia. CONTEMPORARY EXAMPLE:
Sylvie Messinger, publishers' representative.

Syma   A variant spelling of Cyma. *See* Cyma.

Syna   A variant form of Signa. *See* Signa.

Syril   A variant spelling of the masculine Cyril. *See* Cyril (masculine
section). *See also* Cyrilla. CONTEMPORARY EXAMPLE: Syril Hammel,
Brooklyn, New York.

T

Taafe   A variant spelling of Taffy. *See* Taffy. CONTEMPORARY EXAMPLE: Taafe O'Connell, actress.

Tabitha   From the Greek and Aramaic, meaning "a roe, a gazelle." In the New Testament, a charitable person who was brought up by St. Paul. CONTEMPORARY EXAMPLE: Tabitha May Kinsey, photographer.

Tace   A variant form of Tacita. *See* Tacita. Tacye is a variant spelling popular among Quakers.

Tacita   From the Latin *tacitus*, meaning "to be silent."

Tacye   A variant spelling of Tace. *See* Tace.

Taffy   The Welsh form of Vida, which is a form of David. *See* David (masculine section). Taafe is a variant spelling. CONTEMPORARY EXAMPLE: Taffy Pergament, figure skater.

Taga   From the Aramaic and Arabic, meaning "a crown."

Tai   A variant spelling of Thai, meaning "a person from Thailand." CONTEMPORARY EXAMPLE: Tai Babilonia, U.S. figure skater.

Tal   From the Hebrew, meaning "a dew."

Tali   From the Hebrew, meaning "my dew." Akin to Tal. CONTEMPORARY EXAMPLE: Tali Haenosh, Huntsville, Alabama.

Talia   From the Hebrew, meaning "dew." Akin to Tal. Also, from the Aramaic, meaning "a lamb." CONTEMPORARY EXAMPLE: Talia Shire, actress.

Tallula, Tallulah   An American Indian name generally taken to mean "running water." CONTEMPORARY EXAMPLE: Tallulah Bankhead, actress. PLACE-NAME USAGE: Tallula, Georgia.

Talma, Talmit   From the Hebrew, meaning "mound, hill."

Talmor   From the Hebrew, meaning "a heap of myrrh (spice)."

Talor, Talora   From the Hebrew, meaning "dew of the morning."

Talya   A variant spelling of Talia. *See* Talia.

Tamah   From the Hebrew, meaning "whole, perfect."

Tamanique   A name invented by adding a French ending to a form of Tammy. *See* Tammy. CONTEMPORARY EXAMPLE: Tamanique Livermore, El Cajon, California.

Tamar   From the Hebrew, meaning "a date-yielding palm tree." Used commonly as a masculine name.

Tamara, Tamarah   Variant forms of Tamar. *See* Tamar. Also, from the Hindi, meaning "a spice." CONTEMPORARY EXAMPLE: Tamara Heather Ross, Amenia, New York; Tamara Dobson, actress.

Tamarine   A French name adapted from tamarin, a squirrel-like animal native to South America.

Tamath   A variant form of the Arabic *tamasha*, meaning "to walk around." Also, an Indian name for "a spectacle, a performance." CONTEMPORARY EXAMPLE: Tamatha Lynn Edsall, South Portland, Maine.

Tameron   A name invented by substituting a "T" for the "C" of Cameron. CONTEMPORARY EXAMPLE: Tameron M. Wade, Coronado, California.

Tami, Tammy   Feminine forms of Thomas. *See* Thomas (masculine section). Also, pet forms of Tamar, Tamara, and Tamira. CONTEMPORARY EXAMPLE: Tammy Grimes, actress.

Tamzin, Tamzine   Feminine forms of Thomas. *See* Thomas (masculine section).

Tamzon   A feminine form of Tamson. *See* Tamson (masculine section). CONTEMPORARY EXAMPLE: Tamzon E. Richmond, Redwood City, California.

Tana   A variant form of Dana. *See* Dana. CONTEMPORARY EXAMPLE: Tana Carli, Miss Ohio of 1979.

Tangye   From the Old Norse *tengi*, meaning "a dagger." CONTEMPORARY EXAMPLE: Tangye Dunn, Buckeye, Arizona.

Tania   From the Russian, meaning "the fairy queen." Tanya is a variant spelling.

Tanim   A name invented by scrambling the letters of the name Minta. CONTEMPORARY EXAMPLE: Tanim Elaine Sturgill, Lima, Ohio.

Tanith   From the Old Irish *tan*, meaning "an estate." In Gaelic society, a *tanaiste* was the heir of a leader. CONTEMPORARY EXAMPLE: Tanith Lee, author.

Tanka   Probably from the Portuguese *tanque*, meaning "a tank, a pond."

Tansy   A pet form of Anastasia. *See* Anastasia.

Tanya   A variant spelling of Tania. *See* Tania. CONTEMPORARY EXAMPLE: Tanya Tucker, singer.

Tara   Either a French name derived from the Arabic, meaning "a measurement," or from the Aramaic, meaning "to throw" or "to carry." Also, a short form of Taranto, a city in Italy, so named because the spider called tarantula was found nearby. CONTEMPORARY EXAMPLE: Tara Tyson, actress.

Taragabee Meaning uncertain. Probably a form of Tara. *See* Tara. CONTEMPORARY EXAMPLE: Taragabee Hurt, Houston, Texas.

Taryn Probably a variant form of Tara. *See* Tara. Also, an invented name: an adaptation of the masculine Tyrone. CONTEMPORARY EXAMPLE: Taryn Stenman, caterer; Taryn Krol, Southgate, Minnesota.

Tasha A short form of Natasha. *See* Natasha. Or, from the Arabic *tassa*, meaning "a cup." CONTEMPORARY EXAMPLE: Tasha Tudor, author.

Tashua A variant form of Tasha. *See* Tasha. CONTEMPORARY EXAMPLE: Tashua Hyman, Shelton, Connecticut.

Tate From the Anglo-Saxon, meaning "to be cheerful." Used also as a masculine name. SURNAME USAGE: Sharon Tate, actress.

Tatiana A third-century Christian martyr. A favorite Russian name often transcribed as Tanya. CONTEMPORARY EXAMPLE: Tatiana Troyanos, opera singer.

Tatum A variant form of Tate. *See* Tate. CONTEMPORARY EXAMPLE: Tatum O'Neal, actress.

Tauba From the German *taube*, meaning "a dove." A popular Yiddish name. Toby is a variant form. CONTEMPORARY EXAMPLE: Tauba Ingenthron, St. Louis, Missouri.

Tavi A variant form of the masculine form David. *See* David (masculine section). CONTEMPORARY EXAMPLE: Tavi Granger, Marysville, California.

Tavita A pet form of Tavi. *See* Tavi. Akin to Tevita.

Tawana An American Indian name. Meaning unknown. CONTEMPORARY EXAMPLE: Tawana Bernard, Irving, Texas.

Taylor An Anglo-Saxon occupational name, meaning "a tailor." Used also as a masculine name. CONTEMPORARY EXAMPLE: Taylor Caldwell, author. SURNAME USAGE: Elizabeth Taylor, actress.

Tegan From the Celtic, meaning "a doe." Tegan was a queen of ancient Britain.

Teli From the Aramaic and Hebrew, meaning "a lamb." Also, a pet name for Theodora and Thelma. *See* Theodora *and* Thelma.

Tellus From the Latin *telluris*, meaning "the earth." In Roman mythology, the goddess of the earth.

Temima From the Hebrew *tamim*, meaning "whole, honest."

Temira From the Hebrew, meaning "tall." Akin to Timora.

Temperance   From the Latin *temperare*, meaning "to mix in correct proportions." CONTEMPORARY EXAMPLE: Temperance Sue Zann Cullum, Marlow, Oklahoma.

Templa   From the Latin *templum*, meaning "a temple, a sanctuary."

Teresa   The Spanish and Italian form of Theresa. *See* Theresa. Became popular throughout Europe when St. Teresa of Avila's fame carried the name to all Roman Catholic countries beyond the Iberian Peninsula. CONTEMPORARY EXAMPLE: Teresa Brewer, singer.

Teresina, Teresita   Pet forms of Theresa. *See* Theresa.

Teri   A pet form of Theresa. See Theresa. VARIANT SPELLINGS: Terri, Terrie, Terry.

Terranda   From the Latin *terra*, meaning "earth," plus *andr*, meaning "man," hence "man's earth." CONTEMPORARY EXAMPLE: Terranda King, teacher.

Terri, Terrie   Pet forms of Theresa. *See* Theresa.

Terrill   A variant form of Terry. *See* Terry.

Terry   A pet form of Theresa. *See* Theresa.

Tertia   From the Latin *tertius*, meaning "the third."

Teruma   From the Hebrew, meaning "an offering, a gift."

Teshura   From the Hebrew, meaning "a gift."

Tess, Tessie   Pet forms of Theresa. *See* Theresa. CONTEMPORARY EXAMPLE: Tessie O'Shea, entertainer.

Tetty   A pet form of Elizabeth. *See* Elizabeth.

Tevita   A Fijian form of Davida. *See* Davida.

Tex   A nickname bestowed on people from the state of Texas. CONTEMPORARY EXAMPLE: Tex Yuma Heinrich Middlebrooks, Yuma, Arizona.

Thaddea, Thadine   Feminine forms of Thaddeus. *See* Thaddeus (masculine section).

Thalassa   From the Greek, meaning "the sea." CONTEMPORARY EXAMPLE: Thalassa Caruso, gardening expert.

Thalia   From the Greek, meaning "to flourish, to bloom." One of the Greek Muses. Also, a variant spelling of the Hebrew forms Tal and Talia. *See* Tal *and* Talia.

Thana   From the Greek *thanatos*, meaning "death." In Greek mythology, Thanatos is death personified.

Thea   A short form of Althea. *See* Althea. In Greek mythology, the name of a goddess.

Theda   A variant form of Theodora. *See* Theodora. CONTEMPORARY EXAMPLE: Theda Bara, actress.

Thekla   From the Greek, meaning "God-famous." According to legend, Thekla was the first woman martyr, a convert of St. Paul.

Thelma   From the Greek, meaning "a nursling, infant." Assumed to be a name invented by Marie Corelli for the Norwegian heroine of her novel *Thelma: A Society Novel* (1887). Also, a variant form of Selma. CONTEMPORARY EXAMPLE: Thelma Ritter, actress; Thelma Rubin, Wassaic, New York.

Theodora   The feminine form of Theodore. *See* Theodore. Theo is a pet form. CONTEMPORARY EXAMPLE: Theodora Wells, author.

Theodosia   From the Greek, meaning "divine gift." Akin to Theodora.

Theola   From the Greek, meaning "the divine."

Theone   From the Greek, meaning "godly."

Theophania   From the Greek, meaning "a manifestation of God." SURNAME USAGE: Tiffany, Tiffen, Tiffin.

Theophila   From the Greek, meaning "beloved of God."

Thera   A variant form of Theresa. *See* Theresa.

Theresa   From the Greek *therizein*, meaning "to reap." VARIANT FORMS: Tracey, Tracy, Terry (English); Therese (French); Teresa (Spanish and Italian); Theresia, Tressa (German). PET FORMS: Teri, Terri, Terry, Tess, Tessa, Tessie.

Therese   The French form of Theresa. *See* Theresa.

Theryl   An invented name. CONTEMPORARY EXAMPLE: Theryl Penney, author.

Thesia   From the Greek *thesis*, meaning "a position, a proposition." In Greek legend, Theseus is the hero of Attica and king of Athens.

Thetis   From the Greek *thetos*, meaning "dogmatic." In Greek legend, the mother of Achilles. She dipped him into the River Styx when he was an infant to make him invulnerable, but neglected to immerse his heel.

Thirza   A variant spelling of Tirza. *See* Tirza. In the Bible, the name of Abel's wife. Thyrza is a variant spelling used in England.

Thomasa   The feminine form of Thomas. *See* Thomas (masculine section). VARIANT FORMS: Thomasina, Thomasine, Thomassine.

Thomasina   From the Hebrew, meaning "the twin." Thomasa is a variant form. Thomas is the masculine form.

Thomasine, Thomassine   Feminine forms of Thomas. Akin to Thomasina. *See* Thomas (masculine section).

Thora   From the Norse, meaning "the thunderer," a feminine form of Thor, the god of war in Norse mythology.

Thordis   From the Scandinavian, meaning "Thor's spirit."

Thrine   From the Greek, meaning "the pure one."

Thyra   From the Greek, meaning "a door" or "a window." CONTEMPORARY EXAMPLE: Thyra Thomson, Wyoming politician. In Danish mythology, the goddess of dawn.

Thyrza   A variant spelling of Thirza. *See* Thirza.

Tiberia   From the Latin, meaning "of the River Tiber." Named for the first–century Roman emperor Tiberius Claudius Nero Caesar.

Tiffany   A variant form of the Latin *trinitas*, meaning "three, the trinity." Also, from the Greek *theophania*, meaning "manifestation of God." CONTEMPORARY EXAMPLE: Tiffany Bolling, actress. SURNAME USAGE: C.L. Tiffany (1812-1902), U.S. jeweler.

Tilda   A pet form of Mathilda. *See* Mathilda.

Tilla   A variant form of Tillie. *See* Tillie.

Tillamae   A name invented by combining Tilla and Mae. *See* Tilla *and* Mae.

Tillie   A pet form of Mathilda. *See* Mathilda. CONTEMPORARY EXAMPLE: Tillie S. Pina, educator.

Tilly   A variant spelling of Tillie. *See* Tillie.

Timi   A pet form of Timora. *See* Timora.

Timora   From the Hebrew *tamar*, meaning "tall," as the palm (tamar) tree.

Timothea   From the Greek, meaning "honoring God." Timothy is the masculine form.

Tina   A pet form of names ending in "tina," such as Christina and Bettina. *See* Christina *and* Bettina.

Tinkerbelle   The name of a fictional character in *Peter Pan*. CONTEMPORARY EXAMPLE: Tinkerbelle O'Brien, Long Island City, New York.

Tinkle   An invented name suggested by the tinkling of Christmas bells. CONTEMPORARY EXAMPLE: Tinkle Marie Cooper, Columbus, Indiana.

Tira   From the Hebrew, meaning "encampment, enclosure."

Tirza, Tirzah   From the Hebrew, meaning either "a cypress tree" or, from a second root, "she will be willing, desirable." PLACE-NAME USAGE: in the Bible, the capital of Samaria; Tirzah, South Carolina.

Tisha   A pet form of Patricia. *See* Patricia. CONTEMPORARY EXAMPLE:

Tisha Sterling, actress.

Tita   A variant form of Titania. *See* Titania.

Titania   From the Greek, meaning "the great one." In early folklore, the queen of fairyland and the wife of Oberon.

Tivona, Tivoni   From the Hebrew, meaning "a lover of nature."

Toba   A variant spelling of Tova. *See* Tova. Akin to the masculine Tobias.

Tobelle   A Yiddish pet form of Toba. *See* Toba.

Tobey   A variant form of Toba. *See* Toba.

Tobi   A variant spelling of Toby. *See* Toby. CONTEMPORARY EXAMPLE: Tobi Tobias, author.

Tobit   From the Hebrew, meaning "good." In the Apocrypha, the heroine of the Book of Tobit. Mentioned several times in the Bible as a masculine name.

Toby   A variant form of Toba. Tobi is a variant spelling. Tobias is a masculine form. PLACE-NAME USAGE: Toby's Creek, Pennsylvania.

Toinette   A short form of Antoinette. *See* Antoinette.

Tomasa   The Spanish feminine form of Thomas. *See* Thomas (masculine section).

Tommi   A feminine pet form of Thomas. *See* Thomas (masculine section).

Tommianne   A name invented by combining Tommi and Anne. *See* Tommi *and* Anne.

Toni, Tonia, Tony   Pet forms of Antoinette. *See* Antoinette.

Topaza   From the Greek *topazos*, a yellow variety of sapphire.

Torine   A variant form of Torino, the Italian form of Turin, a city in Italy.

Totie   A variant form of Dottie, a pet form of Dorothy. *See* Dorothy. CONTEMPORARY EXAMPLE: Totie Fields, comedienne.

Tottie   A pet form of Charlotte. *See* Charlotte. Also a pet form of Dorothy. *See* Dorothy.

Tourmaline   The French for the precious gem carnelian.

Tova, Tovah   From the Hebrew, meaning "good." Toba is a variant spelling. CONTEMPORARY EXAMPLE: Tovah Feldshuh, actress.

Toyah   From the Scottish *toy*, a woman's headdress with flaps that hang over the shoulder. CONTEMPORARY EXAMPLE: Toyah Dafft, Carrollton, Texas.

Tracey, Tracy   From the Anglo-Saxon, meaning "brave." Also, variant forms of Theresa. *See* Theresa. Used also as masculine names. CONTEMPORARY EXAMPLE: Tracy Austin, tennis player.

Trazon   Origin unknown. CONTEMPORARY EXAMPLE: Trazon Minor, Toledo, Ohio.

Trella   A short form of Estrella, the Spanish form of Esther. *See* Esther.

Trellis   From the Latin *trilix*, meaning "triple-twilled; interwoven; a bower."

Tressa   A German form of Theresa. *See* Theresa.

Tressella   A name invented by combining Tressa and Claudella. *See* Tressa and Claudella. CONTEMPORARY EXAMPLE: Tressella Benson, Louisville, Kentucky.

Tricia   A pet form of Patricia. *See* Patricia. VARIANT FORMS: Tisha, Trish, Trisha. CONTEMPORARY EXAMPLE: Tricia Nixon Cox, President Nixon's daughter.

Trilby   From the Old English, meaning "a soft hat." The title of George du Maurier's novel. CONTEMPORARY EXAMPLE: Trilby S. Redford, Richmond, Virginia.

Trina   A short form of Katrina, a form of Katherine. *See* Katherine.

Trinita   An invented name, meaning "the trinity." Conferred upon Sister M. Trinita Flood, Miami Shores, Florida, when she received the habit of the Sisters of St. Dominic.

Trish, Trisha   Short forms of Patricia. *See* Patricia. Tricia is a variant spelling. CONTEMPORARY EXAMPLE: Trish van Devere, actress.

Tristine   From the Latin *tristis*, meaning "sad." Tristan is a masculine form. CONTEMPORARY EXAMPLE: Tristine Rainer, author.

Trix, Trixie, Trixy   Pet forms of Beatrice and Beatrix. *See* Beatrice *and* Beatrix.

Truda, Trude   Pet forms of Gertrude. *See* Gertrude. CONTEMPORARY EXAMPLE: Trude Weiss-Rosmarin, author.

Trudel   A Dutch contraction of Gertrude. *See* Gertrude.

Trudi, Trudy   Popular pet forms of Gertrude. *See* Gertrude.

Trula   Probably a variant form of Gertrude. *See* Gertrude. CONTEMPORARY EXAMPLE: Trula M. Dresser, Santa Ana, California.

Tryphena   From the Greek, meaning "delicate." In the Bible, mentioned by St. Paul in the Book of Romans.

Tuanette   A pet form of Antoinette. *See* Antoinette. CONTEMPORARY EXAMPLE: Tuanette van Winkle, Billings, Montana.

Tuesday   From the Old English *tiwesdaeg*, meaning "tiu's day." In German mythology, *tiu* (*tiw*) is the god of war and the sky. CONTEMPORARY EXAMPLE: Tuesday Weld, actress.

Turquois, Turquoise   From the Old French *turkeis*, a semiprecious stone originally brought to Europe through Turkey. CONTEMPORARY EXAMPLE: Turquois Erving, wife of basketball star Julius Erving.

Tusnelda   Origin unknown. Nadie is a pet form. CONTEMPORARY EXAMPLE: Tusnelda Kaufmann, Tustin, California.

Twila   From the Middle English *twyll*, meaning "woven of double thread," a cloth woven with parallel lines. CONTEMPORARY EXAMPLE: Twila Rae Williams, Lincoln, Nebraska.

Twyla   A variant spelling of Twila. *See* Twila. CONTEMPORARY EXAMPLE: Twyla Tharp, choreographer.

Tyann   A name invented by combining the masculine Tyrus and Ann. *See* Tyrus (masculine section) *and* Ann. CONTEMPORARY EXAMPLE: Tyann McIntyre, Rensselaer, Indiana.

Tybal, Tyballa   From the Old English *tiber*, meaning "a holy place, a place where sacrifices were brought."

Tyna   A variant form of Tyne. *See* Tyne. CONTEMPORARY EXAMPLE: Tyna Barinaga, badminton champion.

Tyne   From the British *tain*, meaning "a river." Tyna is a variant form. CONTEMPORARY EXAMPLE: Tyne Daly, actress.

Tzigane   From the Hungarian *czigany*, meaning "a gypsy."

Ualani   From the Hawaiian, meaning "heavenly rain."

Uda   A variant form of Uta. *See* Uta.

Ula   A pet form of Ulrica. *See* Ulrica.

Ulani   From the Hawaiian, meaning "gay."

Ulema   From the Arabic *alama*, meaning "to know, to be learned."

Ulla   From the Middle English *ulage*, meaning "to fill (a cask to the brim)." CONTEMPORARY EXAMPLE: Ulla Bergryd, actress.

Ulrica   From the German, meaning "ruler over all." Ulric is the masculine form. PET FORMS: Rica, Rickie, Ricky, Rikki, Rikky.

Ultima   From the Latin *ultimus*, meaning "the end, final."

Una   From the Latin, meaning "the one." VARIANT FORMS: Oona (Irish); Unity (English). A character in Spenser's *Faerie Queene*. CONTEMPORARY EXAMPLE: Una Merkel, actress.

Undina, Undine   From the Latin *unda*, meaning "a wave." In folklore, a female water spirit or nymph who could acquire a soul by marrying a mortal and bearing a child.

Unity   From the Latin *unus*, meaning "one." Became fashionable in the seventeenth century. CONTEMPORARY EXAMPLE: Unity Hall, author. PLACE-NAME USAGE: Unity, Maine.

Urania   From the Greek *ouranos*, meaning "heaven." In Greek mythology, a god who is the personification of the heavens. PLACE-NAME USAGE: Urania, Louisiana.

Urbana, Urbanna   From the Latin *urbs* and *urbanus*, meaning "a city." Urban is the masculine form. PLACE-NAME USAGE: Urbanna, Virginia.

Urit   From the Hebrew *or*, meaning "light."

Urith   A variant spelling of Urit. *See* Urit.

Urilla   Probably a French form of the masculine Uriah, meaning "God is light." *See* Uriah (masculine section). CONTEMPORARY EXAMPLE: Urilla M. Cheverie, North Reading, Massachusetts.

Ursa   From the Latin, meaning "a she-bear."

Ursala   A variant spelling of Ursula. *See* Ursula.

Ursel   A variant form of Ursala. *See* Ursala.

Ursina, Ursine   Variant forms of Ursula. *See* Ursula. PLACE-NAME USAGE: Ursina, Pennsylvania; Ursine, Nevada.

Ursula   A pet form of the Latin *ursa*, meaning "a she-bear." The legend of St. Ursala and her 11,000 virgin companions who were slain by Attila, king of the Huns, was popular in the Middle Ages. VARIANT FORMS: Ursa (Latin); Ursel (English and German); Orsola (Italian). CONTEMPORARY EXAMPLE: Ursula Andress, actress.

Ursule   A variant spelling of Ursula. *See* Ursula. CONTEMPORARY EXAMPLE: Ursule Molinaro, translator.

Urte   From the Latin *urtica*, meaning "a stinging or spiny plant." CONTEMPORARY EXAMPLE: Urte Krefeli, homeopathic practitioner.

Uta   Probably from the Spanish tribal name Yutta, meaning "mountain dwellers." Akin to Utah (the state). CONTEMPORARY EXAMPLE: Uta Hagen, actress.

V

Vaino From the British *ban*, meaning "high." CONTEMPORARY EXAMPLE: Vaino Spencer, lawyer.

Val A pet form of Valda, Valerie, Valentina, and Valentine. *See* Valda, Valerie, Valentina, *and* Valentine.

Valari A variant form of Valerie. *See* Valerie. CONTEMPORARY EXAMPLE: Valari Barocas, publisher.

Valda From the German, meaning "battle heroine." Val is a pet form.

Valencia From the Latin, meaning "strong, vigorous." PLACE-NAME USAGE: cities in Pennsylvania, New Mexico, and California.

Valentia A variant spelling of Valencia. *See* Valencia.

Valentina An Italian form of Valentine. *See* Valentine.

Valentine From the Latin *valens*, meaning "healthy, strong." Used originally as a masculine form. VARIANT FORMS: Valencia, Valentia, Valentina, Valentino. PET FORMS: Val, Vallie. PLACE-NAME USAGE: Valentine, Nebraska, named for E.K. Valentine, a congressman; Valentine, Texas, named in honor of Saint Valentine.

Valentino An Italian form of Valentine. *See* Valentine.

Valeria From the Latin *valere*, meaning "to be strong." Valerie is a variant French form. An early Roman family name. Popular in Italy. CONTEMPORARY EXAMPLE: Valeria Johnson, librarian.

Valerie A French form of the Latin name Valeria, meaning "to be strong."

Valery A variant spelling of Valerie. *See* Valerie.

Valeska From the Slavic, meaning "glory." CONTEMPORARY EXAMPLE: Valeska Klindt, San Jose, California.

Valonia, Vallonia Italian forms of the Greek *balanos*, meaning "an acorn."

Valora From the Latin *valere*, meaning "to be strong." VARIANT FORMS: Valeria, Valerie.

Vana From the British *ban*, meaning "high." Also, a form of the name of the Old Norse goddess Vanadis. CONTEMPORARY EXAMPLE: Vana Gonzales, New York City.

Vanessa   From the Greek, meaning "a butterfly." Also, a name invented by Jonathan Swift in his *Cademus and Vanessa*, from the name Esther Vanhomrigh.

Vania   A feminine form of Ivan. *See* Ivan (masculine section).

Vanora   From the Celtic, meaning "white wave."

Varda   From the Hebrew, meaning "a rose."

Vardia, Vardina   From the Hebrew, meaning "a rose." Akin to Varda.

Vardit   A variant form of Varda. *See* Varda.

Varina   Possibly a variant form of Varuna. *See* Varuna. PLACE-NAME USAGE: Varina, North Carolina.

Varuna   In Hindu mythology, the god of the cosmos. CONTEMPORARY EXAMPLE: Varuna J. Mitchell, Marina, California.

Vashti   From the Persian, meaning "beautiful." In the Bible, the queen of King Ahasuerus of Persia. PLACE-NAME USAGE: Vashti, North Dakota, named for Mollie Vashti Jarvis, wife of an early settler (c. 1916).

Veda   From the Sanskrit, meaning "knowledge." The Veda is one of the sacred books of the Hindus.

Vedis   From the Singhalese, meaning "a hunter."

Vega   From the Arabic, meaning "the falling," referring to a very bright star in the constellation Lyra.

Vela   From the Latin *velle*, meaning "to wish, to desire." Also, a constellation in the Southern Milky Way. Vella is a variant spelling.

Velda, Veleda   From the Middle Dutch, meaning "a field." CONTEMPORARY EXAMPLE: Velda Johnston, novelist.

Velika   From the Slavic, meaning "great."

Velinda   A variant form of Belinda. *See* Belinda.

Vella   A variant spelling of Vela. *See* Vela.

Velma   A pet form of Wilhelmina. *See* Wilhelmina. Vilma is a variant form. CONTEMPORARY EXAMPLE: Velma V. Varner, educator.

Velva   A name derived from "velvet." PLACE-NAME USAGE: Velva, North Dakota.

Velvet   From the Latin *villus*, meaning "shaggy hair, wool."

Vena   From the Latin *vena*, meaning "a vein." CONTEMPORARY EXAMPLE: Vena Garrett, Newport Beach, California.

Venda   From the Latin *venus*, meaning "to love."

Veneta   A variant form of Venetia. *See* Venetia. PLACE-NAME USAGE:

Veneta, Oregon, named for Veneta Hunter, daughter of the town founder.

Venetia From the Latin, meaning "a woman of Venice." Akin to Venita. Also, a Latin form of the Welsh Gwyneth. PLACE-NAME USAGE: an ancient district north of the Po River; a region in northern Italy.

Venita From the Latin, meaning "woman of Venice." CONTEMPORARY EXAMPLE: Venita van Caspel, author.

Venus From the Latin, meaning "to love." In Greek mythology, the goddess of love and beauty.

Ventura From the Spanish, meaning "good fortune." PLACE-NAME USAGE: Ventura, California.

Vera From the Latin *vera* and *verus*, meaning "truth." Also, from the Russian *vjera*, meaning "faith." CONTEMPORARY EXAMPLE: Vera Miles, actress.

Verda A variant form of Verdi. *See* Verdi. Used also as a masculine form.

Verdi From the Old French *verd*, meaning "green, springlike." Used also as a masculine form.

Vered From the Hebrew, meaning "a rose." Used also as a masculine name.

Verena, Verina From the Latin *vera* and *verus*, meaning "truth." Also, from the Latin *venerari*, meaning "to venerate God." Verena was a virgin martyred under Diocletian. CONTEMPORARY EXAMPLE: Verena Schubert, Hidden Hills, California.

Verita From the Latin *veritas*, meaning "truth." VARIANT FORMS: Vera, Verena, Verina, Verity. CONTEMPORARY EXAMPLE: Verita Aalbue, Pueblo, Colorado.

Verity From the Latin *veritas*, meaning "truth." Akin to Verita. CONTEMPORARY EXAMPLE: Verity Bargate, novelist.

Verna From the Latin *veritas*, meaning "truth." VARIANT FORMS: Verena, Verne, Veronica. Vernon is a masculine form. CONTEMPORARY EXAMPLE: Verna Penn, librarian.

Verne, Vernee From the Latin, meaning "green, springlike." Also, variant forms of Verena. *See* Verena. CONTEMPORARY EXAMPLE: Vernee Watson, actress.

Vernie A pet form of Verne. *See* Verne. PLACE-NAME USAGE: Verndale, Minnesota, named for Vernie Smith, granddaughter of an early settler.

Vernique A French form of Verne. *See* Verne.

Vernita A pet form of Verne. *See* Verne.

Vernona A variant form of Verne. *See* Verne. PLACE-NAME USAGE: Vernonia, Oregon, named for Vernona Cherrington, daughter of a town founder.

Veronica From the Latin *veritas*, meaning "truth." Akin to Verity. According to legend, a woman of Jerusalem who wiped the bleeding face of Jesus on the way to Calvary. Vernon is a masculine form. CONTEMPO-RARY EXAMPLE: Veronica Lake, actress. PLACE-NAME USAGE: Verona, Italy.

Versie From the Latin *versus*, meaning "a turning, verse, line, row." CONTEMPORARY EXAMPLE: Versie B. Cook, Ashland, Kentucky.

Vesma From the Latin *vas*, meaning "a vessel, a vase." CONTEMPORA-RY EXAMPLE: Vesma Grinfelds, bowling champion.

Vesna A variant form of Vesma. *See* Vesma. CONTEMPORARY EXAMPLE: Vesna Krmpotic, Yugoslav poet.

Vespera An Old French form of Esther, meaning "a star."

Vesta In Roman mythology, the goddess of fire. PLACE-NAME USAGE: Vesta Temple, Arizona.

Vevay A Celtic name, meaning "a white wave."

Vevila From the Celtic, meaning "harmonious."

Vi A pet form of Violet. *See* Violet.

Vici, Vicki, Vicky Pet forms of Victoria. *See* Victoria. CONTEMPO-RARY EXAMPLE: Vicki Lawrence, actress.

Victoria From the Latin, meaning "victorious." The feminine form of Victor. Queen of Britain and Ireland (1837-1901). VARIANT FORMS: Victoire (French); Vittoria (Italian); Vitoria (Spanish). PET FORMS: Vici, Vicki, Vicky, Victorine, Vikki, Vikkie. PLACE-NAME USAGE: capital of Hong Kong; a region in Australia; a lake in East Africa; cities and sites in Minnesota, Texas, and Kansas.

Victorine A pet form of Victoria. *See* Victoria.

Vida A pet form of Davida. *See* Davida. Also, a variant form of Vita. *See* Vita. PLACE-NAME USAGE: Vida, Oregon, named for Vida Pepiot, daughter of a postmaster.

Vidonia From the Latin, meaning "a vine."

Viena, Vienna From the Middle English *vien* and the Old French *en-vier*, meaning "to invite, to vie with (in competitive games)." PLACE-NAME USAGE: the capital of Austria (spelled Vienna); a city in France (spelled Vienne); Vienna, South Dakota.

Vikki, Vikkie Pet forms of Victoria. *See* Victoria. CONTEMPORARY EX-AMPLE: Vikki Carr, singer.

Vila An Italian form of the Latin *villaticus*, meaning "a country estate, a farm." CONTEMPORARY EXAMPLE: Vila Cristine Servall, Robbins, California.

Vilma   A variant form of Velma. *See* Velma. CONTEMPORARY EXAMPLE: Vilma Jester, New York City.

Vilna   A pet form of Wilhelmina. *See* Wilhelmina. Velma is a variant form. CONTEMPORARY EXAMPLE: Vilna Bergane, publisher.

Vincentia   From the Latin *vincere*, meaning "to conquer." Vincent is the masculine form.

Vinetia   A variant spelling of Venetia. *See* Venetia. CONTEMPORARY EXAMPLE: Vinetia McGreevvy, Cadiz, Ohio.

Vinita   A variant spelling of Venita. *See* Venita. PLACE-NAME USAGE: Vinita, Oklahoma.

Vinnette   A French pet form of Winifred. *See* Winifred. Also, a pet form of Vincentia. *See* Vincentia. CONTEMPORARY EXAMPLE: Vinnette Carrol, theatrical writer and director.

Viola   From the Middle English and Latin, meaning "a violet." A genus of plant with white, blue, purple, or yellow flowers.

Violet   The Old French form of Viola. *See* Viola. Vi is a pet form.

Violeta, Violetta   Italian pet forms of Violet. *See* Violet.

Violette   A pet form of Viola. *See* Viola. CONTEMPORARY EXAMPLE: Violette A. Johnson, attorney.

Viqui   A variant spelling of Vicki. *See* Vicki. CONTEMPORARY EXAMPLE: Viqui Litman, free-lance writer.

Virenda   Origin unknown. CONTEMPORARY EXAMPLE: Virenda Nyberg, author.

Virgie   A pet form of Virginia. *See* Virginia. CONTEMPORARY EXAMPLE: Virgie Husted, East Liverpool, Ohio.

Virgilia   The feminine form of Virgil. *See* Virgil (masculine section). Akin to Virginia.

Virginia   From the Latin *virginitas*, meaning "virgin, pure" or "a maiden." Akin to Virgilia. Virginius was the name of an early Roman family. Virginie is a French form. Popularized by Elizabeth I of England (1533-1603), known as the Virgin Queen. PET FORMS: Ginnie, Ginny, Virgie. PLACE-NAME USAGE: a southern U.S. state; Virgin Islands, West Indies.

Virginie   A French form of Virginia. *See* Virginia.

Viridis   From the Latin *viridis*, meaning "green, youthful, blooming."

Virna   A variant spelling of Verna. *See* Verna. CONTEMPORARY EXAM-

PLE: Virna Osmond, singer.

Vita   From the Latin, meaning "life, animated." VARIANT FORMS: Vida, Vivian, Vivien, Vyvyan.

Viveca   From the Middle Latin *viva voce*, meaning "with living voice, by word of mouth." CONTEMPORARY EXAMPLE: Viveca Lindfors, actress.

Vivevca   From the Latin *vivactus*, meaning "lively."

Vivi   From the Latin *vivus*, meaning "alive." Akin to Vivian. CONTEMPORARY EXAMPLE: Vivi Janiss, actress.

Vivian, Viviana   From the Latin *vivus*, meaning "alive." Akin to Vivi. Viviana appears in twelfth-century England as a hybrid of Vivian. Vivian is also used as a masculine form. In Arthurian legend, Vivian was an enchantress, mistress of Merlin.

Vivien, Vivienne   French forms of Vivian. *See* Vivian.

Volante   An Italian form of the Latin *volare*, meaning "to fly."

Voleta, Voletta   Probably variant forms of Violetta. *See* Violetta.

Vona   Probably a variant form of Wanda. *See* Wanda. PLACE-NAME USAGE: Vona, Colorado, named by P.S. King, town founder, for his niece.

Voncile   Origin unknown. CONTEMPORARY EXAMPLE: Voncile Draper, Covina, California.

Vonda   Probably a variant form of Wanda. *See* Wanda. CONTEMPORARY EXAMPLE: Vonda N. McIntyre, author.

Vondra   An invented name. Meaning unknown. CONTEMPORARY EXAMPLE: Vondra Lynne Day, East Liverpool, Ohio.

Vyonne   Probably a reversal of the syllables in Yvonne. *See* Yvonne CONTEMPORARY EXAMPLE: Vyonne Bowers, Huntington Beach, California.

Vyvyan   A variant spelling of Vivian. *See* Vivian. CONTEMPORARY EXAMPLE: Vyvyan Holland, author.

W

Wacil   From the British *wac*, meaning "weak, small." CONTEMPORARY EXAMPLE: Wacil Johnson, Bainbridge Island, Washington.

Wahalla   Probably a variant form of Valhalla, from the Old Norse, meaning "hall of the slain." In Norse mythology, Valhalla is the great hall where Odin received the soul of war heroes. CONTEMPORARY EXAMPLE: Wahalla Cullum, Quinlan, Texas.

Wahkuna   From the American Indian *warnhu*, meaning "arrow wood."

Waikiki   From the Hawaiian, meaning "spurting water." PLACE-NAME USAGE: a beach in Honolulu, Hawaii.

Wakenda   From the Middle English *waknen*, meaning "to become awake." Also, an American Indian name, meaning "of the world force."

Walda   From the Old English *waeld*, meaning "forest, uncultivated field." Or, from the Old High German *waldan*, meaning "to rule." The feminine form of Waldo.

Wallis   From the British *wall*, meaning "a fortification." Also, from the Old Norse *val*, meaning "a choice, a selection." May also mean "a girl from Wales." CONTEMPORARY EXAMPLE: Wallis Warfield Simpson, the former Duchess of Windsor.

Wanaka   The Hawaiian form of Wanda. *See* Wanda.

Wanda   A Middle English form of the Old Norse *vondr* and the Gothic *wandus*, meaning "a slender, supple shoot; a young tree." VARIANT FORMS: Vonda, Wanaka, Wandis. PLACE-NAME USAGE: Wanda, Montana.

Wandis   A variant form of Wanda. *See* Wanda.

Wanika   The Hawaiian form of Juanita. *See* Juanita.

Wannetta, Wanette   From the Old English *wann*, meaning "young pale one." Also, an adaptation of Juanita. *See* Juanita. PLACE-NAME USAGE: Wanette, Oklahoma.

Wapeka   From the Old English *waepen*, meaning "a weapon." An American Indian name.

Warnette   A name invented by combining Warren and Annette. *See* Warren (masculine section) *and* Annette. CONTEMPORARY EXAMPLE: Warnette Kondo, Santa Clara, California.

Warrene   The feminine form of Warren. *See* Warren (masculine section). CONTEMPORARY EXAMPLE: Warrene Berge, Phoenix, Arizona.

Wasida   From the Old English *waes*, meaning "water." CONTEMPORA-RY EXAMPLE: Wasida Mastalerz, Cumberland, Rhode Island.

Waunena   Possibly from the British *gwaun*, meaning "a meadow." An American Indian name. CONTEMPORARY EXAMPLE: Waunena Williams, Santarosa, California.

Waurene   Possibly a feminine form of Warren. *See* Warren (masculine section). CONTEMPORARY EXAMPLE: Waurene Flannigan, Batesville, Mississippi.

Welcome   From the Old English *willa*, meaning "pleasure," plus *cuma*, meaning "guest," hence "a welcome guest." Used also as a masculine name.

Welthy, Welty   From the Old English *wolcen*, meaning "a cloud," and later, "the sky." CONTEMPORARY EXAMPLE: Welthy Hotmar Weigel, Bowling Green, Kentucky. SURNAME USAGE: Eudora Welty, novelist.

Wenda   From the British *gwen*, meaning "fair."

Wendelin, Wendeline   Pet forms of Wenda. *See* Wenda.

Wendey, Wendi, Wendy   Pet forms of Gwendaline and Wenda. *See* Gwendaline *and* Wenda.

Wenona, Wenonah   From the Old English *wen*, a variant form of *win*, meaning "joy, bliss." Also, an American Indian name, meaning "first-born daughter."

Whaley   From the Old English *wheal*, meaning "a wall." Also, from the Middle English *whal*, meaning "a large fish." CONTEMPORARY EX-AMPLE: Whaley Hunt, salesperson.

Wilda   From the Old English *wil*, meaning "a willow." CONTEMPORA-RY EXAMPLE: Wilda Guerrette, bowling champion.

Wilenda   A name invented by combining William and Brenda. CON-TEMPORARY EXAMPLE: Wilenda June Staselavaag, Spartanburg, South Carolina.

Wilfreda   The feminine form of Wilfred. *See* Wilfred (masculine section).

Wilhelmina   The English and Dutch form of Wilhelm, the German form of William. *See* William (masculine section). VARIANT FORMS: Wilmot (English); Minette (French); Guglielma (Italian); Minka (Polish). PET FORMS: Mimi, Minnette, Mina, Minna, Helma, Velma, Vilma, Vilna, Willa, Willene, Wilmena, Wilma. CONTEMPORARY EXAMPLE: Wilhelmina Helena Pauline Maria (1880-1962), queen of the Netherlands. PLACE-NAME USAGE: Mount Wilhelmina, New Guinea.

Willa   A pet form of Wilhelmina. *See* Wilhelmina. CONTEMPORARY EXAMPLE: Willa Cather, writer.

Willamae   A hybrid name of Willa and Mae. *See* Willa *and* Mae.

Willandra   A name invented by combining William and a form of Andrew. *See* William *and* Andrew. CONTEMPORARY EXAMPLE: Willandra S. Dean, Little Rock, Arkansas.

Willene   A pet form of Wilhelmina. *See* Wilhelmina.

Willeta, Willetta, Willette   Feminine forms of William. *See* William (masculine section).

Willi   A pet form of Wilhelmina. *See* Wilhelmina.

Wilmena   A pet form of Wilhelmina. *See* Wilhelmina.

Wilmet, Wilmette   Pet forms of Wilhelmina. *See* Wilhelmina. PLACE-NAME USAGE: Wilmette, Illinois.

Win   A pet form of Winifred. *See* Winifred.

Winema   An American Indian name, meaning "lady chief."

Winifred   From the Old English, meaning "friend of peace." Also, from the Welsh name Gwenfrewi, meaning "white wave." VARIANT FORMS: Freda, Frieda. PET FORMS: Win, Winnie, Wyn.

Winnie   A pet form of Winifred. *See* Winifred.

Winona   A variant spelling of Wenona. *See* Wenona. PLACE-NAME USAGE: Winona, Minnesota.

Woodren   A feminine form of Woodrow. *See* Woodrow (masculine section). CONTEMPORARY EXAMPLE: Woodren Buchan, Apple Valley, California.

Wyn   A pet form of Gwendaline and Winifred. *See* Gwendaline *and* Winifred.

Wynne, Wynelle, Wynette   Pet forms of Gwendaline and Winifred. *See* Gwendaline *and* Winifred. CONTEMPORARY EXAMPLE: Wynelle S. Deese, psychologist.

Wyome   From the Algonquin Indian language, meaning "large plain." CONTEMPORARY EXAMPLE: Wyome Ruey Smith, Sioux City, Iowa.

Wyomia   A variant form of Wyome. *See* Wyome. CONTEMPORARY EXAMPLE: Wyomia Tyrus, athlete. PLACE-NAME USAGE: the state of Wyoming.

X

Xanthe   From the Greek *xanthas*, meaning "yellow." Xantheine is a yellow pigment present in the cell sap of some plants. PLACE-NAME USAGE: Xanthes, a town in Asia Minor noted for its golden-haired maidens.

Xavier   Used primarily as a masculine name. *See* Xavier (masculine section). PLACE-NAME USAGE: Xavier, Kansas, named for Sister Xavier Ross, founder of the community.

Xena   A variant form of Xenia. *See* Xenia.

Xenia   From the Greek *xenia*, meaning "hospitality," and *xenos*, meaning "a guest, a stranger" (to whom hospitality was extended). Akin to Xena. CONTEMPORARY EXAMPLE: Xenia Ley Parker, author. PLACE-NAME USAGE: cities in Illinois and Ohio.

Ximena   A variant form of Xenia. *See* Xenia.

Xiomara   A variant form of Xenia. *See* Xenia. CONTEMPORARY EXAMPLE: Xiomara Gomez, Laurelton, New York.

Xylia, Xylina   Variant forms of Sylvia. *See* Sylvia.

Xylophila   From the Greek, meaning "lover of forests."

Y

Yaalit A variant form of Yael. *See* Yael.

Yael, Yaela, Yaella Variant spellings of Jael. *See* Jael.

Yaffa From the Hebrew *yafeh*, meaning "beautiful." Akin to Yafit. CONTEMPORARY EXAMPLE: Yaffa Yarkoni, singer. PLACE-NAME USAGE: a city in Israel, also spelled Jaffa and Yafo.

Yafit From the Hebrew *yafeh*, meaning "beautiful." A variant form of Yaffa.

Yakira From the Hebrew, meaning "valuable, precious."

Yardena The feminine form of Yarden. *See* Yarden (masculine section). Also, the feminine Hebraic name for Jordan. *See* Jordan (masculine section).

Yarkona The feminine form of the masculine Yarkon, meaning "green." A bird with golden-green feathers, Yarkona, is found in southern Israel.

Yasmeen A variant form of Jasmine. *See* Jasmine. A Persian flower name. CONTEMPORARY EXAMPLE: Yasmeen Alexis Royal, Elizabeth, New Jersey.

Yasmin, Yasmine Variant spellings of Jasmine. *See* Jasmine. A Persian flower name. CONTEMPORARY EXAMPLE: Yasmin Lee Ratcliff, Norfolk, Virginia.

Yatva From the Hebrew *tov*, meaning "good."

Yedida, Yedidah From the Hebrew, meaning "friend, beloved." CONTEMPORARY EXAMPLE: Yedida K. Stillman, professor.

Yehiela, Yehiella Feminine forms of Yehiel (Jehiel). *See* Yehiel (masculine section).

Yehudit The Hebrew form of Judith. *See* Judith. In the Bible, the wife of Esau.

Yeira From the Hebrew *or*, meaning "light."

Yemima A Hebraic form of Jemima. *See* Jemima.

Yemina From the Hebrew, meaning "right hand." Yemin is a masculine form. *See* Yemin (masculine section).

Yeshisha From the Hebrew, meaning "old." Yeshish is a masculine form.

Yetive From the Tibetan *yeti*, a large, hairy, manlike animal reputed to live in the Himalayas. Yetive is the name of the heroine in George Barr McCutcheon's books about the mythical kingdom of Graustark. CONTEMPORARY EXAMPLE: Yetive Matthews Ashcraft, Uniontown, Pennsylvania.

Yetta A pet form of Henrietta. *See* Henrietta.

Yigaala, Yigala From the Hebrew, meaning "to redeem." Yigal is a masculine form.

Yitta A variant spelling of Yetta. *See* Yetta. CONTEMPORARY EXAMPLE: Yitta Mandelbaum, publicist.

Yma A variant form of Ima. *See* Ima. CONTEMPORARY EXAMPLE: Yma Sumac, singer.

Yochebed, Yocheved, Yoheved Hebraic spellings of Jochebed. *See* Jochebed.

Yolanda, Yolande Possibly, a form of the Old French name Violante, which is a derivative of Viola. *See* Viola. Or, from the Latin, meaning "modest, shy." Also, a variant form of Eolande. *See* Eolande. CONTEMPORARY EXAMPLE: Yolande Gunz, editor.

Yona, Yonah From the Hebrew, meaning "a dove." Jonah is the Anglicized form. Used also as a masculine name.

Yonina, Yonit, Yonita Variant forms of Yonah. *See* Yona.

Yoseb The Tibetan form of Joseph and Josepha. *See* Joseph. CONTEMPORARY EXAMPLE: Yoseb Afsharzadeh, Chico, California.

Yosefa, Yosifa Variant spellings of Josepha, the feminine form of Joseph. *See* Josepha.

Yovela From the Hebrew, meaning "jubilee" or "rejoicing." Yovel is the masculine form.

Yudit A pet form of Yehudit. *See* Yehudit.

Yullis From the Old English *geol* and *iul*, originally the name of a heathen festival. Akin to the Old Norse *jol*, meaning "jolly," and to yule and yuletide. CONTEMPORARY EXAMPLE: Yullis Ruval, actress.

Yuma A tribal name of North American Indians. PLACE-NAME USAGE: Yuma, Arizona.

Yuta A variant form of Yehudit. *See* Yehudit.

Yve A feminine form of Yves. *See* Yves (masculine section). VARIANT FORMS: Yvette, Yvonne.

Yvette A variant French form of Yve. *See* Yve.

Yvonne A variant French form of Yve. *See* Yve. CONTEMPORARY EXAMPLE: Yvonne Lawley, actress.

Z

Zabrina   A variant form of Sabrina. *See* Sabrina. CONTEMPORARY EXAMPLE: Zabrina Faire, author.

Zahava   A variant spelling of Zehava. *See* Zehava.

Zaida   From the Yiddish, meaning "grandfather." Occasionally used as a feminine form.

Zaka, Zakia, Zakit   From the Hebrew, meaning "bright, pure, clear."

Zamoka   From the Hebrew, meaning "a branch." PLACE-NAME USAGE: a Spanish province.

Zamora   A variant form of Zimra. *See* Zimra.

Zandra   A variant form of Sandra. *See* Sandra. CONTEMPORARY EXAMPLE: Zandra Rhodes, designer.

Zaneta   A Russian form of Johanna. *See* Johanna.

Zara, Zarah   Variant forms of Sarah. *See* Sarah. Also, from the Arabic, meaning "dawn." CONTEMPORARY EXAMPLE: Zara Steiner, historian. PLACE-NAME USAGE: Zarah, Kansas.

Zariza, Zeriza   From the Hebrew, meaning "industrious."

Zathara   Meaning unknown. Used in a soap opera that played in Oklahoma in the 1930s. CONTEMPORARY EXAMPLE: Zathara Delaney, Lancaster, California.

Zayit   From the Hebrew, meaning "olive." Used also as a masculine name.

Zaza   From the Hebrew, meaning "movement." CONTEMPORARY EXAMPLE: Zaza H. Duffy, Vancouver, B.C., Canada.

Zazu   A variant form of Zaza. *See* Zaza. CONTEMPORARY EXAMPLE: Zazu Pitts, actress.

Zeena   A variant spelling of Zina. *See* Zina.

Zehara, Zehari   From the Hebrew, meaning "to shine; light, brightness."

Zehava, Zehavi, Zehavit   From the Hebrew, meaning "golden." Zehavi is used also as a masculine name.

Zehira   From the Hebrew, meaning "guarded, protected."

Zehuva   From the Hebrew, meaning "gilded." Akin to Zehava.

Zelda   A variant form of Selda. *See* Selda.

Zelia   From the Latin *zelus*, meaning "zealous."

Zella   A variant form of Zelia. *See* Zelia. CONTEMPORARY EXAMPLE: Zella Sutton, Elizabethtown, Kentucky.

Zelma   A name invented by combining parts of Zaida, Ella, and Mark. CONTEMPORARY EXAMPLE: Zelma M. Anderson, Wallingford, Connecticut.

Zemira, Zemora   From the Hebrew, meaning "a branch." Akin to Zimra. *See* Zimra. Zamora is a variant form.

Zena   A short form of the Persian *zan*, meaning "a woman." CONTEMPORARY EXAMPLE: Zena Sutherland, librarian. PLACE-NAME USAGE: Zena, Oregon, named for Arvezena Cooper, wife of an early settler; Zena, Oklahoma.

Zenana   From the Persian *zan*, meaning "a woman." Akin to Zena.

Zenda   From the Persian *zend*, meaning "sacred."

Zenia   A variant form of Zena. *See* Zena. PLACE-NAME USAGE: Zenia, California.

Zenobia   From the Greek *sema*, meaning "a sign, a symbol." A third-century queen of Palmyra.

Zeona   A variant spelling of Ziona. *See* Ziona. PLACE-NAME USAGE: Zeona, South Dakota.

Zephira   From the Hebrew, meaning "morning." Zephyr is a variant form.

Zephyr   From the Greek, meaning "the west wind." In Greek mythology, Zephyrus was the god of the west wind. CONTEMPORARY EXAMPLE: Zephyr Cooper, educator.

Zeta   From the Hebrew *zayit*, meaning "an olive." Also, the sixth letter of the Greek alphabet. Zetta is a variant spelling.

Zetana   A variant form of Zeta. *See* Zeta.

Zetta   A variant spelling of Zeta. *See* Zeta.

Zeva   From the Hebrew *ze'ev*, meaning "a wolf." Zev is the masculine form. CONTEMPORARY EXAMPLE: Zeva Shapiro, translator.

Zevida, Zevuda   From the Hebrew *zeved*, meaning "a gift."

Zevula   From the Hebrew, meaning "a dwelling place" or "a palace." Zevulun is the masculine equivalent.

Zia   From the Hebrew, meaning "to tremble." PLACE-NAME USAGE: Zia, New Mexico.

Zila, Zilla, Zillah   From the Hebrew *tzel*, meaning "a shadow, shade."

In the Bible, the wife of Lamech. Favorite gypsy names. CONTEMPORARY EXAMPLE: Zillah Richardson, Oceanside, California.

Zili, Zilli   From the Hebrew, meaning "my shadow." Akin to Zila.

Zilpah   From the Hebrew, meaning "dripping, sprinkling." In the Bible, the concubine of Jacob; mother of Gad and Asher.

Zimra   From the Hebrew *zemer*, meaning either "a branch" or "song of praise." VARIANT FORMS: Zamora, Zemira, Zemora.

Zimria, Zimriah   From the Hebrew *zemer*, meaning "a song."

Zina   A variant form of Zinnia. *See* Zinnia. CONTEMPORARY EXAMPLE: Zina Jasper, actress.

Zinaida   A variant form of Zenobia. *See* Zenobia.

Zinnia   A variety of plant with colorful flowers, named for German botanist J.G. Zinn (died 1759). VARIANT FORMS: Zeena, Zina.

Ziona   From the Hebrew, meaning "excellent" or "a sign." Zeona is a variant spelling. Zion is the masculine form.

Zippora, Zipporah   From the Hebrew *tzipor*, meaning "a bird." In the Bible, the wife of Moses, daughter of Jethro.

Zira   From the Hebrew, meaning "an arena."

Zita   A pet form of Theresa. *See* Theresa.

Ziva, Zivit   From the Hebrew, meaning "brightness, splendor." Ziv is a masculine form. CONTEMPORARY EXAMPLE: Ziva Amir, author.

Zoe   From the Greek, meaning "life." In a third–century translation of the Bible by Alexandrian Jews, Eve (Chavah), meaning "life," is translated as Zoe. Used later as a Christian name by Byzantine Greeks. CONTEMPORARY EXAMPLE: Zoe Caldwell, actress.

Zohar   From the Hebrew, meaning "light, brilliance." Used also as a masculine name.

Zoheret   From the Hebrew, meaning "she shines." Akin to Zohar.

Zona   From the Hebrew, meaning "a prostitute." CONTEMPORARY EXAMPLE: Zona Gale, playwright.

Zonya   A variant form of Sonia. *See* Sonia.

Zophia   A variant form of Sophia. *See* Sophia.

Zora   A variant form of Zara. *See* Zara. CONTEMPORARY EXAMPLE: Zora N. Hurston, author.

Zorana   A pet form of Zora. *See* Zora.

Zoreen, Zoreene, Zorene   Pet forms of Zara. *See* Zara.

Zorna   A variant form of Zara. *See* Zara

Zsa Zsa   A pet form of the Hungarian name Zsusanna (Susan). *See* Susan. CONTEMPORARY EXAMPLE: Zsa Zsa Gabor, actress.

Zsusanna   A Hungarian form of Susan. *See* Susan. Zsa Zsa is a pet form.

Zudora   A variant form of the Sanskrit *sudra*, meaning "menial laborer." A sudra is a member of the fourth and lowest Hindu caste. Zudy is a pet form.

Zudy   A pet form of Zudora. *See* Zudora. CONTEMPORARY EXAMPLE: Zudy Brier, San Leandro, California.

Zuelia   A variant form of Zulema. *See* Zulema. CONTEMPORARY EXAMPLE: Zuelia Ann Hurt, needlepoint designer.

Zuleika   A variant form of Zulema. *See* Zulema.

Zulema   From the Arabic name Suleima, and the Hebrew *shalom*, meaning "peace." CONTEMPORARY EXAMPLE: Zulema Dene, actress.

Zulpha   Probably a variant form of Zilpah. *See* Zilpah. CONTEMPORARY EXAMPLES: Zulpha Keatley Snyder, author.

Zylpha   A variant form of Zilpah. *See* Zilpah.

Bibliography

Ames, Winthrop *What Shall We Name the Baby?* New York; Simon & Shuster, 1935.

Bardsley, Charles *English Surnames.* London: Chatto & Windus, 1884.

———*Curiosities of Puritan Nomenclature.* London: 1897.

———*The Romance of the London Directory.* London: 1879.

Baring, Gould S. *Family Names and Their Story.* London: 1932.

Barr, George. *Who's Who in the Bible.* New York: Jonathan David Publishers, 1975.

Blackie, C. *Dictionary of Place Names.* London: John Murray, 1887.

Bowman, William D. *The Story of Surnames.* London: 1932.

Burnham, S.M. *Our Names.* Boston: A. I. Bradley Co., 1900.

Burton, Dorothy. *A New Treasury of Names for the Baby.* New York: Prentice Hall, 1961.

Brown, Driver & Briggs. *Hebrew and English Lexicon of the Old Testament.* New York: Houghton Mifflin Co., 1907.

Edmunds, F. *Traces of History in the Names of Places.* London: Longmans, Green and Co., 1872.

Fisher, Henry W. *Girls' Names.* New York: Fisher's Foreign Letters, Publishers, 1910.

Grussi, A.M. *Chats on Christian Names.* Boston: The Stratford Co. 1925.

Kolatch, Alfred J. *These Are the Names.* New York: Jonathan David, 1948.

———*The Name Dictionary.* New York: Jonathan David, 1967.

———*Names for Boys and Girls.* New York: Jonathan David, 1968.

———*Names for Pets.* New York: Jonathan David, 1971.

———*Who's Who in the Talmud.* New York: Jonathan David, 1964.

Lambert, E. and Pei, M. *Our Names.* New York: Lothrop, 1962.

Latham, Edward *Dictionary of Names, Nicknames, and Surnames.* London: 1904.

Loughead, F. *Dictionary of Given Names.* Glendale, California: Arthur Clark, 1966.

Moody, Sophy *What Is Your Name?* London: Richard Bentley, 1863.

Mordacque, L.H. *History of the Names of Men, Nations and Places.* Vol. I (1862), and Vol. II (1964). London: John Russel Smith, Publisher.

Palmer G., and Lloyd, N., *Exploring Names.* London: Oldham Books, 1964.

Sleigh, L. and Johnson, C. *The Book of Boys.* New York: Thomas Y. Crowell, 1962.

———*The Book of Girls.* New York: Thomas Y. Crowell, 1962.

Smith, Elsdon *American Surnames.* New York: Chilton, 1970.

— — —*Naming Your Baby*. New York: Chilton, 1970.

Stewart, George R. *American Place-Names*. New York: Oxford, 1970.

Swan, H. *Girls' Christian Names*. London.

Taggart, Jean *Pet Names*. New York: Scarecrow Press, 1962.

Wagner, Leopold *Names and Their Meaning*. London: T. Fisher Unwin, 1893.

— — —*More About Names*. London: T. Fisher Unwin, 1893.

Weekley, Ernest *Surnames*. London: John Murray, Second Edition, 1927.

Wells, Evelyn *What to Name the Baby*. New York: Doubleday, 1946.

— — —*A Treasury of Names*. New York: Duell, Sloan & Pearce, 1946.

Withycombe, E.G. *The Oxford Dictionary of English Christian Names*. New York: Oxford University Press, 1945.

Yonge, Charlotte M. *History of Christian Names*. London: MacMillan (1884).